# 1001 GOLF HOLES

## YOU MUST PLAY BEFORE YOU DIE

JEFF BARR GENERAL EDITOR

PREFACE BY ROBERT TRENT JONES JR.

A Quintessence Book

First published in Great Britain in 2005 by Cassell Illustrated,
a division of Octopus Publishing Group Limited
Endeavour House, 189 Shaftesbury Avenue
London, WC2H 8JY
www.octopusbooks.co.uk

An Hachette UK Company
www.hachette.co.uk

ISBN 978 1 84403 741 4
QSS.KGOL

A CIP catalogue record for this book is available from the British Library.

This book was designed and produced by
Quintessence
230 City Road
London EC1V 2TT

First edition published in 2005
This edition first published in 2012

Project Editor: Ruth Patrick
Art Director: Roland Codd
Designers: Ian Hunt, James Lawrence
Creative Director: Richard Dewing
Update Editor: Ruth Patrick
Update Consultant: Jeff Barr
Update Designer: Tea Aganovic
Publishers: Ian Castello-Cortes, Mark Fletcher

Manufactured in Singapore by Pica Digital Pte Ltd.
Printed in China by Midas Printing International Ltd.

With special thanks to Oliver Salzmann, Laura Price, and Rosie Barry
without whom this book would not have been born. Thanks also to Joanna
Morley and Sara Di-Girolamo for their assistance with picture research, and to
all golf clubs who supplied images of golf holes.

# CONTENTS

# PREFACE
## BY ROBERT TRENT JONES JR.

Seeing some of my own work included among the world's best golf holes — placed alongside the all-time greats of the profession — is, of course, deeply satisfying. As a golf course architect though, I dwell less on what we've already done and more on contemplating the challenges our current projects pose. As a young man, working with my father, I saw sites selected mostly on the basis of their natural suitability for a golf course. Now, although we occasionally are privileged to work on a classic links-style site, one comparable to those magical seaside venues where, it is supposed, Scottish shepherds and fishermen hitting rocks with crooks invented the game of golf, it's more typical now that we're asked to design courses on sites where the reasoning behind the venture is, to a large extent, economic.

Japan, for example, which adopted golf with the same energy and enthusiasm it applied to building its might, provided an especially demanding set of architectural and construction challenges for golf course designers in the 1970s and 1980s, when my firm was particularly active there. Rather than using seaside sites on sandy soils, the Japanese developers planned their courses on hills and mountains where the ground was rocky and steep. Arable land in Japan, especially the lowlands where rice is grown, is considered to be sacred, and not available for other land uses. As a consequence, when the people of Japan did embrace golf, the only places where they could find enough land to build courses were in the hills and mountains. Designing a golf course was, therefore, as much an engineering challenge as it was artistic.

Contemporary golf design requires imagination, political savvy, stamina, and determination. Every country and region has its special design requirements, but they all start with what's on the ground. Our design philosophy has always been to use the inherent features of the site to enhance the golf opportunities, rather than to impose an imported style on the site. Our courses don't so much have a look as they have a natural "feel." We make our courses fit their sites, as do the other classic designers whose work is featured in this book.

We learn all we can about a site before design is complete and construction begins — we study the vegetation, the climate, the local building vernacular, the overall location — that is, what surroundings you will see from the tees or other vantage points on the course — but most of all the landforms, the inherent shape of the site. This is the information conveyed by a topographical map, and the information that designers use to make the most of the natural setting in the creation of great courses, time after time.

Designers such as myself hold multiple images of 18-hole tracks in the mind at once during the design stage, comparing one routing concept to another as we seek the best solution. We remember our route plans — comparing one to the other and deciding on the best model for the current site — just as a composer remembers his compositions or a poet the stanzas of his verse.

The ability to hold a conceptual model of one or more landscapes in our minds is essential to golf course architects, just as it is to military leaders. The great American general (and later president), U.S. Grant, could envision an entire battlefield and its various components in his mind as he ordered troop movements during combat. I've always thought Grant would have made a great golf course architect had he lived in another time and place.

Golf design, as with any art form, experiences fads and fashions, but great design is timeless. The strength and beauty of the Old Course at St. Andrews, Scotland, for example, is its subtlety — a series of mysteries slow to reveal themselves. The design principles guiding our work will, we hope, continue to generate holes worthy of respect and admiration.

Designers may have different approaches and employ different principles to their art, but one thing is for sure: the work featured in this book is a selection of the best of the best — snapshots of key moments on the world's key courses. For anyone involved, on whatever level, with golf, this book will long be a source of inspiration, as well as enjoyment.

# INTRODUCTION

I'm quite sure the good people at the publishing house were as surprised by my reaction as I was by their question. Their phone call found a receiver in Orlando:

"Jeff, we're wondering if you would be interested in doing a book entitled *1001 Golf Holes You Must Play Before You Die.*"

I'm sure there was some further discussion, some explanation of the book's concept, but I couldn't comprehend much after hearing the daunting number they were considering. So, trying to sound as calm as possible, I proceeded as if 1001 were a perfectly manageable number, and asked in a near-squeak:

"Did you say 1001?"

That was the beginning of this project — a phone call that almost left me wondering if I were the victim of some sort of intercontinental prank. But once a plan was formulated and a team of experts put together, the writing of this book transformed from daunting to exhilarating. This is my fourth book, and I can honestly say I've never enjoyed a project more, nor been more proud of the final outcome. As I hope you will agree — the photography, information, history, and descriptions of the golf holes included in these pages come together to offer a book that you can revisit for years to come.

Choosing the holes was perhaps the biggest challenge. It is important to note that we are not proclaiming these golf holes to be the 1001 *best* in the world; rather these are 1001 *great* holes that you simply must play. Certainly there are countless other great golf holes that weren't included in this publication, but we could only go 1001 deep. Besides, there's always the sequel. Did someone say 2002?

And, truth be told, debate about the list was a great part of the fun — we hope that our choices will spur further discussion among readers. Certainly, we don't expect you to agree with all 1001 selections. However, we hope that if a favorite hole of yours isn't included, it will at least result in conversation over a post-round mug of ale in the clubhouse.

As general editor and lead writer of *1001 Golf Holes*, it was both thrilling and humbling to work with a team loaded not only with so much golf knowledge but also with writing talent. Kevin Adams, Beth Ann Baldry, Graham Elliott, Rex Hoggard, Terry Jacoby, Kelle Larkin, John Steinbreder, and Alistair Tait were dedicated pros from start to finish. And when you add the contributions of the legions of first-class international golf photographers, it is no wonder the outcome is so monumental.

This book also taught me a lesson: no matter how much you think you already know, there is always room to learn. After 31 years as a golfer and more than 20 as a professional writer, I have accrued a fair amount of insight into the game and where it is played. However, during the months of researching, editing, and writing *1001 Golf Holes*, I quickly realized how much I had left to learn.

This "behind-the-scenes" look at these 1001 venues is what made the creation of this book so enjoyable to me: in addition to the astounding natural beauty of some of the golf courses in this book, we consider the players that marked their greens, the visions that motivated their designers, and the histories that they now hold in their clutches.

I must, in closing, give special thanks to Robert Trent Jones Jr. for his preface. Special thanks also to Kelle, for supporting me throughout this project and in everyday life. Thanks to my daughter, Ashley, for understanding how busy Dad can get. And a sincere thank you to Ruth Patrick, whose professionalism and grace were a constant from hole No. 1 to 1001.

## HOW THIS BOOK IS ORGANIZED

*1001 Golf Holes* is organized into eighteen chapters by hole for easy reference, making navigation through the book simple. The chapters are structured by par — par-3 holes denoted by the yellow fact boxes, par-4 holes by the green fact boxes, and par-5 holes by the gray fact boxes.

The book is your round-the-world ticket to experience key moments from some of the greatest golf courses in existence — at a fraction of the price. It provides an infinite number of virtual rounds — every time you dip into the book, you can soar effortlessly from continent to continent — choosing whichever fantasy combination of 1–18 suits you that day.

Although we have included hundreds of exceptional examples from earlier in the round, you will find that the latter part of the book is proportionally larger, reflecting the emphasis designers place on the later holes and their importance in the round. In order to help you find your way around, we have provided three indices:

- **Course Index** *(Page 8)* An A–Z of the golf courses and holes in the book. Useful if looking up your favorite club — see how many holes are featured at a glance.
- **Designer Index** *(Page 953)* Find out how much of your favorite designer's work is featured.
- **General Index** *(Page 955)* All the information you could possibly wish to look up — all the above, plus players, countries of the world, and much more.

Whether you are an avid golfer or not, the book you now have in front of you is the perfect companion to take you away for a while. So with each turn of the page, feel the manicured tee-box underfoot, the wind blowing back your hair, adjust your grip, and let rip!

**Jeff Barr**

# COURSE INDEX

# TOURNAMENT WINNERS: RYDER CUP AND MAJORS

## RYDER CUP

The winning team is highlighted in **bold**.

| | | | |
|---|---|---|---|
| 1927 | Worcester Country Club | GB 2½ | **USA 9½** |
| 1929 | Moortown Golf Club | **GB 7** | USA 5 |
| 1931 | Scioto Country Club | GB 3 | **USA 9** |
| 1933 | Southport & Ainsdale Golf Club | **GB 6½** | USA 5½ |
| 1935 | Ridgewood Country Club | GB 3 | **USA 9** |
| 1937 | Southport & Ainsdale Golf Club | GB 4 | **USA 8** |
| 1947 | Portland Golf Club | GB 1 | **USA 11** |
| 1949 | Ganton Golf Club | GB 5 | **USA 7** |
| 1951 | Pinehurst Country Club | GB 2½ | **USA 9½** |
| 1953 | Wentworth Club | GB & Ire 5½ | **USA 6½** |
| 1955 | Thunderbird Country Club | GB & Ire 4 | **USA 8** |
| 1957 | Lindrick Golf Club | **GB & Ire 7½** | USA 4½ |
| 1959 | Eldorado Golf Course | GB & Ire 3½ | **USA 8½** |
| 1961 | Royal Lytham & St. Annes | GB & Ire 9½ | **USA 14½** |
| 1963 | East Lake Golf Club | GB & Ire 9 | **USA 23** |
| 1965 | Royal Birkdale Golf Club | GB & Ire 12½ | **USA 19½** |
| 1967 | Champions Club | GB & Ire 8½ | **USA 23½** |
| 1969 | Royal Birkdale Golf Club | GB & Ire 16 | USA 16 |
| 1971 | Old Warson Country Club | GB & Ire 13½ | **USA 18½** |
| 1973 | Muirfield Links | GB & Ire 13 | **USA 19** |
| 1975 | Laurel Valley Golf Club | GB & Ire 11 | **USA 21** |
| 1977 | Royal Lytham & St. Annes | GB & Ire 7½ | **USA 12½** |
| 1979 | The Greenbrier | Europe 11 | **USA 17** |
| 1981 | Walton Heath | Europe 9½ | **USA 18½** |
| 1983 | PGA National | Europe 13½ | **USA 14½** |
| 1985 | The Belfry | **Europe 16½** | USA 11½ |
| 1987 | Muirfield Village Golf Club | **Europe 15** | USA 13 |
| 1989 | The Belfry | Europe 14 | USA 14 |
| 1991 | Kiawah Island | Europe 13½ | **USA 14½** |
| 1993 | The Belfry | Europe 13 | **USA 15** |
| 1995 | Oak Hill Country Club | **Europe 14½** | USA 13½ |
| 1997 | Valderrama | **Europe 14½** | USA 13½ |
| 1999 | Brookline | Europe 13½ | **USA 14½** |
| 2002 | The Belfry | **Europe 15½** | USA 12½ |
| 2004 | Oakland Hills Country Club | **Europe 18½** | USA 9½ |
| 2006 | K-Club | **Europe 18½** | USA 9½ |
| 2008 | Valhalla | Europe 11½ | **USA 16½** |
| 2010 | Celtic Manor | **Europe 14½** | USA 13½ |
| 2012 | Medinah Country Club | | |
| 2014 | Gleneagles, Centenery PGA Course | | |
| 2016 | Hazeltine National Golf Club | | |
| 2018 | Le Golf National | | |
| 2020 | Whistling Straits | | |

## MASTERS

The Masters is held at Augusta National Golf Club every year.

| | | | | | |
|---|---|---|---|---|---|
| 1934 | Horton Smith | 1964 | Arnold Palmer | 1991 | Ian Woosnam |
| 1935 | Gene Sarazen | 1965 | Jack Nicklaus | 1992 | Fred Couples |
| 1936 | Horton Smith | 1966 | Jack Nicklaus | 1993 | Bernhard Langer |
| 1937 | Byron Nelson | 1967 | Gay Brewer Jr. | 1994 | Jose-Maria Olazabal |
| 1938 | Henry Picard | 1968 | Bob Goalby | 1995 | Ben Crenshaw |
| 1939 | Ralph Guldahl | 1969 | George Archer | 1996 | Nick Faldo |
| 1940 | Jimmy Demaret | 1970 | Billy Casper | 1997 | Tiger Woods |
| 1941 | Craig Wood | 1971 | Charles Coody | 1998 | Mark O'Meara |
| 1942 | Byron Nelson | 1972 | Jack Nicklaus | 1999 | Jose-Maria Olazabal |
| 1946 | Herman Keiser | 1973 | Tommy Aaron | 2000 | Vijay Singh |
| 1947 | Jimmy Demaret | 1974 | Gary Player | 2001 | Tiger Woods |
| 1948 | Claude Harmon | 1975 | Jack Nicklaus | 2002 | Tiger Woods |
| 1949 | Sam Snead | 1976 | Raymond Floyd | 2003 | Mike Weir |
| 1950 | Jimmy Demaret | 1977 | Tom Watson | 2004 | Phil Mickelson |
| 1951 | Ben Hogan | 1978 | Gary Player | 2005 | Tiger Woods |
| 1952 | Sam Snead | 1979 | Fuzzy Zoeller | 2006 | Phil Mickelson |
| 1953 | Ben Hogan | 1980 | Seve Ballesteros | 2007 | Zach Johnson |
| 1954 | Sam Snead | 1981 | Tom Watson | 2008 | Trevor Immelman |
| 1955 | Cary Middlecoff | 1982 | Craig Stadler | 2009 | Angel Cabrera |
| 1956 | Jack Burke Jr. | 1983 | Seve Ballesteros | 2010 | Phil Mickelson |
| 1957 | Doug Ford | 1984 | Ben Crenshaw | 2011 | Charl Schwartzel |
| 1958 | Arnold Palmer | 1985 | Bernhard Langer | 2012 | Bubba Watson |
| 1959 | Art Wall Jr. | 1986 | Jack Nicklaus | | |
| 1960 | Arnold Palmer | 1987 | Larry Mize | | |
| 1961 | Gary Player | 1988 | Sandy Lyle | | |
| 1962 | Arnold Palmer | 1989 | Nick Faldo | | |
| 1963 | Jack Nicklaus | 1990 | Nick Faldo | | |

# U.S. OPEN

| Year | Venue | Winner |
|---|---|---|
| 1895 | Newport Country Club | Horace Rawlins |
| 1896 | Shinnecock Hills Golf Club | James Foulis |
| 1897 | Chicago Golf Club | Joe Lloyd |
| 1898 | Myopia Hunt Club | Fred Herd |
| 1899 | Baltimore Country Club, East Course | Willie Smith |
| 1900 | Chicago Golf Club | Harry Vardon |
| 1901 | Myopia Hunt Club | Willie Anderson |
| 1902 | Garden City Golf Club | Laurie Auchterlonie |
| 1903 | Baltusrol Golf Club | Willie Anderson |
| 1904 | Glen View Club | Willie Anderson |
| 1905 | Myopia Hunt Club | Willie Anderson |
| 1906 | Onwentsia Club | Alex Smith |
| 1907 | Philadelphia Cricket Club, St. Martin's Course | Alex Ross |
| 1908 | Myopia Hunt Club | Fred McLeod |
| 1909 | Englewood Golf Club | George Sargent |
| 1910 | Philadelphia Cricket Club, St. Martin's Course | Alex Smith |
| 1911 | Chicago Golf Club | John McDermott |
| 1912 | Country Club of Buffalo | John McDermott |
| 1913 | The Country Club | Francis Ouimet |
| 1914 | Midlothian Country Club | Walter Hagen |
| 1915 | Baltusrol Golf Club | Jerome Travers |
| 1916 | The Minikahda Club | Chick Evans |
| 1919 | Brae Burn Country Club, Main Course | Walter Hagen |
| 1920 | Inverness Club | Edward Ray |
| 1921 | Columbia Country Club | Jim Barnes |
| 1922 | Skokie Country Club | Gene Sarazen |
| 1923 | Inwood Country Club | Bobby Jones |
| 1924 | Oakland Hills Country Club, South Course | Cyril Walker |
| 1925 | Worcester Country Club | Willie Macfarlane |
| 1926 | Scioto Country Club | Bobby Jones |
| 1927 | Oakmont Country Club | Tommy Armour |
| 1928 | Olympia Fields Country Club | Johnny Farrell |
| 1929 | Winged Foot Golf Club, West Course | Bobby Jones |
| 1930 | Interlachen Country Club | Bobby Jones |
| 1931 | Inverness Club | Billy Burke |
| 1932 | Fresh Meadow Country Club | Gene Sarazen |
| 1933 | North Shore Country Club | Johnny Goodman |
| 1934 | Merion Golf Club, East Course | Olin Dutra |
| 1935 | Olympia Fields Country Club | Sam Parks Jr. |
| 1936 | Baltusrol Golf Club, Upper Course | Tony Manero |
| 1937 | Oakland Hills Country Club, South Course | Ralph Guldahl |
| 1938 | Cherry Hills Country Club | Ralph Guldahl |
| 1939 | Philadelphia Country Club | Byron Nelson |
| 1940 | Canterbury Golf Club | Lawson Little |
| 1941 | Colonial Country Club | Craig Wood |
| 1946 | Canterbury Golf Club | Lloyd Mangrum |
| 1947 | St. Louis Country Club | Lew Worsham |
| 1948 | Riviera Country Club | Ben Hogan |
| 1949 | Medinah Country Club, No. 3 Course | Cary Middlecoff |
| 1950 | Merion Golf Club, East Course | Ben Hogan |
| 1951 | Oakland Hills Country Club, South Course | Ben Hogan |
| 1952 | Northwood Club | Julius Boros |
| 1953 | Oakmont Country Club | Ben Hogan |
| 1954 | Baltusrol Golf Club, Lower Course | Ed Furgol |
| 1955 | Olympic Club, Lake Course | Jack Fleck |
| 1956 | Oak Hill Country Club, East Course | Cary Middlecoff |
| 1957 | Inverness Club | Dick Mayer |
| 1958 | Southern Hills Country Club | Tommy Bolt |
| 1959 | Winged Foot Golf Club, West Course | Billy Casper |
| 1960 | Cherry Hills Country Club | Arnold Palmer |
| 1961 | Oakland Hills Country Club, South Course | Gene Littler |
| 1962 | Oakmont Country Club | Jack Nicklaus |
| 1963 | The Country Club | Julius Boros |
| 1964 | Congressional Country Club, Blue Course | Ken Venturi |
| 1965 | Bellerive Country Club | Gary Player |
| 1966 | Olympic Club, Lake Course | Billy Casper |
| 1967 | Baltusrol Golf Club, Lower Course | Jack Nicklaus |
| 1968 | Oak Hill Country Club, East Course | Lee Trevino |
| 1969 | Champions Golf Club, Cypress Creek Course | Orville Moody |
| 1970 | Hazeltine National Golf Club | Tony Jacklin |
| 1971 | Merion Golf Club, East Course | Lee Trevino |
| 1972 | Pebble Beach Golf Links | Jack Nicklaus |
| 1973 | Oakmont Country Club | Johnny Miller |
| 1974 | Winged Foot Golf Club, West Course | Hale Irwin |
| 1975 | Medinah Country Club, No. 3 Course | Lou Graham |
| 1976 | Atlanta Athletic Club, Highlands Course | Jerry Pate |
| 1977 | Southern Hills Country Club | Hubert Green |
| 1978 | Cherry Hills Country Club | Andy North |
| 1979 | Inverness Club | Hale Irwin |
| 1980 | Baltusrol Golf Club, Lower Course | Jack Nicklaus |
| 1981 | Merion Golf Club, East Course | David Graham |
| 1982 | Pebble Beach Golf Links | Tom Watson |
| 1983 | Oakmont Country Club | Larry Nelson |
| 1984 | Winged Foot Golf Club, West Course | Fuzzy Zoeller |
| 1985 | Oakland Hills Country Club, South Course | Andy North |
| 1986 | Shinnecock Hills Golf Club | Raymond Floyd |
| 1987 | Olympic Club, Lake Course | Scott Simpson |
| 1988 | The Country Club | Curtis Strange |
| 1989 | Oak Hill Country Club, East Course | Curtis Strange |
| 1990 | Medinah Country Club, No. 3 Course | Hale Irwin |
| 1991 | Hazeltine National Golf Club | Payne Stewart |
| 1992 | Pebble Beach Golf Links | Tom Kite |
| 1993 | Baltusrol Golf Club, Lower Course | Lee Janzen |
| 1994 | Oakmont Country Club | Ernie Els |
| 1995 | Shinnecock Hills Golf Club | Corey Pavin |
| 1996 | Oakland Hills Country Club, South Course | Steve Jones |
| 1997 | Congressional Country Club, Blue Course | Ernie Els |
| 1998 | Olympic Club, Lake Course | Lee Janzen |
| 1999 | Pinehurst Resort, Course No. 2 | Payne Stewart |
| 2000 | Pebble Beach Golf Links | Tiger Woods |
| 2001 | Southern Hills Country Club | Retief Goosen |
| 2002 | Bethpage State Park, Black Course | Tiger Woods |
| 2003 | Olympia Fields Country Club | Jim Furyk |
| 2004 | Shinnecock Hills Golf Club | Retief Goosen |
| 2005 | Pinehurst Resort, Course No. 2 | Michael Campbell |
| 2006 | Winged Foot Golf Club, West Course | Geoff Ogilvy |
| 2007 | Oakmont Country Club | Angel Cabrera |
| 2008 | Torrey Pines Golf Course | Tiger Woods |
| 2009 | Bethpage State Park, Black Course | Lucas Glover |
| 2010 | Pebble Beach Golf Links | Graeme McDowell |
| 2011 | Congressional Country Club, Blue Course | Rory McIlroy |
| 2012 | Olympic Club, Lake Course | Webb Simpson |
| 2013 | Merion Golf Club, East Course | |
| 2014 | Pinehurst Resort, Course No. 2 | |
| 2015 | Chambers Bay | |
| 2016 | Oakmont Country Club | |
| 2017 | Erin Hills | |
| 2018 | Shinnecock Hills Golf Club | |
| 2019 | Pebble Beach Golf Links | |

13

## OPEN CHAMPIONSHIP

| Year | Venue | Winner |
|---|---|---|
| 1860 | Prestwick Golf Club | Willie Park Sr. |
| 1861 | Prestwick Golf Club | Tom Morris Sr. |
| 1862 | Prestwick Golf Club | Tom Morris Sr. |
| 1863 | Prestwick Golf Club | Willie Park Sr. |
| 1864 | Prestwick Golf Club | Tom Morris Sr. |
| 1865 | Prestwick Golf Club | Andrew Strath |
| 1866 | Prestwick Golf Club | Willie Park Sr. |
| 1867 | Prestwick Golf Club | Tom Morris Sr. |
| 1868 | Prestwick Golf Club | Tom Morris Jr. |
| 1869 | Prestwick Golf Club | Tom Morris Jr. |
| 1870 | Prestwick Golf Club | Tom Morris Jr. |
| 1872 | Prestwick Golf Club | Tom Morris Jr. |
| 1873 | St. Andrews, Old Course | Tom Kidd |
| 1874 | Musselburgh Links | Mungo Park |
| 1875 | Prestwick Golf Club | Willie Park Sr. |
| 1876 | St. Andrews, Old Course | Bob Martin |
| 1877 | Musselburgh Links | Jamie Anderson |
| 1878 | Prestwick Golf Club | Jamie Anderson |
| 1879 | St. Andrews, Old Course | Jamie Anderson |
| 1880 | Musselburgh Links | Bob Ferguson |
| 1881 | Prestwick Golf Club | Bob Ferguson |
| 1882 | St. Andrews, Old Course | Bob Ferguson |
| 1883 | Musselburgh Links | Willie Fernie |
| 1884 | Prestwick Golf Club | Jack Simpson |
| 1885 | St. Andrews, Old Course | Bob Martin |
| 1886 | Musselburgh Links | David Brown |
| 1887 | Prestwick Golf Club | Willie Park Jr. |
| 1888 | St. Andrews, Old Course | Jack Burns |
| 1889 | Musselburgh Links | Willie Park Jr. |
| 1890 | Prestwick Golf Club | John Ball Jr. |
| 1891 | St. Andrews, Old Course | Hugh Kirkaldy |
| 1892 | Muirfield Links | Harold Hilton |
| 1893 | Prestwick Golf Club | William Auchterlonie |
| 1894 | Royal St. George's Golf Club | John Henry Taylor |
| 1895 | St. Andrews, Old Course | John Henry Taylor |
| 1896 | Muirfield Links | Harry Vardon |
| 1897 | Royal Liverpool Golf Club | Harold Hilton |
| 1898 | Prestwick Golf Club | Harry Vardon |
| 1899 | Royal St. George's Golf Club | Harry Vardon |
| 1900 | St. Andrews, Old Course | John Henry Taylor |
| 1901 | Muirfield Links | James Braid |
| 1902 | Royal Liverpool Golf Club | Alexander Herd |
| 1903 | Prestwick Golf Club | Harry Vardon |
| 1904 | Royal St. George's Golf Club | Jack White |
| 1905 | St. Andrews, Old Course | James Braid |
| 1906 | Muirfield Links | James Braid |
| 1907 | Royal Liverpool Golf Club | Arnaud Massy |
| 1908 | Prestwick Golf Club | James Braid |
| 1909 | Royal Cinque Ports Golf Club | John Henry Taylor |
| 1910 | St. Andrews, Old Course | James Braid |
| 1911 | Royal St. George's Golf Club | Harry Vardon |
| 1912 | Muirfield Links | Edward Ray |
| 1913 | Royal Liverpool Golf Club | John Henry Taylor |
| 1914 | Prestwick Golf Club | Harry Vardon |
| 1920 | Royal Cinque Ports Golf Club | George Duncan |
| 1921 | St. Andrews, Old Course | Jock Hutchison |
| 1922 | Royal St. George's Golf Club | Walter Hagen |
| 1923 | Royal Troon Golf Club, Old Course | Arthur Havers |
| 1924 | Royal Liverpool Golf Club | Walter Hagen |
| 1925 | Prestwick Golf Club | Jim Barnes |
| 1926 | Royal Lytham & St. Annes | Bobby Jones |
| 1927 | St. Andrews, Old Course | Bobby Jones |
| 1928 | Royal St. George's Golf Club | Walter Hagen |
| 1929 | Muirfield Links | Walter Hagen |
| 1930 | Royal Liverpool Golf Club | Bobby Jones |
| 1931 | Carnoustie Golf Links, Championship Course | Tommy Armour |
| 1932 | Prince's Golf Club | Gene Sarazen |
| 1933 | St. Andrews, Old Course | Denny Shute |
| 1934 | Royal St. George's Golf Club | Henry Cotton |
| 1935 | Muirfield Links | Alf Perry |
| 1936 | Royal Liverpool Golf Club | Alf Padgham |
| 1937 | Carnoustie Golf Links, Championship Course | Henry Cotton |
| 1938 | Royal St. George's Golf Club | Reg Whitcombe |
| 1939 | St. Andrews, Old Course | Richard Burton |
| 1946 | St. Andrews, Old Course | Sam Snead |
| 1947 | Royal Liverpool Golf Club | Fred Daly |
| 1948 | Muirfield Links | Henry Cotton |
| 1949 | Royal St. George's Golf Club | Bobby Locke |
| 1950 | Royal Troon, Old Course | Bobby Locke |
| 1951 | Royal Portrush Golf Club | Max Faulkner |
| 1952 | Royal Lytham & St. Annes | Bobby Locke |
| 1953 | Carnoustie Golf Links, Championship Course | Ben Hogan |
| 1954 | Royal Birkdale Golf Club | Peter Thomson |
| 1955 | St. Andrews, Old Course | Peter Thomson |
| 1956 | Royal Liverpool Golf Club | Peter Thomson |
| 1957 | St. Andrews, Old Course | Bobby Locke |
| 1958 | Royal Lytham & St. Annes | Peter Thomson |
| 1959 | Muirfield Links | Gary Player |
| 1960 | St. Andrews, Old Course | Kel Nagle |
| 1961 | Royal Birkdale Golf Club | Arnold Palmer |
| 1962 | Royal Troon, Old Course | Arnold Palmer |
| 1963 | Royal Lytham & St. Annes | Bob Charles |
| 1964 | St. Andrews, Old Course | Tony Lema |
| 1965 | Royal Birkdale Golf Club | Peter Thomson |
| 1966 | Muirfield Links | Jack Nicklaus |
| 1967 | Royal Liverpool Golf Club | Roberto DeVicenzo |
| 1968 | Carnoustie Golf Links, Championship Course | Gary Player |
| 1969 | Royal Lytham & St. Annes | Tony Jacklin |
| 1970 | St. Andrews, Old Course | Jack Nicklaus |
| 1971 | Royal Birkdale Golf Club | Lee Trevino |
| 1972 | Muirfield Links | Lee Trevino |
| 1973 | Royal Troon, Old Course | Tom Weiskopf |
| 1974 | Royal Lytham & St. Annes | Gary Player |
| 1975 | Carnoustie Golf Links, Championship Course | Tom Watson |
| 1976 | Royal Birkdale Golf Club | Johnny Miller |
| 1977 | The Westin Turnberry Resort, Ailsa Course | Tom Watson |
| 1978 | St. Andrews, Old Course | Jack Nicklaus |
| 1979 | Royal Lytham & St. Annes | Seve Ballesteros |
| 1980 | Muirfield Links | Tom Watson |
| 1981 | Royal St. George's Golf Club | Bill Rogers |
| 1982 | Royal Troon, Old Course | Tom Watson |
| 1983 | Royal Birkdale Golf Club | Tom Watson |
| 1984 | St. Andrews, Old Course | Seve Ballesteros |
| 1985 | Royal St. George's Golf Club | Sandy Lyle |
| 1986 | The Westin Turnberry Resort, Ailsa Course | Greg Norman |
| 1987 | Muirfield Links | Nick Faldo |
| 1988 | Royal Lytham & St. Annes | Seve Ballesteros |
| 1989 | Royal Troon, Old Course | Mark Calcavecchia |
| 1990 | St. Andrews, Old Course | Nick Faldo |
| 1991 | Royal Birkdale Golf Club | Ian Baker-Finch |
| 1992 | Muirfield Links | Nick Faldo |
| 1993 | Royal St. George's Golf Club | Greg Norman |
| 1994 | The Westin Turnberry Resort, Ailsa Course | Nick Price |
| 1995 | St. Andrews, Old Course | John Daly |

| | | |
|---|---|---|
| 1996 | Royal Lytham & St. Annes | Tom Lehman |
| 1997 | Royal Troon, Old Course | Justin Leonard |
| 1998 | Royal Birkdale Golf Club | Mark O'Meara |
| 1999 | Carnoustie Golf Links, Championship Course | Paul Lawrie |
| 2000 | St. Andrews, Old Course | Tiger Woods |
| 2001 | Royal Lytham & St. Annes | David Duval |
| 2002 | Muirfield Links | Ernie Els |
| 2003 | Royal St. George's Golf Club | Ben Curtis |
| 2004 | Royal Troon, Old Course | Todd Hamilton |
| 2005 | St. Andrews, Old Course | Tiger Woods |
| 2006 | Royal Liverpool Golf Club | Tiger Woods |
| 2007 | Carnoustie Golf Links, Championship Course | Padraig Harrington |
| 2008 | Royal Birkdale Golf Club | Padraig Harrington |
| 2009 | The Westin Turnberry Resort, Ailsa Course | Stewart Cink |
| 2010 | St. Andrews, Old Course | Louis Oosthuizen |
| 2011 | Royal St. George's Golf Club | Darren Clarke |
| 2012 | Royal Lytham & St. Annes | |
| 2013 | Muirfield Links | |
| 2014 | Royal Liverpool Golf Club | |
| 2015 | St. Andrews, Old Course | |

## PGA CHAMPIONSHIP

| | | |
|---|---|---|
| 1916 | Siwanoy Country Club | Jim Barnes |
| 1919 | Engineers Country Club | Jim Barnes |
| 1920 | Flossmoor Country Club | Jock Hutchison |
| 1921 | Inwood Country Club | Walter Hagen |
| 1922 | Oakmont Country Club | Gene Sarazen |
| 1923 | Pelham Country Club | Gene Sarazen |
| 1924 | French Lick Springs Resort, Springs Country Club Course | Walter Hagen |
| 1925 | Olympia Fields Country Club | Walter Hagen |
| 1926 | Salisbury Golf Club now Eisenhower Park, Red Course | Walter Hagen |
| 1927 | Cedar Crest Country Club now Cedar Crest Park | Walter Hagen |
| 1928 | Baltimore Country Club, East Course | Leo Diegel |
| 1929 | Hillcrest Country Club | Leo Diegel |
| 1930 | Fresh Meadow Country Club | Tommy Armour |
| 1931 | Wannamoisett Country Club | Tom Creavy |
| 1932 | Keller Golf Club | Olin Dutra |
| 1933 | Blue Mound Golf & Country Club | Gene Sarazen |
| 1934 | The Park Country Club | Paul Runyan |
| 1935 | Twin Hills Golf & Country Club | Johnny Revolta |
| 1936 | Pinehurst Resort, Course No. 2 | Denny Shute |
| 1937 | Pittsburgh Field Club | Denny Shute |
| 1938 | The Shawnee Inn & Golf Resort | Paul Runyan |
| 1939 | Pomonok Country Club | Henry Picard |
| 1940 | Hershey Country Club, West Course | Byron Nelson |
| 1941 | Cherry Hills Country Club | Vic Ghezzi |
| 1942 | Seaview Country Club | Sam Snead |
| 1944 | Manita Golf and Country Club | Bob Hamilton |
| 1945 | Moraine Country Club | Byron Nelson |
| 1946 | Portland Golf Club | Ben Hogan |
| 1947 | Plum Hollow Country Club | Jim Ferrier |
| 1948 | Norwood Hills Country Club | Ben Hogan |
| 1949 | Hermitage Country Club | Sam Snead |
| 1950 | Scioto Country Club | Chandler Harper |
| 1951 | Oakmont Country Club | Sam Snead |
| 1952 | Big Spring Country Club | Jim Turnesa |
| 1953 | Birmingham Country Club | Walter Burkemo |
| 1954 | Keller Golf Club | Chick Harbert |
| 1955 | Meadowbrook Country Club | Doug Ford |
| 1956 | Blue Hill Country Club | Jack Burke Jr. |
| 1957 | Miami Valley Country Club | Lionel Hebert |
| 1958 | Llanerch Country Club | Dow Finsterwald |
| 1959 | Minneapolis Golf Club | Bob Rosburg |
| 1960 | Firestone Country Club, South Course | Jay Hebert |
| 1961 | Olympia Fields Country Club | Jerry Barber |
| 1962 | Aronimink Golf Club | Gary Player |
| 1963 | Dallas Athletic Club, Blue Course | Jack Nicklaus |
| 1964 | Columbus Country Club | Bobby Nichols |
| 1965 | Laurel Valley Golf Club | Dave Marr |
| 1966 | Firestone Country Club, South Course | Al Geiberger |
| 1967 | Columbine Country Club | Don January |
| 1968 | Pecan Valley Golf Club | Julius Boros |
| 1969 | NCR Country Club, South Course | Raymond Floyd |
| 1970 | Southern Hills Country Club | Dave Stockton |
| 1971 | PGA National Golf Club now BallenIsles Country Club | Jack Nicklaus |
| 1972 | Oakland Hills Country Club, South Course | Gary Player |
| 1973 | Canterbury Golf Club | Jack Nicklaus |
| 1974 | Tanglewood Park, Championship Course | Lee Trevino |
| 1975 | Firestone Country Club, South Course | Jack Nicklaus |
| 1976 | Congressional Country Club, Blue Course | Dave Stockton |
| 1977 | Pebble Beach Golf Links | Lanny Wadkins Jr. |
| 1978 | Oakmont Country Club | John Mahaffey |
| 1979 | Oakland Hills Country Club, South Course | David Graham |
| 1980 | Oak Hill Country Club, East Course | Jack Nicklaus |
| 1981 | Atlanta Athletic Club, Highlands Course | Larry Nelson |
| 1982 | Southern Hills Country Club | Raymond Floyd |
| 1983 | Riviera Country Club | Hal Sutton |
| 1984 | Shoal Creek Golf and Country Club | Lee Trevino |
| 1985 | Cherry Hills Country Club | Hubert Green |
| 1986 | Inverness Club | Bob Tway |
| 1987 | PGA National Resort & Spa | Larry Nelson |
| 1988 | Oak Tree Golf Club | Jeff Sluman |
| 1989 | Kemper Lakes Golf Club | Payne Stewart |
| 1990 | Shoal Creek Golf and Country Club | Wayne Grady |
| 1991 | Crooked Stick Golf Club | John Daly |
| 1992 | Bellerive Country Club | Nick Price |
| 1993 | Inverness Club | Paul Azinger |
| 1994 | Southern Hills Country Club | Nick Price |
| 1995 | Riviera Country Club | Steve Elkington |
| 1996 | Valhalla Golf Club | Mark Brooks |
| 1997 | Winged Foot Golf Club, West Course | Davis Love III |
| 1998 | Sahalee Country Club | Vijay Singh |
| 1999 | Medinah Country Club, No. 3 Course | Tiger Woods |
| 2000 | Valhalla Golf Club | Tiger Woods |
| 2001 | Atlanta Athletic Club, Highlands Course | David Toms |
| 2002 | Hazeltine National Golf Club | Rich Beem |
| 2003 | Oak Hill Country Club, East Course | Shaun Micheel |
| 2004 | Whistling Straits, Straits Course | Vijay Singh |
| 2005 | Baltusrol Golf Club, Lower Course | Phil Mickelson |
| 2006 | Medinah Country Club, No. 3 Course | Tiger Woods |
| 2007 | Southern Hills Country Club | Tiger Woods |
| 2008 | Oakland Hills Country Club, South Course | Padraig Harrington |
| 2009 | Hazeltine National Golf Club | Yong-Eun Yang |
| 2010 | Whistling Straits, Straits Course | Martin Kaymer |
| 2011 | Atlanta Athletic Club, Highlands Course | Keegan Bradley |
| 2012 | Kiawah Island Resort, Ocean Course | |
| 2013 | Oak Hill Country Club, East Course | |
| 2014 | Valhalla Golf Club | |
| 2015 | Whistling Straits, Straits Course | |
| 2016 | Baltusrol Golf Club, Lower Course | |
| 2017 | Quail Hollow Club | |
| 2018 | Bellerive Country Club | |

# Hole ➊

The first hole on any golf course, being the genesis of your round, sets the tone early for exactly what kind of day lies ahead. A birdie on No. 1 and you're cruising; a bogey, and you're scrambling early.

Golf course architects understand this, and many make the first a trifle more forgiving than the following 17. No. 1 is not generally one of the more difficult holes on a golf course, but designers tend to make it one of the more scenic and memorable, if the land allows.

Whether a pretty hole, or a gentle start to your round, the first hole is without question one of the most important on any course.

**LEFT** *The first hole at The Greenbrier, White Sulphur Springs, West Virginia, USA.*

**Course:** Royal Lytham & St. Annes

**Location:** St. Annes-on-Sea, Lancashire, England

**Hole:** No. 1

**Length:** 206 yards

**Par:** 3

**Designer:** George Lowe, Harry S. Colt

**Course Comment:** Right from the beginning, Royal Lytham — still in the British Open Championship rotation — shows itself as golf's quirkiest major championship test, as it is the only one to begin with a par 3. It also has back-to-back par 5s on Nos. 6–7.

# No. ❶ ROYAL LYTHAM & ST. ANNES

One of three par 3s on Royal Lytham and St. Annes, this is no gentle introduction to a round, but rather a warning of what lies ahead. In other words, bunkers — and lots of them. Of Royal Lytham's 197 bunkers, seven of the more severe are found on No. 1 (four on the left, three on the right). Tony Jacklin once called it "a terrible strain" for the game's top players to begin with such a short, diabolical test.

The tee shot must be played through an avenue of trees, with the infamous railway line marking out of bounds down the right side and virtually no bail-out area. If the green isn't hit, trouble no doubt awaits.

As to the adverse effect this opening hole can have on a player's major championship hopes, just ask Grace Park, who was three over on it during the last two rounds of the 2003 Women's British Open. Poor Park bogeyed No. 1 on Saturday, then took double bogey to begin the final round. Sunday's final 17 holes she managed just fine, with four birdies and 13 pars, but she wound up third, two shots shy of champion Annika Sorenstam — the two shots she gave up on No. 1.

A terrible strain indeed. **KA**

## No. ❶ GRAND CYPRESS RESORT

**Course:** Grand Cypress Resort

**Location:** Orlando, Florida, USA

**Hole:** No. 1

**Length:** 362 yards

**Par:** 4

**Designer:** Jack Nicklaus

**Course Comment:** The Grand Cypress Academy of Golf has a permanent teaching facility. They combine innovative computer technology and biomechanics with expert instruction.

Jack Nicklaus designed this course in tribute to the historic St. Andrews in Scotland. It's a links-style design which features pot bunkers and double greens and is packed with undulation.

No. 1 isn't the toughest hole on the course but it's one you are not likely to forget. It won't take you long to discover that Nicklaus has successfully brought St. Andrews to the United States — and not as a computer game. You can actually play this course.

Standing on the first tee, you look out over an enormous fairway. It's so big that it's shared with golfers finishing their round on No. 18 — just like at St. Andrews. The fairway is anywhere between 150 and 200 yards wide with out-of-bounds on the right. There is a burn directly in front of the green — just like at St. Andrews. The green, like the fairway, is large enough to include two holes. Both No. 1 and No. 17 share this massive putting surface — just like at St. Andrews.

The playing conditions on the New Course are typical of the great resort courses in Florida. Perfect. And the challenge that lies ahead of you can't be matched — except at St. Andrews. **TJ**

## No. ❶ ROYAL BELFAST

**Course:** Royal Belfast

**Location:** Belfast, Northern Ireland

**Hole:** No. 1

**Length:** 415 yards

**Par:** 4

**Designer:** Harry S. Colt

**Course Comment:** Founded on Nov. 9 1881, Royal Belfast Golf Club is the oldest club in Ireland and its formation proved to be the inspiration for the growth of the game there.

The Royal Belfast Golf Club is one of only four golf clubs in Ireland that have been honored with the title "Royal," having been visited in 1885 by the Prince of Wales who became the club's first patron.

Like all great golf courses, your round begins in grand style with an inspiring and testing opening hole. There is no easing into a round at Royal Belfast. Your best is required from the first tee on.

And don't forget to pause and reflect. There is a lot of history on this golf course. A lot of people have walked these steps before.

The club professional considers the first hole to be one of the best opening holes in Irish golf — it measures 415 yards from the back tee and is a slight dogleg left. There are bunkers on the inside left at the turn of the dogleg and three more bunkers guard the green.

The fairway rises to the green, which is probably the most difficult on the course. A great start to a great and classic round of Irish golf.

There are three sets of tees, but there is not much difference in length. The shorter tees are only eight yards ahead. The hole has a stroke index of seven. **TJ**

# No. ❶ PGA CATALUNYA (STADIUM COURSE)

**Course:** PGA Catalunya (Stadium Course)

**Location:** Girona, Spain

**Hole:** No. 1

**Length:** 396 yards

**Par:** 4

**Designer:** Neil Coles and Angel Gallardo

**Course Comment:** The PGA Catalunya Stadium Course opened at the end of 1998, and had hosted the Sarazen World Open in 1999 and the Spanish Open in 2000. This made the Stadium the only course to host two European Tour events within ten months of opening.

OPPOSITE  *The first hole at PGA Catalunya.*

When the European Tour started planning the PGA Catalunya Stadium Course before 1990, its goal was to have its own Players Championship Course much like the American PGA Tour has TPC at Sawgrass in Ponte Vedra Beach, Florida. They are even both called the Stadium Course.

What the European Tour lacked in naming originality, it certainly made up for in creating one of the great courses of Europe and among the best of a fine lot in Spain. It took a decade of planning, but they hit the mark.

No. 1 at the Stadium Course is an elevated tee, which gives an outstanding view to a fairway surrounded by a forest of majestic trees. It bends to a dogleg left, and every bit of the slight left-hand turn is stunning.

The play off the tee may just be a 3-wood because there is water on the left some 256 yards away. The safer play is the right side of the fairway, but this creates a longer shot into the green. You can avoid the water this way, but if you are feeling brave and want to cut the corner, bring the water into play and run your ball to its edge.

Then, of course, comes the green. Its elevation changes are rampant, and it truly is an indicator of what waits on the rest of the course. The Stadium's putting surfaces are famous for their slopes and tough reads. **JB**

# No. ❶ YALE GOLF COURSE

**Course:** Yale Golf Course

**Location:** New Haven, Connecticut, USA

**Hole:** No. 1

**Length:** 410 yards

**Par:** 4

**Designer:** Charles Blair Macdonald

**Course Comment:** How did this piece of property become a golf course? In 1924, Mrs. Ray Tompkins wanted something to be built in honor of her husband, so she gave away 700 acres of swamp and woodland on which Yale built the golf course. What an honor.

The first hole (named "Eli") at Yale is a 410-yard par 4 and is the fifth handicap on the course. So like anything else at Yale, it's a tough exam of your skills.

The first views off the tee box are nothing if not intimidating. You won't find many opening tee shots with so much at stake. The tee overlooks Griest Pond and some 170 yards from the back tee you will find the fairway — hopefully, you will find the fairway.

A big drive is required to carry the water and the steep portion of the fairway. You also need a good drive to help avoid a blind second shot. There is some real estate before the fairway, but there also is a nice slope back toward the water.

Several large trees line both sides of the fairway. These timbers can obstruct any shot to a difficult two-tiered green. There is also a fairway bunker along the left side about 160 yards from the green. The bottom of the pin is hidden so your second shot is deceptively long.

The extra large green has a slope that divides the green left into a punchbowl and right into a higher plateau. There are two larger bunkers on the right side of the green and one bunker near the left front. **TJ**

**Course:** Crystal Downs Country Club

**Location:** Frankfort, Michigan, USA

**Hole:** No. 1

**Length:** 460 yards

**Par:** 4

**Designer:** Alister MacKenzie, Perry Maxwell

**Course Comment:** It's the debut hole of 18 that were designed for the thinking player. Tree-lined, hilly fairways characterize it from start to finish. The first hole is a stern reminder of what lies ahead, but its striking views make up for the alarming first tee shot.

## No. ❶ CRYSTAL DOWNS COUNTRY CLUB

So much for a nice, gradual start. The first hole at Crystal Downs is anything but. On a links course situated on a bluff flanked by Lake Michigan and Crystal Lake, this hole's dramatic pitch makes for an impressive taste of Midwestern golf at its scenic best.

The tee box is elevated 60 feet above the fairway, and its panorama is legendary — since 1929, golfers have gazed out at the thick, majestic Michigan woods from the first hole at Crystal Downs.

The wind sweeping off Lake Michigan lends an exotic taste — making this hole much more Scottish in flavor and delightfully more difficult to play than some of the finest on inland courses in the Great Lakes state.

MacKenzie put a devilish twist on this brilliantly conceived hole, with its height and tricky bunker placement, to make sure that no serious golfer would ever walk away bored. More than a good share walk away frustrated but always challenged, so the grandfather of golf architecture achieved his aim with this conceptualization. The green is benched into a dune and protected by two bunkers, putting a frightening finish on a daunting hole.

Crystal Downs is a masterpiece, and No. 1 is its signature. **KLL**

**Course:** Long Cove Club

**Location:** Hilton Head Island, South Carolina, USA

**Hole:** No. 1

**Length:** 423 yards

**Par:** 4

**Designer:** Pete Dye

**Course Comment:** PGA Tour players in town for the MCI Heritage each April often play practice rounds at Long Cove to prepare them for tournament host Harbour Town Golf Links — another Dye design that places a premium on accuracy and shotmaking off the tee.

## No. ❶ LONG COVE CLUB

Although Harbour Town comes first to mind when people think of Hilton Head golf, most serious players consider Long Cove — a private club located only a few miles away — as the island's best overall test. It is a shotmaker's course that demands tee shots that are both lengthy and strategic, especially on the par 4s and 5s, and water comes into play on 12 of 18 holes.

Dye devilishly introduces golfers to these concepts right from the beginning, as all of Long Cove's elements are readily evident on No. 1.

A long dogleg right with a waste bunker and lagoon running the length of the right side, Dye's opening hole delivers a delicious risk-reward scenario on the first drive of the day. There's plenty of room left, but the shortest route to the green and best approach angle is from the right side; important because the green slopes from left to right toward the water.

Long Cove played host to the U.S. Mid-Amateur Championship in 1991 and the U.S. Women's Mid-Amateur Championship in 2003. Because of the skills demanded by No. 1, players in both match play events who were not ready out of the gate found themselves quickly down a hole. **KA**

**Course:** Desert Highlands Golf Club

**Location:** Scottsdale, Arizona, USA

**Hole:** No. 1

**Length:** 356 yards

**Par:** 4

**Designer:** Jack Nicklaus

**Course Comment:** In addition to having the "Golden Bear" as its architect, Desert Highlands' claim to fame is playing host to the original Skins Game in 1983 where Nicklaus, Arnold Palmer, Gary Player, and Tom Watson dueled in the desert sun. The made-for-TV event garnered even more attention when Watson accused Player of improving his lie.

## No. ❶ DESERT HIGHLANDS GOLF CLUB

Desert Highlands, a juxtaposition of grass and sand — good and evil — gets off to a stunning start with a demanding 356-yard par 4. From a granite grotto that shelters the first tee, players are immediately struck by the valley's breathtaking desert view.

It doesn't take long, however, for the fear to set in.

From the Nicklaus tee, players must carry their opening drive 200 yards over an area of desert and rocks to a fairway 125 feet below. A long iron might be in order from the tee as the fairway narrows to 25 yards in the landing zone where bunkers litter the right side. A misfire in either direction will likely result in an unplayable lie as unfriendly desert terrain lines both sides of the fairway. While the first green appears ripe for the taking with no bunkers or water in sight, beware of selecting too much club. Directly beyond the putting surface is a 20-foot drop-off that will undoubtedly lead to a penalty stroke.

After finding the dance floor, players must then negotiate a severely undulating green. Because tricky greens can be found throughout this desert track, players may want to spend time on the club's 18-hole putting course, designed by Gary Panks in 1986, before heading to the first tee. **BB**

**Course:** Royal Melbourne Golf Club (East Course)

**Location:** Black Rock, Victoria, Australia

**Hole:** No. 1

**Length:** 333 yards

**Par:** 4

**Designer:** Alex Russell

**Course Comment:** Architect Alex Russell built the fabled Royal Melbourne West Course to the specifications of the great designer Alister MacKenzie and was then asked to construct the adjoining East layout, which opened in 1932. It was not surprising, then, that the East incorporates so many of MacKenzie's features as they relate to use of the undulating, Sand Belt terrain, the placing of the bunkers and the incorporation of large, sloping greens. And the first hole on that layout is a classic starter.

The opening drive on this short yet treacherous hole does not have to be long, but it must be straight. Try and bite off too much to the right of the dogleg, and you will likely find the mammoth fairway bunker protecting that flank. Pull your tee shot left, and your ball will surely roll down a steep hill into deep rough.

Either way is trouble, and it makes sense to take your most accurate club out of the bag for the drive here. But simply hitting the fairway on No. 1 does not in any way ensure a four, for there is also the matter of the approach. The club needed is usually a wedge, and it must be hit precisely in order to hold a small, slick green guarded by three bunkers.

Yes, Royal Melbourne members say it is easy to make a four on this hole. But, they caution, it is just as possible to post a six, and get your round off to a horrid start. **JS**

RIGHT *Paul Casey of England plays his second shot on the first hole at Royal Melbourne, January 2003.*

OPPOSITE *Craig Parry of Australia tees off on the first hole at Royal Melbourne, December 1998.*

**Course:** The Greenbrier (Old White Course)

**Location:** White Sulphur Springs, West Virginia, USA

**Hole:** No. 1

**Length:** 449 yards

**Par:** 4

**Designer:** Charles Blair Macdonald

**Course Comment:** In 1938, the noted golf course architect Robert Trent Jones chose this hole for the dream 18-hole course he put together for *Town & Country* magazine.

OPPOSITE *The first hole at The Greenbrier.*

## No. ❶ THE GREENBRIER (OLD WHITE COURSE)

The opening hole at the Old White Course is most likely the strongest on the course. Not only did Robert Trent Jones select this 449-yard par 4 as the first hole in his "Dream 18," but also numerous golf enthusiasts have called this hole a masterpiece of first holes.

The hole begins in front of the clubhouse verandah, which makes it a very intimidating shot by itself, but what makes it more difficult is the 100-plus Greenbrier Resort guests watching to see how far and well you hit it. This par-4 demands a straight tee shot and there is no room for error on this rather long test. The hole plays downhill to a fairway which bends directly through two tall stands of trees.

The approach shot most likely will be a long to mid-iron and you must hit an accurate second shot to give yourself a chance at a par. The green, which is framed with bunkers on three sides (left, right, and the middle), is fairly large for an older course. The breaks and speed on this hole are very tricky, no matter where the cup is, and every putt must be judged with pinpoint accuracy.

This is a classic among golf's opening holes and it was a favorite of The Greenbrier's late golf professional, Sam Snead. **GE**

**Course:** Canterbury Golf Club

**Location:** Beachwood, Ohio, USA

**Hole:** No. 1

**Length:** 432 yards

**Par:** 4

**Designer:** Herbert Strong

**Course Comment:** Canterbury is known as a tough place to play for the ladies. It's a par 72 for the men and par 75 for the women. But both genders better bring their A games for this test of golf.

## No. ❶ CANTERBURY GOLF CLUB

Canterbury, located just outside of Cleveland, has a few famous finishing holes, including No. 16 and No. 18. But the toughest hole on the golf course is No. 1.

Sure it's not fair. But who ever said golf was fair? You want to warm up a bit before facing the greatest challenge on the golf course. But Canterbury is one of those courses that doesn't follow the rules. That's what makes it special.

Many of the greens, including the first, are sloped from back to front, so keep your approach shot in front of the hole. It's not too difficult to putt from the back and find yourself off the green. Built in 1992, Canterbury was named one of Ohio's top 25 golf courses by the Ohio Golf Guide. And, No. 1 is a tough way to begin a day on such a splendid course.

The members like to say that no matter how many times you play Canterbury, the course always offers a challenge. Nothing comes easy and each time out is another fight with the scorecard. The course is considered fair and always in excellent condition. It has withstood the test of time. **TJ**

**Course:** Muirfield Links

**Location:** Muirfield, Gullane, Scotland

**Hole:** No. 1

**Length:** 447 yards

**Par:** 4

**Designer:** Old Tom Morris, Harry S. Colt, Tom Simpson

**Course Comment:** Unlike the country clubs of the United States, it's rare for a private club in the U.K. to be closed altogether to visitors, even those that entertain the British Open. There are eight courses on the active Open rotation and as long as you can afford the green fees, you can usually play where legends have walked.

## No. ❶ MUIRFIELD LINKS

There is something magical about standing on the first tee of a golf course that helped shape the game we love. This course wasn't designed by Robert Trent Jones or Jack Nicklaus or Arnold Palmer. This magical place was first laid out in 1744 and when you walk on to that first tee it's difficult to imagine what it was like standing on this spot so long ago.

But every golfer does try to imagine just that. For a brief moment, we take a step back in time and are overcome by the moment at hand: "How many golfers have stood where I now stand?"

This course wasn't constructed using computer software, blueprints, or earth-moving bulldozers. These 18 holes are handmade and the history is simply overwhelming.

There are more famous holes at Muirfield, but none will ever top feeling that wind in your face and grass under your spikes on that first tee. Forget the old movie cliché, "you had me at hello." For these great courses, it's "you had me at No. 1."

The first hole at the famed Muirfield is 447 yards from the tips and is a rather difficult par 4. Considering this is your first swing of the day, this hole isn't easy. It's a dogleg right and you'll need at least a 250-yard rip to reach the break. But you don't need to hit it that far to reach the fairway.

At the 223-yard mark there is a large bunker on the left side of the fairway. Try and avoid that. There are more bunkers further down the fairway to the left and one almost in the middle just before the green. **TJ**

**Course:** Winged Foot Golf Club (West Course)

**Location:** Mamaroneck, New York, USA

**Hole:** No. 1

**Length:** 446 yards

**Par:** 4

**Designer:** A.W. Tillinghast

**Course Comment:** The West Course, which has undergone revisions by George and Tom Fazio, will host its fifth U.S. Open in 2006.

## No. ❶ WINGED FOOT GOLF CLUB (WEST COURSE)

A dramatic opener on a dramatic golf course. And a difficult (the third toughest hole) opener on a difficult golf course. Some even call this the toughest opening hole in the world. Most would be thrilled with a par — or even a bogey at Winged Foot's famed No. 1.

There isn't a hill to be found on the fairway but the green is where your trouble starts. The green is so tough that Jack Nicklaus putted off it in the 1974 U.S. Open. Not easy to do — unless you are at No. 1 at Winged Foot.

Mr. Tillinghast didn't have the greatest piece of property to work with — which makes what he accomplished even more remarkable. The great history of this golf course will always be on your mind as you make your way from the first tee to the 18th green. Claude Harmon holds the course record on both the East and West courses with a pair of 61s. What's even more amazing about Harmon's 61 on the West Course is that his concentration wasn't totally on playing golf. He was listening to the World Series on the radio while making his way around the links.

Like the first hole, the entire course is long and difficult. But there is plenty of variety — and memorable moments — starting with No. 1. **TJ**

---

**Course:** Pine Valley Golf Club

**Location:** Pine Valley, New Jersey, USA

**Hole:** No. 1

**Length:** 427 yards

**Par:** 4

**Designer:** George Crump

**Course Comment:** Pine Valley Golf Club has the highest slope (153) and course ratings (74.1) for men in the continental United States. So New Jersey may be home to Bruce Springsteen, but this course is "the boss" when it comes to difficulty.

## No. ❶ PINE VALLEY GOLF CLUB

Nothing is easy at Pine Valley. And that goes for No. 1. The first challenge at Pine Valley is the third toughest hole on the course. In fact, three of the toughest five holes are among the first seven. So you better be ready to go by the time you slam the trunk.

At 427 yards from the back tees, No. 1 has plenty of length. It's a dogleg right, which means you better have your target-golf swing on-line. If you miss the corner, give yourself another stroke in order to recover.

The trouble begins — but doesn't end — with your approach shot to the green. And at 8,300 square feet, what a green it is. The key here is not to miss the target. Yes, it's a big bull's-eye, but be a little off and you're in big trouble. The fairway rolls right into a "peninsula"-style green with dramatic — and costly — drop-offs on all three sides.

The challenge here is simple. Take a lesser club, play it safe and land it safely at the front of the mammoth green and then two-putt. Or go for the back and risk falling off the green. Certainly, a fun problem to have right off the bat.

Built in 1918, this world-renowned private course is No. 1 on *Golf Magazine*'s "Top 100 Courses in the U.S." **TJ**

**Course:** St. Andrews (Old Course)

**Location:** St. Andrews, Scotland

**Hole:** No. 1

**Length:** 370 yards

**Par:** 4

**Designer:** Old Tom Morris

**Course Comment:** The Balgove course at St. Andrews has nine holes and is essentially for children. During the school holidays an adult may play the Balgove only if accompanied by a child!

BELOW *The first hole at St. Andrews.*

OPPOSITE *Colin Montgomery of Scotland plays his second shot on the first hole at St. Andrews, October 2000.*

# No. ❶ ST. ANDREWS (OLD COURSE)

If you don't have chills standing on the first tee of the most famous golf course in all the world, then you must not have a pulse. For any golf enthusiast, historian or fan, playing this hole is a dream come true, and what you end up putting down on the scorecard is secondary to the memory of the moment. Forget Augusta. Forget Pebble Beach. This is golf's eternal home. Forever sacred. Forever magical.

After you pick your jaw off the grass, it's time to pick a club out of the bag. Pull out the driver and let her ride. The fairway on the first hole is pretty generous. But you do want to lean a little left of center to avoid the out of bounds on the right.

While you stand over your ball in the middle of the fairway, pause for a moment and think of all the players who have stood on this spot. Then avoid the burn which is hard against the front of the green. Club selection will be a medium to long iron. And don't forget to take the wind into account. Many a fine golfer has left his or her second shot short of the green and even short of the Swilcan Burn.

Don't worry about three-putting. You are on the first green of the famous Old Course. Take your time and enjoy the moment. **TJ**

## No. ❶   SALEM COUNTRY CLUB

**Course:** Salem Country Club

**Location:** Peabody, Massachusetts, USA

**Hole:** No. 1

**Length:** 408 yards

**Par:** 4

**Designer:** Donald Ross

**Course Comment:** Donald Ross was a busy man in 1925 when he built Salem Country Club. From 1919 to 1925, five of the seven National Opens were contested on Ross courses. Yet despite his hectic schedule, Ross did not rush through Salem Country Club. His great care and attention to detail are still quite evident today.

With 350 acres of rolling New England land on which to build a course, Donald Ross knew he could create something special. A master of routing a course and picking natural green sites, Salem was a perfect project for Ross. And he created something close to perfect. It all begins at No. 1.

Standing on the elevated tee on the first hole at Salem Country Club is a memory one won't soon forget. The challenge of the hole is laid out in front of you in a clear and stunning way. But from that same spot you also see why the entire course is special. This is not only a snapshot for the first hole, but one for the entire golf course.

With four sets of tees ranging from 327 yards to 408 yards, the first hole is the seventh most difficult on the course according to the scorecard. It is considered by many as one of the best first holes in the United States.

A good solid drive right down the middle of the fairways doesn't mean your work is finished. You will need to contend with two bunkers cut into an upslope about 100 yards in front of the green. If you can land it in between those bunkers, you should get a nice roll onto the green. Don't worry about sand traps. There are none.

Knock it in the hole and take your birdie. Miss the putt and be happy with a two-putt par. And who said golf had to be difficult? **TJ**

## No. ❶   ARONIMINK GOLF CLUB

**Course:** Aronimink Golf Club

**Location:** Newtown Square, Pennsylvania, USA

**Hole:** No. 1

**Length:** 425 yards

**Par:** 4

**Designer:** Donald Ross

**Course Comment:** Classic Ross starting hole offers ample room to drive the ball but players will need to be careful approaching the two-tiered green. Anything short runs the risk of backing off the putting surface and down a large hill. Long, and players face a slippery downhill.

Just a few paces from the tee, a plaque greets players with a telling quote from Donald Ross: "I intended to make this my masterpiece, but not until today did I realize that I built better than I knew."

The quote was taken from a speech Ross gave in 1948, 20 years after completing the layout and just months before his death. Ross, of course, was referring to Aronimink's entire 6,928-yard rolling layout; the par 4 first, however, is simply a perfectly placed microcosm of the masterpiece at large.

Even by today's prodigious standards Aronimink's opening hole can be a haul at 425 yards. In signature Ross style, the Scotsman gives players plenty of room from the tee, with only a single fairway bunker some 80 yards from the green. Instead, Ross defends par around the putting surface, with greenside bunkering, collection areas, and crowned putting surfaces.

The hole plays uphill and requires a mid- to long-iron approach to a two-tiered green that feeds sharply to the left. At the 2003 Senior PGA Championship, the club's first major championship since the 1962 PGA Championship, the hole played well over par (4.24 average). **RH**

**Course:** Prestwick Golf Club (Old Course)

**Location:** Prestwick, Ayrshire, Scotland

**Hole:** No. 1

**Length:** 346 yards

**Par:** 4

**Designer:** Old Tom Morris

**Course Comment:** Prestwick is the birthplace of the British Open, making No. 1 at the Old Course the first hole ever played in Open Championship history.

# No. ❶ PRESTWICK GOLF CLUB
## (OLD COURSE)

Twenty-four British Opens have been played at Prestwick, first when it was a 12-hole layout in 1860, and then after it was expanded to 18 holes in 1883. The shortish first hole has been in its original form for more than 140 years, since its design by Old Tom Morris — who won the British Open four times on the course he conceived.

The first prize for the British Open in Old Tom's day was a red Morocco leather belt worth £25. When Old Tom had worn the belt four times, his son Young Tom Morris won the prized belt three consecutive times. All at Prestwick, and all begun at the historic — and sometimes noisy — first hole. No. 1 is an indicator of the way much of the course appears — kind of an unkempt look that not so much seems like a course built from the land, but one that is actually born from it. It is a course today that remains true to its roots, and the first hole is a prime example.

Railroad tracks run the entire right side of the hole, so a push or a slice might end up on a railway car to some hither land. Like almost all of the fairways at Prestwick, the first is very narrow, and a pull or hook shot ends up in the heather and gorse that make a ball often unfindable, let alone unplayable. Because the hole is relatively short and so dangerously narrow,

a fairway wood off the tee is often the wise play.

With a decent drive, the approach shot is nothing more than a wedge, but it is no bargain. There is a large bunker protecting the front of the green, heather and gorse behind the green, the railroad tracks to the right, and more heather and gorse to the left. An unusual distraction might be the roar of a train just as you are lining up a putt, which makes the undulating green even more difficult to negotiate.

If two pure shots are played, it is possible to complete this hole on par, but that could be said of any hole. The difference with No. 1 at the Old Course at Prestwick is the margin for error. It is so small that one mistake results in a bogey . . . at least. **JB**

**Course:** Royal St. George's Golf Club

**Location:** Sandwich, Kent, England

**Hole:** No. 1

**Length:** 441 yards

**Par:** 4

**Designer:** Laidlaw Purves, Alister MacKenzie, J.J.F. Pennink

**Course Comment:** To the locals, Royal St. George's is just called "Sandwich" because of the neighboring small town by that name. So when you pull up in your car, tell your buddy how much you're looking forward to a Sandwich.

OPPOSITE *Nick Price of Zimbabwe tees off on the first hole at Royal St. George's, July 2003.*

# No. ❶  ROYAL ST. GEORGE'S GOLF CLUB

Selected by the *World Atlas of Golf* as the perfect opening hole in golf, No. 1 at Royal St. George's Golf Club plays between 390 and 441 yards (championship tees) and is the fifth hardest hole on the golf course. There are many more famous holes on the course, including No. 4, No. 14 and No. 15, but this hole rates among the best in all of England.

From the back tees, a 250-yard drive sets you up very well for your second shot. You don't have to be that long off the tee in order to par this hole, but you will face a second shot over 175 yards.

There are dangers along the way. Almost the entire right side has out-of-bounds stakes, but a fairly straight hitter won't have to worry about them. Everyone will have to worry about the bunker in the middle of the fairway about 73 yards from the flag and/or the three bunkers near the green, including one large one directly in front.

The green is big but can be tricky.

The sandhills on the front nine are the largest and trickiest of any British Open course while the fairways are known to be bouncy, giving you plenty of uneven lies and unpredictable bounces. **TJ**

**Course:** Kennemer Golf & Country Club

**Location:** Zandvoort, Holland

**Hole:** No. 1

**Length:** 452 yards

**Par:** 4

**Designer:** Harry S. Colt

**Course Comment:** Golf isn't the only sport for which Zandvoort is noted. The beachside resort town was also the longtime host of the Dutch Grand Prix Formula One race, and Formula Three races are still held there today.

# No. ❶  KENNEMER GOLF & COUNTRY CLUB

This traditional Dutch links course set along the sand dunes beside the North Sea is less than 20 miles west of Amsterdam and was designed by legendary Englishman Harry Shapland Colt. The Colt layout opened in 1928 (the original club was founded in 1910) and is one of the country's finest examples of old-style architecture.

Kennemer's opening hole is long, but fair. Dunes on both sides of the fairway slope toward the middle, offering the chance for a good kick or two off the drive and an excellent opportunity to reach the green in two. The second shot, however, is where you must be careful.

Despite a putting surface that is relatively large and flat, there is still plenty of danger because the entire back and sides of the green are surrounded by thick gorse bushes. Miss the target, and you're likely to lose your golf ball — and at least one early shot off your score. Because of Kennemer's seaside location, correctly judging the ocean winds and selecting the right club are imperative.

Kennemer has served many times as host course for the Ladies Dutch Open, a tournament on the Ladies European Tour. **KA**

# No. ❶ MACHRIHANISH

**Course:** Machrihanish

**Location:** Campbelltown, Argyll, Scotland

**Hole:** No. 1

**Length:** 428 yards

**Par:** 4

**Designer:** Old Tom Morris

**Course Comment:** The course's name is derived from the Scottish term Machair-an-lomain — "field of the shinty." Shinty was a golf precursor played with large clubs curved at one end, similar to the hockey sticks of today. Shinty matches, some with more than 1,000 spectators, formerly took place on the land now occupied by Machrihanish's first hole.

ABOVE *Mrs Cochran (right) and Mrs Quill (left) playing at Machrihanish, June 1927.*

Considered by many to be the finest first hole — and, certainly, the finest opening tee shot — in the world, Machrihanish No. 1 requires golfers to be warmed up and mentally prepared right off the bat. Beach walkers should be prepared as well, as a nearby sign informs them: "Danger, first tee above, please move farther along the beach."

The hole has been given the moniker "Battery," and for obvious reasons. The tee shot must be struck from a narrow patch of land that's nearly been swallowed up by the sea, and the lone chance one has of reaching the green in two is to courageously take the drive over Machrihanish Bay — not an opening salvo for the faint of heart. If all goes well, the ball will find the sloping fairway that runs adjacent to the ocean's edge. Thankfully, the beach is considered a lateral water hazard, and ending up there is no worse than being in one of the right bunkers.

It is a fitting beginning to a secluded, spectacular layout that owes part of its magnetism to its enigmatic isolation at the southwestern corner of the Mull of Kintyre. Machrihanish isn't easy to reach — it's three hours from Glasgow by car — but well worth the drive. The same, of course, could be said for the opening hole alone. **KA**

**Course:** Palmares

**Location:** The Algarve, Portugal

**Hole:** No. 1

**Length:** 457 yards

**Par:** 4

**Designer:** Frank Pennink

**Course Comment:** This is a course that offers some of the best views in all of Portugal, with scenic vistas of both the sea and the Monchique Hills in the distance.

# No. ❶ **PALMARES**

At 457 yards from the back blocks, Palmares' opening hole may seem long. Don't let the yardage fool you. Length is not as big a factor on this hole as it first appears. The first plays from a high tee to a fairway that doglegs to the right. The trick is to get the line of play right off the tee, so it pays to perhaps walk this hole first before you play it.

Getting the line right off the tee is paramount, because the tee shot has to contend with tall pines that come into play. You won't be able to see the green from the tee, since it is tucked away out of view. Get the tee shot right though, and you will be surprised at how little club you have to play for your second considering the length of the hole. Don't worry if you hit a bad tee shot. Stop for a few seconds and enjoy the view down to the holes at the low end of the course with the sea beyond. There is none finer in all of Portugal. **AT**

**Course:** Royal Liverpool (Hoylake)

**Location:** Hoylake, Merseyside, England

**Hole:** No. 1

**Length:** 427 yards

**Par:** 4

**Designer:** Robert Chambers, George Morris

**Course Comment:** History was made at Royal Liverpool (no, not the Beatles) when rules outlining the status of amateur players were first drawn up. So if you are not on one of the professional tours, don't take any prize money or you might lose your amateur eligibility.

# No. ❶   ROYAL LIVERPOOL (HOYLAKE)

The good news about the first hole at Royal Liverpool is it's the only green on the golf course without bunkers surrounding it. The bad news is trying to get to the green in the first place.

Welcome to Hoylake. Hopefully, you took your time warming up on the practice green because you better be ready when you step to the first tee.

The first hole at Hoylake is a sharp dogleg to the right around out-of-bounds on the inside of the fairway. Bring your driver and your confidence to the tee with you because the key to the hole is getting the ball as close to the corner as possible.

Now comes the hard part. From the corner you have about 190 yards to that bunkerless green. Of course, the big hitters can reduce that to 160 yards if they're feeling lucky. Remember, though, out-of-bounds sticks await you down the entire right side of the fairway.

Named "The Course," the opening hole is the fifth hardest at Hoylake according to the scorecard. Located 10 miles southwest of Liverpool on the Wirral Peninsula, Royal Liverpool will host the British Open in 2006. **TJ**

RIGHT *Thomas Bjorn of Denmark plays his second shot on the first hole at Royal Liverpool, February 2003.*

OPPOSITE *A picture of the first international golf match in the world between England and Scotland at Royal Liverpool, which hangs in the clubhouse.*

FIRST INTERNATIONAL GOLF MATCH ENGLAND v. SCOTLAND - HOYLAKE 1902

# No. ❶ VILA SOL

**Course:** Vila Sol

**Location:** The Algarve, Portugal

**Hole:** No. 1

**Length:** 417 yards

**Par:** 4

**Designer:** Donald Steel

**Course Comment:** The first is the start of the most brutal stretch of opening holes in all of Portugal. Get through these and you have a chance to play well.

If there is a harder opening hole in Portugal than the first at Vila Sol, then it has yet to be discovered. Quite simply, this is a hole where most players normally feel happy, even if they walk off with a bogey. Indeed, Vila Sol's first would serve as a pretty good finishing hole rather than an opener.

At first glance the hole seems pretty much straightway. However, the lie of the land is such that getting the ball to stay on the fairway requires a bit of skill. The fairway is tilted left, so that most balls end up in the left-hand rough. Hit the ball too far left and tall pine trees can block the route to the green. Even if the player finds the left-hand portion of the fairway, a large tree blocks the approach.

Even those who can hit a fade off the tee to land the ball softly on the right-hand side of the fairway leave themselves with no easy second shot. A large bunker guards the right-hand corner of the green, which is slightly elevated. Par here will feel like a birdie. **AT**

**Course:** Augusta National Golf Club

**Location:** Augusta, Georgia, USA

**Hole:** No. 1

**Length:** 400 yards

**Par:** 4

**Designer:** Bobby Jones, Alister MacKenzie

**Course Comment:** Augusta National is easily one of the most famous golf courses in the world. This is particularly evident in Japan, where there are several courses that have attempted to duplicate its design.

**BELOW** *Maintaining the grounds at Augusta.*

**OPPOSITE** *Phil Mickelson of the USA plays out of the bunker on the first hole at Augusta, April 2004.*

# No. ❶ AUGUSTA NATIONAL GOLF CLUB

The No. 1 hole at Augusta National is 400 yards from the "Masters" tees, but only 365 yards from the member tees. And for good reason. The members probably need a little more help than those capable of playing from the back tees. But the hole is not easy — from wherever you tee it up.

Remember, you are playing Augusta National, so nothing will be easy. And this first hole helps prepare you for what lurks around the corner. The second hole is the longest (575 yards) and most difficult (No. 1 handicap) on the course. In other words, you better be ready by the time you leave the first green.

Named "Tea Olive," the starting hole at Augusta was lengthened before the 2003 Masters. The fairway breaks to the right with a large and deep bunker on the right-hand side about 300 yards from the tee. So you big hitters be prepared. If you miss to the left off the tee, you can find the trees on this uphill hole. Hoping to avoid both the bunker and trees, many pros opt for a 3-wood on this hole. Why ruin your round on the first shot? Play it safe off the tee. This demanding hole also has a bunker to the left front of the green.

The course has been tweaked over the years, a little bit of rough has been added, and some holes have been lengthened. But Augusta National is still very much as it was when it was created. It's still perfect. And No. 1 is the perfect place to start. **TJ**

## No. ❶ LIONHEAD GOLF & COUNTRY CLUB (LEGENDS COURSE)

**Course:** Lionhead Golf & Country Club (Legends Course)

**Location:** Brampton, Ontario, Canada

**Hole:** No. 1

**Length:** 458 yards

**Par:** 4

**Designer:** Ted Baker

**Course Comment:** This club features two 18-hole courses that have been rated as some of the finest public golf courses in Canada. The Legends Course has the second highest slope (153) rating in North America.

Few courses tab the first hole as their signature hole, but few courses tee up what the Legends Course has to offer. And it won't take long to see that the experts at Lionhead know what they're doing.

This is simply a spectacular golf hole. Looking down from the elevated tee box to the fairway some 50 feet below is something you won't soon forget. Hit your tee shot 235 yards to clear the pond on the left and fairway bunker to the right. There's about 80 yards of the Credit River and some wetlands to carry on your second shot, which, if you hit the landing area, is between 165 and 208 yards to the green. Don't forget the four bunkers acting as the greeting committee in the front of the green.

Laying up is wise if you put your tee shot in the fairway bunker. There are no 150 or 100-yard markers because they would be located in the river. Now it gets tricky. The three-tiered green features many undulations and three putts are common. Many of the greens at the Legends are tricky.

The Credit River meanders through the layout and affects almost every hole on the course. In fact, many golfers "credit" the river for ruining their scorecards. **TJ**

## No. ❶ MOONAH LINKS (OPEN COURSE)

**Course:** Moonah Links (Open Course)

**Location:** Fingal, Victoria, Australia

**Hole:** No. 1

**Length:** 373 yards

**Par:** 4

**Designer:** Peter Thomson, Michael Wolveridge, Ross Perrett

**Course Comment:** This shortish par 4 at the relatively new home of the Australian Golfing Union is a great opener to the first, links-style, stadium course ever built "down under" and the only one designed to host that nation's Open Championship on a regular basis.

You cannot see the sea when you step to the first tee at this course, but you can feel the salty wind that so often blows across the Mornington Peninsula, situated some 90 minutes by car from Melbourne city center.

And you get the sense, from the freshness of those breezes and the very intimidating length of the layout (more than 7,400 yards from the tips), that even the best players will struggle out here. You feel a sudden calm as you start off, however, because hole No. 1 at Moonah Links is a fair starter that gently introduces a golfer to the difficulties that lie ahead.

It's a dogleg left, with a menacing fairway bunker on the left for anyone who hooks his driver, and farther on, a tree on the corner for those who really catch theirs.

The golfer who keeps his tee shot to the right of those hazards is left with a short iron to a rather ample green. But it's a tough one, perched amongst the native Moonah trees and protected in the center front by a deep pot bunker that swallows any errant balls. **JS**

# NATIONAL GOLF LINKS OF AMERICA

**Course:** National Golf Links of America

**Location:** Southampton, New York, USA

**Hole:** No. 1

**Length:** 327 yards

**Par:** 4

**Designer:** Charles Blair Macdonald

**Course Comment:** The National is a Scottish links-style course with many blind shots and many, many sand bunkers — 365 sand bunkers to be exact. Bring a beach towel.

No, this hole isn't very long. But length isn't everything. It's almost nothing at this difficult opening hole at the National Golf Links of America.

This isn't a split fairway, but it might as well be. You have some choices when you stand at the first tee. Take a bigger club and drive the ball to the left side of the fairway just past the bunkers. Here, you will get a look at the flag and the difficult green awaiting you.

Or you can take less club and play it safer down the right side of the fairway. The problem on your second shot however, is that you won't be able to see the hole.

Now, the fun begins. There is no other way to put this: the first green here is one of the toughest in the world. Because of brutal interior contours, the green is tough to manage. And don't trip over the two foot hump that runs through the middle of the green.

When play began in 1909, the course measured 6,100 yards and when Macdonald died in 1939, it measured 6,700 yards. Every hole had had something done to it. But he was one who believed in change. A few things haven't changed. This is still a classic golf course. And the first hole is proof that reaching the green only means you still have a lot of work to do. **TJ**

**Course:** Spyglass Hill Golf Club

**Location:** Pebble Beach, California, USA

**Hole:** No. 1

**Length:** 600 yards

**Par:** 5

**Designer:** Robert Trent Jones Sr.

**Course Comment:** The first hole at Spyglass is the annual starting point of the PGA Tour's AT&T Pebble Beach Pro-Am.

Spyglass Hill takes its name from Robert Louis Stevenson's classic novel, *Treasure Island*, published in 1863. Local legend maintains that Stevenson once wandered the Spyglass area gathering ideas for his novels. A unique aspect of this course is that the holes are named after characters in *Treasure Island*. The first hole, indeed, is named "Treasure Island."

# No. ❶  SPYGLASS HILL GOLF CLUB

The majestic pine that rose from the left side of the fairway, about 150 yards out, when this hole was first built in 1966, is gone. But just because that original signature is no longer part of the landscape, don't think that any of the tradition and majesty have been removed from No. 1.

Three smaller trees sit in its spot, still making golfers wary of playing close enough to shorten the length of this dogleg left. And cutting angles is important on a hole that measures 600 yards. The first tee shot, like the second shots on No. 6 through 18, is played through the Del Monte forest.

After six years of planning, Spyglass Hill opened on March 11, 1966. The first five holes roll through sandy seaside dunes, challenging the golfer to carefully pick the safest path. The following 13 holes are cut through majestic pines with elevated greens and strategically placed bunkers and lakes to grab the errant shot.

The opening challenge is the first of five consecutive holes which feature "target golf," with sand dunes creating serious penalties for mistakes off the tee. The first hole is very long, but at least it gives golfers the benefit of playing downhill. The drive goes through a chute of trees, and if it's too far right, it means hitting out from under the pines. And if you drive too far left, the rough can be treacherous.

Once you negotiate the tee shot, and find an acceptable spot from which to approach the green, it is time to consider the putting surface. There is sandy scrub behind the hole adjacent to the Pacific Ocean, and there are five huge bunkers in front of the green. The green is a protected plateau, rewarding golfers with a wonderful view but a biting challenge. **JB**

## No. ❶   LE QUERCE GOLF CLUB

**Course:** Le Querce Golf Club

**Location:** San Martino, Lazio, Italy

**Hole:** No. 1

**Length:** 541 yards

**Par:** 5

**Designer:** Jim Fazio, George Fazio

**Course Comment:** Le Querce is home to the Italian Golf Federation, which has its training center here.

This course, set in a scenic mountain valley north of Rome, starts off with its most difficult exam. Pass this early test, and you are filled with optimism at the opportunity for a good round. Struggle, and you have the feeling it may be one of those days.

Make sure to take your driver to the range before your round, as the Fazios have demanded accuracy with the first shot of the day. Dense woods to the right and a large bunker on the right side of the fairway make the left side the easy preferred choice for the drive.

The second shot to a narrow, snaking fairway must avoid water on the left and more trees on the right to set up a short approach to an elevated green. Your wedge shot must also stay on target — those that are just short or wide often roll back into one of three bunkers placed strategically around the putting surface.

Le Querce Golf Club played host to the 1991 World Cup of Golf, with the team competition being captured by Sweden's Anders Forsbrand and Per-Ulrik Johansson, and individual medalist honors going to Wales's Ian Woosnam. **KA**

## No. ❶   SAND HILLS GOLF CLUB

**Course:** Sand Hills Golf Club

**Location:** Mullen, Nebraska, USA

**Hole:** No. 1

**Length:** 549 yards

**Par:** 5

**Designer:** Bill Coore, Ben Crenshaw

**Course Comment:** *Golfweek* magazine named this links-style course No. 1 in the category of "America's 100 Best Modern Courses" from 1997 to 1999.

Sand Hills starts as dramatically as it finishes. And there is nothing wrong with what's in between either. The first hole will take your breath away. Standing on the first tee looking out over the winding fairway will get the blood flowing and the spine tingling. It's the start of something very special.

Then comes the hard part. Hitting the ball. From the elevated tee box, you have anywhere between 180 and 200 yards to carry over the junk — it's pretty scenic but if you land in it, it's junk. Make sure your tee shot is not only long but straight. Coore and Crenshaw have placed fairway bunkers on both sides of the landing area in case your ball decides to slice or hook.

Can you reach the green in two? Yes, but only if the wind is behind you. Most players use their second shot to get within 70 to 100 yards of the elevated green. Depending on the wind and the pin placement, you may find it difficult to keep your shot on the green, which is sloped from back to front. There is no men's handicap available for this hole. But you can certainly label it challenging. **TJ**

## No. ❶ BLACKWOLF RUN GOLF CLUB
### (RIVER COURSE)

On a course that boasts a slope of 151, one of the highest ratings in the country, how fitting it is that this tough test of golf starts out with a challenging par 5. This hole isn't nicknamed "Snake" by happenstance.

A solid tee shot right down the middle is your best bet. With the Sheboygan River on the left and trouble on the right, stick to the middle. If you happen to misfire, the left side, even though it appears to be very well guarded by the river, would be your second option. Try to stay out of the rough at whatever cost.

Alison Nicholas, the 1997 U.S. Women's Open champion, said when she played this hole in the 1998 U.S. Women's Open she hit a bad tee shot and was in some long grass that was taller than she was. The green, which is a very large putting area, has a very low profile and flows from right to left. "Snake" should be played as a three-shot hole, which would give you a great chance to make par and move on. **GE**

## No. ❶ DOONBEG

Greg Norman says he was fortunate to design Doonbeg because of the unique nature of the land. And it doesn't get much more unique than the first hole. The problem will be taking your eye off the scenery ahead of you and focusing on that little white ball on the tee. And focus you better, or you will lose that little white ball in the dunes — or pot bunkers — on your second shot.

From the tee, you can see part of the 1.5-mile crescent beach and those massive dunes. If you can avoid the trouble and safely reach the green with your third shot, you will be off to a good start. The large green is guarded — and we mean guarded — on three sides by an enormous dune typical of what you will encounter for the rest of your round.

Although a relative newcomer, the first hole at Doonbeg is already hailed as the best starting hole in Ireland. It's 567 yards from the back championship tee, 522 yards from the yellow tee and 441 yards from the ladies tee. It is considered the third toughest hole on the course.

Opened in July 2002, Doonbeg has been a mixed bag with the public. Initial complaints of the course included "inescapable rough" and "over-the-top green contour." Some even called the crossovers from holes five to six, 14 to 15, and 17 to 18 "dangerous."

But it's hard not to be impressed with the way Norman cut this course into the unique and striking landscape. Its beauty alone makes this a memorable stop on any golf trip. And it all begins at No. 1. **TJ**

# Hole ❷

Here is a chance to continue positive momentum from No. 1, or quickly reverse any negative effects in the event the first was played poorly.

If the natural land allows, course designers, as a general rule, prefer to make the first four holes play in different directions so players have a chance to experience four distinct wind angles early in the round. So, if terrain allows, No. 2 will almost always go in a different direction than the first.

For the player, on a windy day, this opens a new challenge under new conditions. And, on early morning rounds, sun could be an issue because designers generally avoid pointing the first hole due east into the rising sun. This opens up the possibility that No. 2 will be played into the morning sun. Scenic, perhaps, but sometimes distracting.

LEFT  *Tony Johnstone of Zimbabwe plays his second shot on the second hole at Celtic Manor, Coldra Woods, Newport, Gwent, Wales.*

**Course:** Durban Country Club
(Country Club Course)

**Location:** Durban, South Africa

**Hole:** No. 2

**Length:** 176 yards

**Par:** 3

**Designer:** George Waterman,
Laurie Waters

**Course Comment:** Towering dunes
are Durban's signature and the
second tee box is fixed high atop
the tallest. Gladly take par at the
well-guarded second but also take
time to savor the view of the Indian
Ocean and surrounding dunescape.

BELOW *An aerial view of the second
hole at Durban.*

**DURBAN COUNTRY CLUB**
**(COUNTRY CLUB COURSE)**

Much of Durban's Country Club Course was molded from old swampland,
yet from the second tee perched high atop a dune the layout bears no
resemblance to its former incarnation.

No. 2's tee box is the highest point on the course, with wild bush to the
right and the 17th fairway waiting left. There are also views of the Indian
Ocean barely 100 yards away. All this combines to draw attention away from
a tee shot that must carry a small valley fronting the green and avoid one of
the four deep bunkers that guard the smallish putting surface.

Depending on the wind, which normally blows to the northwest, the
key to Durban's second hole is club selection. The downhill tee shot usually
requires a shorter club but players must avoid missing short in the valley.

Members describe their club as a links course with trees but the truth is
the layout — designed by the talented George Waterman and Laurie Waters
and opened in 1922 — is probably closer to a classic American parkland
course, complete with a storied championship history. Durban has hosted
more South African Opens (14) than any other course, including the 2002
championship. **RH**

**Course:** Golf del Sur (Southern Course)

**Location:** Tenerife, Spain

**Hole:** No. 2

**Length:** 193 yards

**Par:** 3

**Designer:** Pepe Gancedo

**Course Comment:** Golf del Sur has been the setting for two golf driving distance records, both of which were set by Britain's Karl Woodward. First he set a new record of 398 yards and then, a few months later, he managed to break the legendary 400-yard barrier with a huge stroke which sent the ball flying 408 yards.

## No. ❷   GOLF DEL SUR (SOUTHERN COURSE)

History is one of the great trademarks at Golf del Sur. One of the oldest and most prestigious courses in Spain, it is a real beauty. One of the many notable holes on this historic track is the second hole on the Southern Course. The hole is a par 3 with a carry of 193 yards from scenic tee to large and undulating green.

The second green is a microcosm of the second hole, indeed of the entire course at Golf del Sur. The difficulty is there — because of a huge bunker in the back. And the beauty is also evident — because of the same bunker. It is filled with black sand, and offers one of the more unique sites from any tee in golf.

And after trudging through (or hopefully past) the black sand bunker, there are 16 more holes with which to contend — and 18 more after that if you play the North Course. If so, the third hole is the trademark of the North. The fairway is pretty wide open but there is a water hazard to the right. And behind the water lies a ravine with an ochre-colored rock face, while to the left is another bunker of black sand. **TJ**

## No. ② WENTWORTH CLUB (WEST COURSE)

One of four excellent par 3s at Wentworth's storied West Course (also known as the Burma Road), No. 2 offers plenty of obstacles between tee and green. The tee shot must be played over a valley to a kidney-shaped plateau green that is set in the side of the hill and guarded by a Spanish oak on the right as well as four deep bunkers — two left and two right. Golfers must be careful not to spin off and back down the steeply banked hill when the pin is in the front. Miss the green and you will no doubt be in some sort of trouble.

No. 2 is the hole where Gary Player began his stunning comeback in the 1965 final of the World Match Play Championship, held annually at the West. Seven down to Tony Lema after 19 holes, Player won at the second and went on to prevail in 37 holes for the first of his five Match Play titles.

Another Match Play master, Seve Ballesteros, who also won the event five times, has this to say about the West: "The Burma Road is one of the few courses with a capacity to extract continually the best from the best . . . The West Course is, for me, the ultimate examination." It's also an apt description of No. 2. **KA**

**Course:** Garda Golf Country Club

**Location:** Soiano del Lago, Italy

**Hole:** No. 2

**Length:** 160 yards

**Par:** 3

**Designer:** Cotton, Penning Steel and Partners

**Course Comment:** Sweeping panoramas of nearby Rocca di Manerba and Lake Garda are Garda Golf's primary draw, but demand of shotmaking is what sets it apart. The par-3 second, for example, is short (160 yards) but requires an extremely precise tee shot if a player is to have any chance at birdie.

## No. ❷ GARDA GOLF COUNTRY CLUB

Sandwiched between the towering Rocca di Manerba — a high promontory dominating the western shore of Lake Garda — and Valtenesi hills, Garda Golf Country Club is an impressive newcomer to a place dominated by the ancient and the par-3 second hole is a perfect example of how the young can sometimes appear aged to perfection.

Garda Golf's No. 2 has the look and, minus the azaleas, feel of Augusta National Golf Club's famous 12th hole, complete with a shallow, kidney-shaped green and looming water hazard fronting the hole. Just 160 yards from the tips, the tee shot is played from a bluff high above the putting surface to a green that has only two real pin positions (front left and back right). Players will need little more than an 8-iron to safely carry the creek that guards the green short. Anything remotely long, however, will leave a demanding, downhill chip to a green that runs quickly to the water.

Built in 1986 by the British team of Cotton, Penning Steel and Partners, Garda Golf has quickly become one of the Continent's top-rated courses. In 1997 and 2003 Garda Golf hosted the PGA European Tour's Italian Open. **RH**

## No. ❷ TPC AT THE CANYONS

**Course:** TPC at the Canyons

**Location:** Las Vegas, Nevada, USA

**Hole:** No. 2

**Length:** 196 yards

**Par:** 3

**Designer:** Bobby Weed

**Course Comment:** With the help of Ray Floyd, Bobby Weed cut a green monster right through the canyons and desert just north of the sparkling lights of Las Vegas. Part of the Tournament Players Club network, TPC at The Canyons is co-host to the PGA Tour's Invensys Classic.

What a sight. The devil to one side. Mother Nature in all her glory to the other. Off in the distance, to the south, shimmers glamorous Las Vegas with all its polished attractions. Look away and the stark mountains and canyons offer a drama all of their own.

That's the view from the TPC at The Canyons.

The view from the second tee is almost as stunning on this par-3 hole, rated the seventh toughest on the scorecard. There are several tees to choose from (110 from the reds to 196 from the tips) but one thing separates all of them from the green — the desert floor.

Let the man tell you about it:

"A dramatic, downhill hole playing to a green flanked by a barranca and protected on the right by a greenside bunker," explains architect Bobby Weed. "This hole plays a bit shorter than its measured distance, so club selection is a premium."

The hole is simply called "The Canyons." And you will know why as soon as you walk up to the tee.

Ray Floyd, a consultant to Weed, says the second hole is among his favorites, even though he quickly adds that there is no real "signature" hole on the course. **TJ**

## No. ❷ GARDEN CITY GOLF CLUB

**Course:** Garden City Golf Club

**Location:** Garden City, New York, USA

**Hole:** No. 2

**Length:** 135 yards

**Par:** 3

**Designer:** Devereux Emmet, Walter Travis

**Course Comment:** Renowned architect Donald Ross praised the newly opened course when he played the 1902 U.S. Open at Garden City. Since that first championship, Garden City has hosted an additional five U.S. Golf Association events.

Often lost amid the clutter of quality metropolitan golf courses, Garden City's timeless simplicity seems to give the layout a potent nudge above many of its other, high-profile counterparts. The simplicity of the par-3 second's understated tee box and long green, for example, is the rule rather than the exception at the Walter Travis-designed gem.

The 135-yard second is framed by an old sand quarry, the property's most prominent natural attribute, on the left. However, most players in an attempt to avoid the quarry hit long and right only to end up in one of the gaping bunkers behind the putting surface.

The green slides from front right to back left and, depending on the wind which blows in off the Hempstead Plain, could play as much as two clubs longer.

Following the 1902 U.S. Open at Garden City, which was originally built in 1901 by Devereux Emmet, the club commissioned Travis, a club member, to redesign the layout in 1926. Travis added 50 bunkers, reworked all 18 greens and added some much-needed length. Since the 2002 U.S. Open, Garden City Golf Club has hosted an additional five U.S. Golf Association championships, including the 1924 Walker Cup. **RH**

**Course:** Medinah Country Club (No. 3 Course)

**Location:** Medinah, Illinois, USA

**Hole:** No. 2

**Length:** 192 yards

**Par:** 3

**Designer:** Tom Bendelow

**Course Comment:** Site of numerous major championships, Medinah will play host to its first Ryder Cup in 2011, and this dangerous par 3 could be an early momentum swinger.

# MEDINAH COUNTRY CLUB
## (NO. 3 COURSE)

Medinah Country Club is known for its prodigious length (7,409 yards from the tips) and narrow fairways lined with thick forests of trees — more than 4,000 of them — but trees aren't the challenge here. Instead, it's water.

This is the only one of Medinah's four par 3s that measures less than 200 yards, although players standing on the tee and looking at the great divide of Lake Kadijah — which they are forced to carry — won't believe it.

The wind will play a major role in club selection. A large bunker front right will swallow any tee shots that fade and come up short, and a pot bunker on the left back will do the same for players who miss long. For those fortunate to make it over the water and avoid the traps, another challenge awaits: the green has two tiers, with pin placement determining where you want your ball to land.

At a course that's known for its tinkering and numerous renovations, No. 2 is the only par 3 that didn't receive a radical makeover by Roger Rulewich before the 1999 PGA Championship. **KA**

# SAUJANA GOLF CLUB
## (PALM COURSE)

**Course:** Saujana Golf Club (Palm Course)

**Location:** Selangor Darul Ehsan, Malaysia

**Hole:** No. 2

**Length:** 216 yards

**Par:** 3

**Designer:** Ronald Fream

**Course Comment:** Adjoining the golf course is a 5-star hotel (Hyatt Regency Saujana) with a comprehensive range of conference and other hotel facilities. You can also find a swimming pool, driving range, and golf school on the property.

BELOW *Paul McGinley of Ireland tees off on the second hole at Saujana, February 2004.*

OPPOSITE *The second hole at Saujana.*

The Saujana Golf Club features two dramatic 18-hole golf courses. The Palm Course, also known as "The Cobra" for its testing and challenging layout, is 6,565 yards off the blue tees and 6,959 yards from the black. The sixth Pharmaton-Saujana Senior Malaysian Open was played at the Palm Course in 2004 with Australian John Clifford coming in at first place, closely followed by Kuo Chie Hsiung of Taiwan. The Bunga Raya, also known as "The Crocodile," is a scenic 18 with a wide expanse of water and undulating greenery that creates a sense of space. At 6,400 yards, it looks deceptively easy but many have regretted underestimating it.

The second hole on the Palm Course is a real Cobra of a hole. The 172-yard (216 yards from the black tees) par-3 second hole has been rated as the most difficult hole in Malaysia. The hole is played over a deep chasm and requires a precise tee shot to reach the correct level of the two-tiered green. Three putting is not uncommon on this extremely undulating and large green. The Palm Course has a 75.1 rating and a 142 slope from the back tees. The Bunga Raya has a 73.9 rating and 138 slope. **TJ**

**Course:** Prairie Dunes Country Club

**Location:** Hutchinson, Kansas, USA

**Hole:** No. 2

**Length:** 161 yards

**Par:** 3

**Designer:** Perry Maxwell

**Course Comment:** During the 2002 U.S. Women's Open, Prairie Dunes' second hole yielded 40 birdies compared with 104 bogeys and nine double bogeys.

# No. ❷ PRAIRIE DUNES COUNTRY CLUB

When Perry Maxwell first set eyes upon the 480-acre canvas of rolling hills he had to craft into this unique, links-style masterpiece in the center of America's heartland, he had this response: "There are 118 holes here . . . and all I have to do is eliminate 100." Thank goodness this wasn't one of them.

The shortest of Prairie Dunes' four par 3s has a raised, two-tiered green that is set on a diagonal angle from the tee box (from front right to back left), making a player first determine the line and then select a club.

Golfers will want to stay below the hole, but that's a dangerous gamble. A diabolical 12-foot-deep bunker guards the front right of the putting surface and two more bunkers loom left. But that's not the worst of it — go long, and you've really got trouble, as Prairie Dunes' infamous native grasses could make for an unplayable lie.

This small Kansas town isn't the place one would expect to find a magnificent layout often compared with some of the best the British Isles have to offer. There's no sea in sight. But No. 2 is one reason five-time British Open champion Tom Watson calls Prairie Dunes "a touch of Scotland in the Land of Oz." **KA**

**Course:** Chicago Golf Club

**Location:** Wheaton, Ilinois, USA

**Hole:** No. 2

**Length:** 440 yards

**Par:** 3

**Designer:** Charles Blair Macdonald, Seth Raynor

**Course Comment:** The club's name is something of a misnomer: the club is located 30 miles west of the downtown Chicago loop.

# No. ❷ CHICAGO GOLF CLUB

This ultra-private club, Chicago's most exclusive, was founded in 1892 and is one of five founding members of the U.S. Golf Association. Its Charles Blair Macdonald course opened in 1895, and is widely credited as being the oldest 18-hole course in the United States.

Macdonald's first work was at Chicago, and it's still considered one of his finest. Born in Chicago to a Scottish father and Canadian mother, Macdonald attended the University of St. Andrews, Scotland, during the mid-1870s, and became entranced with the game during his time at the birthplace of golf.

It comes as no surprise that Macdonald laid out the original course as a tribute to the Old Course at St. Andrews. Nowhere is that link more apparent than Chicago's second hole, a near replica of the St. Andrews' No. 17, the Road Hole, complete with pot bunker short and left of the green.

The Chicago hole, also known as "Road," has a few minor differences. There's no road, and a series of three bunkers rest at the inside corner of the dogleg right rather than the Old Course's trademark railway sheds.

Macdonald protégé Seth Raynor redesigned the course layout in 1923, lengthening the course from 6,200 to 6,545 yards. The course hasn't been altered signicantly since. **KA**

## No. ❷   PETE DYE GOLF CLUB

**Course:** Pete Dye Golf Club

**Location:** Bridgeport, West Virginia, USA

**Hole:** No. 2

**Length:** 435 yards

**Par:** 4

**Designer:** Pete Dye

**Course Comment:** This unique course has a coal-mining theme. For instance, the tee markers are from the coal railroad. The entire course was built on a strip mine and various mining paraphernalia is strewn throughout its design.

Pete Dye was so impressed with the real estate in Clarksburg that he decided to put his name in front of the golf club. "It is 18 of the most exciting and memorable holes that I have ever built on one course," said Dye, who built the course in 1994.

And if you think that's a pretty big statement, check this testimonial: "Nature has created a framework surrounding the course that is truly unforgettable. Each hole is etched into a player's memory providing perhaps the most important testament one can give any golf course . . . total recall of each and every shot at the completion of play and for years to come . . . I am very proud of this golf course and believe it will be recognized as one of the great golf courses of the world."

You certainly aren't going to forget the second hole, the No. 1 handicap and a true challenge from start to finish. The tee shot must clear the creek and rough and land safely on the fairway. **TJ**

## No. ❷   PELICAN WATERS GOLF CLUB

**Course:** Pelican Waters Golf Club

**Location:** Golden Beach, Queensland, Australia

**Hole:** No. 2

**Par:** 4

**Length:** 347 yards

**Designer:** Greg Norman, Bob Harrison

**Course Comment:** Located at the southern end of Queensland's spectacular Sunshine Coast, this course opened in 2000 and quickly became regarded as one of the finest modern tracks in Australia. It's best known for its short par 4s, and the best of that bunch is the superb second hole that is a visual delight and presents classic risk-reward opportunities.

Located in beautiful Golden Beach, Club Pelican is only an hour's drive from Brisbane and is the first golf course designed by Greg Norman in this part of Australia. This is another of those short par 4s that are timeless features on modern and classic courses. Water runs down the entire right side of the second, and it needs to be carried as well to reach the fairway with the tee shot.

The best position for approaching the green is achieved by hitting a long, straight drive along that hazard, but the longer a golfer hits his ball, the more water he has to carry. Conversely, the more a golfer bails out safely to the left, the more he is going to have to do with his second shot.

An above-average drive will leave a player with little more than a pitch to an angled green that has three distinct levels and is guarded on the left by a series of bunkers.

That construction gives the course superintendent and his crew plenty of pin placement options, and gives players a number of very difficult putting possibilities that makes par a very good score here indeed. **JS**

**Course:** Valderrama

**Location:** Andalucia, Spain

**Hole:** No. 2

**Length:** 385 yards

**Par:** 4

**Designer:** Robert Trent Jones Sr.

**Course Comment:** In 1997 the Club hosted the 32nd Ryder Cup, won by Europe in a most thrilling finish. Valderrama remains today the only club ever to have hosted golf's pinnacle event outside its traditional homelands, USA and Britain.

BELOW *Thomas Bjorn of Denmark plays his second shot on the second hole at Valderrama, October 2003.*

OPPOSITE *The second hole at Valderrama.*

# No. ❷  VALDERRAMA

Valderrama is known for its extremely strong finishing holes (the last two are as good as it gets), but the front nine can hold its own with any course around. The par-4 "El Arbol" second hole at Valderrama is one of the more unique holes around.

Don't be fooled by the 385 yards. This is not an easy par. In the landing area a large cork oak dominates the middle of the fairway. Just the sight of this enormous hazard can send shivers up the spine. But it can actually be a help, not a hindrance. Just aim your tee shot at it with a slight draw (the cork oak is 258 yards from the back tees). This will give you the perfect approach to the green because the fairway slopes slightly from right to left.

If the first shot is to the right, the second shot will be difficult at best because of a group of trees that encroaches on the right-hand side of the fairway. There are plenty of trees running along both sides of the fairway and a huge bunker to the left front of the green. If you need some help getting past the giant tree in the fairway, you have six sets of tees to choose from. **TJ**

**Course:** Mangawhai Golf Club

**Location:** Northland, New Zealand

**Hole:** No. 2

**Length:** 387 yards

**Par:** 4

**Designer:** Harry Dale, Geoff Ashe

**Course Comment:** Mangawhai Golf Club is an 18-hole championship course complete with a helicopter pad for guests interested in flying in for a quick round of golf. The club does allow golfers who drive a car to play the course as well.

# No. ❷  MANGAWHAI GOLF CLUB

Mangawhai itself is a secluded little beach resort, nestled between the expanse of the crystal-clear Pacific Ocean and beautiful rolling farmland, and is within easy driving distance of Auckland. The "semi-links" all-weather, 18-hole, 5,978-yard golf course located there was built in 1979 and is one of the best and tougher places to play in New Zealand. At one time in its short history it was voted the toughest in the country. It might have lost that tag but the course certainly hasn't gotten any easier.

Secretary-manager Dave Barlow told the *New Zealand Herald* that he would nominate the second hole, a par 4 of 423 yards off the blue tees, as his favorite. It's the number one stroke hole, doglegged to the right, with a swamp on the left. Miss the fairway to the right and you're amidst the manuka on the dunes. A strong hitter is tempted to cut the corner to tackle the elevated green, which is bunker-free, but has its own challenges.

There is a good amount of fairway at the 148-yard mark, but it is tight at spots. Despite being labeled "difficult," Mangawhai is a fair course. It's also pretty good value — for those not flying in on a helicopter. **TJ**

## No. ❷ TIBURON (BLACK COURSE)

**Course:** Tiburon (Black Course)

**Location:** Naples, Florida, USA

**Hole:** No. 2

**Length:** 436 yards

**Par:** 4

**Designer:** Greg Norman

**Course Comment:** Greg Norman designed it to play like a British Open links course, firm and fast, but without the frustrating thatch of rough. Instead, Norman used waste areas made of a combination of hard sand and crushed shells.

This stunning hole starts with a tee shot through a narrow chute of pines that gives the fairway an ultra-narrow illusion. Once your ball gets through the chute, however, the fairway is quite a bit more generous than meets the eye from the tee. "It's narrow, it's long, and it's one of the toughest and prettiest holes I've ever played," said head pro Corey Schaub, who said seeing the hole was the clincher when he took the job at Tiburon.

Both the Black and Gold courses are nestled in 800 acres of native Florida foliage, which complement the beauty of their natural surroundings. The absence of rough and the meticulously maintained turf throughout both courses present golfers a variety of challenging shots, especially around the greens.

Even though there is no rough, this is a tough course. Greg Norman, the Shark, designed it with a little "bite." Norman has always been a big fan of the British Open links course, so when he set out to design Tiburon he kept that style at the top of his drawing board. He wanted the course firm and fast. He wanted a great challenge. Yet a fair challenge. Like he's done so many times as a player, Norman achieved success. **TJ**

## No. ❷ SUN RIVERS GOLF RESORT

**Course:** Sun Rivers Golf Resort

**Location:** Kamloops, British Columbia, Canada

**Hole:** No. 2

**Length:** 448 yards

**Par:** 4

**Designer:** Graham Cooke

**Course Comment:** *Golf Digest* recognized Sun Rivers Golf Course as the "Best New Golf Course" in western Canada and second overall in Canada in 2003.

Carved out of the sunny benchlands at the base of mounts Peter and Paul, Sun Rivers Championship Golf Course is one of the few "true" desert courses in Canada. And this will become all too apparent when you reach the picturesque No. 2.

The club experts advise golfers to not be distracted by the view — use it for a target instead. A shot toward the church in the distance is ideal. So aim for the steeple and let it rip. Hit the fairway and the ball will roll forever, leaving a short iron into a green that plays 10 yards shorter than your yardage. On your approach shot, beware of the large bunker to the front left of the green and the smaller one to the right front. There are four sets of tees with the closest at 313 yards.

Sun Rivers is the essence of exceptional golf, offering dramatic elevation changes, sagebrush, natural sand dunes, classic bunkering, wide bentgrass fairways, gently contoured greens, and majestic vistas. The par-72 course has a 73.3 rating and a 130 slope. **TJ**

**Course:** Royal Porthcawl Golf Club

**Location:** Porthcawl, Wales

**Hole:** No. 2

**Length:** 454 yards

**Par:** 4

**Designer:** Charles Gibson

**Course Comment:** This could be the home of royalty. After King Edward VII bestowed the honor of royal status on the club in 1909, the Prince of Wales (later the Duke of Windsor) visited the club in 1932.

**BELOW** *A general view of Royal Porthcawl.*

Royal Porthcawl overlooks the Bristol Channel on the Glamorgan Coast between Cardiff and Swansea. Golfers can see the sea on every hole and enjoy memorable views south to Somerset and Exmoor, and northwest across Swansea Bay to the Gower Peninsula. And the golf is on par with the exceptional scenery.

Royal Porthcawl is home to one of the finest second holes in golf. The drive is a long carry that needs to be positioned on the right of the fairway. How long a carry? About 230 to 240 yards to be on the safe side. The second shot into the green requires lots of focus and plenty of accuracy. If you have a tendency to draw or hook the ball, you're out of bounds and out of luck.

Charles Gibson drew up the original design at Royal Porthcawl, but there have been several modifications since then — in 1913 by Henry Colt, Tom Simpson in 1933, and minor changes in 1950 by C.K. Potter and 1986 by Donald Steel. Among a long and impressive list, the Club has hosted the Amateur Championship (five times), the Walker Cup, the Curtis Cup, the European Team Championship, the Home Internationals (eight times), the Vagliano Trophy, the Ladies British Open Amateur Championship, and the Dunlop Masters. **TJ**

**Course:** Ballybunion Golf Club
(Old Course)

**Location:** Ballybunion, County Kerry,
Ireland

**Hole:** No. 2

**Length:** 420 yards

**Par:** 4

**Designer:** Tom Simpson,
Molly Gourlay

**Course Comment:** There is a
small cemetery to the right of
Ballybunion's first hole. It would
be better situated on the second
because many rounds have "died"
on this windswept par 4.

BELOW *The second hole
at Ballybunion.*

OPPOSITE *An aerial view
of Ballybunion.*

No. ❷ **BALLYBUNION GOLF CLUB
(OLD COURSE)**

Ballybunion's second hole features blind shots, almost incessant winds, sweeping cliff-top vistas, and enough dune grass to carpet Connecticut. Everything one would expect from a course five-time British Open champion Tom Watson once described as the "most beautiful test of links golf anywhere in the world."

To be fair, Watson's judgment may be a bit clouded ever since the club named him the millennium captain in 2000.

The challenge of Ballybunion's second hole lies in the approach shot. The fairway is wide and has a slight, hardly noticeable dogleg right. Your tee shot should favor the left side of the fairway to set up the best approach to a green that sits high above the fairway on a plateau.

The green is fronted by a pair of towering dunes and the approach shot must bisect these to have any chance of finding the putting surface. Compounding the challenge, the prevailing wind often requires one to two extra clubs and the elevated green is exposed, making putting difficult.

Following a relatively benign opening hole, the second is followed by an equally taxing, 240-yard par 3 before a fairly easy stretch through the sixth. **RH**

**Course:** Huntsville Golf Club

**Location:** Shavertown, Pennsylvania, USA

**Hole:** No. 2

**Length:** 391 yards

**Par:** 4

**Designer:** Rees Jones

**Course Comment:** Because much of the subsite consisted of siltstone and sandstone, 65,000 cubic yards of rock had to be dynamited to build this course set in the midst of heavily wooded Pennsylvania farmland.

## No. ❷   HUNTSVILLE GOLF CLUB

This relatively short dogleg left — with a drop in elevation of approximately 100 feet — features a view off the tee that's both magnificent and frightening. The view, however, can be deceiving, deluding some into trying to cut the corner, something that often leads to trouble because of four fairway bunkers on the left side of a landing area that's thickly lined with trees. The right side of the fairway is eminently more forgiving, sloping gently toward the center and still providing plenty of distance for golfers to reach the green in two. Bunkers continue to adjoin the fairway leading up to a small, elevated green, where yet more sand awaits, with the largest trap looming to the left to swallow errant approaches.

Although Huntsville, built in 1995, is not as well known as many of the more established layouts included in this list, don't be fooled. Jones has crafted a masterpiece in the rolling Pennsylvania hills near the Poconos. Several rustic barns — one of which can be seen from the second tee — and farmhouses dot the course, making you feel as if this Rees Jones layout has been here much longer than it actually has. **KA**

**Course:** Scioto Country Club

**Location:** Columbus, Ohio, USA

**Hole:** No. 2

**Length:** 460 yards

**Par:** 4

**Designer:** Donald Ross

**Course Comment:** Better bring your "Aim-game" to this tight golf course. The club has hosted many major events, including the 1926 U.S. Open, the 1950 PGA Championship, the 1968 U.S. Amateur and the 1986 Senior Open.

## No. ❷   SCIOTO COUNTRY CLUB

Standing on the tee at Scioto Country Club's second hole is a mixed bag of emotions. You can't take your eyes off the scenery because if you do, you will see the great challenge laid out in front of you. Better take an extra second to admire those old homes lined up along the right side of the fairway. They often look better before you tee off.

This 460-yard par 4 is a slight dogleg to the right and sets up nicely for a little fade off the tee. There is about a 60-yard dip off the tee down to a creek at the bottom and trees line the fairway to the left. It's one of many spectacular views at Scioto. There are two big bunkers on the right side of the fairway about 250 yards from the back tees. Neither bunker is a good place to be on this hole. There are green-side bunkers on the right and left. Again, try and avoid these bunkers as well.

It's a typical Donald Ross green that slopes and is pretty flat except for a slight hill on the back right. Be happy with a par on this hole. **TJ**

**Course:** Walton Heath (Old Course)

**Location:** Walton on the Hill, Tadworth, Surrey, England

**Hole:** No. 2

**Length:** 458 yards

**Par:** 4

**Designer:** Herbert Fowler

**Course Comment:** Walton Heath is the only club in the world to have had a reigning monarch as its captain. In 1935–36 the then Prince of Wales became Edward VII while serving as Walton Heath's captain.

# No. ❷ WALTON HEATH (OLD COURSE)

Walton Heath's two outstanding golf courses have a unique "inland links" feel to them. You will notice the difference right away. There are few trees to worry about but the openness of the course means more wind.

The wind also wreaks havoc on the course, drying out the fairways, creating rock-hard landing areas. It's very difficult to keep even slightly errant tee shots out of the nasty rough.

How bad is the rough? Walton Heath may just have the most heather of any course you will play in Britain. Those beautiful purple flowers love to swallow golf balls.

Holes such as Nos. 5 and 17 attract most of the attention from the experts, but there are other excellent holes. The second hole is a dogleg right par 4 with plenty of places to get in trouble along the way.

A drive off the tee of about 250 yards puts you in good position for your second shot. But the fairway gets quite narrow in the 260–270-yard range. From a good drive spot, you are looking at about 180 yards to the green.

Host to over 60 major championships in its grand history, the courses have been graced by the 1981 Ryder Cup, five European Open Tournaments and 23 *News of the World* Match Play Championships. Notable members have included Winston Churchill, the Prince of Wales and Lloyd George. **TJ**

**Course:** Bay Harbor Golf Club (Preserve Course)

**Location:** Bay Harbor, Michigan, USA

**Hole:** No. 2

**Length:** 341 yards

**Par:** 4

**Designer:** Arthur Hills

**Course Comment:** The three layouts at Bay Harbor combine to form the longest coastline of any course in the United States. The three sets of nine are nothing alike. The Links sit along high bluffs above Lake Michigan; the Quarry is surrounded by cliffs; and the Preserve cuts through the woods.

## No. ❷  BAY HARBOR GOLF CLUB (PRESERVE COURSE)

Arthur Hills has designed many outstanding golf courses throughout the world, but Michigan is where he has been the busiest. And Michigan golfers aren't complaining. Bay Harbor was the talk of Michigan golf long before it opened, and when they cut the ribbon in 1997, few were disappointed.

*Golfweek* magazine had this to say: "Bay Harbor Golf Club is one of the most picturesque golf sites in the country . . . it may be America's most diverse collection of holes." One of the more unique holes at Bay Harbor is No. 2 on the Preserve Course. The tee is angled to an L-shaped fairway with water along the right side that sometimes comes into play.

But keep the driver in the bag on this hole. You need to carry about 185 yards off the tee to clear the water and marsh. But if you go past 245 yards you will need another ball. In other words, drop a nice tee shot about 210 yards in the middle of the L-shaped fairway. From there, it's a chip shot to a double green, which is shared with No. 7. The green has a bunker on the left and is slightly elevated. And don't be short or your ball could roll back into the marsh. **TJ**

**Course:** Aloha Golf Course

**Location:** Málaga, Andalucia, Spain

**Hole:** No. 2

**Length:** 331 yards

**Par:** 4

**Designer:** Javier Arana

**Course Comment:** Short by modern standards, Aloha's rolling terrain and an array of water hazards and slick greens make it one of the country's most demanding layouts. Its opening in 1975 set off a golf course construction boom in the Nueva Andalucia region.

## No. ❷  ALOHA GOLF COURSE

On its scorecard, Aloha Golf Course boasts "a varied combination, where one hole is never like another. Neither long nor short, perfectly kept." The par-4 second is more of the former (as in short) and plenty of the latter.

Immaculately conditioned, Aloha's second plays to only 331 yards, yet a combination of water hazards and ever-present olive trees makes it seem much longer. Dubbed "Uresandi," a Basque word that means a lot of water, the second has no shortage of watery dangers. A large lake awaits errant drives down the left side of the narrow fairway while two smaller, yet just as penal, ponds loom down the right for misplayed approach shots.

Like the rest of the course, No. 2 features a rolling, almost rugged, fairway and bends slightly to the left. The best tee shot should favor the left side. The green is large considering the hole's length and a short iron approach should give players a decent birdie opportunity depending on where the pin is cut.

Located in Spain's southwest Nueva Andalucia region, the Javier Arana-designed Aloha Course opened in 1975 and is credited with providing the spark that ignited the area's golf boom. **RH**

**Course:** Highlands Links

**Location:** Ingonish, Nova Scotia, Canada

**Hole:** No. 2

**Length:** 447 yards

**Par:** 4

**Designer:** Stanley Thompson

**Course Comment:** Reflective of the Celtic heritage that abounds in the Cape Breton Highlands, each hole bears a colorful Scottish name, with signs bearing the monikers in both Gaelic and English. No. 2 is called Tam O'Shanter, after the shape of the green, which is similar to a Scot's bonnet.

# No. ❷  HIGHLANDS LINKS

Part of the stunningly spectacular Cape Breton Highlands National Park, Highlands Links is considered by many to be the finest public course in all of Canada. It is indeed a true national treasure.

Few settings can match the sheer raw beauty of 4,000-square-mile Cape Breton Island, which is nestled between the Atlantic Ocean and the Gulf of St. Lawrence, and is blessed with breathtaking beaches, mountains and river valleys. Other activities are abundant here, from salmon fishing and whale watching to hiking the renowned Cabot Trail, but the golf is hard to beat.

Stanley Thompson, a noted traditionalist, stays true to form on No. 2, letting nature do most of the work. And why not? The downhill hole has approximately 110 feet of elevation change from tee to green. From the towering tee box with a magnificent view of the shoreline, golfers play to a narrow fairway dotted with mounds and contours similar to those found on many links courses in the British Isles. The unpretentious, bunkerless green allows golfers to run their balls onto the putting surface, especially in the summer months.

Nothing fancy, but beautiful in both its scenery and simplicity. **KA**

**Course:** Spyglass Hill Golf Club

**Location:** Pebble Beach, California, USA

**Hole:** No. 2

**Length:** 349 yards

**Par:** 4

**Designer:** Robert Trent Jones Sr.

**Course Comment:** The Northern California Golf Association holds many events here, including the NCGA Amateur, the NCGA Best Ball and the NCGA Public Links Championship.

# No. ❷ SPYGLASS HILL GOLF CLUB

"Billy Bones," as the second hole is named in keeping with the *Treasure Island* theme of this famous golf course, might just be a hint for the unwary. As players attempt to master this difficult hole, they may hear the laughter of pirates in the distance.

OK, maybe not.

Still, after playing the behemoth, 600-yard first hole at Spyglass, golfers might be seeking a bit of the break when they get to the second tee. Sorry, golfers, it might be 251 yards shorter than its predecessor, but it is definitely not short on challenge.

The second hole is surrounded by trouble, with thick, untenable ice plant providing an unwelcome gobble for the wayward shot. Two extremely precise shots are necessary to reach the putting surface in two, and if you escape the ice plant there are still enormous bunkers to deal with. In fact, as you get closer to the greens, you will see that the term "bunker" actually is a misnomer. There really is no separation of the sand in the true bunker sense. It is more a vast area of sand that is shaped and contoured and designed to cause trouble.

Trouble is a catchword at Spyglass, which was designed by Robert Trent Jones Sr. as a part of the master plan for the Pebble Beach oceanfront. S.F.B. Morse, founder of Pebble Beach Company and chairman of the board of Del Monte Properties, envisioned a string of golf courses around Del Monte Forest's shoreline. Morse commissioned Jones to design a course between Cypress Point and Pebble Beach.

Spyglass Hill is rated one of the toughest courses in the world from the back tees, with a course rating of 75.3 and a slope rating of 148. During the 1999 United States Amateur, the stroke average of the field during medal play was nearly 80.

Nicknamed "The Glass," both as a shortened version of Spyglass and in reference to its slick greens, Spyglass Hill offers challenge after challenge. It doesn't take long for a first-time player to find out what's in store. If the 600-yard first hole doesn't grab your attention, then the trouble-filled second will. **JB**

**Course:** Plainfield Country Club

**Location:** Plainfield, New Jersey, USA

**Hole:** No. 2

**Length:** 450 yards

**Par:** 4

**Designer:** Donald Ross

**Course Comment:** Head professional Scott Paris has been playing golf at Plainfield for seven years but still gets nervous when he lines up his approach shot to the second green. "The green plays with your mind. I still feel uncomfortable when I play that hole. It's a great sense of relief when I get on in two," said Paris.

## No. ❷   PLAINFIELD COUNTRY CLUB

Longtime members say the club has a big welcome sign that people can't miss: the first two holes. The opening holes at Plainfield are a 425-yard, par 4 and a 445-yard par 4 . . . from the white tees. "Welcome to Plainfield."

This course is tough. And No. 2 is a perfect example. The second hole has different problems for different players. For the short- to medium-length drivers, there is a bunker on the right side that comes into play about 200 yards off the tee. The big hitters have to worry about two fairway bunkers on the left about 285 yards off the tee.

This is a 450-yard slightly downhill hole with a right-to-left sloped fairway. You need to land your tee shot right of center or use a slight fade. At about 310 yards, the fairway begins a downslope and there is a 35-yard-long fairway bunker along the left side between 85 and 50 yards out from the green, and a big "chipping area" about 20 yards wide along the left-hand side. Try and avoid both of these. The elevated green is a classic Ross design, that slopes from the back right to the front left.

"The first 20 percent of this green is false because of the slope," Paris said. "With normal conditions if you drop a ball here it will roll right off the green. And it's very easy to putt the ball off this green." **TJ**

**Course:** The Greenbrier (Greenbrier Course)

**Location:** White Sulphur Springs, West Virginia, USA

**Hole:** No. 2

**Length:** 403 yards

**Par:** 4

**Designer:** Seth Raynor, George O'Neil

**Course Comment:** The Greenbrier Course is the only resort golf course in the world to be the site of two international cup matches: the Ryder Cup Matches (1979) and the Solheim Cup Matches (1994). Every U.S. president who played golf has played at the Greenbrier.

# No. ❷ THE GREENBRIER
## (GREENBRIER COURSE)

The second hole on the Greenbrier Course is a real gem. Coupled with the beautiful Allegheny Mountains in the background, this fairway, tree-lined on the left, requires an accurate tee shot.

With water in play off the tee for longer hitters, a mid-range fairway shot is the safest place to be. The approach shot must be dead on. Although it will be a short iron, you still need to handle this hole with caution.

Water protects the right front part of the green, and there is a large deep-set bunker in the back left of the green and a smaller one in the front right. The green, which is a peanut shape, is guarded nicely. The surface undulates and every pin placement on this green is tough. The green tends to roll quickly on this hole and it is very easy to three-putt.

Overall this hole requires an accurate tee shot, approach shot, and patience with the putter. Just think — you can master the same hole Sam Snead, the Grand Master of Golf, who came to The Greenbrier in 1935 as the head golf pro, did on occasion. And if you struggle on this hole, the Sam Snead Golf Academy is just around the corner. **GE**

# No. ❷  HAMILTON GOLF & COUNTRY CLUB (SOUTH COURSE)

Golfers fortunate enough to tackle one of Canada's most highly rated courses must try and tame one of Hamilton's toughest holes early in the round. This long dogleg left requires a massive shot off the tee, so players had best get their drivers warmed up in a hurry. A drive of 240 yards is required to get past the dogleg and 300 yards are needed to carry the right-side bunkers. To make matters worse, the prevailing wind often pushes tee shots to the left, causing many shots to land in deep rough left of the tree-lined fairway.

A failure to make it to the fairway's turn, and you might as well play for a bogey 5. The green is slightly elevated, but you don't want to go too long, either. A quick drop-off leads to a hazard just beyond the green.

It's hard to believe there was such a wide gap between visits, but the PGA Tour's Bell Canadian Open returned to Hamilton's venerable layout for the first time in 73 years in 2003. In preparation, the course underwent several changes, including the insertion of several new teeing areas for additional length. Bob Tway won with a 272 total, a full 15 shots lower than Tommy Armour's 287 winning score in 1930. **KA**

| |
|---|
| **Course:** Le Meridien Penina & Resort |
| **Location:** The Algarve, Portugal |
| **Hole:** No. 2 |
| **Length:** 438 yards |
| **Par:** 4 |
| **Designer:** Sir Henry Cotton |
| **Course Comment:** Built on a former rice field, this course has been raised by three feet in recent years to help with perennial drainage problems. |

*OPPOSITE Miguel Angel Jimenez of Spain plays his tee shot on the second hole at Le Meridien Penina, April 2004.*

## No. ❷   LE MERIDIEN PENINA & RESORT

The problem with the second hole is that it comes too early in the round. Normally you want the toughest hole on the course to come about the 14th or 15th hole when you are suitably warmed up. That it comes as early as the second is something of a shock to the system.

The hole doglegs to the left and the ideal tee shot is a draw around the corner of the dogleg. However, this hole is a hooker's nightmare because anything too far left will find the water hazard that runs the entire length of the hole, with the out-of-bounds line beyond that.

A good drive is needed to have any chance of reaching the green. A water hazard fronts the green and the question after a short drive is whether to lay up short of it or try to get a long iron or fairway wood onto the putting surface.

The green does not make the second shot any easier because it is domed, so that anything that lands on the wrong part will be shed off the putting surface. It is also quite undulating, meaning that a bogey is still a distinct possibility for those who do find the putting surface. **AT**

| |
|---|
| **Course:** Westchester Country Club (West Course) |
| **Location:** Rye, New York, USA |
| **Hole:** No. 2 |
| **Length:** 442 yards |
| **Par:** 4 |
| **Designer:** Walter Travis |
| **Course Comment:** Some of the world's finest play this hole every year at the PGA Tour's Buick Classic. No. 2 plays as No. 11 during the PGA Tour event. |

## No. ❷   WESTCHESTER COUNTRY CLUB (WEST COURSE)

This second hole on the West Course is long, downhill and doglegs to the left. No matter what kind of player you may be, a good decision off the tee is critical on this hole. You need pick a good target on your first shot because your ball will drop some 30-plus feet off the tee, and on to the landing area.

Most players lay off the driver to stay short of a stream located 255 yards away, hoping to leave a mid-iron approach shot, which is very tight. Keep it in the fairway, because the rough is challenging. Your approach shot will be to a three-tiered green surrounded by trees on either side and in the rear.

The green, which is very wide and one of the largest on the course, angles from front left to right. The surface is one of the most undulating on the course and no matter where the pin is, it will be challenging. The greens are always kept nice and fast at Westchester so take your time.

The length of the second hole, coupled with the demanding tee shot, the rough, the approach shot, and the undulating green, makes for one of the more challenging holes on the course. **GE**

**Course:** Pinehurst (No. 2 Course)

**Location:** Pinehurst, North Carolina, USA

**Hole:** No. 2

**Length:** 449 yards

**Par:** 4

**Designer:** Donald Ross

**Course Comment:** Ask anyone who's played it what they remember most about No. 2 and the answers will sound eerily similar: the turtle shell greens. Not only do your approach shots here have to hit the green, they also have to hit the right part of the green.

# No. ❷  PINEHURST (NO. 2 COURSE)

Tom Watson once called the second hole on Pinehurst's No. 2 Course one of the best second holes in the world. High praise indeed from one of the game's greats.

After a fairly easy opening hole, things change in a hurry at No. 2. This second hole is a slight dogleg to the right and the target for the tee shot is the left center of the fairway.

However, this approach leaves the player open to knocking it into one of the four fairway bunkers on the left side. In case that's not enough to scare you, don't forget the out of bounds just past the bunkers.

This green lends itself to several good hole locations. If the pin is in the front left and your approach shot is short of the target, the ball will roll off the green. The second green is not an easy target. No. 2 is simply not an easy hole. And Pinehurst No. 2 is not your typical day on the links. It is golf the way it was meant to be played, "the fairest test of championship golf" ever designed by Ross, in his own words. **TJ**

## No. ❷  SAUCON VALLEY COUNTRY CLUB (GRACE COURSE)

**Course:** Saucon Valley Country Club (Grace Course)

**Location:** Bethlehem, Pennsylvania, USA

**Hole:** No. 2

**Length:** 412 yards

**Par:** 4

**Designer:** William Gordon, David Gordon

**Course Comment:** The last three holes on the Grace Course are all difficult par 4s, each one being 437 yards in length or greater. All of the fairways are escorted by trees and the greens are all small.

Saucon Valley Country Club is a 54-hole private country club with three outstanding golf courses. Picking the best hole off these courses is like picking the best Beatles song. The Grace Course features some outstanding holes. No. 14 is a great par 3 and No. 13 is a good, short par 4.

No. 1 is a good opener and No. 18 is a strong finisher. But No. 2 gets the nod. And it's a slight nod. The tee shot on this 412-yard hole is the key. There is a fairway bunker about 180 to 200 yards along the right side. If you land in that bunker, you must lay up in front of the creek that cuts through the fairway about 100 yards before the green.

There is about 25 yards of fairway to the left of that bunker. But if you hit too far left, you will have a tree to contend with on your second shot. Best to be in the fairway. The green is slightly elevated and crowned and is heavily guarded with bunkers. No. 2 on the Old Course is another great hole at Saucon and members could also pick a few "bests" off the Weyhill Course. The best thing about golf is you get to play all 18 at once and don't have to pick just one. **TJ**

## No. ❷  THE THOROUGHBRED GOLF CLUB

**Course:** The Thoroughbred Golf Club

**Location:** Rothbury, Michigan, USA

**Hole:** No. 2

**Length:** 446 yards

**Par:** 4

**Designer:** Arthur Hills

**Course Comment:** The Thoroughbred Golf Club is part of the Double JJ Ranch located on the western side of the state. The picture on the scorecard of the second hole shows a lake along the left side. It's actually a marsh. Either way, you'll need a new ball if you land in it.

After finishing the impressive first hole at the Thoroughbred Golf Club, you take a short drive through the woods to your second hole. The ride usually ends with a "wow" or "awesome" or "I'm going to need more golf balls."

Arthur Hills created magic with his second hole at the Double JJ Ranch. And while some might argue that No. 18 is the better hole, no one will ever forget the first time they ride up on No. 2.

The hole plays anywhere between 349 and 446 yards but you want to play this from the back. It's a challenge you won't want to pass up. Your drive from the elevated back tees must clear a large marsh area to a fairway with a major slope down to the left. If you don't get it up high enough on the fairway, it will roll right into the marsh.

Your second shot is just as important. Likely, you will not have an even lie. And some can't pass up the challenge of cutting the dogleg out and going for the green. The problem is you have to clear a large marsh, and a big tree right at the turn can also come into play.

The smart shot is to knock over the big hill in front of you and let it roll down, giving you a short chip to the green.

After you putt in for your par, take a look back and appreciate what you just accomplished. **TJ**

## No. ❷  PASATIEMPO GOLF CLUB

**Course:** Pasatiempo Golf Club

**Location:** Santa Cruz, California, USA

**Hole:** No. 2

**Length:** 442 yards

**Par:** 4

**Designer:** Alister MacKenzie

**Course Comment:** Alister MacKenzie lived just off hole No. 6, and this was one of his last course designs before he died in 1934 at the age of 63.

The No. 10 handicap on the course doesn't appear too difficult from the tee. But don't let the view fool you. While it's a generous driving hole with plenty of room all around, the fairway does narrow closer to the green. Just remember to be on the right side of this hole. All the way to the pin. With a fairway sloping right to left, keep your drive on the right side or you may end up in some difficult rough. The narrow opening to the green will be your target on the second shot. There is big trouble (as in huge traps) on both sides of the green. If possible, land to the right side of the green.

Here's a tip from member Geoff Fox: "When the course is firm running the ball on from the right front of the green can work well." Today Pasatiempo is recognized throughout the golf industry as one of the top 100 courses in the country. Of all MacKenzie-designed courses, Pasatiempo remains the closest to its original design, with the addition of trees and the reduction in the number of bunkers being the only major changes.

"Pasatiempo is one of the toughest courses I ever played," LPGA star Juli Inkster said. "I'm grateful for all the experience I gained here because, in comparison, most courses are a piece of cake." **TJ**

## No. ❷  THE ESTANCIA CLUB

**Course:** The Estancia Club

**Location:** Scottsdale, Arizona, USA

**Hole:** No. 2

**Length:** 375 yards

**Par:** 4

**Designer:** Tom Fazio

**Course Comment:** The course is situated on the north slope of Pinnacle Peak and every hole, especially No. 2, offers breathtaking desert views. The service at this club, like this hole, is excellent.

This hole is a true test for any golfer. At 375 yards it is a rather short par 4, but don't think just because it is short it is easy. This hole doglegs to the left and a well-placed tee shot is required.

The scenery on this hole can be very distracting. Picture an incredible green fairway placed in the middle of the desert, with cactus and boulders to the left and right just waiting to take your ball.

The second shot is very tricky, depending where the tee shot lands. If you happen to catch the left side of the fairway, you will have a long bunker on the left side of the green to contend with and a small bunker on the right side, but it really should not come into play. If you are hitting your second shot from the right side of the fairway, you will only have to deal with the small bunker on the right, but don't go long and left because you will hit in the sand.

The green is average size, will roll very true and has some severe break, but that all depends on where the cup is. This course is in immaculate shape, as is this hole. **GE**

**Course:** Southern Hills Country Club

**Location:** Tulsa, Oklahoma, USA

**Hole:** No. 2

**Length:** 471 yards

**Par:** 4

**Designer:** Perry Maxwell

**Course Comment:** The land that is now Southern Hills Country Club was donated by oilman Waite Phillips shortly after the crash of the stock market. The clubhouse was constructed in 1936. Perry Maxwell, who designed the Colonial and Prairie Dunes golf courses, was hired to design the Southern Hills golf course.

# No. ❷   SOUTHERN HILLS COUNTRY CLUB

There are some famous par-4 holes at Southern Hills Country Club. No. 12 is spectacular. And No. 18 is one of the best finishing holes in the United States. But don't think all of the gems reside on the back nine. The front nine at Southern Hills has its moments, including the par-4 second hole. From the tips you are looking at 471 yards of real estate before you reach your intended target. The fairway is a slight dogleg left with trees lining it the entire way down.

About 220 yards from the tee is a creek which cuts from the right side to the left at about a 45-degree angle. There are also bunkers just beyond the creek — about 240 to 250 yards to pass the bunkers from the tee.

The green isn't difficult, but is slightly elevated with four bunkers in the shadows. The key to this hole is your tee shot. You need to get it out on the fairway to help reduce a long second shot to the green. Like many of the holes at Southern Hills, its scenery alone is memorable. So there is no need to rush to that back nine. **TJ**

**Course:** Grandview Golf Club
(Mark O'Meara Course)

**Location:** Huntsville, Ontario,
Canada

**Hole:** No. 2

**Length:** 540 yards

**Par:** 5

**Designer:** Mark O'Meara

**Course Comment:** A second 18-hole
course designed by Nancy Lopez and
Curtis Strange is planned for the 36-
hole Grandview Golf Club adjacent
to the 149-room Delta Grandview
Inn in Huntsville.

OPPOSITE *Mark O'Meara, the designer
of the self-titled course at Grandview,
in action during the second round
of the Bell Canadian Open at Royal
Montreal, September 2001.*

## No. ❷ GRANDVIEW GOLF CLUB
### (MARK O'MEARA COURSE)

The Mark O'Meara Course at Grandview Golf Club opened in 2001, signifying the golf course design debut of the PGA Tour star. The 1998 Masters and British Open Champion wanted the first O'Meara design to be on a "beautiful piece of property," and he has made outstanding use of the natural setting.

The second hole at Grandview is its signature.

It's long. And tough. But "grand" in its design with a great "view" from the tee. The trek begins with a demanding tee shot over a ridge framed by rocks and trees. The second shot crosses a dramatic drop-off to a rolling fairway. And the third shot is uphill to a well-protected green.

Get a par here and your round is off to a terrific start. But don't be discouraged with a bogey.

O'Meara's course features a little of everything. It's first of all simply breathtaking in its scenery. There are plenty of trees and granite outcroppings, and the elevation changes offer great views but uneven lies.

Once you leave the clubhouse it doesn't take long to get out into the wild. Hopefully with the wide fairways O'Meara has created, you will only have to look at the wilderness and not play out of it. **TJ**

**Course:** The National Golf Club
(Moonah Course)

**Location:** Cape Schanck, Victoria,
Australia

**Hole:** No. 2

**Length:** 497 yards

**Par:** 5

**Designer:** Greg Norman,
Bob Harrison

**Course Comment:** This hole is
regarded as one of the finest
modern par 5s in Australia and
introduces what many golfers in
Oz believe is as strong a trio of golf
holes as one will find there, with
Nos. 2, 3, and 4.

## No. ❷ THE NATIONAL GOLF CLUB
### (MOONAH COURSE)

Golfers have to hit their tee shots on this meaty par 5 between a pair of ridges and onto an undulating landing area protected by two medium-sized bunkers to the left and an imposingly large one to the right. The direction — and strength — of the wind will determine what they do next.

For most, it's a mid-range iron down the center of the fairway and then a pitch to the green that has a bunker short and right that locals like to say resembles the famed Road Hole bunker in St. Andrews (and is just as tough to get out of). But the prevailing breezes pour out of the south in the Australian summer, making No. 2 a downwind play and creating a very real temptation to go the green in two.

The hole curves slightly to the right after a good drive, turning at the foot of an enormous sand dune, and it makes the most sense for golfers to keep their second shots to the left side of the fairway for a better approach angle to the green. **JS**

ABOVE *Tiger Woods of the USA and caddie Steve Williams look over the second hole at TPC of Boston, September 2001.*

## No. ❷ TPC OF BOSTON

Part of the famous Tournament Players Club network, the TPC of Boston opened in June 2002 and instantly became one of the premier golf clubs in New England. It's everything you would expect. And then some.

The experts at the TPC of Boston advise golfers to bring everything they've got to the par-5 second hole. You are going to have to hit three well-placed shots to score on this hole. One bad one, and you can forget about it. This hole ranges in distance between 437 yards and 554 yards, so you have several options to find your right skill level.

The tee shot is over a small stream with bunkers guarding the landing area to the right. The second shot is a lay up — either that or go in the lake. Your choice. A three-tiered green awaits your third shot, but pay close attention to where the pin is set up. Hit your mark and you're home free. And what if you miss? "Miss and you're looking at a double bogey on the rocks," as they like to say.

The TPC of Boston has achieved designation as a "Certified Audubon Cooperative Sanctuary" by the Audubon Cooperative Sanctuary System (ACSS). It is only the seventh course in Massachusetts and the 460th in the world to receive this honor. **TJ**

**Course:** Kiawah Island
(Ocean Course)

**Location:** Kiawah Island, South
Carolina, USA

**Hole:** No. 2

**Length:** 528 yards

**Par:** 5

**Designer:** Pete Dye

**Course Comment:** With 10 holes
on the Atlantic and the other eight
winding through the surrounding
marshes and dunes, the Ocean
Course offers a natural links-style
setting reminiscent of the great
courses of Scotland.

BELOW *Ian Woosnam of Wales plays
his second shot on the second hole
at Kiawah Island, November 2003.*

# No. ❷ KIAWAH ISLAND (OCEAN COURSE)

The second hole on the Ocean Course at Kiawah Island is as challenging as
it is beautiful. And you won't find many more scenic holes than this second
tee on the Atlantic Ocean. The second fairway, a dogleg left, is one of the
more interesting and demanding on the golf course.

Any drive off the tee more than 175 yards will get you over the marsh
and safely onto the fairway. Now that you are on the plush carpet of the
fairway, you're faced with the all-important decision of how close to the
green you want to be for your third shot.

Option one — usually the best — is to lay up short of the marsh that cuts
right through the fairway. This will leave you with about a 140-yard carry
into the green. Option two — usually reserved for the low-handicap players
— is to fly the marsh and use a short wedge into the long but shallow green.

In 2002, Pete Dye made architectural changes to seven holes on the
Ocean Course. On hole No. 2, the second marsh crossing, which is about 110
yards from the green, was bulk-headed to make it more visible. This change
makes shots less likely to trickle out of play. **TJ**

**Course:** Celtic Manor (Wentwood Hills Course)

**Location:** Coldra Woods, Newport, Gwent, Wales

**Hole:** No. 2

**Length:** 613 yards

**Par:** 5

**Designer:** Robert Trent Jones Jr.

**Course Comment:** Colin Montgomerie is being widely tipped as a strong contender for the captaincy of the European Team for the 2010 Ryder Cup, to be held at Celtic Manor.

BELOW *Andrew Coltart of Scotland plays a shot on the second hole at Celtic Manor, August 2001.*

OPPOSITE *Tony Johnstone of Zimbabwe plays his second shot on the second hole at Celtic Manor, August 2001.*

No. ❷ **CELTIC MANOR**
## (WENTWOOD HILLS COURSE)

The Celtic Manor resort consists of three very different golf courses: Wentwood Hills, Roman Road, and Coldra Woods. All three are very challenging. All three are of the exceptional quality you would expect at a first-rate resort.

The Wentwood Hills Course, the youngest of the three, is the venue for the Wales Open and will also be hosting the Ryder Cup in 2010. The folks at Celtic Manor describe it this way: "A bit of Augusta, a bit of Florida, and a lot of Wales."

The second hole is a bit difficult and a lot long. From the back tees, the scorecard says 613 yards. Big hitters shouldn't have any trouble clearing the bunkers where the fairway gets a little generous.

The woods on the left should force you to the center of the fairways. A safe second shot will be to lay up before the fairway bunkers. For even the longer hitters, the challenge to hit the green in two is almost impossible — unless your name is Tiger.

Your approach shot into the green will require a good, soft touch because the green is surrounded by bunkers and slopes. The green slopes from back to front. **TJ**

**Course:** Sotogrande Club de Golf

**Location:** Sotogrande, Cádiz, Spain

**Hole:** No. 2

**Length:** 517 yards

**Par:** 5

**Designer:** Robert Trent Jones Sr.

**Course Comment:** The name Sotogrande is a combination of the two Spanish words "soto," a riverside meadow abundant with trees and other vegetation, and "grande" which means large.

# No. ❷ SOTOGRANDE CLUB DE GOLF

Robert Trent Jones Sr. once described a golf course as a battleground: "The players attack the course, and it's the architect's obligation to defend it." So, to defend Sotogrande he has strategically placed bunkers and water hazards, and used the general layout of the course itself. This was Jones' first design in Europe. And he nailed a winner on his first swing.

The second is a pretty par 5. As in pretty tough. From the tee, aim your drive to the right of the fairway bunker and play your second shot right of center, as the fairway slopes to the left. The third shot could be the most important on the hole. It requires a lot of precision to this shallow green — there are also plenty of sand traps around the green. If short of the green, the ball will most probably roll back down the slope. If long of the flagstick, you will face a very fast downhill putt. So your best option is to just put it on the green.

Although the course has wide fairways and very little semi-rough on its fairways, its lakes, fast greens, and the strong winds in this area make it a real challenge to the best of players. **TJ**

**Course:** Maidstone Golf Club
(18 Hole Course)

**Location:** East Hampton, New York,
USA

**Hole:** No. 2

**Length:** 537 yards

**Par:** 5

**Designer:** William H. Tucker

**Course Comment:** This club
has been listed by the U.S. Golf
Association as one of the first
100 clubs established in the
United States.

# No. ❷ MAIDSTONE GOLF CLUB
## (18 HOLE COURSE)

The second hole on this world-class track is the No. 1 handicap on the golf course. The quickest way to the green would be taking the road, which runs along the left side of the fairway and is a very intimidating sight. But the road is out of bounds so you will have to advance the ball the old-fashioned way — with a golf club.

When you do finally get to your approach shot, try and be on the right side of the fairway — although there is out-of-bounds on that side as well. The green is designed to best accept an approach from the far right side of the fairway. And you don't have very much room for error when firing into this green.

The green is on a diagonal angle from front right to back left. And don't be long on your approach. A massive bunker takes up a good portion of real estate behind the green. The hole ranges in length from 497 yards (red tees) to 537 (blue).

Built in 1891, the Maidstone club features one regulation 18-hole course and one executive 9-hole course. *Golf Magazine* ranked the private course third in the category of the "Top 100 Courses in the U.S." for 1999. **TJ**

## No. ❷ TRALEE GOLF CLUB

**Course:** Tralee Golf Club

**Location:** County Kerry, Ireland

**Hole:** No. 2

**Length:** 588 yards

**Par:** 5

**Designer:** Arnold Palmer

**Course Comment:** Tralee, which has been hardened over the years by the non-stop pounding of the sea, opens with a few challenging holes. It takes guts to take aim at the No. 2 green, and that is quickly followed by the third hole — a par 3 measuring 201 yards, and just as difficult.

OPPOSITE *The second hole at Tralee.*

Do you want a reason to visit Tralee? Here's a good one. Order a drink and take a seat in the member's lounge and enjoy the view of the Atlantic Ocean and the spectacular Kerry coastline.

Need another reason? How about the golf course. Not a bad place to spend the day. And No. 2 comes early and is a welcome early leg.

From start to finish, the long 588-yard par-5 second hole hugs the coastline and is one of the more memorable holes in Ireland. Each shot on this tough dogleg right requires great skill — if you can take your eye off the scenery long enough to pay attention to the golf.

Named the "Cuilin," this is the longest hole on the course. And you can forget trying to cut the corner on this one. Be very careful with your shot to the green, which sits in the "little corner" of a cliff top.

The third hole, a par 3 in which a rocky cliff comes between the tee and the green, and the eighth are other highlights on a front nine filled with memorable moments.

And when you have putted out, grab the camera and take a snapshot back toward the pin. Hopefully, you will still have the golf ball you started the hole with to put in a nice frame with the photo. **TJ**

## No. ❷ PEACHTREE GOLF CLUB

**Course:** Peachtree Golf Club

**Location:** Atlanta, Georgia, USA

**Hole:** No. 2

**Length:** 534 yards

**Par:** 5

**Designer:** Robert Trent Jones Sr., Bob Jones

**Course Comment:** Peachtree has never played host to a U.S. Open or PGA Championship, and it's a shame. It'd be fun to see the strategy — and the second shots into the green — of the world's top pros on No. 2.

Peachtree may be known for its fast greens and being well bunkered, but surprisingly, what is considered by most to be its best hole has nary a bunker on it.

The hole may be bunkerless — and short by today's par-5 standards — but don't be fooled. There is plenty of danger in the form of not one, but two, water hazards that loom in front of the green — a pond and a creek. While there is the possibility that long hitters can reach the putting surface in two, they must be pinpoint precise to do so, because there's no margin for error. The creek runs diagonally from left to right toward the green, then meanders around its right side. Many a well-struck second (or third) shot navigates the pond, but cannot conquer the creek.

The lay-up shot is no bargain either. Those who place their second shot short of the pond still have almost 150 yards in — and still must face that same confounded creek.

Robert Trent Jones Sr. always said his design philosophy was this: "Each hole should be a difficult par but an easy bogey."

He succeeded on both counts with Peachtree No. 2. **KA**

## No. ❷  KOOYONGA GOLF CLUB

This par-72 track opens in a most unusual way, with two par 5s, and it is the second of those, the 496-yard second, that attracts much of the attention.

Rymill did a brilliant job working his design around this scrubby land, with its tree-lined fairways and small, firm greens, and this hole is regarded as perhaps the best of the bunch. Don't be deceived by the fact that the scorecard indicates it is only the 15th-index hole, or that it is very reachable in two, especially when the wind is blowing.

It is always a tough play, requiring an accurate drive and a precise second shot. No matter what club a player chooses to use from the lush, couch fairways, a deft approach shot is essential when playing to a green that can run as fast as any in Australia when it is in top tournament shape. **JS**

RIGHT *Steve Haskins of the USA plays out of a bunker on the second hole at Kooyonga, February 2003.*

OPPOSITE *Jarrod Moseley of Australia plays out of a bunker on the second hole at Kooyonga, February 2003.*

# Hole ❸

Rarely, because of pace-of-play concerns, will a golf course have a par 3 among its first two holes. This does not mean No. 3 must be a par 3, of course, but if it is, it almost certainly will be the first par 3 of the round. Such examples of this are Mauna Kea's famed third that plays over a jutting finger of the Pacific Ocean on the Big Island of Hawaii; Mount Juliet in Thomastown, Ireland; and Orebro in Vintrosa, Sweden.

The third can be viewed as a "bridge" hole from both the players' and designers' perspectives. No. 3 serves as a bridge from the start of the round to the "meat" of the challenge. If the third is indeed a par 3, often it is the designer taking advantage of a chance to "bridge" two solid pieces of ground over a rougher area — an opportunity afforded by the use of a short tract of land to build a par-3 link between the second and fourth.

LEFT *The third hole at Essex County Club, Manchester-by-the-Sea, Massachusetts, USA.*

**Course:** Indianwood Golf and Country Club (New Course)

**Location:** Lake Orion, Michigan, USA

**Hole:** No. 3

**Length:** 201 yards

**Par:** 3

**Designer:** Bob Cupp, Jerry Pate

**Course Comment:** The pro shop at Indianwood has several photographs of the golf course for sale. Officials at Indianwood say the scenic No. 3 hole on the New Course is the most sold photograph in the clubhouse.

## No. ❸ INDIANWOOD GOLF & COUNTRY CLUB (NEW COURSE)

Selecting the right club on this 201-yard par 3 is very important. It's also not very easy. There are some large pine trees to the right of the tee box that can throw some needles into your decision. Because the pines block the wind at the tee, it's difficult to know what the wind is doing closer to the green. So take that into account when selecting your all-important club. Remember, the bail-out area is to the right.

You don't want to be short on this hole. There are some nasty wetlands to the front and left of an elevated green. Any tee shot short of the green usually hits the bank in the front and rolls back into the wetlands.

You also don't want to be long on this hole. There is a steep slope behind the green but don't expect it to kick your ball onto the green. It's not a backstop. The ball usually will stay up on the bank, forcing you to hit a tough, downhill shot onto the green. And it's easy to hit it bad enough for it to roll right off the green and into the wetlands. In other words, pick the right club. But watch the wind. **TJ**

**Course:** Dunbar Golf Club

**Location:** Dunbar, East Lothian, Scotland

**Hole:** No. 3

**Length:** 173 yards

**Par:** 3

**Designer:** Old Tom Morris

**Course Comment:** The hole is named Jackson's Pennies. Why? About 80 years ago Mr. Jackson, a retired local businessman, sat behind the green and awarded a coin to golfers he considered had played the hole well.

## No. ❸ DUNBAR GOLF CLUB

Situated 30 miles from Edinburgh, the golf course is laid out on the very land where Oliver Cromwell camped prior to the Battle of Dunbar in 1650.

This is one of the most attractive links courses on Scotland's east coast, sprawling out over a narrow piece of property along the striking shoreline. Though not a particularly long course, when the wind is blowing in off the North Sea, which it usually does, Dunbar can be one of Scotland's most difficult tests of the great game.

The third hole shouldn't ruin your round. It's not all that difficult. But there is something about that view that will leave a lasting impression. In fact, many holes on this course have that memorable impact.

Standing on the tee here you see the white fence on the border of the course with the white clubhouse to the back. And behind it all is the North Sea. The course covers 6,404 yards of coastal terrain and you can see it all from No. 3.

The hole is not without challenges. There are six bunkers surrounding the green and if you land in one of them, the view might not be as nice. **TJ**

**Course:** Real Club de Golf de Sevilla

**Location:** Alcala de Guadaira, Spain

**Hole:** No. 3

**Length:** 154 yards

**Par:** 3

**Designer:** José María Olazábal

**Course Comment:** Argentina's Ricardo Gonzalez claimed his third title on the European Tour International Schedule and second title in Spain when he birdied the final hole at Real Club de Golf de Sevilla for a two-stroke victory in the inaugural Open de Sevilla in April 2004.

## No. ❸ REAL CLUB DE GOLF DE SEVILLA

Because Seville's topography is basically plains, the layout is flat. However, Olazábal used plenty of water and sand and planted more than 12,000 trees to make it interesting — and to provide shade. This is a very long golf course with two long par 3s, three doglegs left, two doglegs right, nine lakes, and a lot of shots over water to some really tight pin positions.

Did someone mention water? No. 3 is the perfect example of how wet your scorecard can get at Real Club de Golf. The rather short par 3 — even the pros on the European Tour were only at 168 yards — is one of those all-or-nothing holes. With a waterfall rocketing skyward in the back, the green is almost surrounded by water. There is some bail-out room to the right, but not much. To the right front is a very large sand trap. There are also traps along the back left side of a rather narrow green. There are four sets of tees on the slightly elevated tee box. Remember, there isn't much elevation on this course. It's one of the more scenic holes on the course — unless of course you land in the water. Then your perspective changes. **TJ**

**Course:** Mauna Kea Golf Club

**Location:** Kamuela, Hawaii, USA

**Hole:** No. 3

**Length:** 210 yards

**Par:** 3

**Designer:** Robert Trent Jones Sr.

**Course Comment:** Mauna Kea Golf Club was the first golf course on the Big Island of Hawaii, where golfers play on black lava desert covered with topsoil and turf.

# No. ❸  MAUNA KEA GOLF CLUB

Mauna Kea Golf Club officials say that the oceanside No. 3 is the most photographed golf hole in the world. While the validity of this may be difficult to verify, it certainly is justified if true. Black lava rock, blue ocean, and green turf combine nicely for a splendid photo opportunity, not to mention a terrific setting for a make-or-break golf hole.

This is one of those tee shots you hate to play just once. Even if you are lucky enough to be successful, soaring over ocean and lava to reach the green on your first try, the temptation to tee it up one more time is too strong for some players to resist. Here's a tip for playing No. 3 that goes beyond the usual advisories on how to enjoy a hole. Try to get the first tee time of the day at Mauna Kea and play the first two holes quickly. If you are lucky enough to create some space between yourself and the group behind, then you'll have an opportunity to tee it up a few times on No. 3. Count the first one, of course. But play the next couple just for fun.

It's hard to imagine that this site used to be just a vacant moonscape of a lava field, beautiful in its own right, but nothing that would bring a golf hole to mind. Robert Trent Jones Sr., however, brought this vision to life with a memorable and beautiful test.

The visual splendor of Mauna Kea, with snow-capped mountains and an often-active volcano serving as a distant (and safe) backdrop, is no more evident than on its third hole. As the Pacific surf pounds the lava, players are asked to clear the ocean and land on a green that faces them diagonally. Depending on pin placement, the hole can play anywhere from 182 to 234 yards, although it is listed at 210 yards on the scorecard. The bunkers in front of the green actually are a blessing. Other than the bail-out area on the right side of the ocean, the bunkers are the lone respite from the sea.

The lava might be visually pleasing, but it's not a pretty sight to watch a golf ball carom off the jagged black and plop into the Pacific. **JB**

**Course:** Mount Juliet Golf Club

**Location:** Thomastown, County Kilkenny, Ireland

**Hole:** No. 3

**Length:** 182 yards

**Par:** 3

**Designer:** Jack Nicklaus

**Course Comment:** Jack Nicklaus designed this course with two goals. First, he wanted a course to challenge the professional golfer. Second, he wanted a course that the average golfer would enjoy playing. With the different sets of tees he established, he accomplished both goals.

## No. ❸ MOUNT JULIET GOLF CLUB

Mount Juliet's championship course has quickly become known as the "Augusta" of Europe and is popular with pros, tourists, and hackers alike.

There are many stunning and spectacular holes at Mount Juliet, but the par-3 third hole is one very few golfers ever forget. It's a spectacular view from an elevated tee to a green guarded by a natural stream and lake.

From the tee, you need to carry about 170 yards of water or get another ball out of your bag. It's also a hole in a very difficult stretch. Nicklaus didn't waste any time challenging the golfer. After a subtler opening hole, No. 2 requires accuracy. The third hole forces you to hit the dance floor. And the fourth hole demands perfection from tee to green.

Mount Juliet is recent host to the World Golf Championship — American Express Championship 2002, the Irish Opens of 1993–95 along with the Shell Wonderful World of Golf match between Fred Couples and Tom Watson in 1998. The par-72, 7,200-yard layout includes rolling fairways, many featuring tricky water hazards and contoured greens — all of this blended into the spectacular setting of this famous old Irish estate. **TJ**

## No. ❸  THE GOLF CLUB

**Course:** The Golf Club

**Location:** New Albany, Ohio, USA

**Hole:** No. 3

**Length:** 185 yards

**Par:** 3

**Designer:** Pete Dye

**Course Comment:** The Golf Club, built in the mid-1960s, was the first course on which Pete Dye included his trademark railroad ties.

The Golf Club, one of Pete Dye's earliest designs, has never hosted a major championship or received national television exposure, and unfortunately remains an unknown to many golfers. The club's pure-golf atmosphere, however, speaks volumes, enhanced by a natural setting that includes rolling terrain, huge oaks and a clear-running creek that winds throughout the course.

At first glance, the third appears simple enough, with a pond on the left side running all the way to the edge of the small, round green. But looks can be deceiving. A huge, multileveled bunker complex, bulkheaded by more than 450 railroad ties and mostly unseen from the tee, is located left and back of the putting surface. A bunker 10 to 12 feet deep is embedded left of the green, with another bunker set slightly above stretching all the way behind the putting surface. Stay to the generous landing area right of the green and you've got a chance to kick your ball on for par. Go left, short or long, and bogey — or worse — is a virtual certainty.

Dye says golfers can thank a young Jack Nicklaus for the trickery. He had originally placed four rather ordinary bunkers around the green, but Nicklaus, after inspecting the course during construction, told Dye the hole was dull.

Thanks to Dye's bunker revisions, that's no longer a concern. **KA**

## No. ❸  ST. LOUIS COUNTRY CLUB

**Course:** St. Louis Country Club

**Location:** Clayton, Missouri, USA

**Hole:** No. 3

**Length:** 205 yards

**Par:** 3

**Designer:** Charles Blair Macdonald, Seth Raynor

**Course Comment:** The 1947 U.S. Open, the only one held at St. Louis Country Club, was the first one televised, but only locally.

The uphill view from the tee box is a frightening one, and golfers can't even see the lengthy, 5-foot-deep bunkers that await just beyond the sharp drop on the green's far side.

St. Louis No. 3 contains most of the elements of an Eden-style hole — a false front, a raised green with deep bunkers in the front ridge, a green that slopes from back to front, and dire consequences for those who go long. This hole is made even tougher by its unusual length, which is rare for an Eden, and a small pond located directly in front of the tee box.

The 1947 U.S. Open at St. Louis was won by unheralded club pro Lew Worsham, who ruined what may have been Sam Snead's best chance for an Open title that somehow always managed to elude him. Snead made a clutch 18-footer on the 72nd hole to force an 18-hole playoff. The two golfers came to the last hole tied at two under par, but this time Snead missed a 30-inch shot for par to hand Worsham the victory. In 17 Open starts and 54 rounds, Worsham shot in the 60s only twice — both at St. Louis. **KA**

## No. ❸   ULLNA GOLF CLUB

**Course:** Ullna Golf Club

**Location:** Rosenkalle, Akersberga, Sweden

**Hole:** No. 3

**Length:** 160 yards

**Par:** 3

**Designer:** Sven Tumba

**Course Comment:** Believe it or not, No. 3 is Ullna's No. 18 handicap hole, meaning that the water is often more of a mental obstacle than a physical one.

Since Pete Dye created the famous 17th hole at the TPC of Sawgrass, architects around the world have attempted imitation island greens. This is one of the best, although it comes much earlier in the round and is 25 yards longer. A few other differences: the body of water in front of the green isn't nearly as wide, and rather than a bunker in the right front, Ullna's version has a bunker at the back right. There is also slightly more room to the right and behind the green than Dye's original offers, as well as a small group of trees on the back right side that might prevent your golf ball from bouncing into Lake Ullna.

Ullna has been the site for several top professional events. It is the former host for the PGA European Tour's Scandinavian Enterprise Open, the forerunner to today's Scandinavian Masters, and also was the site of the 1988 World Amateur Team Championship, the HP Open Ladies European Tour event and the SAS Invitational, a team exhibition (Nordic vs. Rest of the World) that featured such stars as Tiger Woods, David Duval, Thomas Bjorn, Colin Montgomerie, and native son Jesper Parnevik. **KA**

## No. ❸   CHEROKEE RUN GOLF CLUB

**Course:** Cherokee Run Golf Club

**Location:** Conyers, Georgia, USA

**Hole:** No. 3

**Length:** 196 yards

**Par:** 3

**Designer:** Arnold Palmer, Ed Seay

**Course Comment:** Cherokee Run Golf Club is located 30 minutes east of Atlanta in the Georgia International Horse Park, which played host to the equestrian and mountain-bike events during the 1996 Summer Olympics.

Arnold Palmer has called Cherokee Run one of the "great golf courses of the world." And Palmer knows a little bit about golf courses. There are four sets of tees on this hole playing to different lengths and difficulty: the Black (196 yards), the Blue (171), the Augusta (140) and the Burgundy (110). This is important because of the elevation change. The tees are up on a hill and the further back you go, the higher on the hill.

Rated as the 11th handicap, No. 3 isn't one of the tougher holes on the golf course but it all depends on your tee shot. In true Palmer style, you must hit a good tee shot to score on this hole. From those back tees, you need to carry the ball at least 190 yards to reach the green. There is a cavernous bunker to the front right of the putting surface that will swallow up anything over in that direction.

Behind the green is a scenic backdrop to this hole. Bunkers are carved right out of the natural fieldstone with rock face leading all the way to the sand. Much prettier when you aren't standing in the trap. The green is tough with a front-to-back slope. **TJ**

**Course:** Aviara Golf Club

**Location:** Carlsbad, California, USA

**Hole:** No. 3

**Length:** 149 yards

**Par:** 3

**Designer:** Arnold Palmer, Ed Seay

**Course Comment:** The Aviara Golf Course is part of the Four Seasons resort and is located north of San Diego overlooking the Batquitos Lagoon in Carlsbad. Framed by abundant native wildflowers, the challenging layout winds through rolling valleys, offers views of the Pacific Ocean, and is considered one of the best-maintained courses in San Diego.

# No. ❸  AVIARA GOLF CLUB

No. 3 isn't going to ruin your scorecard or your round of golf. It might be the second easiest hole on the golf course (according to the scorecard), but this short hole goes a long way in showing why Aviara is considered one of the most scenic golf courses in the United States. There are also two waterfalls on this hole — and two on the par-3 12th.

Your tee shot on this 149-yard hole (and that's from the Palmer tees) requires you to land on a green protected by water hazards in the front and sand bunkers in the back. Usually, the beach comes before the water — but not here.

There is a small pond on the front right of the green and a lake sits to the right, with the water trickling down to a small waterfall. The green is a difficult two-putt, particularly if the pin is in the back left. This hole is easy to play. Hit it on the green and try your best to knock in the hole for birdie — or par. This is one of those all-or-nothing holes. You either hit the green or, as is often the case, reach for another golf ball. Take your time, though. You will want this snapshot to last forever. **TJ**

RIGHT *Ian Poulter of England tees off at Aviara, April 2001.*

**Course:** Woburn Golf Club
(Duke's Course)

**Location:** Milton Keynes,
Buckinghamshire, England

**Hole:** No. 3

**Length:** 134 yards

**Par:** 3

**Designer:** Charles Lawrie

**Course Comment:** The Duke's
Course was designed by Lawrie
in 1974 when the Marquess of
Tavistock decided to bring golf
to the Woburn estate. It now
is one of three Woburn courses,
having been joined by the Duchess
and the Marquess, all ranked
in the top 100 in the British Isles.

**BELOW AND OPPOSITE** *Two views
of the third hole at Woburn.*

# No. ❸ WOBURN GOLF CLUB
## (DUKE'S COURSE)

The Duke's layout at Woburn, considered one of the finest inland courses in Europe, has played host to the PGA European Tour's British Masters on numerous occasions. Pine, silver birch, and chestnut trees line the fairways, and heather, bracken, and gorse add to the course's natural beauty — and often its difficulty.

The famed third hole, with a drop of 100 feet from tee to green, is framed by a sea of beautiful rhododendrons. The tee shot is not a long one, but it must be accurate, as large sand bunkers guard the left side and right front of the green, which slopes severely from back to front. Shots with too much backspin may hit on the putting surface, but quickly will roll back off the front of the green.

In other words, stay below the hole at all costs. Miss even the shortest of putts from above, and there's no telling where your ball will stop.

Some of the world's finest professionals have captured British Masters crowns on the Duke's Course, including Lee Trevino (1985), Seve Ballesteros (1986 and 1991), Mark McNulty (1987), Sandy Lyle (1988), Nick Faldo (1989), Mark James (1990), and Ian Woosnam (1994). **KA**

**Course:** Wannamoisett Country Club

**Location:** Rumford, Rhode Island, USA

**Hole:** No. 3

**Length:** 140 yards

**Par:** 3

**Designer:** Donald Ross

**Course Comment:** The Donald Ross Society thinks so much of Wannamoisett's No. 3 that the hole serves as the model for its logo.

## No. ❸ WANNAMOISETT COUNTRY CLUB

Wannamoisett is a rare par-69 gem that measures less than 6,700 yards and is set on just 104 acres in the heart of New England. This Donald Ross masterpiece — said by many to be the designer's pride and joy — has only one par 5, but the others aren't missed, as more than enough challenge is provided by several long, lauded par 4s and a testy quartet of par 3s, including the vaunted third.

At first glance, the hole might seem a welcome breather after two long, difficult par 4s (the 430-yard first and 475-yard second) to begin the round. But a closer look reveals this is no respite at all. Indeed, the third holds its own with the previous two holes, and not many courses can claim a tougher opening trio than Wannamoisett. On No. 3, two deep bunkers guard the left and front of the tiny green, and attempted bail-outs right are met with a green that slopes steeply away and carries balls well off the putting surface. Many consider the greens at Wannamoisett as Ross's finest collective set anywhere.

The course serves as the host each summer for the Northeast Amateur, one of the most prestigious men's amateur tournaments in the U.S. **KA**

## No. ❸  OREBRO GOLF CLUB

**Course:** Orebro Golf Club

**Location:** Orebro, Vintrosa, Sweden

**Hole:** No. 3

**Length:** 171 yards

**Par:** 3

**Designer:** Nils Skold

**Course Comment:** The Orebro course once was a native habitat for beavers, who kept especially busy in the winding stream and pond near the No. 3 green. Hence the name, the Beaver Hole.

Orebro, located 125 miles west of Stockholm, is one of Sweden's oldest settlements. Though it was largely rebuilt after a fire devastated it in 1854, the city still contains a number of medieval structures, including a castle that dates back to the 13th century, and is the area's primary tourist attraction today.

One of its greatest treasures, however, is Orebro Golf Club, a well-respected inland course with plenty of undulations, set in a country valley at the base of a mountain range.

Golfers must carry two water hazards off the No. 3 tee — a pond and a stream that snakes in front, then left and behind the green. Two large bunkers also lurk in the back to catch shots that go too far. So you don't want to be short, left or long. The safe play is to the right side, which slopes toward the center of the green.

Swede Helen Alfredsson lost to Italy's Federica Dassu in a sudden-death playoff at the 1996 Compaq Open played at Orebro, disappointing the galleries that had gathered hoping for a victory by their native daughter. The Ladies European Tour event is rotated annually among Sweden's top courses. **KA**

## No. ❸  SHAKER HILLS

**Course:** Shaker Hills

**Location:** Harvard, Massachusetts, USA

**Hole:** No. 3

**Length:** 210 yards

**Par:** 3

**Designer:** Brian Silva

**Course Comment:** Shaker Hills, which features many doglegs with tree-lined fairways, puts a demand on accuracy – and length. With many elevated and undulating greens that vary in size and shape, putting is another key to success here.

Shaker Hills is one of the more scenic golf courses in Massachusetts — and there are no shortage of those in this golf-crazy state. No. 3, a 210-yard par 3, would certainly make New England's most scenic 18 holes.

One of the most beautiful — and demanding — holes in the state, No. 3 is one of the signature holes at Shaker Hills. A wide, shallow green offers an inviting target from an elevated, five-tier tee. But dangers are everywhere on this hole. Several sand traps await any long shots, and a small pond lurks to the left of the fairway and green to snare off-line tee shots. Club selection is very important on this hole and can range from lofted woods to mid-irons.

It's better to be a little right than left. At least if you are to the right, you can still use your golf ball. After a short par-4 opening hole, Shaker Hills gets long in a hurry. No. 2 is a 535-yard par 5, No. 4 is a 466-yard par 4 and No. 5 is a 606-yard par 5. In between is the picturesque No. 3, complete with its own difficult challenges. No. 8, a 416-yard par 4, is the other signature hole at Shaker Hills. **TJ**

**Course:** Pine Needles Lodge & Golf Club

**Location:** Southern Pines, North Carolina, USA

**Hole:** No. 3

**Length:** 134 yards

**Par:** 3

**Designer:** Donald Ross

**Course Comment:** Legendary architect Donald Ross always said a good golf hole should be fair, yielding a relatively equal number of birdies and bogeys. He no doubt would be proud of Pine Needles' third hole, which in the 2003 U.S. Women's Open yielded 52 birdies and 53 bogeys.

No. ❸ # PINE NEEDLES LODGE & GOLF CLUB

This hole is the very picture of tranquility, and looks virtually the same as when Pine Needles first opened in 1928. But beware: it can be tougher than it appears. The short, slightly downhill shot seems deceptively easy from the tee box, and because it requires only an 8-iron to a wedge for most players, tempts many to go straight at the flag. However, the green is as narrow as it is deep, has plenty of subtle undulations and is surrounded by a number of hazards, including five bunkers and a small pond that guards the front. Because the green is so deep, club selection can vary by as many as two clubs based on where the pin is placed.

Be especially careful when the pin is on the front portion of the green. If not, you'll wind up in the water or with a difficult, downhill putt. The best strategy is to aim directly for the center of the green — no matter where the pin is located.

Yes, No. 3 can yield its share of birdies, but it can bite you just as easily with bogeys or worse — just the way Donald Ross liked it. **KA**

RIGHT *Karrie Webb of Australia tees off on the third hole at Pine Needles, May 1996.*

**Course:** Torrey Pines (South Course)

**Location:** La Jolla, California, USA

**Hole:** No. 3

**Length:** 198 yards

**Par:** 3

**Designer:** William F. Bell, Rees Jones (redesigned in 2000)

**Course Comment:** You may have some company on this hole. But don't worry, they won't be needing a cart. The par-3 No. 3 on the South Course is a popular spot for paragliders. It's not uncommon to see a few perched above the green as you prepare to tee off.

## No. ❸ TORREY PINES (SOUTH COURSE)

The owners at Torrey Pines need to put up a sign on the third tee on the South Course: Welcome to Torrey Pines, paradise by the sea.

You are going to take plenty of memories home with you from this golf course, but the third tee is going to stick in your mind forever. Just looking at this hole is worth the green fee. Spectacular only begins to describe the hole and no matter how many pictures you see, it must be experienced. This par 3 slopes sharply downhill to the green, which rests on a large cliff directly above the ocean. The dramatic elevation produces plenty of hang time for your tee shot — try to follow your ball if you can take your eyes off the ocean.

At just 198 yards from the back tees, you need to be aware of the unpredictable wind direction and speed. It's usually pretty brisk coming off the ocean and tends to swirl in all kinds of directions. There is a bunker and plenty of trouble to your left. With a wider fairway and some forgiveness, taking aim to the right isn't a bad idea.

Don't aim too long, though. The cliffs and ocean claim anything past the green. **TJ**

**Course:** The Kittansett Club

**Location:** Marion, Massachusetts, USA

**Hole:** No. 3

**Length:** 165 yards

**Par:** 3

**Designer:** William Flynn, Fred Hood

**Course Comment:** This venerable Massachusetts club played host to the Walker Cup in 1953, with the United States taking a 9–3 victory over Great Britain and Ireland.

This picturesque, signature par 3 set on beautiful Buzzards Bay is basically an island hole, with a tee shot that requires golfers to carry a stretch of the water and beach to a green, which is a raised island surrounded completely by sand. Much of your fate will depend on the finicky breezes off the bay — sometimes as much as a four-club wind — and the ebb and flow of the tides. At low tide, a ball can land on the beach, often providing a relatively good lie that allows golfers the chance to still get up and down for par. At high tide, however, you're sunk, as the bay reaches all the way to the edge of the bunker that circles the green. And if you are fortunate enough to find the putting surface, you're not home yet. The green has plenty of contours that can confound even the best putters.

Architect Gil Hanse performed a restoration in the late 1990s that recaptured many of the Kittansett Club's original design features, including restoring bunkers and removing several hundred trees. **KA**

**Course:** Worthington Manor Golf Club

**Location:** Urbana, Maryland, USA

**Hole:** No. 3

**Length:** 430 yards

**Par:** 4

**Designer:** Ault, Clark, and Associates

**Course Comment:** Don't always go by the handicap ratings on your scorecard. No. 3 at Worthington Manor is the No. 2 handicap, but most will tell you it's the hardest hole on the course. Why isn't it the No. 1 handicap? Because the back nine was rated the more difficult, and therefore, the No. 1 handicap must be on the back nine.

BELOW *The third hole at Worthington Manor.*

# No. ❸ WORTHINGTON MANOR GOLF CLUB

This 430-yard par 4 redefines toughness. And if you are even thinking of getting there in two, you better crank it up on the tee.

No. 3 at Worthington Manor requires a straight — and long — drive off the tee. There is a long bunker along the right side of the fairway, which starts at about 200 yards from the back tees.

Now it gets tough. Your second shot — if you are going for it in two — must clear an environmental area which runs in front of the green and is about 20 to 25 yards wide. Getting to the green is impossible if you do not clear this.

The green also is a challenge. There is a bunker on the right side and the green is sloped back with a hump in the middle. There is a hill behind the green that will stop your shot if you are long. But with the green sloping away from you, it's just another challenge on this challenging hole.

With a distinctive slope rating ranging from 116 to 143, the Maryland masterpiece is a true test of golf for all skill levels. It's always in excellent playing condition and one of the best courses in the state. **TJ**

**Course:** Portage Lake

**Location:** Houghton, Michigan, USA

**Hole:** No. 3

**Length:** 372 yards

**Par:** 4

**Designer:** Bob Newcome

**Course Comment:** The Portage Lake Golf Club was established in 1902. One of the oldest courses in Michigan, it was transferred to Michigan Technological University in June 1945. The transfer was handled by the club president, Tom Ristell, of the Portage Lake Golf Club Board of Control for the sum of $1.

# No. ❸  PORTAGE LAKE

Ignore what the scorecard tells you about No. 3 at Portage Lake. While the hole is the ninth handicap (the folks in the pro shop say it's been a long time since that was updated), the hole is one of the tougher on the golf course — "A birdie in a tournament will always win a skin," they like to say.

From an elevated tee you get a nice look at the river that runs along most of the fairway along the right side. The left side is lined with trees but the fairway is pretty open and there are no fairway bunkers to worry about.

So what's the difficulty? Everything slopes toward the river. So if you are not on the left side of the fairway, your ball might end up rolling down to the banks of the river. The only hole with any real elevation to it, No. 3 starts from an elevated tee then rolls back up when you get near the green, which has three bunkers all along the right side. The green slopes from back to front and left to right and is not an easy time.

There are longer holes at Portage Lake but No. 3 has enough tricks and hidden difficulties to make it one of the more challenging on this grand old golf course. **TJ**

**Course:** The Country Club

**Location:** Brookline, Massachusetts, USA

**Hole:** No. 3

**Length:** 444 yards

**Par:** 4

**Designer:** Willie Campbell, William Flynn, Rees Jones

**Course Comment:** The three U.S. Opens played at The Country Club (1913, 1963 and 1988) were decided by playoffs. And all three champions (Francis Oimet, Julius Boros, and Curtis Strange) either had the lead outright or were tied for the lead at the third hole of the final round.

BELOW *Darren Clarke of Northern Ireland plays a shot at The Country Club, September 1999.*

OPPOSITE *Jesper Parnevik of Sweden plays out of the bunker on the third hole at The Country Club, September 1999.*

The Country Club, originally founded in 1882 and recognized by the U.S. Golf Association as one of the first 100 clubs established in the United States, is steeped in history. But it also is a gem that has endured the test of time, as attested to by hosting four U.S. Opens and the raucous 1999 Ryder Cup. With all the world-class competition being held at The Country Club, it feels like it truly belongs to the entire United States.

In fact, The Country Club's importance is pointed out in a book by Professor Richard J. Moss, entitled *The Country Club*. The book highlights the emergence of golf as a sport in America and also the evolution of The Country Club. The story begins with the Country Club of Brookline. There and throughout, Moss describes the varied architectural styles and features of country clubs and explains how their architectural forms reflected their social functions, beginning with Brookline.

The Country Club might be a national monument, but it also is a New England trademark. And the third hole — snaking a trail through natural rock outcroppings — shows just how much this hole exemplifies the natural beauty that is Massachusetts.

The third hole is a dogleg to the right, and that is the target from the tee. The green is invisible from the tee shot, so local knowledge is a definite plus. Once again, advantage New Englanders. From the tee, your landing area is framed by rock outcroppings and rough, so accuracy is at a premium. Once you hit your tee shot and make it to the dogleg, however, you might wish the green remained invisible, because it is one scary sight.

The putting surface is small, sloped, and is heavily guarded on all sides. Bunkers surround the fairway starting about 50 yards short of the green, and the green itself is surrounded. You can't miss left, short, right, or long without having to deal with danger. Sand is in front and on the sides, and there is a road and a pond in the back.

There is history, there is danger, and most of all, there is great golf. A delicious combination in New England, and the third hole is a great example of all three. **JB**

## No. ❸ THE NATIONAL GOLF CLUB
### (MOONAH COURSE)

**Course:** The National Golf Club
(Moonah Course)

**Location:** Cape Schanck, Victoria,
Australia

**Hole:** No. 3

**Length:** 433 yards

**Par:** 4

**Designer:** Greg Norman,
Bob Harrison

**Course Comment:** The winds around
Cape Schanck blow hard and often,
and they are a big reason why most
of the greens built at Moonah have
open fronts, so they may receive
punch-like, links-style approach
shots more easily.

Situated on the rolling farmlands of the Mornington Peninsula overlooking the Bass Strait, the Moonah Course at The National Golf Club is a sight to behold. The natural landscape was crafted by the designers into the outstanding golf course you see today, the third hole demonstrating a perfect example of its hallmark undulations.

The third is a slight dogleg left, and the best place to put your drive is the left center of the fairway, over a series of ridges to a narrow landing area. Do that, and you may well receive a favorable bounce that adds distance to your tee shot and shortens the yardage needed for the approach, which must sail over ridges on both sides of the hole that are covered by groves of Moonahs. Plus, you get a complete view of the green from that vantage.

And it is a tough approach, to a bowl-like, undulating green that doesn't have any bunkers but requires Dave Pelz-like precision with your short game should you miss.

To say it often presents not-so-accurate players with some interesting chipping and putting possibilities on the tightly mown grass all around the green would be an understatement. **JS**

## No. ❸ CHUNG SHAN HOT SPRINGS GOLF CLUB

**Course:** Chung Shan Hot Springs
Golf Club

**Location:** Zhongshan City, China

**Hole:** No. 3

**Length:** 405 yards

**Par:** 4

**Designer:** Arnold Palmer

**Course Comment:** Chung Shan
Hot Springs, which opened for play
in 1984, was the first post-Cultural-
Revolution golf club in China.

Located less than two hours by fast ferry from Hong Kong, Chung Shan enjoys a tranquil setting in the rural heartland of Guangdong Province.

The history of golf in southern China goes back to the late 1890s, when the game was introduced to Hong Kong by British troops. Several golf clubs existed before the Communist takeover in 1949, but were turned into rice paddies after the government dismissed the sport, calling it a "decadent Western pastime."

Palmer's Hot Springs course, which meanders through groves of gum trees, ivy-covered hills, and lily-padded ponds, was aimed at foreigners and American and British expatriates living in Hong Kong. It was built without a single piece of machinery, and 400,000 cubic yards of dirt were moved entirely by hand.

No. 3 is a draw all by itself. The green is hidden from the tee on this dogleg left par 4, but when you reach your ball after your drive, you'll see why this hole is so highly regarded. The slightly elevated, flat green is guarded by a canal and a deep front left bunker. Go too far left of the green, and you're out of bounds. A word of advice: Stay on the right side — both in the fairway and on the green. **KA**

## No. ❸ PINEHURST (NO. 2 COURSE)

**Course:** Pinehurst (No. 2 Course)

**Location:** Pinehurst, North Carolina, USA

**Hole:** No. 3

**Length:** 340 yards

**Par:** 4

**Designer:** Donald Ross

**Course Comment:** This isn't one of the toughest holes at Pinehurst. It's the No. 13 handicap on the scorecard and falls in between one tough stretch. The second hole is very challenging and the fifth (No. 1 handicap) is the most difficult on the course. So take advantage on this one or it could be a long day.

Donald Ross usually likes to give players plenty of room on the fairway. He must have been in a bad mood when he drew up the third hole at Pinehurst No. 2 course.

The fairway on this slight dogleg right is uncharacteristically tight. Ross gives you two options on this hole: lay up in front of the bunker on the right side of the fairway and away from the two sand traps on the left, or just grab the driver and try to clear all of the bunkers setting up for a short chip to the green. The sand traps on the left aren't as far off the tee as the one on the right — where the fairway gets really tight. And there is out-of-bounds along the left side.

What you decide depends a lot on the wind direction and speed — and, of course, how far you can hit it. The safer play is to lay up, but then again, why play Pinehurst No. 2 if you're going to play it safe. Ross did use his trademark back-to-front slope on the green. There are a few bunkers near the green, including a large one to the front right and another good-size one on the left front. **TJ**

ABOVE *The clubhouse at Pinehurst.*

**Course:** Wolf Creek (East Course)

**Location:** Ponoka, Alberta, Canada

**Hole:** No. 3

**Length:** 427 yards

**Par:** 4

**Designer:** Rod Whitman

**Course Comment:** The East Course at Wolf Creek has plenty of bunkers. It's not like they are anti-sand. But you won't find a single grain of sand on the third hole. Not along the fairway. Not next to the green. Whitman must have felt the hole was difficult enough without digging in a bunker or two.

# No. ❸ WOLF CREEK (EAST COURSE)

Standing on the tee at No. 3 is a mixed bag of emotions. It's really not the toughest tee shot you will hit, but visually it can really intimidate you.

This very scenic par 4 also is the most difficult hole on the East Course at Wolf Creek. The dogleg left is 427 yards from the back tees. That intimidating tee shot is uphill over a small gully. The pro-shop experts suggest a 260-yard smack to reach the bend. Otherwise, you aren't getting home in two.

You want to avoid the gully along the left side of the fairway, so keep the ball right to have any shot at the dance floor. Remember, you have been warned.

Trees line the fairway from tee to green — just in case you have trouble keeping your game online. And your approach shot is a little downhill to a green you can't see. Yes, it's one of those blind shots.

Are you starting to figure out why they didn't need sand on this hole? The green shows a little mercy. It does slope a touch, but it's not too difficult. If you can birdie or even par this hole, you are on your way to a good round. **TJ**

---

**Course:** Baltusrol Golf Club (Lower Course)

**Location:** Springfield, New Jersey, USA

**Hole:** No. 3

**Length:** 466 yards

**Par:** 4

**Designer:** A.W. Tillinghast

**Course Comment:** The 39-hole final match between Jeff Quinney and James Driscoll at the 2000 U.S. Amateur tied the longest finale in championship history.

# No. ❸ BALTUSROL GOLF CLUB (LOWER COURSE)

Since hosting its first U.S. Open in 1903, this A.W. Tillinghast design has fostered a rich history by rolling with the times. Lengthened over the years to 7,191 yards, the Lower Course has hosted a national championship in every decade of the 20th century except one, the 1970s.

As time and technology have crept forward, Baltusrol has improved, strengthened and modernized. At the heart of this evolution is the par-4 third hole. The long dogleg left plays 466 yards and even though it's slightly downhill, that advantage does little to ease the hole's difficulty.

A long drive into a relatively open, albeit tree-lined, fairway must be followed by a demanding approach shot to a green that is guarded by a creek in the front and two deep bunkers which lie in wait right of the green. Once on the putting surface, players must negotiate a spine that runs through the middle of the putting surface from front to back, creating sharp breaks on either side.

Few courses can match Baltusrol's championship history. The par-70 layout has hosted 15 U.S. Golf Association championships — only Merion Golf Club in Ardmore, Pennsylvania, has hosted more (16) — including seven U.S. Opens, and the 2005 PGA Championship. **RH**

**Course:** Olympia Fields
(North Course)

**Location:** Olympia Fields, Illinois,
USA

**Hole:** No. 3

**Length:** 439 yards

**Par:** 4

**Designer:** Willie Park Jr.

**Course Comment:** On the scorecard
at Olympia Fields Country Club there
are five sets of tees, including the
"U.S. Open" tees. The No. 3 hole is
439 yards from the championship
tees, but 461 yards from the U.S.
Open tees. The shortest "regular"
tees are 327 yards — quite a
difference, indeed.

**BELOW** *Tiger Woods of the USA plays
a shot on the third hole at Olympia
Fields, June 2003.*

# No. ❸ OLYMPIA FIELDS (NORTH COURSE)

The North Course at Olympia Fields Country Club, host of the 2003 U.S. Open, features 36 holes with many testing and dramatic holes. But it doesn't get much more difficult than this one. This is an uphill, slight dogleg right with a creek running across the fairway about 280 yards from those "U.S. Open" tees.

Your tee shot is the key here. It's very important to keep your drive straight or "on a laser line" as the U.S. Open Web site suggests. Huge oaks line both sides of the fairway. Because of the creek and a large fairway bunker on the left side, the smart golfer will keep his or her driver in the bag. If you hit a good, long iron off the tee, you can leave yourself with a 140-yard second shot.

The relatively shallow green features a lot of side slope. It's difficult to judge the effect of the wind on your approach shot, which may wreak havoc with some players. If you pull or slightly push your second shot, you will find deep, sloping bunkers. And that's big trouble. The South Course, another great challenge, is beautiful and features many large, old trees and scenic views. **TJ**

**Course:** Oakmont Country Club

**Location:** Oakmont, Pennsylvania, USA

**Hole:** No. 3

**Length:** 425 yards

**Par:** 4

**Designer:** Henry and William Fownes

**Course Comment:** Distinctive Church Pew bunkers on this hole are one of the most famous architectural features in the world.

**BELOW** *Arnold Palmer plays his second shot on the third hole at Oakmont, June 1994.*

**OPPOSITE** *The third hole at Oakmont.*

# No. ❸   OAKMONT COUNTRY CLUB

The Fownes's — club founder Henry and his son William — created a great cathedral of golf in 1903, when Oakmont was finished. At the time, it was considered the toughest golf course in the country. That changed 15 years later when Pine Valley opened for play, but Oakmont — with the famed, 2-acre Church Pews between the third and fourth fairways — still is a wonderful place of worship in golf's storied history.

William Fownes was a firm believer that a poor shot should be appropriately penalized, and he had plenty of background upon which to call. He was the first captain of the Walker Cup team in 1922, 12 years after winning the U.S. Amateur Championship. He later became president of the U.S. Golf Association, so no one scoffed when he spoke.

The Church Pews feature eight ridges, each covered with grass, filled with sand in between. Depending on where you land, you may not be able to advance the ball because of the ridges. Sometimes a sideways play is necessary. In more severe cases, going backward is the only option. While the Church Pews are the most daunting hazard on the third hole, there are other obstacles of which to be aware. Three deep bunkers penalize players who stray too far right in their efforts to avoid the Pews.

The green on No. 3 is somewhat forgiving, because it is considerably less undulating than some of the others at Oakmont, but it does slope slightly toward the backside and it is protected on both the right and left sides by severe bunkers.

The third and fourth holes form the dual signature at Oakmont, which has been established as a National Historic Landmark. This hasn't prevented the management at Oakmont from tweaking, however. All the improvements have been necessary, of course. In 1999, a tree-clearing program was completed that brought back some of the open spaces of 1903 and restored the integrity of the original design. Oakmont has played host to the U.S. Amateur Championship, the PGA Championship and seven U.S. Opens. It is the site of what some consider to be the greatest round of golf ever played, a U.S. Open record 63 by the legendary Johnny Miller in the 1973 National Championship's final round. **JB**

## No. ❸ ROYAL ADELAIDE GOLF CLUB

**Course:** Royal Adelaide Golf Club

**Location:** Adelaide, Australia

**Hole:** No. 3

**Length:** 291 yards

**Par:** 4

**Designer:** Alister MacKenzie

**Course Comment:** Nine Australian Opens have been decided at Royal Adelaide — 1910, 1923, 1926, 1929, 1932, 1935, 1938, 1962, and the last in 1998.

This hole is a classic. In fact, it's the only classic at Royal Adelaide because it's the only hole that remains faithful to Alister MacKenzie's original design. Some call it the best hole on the golf course — so read into that what you will (maybe they should have left the rest of the holes alone).

And don't ask Colin Montgomerie about what he thinks. In 1989, Montgomerie put down an eight on his scorecard for this hole (maybe he thinks this hole, too, should be redone).

This is a fairly straight hole with a good-size fairway to take aim at from the tee. But the fairway does tighten up as you move closer to the green. The green is described as "leg of mutton" in shape by the locals. It has an oblique ridge on the left, while on the right, a knoll on the side of the green.

As you might imagine, the green can make or break this hole. You might be thinking eagle when you line up that approach shot, but miss into the thick grass just off the putting surface and that eagle can easily become a seven or eight.

The key shot here is your approach. It can make or break you, with the latter being the more common.

But what fun is playing it safe? Take out your club of choice and challenge this hole. That's why you're here in the first place. **TJ**

## No. ❸ GOLF CLUB DEL SUR (CAMPO NORTE)

**Course:** Golf Club del Sur (Campo Norte)

**Location:** Tenerife, Canary Islands, Spain

**Hole:** No. 3

**Length:** 457 yards

**Par:** 4

**Designer:** José "Pepe" Gancedo

**Course Comment:** In 1995, Golf Club del Sur was the site of a Shell's Wonderful World of Golf match between Ernie Els and Phil Mickelson.

Golf Club del Sur has 27 holes set amid the splendid scenery of Spain's Canary Islands, with the Campo Norte (North Course) one of three nines at the resort.

The Canary Islands make up a volcanic archipelago, having been formed by volcanoes thrusting them up from the floor of the Atlantic, leading many to call the islands the "Children of Fire and the Sea."

Nowhere is that history more evident than Campo Norte's third hole, which features the beauty and lushness of today's islands contrasted with the barren lava wasteland that lines the entire right side and forms the primary hazard on this long par 4.

You definitely want to avoid a slice on your drive, but the left side is no guarantee either, with groups of palm trees preventing an easy approach to a long, narrow green that's also protected by intimidating bunkers with black volcanic sand.

Golf Club del Sur played host to the PGA European Tour's Open de Tenerife in the early 1990s, and the event was won twice by native son José María Olazábal (1989 and 1992). Another Spaniard, Raquel Carriedo, won the Ladies European Tour's Tenerife Ladies Open at del Sur in 2002. **KA**

# ROYAL COUNTY DOWN
## (CHAMPIONSHIP COURSE)

**Course:** Royal County Down (Championship Course)

**Location:** Newcastle, County Down, Ireland

**Hole:** No. 3

**Length:** 474 yards

**Par:** 4

**Designer:** Old Tom Morris

**Course Comment:** You have to have a little faith to play this course. Royal County Down has five tee shots that are either fully or partially blind. To make matters worse, several approach shots must be struck to greens where you might not see the flag.

Before we head out to No. 3 here are a few words from Tom Watson: "My advice to anyone playing this great course is to keep it very straight off the tee — stray from the fairways at your peril!"

Royal County Down, host to the 2007 Walker Cup, is much more than a postcard. It's throwback golf. Traditional in every sense of the word. And bring *all* your clubs because you are going to need them. And a few tricks in the bag wouldn't hurt, either.

From an elevated tee the shorter hitter will tee off with a little target practice; aim right between two sets of fairway bunkers.

The longer hitter can fly the left trap onto a plateau, giving an excellent line to the green. Approaching the green there is a "knuckle" guarding the front left which sends anything short to the right side. Because of a bunker on the left, the only bail-out is pin high right.

This green is one of the fastest on the course and can be tricky to read. Any putt from front to back will break toward the sea. It doesn't get much better than this. Challenging. Scenic. Awesome. **TJ**

**Course:** Wentworth Club
(West Course)

**Location:** Virginia Water, Surrey,
England

**Hole:** No. 3

**Length:** 447 yards

**Par:** 4

**Designer:** Harry S. Colt,
Charles Alison

**Course Comment:** In the last
two of his record three consecutive
Volvo PGA Championship victories
(1998–2000), Colin Montgomerie
was a combined 35 under par
on Wentworth's West Course —
1 over on the tough third hole
and 36 under on the other 17.

## No. ❸ WENTWORTH CLUB (WEST COURSE)

On a course that's often called the Burma Road because of its length and difficulty, no hole fits that description more aptly than No. 3, the No. 1 handicap hole at Wentworth West.

A long shot into a prevailing wind is required off the tee of this uphill grind, and golfers should take pains to avoid the bunker in the right center of the fairway. Getting home in two demands a well-struck iron shot to the proper position on the hole's trademark three-tiered green, guarded by bunkers on the left and right.

Depending on where the pin is placed, the difference in distance from the front tier to the back can be as much as three clubs, and although the tiers on the putting surface have been somewhat softened in recent years, three putts are still a common occurance. A bogey here is no shame, and a par seems more like a birdie.

Just ask the players at the World Match Play Championship, held annually at Wentworth. Since the inaugural event in 1964, more than five times as many bogeys as birdies have been turned in by some of the world's top professionals. **KA**

**OPPOSITE** Colin Montgomerie of
Scotland plays out of a bunker on the
third hole at Wentworth, May 2004.

**RIGHT** The third hole at Wentworth.

**Course:** Lahinch Golf Club

**Location:** Lahinch, County Clare, Ireland

**Hole:** No. 3

**Length:** 420 yards

**Par:** 4

**Designer:** Old Tom Morris, George Gibson, Alister MacKenzie, Martin Hawtree

**Course Comment:** The Old Course at Lahinch has been the home of the South of Ireland Amateur Open, the oldest provincial championship in Ireland, since the event's inception in 1895. Former champions include Padraig Harrington, Darren Clarke and Paul McGinley.

# No. ❸  LAHINCH GOLF CLUB

Lahinch's third hole was formerly the fourth before an intensive renovation by architect Martin Hawtree was completed in 2003. The entire length of No. 3 runs along the shoreline and serves as a delightful yet difficult lead-in to Lahinch's famous pair of blind-shot holes, the Klondyke (par-5 fourth) and the Dell (par-3 fifth), a duo that is revered by some and reviled by many others.

You'd be hard pressed to complain about Lahinch's third, however. From the tee, the terrain rises to the top of an enormous dune slope, with only a well-struck drive reaching the top of the hill. From the high ground, players finally get a glimpse of the well-situated green. To reach it, they must carry their approach over an area of broken ground, humps and hollows that suddenly replaces the fairway. The shallow green offers its own set of problems, sloping sharply away on all sides and being guarded by a hidden bunker at the front left, with the shot made even tougher by the varying winds off the Atlantic.

If you want a romantic links experience, Lahinch is it — an outstanding design, a glorious setting along the sea, a rich history, castle ruins — it even has a group of goats that meander about the dunes. **KA**

**Course:** The Okanagan Golf Club
(The Bear Course)

**Location:** Kelowna, British
Columbia, Canada

**Hole:** No. 3

**Length:** 453 yards

**Par:** 4

**Designer:** Jack Nicklaus

**Course Comment:** The Okanagan
Golf Club is home to two 18-hole
courses. The Quail Course winds
its way around a mountain with
tree-lined fairways. The Bear Course
was designed by Jack Nicklaus
and has several memorable holes,
including No. 3.

## No. ❸ THE OKANAGAN GOLF CLUB
### (THE BEAR COURSE)

The 453-yard par-4 third hole on The Bear is the signature hole, both for its
difficulty and scenic views. From a very elevated tee box, you get an eyeful
of the Okanagan Valley and a glimpse of the danger ahead. This is the third-
hardest hole on the golf course and it has very little to do with length. Play
this hole smart.

Your tee shot drops some 100 feet down the fairway and you've only just
begun your descent. The very tight fairway has a big hill and out of bounds
on the right, and trees and a bunker hugging the left side. Your second shot
also is downhill toward a double-tiered green, protected by a large bunker
to the right front. The folks in the pro shop like to say, "there is trouble
long, trouble left and trouble right." Best advice is to just hit the green.

The green is relatively flat and not too tricky. The tricky part is getting
there. There are four sets of tees ranging from 319 yards to 453. Planned by
Nicklaus Designs and built in 1998, The Bear is an 18-hole, 6,900 yard, par-72
masterpiece. **TJ**

---

**Course:** Waterville Golf Club

**Location:** Waterville, County Kerry,
Ireland

**Hole:** No. 3

**Length:** 417 yards

**Par:** 4

**Designer:** John A. Mulcahy, Eddie
Hackett

**Course Comment:** Waterville is
known for great golf and great
history. On May 21, 1927, Charles A.
Lindbergh reached Waterville on the
first non-stop flight from New York
to Paris. No, he didn't bring his golf
clubs with him.

## No. ❸ WATERVILLE GOLF CLUB

Founded in 1889, Waterville Golf Club is one of the oldest-established golf
clubs in the British Isles. And it's not just one of the best clubs in Ireland,
but one of the best in the world. The front nine holes are considered to be
the easy nine at Waterville. The back nine is tough. OK, it's very tough. But
that doesn't mean there aren't any challenges on the front nine.

The first two holes ease you in a bit, although the second hole is the
longest par 4 on the course at 425 yards. No. 3 officially welcomes you to
Waterville. Called "Innyside," this par 4 is rated the third most difficult hole
on the golf course. The fairway doesn't have a lot of room in the landing
areas, or any areas for that matter. There are bunkers on both sides and an
inlet of a bay on the right. The elbow of the dogleg is about 50 yards in
front of the green, which sits right on the inlet and is protected by another
bunker on the left.

This is simply a great golf hole. And if the wind is kicking up it can be
the most difficult.

The original course on the front side is a par-72, 7,200-yard (6,600 from
the middle tees) links-style layout.

Waterville is so highly challenging that the saying goes: "Whoever can
conquer Waterville can play on any golf course of the world." **TJ**

## NATIONAL GOLF LINKS OF AMERICA

**Course:** National Golf Links of America

**Location:** Southampton, New York, USA

**Hole:** No. 3

**Length:** 426 yards

**Par:** 4

**Designer:** Charles Blair Macdonald

**Course Comment:** This Scottish links-style course is a true classic that features plenty of opportunities to get in trouble. There is water, there are blind shots, and over 350 bunkers. Bring a few extra golf balls.

**BELOW** *The third hole at the National Golf Links of America.*

After a couple of short par 4s (327 and 330 yards from the tips), National Golf Links turns mean. The third hole is the No. 1 handicap on the course and ranges in length between 378 and 426 yards.

Named the "Alps," this was designed with the Alps at Prestwick in mind. Macdonald pulled it off and then some. It doesn't get more memorable than this masterpiece. Your approach shot must carry over a large, fescue-covered hill to a green that is almost 35 yards wide. There is a little bit of room in front in case you miss. But there also are some big, nasty sand traps leading up to the green on both sides of the fairway.

One sand trap is a V-shaped beach that is possibly right in your line to the green about 250 yards from the tee. How blind is this shot? If you stand on the green and look back toward the tee, you will see very little of the fairway. The green is loaded with plenty of ups and downs, so don't think you are home free just because you have reached the green. Three putts (and even the dreaded four putts) are commonplace here. **TJ**

No. ❸ **THE OLYMPIC CLUB** (LAKE COURSE)

**Course:** The Olympic Club (Lake Course)

**Location:** San Francisco, California, USA

**Hole:** No. 3

**Length:** 223 yards

**Par:** 4

**Designer:** Willie Watson, Sam Whiting, Robert Trent Jones Sr.

**Course Comment:** Despite its name, there are no water hazards on the Lake Course (the moniker comes from nearby Lake Merced) and only one fairway bunker.

Although Olympic's final four are feared, the layout's most difficult four-hole stretch may well be holes 2–5, known as Earthquake Corner, a quartet that can make or break rounds right from the outset.

The uphill green on No. 3 slopes from right to left and is tightly guarded by bunkers on both the left and right sides, requiring players to be precise with a long tee shot.

The club has played host to four U.S. Opens (1955, 1966, 1987 and 1998), and was toughened up by Robert Trent Jones Sr. in 1953 in preparation for the 1955 Open, a tournament that will always be remembered for Jack Fleck's shocking upset of the great Ben Hogan. And No. 3 played a crucial role in the outcome of the competition, giving Fleck important early momentum in his playoff victory.

After Hogan craftily struck a 2-iron off the tee to within three feet of the pin, Fleck rolled a 20-footer in the cup for an improbable birdie. Stunned, the usually unflappable Hogan missed his short putt to fall behind and give Fleck much-needed confidence and an early edge in what would prove to be his first professional victory (and one of only three in his career). **KA**

## No. ❸   **PORTSALON GOLF CLUB**

**Course:** Portsalon Golf Club

**Location:** Portsalon, Letterkenny, Donegal, Ireland

**Hole:** No. 3

**Length:** 356 yards

**Par:** 4

**Designer:** Mother Nature, Pat Ruddy

**Course Comment:** This golf club is located in one of Ireland's natural beauty spots, right on the Fanad Peninsula on Lough Swilly between the beach of Ballymostocker Bay and the Knockalla mountains. The beach was recently voted the "second most beautiful beach in the world."

Portsalon used to be one of the best-kept secrets in Irish golf. It still isn't quite as well known as some of the Emerald Isle's other gems, but word is getting out.

Ballybunion and Lahinch, two of the more well-known courses in Ireland, used to be more quaint and charming before the world of golf tourists caught on. This certainly isn't to say that they still aren't great places to play, because they are. But, tee times are definitely more difficult to procure. At Portsalon, the charm still remains, but if you want to get there before the rest of the world catches on, now is the time.

Portsalon, a par 69 that measures just less than 6,000 yards, is a charmer from start to finish. The course is without pretense, yet it is still a wonderful round of golf.

The third hole, a throwback to another era, is a prime example why the world is becoming more aware of Portsalon's magic.

No. 3 has been unchanged since 1891 and is a downhill par 4 played across and along the beach to a green guarded by two ancient rock formations. It's not one of the more difficult holes on the golf course but certainly one of the more scenic on a course packed with natural beauty. **TJ**

## No. ❸   **LINVILLE GOLF CLUB**

**Course:** Linville Golf Club

**Location:** Linville, North Carolina, USA

**Hole:** No. 3

**Length:** 449 yards

**Par:** 4

**Designer:** Donald Ross

**Course Comment:** From the air, the course looks like an irregularly shaped Y, with one arm following Grandmother Creek up through a narrow valley. The longer arm stretches itself toward Lake Kawana.

Somewhat surprisingly to outsiders, Linville is where golf began in North Carolina: Linville's original course, designed and built by the McRae family in 1895, predated the first holes at more famous Pinehurst by at least three years. The McRae course was later replaced with a layout by legendary architect Donald Ross in 1924, and it is one of the country's most revered mountain courses.

In a state filled with Ross designs — 43 to be exact — Linville is one of only 16 that are open to the public. The traditional Ross layout, located in a valley below Grandfather Mountain, features many elevation changes, severely sloping fairways and small, quick greens.

No. 3 is Linville's signature hole, a long par 4 that twice crosses a scenic, trout-filled creek. Golfers must launch a well-struck tee shot over the crest of a hill to a valley, followed by an uphill, long-iron approach that requires the second shot to carry the creek in order to reach a tiny, bunkerless green with plenty of slope.

The course received a recent renovation by architect Bobby Weed that included a new irrigation system, enlarging tee boxes and replacing cart paths and several bridges. **KA**

## No. ❸ CARNOUSTIE GOLF LINKS

**Course:** Carnoustie Golf Links

**Location:** Carnoustie, Angus, Scotland

**Hole:** No. 3

**Length:** 342 yards

**Par:** 4

**Designer:** Allan Robertson, Old Tom Morris

**Course Comment:** Five times Open champion James Braid was commissioned in 1926 to carry out any alterations he felt necessary to turn Carnoustie into a championship golf course. He moved the third tee to its current elevated position on top of the sand dunes.

Named Jockie's Burn, the No. 3 hole at Carnoustie is the highest point on the course and makes for an inspiring and memorable view out over Carnoustie Bay and the North Sea to the right and over the links to the left.

Not only did moving the tee raise the hole to new heights, it turned the previously straight hole into a dogleg. It is now one of the most deceptive holes on the course — as well as being one of the most picturesque.

Here is some wisdom from the club's pros: "If scoring well at the second is like slugging it out with a heavyweight boxer, parring the third is more akin to cracking a safe, requiring patience, guile, and a steady nerve!"

A fairly open view from the tee gives you a nice target to shoot at. But there is trouble lurking in the fairway — two bunkers about 126 yards from the green and another two about 87 yards from the green.

The sloping green is guarded at the front by the mean little Jockie's Burn. The left, with its deep bunker, isn't a much better place to miss. Nor is the right side with its thick vegetation. So keep it straight.

There are five sets of tees, ranging from 301 yards to 342. **TJ**

**Course:** Kingston Heath Golf Club

**Location:** Cheltenham, Victoria, Australia

**Hole:** No. 3

**Length:** 296 yards

**Par:** 4

**Designer:** D.G. Soutar, Alister MacKenzie

**Course Comment:** A short, slight dogleg right, this is a devilishly difficult hole that requires an accurate fairway wood or long iron off the tee and a deft pitch to a small, raised green surrounded by bunkers and backed by a deep depression.

## No. ❸ KINGSTON HEATH GOLF CLUB

Five-times British Open winner Peter Thomson counts Kingston Heath among his favorite courses, and the Australian native lists the par-4 third among the best holes of that track. "Holes of this length are not built anymore," he writes in the club history, describing that development as a "pity" and lauding No. 3 as a true "gem."

Yes, it can be driven from the tee, and even more so in this age of high-tech titanium and long-range urethane. But the penalties for missing this green are very severe, especially when you consider the two bunkers to the left of the putting surface and the five that make up a sinister complex on the right.

The green often is firm and fast, and no one is surprised when seemingly perfect approach shots run off the back. The length of No. 3, or more accurately its lack thereof, make it a brilliant match-play hole, tempting competitors to fade their drivers as closely as possible to the green when a crisply hit four-iron will work just as well. **JS**

**Course:** Dundonald Links

**Location:** Dundonald, Scotland

**Hole:** No. 3

**Length:** 540 yards

**Par:** 5

**Designer:** Kyle Phillips

**Course Comment:** Dundonald Links was inspired by the architecture of the Ayrshire links courses of Prestwick, Western Gales, and Royal Troon, which are all connected by rail line.

# No. ❸ DUNDONALD LINKS

Dundonald Links gained the sometimes-overused term "instant classic" when it opened in 2003, but in this case, the term seems to be more than justified. The course has already hosted qualifying for the Senior British Open, as well as the European Tour School.

It can be called a links course to some degree, but low-trajectory is not always the play. It has very generous landing areas and winding fairways. The further you can drive the ball, the narrower the fairway gets and the greater the reward. Irons off the tee are not a good idea.

The signature hole of the course is perhaps the first of the four par-5 holes — No. 3. It requires a well-struck tee shot to steer clear of a dangerous ditch on the right side of the fairway. The ideal shot is to lay up short of a fairway bunker then play up just short of the ditch on your second shot.

If conditions dictate, those with a little length in their bag might want to go for the green in two. If so, it is imperative to avoid the gorse to the right. But, be aware of the moguls on the green; there is a bunker that is hidden behind the green for anyone not aware. **JB**

**Course:** Prestwick Golf Club
(Old Course)

**Location:** Prestwick, Ayrshire,
Scotland

**Hole:** No. 3

**Length:** 482 yards

**Par:** 5

**Designer:** Old Tom Morris

**Course Comment:** Prestwick has
been the site of many professional
events, and it also has hosted
the British Amateur on a dozen
occasions since 1888.

OPPOSITE *Ian Campbell of Wales
plays out of a bunker at Prestwick,
June 2001.*

BELOW *The third hole at Prestwick.*

# No. ❸ PRESTWICK GOLF CLUB
## (OLD COURSE)

They say competition brings out the best. This can be said in business, of golfers, and in some case, of golf courses. Such is the case with Prestwick Golf Club. The Prestwick Golf Club, located 30 minutes southwest of Glasgow, isn't the only game in town. But it stacks up with the best.

Prestwick shares the prime golf course land of the Ayrshire coast with Turnberry, Kilmarnock (Barassie), Glasgow Gailes, Western Gailes and Irvine Bogside. In fact, it shares its boundaries with Royal Troon. There's plenty to choose from in the area, and the relaxed and friendly atmosphere of Prestwick makes it a great place to play. And so does the great course.

The third hole at Prestwick's Old Course is a 482-yard par 5, and it is placed perfectly in the round. You have two holes with which to warm up and get ready for "The Cardinal," a hole that isn't overly long, but one that is fraught with peril from tee to green.

It is a gradual beginning to the round, starting with the first hole, "Railway," a par 4 that is the ninth toughest hole on the course. Next comes the 167-yard Tunnel hole, which is the second easiest on the Old Course. However, it is advisable that a player is good and limbered after the first two tests, because the The Cardinal is the No. 1 index hole on the Old card.

The third hole takes extreme accuracy on all five shots, and if by chance you attempt to get home in four, you have accomplished a rarity. It isn't the length that protects The Cardinal, but it is the trickling waters of the Pow burn which lines the left of the hole, and which must be carried on the approach. There also are the ever-troublesome swales on each shot, not to mention large bunkers which come into play off the tee.

And even if you don't find one of the man-made hazards, or the meandering waterway, there is brush and gorse and other distasteful destinations for wayward efforts.

The green itself is surrounded by bunkers, swales, and gorse, so a conservative, on-par five shots is the recommended strategy. Take the par, move onto The Bridge hole and take a breath. **JB**

| | |
|---|---|
| **Course:** Troon North Golf Club (Monument Course) | |
| **Location:** Scottsdale, Arizona, USA | |
| **Hole:** No. 3 | |
| **Length:** 564 yards | |
| **Par:** 5 | |
| **Designer:** Tom Weiskopf, Jay Morrish | |
| **Course Comment:** The hole is nicknamed "The Monument," the same moniker given the course. A signature name on a signature hole. | |

No. ❸ **TROON NORTH GOLF CLUB**
**(MONUMENT COURSE)**

The third hole at Troon North's Monument Course is one of a collection of par 5s that attract attention. It probably isn't even the best of the par 5s on the course — that distinction might go to the 11th, nicknamed "The Saddle." But No. 3, nicknamed "The Monument" — after a giant rock on the hole — is another eye-opener.

This par-5, 564-yarder requires you to dodge the giant boulder anchored in the middle of the fairway, 262 yards from the black tees. There are enough obstacles on this hole, and on the course, but the giant boulder is its most famous. During construction, after initial attempts to move the boulder were unsuccessful, and the city of Scottsdale wanted the stone to stay put, designers Tom Weiskopf and Jay Morrish incorporated the natural wonder into the hole. The Monument hole is intriguing, and there are plenty of risk-reward options.

The Monument hole is part of the Troon North Golf Club that stands in the high desert north of Scottsdale, and it represents the hallmark of the desert golf experience, stretching through natural ravines and foothills in the Sonoran desert in the shadow of Pinnacle Peak.

The par-72 Monument Course stretches to 7,028 yards and is the original course on the site. The Pinnacle Course is 7,044 yards and was added in 1995. Both courses will challenge you with natural washes, huge saguaros, arroyos, ironwood, mesquite and lush green fairways, some hidden behind boulders, mounds and bunkers. Then there's the expansive, undulating greens. Many tees seem to be pedestals perched above the fairways.

The challenge and visuals of Troon North are exquisite, and the service is excellent. You are treated right from the moment you arrive at the club, and after playing the 444-yard first and the 172-yard par-3 second, The Monument awaits and it is a pleasure. Three holes in, and you know you are in for a very special round of golf. This club is situated on Dynamite Boulevard, and it offers an explosive golf experience.

Morrish called The Monument one of his favorite courses when he completed the project: "Troon North is certainly a marvelous piece of property and the Monument Course was one of the neatest assignments I've ever had," he said. "The owners left us alone and let us create. They just wanted to know when we were finished." **JB**

**Course:** Crown Colony Country Club

**Location:** Lufkin, Texas, USA

**Hole:** No. 3

**Length:** 583 yards

**Par:** 5

**Designer:** Bruce Devlin, Robert Von Hagge

**Course Comment:** Lufkin is all about the outdoors, and we're not just talking golf. The city is located between the Davy Crockett National Forest and the Angelina National Forest, and also nearby is the renowned bass fishing of Lake Sam Rayburn, with more than 570 miles of shoreline.

## No. ❸ CROWN COLONY COUNTRY CLUB

Because of the exclusive nature of Crown Colony Country Club, not many souls are fortunate enough to take a shot at this course set amid the beautiful Piney Woods of east Texas. But it's considered by many to be one of the top layouts in a state where just about all things big and tough are revered.

Crown Colony No. 3 certainly fits the bill. There may not be a harder hole in the great state of Texas. From start to finish, this long par 5 offers plenty of trouble and the opportunity to mark down a well-earned par.

From the tips, the tee shot requires a 225-yard carry over a winding lake that continues down the entire left side of the hole, then wraps behind the peninsula green. The fairway slopes from right to left toward the water and becomes narrower as you get closer to the green, with the smart play being to lay up about 140 yards out to set up your third shot to the L-shaped putting surface. There's not much margin for error — in addition to the water left and long, the green also is guarded by a front right bunker that discourages bail-outs.

Rare is the cowboy who can reach this green in two. **KA**

| |
|---|
| **Course:** Sycamore Hills (South Course) |
| **Location:** Macomb, Michigan, USA |
| **Hole:** No. 3 |
| **Length:** 475 yards |
| **Par:** 5 |
| **Designer:** Jerry Matthews |
| **Course Comment:** There is a sign posted on this hole at the turn of this 475-yard dogleg. It reads: "127 yards to the river along centerline of fairway." And make sure you add another 30 yards to carry the river. |

# No. ❸ SYCAMORE HILLS (SOUTH COURSE)

This popular up-scale club is a sand wedge north of Detroit and has three nine-hole courses. The South is the more challenging of the group because it is heavily wooded with very narrow fairways. The par-5 third hole is a perfect example of wooded. And narrow.

From the tips, this hole is simply a challenge for any level of golfer. You are teeing off with woods on both sides. Hit it right and you'll never find your ball. Hit it left and you may find your ball — but wish you hadn't.

The tee shot must carry over 225 yards from the back in order to reach the elbow. And forget about going for this in two. Save your heroic attempts for another hole.

Depending on where your tee shot lands, you will most likely need another 130 to 160 yards just to clear the Clinton River. As if narrow and wooded weren't enough, Jerry Matthews decided to throw a river into the mix. Actually, Mother Nature provided the river. Matthews just makes you hit over it.

And the river can come into play off the tee if you hit it too far right. Just thought we should mention that. Three fairway bunkers are on the other side of the river to the right. And two bunkers guard the large green. **TJ**

| |
|---|
| **Course:** The Baltray |
| **Location:** Baltray, Drogheda, County Louth, Ireland |
| **Hole:** No. 3 |
| **Length:** 544 yards |
| **Par:** 5 |
| **Designer:** Tom Simpson |
| **Course Comment:** Also known as County Louth, Baltray is considered one of the great courses in Ireland. It's sandwiched between Royal County Down at Newcastle and Portmarnock to the north of Dublin and belongs on any list of great Ireland courses. |

# No. ❸ THE BALTRAY

Many golf courses — even the great ones — go through many changes over the years. Baltray is no different, although not to the extent of most. And for good reason. There really isn't much worth changing. And there are certain signs still visible of the great work performed by Tom Simpson way back in 1892.

You don't have to go much further than the par-5 third hole. His authentic stamp is detectable on this long and challenging hole. And it is challenging in so many ways. First, it's long and you have to deal with the wind. Second, your third shot is a blind shot over a knoll. And third, you're trying to land the ball on a very small green.

With its 6,783 yards, the course has a considerable length, especially when you consider the natural hazards of a links: blowing winds and heavy rough. And these two factors should not be ignored, because they are responsible for your score at the end of the game. In an article in 1962 in the *Golfers Companion* the course was described as "natural unspoilt seaside territory with towering sand hills, murderous rough, and a rating of long holes that call for powerful hitting." **TJ**

**Course:** The De Vere Belfry (Brabazon Course)

**Location:** Wishaw, Warwickshire, England

**Hole:** No. 3

**Length:** 538 yards

**Par:** 5

**Designer:** Dave Thomas, Peter Alliss

**Course Comment:** Prior to the 2001 Ryder Cup, the third hole became a dogleg right to left par 5 with new bunkers around the green. The once plain par 4 is now one of the best holes on the course.

The Belfry Golf Club is home to the Derby Course and the PGA National Course.

# No. ❸ THE DE VERE BELFRY
## (BRABAZON COURSE)

Reaching this hole in two is tough, but possible. For starters, a drive down the left side of the fairway, avoiding the large fairway bunker, gives you a shot. If you get in the rough or bunker or trees, you can forget about it.

You also must be a pretty big hitter. The goal is to get your second shot to within 200 to 230 yards. A poor drive short of the 280-yard mark will force a lay-up shot with a mid-iron and then a chip shot to the green.

The long second shot to the green is for those who trust their fairway wood. Here are the problems as you line up the big shot. The green is narrow and slopes heavily. You have to clear water. And avoid a bunker that could easily cost you two strokes. If this doesn't scare you, swing away. And good luck.

There is plenty of water on this golf course, including the third hole. With water on the front and left side of the green, you are more than likely going to have to clear the water to land the green. And it's better to be right than left on this hole. **TJ**

**Course:** Alwoodley Golf Club

**Location:** Leeds, Yorkshire, England

**Hole:** No. 3

**Length:** 510 yards

**Par:** 5

**Designer:** Harry S. Colt, Alister MacKenzie

**Course Comment:** Alwoodley was famed architect Alister MacKenzie's first design; it opened in 1907, and is one of Britain's most excellent inland designs.

# No. ❸ ALWOODLEY GOLF CLUB

You could say that Alwoodley Golf Club was the result of the meeting of minds. Two great golf minds, about the same age and who both studied at Cambridge, came together to first discuss Alwoodley and then collaborate on its construction.

Alister MacKenzie was the secretary at Alwoodley, and Harry S. Colt — already an established course architect — was hired to design the golf course. But when Colt and MacKenzie met to discuss the course, Colt immediately persuaded MacKenzie to help him design the course. It was the start of a most influential career in course architecture.

MacKenzie left his medical practice and spent the next quarter century building golf courses throughout the world. Some of his masterpieces include Augusta National, Royal Melbourne and Crystal Downs, but none of them would have been possible if it weren't for a persuasive conversation with a fellow Cambridge grad.

The course layout at Alwoodley forms part of Wigton Moor and features soft fairways cutting through heather, whins, and shrubs. In addition to its scenic beauty, the course is strategically bunkered and has undulating and interesting greens.

And the third hole at Alwoodley, while not the most beautiful or even most challenging hole designed by MacKenzie, remains an interesting hole. First is the drive, which must carry over the 16th fairway to fall to the third. Crossing fairways are rare anywhere in golf, much less on a course so respected as Alwoodley. Little more than 200 yards from the tee is the only hazard on the third hole, a bunker that poses very little hazard at all. It frames the landing area, and adds perspective off the tee, but its main effect is cosmetic.

All of this seeming simplicity is anything but. It is a subtle hole that is made more difficult by the false sense of security it provides. Colt and MacKenzie knew of the prevailing wind that almost always is at the golfer's back on No. 3, and with a canting fairway preceding a sloping green, the second shot must be perfectly placed in order to allow the third to get close to the hole.

The third green is unaltered since it was built in 1907. In fact, all the greens on the course are still to the original design, with the exception of the 10th and 11th, which have been slightly reworked. **JB**

OPPOSITE *Two views of the third hole at Alwoodley.*

**Course:** Durban Country Club
(Country Club Course)

**Location:** Durban, Natal,
South Africa

**Hole:** No. 3

**Length:** 513 yards

**Par:** 5

**Designer:** George Waterman,
Laurie Waters

**Course Comment:** At Durban,
Gary Player captured the first of
his 13 South African Opens, an event
that is older than the U.S. Open.
He also holds the course record,
a 64 shot in 1969.

## No. ❸ DURBAN COUNTRY CLUB
### (COUNTRY CLUB COURSE)

There are few more frightening sights in golf than standing on the third tee at Durban, elevated 60 feet above a dunes-laden layer of green that is difficult to describe. Architect Tom Doak gave it a shot, saying it looked like you were "looking down the barrel of a gun." Doak may have been overstating the danger more than a little, but in golf terms it was only a slight exaggeration.

The third hole is the most famous hole on South Africa's most famous course. It is in a valley, and the lumpy look comes from the countless dunes that fill the fairway. The hole is submerged in the valley (all except the tee), and although it is a straight line, when viewing all the dunes it is impossible to think of this fairway as a direct path to anything.

A drive in the fairway is absolutely essential to success, but still no guarantee. Yes, you avoid the thick brush on the right and the dunes on the left if you keep it in the fairway, but there still is that bunker that juts ever so subtly into the left side of the fairway, just about the distance a long hitter will end up.

Then comes the decision about whether to go for the green in two. The distance isn't a deterrent for today's top players, but it is a risk-reward shot with the emphasis on risk. The green is raised and sloped, and if the shot doesn't come in softly, it more than likely will end up in the dune to the rear of the green. If that happens, par becomes extremely difficult.

The third hole at Durban, a tough chore on the calmest of days, is even more difficult when the ocean breezes are kicking — which, as you might have guessed, is almost always.

The golf tradition in South Africa is storied and goes back decades. The country has produced great champions such as Gary Player and Ernie Els. But, of all the great gifts South Africa has given to the game of golf, the magnificent third hole at Durban may be its finest. **JB**

**Course:** El Saler Golf Club

**Location:** Olivia, Valencia, Spain

**Hole:** No. 3

**Length:** 534 yards

**Par:** 5

**Designer:** Javier Arana

**Course Comment:** El Saler has been the site of many Spanish Opens and it is considered one of the top two golf courses in continental Europe.

# No. ❸  EL SALER GOLF CLUB

This area in the mideastern region of Spain might get overlooked because of the vast (and very deserved) attention given to Costa del Sol to the south. Valencia may not have the concentration of golf courses enjoyed by Costa del Sol, but what it lacks in volume it makes up for with the shining star of El Saler Golf Club.

Javier Arana took his golf very seriously, and he understood the great traditions of the game when he designed El Saler. The course, which Arana designed as a tribute to the way the game is played in Scotland, generally is considered a rival to Valderrama as the finest course in Europe.

Even though the course is laid out in links style, it offers a rather unique brand of parkland design as well. Ten of the holes, in fact, run through forest, while the other eight are seaside on the Golfo de Valencia.

The par-5 third hole is one of the inland holes, taking a northward dogleg left through the oaks and pines. It is not overly long at 534 yards, but reaching the green in two is no bargain. First, a solid drive is necessary to make it to the dogleg. So length is an issue. Next, accuracy off the tee is a must because of the bunkers and the ever-present forest through which the fairway is pierced. Cutting the dogleg is an option for big hitters, but falling short of your target forfeits any chance at a good score.

Say you are one of those long hitters, and you have successfully negotiated the dogleg on your drive. Still, there is anywhere from 240 to 260 yards left to the green, which is protected by a huge, oblong bunker in the front and on the right and a smaller bunker on the left.

**BELOW** *Darren Clarke of Northern Ireland watches his third shot on the third hole at El Saler, April 2001.*

The green, like the bunker on the right, is oblong, it is canted slightly, and is diagonal to the fairway which makes a delicate approach necessary, particularly if the pin is placed up front. You can blast away a bit more if the pin is in the back — but make sure you're straight, or the big bunker awaits your shot.

There is trouble and there is beauty, but the best feature at El Saler's third is the decision-making it forces. Thought is required on this hole, just the way Javier Arana planned it. **JB**

**Course:** Essex County Club

**Location:** Manchester-by-the-Sea, Massachusetts, USA

**Hole:** No. 3

**Length:** 625 yards

**Par:** 5

**Designer:** Donald Ross

**Course Comment:** The green on Essex No. 3, which dates to 1893, is said to be the oldest in continuous use in North America.

# No. ❸ ESSEX COUNTY CLUB

This mammoth hole contains plenty of elements to keep it from feeling simply like a long grind. Indeed, its length is not the only obstacle golfers face in their quest for par.

The first is the "transition area" that contains sand, rocks and thick fauna and is located near the landing area for many drives. Then there's the stream on the left and the gargantuan bunker on the right, just part of the creative fairway bunkering that breaks up the long haul to the green.

Three strong shots are a must to reach the putting surface in regulation. The "bathtub" green has its own protections, most notably the three-foot-deep depression at the front left and a deep pot bunker at the back right to catch shots that go awry.

Essex County received special care from Ross for a good reason. After being hired as the architect in 1908 to convert the nine-hole layout into an 18-hole championship track, Ross lived on the course for four years (1909–13) in a house located near a massive bunker that cuts across the 15th and 16th holes. He finished several holes each year, tinkering with the layout and improving it constantly. His work wasn't fully completed until 1917. **KA**

# Hole ④

Warm-up is definitely over by No. 4. Players are loose, limber and have a good idea of what kind of form they are in by the fourth. Course architects understand this when they design the holes.

It is no accident that the fourth holes are some of the more demanding on a golf course. A player should be ready to face any challenge by the time the fourth hole rolls around.

The Dunes at Maui Lani Golf Course in Kahului, Hawaii, for instance, features a 509-yard par-4 fourth that is the fourth-toughest hole on the course and the second toughest on the front nine. This hole follows a par 3 that is the easiest hole on the course, and the contrast is not a challenge that a fair architect would throw at a player before he or she has been braced by preparation.

**LEFT** *The fourth hole at Banff Springs, Alberta, Canada.*

**Course:** Baltusrol (Lower Course)

**Location:** Springfield, New Jersey, USA

**Hole:** No. 4

**Length:** 194 yards

**Par:** 3

**Designer:** A.W. Tillinghast

**Course Comment:** Robert Trent Jones Sr. remodeled the Lower Course in 1954. Jack Nicklaus, who won the U.S. Open at Baltusrol in 1967 and 1980, lists No. 4 as his favorite Jones-designed hole.

BELOW *The fourth hole at Baltusrol.*

OPPOSITE *Dan Forsman of the USA plays out of a bunker at Baltusrol, June 1993.*

# No. ❹ BALTUSROL (LOWER COURSE)

Built on farmland owned by Baltus Roll in the late 1800s, the New Jersey property has hosted 15 national championships over the last 100-plus years. Seven U.S. Opens and two Women's Opens have been contested at Baltusrol, with legends such as Nicklaus and Mickey Wright among those victorious in Springfield. During that time the Lower Course's famed fourth hole has claimed countless victims.

While the hole offers a spectacular view of the clubhouse, players often have difficulty appreciating the scene with a water hazard staring them in the face. Separating the two-tiered green from the hazard is an unforgiving stone wall. There is no safety net between green and pond — precision is essential. Of course, landing safely on dry land is only half the battle. The shallow green's two levels offer a variety of pin placements and numerous side hill putts.

When Jones redesigned the hole prior to the 1954 U.S. Open, members claimed the hole was too difficult. In response Jones invited the club professional and two members to play along with him on the par 3. From the 165-yard member's tee, the club pro and members hit the green in regulation. Playing the hole for the first time, Jones struck a 4-iron that bounced on the green and rolled into the cup. He then turned to his playing partners and said, "Gentlemen, the hole is fair. Eminently fair." **BB**

**Course:** Kananaskis Country Golf Course (Mount Kidd Course)

**Location:** Alberta, Canada

**Hole:** No. 4

**Length:** 197 yards

**Par:** 3

**Designer:** Robert Trent Jones Sr.

**Course Comment:** Golfers find themselves in scenic paradise at the Mount Kidd Course, one of two tucked into the heart of the Canadian Rockies at the Kananaskis Country Golf Course.

# No. ❹ KANANASKIS COUNTRY GOLF COURSE (MOUNT KIDD COURSE)

At more than 5,000 feet above sea level, the air is thinner, so naturally the ball goes farther as it's hit from the tee at the rugged and beautiful fourth. This par-3 creation is one of 20 on the 36-hole course where water comes into play. Large, elevated greens benchmark this jewel; the meandering Kananaskis River and surrounding jagged peaks of Mount Kidd and Mount Lorette make it a dramatically esthetic must-play.

The puzzle of strategically placing holes on a course while taking advantage of visually spectacular terrain is an art — and nowhere is Robert Trent Jones Sr.'s brilliant sculpture more evident than at the fourth hole. This hole seems to be carved straight from the wilderness — it's graced with a tricky bend and three bunkers which surround the prize, so your aim had better be sharp.

The fourth hole is a stunning example of Canadian golf with a rugged infrastructure that dictates both strategic play and some deep breaths of mountain air between shots. This hole is known for its beauty, so tuck a camera into your bag and admire the view while you plot your strategy. **KLL**

OPPOSITE *The fourth hole at Kananaskis.*

**Course:** Greystone Golf Club

**Location:** White Hall, Maryland, USA

**Hole:** No. 4

**Length:** 192 yards

**Par:** 3

**Designer:** Joe Lee

**Course Comment:** This 18-hole course is situated in a large and scenic valley that is surrounded by 200- and 300-acre farms, and features picturesque views of the area. Greystone is located on 215 acres of rolling hills, 20 minutes north of the Beltway.

# No. ❹ GREYSTONE GOLF CLUB

The course is laid out through tall trees and wetlands, with 140 feet of elevation changes, seven ponds, and more than 80 bunkers.

It's a popular place to play golf, which is why the front nine was recently altered to allow for better course management during periods of heavy use — weekends and holidays.

The 192-yard par 4 is the signature hole on the course. It features water to the left of the green. The other side is no bargain, either. There is out-of-bounds and trees to the right, with a large sand bunker in front and behind the green.

You can play it safe. There is a bail-out fairway about 160 yards from the back tees. There are five sets of tees ranging from 105 to 192 yards.

The green, like many here at Greystone, can be fast and tricky. So take an extra second to line up that birdie putt.

Other memorable holes include the 402-yard seventh where the ideal line is to carry the hazards in one, and the 149-yard 14th to an undulating green guarded by deep bunkers.

The *Baltimore Sun* calls Greystone "one of the top courses in the greater Baltimore area, regardless of price." **TJ**

**Course:** Ganton Golf Club

**Location:** Ganton, Yorkshire, England

**Hole:** No. 4

**Length:** 406 yards

**Par:** 3

**Designer:** Tom Chisolm, Harry Vardon, Ted Ray, James Braid, Harry S. Colt

**Course Comment:** During his seven-year stay as Ganton's professional (1896–1903), Harry Vardon won the first three of his six British Open championships and one U.S. Open title (1900).

BELOW *David Inglis of the USA plays on the fourth hole at Ganton, September 2003.*

OPPOSITE *The fourth hole at Ganton.*

# No. ❹  GANTON GOLF CLUB

Ganton is a course that's known for its wide-open heathland, impenetrable gorse and perhaps most of all for its deep, punishing bunkers. All of those elements come into play on the long, par-3 fourth.

The tee shot is the easiest part of the hole, with plenty of fairway to accept your drive. But the approach is significantly more difficult, requiring your ball to be hit across a shallow valley to a plateau green guarded by gorse in the back, a bunker on the right, and a steep drop-off on the left. There also is a deep swale on the right rear portion of the putting surface that players should take care to avoid.

Gary Player once said of Ganton that it was the only inland layout worthy of holding the British Open Championship. It is the only inland course to hold the British Amateur three times (1964, 1977, and 1991), and also has played host to the Ryder Cup (1949), and more recently the Curtis Cup (2000) and Walker Cup (2003), one of only three courses — along with Royal Birkdale and Muirfield — to hold all three team competitions. **KA**

**Course:** National Golf Links of America

**Location:** Southampton, New York, USA

**Hole:** No. 4

**Length:** 190 yards

**Par:** 3

**Designer:** Charles Blair Macdonald

**Course Comment:** The difference between the highest point and the lowest point on the green at No. 4 is a whopping five feet.

# No. ❹ NATIONAL GOLF LINKS OF AMERICA

The National Golf Links of America is filled with some of the greatest replica holes the United States has to offer. Some would say that Charles Blair Macdonald simply took other architects' designs and made them his own. But, even though Macdonald took holes such as the Eden and the Road holes from St. Andrews, and the Alps hole from Prestwick, and brought his renditions to the National, he put his own signature on them to achieve a unique greatness.

The finest of these "knock-offs" is the par-3 fourth, which features the famous Redan design first executed to such perfection at Scotland's North Berwick. Certainly the design principle — based on wartime strategy which employed deep trenches in the front of a protected area — was not Macdonald's. But, like the other mimicry he performed at the National, Macdonald made up for any lack of originality with respect to the original design and a dedication to improving it.

When the great architect was finished and the National Golf Links of America was opened for play in 1911, some said it was the finest golf course in the United States. And, today, it still holds its place among the nation's best. The fourth hole is one of the big reasons why.

The Redan design came naturally at No. 4 because the land already was formed perfectly. From an elevated tee, players look down at the diagonal green, which is protected in the front by a huge and nasty sand pit and is surrounded by four other prominent bunkers. The hole can be conquered, but execution must be exact.

Going straight to the pin is a bold move, reserved for the best players of the game. The back right of the green is the "safe" play, but still, that

requires a 200-yard carry and precise aim. The sight from the tee is enough to make the unsure player a bit wary, but it is a sight designed to entice bravado. There is a bail-out area to the right of the green, but if you come to play this wonderful Redan with the idea of foregoing a true attack, what's the use? Swing away, it is advised, but do so with caution. **JB**

# RAJAPRUEK CLUB AT NORTH PARK

**Course:** Rajapruek Club at North Park

**Location:** Bangkok, Thailand

**Hole:** No. 4

**Length:** 214 yards

**Par:** 3

**Designer:** Robert Moore, JMP Golf Design

**Course Comment:** Golf was first played in Thailand in the 1920s at the old Royal Hua Hin course by the king and other members of royalty and aristocracy. The country has more than 200 golf courses today.

Rajapruek — one of Bangkok's most elite sports clubs — is 20 minutes from the center of bustling Bangkok, but out on the course it seems a world away with its lush, picturesque scenery and dramatic elevations, rare for this part of the world.

Although they began with a flat, seasonally flooded site, the designers achieved the elevation changes by using dewatering pumps to lower the water table and pump storm water to the surrounding klongs, or canals, giving them elevation differences of almost 35 feet and providing spectacular views from much of the golf course. That alone differentiates Rajapruek from other relatively flat courses in the region.

The fourth hole is a long par 3 that requires a strong tee shot to carry a lake, and features a sloping (right to left) green set in an amphitheater with a raised backdrop of colorful ornamental plantings. A deep bunker winds around the left side of the green from front to back, making the right side the preferred target area. Miss too far right, however, and your ball will land in a series of hollows and mounds that will make it difficult to get up and down. **KA**

# OAK TREE GOLF CLUB

**Course:** Oak Tree Golf Club

**Location:** Edmond, Oklahoma, USA

**Hole:** No. 4

**Length:** 200 yards

**Par:** 3

**Designer:** Pete Dye

**Course Comment:** Oak Tree is a relentless 18 holes of bent grass fairways and serious water play. The fourth is an example where the tee shot must carry water. It's nickname, in fact, is Waterloo.

A tee shot over water benchmarks No.4 at Oak Tree. All but 10 of this hole's 200 yards are played over water — demanding a flawless swing on a memorable hole. Aim is crucial and there is very little room for error.

On the first three holes of a difficult front nine, the Oklahoma breezes complicate each tee, and the bumps and hollows of the opening three gradually lead to the magical fourth.

A vicious downhill slope on the green and strategic bunkering on this distinguished and highly photographed hole make it a challenge even once you reach the putting surface. Serious players love the challenge of hole 4, and its designer used Mother Nature to play up its severity — No. 4 just wouldn't be the same without wind.

Is target golf your game? Are you a master of heroic shots? Even if you're not, you'll enjoy No. 4. Are you ready to shoot to one of the finest holes on Pete Dye's most distinguished piece of inland work? This is a bear of a course and the treacherous fourth gives the track its claws. **KLL**

**Course:** Cruden Bay Golf Club

**Location:** Cruden Bay, Aberdeenshire, Scotland

**Hole:** No. 4

**Length:** 193 yards

**Par:** 3

**Designer:** Old Tom Morris (1899), Tom Simpson, Herbert Fowler (1926)

**Course Comment:** Golf has been played on the land around Cruden Bay since 1791 but the original layout traces back to Old Tom Morris's design in 1899. The inner nine-hole Ladies Course was redesigned in 1926 and was renamed the St. Olaf Course.

**BELOW AND OPPOSITE** *Two views of the fourth hole at Cruden Bay.*

# No. ❹  CRUDEN BAY GOLF CLUB

Cruden Bay, quirky, short, and considered by many the most understated of Scotland's great links courses, is nothing if not subtle. Each hole features numerous targets, some deceptively situated, but there nevertheless. Yet these targets, once defined, are the key to Cruden Bay.

The desired target for the par-3 fourth, for example, could be a small, grassy knob just beyond the putting surface. This line takes players over a deep pot bunker, the hole's only bunker, and brings out-of-bounds down the left side into play. Or, if the hole is playing into the prevailing wind, players may want to aim down the right side in an attempt to avoid the deep grassy hollow that stretches from the tee box to the green.

Whatever the target, anything which reaches the putting surface should be considered a triumph. Short tee shots are destined to be swallowed up by a steep false front that feeds into the hollow below. Anything long will result in an awkward chip from the dunes.

The fourth, named Port Erroll after the small village adjacent to the course, is situated at a crucial juncture as the links makes its turn toward the Bay of Cruden for a dramatic, three-hole, seaside run. **RH**

## No. ❹ TERRACE DOWNS

**Course:** Terrace Downs

**Location:** Rakaia Gorge, Darfield, New Zealand

**Hole:** No. 4

**Length:** 191 yards

**Par:** 3

**Designer:** David Cox, Sid Puddicombe, Noel Bain, Fin Hobbs

**Course Comment:** A 50-minute scenic drive from Christchurch International Airport through the Canterbury foothills, will lead you to the unique recreation destination of Terrace Downs High Country Resort.

The fourth hole is a firm favorite of many golfers on this stunning course. The fourth is a "cheeky" par 3 that requires a fair amount of confidence coupled with a good iron shot to carry the lake protecting the front of the green. From the back tee it is 191 yards in length. You really better have some confidence to take aim from back there. A lot can happen on the way to the green.

With the pin placed at front left, only a very accurate shot will get close.

The safe — notice, we didn't say smart — option is short and right. But most players prefer to take their chance on landing one on the green. This is why golf is so much fun — the challenge.

The center back and right sides of the green are bunkers that can leave a difficult shot onto the putting surface. The green is no help either, sloping away and toward the water.

The 10th hole is another outstanding par 3. Pay for 18 holes and you get to play them both.

Jim Webster, editor of *Golf Australia*, had the following to say about the course: "Terrace Downs is enrapturing, a course that one can play day in and day out."

Just don't forget to bring some extra golf balls. **TJ**

**Course:** Banff Springs Golf Course

**Location:** Alberta, Canada

**Hole:** No. 4

**Length:** 192 yards

**Par:** 3

**Designer:** Stanley Thompson

**Course Comment:** Banff Springs opened in 1928 and was the first golf course in the world that cost more than $1 million to construct.

# No. ❹ BANFF SPRINGS GOLF COURSE

She is called the Devil's Cauldron, and although the name is designed to evoke images of fright when trying to master perhaps the most beautiful hole in the world, it seems a bit misplaced. Yes, there is danger at Banff Springs' fourth hole, but it is far outweighed by the panorama of Canada's Rocky Mountains. The hole may be devilish to play, but it looks like it was dropped straight from heaven.

There are so many reasons to love this hole on first glance, and even more when studying it a bit. It is breathtaking to look at, the strategy is brilliant, and it tricks you if you let it.

The green is small and round, protected by six bunkers and enveloped by towering trees. Even more majestic than the spruce and firs is the awesome splendor of Mount Rundle, which acts as a backdrop and dwarfs all else. The granite cliffs are as impressive a view off the tee as you will find anywhere in the world.

The tee is elevated 70 feet above the green, with a sparkling glacial lake in between. The lake and the hole share the aforementioned moniker: the Devil's Cauldron. There is nothing but lake between tee and green, and the only bail-out is to the right side of the putting surface. Even if your tee shot hits the green, a steep bank in the front does not guarantee that the ball will remain dry.

Canadian legend Stanley Thompson designed the course, and No. 4 wasn't even part of the original layout. When the glacial lake was formed in 1927, Thompson changed the design to incorporate it into the course.

Thompson not only added beauty with No. 4, but also a little mischief. He created an optical illusion for the player on the tee. When the pin is placed to the front of the green, the bunkers in the front make the hole appear closer than it really is. And when the pin is in the back, the upsloping bunkers in the rear make the target appear farther.

On second thought, when dealing with optical illusion, bunkers, steep banks, elevation changes, and a lake from tee to green, maybe the name Devil's Cauldron fits after all. **JB**

**OPPOSITE** *The fourth hole at Banff Springs.*

## No. ❹ PAINTED DESERT GOLF CLUB

**Course:** Painted Desert Golf Club

**Location:** Las Vegas, Nevada, USA

**Hole:** No. 4

**Length:** 180 yards

**Par:** 3

**Designers:** Jay Morrish

**Course Comment:** There is a love/hate relationship between the No. 4 hole and the management staff at Painted Desert. While the hole is both scenic and challenging, it results in a lot of slow play. When Painted Desert is busy, you can be sure there is a little backup at No. 4. So do the general manager a favor, knock it on the green and tap in your birdie — and then move along.

This is where it all got started — and it wasn't that long ago. Painted Desert, built in 1982, was the first of the desert courses in Las Vegas. Now they build golf courses faster than they build casinos.

The course features a great contrast of desert areas and lush green fairways, lending both beauty and challenge to your day on the links. Painted Desert's tee boxes and fairways are separated by native desert vegetation, including cactus and mesquite.

No. 4 is one of the best par-3 holes in Vegas — no matter how many more they keep building. And don't focus on the fountain in the pond to the left. You need all your concentration to survive this hole.

The lake does come into play on this hole, extending from the front to the left side of the green. There also is a huge bunker on the right side of the green that is as visually intimidating as the water.

The pin can be either behind the bunker or behind the water. The green front is small and it opens to the right in back of the water. There is also a very small bunker (about eight feet wide) on the left side of the green and it's not a bad place to be. It's better than being in the water. **KLL**

**Course:** Presidio Golf Course

**Location:** San Francisco, California, USA

**Hole:** No. 4

**Length:** 140 yards

**Par:** 3

**Designer:** Arnold Palmer

**Course Comment:** As anyone who has ever visited San Francisco will tell you, it can get pretty chilly. It's so cold, they should consider putting heat lamps on the golf course. Sorry, but that was not a bad joke. It wasn't even a joke. Presidio has heat lamps on fans located around the No. 4 green because the big trees around it block any kind of air flow.

## No. ❹  PRESIDIO GOLF COURSE

Newly rejuvenated and opened to the public under the watchful eye of Arnold Palmer Golf Management, the course is located in the heart of San Francisco just 10 minutes from downtown. Presidio, "rich with history, beauty and possibilities," is a popular place for a round of golf, averaging about 80,000 rounds a year.

One of the holes a good majority of those remember is No. 4, a 140-yard par 3 with trouble all over, especially around the green.

From the tee, you need to hit a fade or a very straight ball on this hole, which is the most photographed on the course. Standing on the tee you will see why so much film has been used on this spot.

The green, which is 50 feet downhill, is the signature on this hole. And it used to be a much smaller signature.

At 7,000 square feet, the green is the largest on the golf course. But the bunkers total about 4,000 square feet. It was only recently that these numbers were practically reversed, increasing the size of the green to what it is now.

The six bunkers completely surround the green — like soldiers standing guard. And rarely does a foursome pass through where at least one doesn't end up getting sand in their shoes. **TJ**

**Course:** Vilamoura Golf Club (Old Course)

**Location:** The Algarve, Portugal

**Hole:** No. 4

**Length:** 178 yards

**Par:** 3

**Designer:** Frank Pennink

**Course Comment:** It's not unusual to see packs of wild dogs running around the Old Course at Vilamoura.

## No. ❹  VILAMOURA GOLF CLUB (OLD COURSE)

It is a credit to designer Frank Pennink that the Old Course has stood the test of time even though many new courses have sprung up in The Algarve since this layout was first opened in 1969.

There is no trickery to the Old Course. What you see is what you get. So it is with the par-3 fourth hole. Normally this is a hole that calls for nothing more than a short iron off the tee from the visitor's tees. Play it off the back and it becomes more testing, calling for a medium or even a long iron if it is into the wind. The hole is defended by two features: a water hazard that fronts the green, and a large umbrella pine standing on the right-hand side of the green. Underclub and you get wet, hit a fade or a push and the tree comes into play.

The ideal shot is a fade that starts on the left-hand edge of the green and moves from left to right into the heart of the green. However, this raised green has so many subtle borrows that even those who hit the green can walk off with a bogey after a three putt. **AT**

## No. ❹ RIVIERA COUNTRY CLUB

**Course:** Riviera Country Club

**Location:** Pacific Palisades, California, USA

**Hole:** No. 4

**Length:** 236 yards

**Par:** 3

**Designer:** George C. Thomas Jr.

**Course Comment:** Ben Hogan once called No. 4 at Riviera Country Club the best par 3 in golf. Today, many would disagree — some would even suggest it's not the best par 3 at Riviera. But let's give Hogan some due. He did know a small amount about golf.

Making a par-3 hole stand out is not an easy task. But George Thomas, considered by many as one of the greatest designers of all time, pulled it off at Riviera.

As soon as you step on this course you realize it is something special. By the time you finish the impressive third hole and reach the tee at No. 4, you understand what all the fuss is about. Of course, avoiding that big bunker you can't keep your eyes off would certainly go a long way in enhancing your enjoyment.

Look at the size of that thing. Was there any sand left for the beaches along the Pacific?

"Yeah, that's a big one," said one of the starters. "I would say it's 25 feet long, if not more. And about 20 feet wide. You can get lost in there."

It won't add to your enjoyment — but it will add to your scorecard if you land in it. The safe play on this 236-yard hole usually into the wind is to the right of the bunker. You can get some friendly rolls from that right side. And even if you are in the rough over there, it's not a bad chip to the green.

The starter had this warning about the green: "It's very fast and can roll right off so be careful. It moves pretty quick right to left."

Left. Right toward the beach. **TJ**

**Course:** Royal County Down

**Location:** Newcastle, County Down, Northern Ireland

**Hole:** No. 4

**Length:** 212 yards

**Par:** 3

**Designer:** Old Tom Morris

**Course Comment:** County Down was likely the first links layout with both nines starting and finishing at the clubhouse. Prior to this, courses consisted of nine holes out, then nine holes back.

BELOW *Ian Stanley of Australia plays out of a bunker on the fourth hole at Royal County Down, July 2000.*

OPPOSITE *The fourth hole at Royal County Down.*

# No. ❹  ROYAL COUNTY DOWN

Royal County Down's fourth hole is an important part of what many consider the finest front nine anywhere. The horizon-spanning view from the hillside back tee includes the beautiful towering mountains of Mourne, 10 bunkers, a sea of gorse, and Dundrum Bay, an inlet of the Irish Sea. It is among the most breathtaking yet tranquil settings in the world of golf. It also is one of the most frightening shots you'll ever hit.

The green itself is long and narrow, rising slightly from front to back with large drop-offs at either side and to the rear, leaving golfers a rather small safe haven at the front of the putting surface. Miss the green, and you're guaranteed a difficult chip shot at best. A final tip: putts running from front to back will move toward the sea.

What was Old Tom Morris's fee to design out the championship course at County Down? A mere four gold guineas, or about 4.2 pounds. A bargain by any standard, even in 1889, but especially for a layout counted by most as one of the top three courses in Europe, if not the world. **KA**

**Course:** Playacar Golf Course

**Location:** Playa Del Carmen, Mexico

**Hole:** No. 4

**Length:** 342 yards

**Par:** 4

**Designer:** Robert von Hagge

**Course Comment:** Playacar and Moon Palace are about 50 miles apart but both are owned and operated by Palace Resorts. Both courses are known for their challenges and excellent playing conditions.

## No. ❹ PLAYACAR GOLF COURSE

Don't be fooled by the length and don't think you can drive this hole from the tee. It's impossible to do. So settle down and try to reach it in two, because even that isn't easy to accomplish on this 342-yard par 4.

Your ideal tee shot is a 6-iron. There is no need to blast away on this hole. A good, medium-to-long iron will get you to the bend so you can see the green on this dogleg left.

Once you can see the green, you can see the trouble.

About 90 yards before the green is a big slope downhill, and in front of the green is a wall that fronts the putting surface. You don't want to be hitting off that downhill lie and you certainly don't want to hit the wall.

But don't be long, either. Behind the green are a couple of traps that create quite a problem when you are trying to get up and down.

The green is pretty flat, but it is small. If you can get to the green in two, this becomes a real birdie opportunity. Getting there in two is the problem.

Both Playacar and Moon Palace are among the top 10 courses in Mexico. You can't go wrong with either venue when it comes to golf. **AT**

OPPOSITE *Two views of the fourth hole at Playacar.*

**Course:** Inverness Club

**Location:** Toledo, Ohio, USA

**Hole:** No. 4

**Length:** 466 yards

**Par:** 4

**Designer:** Donald Ross

**Course Comment:** There is quite a bit of difference in tee boxes at Inverness. For example, the No. 4 hole has five choices, ranging from the green tees (341 yards) to the black tees (466 yards). No. 4 is also the No. 3 handicap hole.

## No. ❹ INVERNESS CLUB

Inverness has hosted numerous PGA Championships and U.S. Opens and the narrow course's five finishing holes are known as "Murderers' Row." But there is nothing easy about the front nine, either. Just check out No. 4.

The first of several excellent, long par-4 holes, No. 4 is classically beautiful and challenging, which typically plays into the prevailing wind.

A well-struck driver off the tee will leave a long- to mid-iron approach into a slightly elevated green, which sits atop a plateau. The green slopes from front right to back left, creating numerous challenging hole positions.

As you can see, you don't have to wait until the back nine to get into serious trouble.

The players of the 1931 U.S. Open took up a collection and presented the club with a huge cathedral chime clock on the final day of the tournament. The clock is still there today, its inscription bearing witness to the beginning of a new era of golf. It reads: "God measures men by what they are, Not by what they in wealth possess, This vibrant message chimes afar, The voice of Inverness." **TJ**

**Course:** Spyglass Hill Golf Club

**Location:** Pebble Beach, California, USA

**Hole:** No. 4

**Length:** 365 yards

**Par:** 4

**Designer:** Robert Trent Jones Sr.

**Course Comment:** The fourth green, encircled in ice plant, is said to be the course's most photographed. Spyglass Hill is rated one of the toughest courses in the world from the championship tees, boasting a course rating of 75.3 and a slope rating of 148.

BELOW *Mike Weir of Canada plays at Spyglass Hill, February 2003.*

OPPOSITE *The fourth hole at Spyglass Hill.*

# No. ❹  SPYGLASS HILL GOLF CLUB

The term "links-style course" is so overused (not to mention misused) in the United States as to render its mention incredible. So many courses claim to be links-style, when in fact they are lucky to approach faux-links. And most times, even that is a stretch.

There are exceptions, of course. There are occasional courses, or more accurately, holes that achieve the true essence of links golf — giving credence to the claim that a links-style course was both the goal and the accomplishment.

The short, par-4 fourth at Spyglass Hill is one of the holes in America that can legitimately call itself a true links-style hole. Robert Trent Jones Sr. set out to create it as such, and he achieved his aim. Bushels and bushels of ice plant lining the fairway helped Jones's cause. Natural brush and sea oats, and undisturbed scrub and sand also pitched in. As with most of the best holes in the world, nature provides most of the splendor. The designer just helps it along. Such is the case with the fourth at Spyglass.

The hole is a dogleg left, which drifts downhill and slopes toward the ocean on the right side of the fairway. The safe play is to the right side, which is the widest landing area to be found. But this brings into play many of the hazards in front of the hole. If you are brave off the tee and hit to the narrow left side, it will give you a less perilous approach. This is not an issue of length, but the thought process involved. This hole requires decisions. You don't grip and rip at No. 4. You stop and think.

The green is oblong and diagonal. It also is very narrow. It is deceptively warm, with its tucked-in appearance and friendly, natural look. However, it takes a pure shot to hold the skinny patch of green. And because the putting surface is so very long, reaching it is no guarantee at all of a two-putt.

Yes, this is a true links hole, with the sound of the ocean blasting just off the green. Jones achieved his goal of a links-style course, and he also accomplished something else: he created a golf hole that is a whole lot of fun to play. **JB**

**Course:** Bandon Dunes (Legends Course)

**Location:** Bandon, Oregon, USA

**Hole:** No. 4

**Length:** 410 yards

**Par:** 4

**Designer:** David McLay Kidd

**Course Comment:** The panoramic setting gets most of the attention at Bandon Dunes but the layout's true gift may be its design. With open fairways and subtle greens, Bandon is an eminently playable course even in the fiercest of winds.

# No. ❹ BANDON DUNES (LEGENDS COURSE)

It's the visuals at Bandon Dunes that have the ability to all at once soothe and startle, tantalize and terrify. Sweeping ocean vistas and towering dunes combine with looming hazards and incessant winds in a harmonized symphony of sweet and sour.

The visual from the fourth tee box, for example, is a seemingly endless field of native grasses with just a hint of the emerald-green fairway in the distance. In fact, from the back tees not even the fairway is visible. An isolated bunker down the left side is the desired target into a deceptively large driving area.

Once in the fairway the hole sweeps right to a large, angled green protected by deep bunkers front left and the Pacific Ocean long. The hole usually plays into the ocean breeze and most players will have a mid-iron in. A low, running shot up the right side is the best approach. Anything short and right is safe but players will face a difficult chip over a ridge if the pin is cut back left.

Kidd intended the fourth to be the player's first introduction to the Pacific Ocean and what a welcome it is. The fourth sets the stage for a dramatic swing along the coastal cliffs on Nos. 5 and 6. In total, Bandon Dunes features seven holes that run along the edge of the bluff. **RH**

**Course:** Glen Eagles Golf Club
(Blue Course)

**Location:** Bolton, Ontario, Canada

**Hole:** No. 4

**Length:** 436 yards

**Par:** 4

**Designer:** René Muylaert

**Course Comment:** When you play this par 4 watch out for the lady in the big white dress and the guy in the tux. No. 4 is such a scenic hole, it's become a popular photo spot for weddings. And don't be checking out anyone in the wedding party—you have plenty of other things to be thinking about on this hole.

# No. ❹ GLEN EAGLES GOLF CLUB
## (BLUE COURSE)

The signature hole on the Blue Course is the tough No. 4, a 436-yard dogleg left featuring an elevated tee. It's one of the more difficult holes at Glen Eagles, especially when you are teeing it up from the back tees. Let's face it, from the reds (337 yards) it's not that tough.

The tee is elevated about 25 feet above the fairway and you must carry the pond. From the back tees, you need to smack it about 200 yards to reach the fairway — and another 30 yards or so to reach the turn.

There is some swampland along the left side of the fairway. The advice from the clubhouse is to hit it long and hit it right — which gives you a better shot at the green.

The green has three grass bunkers and some trees to the back and a sand bunker along the front left side.

You might not par this hole, but you will certainly remember it. And remember to bring some rice to toss at the happy couple.

Located about 20 minutes from the west side of Toronto, Glen Eagles is a 27-hole championship course with natural terrain of high hills, vistas, and valleys. **TJ**

---

**Course:** Seminole Golf Club

**Location:** North Palm Beach, Florida, USA

**Hole:** No. 4

**Length:** 450 yards

**Par:** 4

**Designers:** Peter Thomson, Michael Wolveridge, Ross Perrett

**Course Comment:** The scorecard says 450 yards from the back tees. But the scorecard doesn't mention the wind. And when it's blowing off the ocean you will want to add more yards and more club on this scenic hole on this scenic golf course.

# No. ❹ SEMINOLE GOLF CLUB

The green on this 450-yard par 4 sits on the second-highest elevation on the golf course and the wind can really whip around up there, especially later in the day. So take this into account when reaching into the bag.

From the back tee, you have to carry about 180 to 200 yards of sandy marsh to reach the fairway. You can play it out of the sand, but as they say in the pro shop, "it's not a lot of fun."

There is a large bunker on the left and that same sandy waste area on the right. Big hitters should note the pot bunker on the right side about 285 yards from the back tees. Note it, then avoid it.

From the pot bunker, it's about 170 yards and a little valley between you and the elevated green. There also are four or five bunkers about 40 to 60 yards from the green you should try to avoid.

The green slopes back to front with a short "false" green on the front, two bunkers to the right, and one to the left.

And don't forget to stop and enjoy the view from the green. It's well worth the climb. **TJ**

**Course:** Royal St. George's Golf Club

**Location:** Sandwich, Kent, England

**Hole:** No. 4

**Length:** 470 yards

**Par:** 4

**Designer:** Laidlaw Purves, Alister MacKenzie, J.J.F. Pennink

**Course Comment:** Royal St. George's played host to the 2003 British Open, which featured perhaps the biggest surprise winner in the history of the tournament when little-known Ben Curtis walked away with the Claret Jug.

## No. ❹ ROYAL ST. GEORGE'S GOLF CLUB

The fourth hole at Royal St. George's (or Sandwich, to the locals) is a gargantuan test of golf on one of the most respected courses in the world. Its length and its potential pitfalls combine to make par an extremely fortunate score. In fact, none but the best golfers should consider this a par 4. Mid-range handicappers should stand on the tee, enjoy the visuals, play the hole as a par 5 and enjoy themselves.

Consider the name of the landing area off the tee, "Elysian Fields," which is supposed to emit a peaceful feeling once a player arrives. However, mere survival might be the genuine emotion after hitting a tee shot next to an enormous bunker. Add the 185-yard carry over brush and heather to the narrow fairway, and a feeling of peace may just have to wait a moment.

There are bunkers on the right side, and there is another on the left at 257 yards. If you happen to land parallel to the left bunker — the ideal spot for most players — that still leaves you with nearly 190 yards into the green. Even players who hit it in the 300-yard range must be careful off the tee. Yes, they can clear the bunkers with no problem, but there is a large hollow that is about 35 yards in the area where the big hitters would land.

So the second shot is nearly guaranteed to be at least a mid-range iron for even the top players, and this is trouble because the green is small. If a player comes in hot on his approach, there is even more danger, because if you happen to miss the bunker behind the green you go out of bounds.

Royal St. George's is a private club, but guests are welcome on weekdays and non-holidays. And it is worth a call ahead to get a tee time to play not only the difficult fourth hole, but the rest of the course. Any venue that has hosted tournaments such as the British Open, the Walker Cup, the British and English Amateurs, and the European PGA Championship is a course worth playing and remembering. **JB**

**BELOW** *The fourth hole at Royal St. George's.*

**OPPOSITE** *One of the problematic bunkers on the fourth hole at Royal St. George's.*

# KIAWAH ISLAND RESORT
## (OCEAN COURSE)

**Course:** Kiawah Island Resort (Ocean Course)

**Location:** Kiawah Island, South Carolina, USA

**Hole:** No. 4

**Length:** 432 yards

**Par:** 4

**Designer:** Pete Dye

**Course Comment:** Although Pete Dye's original idea was to sit the course back behind the dunes, Dye's wife, Alice, suggested raising the entire layout to allow for an unobstructed view of Kiawah's pristine shoreline.

This relatively young Pete Dye layout (1991) already has been the site of three major professional events: the 1991 "War by the Shore" Ryder Cup and the 1997 and 2003 World Cups. But with all 18 holes set among the sand dunes and offering panoramic views of the Atlantic, it's likely the Ocean Course would have earned widespread acclaim had no tournament ever been played along its South Carolina shores.

Dye has returned here several times to soften the layout from the devastating difficulty it presented to the world's top players during the 1991 Ryder Cup. The treacherous fourth, however, as the No. 1 handicap hole, still has retained plenty of its severity.

The drive is daunting, but the fairway has more room to the right than it appears from the tee. A tee shot too far left, though, will run through the fairway and into the Lowcountry saltwater marshes.

The putting surface is guarded by a front right waste area for shots that come up short, and for those that go too long, mounds of dunes wait behind the green. Club selection will play a vital role on a hole — and course — that can change almost instantly depending on the ocean winds. **KA**

## No. 4   **DESERT PINES GOLF CLUB**

**Course:** Desert Pines Golf Club

**Location:** Las Vegas, Nevada, USA

**Hole:** No. 4

**Length:** 322 yards

**Par:** 4

**Designer:** Dye Designs International

**Course Comment:** Las Vegas likes duplication. Look at the casinos. Where else can you find New York, Paris, a castle, and a pyramid all in one place? This philosophy isn't exclusive to the mega-hotels. With more than 2,000 pine trees lining the championship golf course, Desert Pines has a "Carolina" look and feel to it. Welcome to Pinehurst — just 15 minutes from the strip.

This short par 4, called "The Narrows," measures 322 yards from the back tees. Water is along the right side with pine trees beyond that. The fairway, which does open up past the water, ends about 58 yards before the green.

The experts in the clubhouse say that the water shouldn't come into play. The key word being "shouldn't." But it doesn't always work out.

The rough in front of the green is tall, hilly, and not the best place to be in Las Vegas.

No. 4 is one of those holes with trouble lurking around every corner.

This is a real easy hole if you hit it straight off the tee. You can even get away with using an iron to get it into the fairway. Play this hole smart and you'll be fine.

The par-71 course measures about 6,800 yards and forces even the best golfers to think. Most of the fairways are narrow and water is plentiful. The short holes can tease you into going for the green when a smarter play would have been to lay up.

Save your gambling for the strip. Unless of course you feel lucky. **TJ**

## No. 4   **ELMBROOK GOLF COURSE**

**Course:** Elmbrook Golf Course

**Location:** Traverse City, Michigan, USA

**Hole:** No. 4

**Length:** 374 yards

**Par:** 4

**Designer:** Verner Nelson

**Course Comment:** Another interesting hole at Elmbrook is the third hole. Not because it's a challenging hole, but because the green is shaped like the state of Michigan and the bunkers around it resemble the Great Lakes.

Elmbrook opened in 1964 and is among the oldest of Michigan's public courses. Situated on high rolling terrain, the course offers panoramic views of the Grand Traverse Bays.

Verner Nelson designed the course in 1964 but he left most of the design to Mother Nature. They didn't exactly bring in bulldozers and move the earth. Instead, Nelson, whose son and daughter still own the course, followed the land.

And Mother Nature can be a pretty good designer where golf courses are concerned. No. 4 is a perfect example.

This short par 4 is a sharp dogleg right from an elevated tee to an elevated green. In between is where the fun is. League members and regulars love this hole because it was built with a little forgiveness in mind.

The fairway is actually a valley with mounds or hills running along both sides all the way to the green. Hit it a little to the left and the hill often kicks it back to the fairway. Same thing if you are to the right.

The hole is very reachable in two. It's not a bad idea to keep your driver in the bag and use an iron off the tee.

It's not the toughest hole on the course, but the locals call it one of the more interesting. **TJ**

**Course:** Yale University Golf Course

**Location:** New Haven, Connecticut, USA

**Hole:** No. 4

**Length:** 443 yards

**Par:** 4

**Designer:** Charles Blair Macdonald, Seth Raynor

**Course Comment:** The fourth hole at Yale isn't exactly a "knock-off" of the 17th at St. Andrews Old Course, but the similarities are inescapable.

# No. ❹   YALE UNIVERSITY GOLF COURSE

The hallowed hallways at Yale University are rife with academia, making way for some of the most scholarly students and professors in the world. Certainly, when one speaks of Yale, one conjures a picture of intelligence. There is another, perhaps lesser known offering the institution makes to history: It was the first university in the United States to build a quality golf course on its grounds.

In 1925, when Charles Blair Macdonald and Seth Raynor pooled their architectural abilities in New Haven, the only other university in the world that had a top-notch golf course was St. Andrews in Scotland. There were other universities that had golf courses, but none that were worthy of first-rate competition.

The course at Yale changed all that, and it stands today, 80 years later, as a testament to the wealth of talent possessed by its two designers. This was a collaboration of mentor and protégé, with Raynor being the follower in this pair of geniuses. And, just as Raynor mimicked many of Macdonald's architectural tendencies, adding personal touches to make them his own, so does the fourth hole at Yale take characteristics from one of the greatest holes in the world — No. 17 at St. Andrews. The Road hole.

As on the Road hole, there is danger on the right side at Yale's fourth (a railroad shed at St. Andrews, a pond in New Haven), but the more risk a player is willing to take, the more the reward on the approach. The closer you drive to the right-side peril, the more comfortable the ensuing entrance to the green.

There are four bunkers surrounding the green, but the only one that really comes into play is the deep trap up front, which serves as ample protection to the center of the green. The bunker in the front bears another striking similarity to the Road hole, mimicking the famed Road bunker. There is one more bunker to the right and two to the left which frame the putting surface, but they only would catch the most errant of shots.

As you might expect at Yale, it takes a very smart play indeed to get home in two. The green itself is fairly straightforward, so if you do succeed in regulation, you could set yourself up for a fair shot at birdie. Certainly, three-putts should be rare. **JB**

**Course:** Clearwater Bay Golf & Country Club

**Location:** Sai Kung, New Territories, Hong Kong, China

**Hole:** No. 4

**Length:** 405 yards

**Par:** 4

**Designer:** T. Sawai, A. Furukawa

**Course Comment:** Clearwater Bay Golf & Country Club has hosted international events including the Omega PGA Championships and the Star Alliance Open.

# No. ❹ CLEARWATER BAY GOLF & COUNTRY CLUB

Clearwater Bay is to Asia what Augusta National, or perhaps, Pinehurst No. 2, is to the United States. Quite simply, it is one of the premier courses in Hong Kong, and beyond that, the Asian continent. It is a links-style course, yet not quite 100 percent links in design. The fairways are narrow, the winds blow in from the sea, the roughs are treacherous, and the putting surfaces challenging.

The course is divided into two distinct nines. There is the Ocean Nine and the Highland Nine, with the differences being obvious. The vistas on both nines are amazing, but one side offers visions of the crashing tide, the other offers mounds, and rough and lush green fairway. But the similarity between the two is that you can enjoy the mountains no matter where you are on the course.

The fourth hole at Clearwater Bay is straightforward enough, and actually it isn't even one of the more difficult challenges at the course. But, there is one small catch: you must fire a shot over a cliff. A rare condition to face on any course in the world.

Get over the cliff in good shape, and you've got No. 4 licked. But, if your ball doesn't land on safe ground, a penalty is in order and par is lost.

So, enjoy the view.

But watch your step. **JB**

**Course:** The Olympic Club
(Lake Course)

**Location:** San Francisco, California,
USA

**Hole:** No. 4

**Length:** 438 yards

**Par:** 4

**Designer:** Sam Whiting

**Course Comment:** How tough is
No. 4 at the famed Olympic Club?
Our expert in the pro shop had this
to say: "It's no cake walk. One of the
tougher holes out here. In fact, holes
two through six are so tough, you
might just want to walk off after
only nine holes."

# No. ❹ THE OLYMPIC CLUB
## (LAKE COURSE)

The San Francisco Olympic Club is the oldest athletic club in the United States. It was founded on May 6 1860, downtown in the still-new city by 23 young men of varying walks of life, from artists to adventurers.

The adventure really begins on the par-4 fourth hole at Olympic. Most of the time, it's an adventure the golfer doesn't win.

The No. 1 handicap hole on the Lake Course, this 438-yard masterpiece, is a dogleg left with a fairway that slopes down and away to the right. In other words, it slopes away from the direction you want to go — which is left around the dogleg.

There are two bunkers about 20 to 30 yards short of the green on both the left and right side of the fairway. Getting to the green is very difficult — and once you're there you will wonder why you tried to get there so fast.

The green slopes slightly off to the right, so take that into account when you line up the approach shot. The front part of the green is sloped. If you hit the so-called false green, your ball will roll right back toward you and end up on the fringe or, even worse, the rough.

As the host site for a number of major championships, including four U.S. Opens, this outstanding course speaks for itself. With no water hazards in play and only one fairway bunker, your only problem becomes the thick rough and dense tree lines. An extremely exclusive club, only members and their guests are permitted to play this pristine course. **TJ**

**Course:** The National Golf Club
(Moonah Course)

**Location:** Cape Schanck, Victoria,
Australia

**Hole:** No. 4

**Length:** 444 yards

**Par:** 4

**Designer:** Greg Norman,
Bob Harrison

**Course Comment:** The No. 1 index
hole on the course is as tough as it is
scenic, and it makes everyone's list
of the best — and most difficult —
modern par 4s in Australia.

# No. ❹ THE NATIONAL GOLF CLUB
## (MOONAH COURSE)

The tee shot delights on this hole, as it must be hit from a large, elevated dune through a narrow opening in the Moonah trees onto a plateau landing area replete with undulations and bordered on both sides by more dangerous sand dunes.

Length is key here, however, and even a terrific view cannot make up for a less-than-powerful drive. Most golfers will invariably face a longish approach shot at No. 4, and they can make things somewhat easier by keeping their balls on the right side of the fairway; that position will usually give them flatter lies and a more open angle from which they can attack the slightly elevated green.

But they must be careful to stay right with those shots as well, and pay special heed to the two bunkers flanking the putting surface ominously on the left. **JS**

**Course:** Firestone Country Club (South Course)

**Location:** Akron, Ohio, USA

**Hole:** No. 4

**Length:** 471 yards

**Par:** 4

**Designer:** Bert Way, Robert Trent Jones Sr.

**Course Comment:** A couple of legends have taken a swing at improving Firestone's South Course. Robert Trent Jones redesigned the South Course in 1959, followed by Jack Nicklaus in 1986.

# No. ❹  FIRESTONE COUNTRY CLUB
## (SOUTH COURSE)

The fabled Firestone Country Club has a rich history of testing the elite golfers. If country clubs were high-school courses, Firestone's South trek would be advance calculus. In other words, there are no gimmies, especially on a course nicknamed "The Monster."

Noted for its length, the par-70, 7,283-yard South Course includes a series of challenging and intimidating, long par-4 holes and one of the longest par 5s anywhere.

It doesn't get much tougher than No. 4. And this hole can trick you. Because from the tee, it doesn't look like the most difficult hole in the world. In fact, it looks rather easy. Until you have to hit the ball.

An accurate tee shot is required to hit the right-to-left sloping fairway. The second shot must come in high to hold the elevated green. Par is always a good score — even for the game's elite.

All the hole asks you to do is hit a long and straight tee shot followed by an approach shot that must be high enough to hold the green. Easier said than done — which is another nickname associated with Firestone Country Club's South Course.

The 4th hole is a 471-yard monster. When Robert Trent Jones redesigned Firestone into The Monster in 1959, this hole made par not only acceptable but welcome. **TJ**

**Course:** The Country Club

**Location:** Brookline, Massachusetts, USA

**Hole:** No. 4

**Length:** 334 yards

**Par:** 4

**Designer:** Willie Campbell, William S. Flynn, Rees Jones

**Course Comment:** The Country Club was the site of perhaps one of the most controversial Ryder Cup matches ever played. In 1999, there was a raucous U.S. celebration that irked many Europeans, but that was far away from the fourth hole, which was the site of drama during the matches — because many players went for the par-4 green off the tee.

# No. ❹  THE COUNTRY CLUB

Now, this . . . is a fun golf hole.

At 334 yards, it is an incredibly short par 4. The average Joe still would maintain his sanity and play it as a two-shot hole. Even that makes it excitingly dangerous with all the possible pitfalls along the way. But when the best of the best visit The Country Club, the drama — and yes, fun — is taken to another level.

The world's top players often stare down No. 4, pull out the big stick, and eye the green in one. They are awarded occasionally with a rare chance at eagle on a par-4 hole. More often, even the best and those filled most with bravado are left with a humbling walk toward shin-high rough and a new grip on reality.

"Shoulda played it safe," is perhaps the most-heard refrain coming off the fourth tee at The Country Club.

Here's why the regret: it's so tempting to grab a driver and let it rip off such a short hole, but there's so much to lose. The shot is blind, forcing even the biggest hitters to just pick an aiming point and hope for the best. Faith can apply itself successfully in many facets of life, but it often isn't the best road to paradise on The Country Club's fourth.

Even if the aiming point proves sound, and you pipe it on course, your tee shot must traverse a ridge. So you've hit the best shot you know how to hit, and you're still not sure that it's what you've wanted to do. Faith, once again, is called upon. You look at your caddie, or your playing partner, and they look back. Neither of you knowing if success has been achieved. A fun hole, but perhaps too much mystery when going for the green in one.

Until now, we've talked of this hole in the context of the big boys, those who would dare take on 334 yards in one shot. But, there is peril in The Country Club's fourth even for those who would hit iron off the tee. Perhaps less than taking aim at the green, but there are still dangers for the safe player. Six bunkers surround the putting surface, and the rough is so penal that it almost guarantees a one-stroke addition to your card.

The green is but 40 feet wide. So, no matter how you get there, it pays to be precise. At least, at this wonderfully enticingly dangerous hole, a two-putt should be close to automatic. Fun, don't you think? **JB**

**Course:** Le Robinie Golf Club

**Location:** Olona, Lombardia, Italy

**Hole:** No. 4

**Length:** 417 yards

**Par:** 4

**Designer:** Jack Nicklaus

**Course Comment:** Le Robinie, located midway between the cities of Milan and Varese, is the only Jack Nicklaus design in Italy.

# No. ❹  LE ROBINIE GOLF CLUB

In the Lombardy region of northern Italy, made famous for its shimmering lakes and sumptuous wines, Jack Nicklaus created a peaceful, green oasis that sits at the doorstep of bustling Milan and at the foot of the magnificent Italian Alps.

Nicklaus incorporated many techniques of modern American golf design on what had been a rather flat piece of property, using extensive excavation work to sculpt a layout with numerous water hazards, bunkers, and contours, as well as natural-looking amphitheaters that surround many of the holes.

The fourth hole, Nicklaus' finest at Le Robinie, has all of these elements, and the slight dogleg right offers players an interesting risk-reward scenario. The fairway contains plenty of mounds and undulations, and slopes gently toward a pond on the right.

The real risk, however, is on the approach, as a series of deep, terraced bunkers lies just short and right of the shallow green, which sits on a plateau. Better players often favor the right side of the fairway because it makes the hole shorter. The safe play, however, is to the longer left side, allowing a much better chance to avoid the imposing bunker complex. **KA**

**Course:** Castelgandolfo Country Club

**Location:** Castelgandolfo, Lazio, Italy

**Hole:** No. 4

**Length:** 411 yards

**Par:** 4

**Designer:** Robert Trent Jones Sr.

**Course Comment:** The nearby medieval town of Castel Gandolfo is known primarily for being the Pope's summer residence. The original palace was built in 1624 and has been used by pontiffs ever since.

# No. ❹  CASTELGANDOLFO COUNTRY CLUB

This outstanding course, with a restored 17th-century villa as its clubhouse, sits in a volcanic crater near the hilltop resort of Castel Gandolfo, located approximately 15 miles southeast of Rome. American architect Robert Trent Jones Sr. was provided with one of the most unique and lovely settings in all of golf — an extinct volcano that millions of years later has become lush, fertile terrain. A lake that had formed in the volcanic crater was drained by the hydraulic engineers of ancient Rome, who created a network of trench ducts that remain in use today.

With all this to work with, Jones didn't disappoint, creating a marvelous design in the midst of century-old mediterranean olives, pines, cypresses, mimosas, and citrus trees.

Castelgandolfo's fourth hole is its hardest, but also one of its most scenic. The tee shot is hit to a gradually narrowing fairway, with several trees providing an obstacle on the left. Two lakes encroach upon the approach, pinching the fairway so that only a thin peninsula leads up to the shallow, slightly elevated putting surface, which is guarded by a pair of nasty bunkers.

Make sure you hit a good drive. You'll need it to have any chance at making the well-protected green with your second shot. **KA**

## No. ❹ FISHERS ISLAND CLUB

**Course:** Fishers Island Club

**Location:** Fishers Island, New York, USA

**Hole:** No. 4

**Length:** 397 yards

**Par:** 4

**Designer:** Seth Raynor

**Course Comment:** Although Fishers Island is claimed by New York, it is actually located just off the Connecticut shore, near New London.

Taking the ferry to Fishers Island Club, a secluded haunt surrounded by the waters of Long Island Sound, might be worth it just for the opportunity to play the club's fourth hole, considered one of Seth Raynor's best.

The hole features no bunkers and the only blind shot on the course, to a green that juts into the sound and is intimidating, to say the least. Maybe it's best you can't see all the obstacles the extreme uphill approach must avoid. The punchbowl green is huge — 12,000 square feet — but it's only fair, because you'll likely need all of it. The fickle winds off the sound are often hard to judge, making club selection difficult. Come up short, and your shot will roll back down the hill. Fly it long, and an even worse fate awaits on the other side, which appears to drop off into the ocean.

Fishers Island has been called the "Cypress Point of the East," a name that isn't bestowed lightly. Because of excellent Raynor holes such as the fourth, Fishers Island is worthy. There are few islands — if any — where a golfer would rather be marooned. **KA**

**Course:** Rye Golf Club

**Location:** Rye, East Sussex, England

**Hole:** No. 4

**Length:** 410 yards

**Par:** 4

**Designer:** Harry S. Colt

**Course Comment:** The first competition at Rye Golf Club took place in February 1894. A rarity — women members were admitted from the start, and by 1905 there were 490 members, 60 of them women.

OPPOSITE *The fourth hole at Rye Golf Club.*

## No. ❹ RYE GOLF CLUB

Most times, the most difficult part about playing a golf course is charting a fine score, perhaps carding a couple of birdies or maybe even an eagle. At Rye Golf Club, however, the hardest test may just be getting on the course.

Visitors are asked to call the secretary ahead of time, and it is a very difficult sell to be invited for a round without a member's introduction.

You get the idea. If you get on the course, enjoy your round. There is plenty of opportunity to have a good time, because it is indeed a wonderful course with plenty of history to offer.

No. 4, at 410 yards, is not made difficult by its length. But its routing makes it a nearly impossible fairway. Its aiming point rests atop a sand dune from start to finish, and if either your drive or approach goes anything but straight, it will stray from the top of the dune, and absolute devilish results await you.

Don't think there is any break once you reach the green. The putting surface itself also rests atop the same dune, and any approach missing to the right will fall away and leave you with a wedge or run-up rather than a putt on your third shot.

The green is sloped right toward you, so you better make it up to the hole, or the ball might find its way right back to your feet. This hole is 410 yards of pure torture if you do not play it right. But, if you do, pocket a par and pat yourself on the back (for the par and for getting on the course). **JB**

---

**Course:** The Dunes Golf Links

**Location:** Rye, Victoria, Australia

**Hole:** No. 4

**Length:** 343 yards

**Par:** 4

**Designer:** Tony Cashmore

**Course Comment:** Set on roughly 370 acres of rolling sand hills in "The Cups" region of the Mornington Peninsula, The Dunes is a true links with natural bunkering, native grasses, testy undulations, and the sorts of sea breezes that make a coastal course so enjoyable — and challenging.

## No. ❹ THE DUNES GOLF LINKS

The Dunes was designed by Tony Cashmore in 1997 and has since firmly established its place as one of the best public access courses in Australia. In *Golf Australia* magazine's 2004 survey of the 50 best golf courses in Australia, The Dunes came in at 15th place.

The fourth hole is a fabulous par 4, short and testy, and just one more example of why size does not really matter in golf.

You hit your drive from an elevated tee to a fairway of Santa Ana couch grass, and the optimum play is to place that ball over the fairway bunkers on the right side in order to set up the easiest possible second shot, usually a very short iron. Yes, golfers can bail out to the left with their tee shots, but that can make for a longer — and often more difficult — approach to a very small green.

And it is a very tough green to hold, perched as it is atop a ledge and set at a side angle. There is heavy bunkering on the left, and a steep drop-off in the back that seems to yank balls right off the putting surface. **JS**

**Course:** The Jockey Club Kau Sai Chau Golf Course (North Course)

**Location:** Sai Kung, New Territories, Hong Kong, China

**Hole:** No. 4

**Length:** 401 yards

**Par:** 4

**Designer:** Gary Player

**Course Comment:** A word of caution before taking on Kau Sai Chau Golf Course. This is a very difficult course and even more difficult to walk. If you are not in shape, make other plans like getting a caddy.

## No. ❹ THE JOCKEY CLUB KAU SAI CHAU GOLF COURSE (NORTH COURSE)

Located at the northern end of Kau Sai Chau Island, Kau Sai Chau is the one and only public golf course in Hong Kong and is one of the most scenic courses in all of Asia.

Remember, there is another course at Kau Sai Chau. The South Course, called "player friendlier," is a little easier to play. But if you want the challenge of taking on one of the toughest courses in Hong Kong, give the North your best shot. But, you've been warned.

The third and fourth holes are a pretty strong combo. The par-3 third is one of the toughest, but most beautiful holes on the North Course.

Walking up to the tee at No. 4 is a very intimidating sight. This slight dogleg left has a bunker at the left, right at the elbow. Big hitters should clear this with very little problem — even from the back tees.

The fairway is fairly wide on this No. 3 handicap hole. This smaller green is surrounded — and we mean surrounded — by six bunkers.

This hole is tough enough, but even more difficult when the wind kicks up. In fact, this description is true for the majority of the holes on the North Course. **TJ**

**Course:** Myopia Hunt Club

**Location:** South Hamilton, Massachusetts, USA

**Hole:** No. 4

**Length:** 392 yards

**Par:** 4

**Designer:** Herbert Leeds

**Course Comment:** This isn't a comment, but a warning. The green is where this No. 4 handicap hole gets tricky. It is severely pitched back to front and left to right. And most of the time you will need a wedge to get the ball to stay on the dance floor.

## No. ❹ MYOPIA HUNT CLUB

This course has a little bit of everything.

It has history. The 1898, 1901, 1905, and 1908 U.S. Opens were played here.

It has recognition. This is the only course in the United States to have been listed by *Golf Magazine* as having two of this country's top 100 signature holes (No. 9 and No. 4).

And it has a great story to tell: in 1901, Willie Anderson won the U.S. Open at Myopia with the highest winning total since the Open was expanded to 72 holes — a record that still stands.

Myopia, though, is first and foremost a great golf course. No. 4 is a prime example of why. Named Miles River — because the Miles River runs next to it — this difficult dogleg left has changed quite a bit since Anderson's playoff victory. Yes, it's gotten a little easier. Although easier is a bad choice of words.

From the back tees, you need a 225-yard drive to reach the corner. There is marsh and the Miles River along the left side. Starting at about 50 yards from the green are four bunkers and a pot bunker.

And to re-emphasize the previous warning, get your approach shot in the air and try to land it to the right side. **TJ**

**Course:** Whispering Pines

**Location:** Pinckney, Michigan, USA

**Hole:** No. 4

**Length:** 315 yards

**Par:** 4

**Designer:** Don Moon

**Course Comment:** How difficult is this course? There are some very good golf courses in southeastern Michigan, but very few as tough as Whispering Pines. Many in the area say it's even tougher than the TPC of Michigan in nearby Dearborn.

## No. ❹ WHISPERING PINES

There are tougher holes at Whispering Pines. And there are more scenic holes at Whispering Pines. But you aren't going to forget No. 4.

Whispering Pines, located north of Ann Arbor, is known for some tight, tree-lined fairways. You will notice the reputation is earned on the first tee. The fourth fairway is equally as challenging.

Your tee shot better get airborne as you look up to the fairway on this rather short but tricky par 4. You are looking at around 75 feet of a climb off the tee on this slight dogleg right to a crowned green.

There are those nasty pines (yes, the whispering kind) on both sides of the fairway, although they are not as thick on the right. The ideal tee shot is about 180 to 200 yards, which would leave you with a wedge to the green.

Your approach shot can be anything but long. There is a huge drop-off directly behind the green. It's such a big drop-off that you will likely need another ball.

The green is fairly long from front to back with a sand trap on the front-left side. There also is about 15 feet of false green along the front where your ball will roll back off the putting surface. The green is slightly sloped but not too difficult.

This hole can be very easy. Or it can ruin your scorecard. **TJ**

**Course:** Valderrama Golf Club

**Location:** Cadiz, Spain

**Hole:** No. 4

**Length:** 535 yards

**Par:** 5

**Designer:** Robert Trent Jones Sr.

**Course Comment:** The fourth is without a doubt the signature hole at Valderrama, a course that has played host to the Ryder Cup, the WGC–American Express Championship, and annually stages the PGA European Tour's Volvo Masters.

# No. ❹  VALDERRAMA GOLF CLUB

The famed fourth is the best hole at the best course in Continental Europe. Does that make it the best hole on the continent? Debatable perhaps, but when bringing up Europe's best, Valderrama's par-5 fourth must enter the conversation. Forcefully.

The Ryder Cup matches have been held on continental European soil just once — and Valderrama was the site. Of course, there is risk when blazing a trail, but reward when that trail proves as glorious as this wonder of a golf course. Risk-reward, much like Valderrama — particularly No. 4.

The fourth is a short hole — at 535 yards, length alone would never be an issue for the best players in the world aiming at the green in two. But, as with virtually all of Robert Trent Jones Sr.'s par-5 designs, there is far more than power required. The risk is the left side of the fairway, which abuts a tantalizing cluster of bunkers. There is a safer play to the right side of the fairway, but safety forfeits the possible reward of going for the green in two.

So, ignore your view from the elevated tee. It looks for all the world like you want to be on the right side of the fairway. There's no danger there. But, landing on the right off the tee means laying up in two, because there is watery protection behind and to the right-hand side of the green. As counterproductive as it sounds, a player must look at those bunkers on the left and aim right at them. Come close to the bunkers — without going in them — and a fairly accessible second shot to the green remains. The water is taken out of play, and a straight shot down the oak-lined fairway is yours for the taking — if you so choose.

The path to the green gets tantalizingly narrow at its conclusion, but the only way to find it is from the left. And, even making the green on the second shot is no guarantee of birdie.

The distance is deceiving, as is the open view from the tee. The fourth, though shortish, is played as a three-shot hole. No. 4 at Valderrama has been more than a match for the best in the game. **JB**

OPPOSITE  *Colin Montgomery of Scotland tees off on the fourth hole at Valderrama, November 2002.*

**Course:** The National Golf Club of Canada

**Location:** Woodbridge, Ontario, Canada

**Hole:** No. 4

**Length:** 600 yards

**Par:** 5

**Designer:** George Fazio, Tom Fazio

**Course Comment:** Lee Trevino won the 1979 Canadian PGA held at The National with a score of 1 over par 285. It was half of an impressive Canadian double for Trevino, who also captured the PGA Tour's Canadian Open that same year at Glen Abbey.

## No. ❹  THE NATIONAL GOLF CLUB OF CANADA

Considered by many to be Canada's top course, the ultra-private National Golf Club is a parkland-style layout set amid rolling, wooded terrain north of Toronto.

The long par-5 fourth, a slight dogleg left, was extended to 600 yards (from 581) by Tom Fazio in fall 2004, 30 years after he and his uncle first opened the course. But the hole's length is the least of a golfer's worries.

A creek cuts immediately in front of the tee box and winds down the right side until forming a large pond about 260 yards from the tee. The preferred landing area is only 25 yards wide at its narrowest point between the water on the right, and a long, narrow bunker and a pair of willow trees slightly farther up on the left. The creek then comes back to play on the second shot, again crossing the fairway 150 yards out — challenging players to cross it on their second shots or forcing them to lay up.

The green is no easier. A complex of six deep bunkers (four left, two right) surround a tiny, elevated putting surface that, despite measuring only 24 paces deep, contains three shelves.

Earn par here, and you can be assured it was no fluke.  **KA**

---

**Course:** Atlantic Beach Golf Course

**Location:** Melkbosstrand, Cape Town, South Africa

**Hole:** No. 4

**Length:** 499 yards

**Par:** 5

**Designer:** Golf Data Inc.

**Course Comment:** The Atlantic Beach Golf Course is two courses in one. On calm days you can play your normal loft shot or on windy days you can use firm turf to play low-running shots beneath the wind.

## No. ❹  ATLANTIC BEACH GOLF COURSE

Situated along the shore of Table Bay, Atlantic Beach is an easy 20-minute drive along the coast to the heart of South Africa's premier city. And it's well worth the trip. Actually, playing the fourth hole is worth the trip.

It is one of the course's most challenging holes. Don't, however, be put off by the fact that you can't see where your tee shot should land — aim just slightly to the right of the cable station on the top right corner of Table Mountain and you should be all right.

By the time you reach the fourth, you should trust your swing. Or not. The four sets of tees start at 386 yards.

Play your second to the left of the fairway bunker, leaving a short iron to the green. If you are level with the bunker, the third shot is steeply uphill so take one more club than you think.

You will, of course, be forgiven if you find your concentration slipping a bit on the green. Your attention is likely to be drawn to the magnificent views of Table Bay and Robben Island in the distance.

But try and focus. You can take pictures when you're done.  **TJ**

**Course:** Royal Melbourne Golf Club (West Course)

**Location:** Black Rock, Victoria, Australia

**Hole:** No. 4

**Length:** 473 yards

**Par:** 5

**Designer:** Alister MacKenzie

**Course Comment:** The fourth at this classic track is regarded as perhaps the finest par 5 in all Australia and kicks off what may golfers believe is the best stretch of holes in that land, Nos. 4, 5, and 6. It is as scenic as it is challenging, and the gaping bunkers around the green are reminiscent of those found at MacKenzie's American masterpiece, Augusta National.

## No. ❹ ROYAL MELBOURNE GOLF CLUB (WEST COURSE)

The drive on this hole requires a tee shot over a trio of bunkers, the farthest of which is roughly 180 yards away. Options abound for the next play on this dogleg right.

Big hitters can carry their second shots to the green, but accuracy is key, as the putting area boasts a vast bunker to the right and a smaller one to the left. For those laying up, the greatest potential is on the right, where a pair of wonderful MacKenzie fairway bunkers loom just a sand wedge away from the green. But that can seem a very green distance to a golfer who has the misfortune of putting his ball in that spot.

And even the player who gets on in two or three generally faces a tough three-putt on a green that has more than its fair share of undulations and difficult pin placements.

The scorecard says No. 4 on the West Course is the 18th handicap hole, and the feeling at first glance is that it should be a cakewalk. But nothing can be further from the truth. **JS**

RIGHT *Nick Faldo of England plays a shot on the fourth hole at Royal Melbourne, February 2003.*

**Course:** Mountaintop Golf & Lake Club

**Location:** Cashiers, North Carolina, USA

**Hole:** No. 4

**Length:** 646 yards

**Par:** 5

**Designer:** Tom Fazio

**Course Comment:** Mountaintop is the sixth course Fazio designed for the Discovery Land Company and is a 1½-hour drive from his home in Hendersonville, North Carolina.

# No. ❹ MOUNTAINTOP GOLF & LAKE CLUB

Six hundred and forty six yards? The toughest hole on the course? You get the idea why No. 4 is being highlighted at Mountaintop Golf & Lake Club.

The 2007 layout boasts many splendid holes, but none as difficult or complex or breathtaking as the magnificent 4th. With so much yardage with which to work, you would think that Tom Fazio would throw a little bit of everything at the golfer. If that were your guess, you would be right.

The tee shot must carry the frightening wetlands of Hurricane Lake. In any other setting, the wetlands would be a remarkable sight, but when you are hitting a golf ball, they are daunting to say the least. On your second shot — and it's got to be long, a recurring theme with this hole — you face a dogleg right. And then it keeps going right, and it keeps going long.

It sounds monotonous, but this hole is anything but. It's a wonder from start to finish. The fairway gives you some room to operate off the tee, but then gets narrower as you go. So not only do you have to be long, you also must be accurate all the way to the green. The right center of the fairway is the play off the tee, but there is a large bunker on the right, and a couple more further down on the left with which to contend.

Mountaintop Golf & Lake Club is a beautiful golf course from start to finish, but when debating the best hole, the discussion is short. Unlike No. 4, which is long. Long and lovely. **JB**

**Course:** Ballyneal Golf and Hunt Club

**Location:** Holyoke, Colorado, USA

**Hole:** No. 4

**Length:** 573 yards

**Par:** 5

**Designer:** Tom Doak

**Course Comment:** Owners Rupert and Jim O'Neal originally raised pheasants on the property for their hunting club. But, in 1995, when Sand Hills Golf Club opened about three hours away in Mullen, Nebraska, the O'Neals were inspired to open a wonderful golf course on similar property adjacent to their own land.

## No. ❹ BALLYNEAL GOLF & HUNT CLUB

They call this region of Colorado "Chop Hills," with its bumps and moguls and exposed, treeless expanses. And, as much as any hole at Ballyneal, the tempting par-5, fourth hole at this 2006 layout offers vast examples of the natural beauty of the area, while allowing the contours of the land to dictate direction and strategy.

Strategy is one thing on No. 4, and panorama is quite another. Making the ascension up the ridge from the third green to the fourth tee offers a great look at Chop Hills — wind whipping, grasses bending, fairway beckoning.

At 573 yards, the No. 4 green can be reached in two when the wind is right. But, regardless of wind speed or direction, it will take two perfect shots to be putting for eagle. Off the tee, the left edge of a bunker far down the right side of the fairway is a good point at which to aim. It is important to stay right, because anything just a touch left will likely find vegetation because of the angle and undulation of the fairway.

The conservative player should hit to the left side of the fairway with their second shot rather than risk jamming up to the contoured green for a difficult chip up. But the big hitter has a shot at the large, undulating green with his or her second shot. **JB**

## No. ❹  DOMAINE IMPERIAL GOLF CLUB

**Course:** Domaine Imperial Golf Club

**Location:** Gland, Geneva, Switzerland

**Hole:** No. 4

**Length:** 589 yards

**Par:** 5

**Designer:** Pete Dye

**Course Comment:** Domaine Imperial's striking clubhouse, which dates to the 17th century, is the former home of Prince Jerome Napoleon, a descendant of Napolean Bonaparte.

Sitting on an exceptional site on the border of Lake Geneva, near the foot of the magnificent Swiss Alps, is the lone Pete Dye-designed golf course in Europe. If Dye had to do just one, the legendary architect made it a good one, as his American-style effort is ranked by many as the top layout in Switzerland. And if you just had to pick one hole at Domaine Imperial, the par-5 fourth would most definitely be it, for it contains elements that test each part of your game.

The long dogleg right features a fairway that narrows considerably at the spot where the hole bends, measuring no more than 15 yards wide at its thinnest point, and being pinched by tall heather grass on one side and out-of-bounds on the right.

Once safely past the turn, golfers are confronted with an altogether different set of problems, with a second shot that must avoid a long, narrow bunker and a green that is framed beautifully by trees and guarded by an array of small pot bunkers.

This is Dye at his devious, delightful best. **KA**

## No. ❹  LOS LEONES GOLF CLUB

**Course:** Los Leones Golf Club

**Location:** Santiago, Chile

**Hole:** No. 4

**Length:** 560 yards

**Par:** 5

**Designer:** Alister MacKenzie

**Course Comment:** One of 58 courses in Chile, the Los Leones Golf Club (Course of the Lions) opened in 1921.

Golf in Chile dates from the second half of the 19th century when a group of Englishmen brought it with them. It continued to expand as more expatriate Englishmen moved to Chile, and after Valparaiso, Santiago was next in line. In 1921, Los Leones was built in Santiago, and it was by far the best course in the country. Los Leones has, after all this time, maintained its place at the top of the Chilean list.

And atop the Los Leones roster of quality holes sits the par-5 fourth, which at first appears to be straightforward and rather plain, but upon further inspection, proves its mettle.

The hole is straight, there is but one bunker, and it runs adjacent to one of the busiest streets in Santiago. All of this aside, it remains a beauty. Tall, shining city buildings give you the feeling that you're playing a round right in the middle of town. A completely different feeling than most are used to when playing golf, but the unique nature of the ambience is memorable enough to be named in our list of 1001 holes.

There is out-of-bounds and water to the right, but, of course, the right side is where you want to be off the tee. The left side looks safer, but it doesn't afford the proper angle for your second shot — whether you plan to go for the green or to lay up.

All 58 courses in Chile are resort courses and cannot be played unless you are a guest at one of the hotels affiliated with the course. Green fees are reasonable, at about $70 per 18. **JB**

**Course:** Bukit Pelangi Resort
(Rainbow Hills Course)

**Location:** Bogor, Indonesia

**Hole:** No. 4

**Length:** 538 yards

**Par:** 5

**Designer:** Robert Moore,
JMP Golf Design

**Course Comment:** Bogor has been called the "lightning strike capital of the world," so make sure to take cover if you're caught in a storm at Rainbow Hills. The course contains dozens of lightning arrestors.

# No. ❹ BUKIT PELANGI RESORT
## (RAINBOW HILLS COURSE)

Set in the hilly highlands south of Jakarta, Rainbow Hills features plenty of waterfalls, cascades, and rocks – many of them integral to the golf holes. Oddly enough, the dogleg left fourth hole doesn't include any of those features, save for one small boulder stationed in the fairway. But be thankful – this par 5 is challenging enough without them.

From the elevated tees, golfers may survey the entire hole — that is, if they can take their eyes off the mountain views in the distance. Big hitters can reach the green in two, although fairway bunkers tighten the fairway on long drives. The second shot provides even more of a risk-reward decision, as players can either choose to lay up high and right to a larger fairway, or hit more of a straight shot toward the green by landing it in a narrow, lower fairway. The risk? The lower landing area skirts a steep hillside that drops to a river below.

All that, and the hole's best feature still remains — a green that's perched on a narrow ridge and protected even further by a false front and a bunker on the left. The scenery's not bad at the end of the hole, either. On clear days, golfers can glimpse Jakarta — some 40 miles away. **KA**

---

**Course:** World Woods (Pine Barrens Course)

**Location:** Brooksville, Florida, USA

**Hole:** No. 4

**Length:** 494 yards

**Par:** 5

**Designer:** Tom Fazio

**Course Comment:** There are plenty of pine trees on the World Woods course. And plenty of barren waste areas. So someone came up with the name Pine Barrens. I guess it's better than Pine Waste.

# No. ❹ WORLD WOODS
## (PINE BARRENS COURSE)

According to golf shop personnel at World Woods, the Pine Barrens Course is "a visually stunning blend of native terrain and golf course design."

If anything, that's an understatement.

A dramatic and beautiful risk-reward tee shot awaits you on this 494-yard par 5. The option is a safe play lay-up down the left or the bold play is to grab the big driver and attempt to carry the waste area on the right.

If you can carry the waste area, the elevated green is certainly reachable in two.

The waste area runs the entire length of the hole and really cuts into the fairway at the start and finish of the hole. So your tee shot and approach shot to the green are crucial.

But the other side wasn't "left" out when it comes to trouble. There is a section of waste area that could come into play either on your first or second shot, and a bunker closer to the green.

The four sets of tees range from 406 to the tournament tees of 494.

This is a fun and challenging hole on a golf course filled with both. And it is quite stunning. **TJ**

**Course:** Bethpage State Park (Black Course)

**Location:** Farmingdale, New York, USA

**Hole:** No. 4

**Length:** 522 yards

**Par:** 5

**Designer:** A.W. Tillinghast, Rees Jones

**Course Comment:** Bethpage Black played host to the 2002 U.S. Open, yet the green fees are less than $50 per round. The 2002 Open was sometimes raucous, but was considered one of the most successful and celebrated the U.S. Golf Association has ever staged.

# No. ❹ BETHPAGE STATE PARK
## (BLACK COURSE)

Bethpage Black opened in 1936 and immediately became known in the New York City area as one of the toughest courses this side of Pine Valley. Its reputation gradually spread westward, as word of its difficulty and beauty spread rapidly throughout the country. But the pace of the word-of-mouth, decades-long story of Bethpage Black increased immensely in 2002, when a terrific U.S. Open was held at the purely public facility.

The Black Course is one of five at the State Park, and the other four have solid characteristics in their own right. But imagine if Babe Ruth — another New York heavy hitter who was in his heyday a few years before Bethpage Black opened — had four younger brothers who each hit 300. They might be fine players, but, hey, Babe Ruth is Babe Ruth.

Bethpage Black, like Babe Ruth, is one of the best that ever was. And the par-5 fourth is one of its most distinctive challenges. There are more beautiful par 5s in the world, but most call upon the help of mountains or ocean to enhance their elegance. The Black's fourth is the purest of pure parkland golf, providing inland splendor and calling for both Ruthian power and a discerning eye for strategy.

The tee at No. 4 is elevated, and the view is magnificent. There are no blind shots on No. 4 — you see the challenge directly in front of you. The fairway is open enough, and framed by large trees. But the highlight of the fourth hole is its bunkering, particularly the terrific cross bunker — an A.W. Tillinghast staple.

The green could be reachable in two, but a longer drive is required and the only route to the green is directly over the severe bunkering surrounding the green. The best angle to the green is a pitch from the right side on your third shot, but of course if you do that, you are talking about laying up on your second shot.

The green slopes away from the player, and it is some 30 feet higher than the ground from which you approach. No easy target, and even if you hit it, you better come in soft.

Power and strategy in a parkland setting. The fourth at Bethpage Black is a wonderful place to play ball. **JB**

## No. ❹ CASTRO MARIM

**Course:** Castro Marim

**Location:** Castro Marim, The Algarve, Portugal

**Hole:** No. 4

**Length:** 548 yards

**Par:** 5

**Designer:** Terry Murray

**Course Comment:** Castro Marim is one of the most easterly courses on The Algarve with good views toward nearby Spain.

The fourth hole at Castro Marim features a tee shot played from an elevated tee to low-lying fairway. It's a common occurrence on this compact course close to the Spanish border.

The drive needs to be thought through carefully. The hole doglegs left, but unlike most doglegs you can't just stand up and blast away at the widest part of the fairway. A lake lies beyond the dogleg on the right of the fairway, and a shot hit too long, or pushed slightly, can end up in the water.

The ideal line is to try to keep as tight to the corner of the dogleg as possible, leaving a better chance of getting close to the green on the second shot.

The problem with the second shot is that it has to be played uphill, making the shot longer. Even those who lay up will still face a second shot played uphill to a green that is well protected by a bunker, young pine trees, and the natural slope of the land.

Finding the putting surface isn't easy, so pray your wedge play is sharp when you arrive at Castro Marim's par-5 fourth. **AT**

## No. ❹ THE DUNES AT MAUI LANI GOLF COURSE

**Course:** The Dunes at Maui Lani Golf Course

**Location:** Kahului, Hawaii, USA

**Hole:** No. 4

**Length:** 509 yards

**Par:** 5

**Designer:** Robin Nelson

**Course Comment:** Located on Maui's north coast, The Dunes at Maui Lani Golf Course is a championship links-style layout which opened in January 1999. The course is constructed over natural dunes created when the island of Maui was formed.

This is the first of the many dynamic Dunes holes where looks can be deceiving. Not only is the entire hole narrow, but each shot must be thought out for placement.

Our host in the clubhouse called this the ultimate "golfer's hole" because "you can hit a great tee shot and still end up with a birdie or a double eagle."

A good tee shot should carry about 226 yards to clear the left fairway bunkers and the valley. Anything shorter and forget about going for the green. Anything left of this group of four sand traps is into the woods; anything too far right is into a steep sand dune.

The second shot is between the kiawe trees on the left and a huge chasm to the right. The green will tempt the long hitters to go for it in two, but the face of the slope for the perched green is dominated by deep sod-revetted bunkers.

The green surface is hidden from view, and a false tongue on the putting surface can be deceiving. An approach hit on this portion may roll down the slope and well back into the fairway.

Our clubhouse host says there are 18 signatures holes at The Dunes. "We really have 18 different types of hole," he said. **TJ**

# Hole ⑤

A general rule of thumb that is followed pretty consistently by great courses throughout the world is that the difficult holes come in clusters. One of the tough stretches of holes tends to be Nos. 2–5, and as the finisher in the first four-hole run of difficult challenges, fifth holes throughout the world sometimes are bears.

The fifth hole at Mid Ocean Club in Bermuda is the only hole on the course that requires both a carry over water *and* a severe dogleg before reaching the green. The 470-yard par-4 fifth at Colonial Country Club in Fort Worth, Texas, is the third-hardest hole on the course and the second most difficult on the outward nine.

**LEFT** *The fifth hole at Bethpage State Park, Farmingdale, New York, USA.*

**Course:** Pumpkin Ridge (Witch Hollow Course)

**Location:** North Plains, Oregon, USA

**Hole:** No. 5

**Length:** 211 yards

**Par:** 3

**Designer:** Bob Cupp

**Course Comment:** Pumpkin Ridge was the site of the Nike Tour Championship in 1993 and 1994, and the site of the 1996 United States Amateur Championship, where Tiger Woods won his third straight Amateur Championship. The U.S. Women's Open was played here in 1997.

OPPOSITE *The fifth hole at Pumpkin Ridge.*

# No. ❺ PUMPKIN RIDGE
## (WITCH HOLLOW COURSE)

The back nine on Witch Hollow has three par 3s and the greens are generally very fast. But the front nine is where Witch Hollow's signature holes can be found.

The par-3 No. 5 is not only the most photographed hole at Pumpkin Ridge, but the most difficult as well. In other words, it's pretty (and) tough.

At 211 yards, it is mighty long for a par 3. But there is more to this hole than distance from tee to green. Water comes into play to the front of the green, and if the flag is in the back right, your target becomes much smaller. Behind is a series of bunkers and hills, also making a long shot risky.

The green might look easy but you have to putt with confidence. Don't ignore the gentle slope of the green. If you are long and playing from the back mounds, this green can destroy you.

There really is no better sight at Pumpkin Ridge than seeing your white ball climb over the water, descend just before those three bunkers, and land on the green.

This is one of those holes where the only decision is what club to use. You have to line it up and shoot for the flag. And hope for the best on Pumpkin Ridge's best. **TJ**

**Course:** Keystone Ranch (Ranch Course)

**Location:** Keystone, Colorado, USA

**Hole:** No. 5

**Length:** 190 yards

**Par:** 3

**Designer:** Robert Trent Jones Jr.

**Course Comment:** This mountain course, which is part of the Keystone Resort, is located at 9,300 feet above sea level, making it the second-highest course in the U.S. The River Course at Keystone was added in 2000.

# No. ❺ KEYSTONE RANCH (RANCH COURSE)

It's so easy for the scorecard to trick you. Doesn't look all that tough on paper, you say? Well, let's take a walk out to the tee and see if you still feel the same way.

Welcome to No. 5, the club's signature hole. Why are you shaking?

You must clear plenty of "meadowland" to reach this island green, which is surrounded by bunkers. There is a big one to the right, one behind and a small one at the center front.

There is some fairway to work with in front of the green, but other than that, you are either dancing or in some very big trouble. It's not rated very difficult on the scorecard — but can you really trust those things?

You also get a good view of the historic Ranch barn on this hole. Try not to hit it in there.

Winding through lodgepole pines, around sage meadows and across a nine-acre lake, this par-72 course features slight elevation changes and many bunkers.

Designed by Robert Trent Jones Jr., Keystone Ranch golf course follows the legendary links style of a Scottish course on the front nine, while the back half presents a traditional mountain valley layout.

Pay for 18 and you get to play both. **TJ**

**Course:** Ballyliffin (Old Links)

**Location:** Ballyliffin, Inishowen, County Donegal, Ireland

**Hole:** No. 5

**Length:** 176 yards

**Par:** 3

**Designers:** Eddie Hackett, Messrs Lawrie and Pennick, Martin Hopkins

**Course Comment:** The principal architect of the links was Mother Nature. The course rests peacefully between the ocean, hills, and endless stretches of dunes.

## No. ➎ BALLYLIFFIN (OLD LINKS)

It was once the best kept secret in golf, but Ballyliffin is now being described as "the Ballybunion of the North."

Located up near Malin Head on Donegal's Inishowen Peninsula, Ireland's most northerly links rests on 365 acres of dunes. On one side are the rolling hills, and to the other side are the rolling waves of the Atlantic Ocean.

One of the more legendary holes on Ballyliffin's Old Links course is undoubtedly the par-3 fifth, or "The Tank," as it is known. Right away you know you are in trouble. Any hole dubbed "The Tank" can't be easy. Do you reach for a golf club or a helmet?

It's a hole that probably equally inspires both love and hate in golfers. Which side you come down on depends a lot on what you write down on the scorecard.

The green enjoys a stage-like setting perched between two large sand hills. Only the perfectly judged tee shot will find the sanctuary of the putting surface.

So when you roll up onto "The Tank" you better be perfect.

Another great par-3 hole is No. 7, which is played from the top of the sand dune to a green guarded by bunkers on three sides and a lake on the other. **TJ**

## No. ❺ GLENEAGLES (KING'S COURSE)

**Course:** Gleneagles (King's Course)

**Location:** Auchterarder, Perthshire, Scotland

**Hole:** No. 5

**Length:** 178 yards

**Par:** 3

**Designer:** James Braid

**Course Comment:** The fifth hole on the King's Course is called "Het Girdle," meaning hot griddle or skillet. If not struck to perfection, the ball can slip off the green as oil on the hot plate.

James Braid named these 18 holes the King's Course for a reason. These were designed to challenge the best players. And challenge on every shot. So you better not only be good off the tee, but solid in the fairway and proficient around the greens.

The fifth hole on the King's Course is a hole where one simple mistake can cost you more than one stroke. It's very easy to "slide off the hot plate."

There are five sets of tees starting at 114 yards, and several sections of the tee boxes do not face the green directly. Of course that's not fair. But what in golf is fair? That's why we love it. All you have to do is be sure to check that you line up properly. Check the footwork and let it fly.

But the tee box is the least of your concerns. You either hit this well-protected plateau green or you roll off and down. Way down. And usually into one of the bunkers.

Trying to blast out of one of those bunkers with the putting surface practically straight up above you is a very nerve-racking shot. Getting up and down in two from there is quite an accomplishment. This long, but narrow green slopes from front to back, making things even more tricky. **TJ**

## No. ❺ CAMARGO CLUB

**Course:** Camargo Club

**Location:** Cincinnati, Ohio, USA

**Hole:** No. 5

**Length:** 179 yards

**Par:** 3

**Designer:** Seth Raynor

**Course Comment:** The fifth hole at Camargo Club is modeled after No. 11 at St. Andrews and is one of the prettier holes on a golf course filled with beauty. Many of the holes at Camargo are taken from the pages of the old Scottish-Irish golf courses.

This is not an easy target to hit. And you better be close to the bull's-eye or off the green you go. The 179-yard par 3 is one of the best Eden holes in the United States. It has a plateau green with a Strath bunker and a hill bunker about 20 feet below a green that is usually firm and difficult.

There is a bunker that wraps around the right side all the way to the back. The green is wider at the left and you must bring your tee shot in high to have a good shot at birdie.

Built in 1925, Camargo is one of Raynor's last courses and he certainly left his mark. He liked to create similar types of par-3 holes at his courses and really created a group of outstanding one-shot holes here.

Some experts would say that Camargo is on the shortlist of courses with the best short holes. The group has variety and character.

Raynor, who once moved dirt for the great Charles Blair Macdonald, never forgot where he came from. In fact, Raynor was influential in Macdonald's career as well.

But every course Raynor designed had that Macdonald touch. And Camargo is certainly one of them. Members of the club like to keep a low profile. As the saying goes, if you start telling everyone about your well-kept secret, it's no longer a secret. **TJ**

**Course:** Loch Lomond

**Location:** Luss, Dunbartonshire, Scotland

**Hole:** No. 5

**Length:** 190 yards

**Par:** 3

**Designer:** Tom Weiskopf, Jay Morrish

**Course Comment:** Loch Lomond's clubhouse, Rossdhu, is a Georgian manor home constructed in 1773, exactly 200 years before architect Tom Weiskopf won the British Open Championship at Royal Troon.

**BELOW** *The fifth hole at Loch Lomond.*

**OPPOSITE** *Lee Westwood of England tees off on the fifth hole at Loch Lomond, July 2003.*

# No. ❺ LOCH LOMOND

Set on the banks of beautiful Loch Lomond, only 25 minutes from Glasgow, this course brought the best of American architecture to the birthplace of golf. The scenic fifth hole gives golfers their first wide-open glimpse of the loch, which provides a scenic setting behind a green that is quite spectacular in its own right.

The long, narrow putting surface is protected by large bunker complexes on both sides, and has two shelves — high on the front, then sloping downward about halfway back. Because of the length of the green, the pin placement can affect club selection by as many as four clubs, and at times, the wind blows in hard off the water, making the choice even more difficult.

If you're going to miss the green, don't miss it left. Getting close from the left-hand bunkers is virtually impossible because of the slope of the putting surface. From the right side, at least you have a chance.

Loch Lomond is the annual host for the European Tour's Scottish Open, played as the lead-in for the British Open in recent years. As such, it has an impressive list of past winners, including Ernie Els (2003, 2000), Retief Goosen (2001), Colin Montgomerie (1999), Lee Westwood (1998), and Tom Lehman (1997). **KA**

**Course:** The National Golf Club (Moonah Course)

**Location:** Cape Schanck, Victoria, Australia

**Hole:** No. 5

**Length:** 165 yards

**Par:** 3

**Designer:** Greg Norman, Bob Harrison

**Course Comment:** Opened in 2000, the Moonah at the National Golf Club has a fabulous collection of par 3s, and the best of that bunch is the 165-yard fifth.

## No. ❺ THE NATIONAL GOLF CLUB
### (MOONAH COURSE)

The Moonah Course at The National Golf Club is something special. A combination of the work of our designers, Greg Norman and Bob Harrison, and, of course, Mother Nature herself, it is a firm favorite with golfers around the globe. As Bob Harrison says, "There were natural golf holes everywhere and our task was to select the best ones and link them together to form an inspiring and memorable course."

Hole No. 5 sits atop the ridge of a sand dune at the highest part of the course, making it especially vulnerable to the prevailing cross winds that so often blow across the peninsula, and especially tough on even the lowest handicap players.

The green, which slopes sharply to the left, is guarded on that side by four bunkers, and any miss there will almost surely result in bogey — or worse. It is not nearly so difficult to recover from miscues to the right, but any chips hit too hard will likely skitter across the green and fall off to that dreaded abyss on the other side. Not even the gorgeous views of that spectacular par 3 can soothe the angst of the golfer who fails to put his tee shot on the green. **JS**

**BELOW** *Craig Parry of Australia tees off on the fifth hole at The National Golf Club, December 2003.*

**Course:** Royal Lytham & St. Annes

**Location:** St. Annes-on-Sea, Lancashire, England

**Hole:** No. 5

**Length:** 210 yards

**Par:** 3

**Designer:** Harry S. Colt

**Course Comment:** Royal Lytham and St. Annes has been the host venue for 10 Open Championships with the first winner being Bobby Jones in 1926 and the most recent, David Duval in 2001. The club has also hosted two Ryder Cups.

This historic course (is there a course in Britain that isn't historic?) is within one mile of the center of St. Annes on Sea. Royal Lytham is a links course with two strange aspects — it is a links course but there is no sea in view and the course opens with a par 3.

Since your first shot of the round requires hitting the green, you should be ready to go by the time you reach the 210-yard No. 5. The longest of the par 3s demands an arrow-straight tee shot to avoid the bunkers that cluster around the green.

There are four sand traps to the left of the green and two more on the right side. The two on the right are more to the front of the green. So of the 197 bunkers on the golf course, six are around the No. 5 green.

Moreover, there is a stretch of "dead ground" in front of the green that is deceptive and makes the hole play longer than it appears.

There are four sets of tees, starting at 147 yards, so if the great length from the tips bothers you, there are a few other shorter options.

Royal Lytham may be surrounded by suburban homes, but the locals are proud to call this course their golfing home. And there is plenty of charm to go round. **TJ**

**Course:** Royal Worlington
and Newmarket Golf Club

**Location:** Worlington, Bury
St. Edmunds, Suffolk, England

**Hole:** No. 5

**Length:** 157 yards

**Par:** 3

**Designer:** Captain A.M. Ross

**Course Comment:** Royal Worlington
and Newmarket is the home course
for the Cambridge University Golf
Club. The relationship began in 1896,
three years after the course opened,
when the Cambridge squad came to
Worlington for a match against the
home club. The captain of that
Cambridge team? Noted golf writer
Bernard Darwin.

No. ⑤ **ROYAL WORLINGTON AND NEWMARKET GOLF CLUB**

Royal Worlington has received accolades as the best nine-hole course in the world, and there's little to argue. This quirky gem has a unique charm — along with some of the finest green complexes in England.

The par-3 fifth is the most well known of Royal Worlington's nifty nine, a bunkerless terror that requires the tee shot to be played across the fourth green to a long, narrow, three-tiered putting surface that drops off sharply on both sides into trouble. On the left sits a deep, grassy pit that once was a water hazard, and on the right, a winding stream. Going long can bring problems as well, as a group of fir trees stands back of the green.

There is no easy up-and-down here. A soft touch is required to keep chips on one side from running down the slope on the other.

Perhaps another renowned golf writer, Henry Longhurst, who played the hole as a Cambridge undergraduate, said it best: "Many is the man who, alternatively fluffing his pitch and watching the ball roll ignominiously back and then, determined to be up, hitting it over the green and down the other side, has passed to and fro half a dozen times." **KA**

**Course:** Royal Melbourne Golf Club (West Course)

**Location:** Black Rock, Melbourne, Australia

**Hole:** No. 5

**Length:** 176 yards

**Par:** 3

**Designer:** Alister MacKenzie, Alex Russell

**Course Comment:** Royal Melbourne Golf Club, which has existed continuously since 1891, is regarded as the oldest golf club in Australia. It was the site of the 1998 President's Cup.

No. ❺ **ROYAL MELBOURNE GOLF CLUB (WEST COURSE)**

The Royal Melbourne Golf Club has a mission statement, if you will, that is hung in the clubhouse, displayed in advertising, and posted on its Web site. That statement is simple: "The aim of the Royal Melbourne Golf Club is to maintain the characteristics and challenges of the course proposed by Dr. Alister MacKenzie when he designed the course in 1926." The par-3 fifth on the West Course is one of the holes that helps Royal Melbourne succeed in its mission.

MacKenzie took on the help of 1924 Australian Open champion Alex Russell when designing the West Course, which opened in 1931 and is one of Australia's finest. The fifth hole, with rolling mounds, heather, and bending oaks and tea trees, is among the course's finest.

Accuracy and the correct choice of middle iron is necessary to cross a valley to the green, which is fortified heavily by five huge bunkers. The carry over the valley is 170 yards, and if you don't land on the green, you more than likely will be dealing with bracken, sand, or heather — none of which is a bargain from which to strike a golf ball.

Simply hitting the green from the tee is no guarantee that the ball will stay put. The front portion of the green is sloped downward and because it

*BELOW Nick Faldo of England plays his second shot on the fifth hole at Royal Melbourne, February 2002.*

usually is shaved, balls that land in the front are more than likely to roll off the green. This is a favorite trick of MacKenzie's. Fortunately, the area in the front of the green is lush turf, but, still, you won't be putting for birdie. If the pin is placed toward the right front, there is scarcely any room between the pin and the bunkers. So a short shot will have you hitting from deep sand with steep faces.

Royal Melbourne is a private golf course, but it is possible to gain access with a current membership at a recognized golf club and a letter of introduction from the home club. It may seem like a lot to go through to gain entry to a golf course, but Royal Melbourne is worth the formality. **JB**

## No. ❺ PARQUE DA FLORESTA

**Course:** Parque da Floresta

**Location:** The Algarve, Portugal

**Hole:** No. 5

**Length:** 123 yards

**Par:** 3

**Designer:** Pepe Gancedo

**Course Comment:** Parque da Floresta has been much altered since it was first opened in 1987 to take some of the sting out of what, for many, was an almost unplayable course.

If you hear about the Algarve, you tend to think of secluded beaches, the crystal-clear Atlantic Ocean, brilliant sunshine, and gently undulating countryside — the perfect setting for a golf course.

It's hard though, to think of The Algarve having its very own Postage Stamp hole like the eighth at Royal Troon on Scotland's Ayrshire coastline, but Parque da Floresta has just that. It's a toss-up to determine which one is tougher.

The fifth may only measure 123 yards, four yards shorter than the Troon version, but it is one of the most daunting tee shots to be found anywhere. Played from a high tee to a green well below you, and astride the crest of a mound, this tee shot is absolutely perilous in a cross wind. Anything too long or wide left and the ball is a goner. Thankfully four bunkers surround the green to stop any ball from getting lost down the steep slopes which surround the green. There is room on the right-hand side of the green and that is a wise place to aim for, especially when the pin is left. Like its namesake, it pays just to get the ball on the green here, two putt and get to the next tee. **AT**

## No. ❺ LAHINCH

**Course:** Lahinch

**Location:** Lahinch, County Clare, Ireland

**Hole:** No. 5

**Length:** 154 yards

**Par:** 3

**Designer:** Old Tom Morris, Alister MacKenzie

**Course Comment:** After helping reshape Lahinch in 1927, Alister Mackenzie went on to design Augusta National, Pebble Beach, and Cypress Point among others in the United States, and Royal Melbourne in Australia.

Only one designer was right to lay out the 18 holes at Lahinch. Old Tom Morris, of St. Andrews fame, was that man. What better choice was there?

Considered one of the best of his time, Morris went to work but quickly discovered most of the job had already been done for him. After finishing the work, Morris said, "I consider the links is as fine a natural course as it has ever been my good fortune to play over."

He wanted the credit to go where it belonged.

While many of the holes have been redone over time, No. 5 is still a Morris signature design. You don't change something as unique as the famous "Dell" hole.

At 154 yards, you won't need to rip this tee shot. Quite the contrary, this hole requires touch, not brawn. It also requires the right club and a little bit of faith. You won't see the green from the tee no matter how hard you try.

This very different golf hole requires you to aim for the white stone on the hill and trust your yardage. You won't know how you did until you pull up to the green.

The green is dug deep into the surrounding dunes. It's not out of the question to get some friendly bounces. It's also not uncommon to find the sand trap. This is a hole you will never forget. **TJ**

**Course:** Formby Golf Club

**Location:** Formby, Merseyside, England

**Hole:** No. 5

**Length:** 162 yards

**Par:** 3

**Designer:** Willie Park, Frank Pennink

**Course Comment:** What a history you will find here. Take the clubhouse, for example. They turned a shack into a modern clubhouse only to see it burn down in 1899. That's when the clubhouse you now walk through was built.

## No. ❺  FORMBY GOLF CLUB

The Formby Golf Club, located within the sandhills and pine woods of Formby, Merseyside, is a golf course worth remembering forever. It's one which will become the benchmark to which you compare other courses.

If your game is accuracy, you should do very well here. If it is not, trouble will be found all over the golf course. Thick heather in the rough can make for a rough scorecard.

Nowhere on the course is this more true than on No. 5.

Here is the tip from the pros at the club regarding this formidable and scenic hole: "Only the perfect tee shot is good enough."

In other words, all you have to be is flawless on this hole and you will be fine. The scary part is, they aren't kidding. If you are just a little off on your tee shot, then trouble lurks.

The fun begins at the tee. Usually, you aren't going to see the bottom of the flag so distance becomes tricky.

At 162 yards, it's not an overly long hole, but with sandhills right and two bunkers left, you better be straight. The green slopes down toward the beautiful pines along the left side. **TJ**

**Course:** Royal Dornoch

**Location:** Dornoch, Sutherland, Scotland

**Hole:** No. 5

**Length:** 354 yards

**Par:** 4

**Designer:** Old Tom Morris

**Course Comment:** Royal Dornoch is a private club but built on public land so visitors are welcome. It's not uncommon to see people walking their dogs, cycling, or wandering along a path up above.

BELOW AND OPPOSITE *Two views of the fifth hole at Royal Dornoch.*

# No. ❺   ROYAL DORNOCH

The secretary of Dornoch welcomes visitors with this greeting: "Dornoch is considered the finest northerly course in the world, and no other course offers as delicious a feeling of getting away from it all or better provides the pieces of natural seaside beauty, challenge and enjoyment and shot values."

That's pretty big stuff. But Mr. Secretary knows full well, as do millions of golfers, that Dornoch lives up to the challenge.

Speaking of challenges, the fifth hole known as the "Hilton," is one of the more delicious ones on the course.

The tee box is perched about 40 feet above the fairway, so keep this in mind when making a club selection. The hillside along the left is not the place to be. But because the fairway slopes left to right, you will want to play your drive along the left side and play the roll. Watch out for the three bunkers and the mounds covered with rough grass.

Your approach shot is to a kidney-shaped plateau green. Don't be short or you will find yourself in a bunker along the front slope. But don't be long, either. A slope at the rear of the green into the long grasses makes for a tough up-and-down. The position of the flag can alter how you best approach this hole. **TJ**

## No. ❺  CABO REAL GOLF CLUB

**Course:** Cabo Real Golf Club

**Location:** Los Cabos, Mexico

**Hole:** No. 5

**Length:** 454 yards

**Par:** 4

**Designer:** Robert Trent Jones Jr.

**Course Comment:** Opened in 1993, Cabo Real gained notoriety in 1999 when it hosted the Senior Slam. Players praised the variety of shotmaking the course demanded and especially enjoyed whale watching from the seaside 15th during the tournament.

The southern tip of Baja is replete with golf holes seemingly designed with the singular purpose of providing a player with a postcard-perfect scene. Although it is a worthy accomplishment considering the striking contrast of ocean and desert, what sometimes is lacking is a hole that challenges a player's skill as well as their senses. It's a curious truth that puts Cabo Real Golf Club's fifth hole in select company.

The 454-yard, uphill par 4 is a challenge from tee to green. A forced carry over desert demands a long, accurate drive to a narrow fairway. Anything short is lost. Players also must contend with a large, clover-shaped fairway bunker down the right.

From the fairway, the approach is long and, if the pin is positioned to the left, must carry another desert waste area to a shallow putting surface. The best place to miss is right, where players have a relatively routine chip up a slope to a straightforward putting surface. It's a rare break on what is otherwise a demanding hole.

Once on the green, which is one of the highest points on the course, players are awarded with an almost endless view of the Sea of Cortez to the east and mountains to the west. **RH**

## No. ❺  BOSTON GOLF CLUB

**Course:** Boston Golf Club

**Location:** Hingham, Massachusetts, USA

**Hole:** No. 5

**Length:** 317 yards

**Par:** 4

**Designer:** Gil Hanse

**Course Comment:** Get out your walking shoes! Boston Golf Club is a walking-only course.

You will not find any golf carts on the property at Boston Golf Club. The course is rife with trails and rustic spots that make it a walker's paradise. It might leave you a bit tuckered out at 7,020 yards, but the hole we speak of here — the short fifth — is a quick, brisk walk. Provided, of course, you don't lose your golf ball.

Keeping the ball visible can be a challenge on Boston Golf Club's fifth hole, even though the par-4 on this 2005 layout is just 317 yards long. That is almost unheard-of brevity in today's game, but distance alone does not tell the story. There are plenty of golfers out there who can hit a ball 317 yards, but not too many of them can make it stick on the No. 5 green.

Here's why: The "Shipwreck" carries over dense scrub pine to a quickly elevated fairway. The green is on the right side, which doesn't sound difficult at 317 yards. But hitting anywhere close to the right off the tee can be a downright disaster. There are sandy waste areas everywhere, natural grasses, hills, scraggly bunkers, you name it.

Sure, if you can carry all that, the green awaits. But, it is a mere vertical ribbon that does not offer much. Instead of going for the green, the best play is to fire away to the top of the hill, which leaves a short iron into the green. You do not want to hit too far off the tee, in fact, because the angle becomes much more difficult into the ultra-skinny green. **JB**

**THIRTEENTH BEACH GOLF LINKS**

**Course:** Thirteenth Beach Golf Links

**Location:** Barwon Heads, Victoria, Australia

**Hole:** No. 5

**Length:** 343 yards

**Par:** 4

**Designer:** Tony Cashmore

**Course Comment:** The site of this layout was once an asparagus farm and then a cattle ranch before being transformed into a stunning links by architect Tony Cashmore in 2001. Tom Watson was so taken with the setting that he once described it as "as good a piece of golf land as I have seen anywhere."

Thirteenth Beach gets its moniker from a nearby surf beach on this peninsula on Melbourne's Port Philip Bay, but it is making waves these days for an entirely different reason, and that is as the site of a much-lauded golf course.

Among the holes most favored there is the very driveable fifth. The temptation to rare back with a monster tee shot is often great. It has something to do with a breeze that frequently blows at the golfer's back, and also with the excitement of seeing the beautiful dunes land stretching out in front. A creek also lends a scenic touch, as do the tall strands of bleached-out grasses, provided, of course, that one steers clear of both those hazards. Again, accuracy is key, and nothing more than a fairway wood or long iron is needed to ensure, in most cases, a 115-yard pitching wedge to a tiered green. **JS**

BELOW *Laura Davis of England tees off on the fifth hole at Sunningdale, August 2001.*

OPPOSITE *The fifth hole at Sunningdale.*

# No. ❺  SUNNINGDALE GOLF CLUB
## (OLD COURSE)

There is an occasional danger when a top player turns his eye on course design. Some are less than inclined to put full effort forth, relying instead on assistants and then simply branding his famous name on the layout. But this was not the case when Sunningdale was conceived at the turn of the century. The original design of the Old Course was initiated by Willie Park Jr., a skilled player who twice won the British Open. He was engaged by the original committee of the club in 1900, and the Old Course opened for play in 1901.

Obviously, Park put forth a solid effort at Sunningdale — the Old Course has stood the test of time for more than 90 years. Park's Old Course is the more famous of the two Sunningdale tracks, but only acquired the title of Old when the New Course, designed by Harry Colt, was opened in 1923.

Both courses have their own individual characteristics but form a perfectly matched 36 holes. The Old Course, with 103 bunkers, is more tree-lined with pine, birch, and oak lining the heather, and culminating with the famous 18th hole and the final green below the "Sunningdale Oak Tree."

The fifth hole at Sunningdale's Old might not have the famed oak, but with its heather-laden carries and still more heather enveloping the fairways at their borders, No. 5 is a perfect exemplification of what makes Sunningdale famous — as being one of the finest inland or "heathland" golf courses in the world.

By its nature, heathland golf has no sea with which to work, so Park had to rely on the natural inland beauty. No. 5 has plenty, and Park played it just right. Golden-green heather is everywhere and is clearly visible in front and on all sides from the elevated tee.

After your tee shot carries the strand of heather in front, you see still more heather to the sides, and further back, the rich oak forest. The aiming point off the tee is the left half of the fairway, which avoids the dangerous bunkers. To get home in two, the approach must either be played as a run-up shot right of the bunkers, or as a delicate pitch over a pond. Either way, it takes a deft touch to get the ball close enough to the hole to have a legitimate shot at birdie. **JB**

**Course:** Bandon Dunes (Bandon Dunes Course)

**Location:** Bandon, Oregon, USA

**Hole:** No. 5

**Length:** 428 yards

**Par:** 4

**Designer:** David McLay Kidd

**Course Comment:** Opened in the spring of 1999, the resort at Bandon Dunes is quite a different place than other West Coast players, like Pebble Beach. For example, no power carts. In the pure sense of the phrase golf tradition, golfers walk. Like it was meant to be.

# No. ❺  BANDON DUNES
## (BANDON DUNES COURSE)

First, an opening statement from the designer, David McLay Kidd: "From the moment I stepped out on these wild, wind-shaped sand dunes, I knew this would be the opportunity of a lifetime. The owner, Mike Keiser, wanted something authentic and true to the Scottish tradition. My reply was, 'No real estate, no golf carts, no clubhouse on the beach.'"

Both the Bandon Dunes Course and Pacific Dunes Course feature stirring holes along the seashore (there are 12 holes where the sea is a major player). Bandon Dunes is a links course built on a beautiful stretch of sand dunes, 100 feet above the Pacific Ocean on the Southern Oregon Coast.

The view on this 428-yard par 4 can be best described as dramatic. Or maybe breathtaking? How about amazing? Pick your adjective, because No. 5 is better experienced than described.

OK, now back to the golf. If you can remove your attention from the breathtaking scenery long enough to concentrate on your tee shot, drive the ball into the right half of the split fairway. Since the hole will play directly against the prevailing wind, it may be necessary to consider conceding this as a three-shot hole, rather than risking a big number.

The fairway is very tight leading up to the green and there is plenty of trouble all over. But the golf doesn't really matter on this hole. You will certainly remember this hole, regardless of your score. **TJ**

**Course:** Cabo del Sol Golf Club (Ocean Course)

**Location:** Los Cabos, Mexico

**Hole:** No. 5

**Length:** 458 yards

**Par:** 4

**Designer:** Jack Nicklaus

**Course Comment:** A large mound behind the green was removed, expanding the view of the Sea of Cortez and creating an imposing visual for players looking down from an elevated fairway to a hole that seems to run into the clear waters.

## No. ❺ CABO DEL SOL GOLF CLUB (OCEAN COURSE)

Cabo del Sol architect Jack Nicklaus has deservedly dubbed the ocean-side course's closing stretch the "finest finishing holes in all of golf." And while it's difficult to argue with golf's Golden Bear, Cabo del Sol's director of golf Brad Wheatley offers this humble rejoinder: "16, 17, and 18 are wonderful but I really think [Nos.] 5, 6, and 7 are Cabo del Sol's heart and soul."

Cabo del Sol's sixth and seventh holes are par 3s that hug the Sea of Cortez and, depending on the wind, usually require little more than a 7-iron to reach the green. The par-4 fifth, however, is a complete test of a player's game, mettle, and senses.

The fifth's tee shot must carry a desert waste area to a fairway protected by a large bunker positioned directly in front of the tee box. Tee shots played to the right of the looming hazard dramatically reduce the length of the hole but run the risk of finding the desert. Although playing left of the fairway bunker is safer, it leaves a long, downhill approach to a large, rolling green. **RH**

**Course:** The Raven at South Mountain

**Location:** Phoenix, Arizona, USA

**Hole:** No. 5

**Length:** 324 yards

**Par:** 4

**Designer:** Gary Panks, David Graham

**Course Comment:** The Raven Golf Club at South Mountain in Phoenix, Arizona, distinguishes itself each year as one of the premier Arizona golf experiences. The 7,078-yard layout features plush, rolling fairways framed by thousands of mature pines that were imported from Georgia in 1994.

## No. ❺ THE RAVEN AT SOUTH MOUNTAIN

This par 4 is one of the more unique holes on a golf course that could trademark the word unique. Forget the country-club atmosphere, the first-rate course conditions, and the warm Arizona air for just one moment. Step back off the tee and really look over this hole.

The view is part frightening. Part intimidating. Part exhilarating. And it's definitely all good.

This is regarded as the toughest hole on the South Mountain course and is one of the Raven's signature holes — there are plenty worthy of that title.

The safe play off the tee on this hole is a middle iron, laying up just short of the fairway bunkers on this big-time dogleg right.

If you are looking to add a birdie to your scorecard, then play a long iron to the left of the bunkers, which are scattered all over the right side of the fairway, almost from tee to green.

There isn't much trouble on the left, but the hole plays much longer the further left you go.

To make matters much worse — or more challenging, based on your perspective — the designers created a two-tiered green with a false front. So don't be short, or you will roll right back onto the fairway — or in the bunker. **TJ**

**Course:** Old Sandwich Golf Club

**Location:** Plymouth, Massachusetts, USA

**Hole:** No. 5

**Length:** 336 yards

**Par:** 4

**Designer:** Bill Coore and Ben Crenshaw

**Course Comment:** Old Sandwich Golf Club is located in a historic area along the oldest unpaved, continuously operated road in the United States – Old Sandwich Road.

# No. ❺ OLD SANDWICH GOLF CLUB

It is not an exaggeration to say that the 5th hole at Old Sandwich may just be one of the finest short par 4s in America. And, by short, we mean short. But, indeed, the fifth measures up.

No. 5 is magnificent in that you cross an enormous ravine to a diagonal stripe of a fairway stuffed full of gigantic mounds. The hole's length may be diminutive, but the subsequent fairway bounces most certainly are not.

The hole looks like it has been lifted straight from a Scottish postcard. The ravine and the moguls make this true, and it is accentuated further by the bunkers carved into the side of a hill in the left of the fairway.

The bunkers are there to keep players from simply having a safe layup to the green. The first bunker requires a 215-yard carry from the tee, the second a 235-yard carry, and the third a 258-yard shot. Doesn't sound like much, but these are the ideal spots from which to approach the green.

The hole cuts sharply to the left, and the most nervy, big-hitting players can make a run for the green or hug the left side for a short shot to the green. However, the middle of the fairway is the safe play because you never know where the contours are going to take you if you miss the green. The green is contoured, and is downhill from the fairway. **JB**

**Course:** Bethpage State Park (Black Course)

**Location:** Farmingdale, New York, USA

**Hole:** No. 5

**Length:** 451 yards

**Par:** 4

**Designer:** A.W. Tillinghast, Rees Jones

**Course Comment:** They say Sam Snead walked off this hole during an exhibition in the 1940s, enraged and just a touch belittled.

BELOW AND OPPOSITE *Two views of the fifth hole at Bethpage State Park.*

# No. ❺ BETHPAGE STATE PARK
## (BLACK COURSE)

Bethpage Black is often called the best bargain in golf. And the unbelievable fifth is a postcard-advertisement of the New York course's greatness. The hole is an example of a course that offers as good a deal as there is in golf. But, after playing the beautiful yet treacherous fifth, the word "bargain" might not leap to your lips. There is nothing cheap about the scenic fifth.

Many call No. 5 at Bethpage Black the best hole on the course. And if that is true, a case could be made that it is the best hole in American public golf. Because Bethpage Black, after playing host to the 2002 U.S. Open, has now become the most famous public golf course in the United States.

Like the entire course, the fifth hole is as attractive as it is excruciating. Blast away on the tee, yet avoid the grotesque fingers of sand that invite tee shots that stray right. Steer free of the danger and manicure awaits, lending a mid-iron challenge to a green that appears to be choked by slopes and trees.

Accuracy works, but in its utmost form. Like almost all of the holes on the Black Course, the "ladies" tees are used by men. Nothing emasculating or embarrassing here, unless, of course, your name is Sam Snead. Do you believe he walked off this hole?

You can see the green up there somewhere. You're sure of it. But, damned if you can figure out how to get there. This is a par-4 hole, long of course at 451 yards, but it is a par-4 hole. Truth be told, however, only the best of the best can expect to get there in two. If you play to scratch, have at it. Any player with a handicap of more than 5 better consider this hole a par 5.

The fifth, like the rest of the course, is a great hole to play. But, that's the key: you must know how to play. No. 5 at the Black Course was tough enough before the U.S. Open came around in 2002, but after the renovations it turned from tough to nearly unbearable.

It is gorgeous, nearly perfect, in fact. But it also is a monster. Come to the fifth at Bethpage Black with your best game in tow.

But leave your ego at home. **JB**

**Course:** Blackwolf Run Golf Club (River Course)

**Location:** Kohler, Wisconsin, USA

**Hole:** No. 5

**Length:** 419 yards

**Par:** 4

**Designers:** Pete Dye

**Course Comment:** In its first major championship, the River Course was the site of one of the most dramatic playoffs in women's history. Se Ri Pak and amateur Jenny Chuasiriporn finished 72 holes tied at 290 and both shot 73 in Monday's 18-hole playoff. Pak eventually prevailed, making birdie at the second sudden-death playoff hole.

# No. ❺ BLACKWOLF RUN GOLF CLUB (RIVER COURSE)

There is no accounting for the Wisconsin sense of humor. These are the same people, after all, who don "cheesehead" hats and brave sub-freezing temperatures each winter to cheer for a team that hasn't won a Super Bowl since 1996.

In typical Wisconsin whimsy, the fifth hole at Blackwolf Run is curiously dubbed "Made in Heaven." A better title for the hazard-strewn par 4 would be "Produced in Purgatory."

From the elevated tee, the Sheboygan River, which winds through the entire course, flows down the right side of the hole. Just left of the river looms a bunker that runs 50 yards down the right side of the fairway. With those dangers in mind, the best drive is down the left toward the smaller fairway bunkers carved into the hill to a rolling fairway.

Similarly, the best approach to the oval-shaped green, which juts 25 feet above the fairway, is down the left side but anything long will leave an exacting downhill chip to a green that angles from left to right and feeds sharply toward the river. Avoid missing approach shots right, for this will send shots caroming into a deep valley and all but guarantee a bogey or worse. **RH**

**Course:** Nairn Golf Club

**Location:** Nairnshire, Scotland

**Hole:** No. 5

**Length:** 390 yards

**Par:** 4

**Designer:** Andrew Simpson, Old Tom Morris, James Braid

**Course Comment:** In 1987 the club celebrated its centenary and played host to both men's and ladies' Scottish Amateur Championships.

Nairn is very much a traditional links with the opening holes stretching out along the shoreline. Accuracy is much more important than length on this Scottish masterpiece.

The front nine is the shorter of the two, although the prevailing south-westerly wind can make this the bigger challenge. The par-4 fifth hole, named "Nets," is no exception to the rule. The wind can easily blow away a good round.

This is simply a very good short par 4.

One reason it's good is because it's hard — starting at the tee. The sea rests along the right side and a bunker rests along the left edge. Down the middle is your play here.

With a good drive in the bag, you look over a short iron shot to a small elevated green. This green is heavily guarded — a miss here and you'll be doing more than shaking your head. One suggestion: don't be long.

Like most of the holes on the front nine, there are spectacular views of the sea. But try and stay focused on the golf course or you might not remember anything but that high number on your card. **TJ**

**Course:** Walton Heath (Old Course)

**Location:** Walton on the Hill, Tadworth, Surrey, England

**Hole:** No. 5

**Length:** 437 yards

**Par:** 4

**Designer:** Herbert Fowler

**Course Comment:** Walton Heath has the unique distinction of being the only club in England to have had a reigning monarch as captain. The then-Prince of Wales became King Edward VIII during his captaincy in 1935–36. Other former members include David Lloyd George and Sir Winston Churchill.

No. **⑤** **WALTON HEATH**
## (OLD COURSE)

Walton Heath's Old Course opened for play in 1904, with an appealing exhibition match between the legendary triumvirate of Harry Vardon, J.H. Taylor, and James Braid. With its expertly crafted layout in the beautiful heathland of the Surrey countryside, it has been considered one of England's top courses ever since.

The fairway of the fifth hole is surrounded by heather, and turns to the left as it nears the green, making the fairway's right side the preferred angle for the approach. The slightly elevated, heavily contoured green is guarded by a pair of deep bunkers (one left and one right). Walton Heath was the site of the 1981 Ryder Cup, in which the United States squad — considered one of the best ever in the competition, with a combined 36 majors to its credit — defeated Europe 18½–9½, the European side's worst-ever loss on British soil. The event had originally been scheduled for The Belfry, but its condition was poor and so Walton Heath was arranged as a late replacement and served more than admirably.

The club also played host to several European Opens, including the inaugural event in 1978 won by American Bobby Wadkins. **KA**

**BELOW AND OPPOSITE** *Two views of the fifth hole at Walton Heath.*

**Course:** Kaanapali Golf Course (North Course)

**Location:** Lahaina, Maui, Hawaii, USA

**Hole:** No. 5

**Length:** 473 yards

**Par:** 4

**Designer:** Robert Trent Jones Sr.

**Course Comment:** Despite designing some of the world's greatest golf courses, Robert Trent Jones Sr. designed only two courses in Hawaii, including Kaanapali, which opened in 1962. No. 5 is the signature hole at Kaanapali, and the No. 1 handicap hole.

## No. ❺ KAANAPALI GOLF COURSE (NORTH COURSE)

The North Course begins at sea level with a par-5 hole extending 550 yards. The course hugs the shoreline before winding its way to the West Maui Mountain foothills.

Speaking of hugging the shoreline, let's stroll out to No. 5. And bring your beach blanket.

This slight dogleg left is long, challenging, and scenic. The second half of the hole features the ocean to your right and more water to the left of the green. The scenery speaks for itself. But this is a great golf hole.

There are fairway bunkers on the left, just at where the fairway breaks. Long hitters should be able to carry the bunkers and set up nicely for their approach shot.

But watch out for the wind. It's already a long hole and when there is a wind in your face, it plays even longer.

Your best approach to the green is from the left side of the fairway. There are green-side bunkers on the right front and left front and one to the back left.

Even the course pros think this is a tough golf hole: "par here is a great score." **TJ**

---

**Course:** Durban Country Club

**Location:** Durban, South Africa

**Hole:** No. 5

**Length:** 461 yards

**Par:** 4

**Designer:** George Waterman, Laurie Waters

**Course Comment:** Native son Gary Player won the first of his 13 South African Opens in 1956 at Durban, and later set the course record of 64 in 1969.

## No. ❺ DURBAN COUNTRY CLUB

Few courses start out with a tougher stretch than Durban Country Club, an elite seaside course located along the shores of the Indian Ocean. The course features an abundance of thick, colorful foliage, virtually every tropical plant imaginable, and indigenous, mature trees — including many filled with monkeys. No. 5 is the finale of a trio of highly ranked holes, along with the par-3 second and world-renowned par-5 third. The fifth may be the least spectacular of the three to look at, but make no mistake: it can be every bit as challenging.

The longest par 4 on the course, it is shielded from the ocean winds by trees lining the fairway. The landing area for the drive is narrow and contains many slopes and undulations that make finding a level lie for the approach difficult. Miss the fairway too far right, and your ball will roll off steep mounds into the tropical forest, perhaps never to be seen again. The green is guarded by a pair of well-placed bunkers, but go too long in an effort to avoid the sand and more trouble awaits: the green complex drops off sharply into a thick jungle. **KA**

**Course:** Hyatt Regency Coolum
Golf Course

**Location:** Coolum Beach,
Queensland, Australia

**Hole:** No. 5

**Length:** 349 yards

**Par:** 4

**Designer:** Robert Trent Jones Jr.

**Course Comment:** This layout on
Queensland's Sunshine Coast basks
in the shadow of Mount Coolum,
which, according to Aboriginal
legend, was formed by the gods
after a warrior of that same name
was killed while fighting for a young
woman. In addition to being a key
part of the five-star Hyatt Regency
Resort there, the course also serves
as home of the Australian PGA
Championship.

BELOW *Adam Smith of Australia
plays his second shot on the fifth
hole at Coolum, December 2003.*

# No. ❺  HYATT REGENCY COOLUM GOLF COURSE

The fifth at Coolum is one of those terrific short par 4s that always seem to play much harder in reality than they actually do on the card. Though it measures only 349 yards from the back tees and has nary a bunker, it nonetheless presents a very good test of accuracy and guile. Most players will hit a 3-wood or long iron off the tee of this dogleg right, in hopes of keeping their drives away from the treacherous bush land on the left and the swampy hazard on the right.

That accomplished, they need only a short iron to a relatively flat green fronted by water ready to swallow any less-than-perfect approaches.

The Hyatt Regency Coolum is featured in *Golf Magazine*'s top 50 courses in Australia — up there with greats such as Royal Melbourne and Ellerston. The glittering Pacific Ocean on one side and the natural Coolum bushland on the other, combined with the subtropical temperatures of the Sunshine Coast, make Coolum a joy to play. **JS**

**Course:** Mid Ocean Club

**Location:** Tucker's Town, Bermuda

**Hole:** No. 5

**Length:** 433 yards

**Par:** 4

**Designer:** Charles Blair Macdonald

**Course Comment:** Bermuda has just eight golf courses, but that's enough to make the sparsely populated group of islands the home of the most golf courses per capita of any place on earth.

OK, quick. Where is Bermuda?

Perhaps you knew, but somehow it seems odd to describe this group of British colony islands as just a quick left turn from North Carolina. Back when Charles Blair Macdonald designed the Mid Ocean Club, however, the 480-mile jaunt from the East Coast of the United States to Bermuda was more than just a slight inconvenience.

It took some time to make it to the islands. And Macdonald wanted to make sure that golfers had a reason to go out of their way. The Mid Ocean Club, with the fifth hole as its beacon, more than made the trip worthwhile.

And today, with the islands' build-up and the advent of a quick jet trip, the journey to this magical golf destination is barely more than a hiccup. And more than worthy of a quick trip from the East Coast.

The fifth hole at the Mid Ocean is a majestic Cape layout, with its tee elevated and the first challenge requiring a shot over Mangrove Lake. Like all Cape holes — a Macdonald original — the fifth allows you to bite off as much of the turn over water as you dare. The 433-yard distance at Mid Ocean's fifth might not seem daunting, but it is a decision-maker's hole. Safe to the right and make the second shot eternal . . . or gamble to the left, stay dry if you can, and cut the corner?

As you stand upon the lifted tee, looking out upon your challenge, it's a question that is almost audible. Can you cut the corner? How close do you dare? How are you feeling today? Why did you make the trip?

Perhaps we're being just a touch dramatic, but you get the idea. This hole is a challenge from the moment you get to the tee box.

Landing in the fairway is a success story, to be sure, but it doesn't guarantee complete victory. The green at No. 5 is well protected either side by two very deep, enlongated bunkers. The green has two levels, and its unintelligible shape makes for a possibility of wicked pin placements, depending on the superintendent's mood.

Good luck. **JB**

## No. ❺ ELLERSTON GOLF COURSE

**Course:** Ellerston Golf Course

**Location:** Upper Hunter Valley, New South Wales, Australia

**Hole:** No. 5

**Length:** 434 yards

**Par:** 4

**Designers:** Greg Norman, Bob Harrison

**Course Comment:** Ellerston is not only regarded as the most difficult modern course in Australia, but also the most exclusive. Owned by media magnate Kerry Packer, who is considered Australia's wealthiest man, and built on his 70,000-acre private estate, it is said to record roughly 50 rounds a year.

The course only opened in 2001, but it took no time at all for it to rise to the top of Australia's best golf course lists and have its name uttered among greats such as Royal Melbourne, Kingston Heath and New South Wales.

And those who have been lucky enough to play Ellerston have no argument with that ranking. Perhaps it is best known for its brutal par 4s, and the fifth hole is often lauded as being the finest on this layout, if not the entire country.

The hole begins with a fairly straightforward drive to a wide landing area guarded on the right by a tributary of Pages Creek. The creek then makes a series of horseshoe-like bends, finally snaking around a very undulating green that invariably putts true and fast.

The forgiving side of the putting surface here is the left, which is wide open. But any player going for the right will be faced with a much tighter landing area as well as the hazards of the creek that present problems for only slightly errant balls both back and front. **JS**

## No. ❺ THE FORTRESS

**Course:** The Fortress

**Location:** Frankenmuth, Michigan, USA

**Hole:** No. 5

**Length:** 353 yards

**Par:** 4

**Designer:** Dick Nugent

**Course Comment:** Designed in 1992, The Fortress reflects characteristics of golf's early Scottish origins. Fescue-covered mounds reveal well-guarded, sectioned greens. Bentgrass tees, greens, and fairways surround 75 bunkers.

Frankenmuth is a very popular tourist spot in the midwest, known for its German origins, outstanding chicken dinners, and delicious homemade fudge. In 1992, golf became part of the attraction, when The Fortress Golf Course opened.

The fifth hole, a 353-yard par 4, is one of the better holes on a course known as much for its excellent conditions as its challenging golf. The key to this hole starts at the tee. You not only have to hit it straight, but you want to be on the right side of this rather straight fairway. The second shot is longer than it looks and there is trouble ahead, including a large bunker along the left side that begins well out in the fairway. There also are green-side bunkers to the left and right.

How tough is this golf course? No. 5 is the 18 handicap. In other words, it doesn't get any easier than this. There are three sets of tees on No. 5, starting at 275 yards. The Fortress encompasses 6,813 yards of formidable play on an 18-hole, par-72 course. About 25,000 rounds of golf are played on the course every season. **TJ**

**Course:** Crystal Downs Country Club

**Location:** Frankfort, Michigan, USA

**Hole:** No. 5

**Length:** 353 yards

**Par:** 4

**Designer:** Alister MacKenzie

**Course Comment:** OK, so this isn't about golf. But you are within a quick drive of the cherry capital of the world, Traverse City. The annual Cherry Festival in June is a great time to visit.

## No. ❺ CRYSTAL DOWNS COUNTRY CLUB

When they speak of Northern Michigan, the locals call it "Up North." Those who once lived there and moved away call it "God's Country." And those who play golf, who choose to traverse up past the middle of the state shaped like a mitten, will know they have visited a golf Mecca. Don't think you are being led astray. This is not hyperbole. Northern Michigan, Crystal Down, No. 5, is as good as it gets.

The fifth at Crystal Downs is a peek at Northern Michigan golf. There are trees. There are changes of color. But these are seasonal experiences. The view from the tee — where the top of the flag is barely visible over the top of a thick ridge that includes a precarious bunker — is consistent all year.

This is a hole with a humpback — you can see the flag over the hump, but you can't quite get there. And, the scruffy bunch of three bunkers halfway up the ridge makes strategy more important than power.

MacKenzie was a master of employing the land, particularly when the land included slopes and moguls. Natural contours make it beautiful, yet rugged challenge is more the theme.

The best line off the tee is over a large tree right of the bunkers, forcing power and accuracy, not to mention height. The perfect drive affords proper angle to the green, which falls left to right, toward a collection four bunkers. This is a flat green, with the pesky exception of a bowl center right. No bargain, the fifth. Mecca, or no. **JB**

**Course:** Colonial Country Club

**Location:** Fort Worth, Texas, USA

**Hole:** No. 5

**Length:** 470 yards

**Par:** 4

**Designer:** John Bredemus, Perry Maxwell

**Course Comment:** Annika Sorenstam made seven bogeys when she missed the cut at the 2003 Colonial. She played the fifth twice and made bogey each time. It was the first PGA Tour event played by a woman in 58 years.

# No. ❺  COLONIAL COUNTRY CLUB

This hole is nicknamed "Death Valley," and this isn't just for the normal player. The world's best understand the difficulty of the fifth at Colonial. Here's where the best shots in the world go to die. Kenny Perry won the 2003 Colonial by six strokes, but still managed to make birdie on No. 5 just once in four rounds.

In other words, make par at No. 5, go on to No. 6 and be happy.

Colonial was Ben Hogan's home. If St. Andrews was golf's birthplace, and Augusta its showcase, then Fort Worth — with Hogan's beloved Colonial at its forefront — is its soul. Colonial's original layout is credited to John Bredemus, a rather unusual sort who sometimes sought refuge in the tops of trees, but Perry Maxwell brought the track to its current form in 1940, just five years after Bredemus' design.

Hogan's office, with "Henny Bogan" still on the desk, sits in memoriam to this day. There is much reverence here, but there is no safety, particularly at the fifth.

Like virtually every hole in this collection of 1001, the fifth at Colonial is trouble. From start-to-finish, from left-to-right, be-careful-enjoy-yourself trouble. This is a long hole that would be difficult for the mid-range handicapper if it were straight as an arrow. But toss in the dogleg right and a ditch on the left with trees wherever you look, and you've got a hole of which even Henny Bogan would be wary.

The length and the dogleg might be challenge enough. But you toss in a wind that almost always blows from left to right, and the devilish fifth's difficulty becomes the stuff of legend. If the wind is blowing as it almost always does, you must take your tee shot over the historic oaks to the left and play a little fade to the middle of the fairway.

Then there's the green. Often exalted as a majestic finisher to a hole, a putting surface can serve as a glorious finishing spot. But the green at Colonial's fifth is anything but. It is anticlimactic, yet devious. There are some traps, some trees, and it looks innocent enough. But the approach is treacherous — it is a shot seemingly bereft of safety. **JB**

**Course:** Pinehurst (No. 2 Course)

**Location:** Pinehurst, North Carolina, USA

**Hole:** No. 5

**Length:** 482 yards

**Par:** 4

**Designer:** Donald Ross

**Course Comment:** The U.S. Open tees, created in 1999, turn one of Pinehurst No. 2's most genteel holes into a monster. Payne Stewart won his second U.S. Open of the decade when he captured the national championship here in 1999. He died later the same year in an airplane accident.

**BELOW** *The Putter Boy statue at Pinehurst.*

**OPPOSITE** *The fifth hole at Pinehurst.*

# No. ❺ PINEHURST (NO. 2 COURSE)

Imagine a golf course, playing an entire round where you felt as if you were putting on an upside-down bowl. A bowl made of the slickest ceramic available, with the most curvaceous slopes you could contrive. This is Pinehurst No. 2. And this is the 482-yard fifth.

Tommy Armour, one of the game's great champions, said: "The man who doesn't feel emotionally stirred when he plays golf at Pinehurst beneath those clear blue skies and with the pine fragrance in his nostrils is one who should be ruled out of golf for life. It's the kind of course that gets into the blood of an old trooper."

Armour was one of the great old troopers of golf. And Pinehurst No. 2 is one of the great old golf courses. The resort was established in 1894, and there are eight courses on the property. However, there is only one must-play. And that's No. 2.

The 482-yard behemoth of a par 4 at No. 5 is among the most arduous adventures on the famed No. 2. Even without the daunting yardage, you'd have a challenge. Length added in, most players don't consider this a real par 4. If you make par here, unless you're playing to scratch, consider it a birdie.

Yes, the landing area looks fairly receptive off the tee. But, it's a deceptive receptive. It appears as if there's plenty of room to land, which is true, but if you don't land on the right side of the fairway, you can forget about having a plausible angle toward the green.

Even with the proper path to the putting surface, the nasty contours of No. 2's greens await. These are without a doubt among the most difficult approach shots in the world. The fifth hole is no exception to this rule.

The fifth is also an exemplification of the No. 2 course's difficulty. No. 5 played as the toughest hole on the course in the 1999 U.S. Open, in large part because even a perfect tee shot and a well-struck approach did not necessarily result in finishing on par. **JB**

## No. ❺ OLD MEMORIAL GOLF CLUB

**Course:** Old Memorial Golf Club

**Location:** Tampa, Florida, USA

**Hole:** No. 5

**Length:** 459 yards

**Par:** 4

**Designer:** Steve Smyers

**Course Comment:** In the honor of tradition — the course is called Old Memorial, after all — caddies are mandatory. However, power carts are available for individuals with disabilities.

The fifth hole, 459 yards from the back tees, is the toughest on the Old Memorial course. With a lake running along the left side, it's also scenic. But don't bother admiring the scenery on this hole. There is too much work to be done.

Your tee shot from an elevated tee is the first challenge. Remember, there is a lake running along the fairway on the left. And there is rough on the other side. From the tee to the break in the dogleg is about 320 yards.

But, believe it or not, the green is reachable in two. With a good wind behind you — which is often the case — and if the course is firm, you could get it there.

For most people, though, a drive of 270 yards will still work. From there, you are looking at 170 to 180 yards to the green. But you must carry water — yes, the lake is back.

There is also trouble leading up to the pin. From about 100 yards from the green, three bunkers on the right escort you to the dance floor. And they are very deep bunkers.

And don't be long on this hole. There are only about 10 yards of real estate from behind the green to out-of-bounds markers. So make sure you have the right distance on your approach shot and pick the right club.

The layout of this exclusive course is wide open and flat, with enough yardage to test even the longest hitters. No. 5 is a perfect example. **TJ**

**Course:** The Homestead (Cascades Course)

**Location:** Hot Springs, Virginia, USA

**Hole:** No. 5

**Length:** 575 yards

**Par:** 5

**Designer:** William S. Flynn

**Course Comment:** There are plenty of great views on the Cascades Course at The Homestead, a popular resort in the Allegheny Mountains. But one of the prettiest sights of all is standing in the fairway about 150 yards from the green on the fifth hole. Standing on a hill, the green below and all its natural surroundings will make you want to reach for the camera. Reach for an 8-iron instead and drop one on the green.

# No. ❺ THE HOMESTEAD (CASCADES COURSE)

The Homestead is "home" to three outstanding golf courses. The Lower Cascades Course features open fairways and large, bentgrass greens. The Old Course has had extensive renovations by William Flynn and, more recently, by Rees Jones. The Cascades Course, the crown jewel of the three, was redesigned by Robert Trent Jones Sr. in 1961. One of the more challenging holes on the Cascades is No. 5. The 575-yard par-5 hole is named "Marathon." And it's one long trek from tee to green.

From a slightly elevated tee, you need to hit your tee shot about 270 yards to safely reach the landing area below. Your second shot is the key. This blind, uphill shot will make or break your score. You need to rip it about 220 yards to clear rough that separates the two landing areas. This will leave you with a nice "chip" shot of about 70 to 80 yards to the green. The putting surface slopes back to front and has a little crown in the middle. There are not a lot of flat areas on this green.

The Cascades Course has played host to two U.S. Women's Amateur Championships, a Curtis Cup match, and the 1967 U.S. Women's Open. **TJ**

**FOTA ISLAND GOLF CLUB**
**(DEERPARK COURSE)**

**Course:** Fota Island Golf Club
(Deerpark Course)

**Location:** Fota Island, Cork, Ireland

**Hole:** No. 5

**Length:** 544 yards

**Par:** 5

**Designer:** Robert Trent Jones Jr.

**Course Comment:** They may be a bit biased, but club staffers call Fota Island the best golf resort in Ireland. It has played host to the Irish Club Professional Championship, The Irish PGA Championship, and three Irish Amateur Opens. Then came the Irish Open in 2001 and 2002. Then in 2011, came the PGA EuroPro Audi Cork Irish Masters.

The Deerpark Course was the host to the Irish Open in 2001 and 2002 and it is little wonder why. There is challenge from start to finish, and the variety of holes leaves players guessing from tee to tee.

There are no "up-and-back" holes, and it is a "thinking player's" course every step of the way. A perfect example of this is the par-5, No. 5 that measures exactly 544 yards from the back tees.

It is a very reachable hole as far as distance is concerned, but the configuration of the hole makes it anything but. You must drive from an "island" driving area to a perpendicular landing stretch that takes a severe right turn to the landing area.

If you drive too short, you have not made the landing area, and if you drive too long, you have driven through it into the trees. The drive is not made any easier by the fact that it is downhill all the way. You must judge your drive properly to avoid misjudging the perpendicular fairway. The downhill slope can take you straight into trouble and rob you of any chance at par.

Trouble is everywhere but in the middle of the fairway. Then, your second takes you to the end of the green, where you have to take a left turn to get to the putting surface. A strategic, risk-reward hole all the way down that is a joy to play. A par here is an achievement. It is makeable, but an achievement, nonetheless. **JB**

**Course:** Kapalua Golf Club (Plantation Course)

**Location:** Kapalua, Maui, Hawaii

**Hole:** No. 5

**Length:** 532 yards

**Par:** 5

**Designer:** Ben Crenshaw, Bill Coore

**Course Comment:** Kapalua plays host each year to the Mercedes Championships, an elite field that includes only PGA Tour winners from the previous year.

BELOW *Tiger Woods of the USA tees off on the fifth hole at Kapalua, January 2004.*

OPPOSITE *The fifth hole at Kapalua.*

## No. ❺ KAPALUA GOLF CLUB
### (PLANTATION COURSE)

Most "Cape" holes are par 4s, but Crenshaw and Coore have brought the architectural concept to a beautiful par 5 at Kapalua, a unique par-73 course laid out amid natural geographic formations and former pineapple plantation fields. The extra shot makes the challenge of this cape — and the thrills — even more enticing.

A canyon filled with tropical vegetation lines the entire right side of the hole, which slopes from left to right all the way to the green, meaning even the straightest of drives often bounds right, forcing a carry over the chasm to reach the green in two. Players who hit good drives will no doubt be tempted because of the hole's relatively short length, but they had best be precise: two perfect shots are required.

Golfers who go the more conventional route will stay left, left and left: a drive down the left side to avoid the gorge, a second-shot long iron or fairway wood to the left side of the fairway and a short iron to the left portion of the green, which is protected by a group of bunkers on the right and rear. **KA**

**ABOVE** *Robert Karlsson of Sweden plays his second shot on the fifth hole at New South Wales, February 2003.*

## No. ❺  NEW SOUTH WALES

The first of back-to-back magnificent holes along the Pacific Ocean and the Cape Banks on Australia's spectacular eastern coast, this relatively short par 5 serves as a worthy lead-in to New South Wales' well-known par-3 sixth.

The blind tee shot must rise over a ridge approximately 250 yards from the tee. Once there, the plateau fairway landing area offers a splendid view of the rugged, rocky Pacific shoreline and the cliffside green below. Depending on the strength of the wind off the ocean, long drivers have a chance to reach the green in two on the downhill approach. But beware: there's not much room for error. The fairway tightens considerably as it reaches the hole, and the putting surface, which slopes from front to back, is fiercely guarded by a pair of bunkers left and front right.

Enjoy the view and the building anticipation of tackling the following hole, which can be seen off to the right. But don't dare take the fifth for granted. Let up your guard even a little, and you'll be left with a high score here. Then playing the sixth won't be nearly as pleasant. **KA**

## No. ❺  THE BOULDERS (SOUTH COURSE)

**Course:** The Boulders (South Course)

**Location:** Carefree, Arizona, USA

**Hole:** No. 5

**Length:** 545 yards

**Par:** 5

**Designer:** Jay Morrish

**Course Comment:** This 36-hole golf resort gets its name from the precariously balanced, 12-million-year-old granite boulder formations that dot the surrounding desert landscape.

No. 5 at the Boulders, a course nestled in the unique serenity of the high Sonoran desert, immediately presents players with the choice of whether to play this hole conservatively or throw caution to the desert wind.

A dry creek bed crosses the fairway and requires a carry of at least 230 yards to reach the narrow landing strip on the other side. A much shorter landing area in front of the creek bed to the right offers a safer route with an iron but will end any shot of reaching the green in two. And even that shot carries its own risk: go too long, too left or too right and you'll still be in the hazard.

It's not much easier from there. The fairway pinches in considerably as it reaches the elevated green, which is framed at the back by several clusters of boulders rising into the sky. Even more worrisome is the group of bunkers on the front left and all the way around the right side of the narrow, curving green, although they may at least save you from the harshness of the encroaching desert.

To have a chance at a two-putt, you must land on the tier where the pin is. Otherwise, bogey — or worse — is a distinct possibility. **KA**

## No. ❺  MILLBROOK

**Course:** Millbrook

**Location:** Arrowtown, New Zealand

**Hole:** No. 5

**Length:** 550 yards

**Par:** 5

**Designer:** Bob Charles

**Course Comment:** Charles said the 434-yard par-4 hole, which features an elevated green and an excellent view of the Remarkables range, is his favorite hole. But there is no doubt that No. 5 is the toughest.

Millbrook has many highlights but it doesn't get any better than an impressive trifecta starting with No. 4 and finishing at No. 6. In between is the big boy, the longest hole on the course, checking in at 550 yards off the back tees. This dogleg right features two nasty bunkers along the fairway guarding the tempting shortcut. Come up short and you'll land on one of New Zealand's new popular beaches. It doesn't get easier.

Two ponds, make that two very large ponds, await your wayward second shot along the right side. And once you find the green, it's no day at the beach either. There is a bunker along the left side that often gathers golf balls from sloping terrain just off the green.

Charles, one of New Zealand's greatest golfers, has this to say about the masterpiece he helped create: "When I first visited the site . . . I realized I had been given something special to work with. Nestled in the Wakatipu Basin, surrounded by the spectacular Remarkables, the terrain lent itself so naturally to the game of golf that it was only on one hole that any earth moving was required. Thus, like most great golf courses in the world, it has been largely laid on the natural landscape." **TJ**

# Hole ⑥

If you're in need of a breather, a chance
to regroup, often No. 6 affords the
opportunity. If architects follow the general
rule that Nos. 2–5 are the most difficult
holes on the front side, then they more
than likely also follow that up with
an easier pair on Nos. 6 and 7.

No. 6 at Seminole Country Club in North
Palm Beach, Florida, for instance, is one of
the best holes on the course and makes our
list of 1001 you must play, yet is also only
the seventh toughest on the course. And
No. 6 at Penha Longa in Lisboa, Portugal,
while clearly the layout's signature hole,
is handicapped no higher than the sixth
hardest on the course. And, as a general
rule, these two are tougher than most
sixth holes tend to be.

So, if you're going well, you've got a
good chance to keep it going at No. 6. Or
if you need a reversal of poor fortune, this
is the time.

LEFT *The sixth hole at Wasioto Winds,
Pineville, Kentucky, USA.*

**Course:** Worthington Manor Golf Club

**Location:** Urbana, Maryland, USA

**Hole:** No. 6

**Length:** 198 yards

**Par:** 3

**Designer:** Ault, Clark, & Associates

**Course Comment:** This course is a rarity in today's golf-crazy environment. It's actually reasonably priced for such an elite and professional-style golf course. So if you want to play a great course without going broke, this is a good bet.

BELOW *The sixth hole at Worthington Manor.*

# No. ❻ WORTHINGTON MANOR GOLF CLUB

The signature hole at Worthington Manor is the 198-yard, par-3 sixth hole, which requires a tee shot over water to a heavily guarded green. And we mean heavily guarded.

This is one of the more imposing-looking par-3 holes you will face all year. The green isn't on an island, but water surrounds the dance floor on three sides. The bail-out is long, although there are traps seemingly everywhere on this hole. A couple of large ones await in the front.

The green is fairly large and doesn't have the slope that many of the others have. Putting isn't the problem on this hole. Getting to the green is the problem.

This is one of several great par-3 holes at Worthington Manor. The par-3 No. 17, which requires a tee shot over a ravine, is another spectacular hole.

The course was named the Maryland "Course of the Year" in 2000 by the National Golf Course Owners' Association and is a frequent site for U.S. Open qualifying. Worthington Manor has become known in the area for its country club atmosphere, outstanding service, and top golf course. **TJ**

## No. ❻ YEAMANS HALL CLUB

**Course:** Yeamans Hall Club

**Location:** Hanahan, South Carolina, USA

**Hole:** No. 6

**Length:** 180 yards

**Par:** 3

**Designer:** Seth Raynor, Tom Doak

**Course Comment:** Tom Doak's restoration in 1998 added approximately 64,000 square feet to Yeamans Hall's greens, increasing the total square footage from about 80,000 to approximately 144,000.

In the mid-1980s, Yeamans Hall, a traditional old classic track set in the Lowcountry of South Carolina near Charleston, was a relatively forgotten Seth Raynor design. The original green contours and bunker schemes had been lost to time — the course opened in 1925 — and a lack of attention. Today, thanks to a gradual transformation that began in the late 1980s and culminated in a Tom Doak restoration in 1998, the course is one of Raynor's more revered layouts anywhere.

No. 6 is a classic Redan hole that requires an almost perfect draw into the narrow green, which slopes from right to left and is surrounded by beautiful magnolias and native live oaks, complete with hanging moss.

Doak's restorative efforts were key at the sixth, where he sharpened contours in the green and reinstated several yards of putting surface that had disappeared in previous decades. The latter change brought a trio of deep bunkers at the rear of the hole back into play, as the edge of the green slopes sharply into the sand. Before, a ball hit too long had a good possibility of staying out of the bunkers. Now the chances for a similar fate might aptly be called slim and none. **KA**

## No. ❻ THAI COUNTRY CLUB

**Course:** Thai Country Club

**Location:** Chachoengsao, Thailand

**Hole:** No. 6

**Length:** 218 yards

**Par:** 3

**Designer:** Denis Griffiths

**Course Comment:** No. 6, Thai Country Club's signature hole, played the toughest in relation to par during the 1997 Asian Honda Classic.

Thai Country Club, one of Thailand's most prestigious and well-kept courses, opened in 1996, and received widespread acclaim from a pair of professional events held there during its first two years. A young Tiger Woods won the 1997 Asian Honda Classic by 10 strokes at 20-under-par 268, and the course also hosted the second round of the 1998 Johnnie Walker Super Tour, which Vijay Singh won with a 66 — two shots better than Ernie Els and Jesper Parnevik.

The best play on this long, scenic par 3 is an arrow-straight tee shot that avoids a shimmering lake and lands on the left portion of the green, which slopes from back to front.

Go left, and several severe grass indentions and undulations will make for a difficult up-and-down. Go long and a pair of side-by-side bunkers await, with the slope of the green making it exceedingly difficult to hold the ensuing sand shot to the putting surface. Go short and right, and your ball will land in a huge bunker or the water. It's one case where you'll happily choose the sand.

The front right bunker, by the way, is shaped like the head of a shamrock, and it's a good thing. On this hole, golfers need all the luck they can get. **KA**

## No. ❻ ELLERSTON GOLF COURSE

**Course:** Ellerston Golf Course

**Location:** Upper Hunter Valley, New South Wales, Australia

**Hole:** No. 6

**Length:** 164 yards

**Par:** 3

**Designer:** Greg Norman, Bob Harrison

**Course Comment:** Length is what most people first think about when talk turns to this superb design, but the par 3s at Ellerston deserve as much attention and acclaim, especially No. 6.

You hit your drive on this scenic gem from an elevated tee, with the Ellerston Mountains looming in the background. Golfers should play their shot, usually a short iron, along a diagonal section of a creek that runs in front of the landing area from right to left and eventually wraps itself around the green.

The green is set in a low-lying spot on the left, and the right side of the hole is pocked with a quartet of treacherous bunkers and slopes sharply toward the putting surface. Any misses to that side often result in the most difficult of leaves, especially given the speed of the greens at Ellerston and the tricky undulations that frequently funnel balls toward the water.

The bunker that is farthest away is the worse, and anyone carding a four from that position is doing quite well. Perhaps the most sensible play is a high fade (for righties) off the tee, avoiding the trouble on the right entirely. **JS**

**Course:** Crooked Stick Golf Club

**Location:** Carmel, Indiana, USA

**Hole:** No. 6

**Length:** 183 yards

**Par:** 3

**Designer:** Pete Dye

**Course Comment:** The home of the 1993 LPGA U.S. Open, Crooked Stick is a long and difficult Scottish links-style course with plenty of character, rolling terrain, and large greens. The course is considered one of Indianapolis' top places to play and one of Pete Dye's best designs.

# No. ❻  CROOKED STICK GOLF CLUB

Pete Dye certainly lives up to his "Dye-abolical" nickname with Crooked Stick. Just ask the ladies. Lauri Merten won the U.S. Open here in 1993 when she birdied the final hole and finished with a score of 280 (70 average).

And these are the professionals. They play golf for a living. Most likely, you don't.

No. 6 is as pretty as it is difficult. And it has the Dye touch.

Standing on a slightly elevated tee (just a few feet so not too much) you have a good 183 yards from the back tees to the kidney-shaped green. The good news is there are no bunkers on this hole. The bad news is the creek and a large tree on the right side of the fairway. The creek is not a good place to be, even though you might like the railroad ties (a Pete Dye trademark) that line the wall or the covered bridge that goes over the water.

The difficulty of this hole increases as the pin placement increases toward the front. The green has a ridge in the middle, creating almost a two-green effect. If the pin is in the front, you have to flirt more with the water. If it's in the back, the water becomes a little less of a factor — the key word being little.

Is this a tough hole? "It can be," is the answer given by our friend back in the clubhouse. **TJ**

**Course:** Winged Foot Golf Club (East Course)

**Location:** Mamaroneck, New York, USA

**Hole:** No. 6

**Length:** 194 yards

**Par:** 3

**Designer:** A.W. Tillinghast

**Course Comment:** The East Course has played host to several national championships of its own: the U.S. Women's Open in 1957 and 1972, and the inaugural U.S. Senior Open in 1980.

**ABOVE** *Davis Love III of the USA plays a shot at Winged Foot, August 1997.*

## No. ❻  WINGED FOOT GOLF CLUB (EAST COURSE)

The East Course is tighter and shorter than Winged Foot's more famous West Course, which has received widespread recognition from playing host to several U.S. Opens with popular and worthy champions (Bobby Jones in 1929, Billy Casper in 1959, Hale Irwin in 1974, and Fuzzy Zoeller in 1984) as well as the 1997 PGA Championship, in which Davis Love III captured his first major title. Despite the East track's lack of recognition nationally, ask Winged Foot members and they'll tell you it is every bit as tough as its counterpart. Together, the two courses are often called "America's Best 36 Holes."

You won't have any argument after playing East No. 6, a devilish par 3 that A.W. Tillinghast appropriately named "Trouble."

The elevated green is protected on three sides (left, right, back) by bunkers — including a pair of gaping bunkers on the left — and slopes from back to front with a drop of at least four feet. Take care to stay below the hole with the tee shot, as it is not uncommon to see putts from above roll off the green. Even two-footers aren't a sure thing, and if they don't find the cup, an even longer putt is often required coming back. **KA**

**Course:** Fox Chapel Golf Club

**Location:** Pittsburgh, Pennsylvania, USA

**Hole:** No. 6

**Length:** 192 yards

**Par:** 3

**Designer:** Seth Raynor

**Course Comment:** The par 3 proved to be a critical turning point for the U.S. team at the 2002 Curtis Cup match. The Americans played the hole in one over in the second day singles matches while the Great Britain and Ireland squad were a stroke higher.

# No. ❻ FOX CHAPEL GOLF CLUB

In a city that is defined by its steel industry, Fox Chapel Golf Club stands as a subtle and serene reminder of gentler times. From its white-stucco clubhouse to its perfectly organized design, the Seth Raynor layout exists in quiet contrast to its blue-collar surroundings.

Subtle is the rule at Fox Chapel and few holes manifest that more than the par-3 sixth. At 192 yards the hole is a copy of the original Redan, the 15th hole on North Berwick Golf Club's West Course in Scotland.

As was the case with many of Fox Chapel's holes, time had softened most of Raynor's peculiar edges, so prior to the 2002 Curtis Cup match at Fox Chapel, the club commissioned architect Brian Silva to return the layout to its original form.

The sixth was at the heart of Silva's renovations. He recontoured the face of the deep bunker that guards the right side of the elevated green and changed the mowing patterns around the putting surface to allow the ball to bounce more freely on to the putting surface, the central element of Redan slopes.

The new mowing patterns are especially noticeable on the left side of the green, which slopes dramatically skyward. **RH**

---

**Course:** Greywolf

**Location:** Kamloops, British Columbia, Canada

**Hole:** No. 6

**Length:** 200 yards

**Par:** 3

**Designer:** Doug Carrick

**Course Comment:** There is a reason this hole is called the Cliffhanger. OK, there are two reasons. One is the obvious. The green is perched on a breathtaking cliff. The second is that this hole is not easy — it's as dramatic as it gets in the game of golf.

# No. ❻ GREYWOLF

Here are a few of the words that echo through the valleys of Canada's Purcell Mountains when golfers start talking about Greywolf: spectacular, inspirational, dramatic, and breathtaking. Oh yeah, and tough.

Named "Cliffhanger," this 200-yard par 3 is worth every dollar you hand over in the pro-shop.

It all starts with a spectacular carry — hopefully — over Hopeful Canyon. The vertical rock cliffs that guard the front and left side of the green are joined by a severe drop off the back.

When selecting a club at the tee you better take into consideration the swirling winds through the Toby Creek valley. If you hit two balls into the canyon, rules say you must take your third shot from the drop area right of the green.

There are also two bunkers to the right front of the green.

Your putting will take a backseat to the view. Grab the camera and take a few shots of the spectacular scenery.

There are four sets of tees starting at 142 yards.

In 2003, *Golf Digest* rated Greywolf as the No. 1 course in British Columbia. And considering some of their neighbors, that's a pretty big-time honor. **TJ**

**Course:** Royal Dornoch

**Location:** Dornoch, Sutherland, Scotland

**Hole:** No. 6

**Length:** 163 yards

**Par:** 3

**Designer:** Old Tom Morris

**Course Comment:** Tom Watson, now an honorary member of Royal Dornoch, first played the course in 1980, the year he won the first of his five British Opens, and declared it "the most fun I've ever had on a golf course." Other honorary members include Prince Andrew and Ben Crenshaw.

# No. ❻ ROYAL DORNOCH

Stand on the tee of Royal Dornoch's sixth hole, in the midst of some of the most splendid scenery Scotland has to offer, and you're confronted with two seas. The lapping waters of the North Sea are visible on the horizon to the right, and in front of you lies a spectacular sea of whin (gorse bushes which produce gorgeous yellow flowers in the spring).

The first sea doesn't come into play on this devious one-shot gem, which is aptly named "Whinny Brae." The latter most definitely does, forming an impenetrable fortress to the left and rear of the plateau green that's set into a hillside full of the thick vegetation.

Attempt to steer your tee shot right, away from the obvious trouble, and you'll discover the whin isn't the only thing protecting the putting surface, which tilts severely from left to right and culminates in a steep 12-foot fall at the rear and right sides. There's also a large bunker at the right front to catch those coming up short.

The preferred ball placement is the left side of the green, but pull it ever so slightly and three tiny bunkers await. Land in one of those, and the slope of the green makes it almost impossible to get up and down for par. **KA**

**Course:** New South Wales Golf Club

**Location:** La Perouse, Sydney, Australia

**Hole:** No. 6

**Length:** 193 yards

**Par:** 3

**Designers:** Alister MacKenzie, Eric Apperly

**Course Comment:** The par 3s (including the western-pointing sixth) and par 5s run to all four points of the compass. Thirteen holes have views of the Pacific Ocean where it meets Cape Banks – a body of water sailed by Captain Cook as he made his way to Botany Bay.

BELOW *Paul Casey of England plays his second shot on the sixth hole at New South Wales, February 2003.*

# No. ❻  NEW SOUTH WALES GOLF CLUB

There is plenty to avoid at the picturesque sixth hole at New South Wales Golf Club. Watch out for the sloping left of the green, as well as the bunkers to the left and to the right. Oh, and also be careful for the trip from tee to green. The tee on the par 3 is an island in the Pacific Ocean that requires a 193-yard carry back to the mainland. But, more important than what you should avoid is what you should take in: the most striking hole on one of the most uniquely beautiful golf courses in the world.

Depending on what ranking you follow, New South Wales is in the top three places to play in Australia and among the top 100 courses in the world. It has been one of Australia's premier courses since it opened in 1928, and there is no question when discussing the issue of which hole is its signature. No. 6, it is.

Ironically, the sixth was not the work of the original designer, Alister MacKenzie. Rather, photographic evidence shows that for the first 19 years of the course's existence, the fifth hole was followed by what is today the seventh. Eric Apperly designed and added the sixth hole to the course in 1947, taking advantage of a unique chance to bring a detached piece of land into the course.

Apperly brought the rocky cove into play as a short hole, including the island tee. The Australian amateur golfer had vision enough to use this natural setting as one of the more unique and beautiful holes you'll find. To get to the tee, you must go over a bridge to a reef. The ocean sits to your left, and there is a bail-out area to the right. However, if you play too safely and land wayward right, the green slants away from you and makes it almost impossible to keep your second shot close to the hole. Goodbye par opportunity.

The course is a links-style beauty with bentgrass greens and couch fairways set amid hills and valleys abutting Australia's Pacific coast, but it is also just 20 minutes from Sydney's downtown area. **JB**

# No. ❻ WASIOTO WINDS GOLF COURSE

Kentucky has long been famed for bluegrass, bourbon, beautiful mountains, and thoroughbreds. And, spurred by a renewed interest from the State Park system, golf is now also becoming a larger part of Kentucky's recreational reputation and tourism industry.

Wasioto Winds Golf Course is as beautiful a golf course as there is in Kentucky, situated on the lower edge of Pine Mountain near Cumberland Gap on the state's eastern border, where Daniel Boone led early settlers across the Appalachian Mountains. The course in Pine Mountain State Park used to be just a nine-holer, but $10 million and a new dedication to golf have turned it into a gem.

"This is a beautiful area for golf," said Donnie Caldwell, assistant pro at Wasioto Winds. "There are mountains everywhere you look, the course is completely bentgrass — tees, fairways and greens — and the maintenance is as good as you're going to find."

Caldwell might be a bit biased when talking of course maintenance. His older brother Ronnie Caldwell is the superintendent at Wasioto Winds.

Some consider the 12th hole Wasioto Winds' signature, and the stern 455-yard par 4 indeed is a challenging gem. But the 13th is a brilliant hole, as well. From the back tees, it is a 258-yard par 3 with a tee box elevated some 80 feet. The 12th and 13th provide one of the toughest and prettiest back-to-back holes you are going to find.

"The course eases you in a little with a short par 4 to start, and then a par 5 on No. 2," Donnie Caldwell said. "But, by the time you get into the meat of it, you know you've got a test on your hands."

Wasioto Winds is the home of Kentucky's only active First Tee program, and 450 local youngsters participate regularly. There is a well-kept, four-hole short course for First Tee participants that was designed by course personnel. **JB**

## No. ⑥ THE CREEK CLUB

**Course:** The Creek Club

**Location:** Locust Valley, New York, USA

**Hole:** No 6

**Length:** 453 yards

**Par:** 4

**Designer:** Charles Blair Macdonald, Seth Raynor

**Course Comment:** Nicknamed "Sound View," No. 6 is not only one of the most esthetically pleasing holes on the course, but it also offers the best views of the Long Island Sound.

After playing a few of the more forgiving holes (Nos. 1–5), the real fun begins at No. 6 and continues over the next 12 holes. No. 6 is a downhill par 4, which has a slight dogleg to the left. The drive on this fairly long hole is very important. Any players should check the wind before teeing off because a miss to the right will find some unplayable fescue grass, and a miss to the left finds trees.

Most players face a mid-iron approach shot from about 175 yards and under. The second shot is very important because an accurate shot to the typical Charles Blair Macdonald and Seth Raynor punchbowl green will be rewarding. Players tend to stay clear of the right side of the green because a miss to the right finds a big, deep bunker. The walls are at least 10 feet high and if your ball finds the right bunker an up-and-down will be a miracle. Most players aim for the left side of the green.

The green itself is big and everything funnels down to the middle, where the pin is usually located.

Overall this hole is a classic masterpiece: it offers the best views of the Long Island Sound on the course and is a true test for any player. **GE**

## No. ⑥ EAGLE POINT GOLF & COUNTRY CLUB

**Course:** Eagle Point Golf & Country Club

**Location:** Kamloops, British Columbia, Canada

**Hole:** No. 6

**Length:** 399 yards

**Par:** 4

**Designer:** Robert Heaslip & Associates

**Course Comment:** The course is nestled in a pine forest on natural rolling terrain and is carved into the undulating topography. Each hole offers exciting challenges and spectacular views of the area.

This is a fairly straight par 4 heading uphill with a large pond that cuts right into the fairway about 150 yards from the green. There is plenty of fairway to work with before the water. It does get a little narrow as you head toward the green.

Here is some advice from the Eagle Point professional: "Unless you're a huge hitter put the woods away. It's about 250 yards to carry the water. A longish iron will put you short of the water and looking up at the green."

The water runs about 50 yards in length, so anywhere between 100 and 150 yards out from the green is the potential to get wet. The good-sized green has a large bunker to the left that actually begins in the fairway.

There are five sets of tees to help accommodate all levels of players. The front tees or red tees are 324 yards. The championship tees sit back some 399 yards.

The par-72 course encompasses 165 acres with a total length of 6,762 yards from the championship tees. With a choice of five tees on every hole, the course provides both challenge and enjoyment for all skill levels.

In 1992 the course co-hosted its first national tournament, the Canadian Senior Championship. **TJ**

**Course:** Kingston Heath Golf Club

**Location:** Cheltenham, Melbourne, Australia

**Hole:** No. 6

**Length:** 431 yards

**Par:** 4

**Designer:** Dan Soutar, Alister MacKenzie

**Course Comment:** When Kingston Heath opened in 1925, it was the longest course in Australia at almost 6,600 yards. The par-82 layout included an amazing 12 par 5s and only two par 3s.

BELOW *Jason Norris of Australia plays a shot on the sixth hole at Kingston Heath, January 2004.*

Soutar routed and designed most of the layout, but Kingston Heath's outstanding bunker work, considered some of the finest in the world, was devised by Alister MacKenzie.

The good doctor's work certainly comes into play on the long, par-4 sixth — with both the drive and the approach affected. The uphill tee shot must split a fairway bunker to the left and a nasty grouping of bunkers on the right. A drive on the left side of the fairway gives the best chance for an approach that can avoid another intimidating array of bunkers that cuts into the fairway and protects the right and front of the contoured putting surface. A horseshoe-shaped bunker also awaits several yards short of the green on the left side, often frustrating those who attempt to lay up and avoid the trouble on the right.

The course has played host to numerous Australian Opens, including 2000, when native son Aaron Baddeley won his second consecutive Open title, helped by an early par save on No. 6 in the final round. Baddeley hit into two traps, pulling his drive into the left fairway bunker, then playing out into another greenside hazard, but still managed to get up-and-down from 10 feet — a rare feat on this hole. **KA**

**Course:** Rosapenna Hotel & Golf Resort (Sandy Hills Course)

**Location:** Downings, Co. Donegal, Ireland

**Hole:** No. 6

**Length:** 420 yards

**Par:** 4

**Designer:** Pat Ruddy

**Course Comment:** Pat Ruddy was a golf writer who later tried his hand at architecture. You could say the transformation was a success because he blew away the golf world with his efforts at The European Club.

*OPPOSITE The sixth hole at Rosapenna.*

# No. ❻ ROSAPENNA HOTEL & GOLF RESORT (SANDY HILLS COURSE)

The wonderful thing about a course such as Rosapenna's Sandy Hills Course is that it is still being shaped today. When it is funneling through dunes so close to the Atlantic Ocean, and the winds are such an active part of the golf, the holes are changing literally day to day.

There may not be one single weak hole on the course, but what many golf enthusiasts agree is the best of the best at Sandy Hills is the stupendous, par-4 sixth. It features an uphill tee shot that must reach the top of a hill before the fairway crashes down to a welcoming green.

The green is a welcome sight after reaching the top of the fairway, and this is emphasized even more because it is framed wonderfully by water and the Muckish Mountain. It is at the southern end of the course, and it offers a postcard view of the mountain from the tee.

The green is such that the bay is the backdrop of the hole, and it undoubtedly is the most beautiful hole on a most beautiful course. No. 6 is a difficult test of a golf hole with its dunes and tumbles, its elevation changes, and its wind. But the most amazing part of the hole is the visual aspect. The combination of beauty and skill makes it one to remember.

The Sandy Hills Course just adds to the long history at Rosapenna where the original course was designed by Old Tom Morris in 1891. Harry Vardon and James Braid also did work on the course in later years. **JB**

---

**Course:** Royal Antwerp

**Location:** Kapellen, Belgium

**Hole:** No. 6

**Length:** 424 yards

**Par:** 4

**Designer:** Willie Park Jr., Tom Simpson

**Course Comment:** Besides Golf de Pau (in France), the Royal Antwerp Golf Club is one of the oldest established golf courses in Europe, dating to 1888, when it was constructed by Willie Park in an area of woodland, 12 miles north of Antwerp.

# No. ❻ ROYAL ANTWERP

This is an introduction from the pros at the club: "In general the greens are well guarded and relatively small with some dogleg holes such as the 6th, 9th, 10th, and 14th being particularly difficult. As you can well imagine this golf course has considerable charm and provides players with a very pleasant and challenging experience."

Charm. Challenging. Pleasant. Grab the clubs, let's play 36. Actually, you just need to play one to get the feel of this golf course. Of course, that will make you want to play the rest. But this one, No. 6, is something special.

The dogleg right has plenty of teeth to it, including a long drive to get the turn. There is a short bunker along the left side that you should carry off the tee. There is also a large bunker on the right side of the green.

Like most of the holes on the championship course, wind plays a factor. So let that influence your club selection.

This golf course has that classic feel to it. You will see plenty of trees. Plenty of bunkers. And plenty of trouble. Being somewhat accurate is very important here. This old course forces you to play the game in a straightforward style. **TJ**

**Course:** Lahinch

**Location:** Lahinch, County Clare, Ireland

**Hole:** No. 6

**Length:** 424 yards

**Par:** 4

**Designer:** Old Tom Morris, Alister MacKenzie

**Course Comment:** Like most courses its age, Lahinch has seen plenty of change over the years. Old Tom Morris laid out the original course in 1892 but the track quickly changed in 1907. In 1927, the club brought in Alister MacKenzie to make a number of major changes.

## No. ❻ LAHINCH

No. 6 at Lahinch takes a back seat to no hole on the golf course, and that includes the more famous "Dell" hole just before it. It's a back-to-back experience — as good a one-two punch as can be found in Ireland.

Like at No. 5, you get another blind shot off the tee, this one going uphill. You should be used to these by this point. But just wait until you see what's ahead. It's certainly worth the wait and the greens fee. The fairway bends ever so slightly before you are greeted by the wind, mist, and spectacular view of the Atlantic. Golf almost seems meaningless at this point. We said "almost."

This par 4 is 424 yards of into-the-wind golf. And we are not talking about a summer breeze. This is a breeze with teeth. And there are bunkers lining both sides of the fairway.

Your approach shot is over a cavernous mine and down to the green with the sea in the background. It's a look you aren't likely to forget soon.

A new green (see the course comment about changing older courses) presents a spectacular postcard of sea with its rolling mounds and deep and dangerous bunkers.

As if this famous track wasn't enough to satisfy the thirst of Irish golfers, Lahinch Golf Club added another 18-hole course in 1975 — the Castle Course designed by Commander John D. Harris. **TJ**

## No. ❻ DINARD GOLF CLUB

**Course:** Dinard Golf Club

**Location:** Saint-Briac-sur-Mer, Brittany, France

**Hole:** No. 6

**Length:** 339 yards

**Par:** 4

**Designer:** Tom Dunn, Willie Park Jr.

**Course Comment:** Saint-Briac-sur-Mer serves as a charming complement to the delightfulness of Dinard Golf Club. Saint-Briac is a quaint fishing village with picturesque, narrow streets and a preserved old quarters.

When you conjure up great links golf in Europe, France probably doesn't immediately come to mind. But one round at Dinard Golf Club — France's second-oldest course — might just change your thinking.

Dinard, built by Scotsman Tom Dunn in 1887, isn't long: its par is 68 and its yardage only 5,748. But what it lacks in length, it more than makes up for in beauty, thanks to its cliffside setting on France's rugged and rocky Emerald Coast.

The sixth hole has one of the course's most spectacular views — and one of the scariest tee shots any golfer will ever want to tackle. The drive must be hit downhill to a narrow, wildly undulating fairway, with the numerous mounds and valleys making it difficult to find a flat landing area for the approach. Still, it's better than the alternative, which is to send your tee shot right of the rail fence that separates safety from disaster — the thick heather grasses and small cliffs that slope to the crashing sea below.

The short, uphill second shot should also be hit precisely. The green has a steep front face that must be carried and is surrounded by thick rough and more undulations. **KA**

## No. ❻ NEWCASTLE FERN BAY

**Course:** Newcastle Fern Bay

**Location:** Stockton, New South Wales, Australia

**Hole:** No. 6

**Length:** 400 yards

**Par:** 4

**Designer:** Eric Apperley

**Course Comment:** Located two hours north of Sydney on the east coast of Australia, Newcastle Fern Bay is worth the trip. Why? Glad you asked. Because it's different. And unique; enjoyable courses aren't always easy to find.

No. 6 at Newcastle is a special hole on a special golf course. No longer is this the hidden gem. The word is now officially out that this course — and this hole, in particular — is a throwback to traditional golf.

The pressure on No. 6 begins at the tee. The drive must be very straight to avoid the steep hill and the trees along the left side, and the slope on the right side which guides the ball into rough and more trees. You must keep your drive to the right of the sand dune.

The second shot must hit the elevated green on the fly to avoid the severe penalty of a short shot running 20 or 30 yards back down the hill. There also are two bunkers along the right side of the green.

From within 100 yards you better be in the middle or left side of the fairway or your ball could roll into the right rough. The fairway slopes severely from left to right.

The slope on the green results in plenty of three-putts on this hole, which despite its difficulty, is still a favorite of many members and visitors.

The great slopes on the green and fairway are typical of the topography found at Newcastle. **TJ**

**Course:** Saint-Nom-La-Breteche Golf Club (Red Course)

**Location:** St.-Nom-La-Breteche, France

**Hole:** No. 6

**Length:** 439 yards

**Par:** 4

**Designer:** F.W. Hawtree, Pier Mancenelli

**Course Comment:** When the PGA European Tour holds the Trophée Lancôme each year, the nines are reversed and this hole plays as No. 15. Tony Jacklin won the first Trophée Lancôme in 1970.

BELOW *Justin Rose of England, Colin Montgomerie of Scotland, and caddie Phil Mobley walk across a bridge on the sixth hole at Saint-Nom-La-Breteche, September 2003.*

OPPOSITE *Colin Montgomerie of Scotland plays a shot on the sixth hole at Saint-Nom-La-Breteche, September 2003.*

# SAINT-NOM-LA-BRETECHE GOLF CLUB (RED COURSE)

If you are making a quick trip to Paris, it doesn't necessarily mean you have to leave your golf clubs at home. Enjoy the Louvre and the Eiffel Tower. But, also a sightseer's paradise if you happen to have a bag in the trunk, is the Saint-Nom-La-Breteche Golf Club.

The club is beautifully converted from the spacious grounds of an old 17th-century château villa. It has been transformed into two 18-hole courses in the forests and fruit orchards of the original grounds. The Red Course is the premier track on the grounds and one of the premier layouts in Europe.

Saint-Nom-La-Breteche is located not far from the Château de Versailles — the palatial home of King Louis XIV. The course was designed in 1950, inspired by the huge golf-course concept common in the United States at the time. It opened for play in 1959 and set the stage for major national and international events. The Red Course — the work of English golf architect Fred Hawtree — has played host to the World Cup of Golf in 1963, the French Open in 1965 and 1969, and most prominently the Trophée Lancôme golf tournament since 1970,

The Hall of Fame list of Lancôme winners includes Arnold Palmer, Johnny Miller, Gary Player, Lee Trevino, Seve Ballesteros, and Nick Price.

France's Catherine Lacoste, U.S. Women's Open champion in 1967, was instrumental in making Saint-Nom-La-Breteche one of France's top clubs.

And the tree-lined sixth, which turns right slowly but forcefully, is one of the best holes on one of France's showcase courses.

It is imperative to drive the ball to the right side of the fairway to avoid the bunkers on the left side at No. 6. Yet, you must drive it long enough to turn so you are past the hole's shoulder on the right. The green is surrounded by deep bunkers, rough, and pines on No. 6, and a well-placed drive for the golfing professionals between two strategically placed bunkers leaves a short-to-medium iron into a long and narrow green.

The sixth is surrounded by a great variety of hardwoods as well as the original fruit-bearing trees that make up the estate of this former French villa. **JB**

**Course:** PohlCat

**Location:** Mt. Pleasant, Michigan, USA

**Hole:** No. 6

**Length:** 310 yards

**Par:** 4

**Designer:** Dan Pohl

**Course Comment:** When the general manager was doing a little marketing for the course, he mentioned the 100-year-old oak trees in the brochure, including the big one on No. 6. A few years later a tree expert came out to the course and informed him that those trees were more than 200 years old.

# No. ❻  POHLCAT

PohlCat, located in the center of the state, is a championship-style course played over and around the scenic 100-foot wide Chippewa River. It was designed by former PGA Tour pro and Mt. Pleasant native Dan Pohl.

And Pohl combined both of his titles to make this course. There are plenty of similarities between the great PGA Tour courses and the PohlCat. And there is plenty of Mt. Pleasant found around these 18 holes.

No. 6 is a 310-yard par-4 dogleg right and a perfect example of how good the PohlCat plays. This is a short yet difficult hole with "plenty of risk and reward." You can risk it and go for the green from the tee. This requires clearing the 200-year-old red oak in the right side and avoiding the water on the right, the four grass bunkers in the front and the sand bunkers on the sides. All of this to a very small, three-tiered green.

The grass bunkers, which are very thick, are difficult to play out of because you can't get your club on the ball.

When the PohlCat first opened in 1992, it created a golf buzz throughout the state. Around this time in Michigan, golf courses were being built as if they were on an assembly line. You couldn't swing a golf club without hitting a new course. And these were first-rate courses, with the top designers leading the way. The PohlCat is still a major player today. **TJ**

**Course:** Quaker Ridge Golf Club

**Location:** Scarsdale, New York, USA

**Hole:** No. 6

**Length:** 446 yards

**Par:** 4

**Designer:** A.W. Tillinghast

**Course Comment:** Though the course seems clearly deserving, being consistently rated by various publications as among the nation's best, it has never hosted a major championship. However, the Walker Cup was held at Quaker Ridge in 1997.

# No. ❻ QUAKER RIDGE GOLF CLUB

John Duncan Dunn first crafted Quaker Ridge as a nine-hole course through 112 acres of New York forest in 1915, but it was the brilliance of A.W. Tillinghast that three years later brought the course to life.

Tillinghast was a true genius of design, and a lover of golf's purity. He drew from the legends of his time, including Old Tom Morris. Of a round with Old Tom, Tillinghast once wrote: "Playing around the Old Course at St. Andrews with the patriarch made me feel as though my own game must seem glaringly new, just like walking up the church aisle in new, squeaky boots, but this feeling soon vanished. The old man and I were just boys together, for such is golf and such was Old Tom Morris."

Tillinghast was hired by a small group called Quaker Ridge Golf Club in 1916, added nine holes and drastically reworked seven of the original holes, including the 446-yard sixth.

The result was a dynamic golf course that opened in 1918, and is now regarded as a Tillinghast original — fitting into his portfolio quite nicely with nearby Winged Foot. The famed architect brought toughness with him when he designed Quaker Ridge. The yardage at No. 6 makes it the longest of the par 4s at his Scarsdale design. Quaker Ridge is famed for its rigid par-4 holes, and the sixth, "Tilly the Terror," is the sternest of the bunch.

Not only is Quaker Ridge's sixth demanding due to length, it is also the tightest drive of any par 4 on the course. Slopes down the right with grass kept long and perilous, and trees whose branches are left to dangle tantalizingly over the edges of the fairway, choke the landing area to a visual that is fairly miniscule. It takes about 20 steps to get from one side of the fairway to the other, and the trees and grass on the sides make it appear even more narrow.

The thin strand of fairway is made even more difficult to hold and/or negotiate because of its right-to-left cant. Even though this hole is fairly lengthy at 446 yards, it isn't just a blast-away tee shot. Players are forced to keep the drive under control, not going too far for fear of hitting through the fairway.

The approach is generally made with a mid- to long-iron shot on uneven ground to a green that isn't quite large enough for comfort. Tilly is quite terror-filled, indeed. **JB**

## No. ⑥  PONT ROYAL GOLF CLUB

**Course:** Pont Royal Golf Club

**Location:** Mallemort, France

**Hole:** No. 6

**Length:** 339 yards

**Par:** 4

**Designer:** Seve Ballesteros

**Course Comment:** Ballesteros, the swashbuckling Spaniard, is one of the legends of the PGA European Tour. He was instrumental in the popularization of the tour in the late 1970s and early 1980s. If the scenic Pont Royal Golf Club is any indication, Ballesteros is looking to make just as big a mark as an architect as he has as a player.

The sixth hole at Pont Royal is extremely short for a par 4, particularly with today's technology that allows golf balls to be driven an alarming distance. But, even though it is the shortest par 4 featured in this book, don't let that fool you into thinking the challenge is belittled.

This dogleg left forces a carry of about 220 yards to reach the fairway, and there is a bunker on the right side at about 270 yards. It is one of six bunkers on the hole, each strategically placed to protect the integrity of the par 4. Even though this is a short hole, it is tough because the tee shot must be nearly perfect in order to avoid trouble.

Big hitters may try to fly the dogleg and go directly toward the green, but that would take a nearly perfect shot of more than 300 yards. It is best to take out a fairway wood, or perhaps even an iron, and aim for the middle of the fairway to allow for a kind approach into the kidney-shaped green.

Before you even play the hole, however, it is best to take a moment on the highly elevated tee to enjoy an amazing 360-degree panoramic view. To the north is the village of Mallemort, perched on its rocky spur; then there is the Durance Valley, the soft curves of the Luberon and the Chaine de la Trevaresse mountain chain heading toward Aix en Provence.

The sixth hole at Pont Royal may be short in distance, but it is not short on challenge, beauty, and intrigue. **JB**

**Course:** Seminole Golf Club

**Location:** North Palm Beach, Florida, USA

**Hole:** No. 6

**Length:** 385 yards

**Par:** 4

**Designer:** Donald Ross

**Course Comment:** If the greenkeeper is in a particularly beguiling mood, he can place the pin in the back of the green. This gives the player a view that makes him wonder if the hole is even on the green. It appears that the pin is just sticking out of an acre of sand.

## No. ❻ SEMINOLE GOLF CLUB

Ben Hogan loved the sixth at Seminole, but other than perhaps a touch of masochism, one must wonder why. This par-4 hole is short but devilish.

The green slopes from left to right, and the first impression when looking at the protective bunkers might indicate that the left side of the fairway is the optimum route from which to approach the putting surface. But first impressions can be imprecise.

If a player attempts to land on the left side of the fairway, the slope to the right makes it virtually impossible to hold in the desired position. Even if the ball somehow stays on the left, the cant of the fairway leaves a treacherous stance. If a player decides to go the right side, there is a level stance waiting on the approach. But the margin for error is miniscule because the green is positioned diagonally from that angle and appears as a sliver from the right side of the fairway.

The sixth hole is one of 14 at Seminole that touch on two lines of dunes that surround the property. The routing is Seminole's highlight, and it is a prime example of Donald Ross's brilliance. The layout takes full advantage of a ridge of dunes to the west, and the dunes along the Atlantic Ocean to the east. In the middle lie the necessary ponds to handle the drainage.

Seminole, including the sixth hole, is a testament to Ross's talents. It is an original, reminding you of no other course. Ross did not force-feed his vision onto the course, rather he allowed the lay of the land to inspire his soul. Perhaps this is why Hogan loved Seminole's sixth so much. **JB**

**Course:** The Berkshire Golf Club (Red Course)

**Location:** Ascot, Berkshire, England

**Hole:** No. 6

**Length:** 360 yards

**Par:** 4

**Designer:** Herbert Fowler

**Course Comment:** Before the course fully matured, skilled players would attempt to cut the corner on this, removing some 80 yards from its distance. A shot at the green was possible for the big hitters, but now — with the maturation of pines on the right side of the dogleg right, the corner is sufficiently guarded.

No. ❻　## THE BERKSHIRE GOLF CLUB (RED COURSE)

Herbert Fowler is an oft-overlooked figure in the world of golf course architecture, even though he was an instrumental figure in his day, being recognized then as one of the first to lead the trend toward natural design. His follow-the-land style still incorporated enough imagination to remove golf-course architecture from the rudimentary designs of the earlier 1800s.

Fowler lived from 1856 to 1941, but his legacy continues today. Walton Heath in England and Cruden Bay in Scotland were some of Fowler's more famous designs. Berkshire, an inland heathlands course, is much like the man who conceived it: it is sometimes overlooked.

But when you play Berkshire's Red, there is one hole you are sure not to overlook – the short, par-4 sixth. Well, it's not as short as it used to be. No longer can you cut the corner on this sharp dogleg right. Now your tee shot must be played straight down the middle of the fairway. Not only must the drive be strong enough to get past the corner of the tree-lined fairway, but it must also carry a ditch or there's real trouble to be found.

This hole, even played down the fairway and taking the dogleg, isn't overly long at 360 yards, but the approach can be arduous and play much longer. The illusion of length comes into play because the shot to the green

is almost always into the wind, and it's generally more than just a gentle breeze. And the shot is uphill, so between the winds and the lay of the land, the approach shot must be clubbed-up about two clubs. The scorecard says 360, but you'll feel like you've bitten off more than that by the time you reach the green.

In addition to the natural beauty, Fowler advocated building difficult but not impossible courses, believing that they provided most enjoyment over repeated visits. The sixth at Berkshire's Red fits that philosophy — difficult because of the dogleg and the wind, but not quite impossible because the length is reasonable.

Fowler designed courses hoping people would play them regularly. Holes such as the sixth at Berkshire Red are good reasons to return. **JB**

**Course:** Royal Melbourne Golf Club (West Course)

**Location:** Black Rock, Melbourne, Australia

**Hole:** No. 6

**Length:** 428 yards

**Par:** 4

**Designer:** Alister MacKenzie, Alex Russell

**Course Comment:** When major championships are held at Royal Melbourne, a composite course comprising 12 holes from the West Course and six holes from the East is employed to keep spectators from having to cross the road. The sixth hole on the West Course is also the sixth hole on the Composite.

In 1926, Mackenzie made a six-week journey to Australia that has left a legacy going on 80 years. He either designed, improved, or enhanced eight golf courses in that stay. Among his original designs was Royal Melbourne West, perhaps the great one's crowning achievement.

OPPOSITE *Richard Green of Australia plays a shot at Royal Melbourne, February 2004.*

## No. ❻ ROYAL MELBOURNE GOLF CLUB (WEST COURSE)

Dr. Alister MacKenzie was without question one of the greatest architects in golf's long and storied history. But he has always been something of a question mark. He graduated from medical school, but he never worked as a doctor. He designed wonderful golf courses, but he couldn't play a lick. He was among the best course architects ever, creating masterpiece after masterpiece, but he was nearly penniless when he died.

All these puzzles aside, however, there is no mystery when it comes to one thing: Alister MacKenzie could design the hell out of a golf course. And the sixth hole at Royal Melbourne's West Course is 428 yards of tea tree-lined, heather-filled, ultra-compelling evidence.

Royal Melbourne's West Course is consistently rated among the best layouts on earth. And the sixth hole is generally regarded as its finest hole. So, using standard logic, we are dealing with one of the best golf holes in the world. Perhaps the world's best par 4.

The tee is elevated and immersed in tea trees, giving a splendid view of a fairway that falls sharply and doglegs right at just over 200 yards. The dogleg is forced by a collection of Old World-style bunkers, scraggly and daunting and to be avoided at all cost.

Even with a perfect tee shot that avoids the bunkers, a player is then faced with an uphill approach to a multi-tiered green surrounded by bunkers — including a monster in front. Royal Melbourne is legendary for its green speed, and with the slopes and tiers on the No. 6 putting surface, it is one of the toughest greens on a course loaded with fast challenges.

Greg Norman, the finest golfer Australia has ever produced, lists Royal Melbourne as his favorite course in the world. **JB**

**Course:** Navatanee Country Club

**Location:** Bangkok, Thailand

**Hole:** No. 6

**Length:** 457 yards

**Par:** 4

**Designer:** Robert Trent Jones Jr.

**Course Comment:** Thailand's first golf course designed by a foreign architect. The course was created especially for the 1975 World Cup and has since become a golfing Mecca for first-time visitors to the country.

## No. ❻ NAVATANEE COUNTRY CLUB

Navatanee Country Club offers a tranquil retreat full of mature trees and beautiful shrubs. Bountiful greenery is the first thing players might notice, but there is much more than leaves and needles to this course.

Virtually every green is well-protected by bunkers, including the lengthy, par-4 sixth's, which is also undulating and offers little relief on the slopes surrounding the putting surface.

There is a mix of wide and narrow fairways, with water coming into play on five holes, including No. 6.

The sixth hole and the par-5 ninth hole (559 yards from the back tees) across the lake are among the best in the country.

In 1997, the course was newly opened after the renovation of all holes in order to improve the water drainage system. **TJ**

**Course:** Mauna Kea Golf Club

**Location:** Kamuela, Hawaii, USA

**Hole:** No. 6

**Length:** 344 yards

**Par:** 4

**Designers:** Robert Trent Jones Sr.

**Course Comment:** Mauna Kea means "White Mountain" in Hawaiian.

# No. ❻   MAUNA KEA GOLF CLUB

This resort course, financed by hotelier Laurence S. Rockefeller, was built in 1964 to serve as an attraction for guests at his new hotel of the same name. It was one of the first true championship layouts in Hawaii and set the standard for the great island courses that followed.

Still considered one of the state's top tracks, it sits on hilly oceanside terrain that offers spectacular vistas of the Pacific Ocean and the snow-capped Mauna Kea Volcano.

Despite its length, the sneaky sixth hole has plenty of defenses. The tee box offers a view of the Pacific in the distant background, but golfers would be well advised to keep their minds centered on the demands of the opening shot, as a precisely placed downhill drive is required on this short dogleg left.

The fairway — lined on the right by groups of palm trees and on the left by thicker vegetation and black lava — curves and pinches tightly near the turn toward the green, with bunkers coming into play on both the left and right sides of the fairway. The approach, while relatively short, leads back uphill to a large, tiered green that is protected by a large bunker right front and a smaller one to the left. **KA**

# No. ⑥ ROYAL BIRKDALE

**Course:** Royal Birkdale

**Location:** Birkdale, Southport, England

**Hole:** No. 6

**Length:** 460 yards

**Par:** 4

**Designer:** George Lowe, F.F. Hawtree, F.W. Hawtree

**Course Comment:** Because the course is so wide open there are no blind shots to be found. Laid out, around, and through a wasteland of sand dunes, this course has the perfect terrain for a links course. And the dunes are quite large.

Only eventual champion Mark O'Meara and his playoff challenger Brian Watts were able to match par over four rounds of a demanding Royal Birkdale course in the 1998 British Open, which featured gales, torrential rain, and brilliant sunshine. So you can be sure this is a solid test of the great game of golf.

And No. 6 is a good example of how challenging this course can be — even when the weather is on your side.

This is generally regarded as one of the finest golf holes in the world, calling for both length and judgment. A true test to challenge even the complete player.

The hole is played along a valley crossed by a ridge a little beyond halfway, which contains a large bunker. Hit it long and you've found this bunker, which isn't hard to find, but is hard to get out of. From here, take a turn to the right. Here you will find the green and its bunker to the right.

The new green here requires good placement off the tee. A long drive to the left will miss the fairway bunker, but won't do you any favors on the next shot. But a short drive will only mean a blind second shot.

Take your time here. Plan each shot accordingly and play smart. This isn't the place to roll the dice. **TJ**

**Course:** Fancourt Country Club (Montagu Course)

**Location:** Blanco, South Africa

**Hole:** No. 6

**Length:** 456 yards

**Par:** 4

**Designer:** Gary Player, David McLay Kidd

**Course Comment:** Ernie Els owns a waterfront home a short drive away from Fancourt, where he and Tiger Woods dueled to a playoff draw at the 2003 Presidents Cup.

BELOW *Tiger Woods of the USA plays a shot from a bunker on the sixth hole at Fancourt, November 2003.*

# No. ❻ FANCOURT COUNTRY CLUB
## (MONTAGU COURSE)

The Fancourt Hotel and Country Club Estate, located near the coastline of the Indian Ocean and along South Africa's spectacular Garden Route, received notice throughout the golf world while its Links Course served as host site of the 2003 Presidents Cup. But the Links layout is one of just four outstanding courses at the resort.

The Montagu, which sits at the foot of the Outeniqua Mountains and was originally designed by the revered Gary Player, received an extensive makeover from renowned Scottish architect David McLay Kidd in 2004, and in the process, its No. 6 signature hole was made even more challenging.

The sixth was lengthened more than 20 yards (from 435 to 456) and the dramatic, downhill tee shot — already demanding — is now downright rigorous with the addition of two strategically placed bunkers to a fairway that was already lined by thick woods and a creek on the left.

The stream crosses the fairway in front of the green and has been widened by more than 25 yards. That makes club selection crucial on a second shot that must carry the water in front of the putting surface while also avoiding the foliage and bunkers behind it. **KA**

## No. ❻ EL SALER

**Course:** El Saler

**Location:** Valencia, Spain

**Hole:** No. 6

**Length:** 442 yards

**Par:** 4

**Designer:** Javier Arana

**Course Comment:** Located near Valencia, El Saler is the third-ranked golf course in the country, and although there are no true links courses in Spain, this one is as close as it gets.

The El Saler course is situated in the Albufera Nature Park on the shores of the Mediterranean, just south of the city of Valencia.

It is laid out on terrain dotted with pine trees and sand dunes, with the last few holes looking very much like a typical English course. Javier Arana designed this 18-hole course with outstanding fairways and ample greens. Several golf publications have classified it among the top-ranking European courses, and it is listed as number 29 on the world level.

When the wind blows it is as tough as many of the Scottish courses. It's also a very tricky course with some very tight holes.

And No. 6 is as tough as it gets.

One of the longest and most difficult holes at El Saler, it's a good drive to get to the turn on this dogleg left, and there are two bunkers to the left and right front of the green in case you are short on your approach shot.

The entrance to the green is very narrow and is protected by the two bunkers. You always need a long second shot.

This also is one of many pretty holes on the course.

El Saler has hosted a number of Spanish Opens. **TJ**

## No. ❻ RIDGEWOOD COUNTRY CLUB
### (CENTER COURSE)

**Course:** Ridgewood Country Club (Center Course)

**Location:** Ridgewood, New Jersey, USA

**Hole:** No. 6

**Length:** 291 yards

**Par:** 4

**Designer:** A.W. Tillinghast

**Course Comment:** Back in the day, this hole was even tougher than it is now. But the club decided to trim back some trees along the right fairway and make it more open on that side. Trees still very much line the left side.

This club offers three nine-hole courses that are played in three 18-hole combinations. The West/East Course is the most challenging, but the Center/West Course can also be very difficult. A good example of the challenge is No. 6 on the Center Course. It's the signature hole, a 291-yard par 4 playing very much uphill.

This is one of those holes where you pause for a brief moment at the tee. No, you are not waiting for the beer cart. You are deciding how to play this hole. The big hitters — and the ones with more moxie — will pull out the driver and go for the green. Putting for eagle is certainly tempting.

But to reach the green from the tee you must fly it all the way uphill to a very small green. Another distraction are the seven bunkers and heavy rough protecting the green from such acts of heroism as going for it in one.

A safe play — for the very few that will take the smart road — is to use an iron and knock it right down the middle. There are bunkers on both sides of the fairway. From the middle, you can use a wedge to the green.

This hole plays tough because of the uphill shot and the bunkers. But the real trouble is on the green. And hitting the green. It's one of the smaller on the golf course and it has plenty of breaks built in. **TJ**

**Course:** Pumpkin Ridge (Witch Hollow Course)

**Location:** North Plains, Oregon, USA

**Hole:** No. 6

**Length:** 453 yards

**Par:** 4

**Designer:** Bob Cupp

**Course Comment:** There are golf holes that make us mad. There are golf holes that cause great angst and frustration. But No. 6 at Pumpkin Ridge is one of those holes that brings golfers back.

**BELOW** *Natalie Gulbris of the USA and her caddie on the sixth hole at Pumpkin Ridge, July 2003.*

**OPPOSITE** *Alison Nicholas of England plays a shot on the sixth hole at Pumpkin Ridge, July 1997.*

## No. ❻ PUMPKIN RIDGE
### (WITCH HOLLOW COURSE)

This hole is tough. And if you think we are making this up, just ask the ladies. It played the toughest during the 1997 U.S. Women's Open. And remember, they're professionals. So once again, this hole is tough.

The experts at Pumpkin Ridge say if you "listen to the bunker" through the fairway, you can cut a club or two off your approach if you turn it left and hit it far enough. In other words, if you can cut the corner you cut some distance off on your second shot. The big problem on an otherwise pretty open tee shot is a bunker on the right side just at the elbow of the dogleg.

Put your thinking cap on for the second shot. Because of the break in the green that you can see from the fairway, the back section of the green rises up and is very steep. There is also a small pond to the front left of the green with a bunker to the back left side. If you are going to miss, make sure you miss right.

Like all of the holes here, No. 6 sure is pretty, especially standing out in the middle of the fairway looking into the green with the big pines all around. Trust your game or play it safe. Or better yet, trust your game *and* play it safe. Remember, this is a tough hole. **TJ**

**Course:** The Wilds Golf Club

**Location:** Prior Lake, Minnesota, USA

**Hole:** No. 6

**Length:** 460 yards

**Par:** 4

**Designer:** Tom Weiskopf, Jay Morrish

**Course Comment:** The Wilds Golf Club is nestled in a breathtaking natural setting of Ponderosa pines, hardwoods, wetlands, and wildlife habitats just a short drive from the Twin Cities. And you might recognize the sand from TV. The bunkers are lined with the same sparkling white sand from Ohio that is used at Augusta National.

# No. ❻  THE WILDS GOLF CLUB

The sixth hole at the Wilds is a 460-yard par 4 and Tom Weiskopf's favorite hole on the golf course.

"This double fairway creates a wonderful strategy," Weiskopf said. "The right side offers an easier tee shot but a more difficult approach. The left side is narrower off the tee but provides a better angle into the green."

Like the man said, you have options.

The left side of the fairway has bunkers on the right side starting at about 242 yards from the back tees. The right side of the fairway has bunkers along the left side.

Farther down, a large pot bunker comes into play from both sides. It's about 80 yards from the green. There is also a sand trap on the right side of the green.

Because of the split fairway, this is a unique hole and one you won't soon forget. It's also a very scenic hole.

In 1984, Weiskopf became a golf-course design consultant with architect Jay Morrish. This team has designed and built courses from Scottsdale to Hawaii to Scotland — some 18 in all — several voted among the 100 best courses in the world. **TJ**

## No. ❻  THE DUNES AT KAMLOOPS

**Course:** The Dunes at Kamloops

**Location:** Kamloops, British Columbia, Canada

**Hole:** No. 6

**Length:** 571 yards

**Par:** 5

**Designer:** Graham Cooke

**Course Comment:** The Dunes at Kamloops truly is nature's golf course. Lush fairways carve through the sand that was once the riverbed of the North Thompson and features wild fescue and wheat grass — and plenty of dunes.

You need power and grace to defeat this golf hole, which will be one of many memories you take home with you from this spectacular golf course.

The split-level fairway with all of the high mounds will have you shaking your head at the tee. And don't forget it's 571 yards from tee to green so you can't be laying up on your drive.

The fairway isn't what you would call generous so most players will need to hit two good shots before facing the challenges on the approach. The good news is there are no fairway bunkers to concern yourself with. The fairway isn't really a true dogleg but it does move from left to right. The elevated green demands accuracy and confidence of the approach shot. Miss on the approach and your trouble is just beginning. Deep bunkers protect this hole like a mother would a baby. And that bunker to the left front is no baby. It begins well out in the fairway and extends to the middle of the green.

Other bunkers around the green include one to the right and one behind. There are four sets of tees here, starting at 490 yards (red). **TJ**

## No. ❻  NCR COUNTRY CLUB

**Course:** NCR Country Club

**Location:** Dayton, Ohio, USA

**Hole:** No. 6

**Length:** 548 yards

**Par:** 5

**Designer:** Dick Wilson

**Course Comment:** NCR Country Club is unique in that it is owned by the NCR Employees Benefit Association. Even today, employees of NCR Corporation have no initiation fee.

Despite its relatively short length, this tough par 5 is extremely difficult to reach in two because of Dick Wilson's ingenious bunker design surrounding the green. No less than six bunkers encircle the green, making it very challenging to land a fairway wood or long iron on the rather small area.

Adding to the difficulty, the fairway narrows considerably as it reaches the green and has a severe right to left slope, sending shots that come up short and left bounding into trees on the left. And the thick woods lining the entire right side of the hole encroach farther into the fairway just before the green. For good measure, another pair of bunkers sit at that spot, although that may be a blessing as they save some balls from being lost in the woods. The smart play is to lay up well in front of the trouble and hit a high short iron or wedge onto the green.

NCR has played host to two major championships — the 1969 PGA Championship won by Raymond Floyd and the 1986 U.S. Women's Open won by Jane Geddes — and will welcome another major tournament in 2005, the U.S. Senior Open. **KA**

# No. ❻ BAY HILL CLUB AND LODGE

Arnold Palmer owns the courses at Bay Hill and is the president. Just like his golf game, these courses are measuring sticks for great golf courses. Bay Hill is the annual host for the PGA Tour's Bay Hill Invitational.

Developed from a Florida orange grove near Orlando, this course was originally designed by Dick Wilson. Palmer liked the course so much he bought it. Then, with the help of Ed Seay, the King turned a good course into a great course.

An example of just how tough this course can be is the par-5 sixth hole. The 543-yard hole is a long dogleg left. John Daly recorded an 18 here in 1998. Even Arnold Palmer, the King himself, took a 10 on this hole.

The hole rolls counter clockwise around the largest lake on the layout. This is the ultimate water hole. From the tee, you decide how much water you want to fly over. A good drive is anywhere around 250 yards. If you can knock it out there around 280 yards, you can go for the green in two.

Most players will lay up with their second shot. Water is still on the left — in fact, it's always on the left on this hole. And there are bunkers on the right with a small runway leading to the green. If you lay up, you are looking at a wedge to a long and narrow green, protected by front bunkers on both sides.

No. 6 is the toughest hole at Bay Hill. And one of the more enjoyable ones — if you can manage to stay dry. **TJ**

**Course:** Carnoustie Golf Links

**Location:** Carnoustie, Angus, Scotland

**Hole:** No. 6

**Length:** 490 yards

**Par:** 5

**Designer:** Allan Robertson, Old Tom Morris, James Braid

**Course Comment:** Carnoustie will play host to the 2007 British Open. The last time the Open was staged here in 1999, Frenchman Jean van de Velde suffered an infamous collapse and lost to Paul Lawrie in a four-hole playoff.

# No. ❻ CARNOUSTIE GOLF LINKS

Carnoustie is not elegant. It is not genteel. It is a most brutal test of golf survival, employing all the elements of Scotland to force a golfer to dig deep to prevail. Think about this: the last time the British Open was held here in 1999, the score at the end of regulation play for the three players who went into a playoff was six over par. The top players in the world. Six over. Gives you an idea of what you're facing at Carnoustie.

Nowhere on the golf course will you find a picture that portrays Carnoustie's challenge better than at the "Long," the course's sixth. The Long got even longer for the 1999 Open. Normally playing to 490 yards, officials added 88 yards to a hole that was already a challenge.

But difficulty is nothing new at Carnoustie. In fact, nothing much is new here. This is one of the oldest sites for golf in the world, with records showing the game was being played here as early as 1520. There is a debate over when golf was first played in Scotland, but there is no argument about the history and lore of Carnoustie, which was laid out hundreds of years ago near the mouth of the Firth of Tay. Three of golf's great early luminaries had a hand in Carnoustie's design, including golf's first professional, Allan Robertson; one of the game's first great champions, Old Tom Morris; and one of Scotland's most prolific course builders, James Braid.

They worked their magic at No. 6, where two cavernous bunkers — one behind the other — await 200 yards off the tee to the left. On the opposite side of the fairway is a nasty-looking animal of a bunker, with steep walls of sod that provide a virtual automatic addition to your scorecard.

Horrid sand bunkers, the trickling Jockie's Burn and a diagonal green that provides a tiny approach angle make the rest of the hole as treacherous as its beginning. Toss in the ever-present wind, and the roller-coaster green that provides some devilish pin possibilities, and the Long becomes as difficult as it is historical. **JB**

**BELOW AND OPPOSITE** *Two views of the sixth hole at Carnoustie.*

**Course:** The Wisely (Mill Course)

**Location:** Ripley, Surrey, England

**Hole:** No. 6

**Length:** 520 yards

**Par:** 5

**Designer:** Robert Trent Jones Jr.

**Course Comment:** The club is tucked away behind the Royal Horticultural Society's gardens, and there has been a strong connection between The Wisely golf course and the horticultural society since the course's inception in 1991.

## No. ❻ THE WISELY (MILL COURSE)

When there is such a strong connection between a Royal Horticultural Society garden (RHS Garden Wisley) and a golf course, it sometimes can be forgotten that the golf course need be more than a display of fine flowers and vegetation. While that part of the equation certainly is not forgotten at The Wisely, Robert Trent Jones Jr. also made sure that the course also stood the test as a wonderful piece of golf strategy.

All in all, it is a beautiful teaming of nature, botanical handiwork, and golf. Suffice to say, it works.

There are three nine-hole courses at the Wisely — the Church, the Garden, and the Mill — and it's tough to say which combination is best. For sheer strategy, we will choose the Garden and Mill today, and for the top hole on the course, the par-5 No. 6 at the Mill gets the nod. We pick the Garden Course simply because there are lakes placed strategically placed throughout the Garden layout that forces them to come into play on eight of the holes. Then you add the elements of the sixth at the Mill that complement the Garden and you have quite a matchup indeed.

Take the Mill's sixth, that forces the player to make two crossings of the River Wey, once with the approach shot to the diagonal green. The drive is 520 yards away, and when you are looking at two river runs through the fairway, it is quite an intimidating site. It reminds slightly of the 17th at Carnoustie (see page 816). Trent Jones does not say that is his inspiration, but the similarity is striking and unforgettable.

And don't forget that professionals Colin Montgomerie, Niclas Fasth, and Paul Casey are members. There is a reason why — The Wisley is a great place to play. **JB**

**Course:** Royal Troon Golf Club (Old Course)

**Location:** Troon, Ayrshire, Scotland

**Hole:** No. 6

**Length:** 599 yards

**Par:** 5

**Designer:** Willie Fernie, James Braid

**Course Comment:** The Old Course at Royal Troon has played host to seven British Opens, with champions Arthur Avers (1923), Bobby Lock (1950), Arnold Palmer (1962), Tom Weiskopf (1973), Tom Watson (1982), Mark Calcavecchia (1989), and Justin Leonard (1997) prevailing.

**BELOW AND OPPOSITE** *Two views of the sixth hole at Royal Troon.*

# No. ❻ ROYAL TROON GOLF CLUB
## (OLD COURSE)

Royal Troon's Old Course enjoys its distinction of having both the longest and the shortest holes in the rotation of courses used for the British Open. The famed "Postage Stamp" eighth at 123 yards remains the shortest in the rota with very little change, but the 599-yard sixth has had to stay up with the times to remain the Open's longest hole.

At 577 yards it was the longest in the rotation, but Carnoustie's sixth was lengthened from 490 yards to 578 for the 1999 Open Championship. However, Royal Troon has now extended the challenge at its sixth to 599. Six hundred, anyone?

An uncompromising tee shot is necessary to land between the fairway bunkers to the left and right. And avoid them you must, because they are cavernous sand pits that refuse to be ignored. If you steer clear of the bunkers, you're looking at a second shot, using a fairway wood, that needs to be aimed slightly left to avoid the bunker on the right, which will put you in perfect position for a soft pitch to a long and narrow green.

The green itself is beautifully framed by sand dunes on both sides with out-of-bounds at the back of the green. The gnarly rough on the right of the hole should be left alone, for venturing into that area will almost certainly add at least one stroke to your score.

It is a long and difficult hole, and it is little wonder that Royal Troon personnel want to maintain its tradition as the British Open's longest. For at Royal Troon, it's all about tradition.

Founded on March 16, 1878, by a scant collection of enthusiasts, Troon Golf Club soon outgrew its purely local reputation. By 1880 the club had six holes, and by 1888 it was an 18-hole track measuring — according to records — "3 miles, 1 furlong and 156 yards."

It has evolved into one of Britain's toughest courses. By the 1997 Open, the course stretched to over 7,000 yards. And as difficult as No. 6 is, the real challenge on this course is still a few holes away. The inward nine at Royal Troon is widely accepted as the most demanding of any course on the championship rota. **JB**

**Course:** Penha Longa (Atlantic Course)

**Location:** Linho, Lisboa, Portugal

**Hole:** No. 6

**Length:** 501 yards

**Par:** 5

**Designer:** Robert Trent Jones Jr.

**Course Comment:** Penha Longa is 30 minutes from Lisbon airport and 10 minutes from Estoril and Cascais. These 27 holes of outstanding golf are situated at the foot of the Sintra hills, and part of the Sintra Cascais Natural Park.

BELOW *Van Philips of England plays out of a bunker at Penha Longa, April 1999.*

## No. ❻ PENHA LONGA (ATLANTIC COURSE)

At just three feet over 500 yards, this par 5 isn't very long. But don't let the number on the scorecard fool you. Numbers don't always tell the whole story and you can be sure Mr. Jones threw in plenty of challenges.

Trouble lurks all the way down from tee to green. There are large bunkers to catch a sliced tee shot and a huge lake on the left side of the green. It's very important to keep well right with your second shot if you are not going for the green.

Like most of the holes at Penha Longa, No. 6 features many wonderful snapshots of the area.

Built in 1992, the Atlantic Course at Penha Longa offers a challenge to all golfers, as well as breathtaking views of the ocean with Estoril and Cascais in the foreground, and also of the Sintra Hills.

Penha Longa, which means long rock, features a 177-room hotel. The resort also includes a nine-hole golf course called the Mosteiro, which was also designed by Robert Trent Jones Jr.. Opened in 1995, the course spreads around the historical part of the resort and is the perfect complement to the Atlantic Course. **TJ**

## No. ⑥ SALGADOS

**Course:** Salgados

**Location:** Albufeira, The Algarve, Portugal

**Hole:** No. 6

**Length:** 563 yards

**Par:** 5

**Designer:** Vasconselos, R. Muir-Graves

**Course Comment:** If you feel like you are playing somewhere in Florida, then don't worry. You are not the first. Water features prominently in this flat course built on land reclaimed from the sea.

The main key to playing the sixth hole at Salgados is to keep the ball dry. Water runs along the entire right-hand side of the fairway, and the hole can be a slicer's nightmare.

The fairway seems generous enough off the tee, but the water to the right forces players to aim left. Big hitters can reach the green in two if they are playing off forward tees. However, that calls for a tee shot played as close to the water hazard as possible, leaving a fairway wood shot over the full expanse of the water hazard to a green that angles away from you.

The safest option is to treat this hole as a dangerous three-shotter and play down the left-hand side of the fairway, leaving a fairly straightforward short iron to the green.

A par on this hole will be a huge psychological boost, because the next is a testing par 4 of 454 yards. And the last thing you want to do is play that hole with a bogey or double bogey hanging over your head. **AT**

## No. ⑥ BALTIMORE COUNTRY CLUB (EAST COURSE)

**Course:** Baltimore Country Club (East Course)

**Location:** Timonium, Maryland, USA

**Hole:** No. 6

**Length:** 583 yards

**Par:** 5

**Designer:** A.W. Tillinghast

**Course Comment:** Watch out for the red barn! No. 6 at Baltimore Country Club is known for the red barn that sits at the turn of the dogleg left. There are a few windows on the old restored barn, but don't worry about shattered glass. The windows are protected from flying white objects.

Few would disagree that the Baltimore Country Club's East Course is the best 18 holes in Maryland. And considering all the great courses in the state, that's quite a statement. The East Course, also known as Five Farms, is northwest of Baltimore and was designed in 1922 by A.W. Tillinghast, restored by Brian Silva in 1991, and revised by Keith Foster in 2002.

The classic Tillinghast touch is evident on all 18 holes. The highlights on the course are the par 5s (Nos. 6 and 14), two of Tillinghast's best.

The sixth hole is a dogleg left with a wonderful target to shoot for (actually, over) from the tee — a big red barn, right at the turn. In fact, there is only about 10 yards of rough between the building and the fairway.

The big hitters will fly their tee shot right over the structure. It's about a 240-yard carry to pass the barn. You can reach this green in two but you better have two long shots in your bag.

About 160 to 170 yards out from the green is a group of bunkers which cut right through the middle of the fairway. The green is very small and narrow with bunkers on the right and left side. A large bunker on the right starts about 10 yards out from the green and goes all the way to the back so you'll need to be accurate. **TJ**

**LOCH LOMOND GOLF CLUB**

**Course:** Loch Lomond Golf Club

**Location:** Luss, Dunbartonshire, Scotland

**Hole:** No. 6

**Length:** 625 yards

**Par:** 5

**Designer:** Tom Weiskopf, Jay Morrish

**Course Comment:** This monster of a par 5 is a true three-shotter even for the world's best players. in the 2003 Scottish Open, for instance, the score average for the week on No. 6 was 5.007, and no player managed an eagle. A combined 18 eagles were scored on Loch Lomond's two other par 5s.

**OPPOSITE** *Ernie Els plays a shot on the sixth hole at Loch Lomond, July 2003.*

**BELOW** *The sixth hole at Loch Lomond.*

Believed to be the longest hole in Scotland, Loch Lomond's scenic sixth hole stretches along the shoreline of the course's namesake, offering marvelous views of the water and the magnificent mountains in the distance.

Golfers, however, should strive to keep their minds on the task at hand, because it is a formidable one. The tee shot, hit from a small box almost touching the loch, is not overly difficult, and should be kept to the right side of the fairway to avoid tangling with a group of trees that encroach on the left.

The second shot, affected by a formidable cross-bunker right center, provides a multitude of options. Players can try to carry it and thereby shorten their approach, play to the narrow strip of fairway left of the bunker, or lay up short of the bunker and have an even longer shot into one of Loch Lomond's smaller greens. The slightly raised, but relatively flat putting surface is protected by deep bunkers at the front right and left rear. Go too far right on the approach and a stately old oak — one of many that line the hole — comes into play.

Enjoy the spectacular scenery, and most definitely enjoy a par. **KA**

**Course:** Saucon Valley Country Club (Old Course)

**Location:** Bethlehem, Pennsylvania, USA

**Hole:** No. 6

**Length:** 582 yards

**Par:** 5

**Designer:** Herbert Strong, Perry Maxwell

**Course Comment:** Saucon Valley played host to the U.S. Senior Open in 1992 and again in 2000.

No. ❻ **SAUCON VALLEY COUNTRY CLUB**
**(OLD COURSE)**

Saucon Valley has 54 holes of golf, and all three courses are full of character. And it is remarkable that when asked about which star shines brightest at Saucon Valley, the venerable Old Course isn't even your answer. The Grace Course gets most of the acclaim at this Bethlehem, Pennsylvania, golf haven, but No. 6 at the Old Course is one of the reasons that the original 1922 beauty can't be ignored. The meaty sixth is as rich in personality as you'll find on the Old layout.

The Old Course was designed in 1922 and revised by Perry Maxwell, resulting in some bold greens, including the one at the mighty sixth. The par-5 holes stand out in the routing, and No. 6 is a prime example of why Saucon Valley is widely acclaimed. The Old Course's sixth hole is a virtual forest, save for the glistening green fairway piercing through the trees. There are said to be approximately 10,000 trees on the property, but to golfers at the sixth, it might seem that there are 10,000 on this par-5 beauty alone.

The sixth hole doglegs sternly right, and it is essential to get to a position to be able to turn the corner on your second shot. The second is important because it sets up the proper angle to the third shot to the green. It must carry a series of bunkers and scrub patches and make a line to the left side of the fairway. From there, the approach isn't impeded by trees on the right.

Trees sometimes can be an issue at golf courses, but Saucon Valley ground crews understand the need to keep them under control. And officials at Saucon Valley are also committed to maintaining as much as the original character of the course as possible. In 2004, they spent more than $250,000 to stem erosion from Saucon Creek that traverses through the property. It was altering the layout, as well as endangering the integrity of the land.

Saucon Valley staff are also committed to the very elements that make all three courses such a natural environment for playing golf. They were seeking a grant that, when added to the money that the club had already spent, would result in $900,000 worth of work being done on Saucon Creek to help protect rich schools of brown trout.

You might feel unprotected and on your own when battling the dogleg sixth, but rest assured, Saucon Valley is being taken care of. **JB**

OPPOSITE *Hale Urwin and his caddie walk across a bridge at Saucon Valley, July 2000.*

# Hole ⑦

By the time you reach the seventh hole, all mystery should be gone. By now, you know what kind of day you're having, whether you have a chance to go low, or whether you might just enjoy the scenery the rest of the way in. Whichever is the case, you are now beginning the final leg of your outward nine.

Often the seventh, as with the preceding sixth, is a breather hole. The 107-yard seventh at Pebble Beach is the shortest hole listed among our 1001. With the winds and the sea, it isn't exactly a piece of cake, but Pebble's seventh offers a relaxing moment or two. Such is the case at many No. 7s throughout the world.

**LEFT** *The seventh hole at Pebble Beach, California, USA.*

**Course:** The Country Club
(Open Course)

**Location:** Brookline, Massachusetts,
USA

**Hole:** No. 7

**Length:** 195 yards

**Par:** 3

**Designer:** Willie Campbell

**Course Comment:** No. 7 is tough.
Even the best players in the world
have a tough time on No. 7. It was
the hardest hole in relation to par
at the U.S. Open in 1988. So if you
can par this hole, consider yourself
a pro. Or lucky.

# No. ❼ THE COUNTRY CLUB (OPEN COURSE)

This par 3 is called the "Oldest Hole" for a reason. It's the only hole on the golf course that remains from the original six holes built in 1893.

Playing this hole depends on where the pin sits on this difficult double-plateau green. The green is set at a 45-degree left-to-right angle as you stand on the tee and plan your approach. If you can hit a high fade, pull it out of your bag and use it. This hole begs for a high fade.

But if the hole is in the front plateau, you must land the ball short of the green. Don't worry. Usually, the ground is in perfect shape to give you the little roll you need.

If you are a little off line from the tee you do need to worry about the two bunkers. One is to the front left and is very big. A smaller one sits to the right of the green. Both are big trouble.

Like all of the holes at Brookline, large trees provide a scenic backdrop to the hole. And don't forget to take note of the great history. The club, formed in 1882, has hosted the U.S. Open in 1913 (Francis Ouimet), 1963 (Julius Boros) and 1988 (Curtis Strange). **TJ**

**Course:** Nirwana Bali

**Location:** Bali, Indonesia

**Hole:** No. 7

**Length:** 185 yards

**Par:** 3

**Designer:** Greg Norman,
Bob Harrison

**Course Comment:** No. 7 is very
similar to the third hole at Mauna
Kea on the Big Island of Hawaii (also
included in this book), even though
they are designed by different
architects in different eras, and
on different continents.

# No. ❼ NIRWANA BALI

Surely, this is one of the least publicized of the 1001 holes covered in this book. It certainly is one of the most remote, which works two ways. Yes, it takes a great deal of effort to get to Bali, Indonesia, to play the splendid seventh hole at Nirwana Bali. But, because of the effort involved, you probably are going to stay at least a week at Nirwana Resort, which gives plenty of opportunities to play the hole again and again.

The seventh, like the rest of the holes at Nirwana Bali, doesn't get old, even after playing it for several consecutive days. Greg Norman and Bob Harrison offer different strategies and angles depending on pin placements. This is the case on virtually every hole, including No. 7. This hole becomes even trickier still, because you must always deal with ocean breezes. The wind is constant; it varies only in degree.

This hole is incredibly scenic. The tee box juts into the ocean, and your tee shot carries beach and water all the way to the green. The putting surface sits atop a cliff, and the hole's backdrop includes a temple that is perched upon its own jutting rock formation a few hundreds yards down the coast. **JB**

**Course:** Whistling Straits
(Straits Course)

**Location:** Kohler, Wisconsin, USA

**Hole:** No. 7

**Length:** 214 yards

**Par:** 3

**Designer:** Pete Dye

**Course Comment:** It didn't take
long for this course to jump into
the national spotlight. The Straits
Course was selected as the site of
the 2004 PGA Championship just
two years after opening.

# No. ❼  WHISTLING STRAITS
## (STRAITS COURSE)

Named "Shipwreck," this par 3 hugs the Lake Michigan shoreline to the right. Try to admire the scenery and not join it. Keeping dry is important on this hole. You don't have to fly the water, but it's very intimidating.

Along the right side of the green, wedged between the beach and the green is a bunker. So from right to left it goes water, beach, man-made beach. Hitting left is drier, but not much better. The left side is protected by a large hillside layered with bunkers leaving a very difficult second shot. The hosts suggest that "laying up short for a chip shot is not a bad play." It might not be a bad play, but you don't play one of the greatest holes in the world to lay up.

The course plays from near lake level to panoramic bluff elevations 50 feet over the fairways. Golfers are sure to remember the spectacular vistas of Lake Michigan from all 18 holes, the fescue fairways and the massive sand-dune bunkers — especially the ones they land in. The course layout weaves 14 holes in nearly uninterrupted sequence along the two miles of lakefront. *Golfweek* magazine named the Straits Course the top resort course in the nation and 11th on its notable roster of "The 100 Best Modern Courses" in March 1999. **TJ**

**Course:** Pebble Beach Golf Links

**Location:** No. 7

**Hole:** Pebble Beach, California

**Length:** 107 yards

**Par:** 3

**Designer:** Jack Neville, Douglas Grant, H. Chandler Egan

**Course Comment:** After missing the seventh green by 25 yards in gale-force winds, Tom Kite holed out for a birdie and went on to win the 1992 U.S. Open.

## No. ❼ PEBBLE BEACH GOLF LINKS

The seventh is the shortest hole at Pebble Beach Golf Links, not to mention the shortest of the 1001 holes covered in this book, but by no means does that diminish its sense of belonging in this collection. It is but a tiny gem on what many call the best golf course in America, but it sparkles quaintly next to the sea.

Pebble Beach is the site of the AT&T National Pro-Am, and the PGA Tour's annual visit offers fans throughout the country a chance to get a glimpse of one of the nation's true wonders. The U.S. Opens that have been held at Pebble also give television viewers a treat, but through a small screen is no way to get a feel for Pebble Beach. Playing the course costs a small fortune, but if you can afford it (and gain access) it is a once-in-a-lifetime experience that you will never forget. And among the memories will be the seventh hole. It takes up a mere speck of Pebble's real estate, but it definitely is prime ground.

After coming off the long sixth hole, the contrast of the seventh's challenge is simultaneously daunting and thrilling. Standing on the seventh tee, the pounding surf of Monterey Bay roars all around. The waves crash below you, behind you and to your right. The green ahead is small at 2,000 square feet (only 24 feet wide), and it looks smaller with the bay as its backdrop. The green is protected by five large bunkers which completely surround the putting surface, so precision is essential.

In calm conditions, a player might scoff at a 107-yard hole, take out a wedge and casually loft his ball close to the pin. But Pebble's seventh is rarely without the addition of a gusting wind. And, if a storm happens to be brewing, it can make up to a four- or even five-club difference when standing on the tee. With the postage stamp of a green ahead and trouble virtually everywhere else, there is no margin for error. In fact, in particularly vehement conditions, the safest play sometimes is intentionally landing in one of the bunkers.

The hole definitely is a contrast to the more lengthy challenges at Pebble Beach, but that doesn't mean it offers an escape. **JB**

**BELOW AND OPPOSITE** *Two views of the seventh hole at Pebble Beach.*

**Course:** Royal Liverpool (Hoylake)

**Location:** Hoylake, Merseyside, England

**Hole:** No. 7

**Length:** 196 yards

**Par:** 3

**Designer:** Robert Chambers, George Morris.

**Course Comment:** Royal Liverpool Golf Club is among the toughest and most demanding of the great seaside championship links of Britain. It's also one of the oldest. Built in 1869, on what was then the racecourse of the Liverpool Hunt Club, Hoylake is the oldest of all the English seaside courses with the exception of Westward Ho! in Devon.

# No. ❼  ROYAL LIVERPOOL (HOYLAKE)

Royal Liverpool presents both history and a challenging golf course. First, some history. It was at Hoylake back in 1930 that the legendary Bobby Jones won the second leg of the Grand Slam when he won the Amateur and Open Championships of both Britain and the United States in the same year.

Now the golf course. And one of the best holes at Royal Liverpool — or in all of England for that matter — is the 196-yard par 3. Named "Dowie," this hole was once described as "a reason to get to the 18th." This hole is a classic example of how a modern-day golf architect can take a very flat piece of land and transform it into a wonderful par 3 while still maintaining the feel that the hole has always had.

This more up-to-date par 3 has two sand bunkers guarding the right and left front of the long and narrow green. There also is a large marsh between the tee and the green, which shouldn't come into play. But what might come into play are the sand hills on the right, the humps and hollows all around, and the out-of-bounds markers to the left of the green.

If they do come into play, you might consider this hole a reason to get to the 18th.

We will leave you with another historical footnote. For the first seven years of its existence, the land doubled as a golf course and a race track and Hoylake's racing heritage is marked to this day by the names of the first and 18th holes, Course, and Stand. **TJ**

**Course:** San Francisco Golf Club

**Location:** San Francisco, California, USA

**Hole:** No. 7

**Length:** 190 yards

**Par:** 3

**Designer:** A.W. Tillinghast

**Course Comment:** San Francisco Golf Club, founded in 1895, is recognized by the U.S. Golf Association as being one of the first 100 golf clubs in the country, one of only a few West Coast clubs on the list.

# No. ❼ SAN FRANCISCO GOLF CLUB

San Francisco Golf Club No. 7 — called the "Duel Hole" — has some history to it, and we're not just talking golf. In a small clearing beyond a line of trees adjacent to the seventh green sit two small granite markers signifying the spots where U.S. Senator David C. Broderick and California Supreme Court Justice David S. Terry stood when they fought the last legal duel in California on September 13, 1859. The two Democrats — at odds because of disparaging remarks each had made about the other — stood back to back, then took ten paces each before turning and firing. Broderick's gun discharged a second early, and Terry quickly shot the senator, the bullet entering at the right lapel of his coat and puncturing a lung. Broderick died three days later.

The golf hole itself is a true gem that manages not to be overshadowed by this historical event. The downhill par 3 requires a tee shot to a green that is protected by a series of bunkers on the left and front right. Approximately halfway up the green, a huge ridge runs all the way across the putting surface, making it vital to place the ball on the section where the pin is located. **KA**

---

**Course:** Kauri Cliffs

**Location:** Matauri Bay, Northland, New Zealand

**Hole:** No. 7

**Length:** 186 yards

**Par:** 3

**Designer:** David Harman

**Course Comment:** "Right from the beginning we knew we had a very special piece of property. The natural beauty is just astounding throughout so our real goal was to create a very special golf course that people from all over the world will come in and enjoy," said David Harman. Mission accomplished.

# No. ❼ KAURI CLIFFS

Kauri Cliffs is a 4,000-acre farm and this special golf course is just a small part of the property. And what a piece of property it is. Forget the views for a moment, Kauri Cliffs is one of the best-maintained courses in the country.

Fifteen of the holes at Kauri Cliffs overlook the Pacific Ocean. And six of them jag along the edges of the cliffs themselves. Welcome to the famed No. 7. Pebble Beach wishes it had a hole so dramatic.

You better pick the right club here or you will get an up-close view of the cliffs watching your ball bounce off them and fall to the ocean below. This is a demanding par 3 so don't take too long admiring the awesome view.

There are five sets of tees that move closer and offer less carry off the cliff. From the shortest tee (85 yards), you only have a short sliver of the cliff to carry. From the other four, though, there is no choice of laying up. To make it even tougher, there are two bunkers directly in front of the green — right between the putting surface and the edge of the cliff. The green is extremely difficult. If the flag is in the back, you better land your tee shot on the back part.

Years from now you probably won't remember your score on this hole. But you certainly won't ever forget the view. **TJ**

**Course:** Vale do Lobo Golf Club
(Royal Course)

**Location:** Almansil, Portugal

**Hole:** No. 7

**Length:** 196 yards

**Par:** 3

**Designer:** Sir Henry Cotton,
Rocky Roquemore

**Course Comment:** The seventh hole
of Cotton's original Yellow Course
design actually plays as the 16th
on the Championship Course and
is one of the most photographed
holes in Europe.

# No. ❼  VALE DO LOBO GOLF CLUB
## (ROYAL COURSE)

Sir Henry Cotton fell in love with Portugal's coastline — The Algarve, in particular — upon his first sighting of the rocky seaside region in 1966. Cotton had been the best British golfer in the 1930s and 1940s, and now — decades later — he also was a respected golf-course architect. His work on The Algarve was said to be Cotton's favorite, and the seventh hole at Vale do Lobo's Royal Course was among his masterpieces.

Set amid orange, fig, and olive trees with rolling pine-covered terrain one side and ocean and orange rock cliffs on the other, the first par 3 on the Royal Course doesn't come until the seventh hole. But it is well worth the wait. The hole makes a bold statement upon first glance: This is the signature hole.

The Vale do Lobo Royal Course combines the former Yellow nine-hole course designed by Henry Cotton and nine new holes adapted by Rocky Roquemore from Cotton's original plan. But the magical seventh hole was unchanged (except it plays as No. 16 on the championship design). It is original Cotton.

The seaside tee is one-of-a-kind. The Atlantic waves hit the beach far below and to the left, and there are seaside cliffs that fall down to the beach in between tee and green.

The seventh is one of a collection of three par-3 holes on the Royal Course that are unparalleled in the region. Attention to detail and concern for the natural environment play a major part in the Royal Course design with wild flowers planted around the lakes and care given to preserve as much of the natural forest as possible.

Every hole on the Vale do Lobo Royal Course has a personality of its own and is its own individual memorable experience. Roquemore has cleverly stayed away from clashing visuals, no small challenge on a layout with so much distinct natural beauty. This course is loaded with acres of interrupted terrain, long, challenging holes, and plenty of sand and water.

Cotton didn't take long to warm up to The Algarve when he arrived nearly 40 years ago. And the golfers who have visited the region since are mighty thankful for his contributions. **JB**

**Course:** Mauna Lani Resort
(South Course)

**Location:** Kohala Coast, Hawaii, USA

**Hole:** No. 7

**Length:** 214 yards

**Par:** 3

**Designer:** H. Flint, R. F. Cain,
R. Nelson

**Course Comment:** There are breathtaking views. Then there are breathtaking views in Hawaii. That's called raising the bar. And No. 7 and No. 15 on the South Course at Mauna Lani Resort tee up some spectacular views of the Pacific Ocean.

# No. ❼  MAUNA LANI RESORT
## (SOUTH COURSE)

During the winter months on the par-3 seventh hole on Mauna Lani's South Course, you can see humpback whales migrating offshore, which, some would say, is reason enough to visit. Then there's the fantastic golf.

While most of the photographers head to the famous 15th hole — it's one of the most photographed holes in the world — No. 7 with its windswept Kiawes backdrop is also worth a picture or two. It might also be worth a golf ball or two, if you know what we mean.

This is what the locals call a charming downhill par 3. From the back tees, your tee shot must carry over 200 yards of shoreline lava cliff. It's safe to say you might want to avoid any cliffs, let alone lava cliffs. It might be difficult to get a good lie.

It's important to try and judge the wind. You certainly will feel it on this hole. And once you reach the green, remember that the ripples mirror the ocean waves.

Here's some more advice to take with you. Don't go left of the large two-tiered green. Your hazards include sand, lava, and the big blue ocean. And in the winter, whales. **TJ**

---

**Course:** Golf Club Hubbelrath
(East Course)

**Location:** Düsseldorf, N. Rhine-Westphalia, Germany

**Hole:** No. 7

**Length:** 175 yards

**Par:** 3

**Designer:** Bernhard von Limburger

**Course Comment:** Hubbelrath has built a steady membership since it opened in 1961. The course currently has about 1,750 members, making it the largest club in Germany.

# No. ❼  GOLF CLUB HUBBELRATH
## (EAST COURSE)

Located conveniently between bustling Düsseldorf and the Bergi country, the East Course at Golf Club Hubbelrath was created to challenge and entertain within the demanding constraints of a busy schedule.

The economy of time played a central role in the club's development, which is why the Hubbelrath's West Course plays to an abbreviated 4,374 yards and a par of 66. At Hubbelrath, time is of the essence.

Despite its hurried reputation, however, players may want to slow the pace at the East Course's par-3 seventh hole.

The 175-yard hole plays to a green protected by a pair of deep ponds and a dense wooded area guarding the entire left side. From the tee, the best play is directly between a pair of deep greenside bunkers to a rolling putting surface which, depending on where the pin is cut, will not always take players at the hole.

Although shots left of the green run the risk of finding the water hazard, beware misses to the right which, if overplayed, may carom off the side of the putting surface and into a deep collection area. Saving par from the collection area or one of the greenside bunkers may leave players out of luck if not out of time. **RH**

## No. ❼ REDTAIL GOLF CLUB

**Course:** Redtail Golf Club

**Location:** Port Stanley, Ontario, Canada

**Hole:** No. 7

**Length:** 220 yards

**Par:** 3

**Designer:** Steel & Associates

**Course Comment:** Throughout the layout, Steel & Associates allowed the land to dictate the design and simple, subtle putting surfaces to protect par. The seventh, for example, is the layout's first par 3 and is followed by three more par 3s over the next seven holes. Nor did the architects have any use for contrived hazards. Redtail has less than 30 bunkers and none at the seventh.

Cleaved from land dotted with deep ravines and rolling woodlands, it stands to reason that a review of any hole at Redtail Golf Club would begin and end with topography that is equally suited for wildlife watching or golf.

Mention Redtail's par-3 seventh, for example, and the conversation should by all rights fixate on the ominous gully and 200-yard carry that must be negotiated from the tee. As is almost always the case at Redtail, however, the real challenge doesn't begin until a player has reached the putting surface.

Although the seventh's ravine, which curls around from the front of the green to the back right, is visually intimidating, avoiding its depths usually leads to more trouble. The fainthearted will often attempt to stay clear of the hazard, a survival instinct that likely produces a pulled tee shot to the left. From here, just keeping the ball on the tilted putting surface is the primary concern.

The seventh's putting surface slopes from left to right which makes any tee shot missed left an almost guaranteed bogey. Even more troubling is a pin position cut to the far right of the green, forcing players to either flirt with the ravine or face an improbable two-putt from left of the hole. **RH**

# No. ❼   EL RINCON GOLF CLUB

In 1957, a group of eight Columbians joined forces to establish a golf club in the middle of the Andes Mountains. They found 87 ½ prime acres that were being auctioned in the Bogota savanna for 1,698 pesos per acre. The group purchased the land and in 1963 paid Robert Trent Jones Sr. $26,000 to design the golf course. Some four decades later, you could say these visionaries got their money's worth.

El Rincon Golf Club, with its spruce and pine trees, eucaplytus groves, water hazards, and wonderful golf holes, is an outstanding portrait of golf. And the seventh hole is among the artist's master strokes.

The seventh hole is a test of accuracy and precision, requiring keen direction in a setting of green so lush as to be nearly texturous. The par-3 seventh is only 179 yards, and it plays shorter still when you consider that the course is built about 1 ½ miles above sea level. The ball travels much further, and it makes the seventh hole even more sensitive to an error in club selection.

The tee is large, and depending on where the markers are placed, can offer several looks at the green. A lake separates tee from putting surface, requiring a full carry to get home. A ball struck too timidly will find the water hazard, falling short of the green that is supported with a brick stone wall. Too brave an effort, or one errant to either side, will land in one of three bunkers surrounding the putting surface.

The Bogota River serves as El Rincon's eastern boundry, and a bridge was constructed in 1965 to allow passage to and from the course. But beware when crossing that bridge. A stern, yet beautiful test awaits on the other side. **JB**

# No. ❼   THIRTEENTH BEACH GOLF LINKS

Drives on this hole are hit from a stunning tee built on a rugged sand dune overlooking Murtnaghurt Lagoon.

To the left of the green is a small sand dune with two bunkers carved out of its side, and the right side is protected by another collection of hazards, including a large, deep bunker in the back. A tight apron in front of the green allows golfers to run their tee shots onto the putting surface, but the best way to ensure par is to settle a long iron onto the green and hope for a two-putt.

As is the case with any coastal course, wind regularly comes into play, and golfers can hit as much as a 3-wood, or as little as an 8-iron, to this target. **JS**

**Course:** Stoke Park Golf Club

**Location:** Stoke Poges, Buckinghamshire, England

**Hole:** No. 7

**Length:** 172 yards

**Par:** 3

**Designer:** Harry S. Colt

**Course Comment:** Not many clubs can say this: "With a recorded history of more than nine hundred years, the 350-acre estate provides a unique combination of the traditions of a great members' club and the best of today's sporting, leisure, entertaining, and hotel facilities."

## No. ❼ STOKE PARK GOLF CLUB

Have you ever played the 12th hole at Augusta National? If so, the seventh at Stoke Park Golf Club should look very familiar. "When Harry S. Colt designed what was then Stoke Poges Club (which opened in 1908), Alister MacKenzie was his assistant," Stuart Collier, head golf professional at Stoke Park, told worldgolf.com's Tom LaMarre. "MacKenzie used the design from our No. 7 for No. 12 at Augusta."

"If you put pictures of the holes side by side, you might or might not see the resemblance," Collier continued. "But they play very similarly. It's a three-club green, depending on the wind, which makes for a very scary tee shot. Anything that leaks right is in the stream, left is in the bunker, and long is real trouble in the bushes or the back trap leaving a bunker shot downhill with water behind."

If you land in the left bunker, you can forget about par. And the green may look easy but there are subtle slopes to be concerned about. Be happy with par or even bogey on this hole. **TJ**

**Course:** Hunter's Station

**Location:** Forest County, Tionesta, Pennsylvania, USA

**Hole:** No. 7

**Length:** 167 yards

**Par:** 3

**Designer:** Jack Sherman

**Course Comment:** Fred Birkmore, director of operations for Whole World Travel in London, had this to say about No. 7 at Hunter's Station: "This is the prettiest hole I have ever seen."

# No. ❼ HUNTER'S STATION

If we cut back a bit on our list and went with the best 101 golf holes in the world, No. 7 at Hunter's Station would still be standing. It doesn't get any better than this.

Here is what Chris Roddell of midatlanticgolf.com said about this hole: "It's rare that a golf hole transcends its utilitarian origins and becomes an honest-to-goodness tourist attraction, a place where even non-golfers will trek to marvel at its beauty."

Pretty good stuff. It doesn't hurt a writer's confidence when there is no way to overdescribe the beauty of something. There are few adjectives that do this hole justice.

Standing on the tee you have a 170-foot drop down to the green. Standing on the tee you have to figure out what club to use on this 167-yard hole that plays more like 145 yards. Standing on the tee you have to find some way to take your eyes off the amazing view in front of you.

Describing the picture doesn't do it justice. How do you describe standing on a hilltop looking over a valley where you can see a good ten miles of the meandering Allegheny River cutting through the heavy forest?

You can't. But we can tell you not to hit long on this hole. Just three feet behind the edge of the green is a good 100-foot drop off. Woods also can come into play if you are left or right of the hole. **TJ**

**Course:** Alto Golf

**Location:** The Algarve, Portugal

**Hole:** No. 7

**Length:** 220 yards

**Par:** 3

**Designer:** Sir Henry Cotton

**Course Comment:** Alto Golf lies near the site of Portugal's first golf course, a 9-hole sand green course that no longer exists.

# No. ❼ ALTO GOLF

Alto is packed into two small parcels of land containing each nine. This is pure parkland golf and the tight confines call for accurate tee shots and approaches. Nowhere is this more noticeable than on the par-3 seventh. If you get a whiff of Pinehurst on this hole then it is because of the green.

The green is like an upturned saucer, like many of the putting surfaces here. Getting the ball to stay on this particular green is difficult, especially when you are faced with a tee shot of 220 yards off the back tees.

Those who come up short of the green will have to try to avoid bunkers left and right. Getting up and down in two from these sand traps is made all the more difficult because of the green configuration. Anyone who has a touch of Phil Mickelson should be okay. Others should settle for bogey and get to the next tee.

Chipping is also a problem here since the shape of the green will force the golfer to use a bit of imagination to get the ball close to the hole. A three is most acceptable on this hole, maybe even a bit of a bonus. **AT**

**Course:** The National Golf Club (Old Course)

**Location:** Cape Schanck, Victoria, Australia

**Hole:** No. 7

**Length:** 152 yards

**Par:** 3

**Designer:** Robert Trent Jones Jr.

**Course Comment:** The No. 7 hole at The National was formerly the second hole before the club's new clubhouse was built and the course was rerouted.

## No. ❼ THE NATIONAL GOLF CLUB (OLD COURSE)

Situated on rugged sand dunes high above a pair of national parks along Victoria's Mornington Peninsula, The National Golf Club offers stunning views of the rugged Australian coastline.

Perhaps none is more spectacular than that offered from the clifftop tee box of The National's signature seventh hole, where golfers are treated to marvelous vistas of Bass Strait, Port Phillip Bay, and on clear mornings, the Melbourne city skyline.

However, players must quickly turn their attention to the downhill tee shot, which must be hit over a ravine filled with trees. The distance is relatively short, but the target is small — a green that's wide but not very deep. The green is further guarded by a deep bunker and more thick vegetation at the rear, and a spine that runs across the entire front right of the putting surface.

On this hole, club selection is crucial, as anything short, long, or left will be lost. With the prevailing wind blowing in, the hole plays much more difficult, so take an extra club — or three. Designer Robert Trent Jones Jr. wasn't talking just about the seventh hole when he said The National could be "a lion in the wind or a lamb on a clear, sunny day," but he could have been. **KA**

**Course:** The Hills Country Club (The Hills Course)

**Location:** Lakeway, Texas, USA

**Hole:** No. 7

**Length:** 204 yards

**Par:** 3

**Designer:** Jack Nicklaus

**Course Comment:** The town of Lakeway, about 20 miles north of Austin, gets its name from its location on Lake Travis, a 64-mile-long, 19,000-acre reservoir created from the waters of the Colorado River.

## No. ❼ THE HILLS COUNTRY CLUB (THE HILLS COURSE)

Considered by many to be the best par 3 in the great state of Texas, No. 7 at The Hills Country Club is a picturesque hole that features a 25-foot waterfall over a limestone cliff that's located directly in front of the green.

At least it's picturesque if you're playing from the forward (89 yards), middle (134 yards), or blue tees (151 yards). From the 204-yard back tees, the view isn't quite as spectacular as it is downright scary, especially when you're playing into the prevailing headwind. Make sure to take plenty of club. Even if you manage to make it over the cascades, however, there's no guarantee of par.

The green, which slopes from right to left, is very shallow and protected by a pair of bunkers in the rear, forcing a golfer who lands in one of them to face an intimidating sand shot back toward the falls.

To give a true picture of the severity of the tee shot, at one point, the club's maintenance staff was forced to put artificial turf at the drop area on No. 7. So many drops were being taken that it simply was impossible to grow real grass there. **KA**

# No. ❼ CASA DE CAMPO GOLF CLUB
## (TEETH OF THE DOG)

World-renowned designer Pete Dye took two years to create Teeth of the Dog before it opened in 1969. The seventh hole, a monster par 3, is one of seven holes on the course that overlooks the Caribbean Sea. It is one of the most distinctive holes on a course that Dye has called his favorite design.

The name "Teeth of the Dog" is derived from the sharp points of the coral formations along the shoreline, like those adjacent to No. 7, but it could just as easily come from the difficulty of the course.

The seventh, at 225 yards, is long for a par 3, and it becomes even more daunting because part of that 225 yards is over the sea. The tee is situated at the edge of the Caribbean and the green is surrounded by sand, giving it the appearance that it actually is cut into the beach. There also are grass bunkers thrown in for good measure, and the rough is downright ornery.

Dye's trademark railroad ties barely make an appearance on Teeth of the Dog. In fact there are none on No. 7, but many of his other staples come into play. The seventh includes waste bunkers, a contoured and elevated green, and trees that don't quite come into play (but could if you are wayward off the tee). Toss in the trade winds that arise without warning, and the hole's difficulty increases dramatically.

Originally, plans called for just a nine-hole course on the Casa de Campo resort, but when Dye scouted the property from a motorboat in the Caribbean, he proclaimed it, "the most beautiful seaside location for golf that I have ever seen," the project became more ambitious. And, Dye's ambition — and patience — paid off. The seventh hole is a prime example. **JB**

# No. ❼ NEWCASTLE GOLF CLUB

The tee for this 155-yarder stands on the highest point of the front nine of this layout, which is located near the Hunter River about a two-hour drive from Sydney.

It requires a mid- to short-iron to a green that is guarded on the right by two bunkers, and pitches considerably from front to back. It is essential for any tee shot to clear the trouble in front, but trouble awaits the player who goes long and watches his shot run off the back.

An up-and-down from that position is among the toughest plays on this celebrated track, and one that should be avoided at all costs.

The seventh is a true signature hole, perhaps the best at Newcastle and one that noted architect Tom Doak puts on his list of the best 18 holes in the world outside the United States and the British Isles. **JS**

**Course:** Ganton Golf Club

**Location:** Ganton, North Yorkshire, England

**Hole:** No. 7

**Length:** 435 yards

**Par:** 4

**Designer:** Tom Chisolm, Harry Vardon, Ted Ray, James Braid, Harry S. Colt

**Course Comment:** Thousands of years previously this site was an inlet from the North Sea, and the natural sandy subsoil was an ideal place to develop a course.

**BELOW** *Trip Kuehne of the USA plays out of a bunker on the seventh hole at Ganton, September 2003.*

# No. ❼  GANTON GOLF CLUB

Some amazing statements have been made about this remarkable golf course, but Peter Alliss sums it up best when he says, "There are few better places to play golf than at Ganton with its unmistakable air of quality, charm, and challenge."

Those who have played Ganton — which hosted the 2003 Walker Cup — understand that the layout puts a premium on accuracy rather than length. So, for the most part, keep the driver in the bag.

Ganton has few peers when it comes to bunkers. According to the club's web site: "A player who is bunkered is punished for his error." In an age when golf designers are making bunkers less penal, this is a most welcome feature indeed.

This talk of bunkers brings us perfectly to the seventh hole, which is often called "one of the most attractively bunkered holes in the world."

This difficult dogleg right has four bunkers guarding the inside. There is a bunker about 50 to 60 yards shy of the green that you really should avoid. Two deep bunkers cut into the green on the left and another one guards the right side.

According to golfclubatlas.com, the seventh hole at Ganton is cleverly bunkered, forcing golfers into a position where they have to play risk-reward shots: "Just the way a dogleg hole should be bunkered as there is a decided advantage, in terms of both distance and angle of approach, to hugging the bunkers at the corner." **TJ**

| |
|---|
| **Course:** St. George's Golf & Country Club |
| **Location:** Toronto, Ontario, Canada |
| **Hole:** No. 7 |
| **Length:** 446 yards |
| **Par:** 4 |
| **Designer:** Stanley Thompson |
| **Course Comment:** St. George's has hosted four Canadian Opens, a tournament which serves as the country's national championship, and its only PGA Tour stop. When Glen Abbey Golf Club in Toronto was built, it was supposed to host all the Canadian Opens. But St. George's was missed by players and fans, so it was returned to the rota. |

# No. ❼ ST. GEORGE'S GOLF & COUNTRY CLUB

With more than 650 courses, Ontario is one of the most highly concentrated golfing regions in North America. Canada as a whole may not receive the recognition it deserves for both its rich golf heritage and the country's current fervor for the game.

Nowhere is the Canadian golf heritage more evident than at Royal St. George's. In 1929, B. L. Anderson, the chief executive officer of the Royal Canadian Golf Association, wrote:

"Golf, like music, cannot be faked or muddled through. You have to do it right, and do it yourself; you have to deliver the goods or it doesn't go. There is an element of luck in golf but it will not carry you through the 18 holes at Royal York [now St. George's]. The course isn't built that way. There has to be a standard of measurement in everything. The Royal York will measure your golf game. It is a real test of golf."

The most difficult test on the course is the 446-yard seventh, rated the No. 1 handicap on the scorecard. The length is enough of a challenge for most players, but when you consider the fact that it plays uphill every step of the way from tee to green, the hole plays as a par 5 for mid-range handicappers or higher.

There are smatterings of bunkers on either side of the fairway, but they shouldn't come into play. The fairways are wide; the protection on this hole is the length and the uphill slope. Once at the conclusion, however, the test isn't over by any means. The green is fairly large, but is among the course's most curvaceous.

No. 7 has been the hardest hole at St. George's in its more than 75 years of existence. In 1909 Robert Home Smith, an accomplished builder from Stratford, began acquiring lands near the banks of the Humber River for real estate development. 18 years later, he decided a golf course would be a good way to add value to the property.

Smith brought in Thompson, one of North America's most renowned golf course architects, to construct an 18-hole championship course. By 1929 the golf course was completed, and it stands today as one of the most cherished in Canada. **JB**

# ROYAL TROON GOLF CLUB
## (OLD COURSE)

**Course:** Royal Troon Golf Club (Old Course)

**Location:** Troon, Ayrshire, Scotland

**Hole:** No. 7

**Length:** 403 yards

**Par:** 4

**Designer:** C. Hunter, W. Fernie

**Course Comment:** Royal Troon is considered the best of all the excellent courses that run in the dunes along the Ayrshire coast, overlooking the lower reaches of the Firth of Clyde.

Tel-El-Kebir is the name of the seventh hole on the Old Course and named after a battle fought in 1882 just before the hole was created. And you are in for a real battle on this hole. The seventh is a magnificent golfing hole and is played from an elevated tee perched on top of the dunes. The fairway doglegs sharply to the right with a sandhill and bunker set into the angle of the dogleg.

The bunkers are about 240 yards out on both sides. A tee shot of around 270 yards gives you a shot at the green. If you hook the ball, you can expect to land somewhere in the bunkers along the left side of the fairway. A lofted iron will send the ball over a slight gully to a well-trapped green set between two imposing sandhills. The narrow green has traps on both sides and plenty of trouble to the back.

This hole plays much easier from the forward tees which are 354 yards. The ladies tees are 348 yards. As you can see, this is a battle that will be tough to win from whichever tees you choose. **TJ**

**Course:** Ballybunion Golf Club
(Old Course)

**Location:** Ballybunion, County Kerry,
Ireland

**Hole:** No. 7

**Length:** 432 yards

**Par:** 4

**Designer:** Tom Simpson,
Molly Gourlay

**Course Comment:** Rated as one
of the world's best golf courses,
Ballybunion is hailed for its expert
exploitation of the natural
undulations.

### No. ❼ BALLYBUNION GOLF CLUB (OLD COURSE)

So many times a newcomer attempts to capture the magic of Ballybunion's Old Course and so many times they fall short. A masterpiece amid rolling dunes, a beautiful test of pure links golf, a priceless gift — all wonderful accolades but somehow wanting. Five-time British Open champion Tom Watson may have paid the undisputed lady of Irish links the ultimate compliment: "Ballybunion is a course on which many golf architects should live and play before they build a golf course," said Watson, Ballybunion's millennium captain who was commissioned by the club in 1995 to give the ancient course a modern edge.

The par-4 seventh hole plays an intimidating 432 yards and often gets lost among the more talked about holes at Ballybunion, but it may well have been the impetus behind Watson's comments. The seventh is, by almost all accounts, an architectural gem.

No. 7 is a subtle dogleg to the right, and tee shots are best played away from the ocean, which runs down the length of the right side. Too far left, however, and players face a more demanding second shot to a slightly elevated green which is protected by large mounding. The putting surface also sits perilously close to the edge of the cliff and second shots are made even more challenging by a large mound in the fairway. **RH**

**BELOW AND OPPOSITE** *Two views of the seventh hole at Ballybunion.*

**Course:** Castle Stuart Golf Links

**Location:** Inverness, Highland, Scotland

**Hole:** No. 7

**Length:** 461 yards

**Par:** 4

**Designer:** Mark Parsinen, Gil Hanse

**Course Comment:** It hasn't taken long: Castle Stuart was named Golf Magazine's Top New International Winner when it opened in 2009, and two years later played host to the 2011 Barclays Scottish Open.

# No. ❼ CASTLE STUART

The seventh hole at Castle Stuart includes a design concept that is at once intimidating and descriptive of the good time available at both the hole and the course: the "infinity green," where it appears there is no end in sight. The putting surface is on a higher plane than the rest of the hole, and it has been described as being "etched on the edge of outer space."

The intimidation factor is obvious as you look from the fairway, in that there is no visible way of stopping the ball. But, the descriptive feature is a bit more subtle. The amount of enjoyment available on this par 4, much like the rest of Castle Stuart, reaches near infinity.

The 461-yard gem tiptoes its way along the top of a sea cliff, and if this—and the infinity green—isn't indication enough that you are playing one tough golf hole, than take a look at the score card. No. 7 is listed as the toughest hole on the course.

A cavernous hollow protects the left side of the hole, which is the correct play for aggressive players. The hollow actually works in the players' favor because it funnels shots to the left side of the green.

There are bunkers on the left side of the green and small depressions on the right. And, as you approach the infinity green, don't overlook the backdrop of the Banchory Point lighthouse. **JB**

**Course:** Double Eagle Golf Club

**Location:** Galena, Ohio, USA

**Hole:** No. 7

**Length:** 380 yards

**Par:** 4

**Designer:** Tom Weiskopf, Jay Morrish

**Course Comment:** This golf club is like two courses in one. Built on 350 acres of natural land, the course weaves in and out of what once was farmland and forest areas before returning to the wide-open fairways of the early holes.

# No. ❼ DOUBLE EAGLE GOLF CLUB

First a story. A few years ago, USGA official Tom Meeks came out to rate the Double Eagle Club. Meeks said he liked the course but before they could go ahead with tournament plans, No. 7 would have to change. He felt that the access to the green was too narrow. The owner of Double Eagle said that the trees were staying, even if it cost him USGA events. Less than two weeks later a severe storm blew through the area and took down the three trees. The USGA gets what they want one way or another. Since then, several U.S. Open qualifiers have been played at Double Eagle.

This 380-yard par-4 hole features a tight tee shot, but you don't have to hit it far. In fact, you better not hit it far. About 260 yards from the back tees is a ravine so you will have to lay up if you are a big hitter. The pin placement dictates where you want to drive the ball. If the pin is on the left side of the green you want to be on the right side of the fairway. If the flag is on the right side of the green, keep it left in the fairway. This hole is on the heavily wooded section of the golf course. It used to be more wooded, until Mother Nature (or the USGA) blew a few over. **TJ**

**Course:** DragonRidge Golf & Country Club

**Location:** Henderson, Nevada, USA

**Hole:** No. 7

**Length:** 441 yards

**Par:** 4

**Designer:** Jay Morrish

**Course Comment:** Don't bet with any of the members when you play their course. Split fairways that incorporate the natural desert mountain surroundings and blind shots off the tee give the players paying the dues a great advantage over course rookies.

OPPOSITE *The seventh hole at DragonRidge.*

## No. ❼ DRAGONRIDGE GOLF & COUNTRY CLUB

Built in 2000, DragonRidge Country Club has already joined the ranks as one of the premier golf courses in the Las Vegas/Henderson area. The course was sculpted out of the McCullough Mountains, which is said to have the most beautiful views of the entire Las Vegas valley.

The seventh hole is not only beautiful but very tough. Among the most difficult holes at DragonRidge, the signature par-4 seventh plays 441 yards from the tips and is very intimidating from start to finish. A well-placed tee shot to a landing area that gradually narrows is a must if you are going to par this hole.

The second is uphill to a shallow green protected by a bunker front and a creek behind that collects to the breathtaking water hazard that protects the right side. You can shorten the length of this long par 4 by either playing from one of the shorter tees, or favoring the right side of the fairway off the tee.

Either way, be wary of the water hazard on the right. The green is deep so use enough club on your approach to compensate for the elevated green. DragonRidge Country Club has been selected more than once by the Tiger Woods Foundation to host its annual Tiger Jam event. **TJ**

**Course:** Tomson Golf Club

**Location:** Pudong, Shanghai, China

**Hole:** No. 7

**Length:** 388 yards

**Par:** 4

**Designer:** Shunsuke Kato

**Course Comment:** According to the *Asia Times*, almost half of China's more than 200 golf courses are running a deficit, as hasty golf-course development, coupled with the country's immature market, have led to blind land requisition and unbalanced consumption.

## No. ❼ TOMSON GOLF CLUB

Two decades after the opening of the country's first golf course in 1984, China now ranks fifth in the world and second in Asia in terms of the number of courses. And the game's popularity is on the rise. In addition to China's more than 200 golf links, 500 to 1,000 more are under construction.

Tomson Golf Club, one of the leading golf clubs in Shanghai, is a good example of the tough golf economy in China. Its annual revenue from membership fees, golf fees, and relevant catering income only reaches around 20 million yuan, indicating a tight margin for profits, according to the *Asia Times*. Tomson Golf Club is one of China's top places to play — despite the tough economy.

The 388-yard par 4 is a good example of both the quality and challenge found at Tomson. Coming out of a narrow shoot, you have to drive the ball a good way to clear both sand and a creek that runs right through the fairway. There is a good size landing area after the creek and before a large bunker on the left side. Your second shot is even harder. There is a bunker before the green on the right side and the fairway is razor thin leading up to the green. The large green has dangerous bunkers behind, and a pot bunker just in front. **TJ**

**Course:** The Olympic Club
(Lake Course)

**Location:** San Francisco, California,
USA

**Hole:** No. 7

**Length:** 288 yards

**Par:** 4

**Designer:** Sam Whiting

**Course Comment:** The green at
the seventh hole on the Lake Course
would make any list of the toughest
greens in the world. Just ask John
Daly. During the final round of the
1998 U.S. Open, Daly hit a 3-wood to
the green and ended up with a six.

## No. ❼ THE OLYMPIC CLUB (LAKE COURSE)

This club, which hosted the U.S. Open in 1955, 1966, 1987, and 1998, is known for its spectacular views of the Golden Gate Bridge. But you don't have to look that far to see something spectacular. The golf course laid out in front of you certainly would qualify. And No. 7 is spectacular, memorable, and very difficult. This is one of those holes you must experience. There is much more elevation than you see from television. It's 288 yards from the back tees and a lot of that is uphill.

From the tips, you need to drive the ball 175 yards to reach a level area of the fairway. From this point, the way to the hole is a steady climb. Your approach shot to the green is crucial. It's important to be on the tier that the flag is on or you are looking at a difficult time. And they aren't kidding when they call this a three-tiered green. There are six to eight steps between the flat spots on each tier. It slopes back and away to the right and it's not uncommon to putt yourself right off the green. So don't be fooled by the yardage on this hole. Your work doesn't begin until you reach the green. **TJ**

**Course:** Conestoga Golf Club

**Location:** Mesquite, Nevada, USA

**Hole:** No. 7

**Length:** 324 yards

**Par:** 4

**Designer:** Gary Panks

**Course Comment:** OK, shrub lovers, here's a collection of what you'll find in Conestoga's desert: Baja fairy duster, brittle bush, bird of paradise, firecracker penstemon, silver cassia, and creosote bush. Not to mention a cactus or two.

# No. ❼  CONESTOGA GOLF CLUB

Conestoga is located just one hour north of Las Vegas, and while it may be a gamble in Sin City, there is no hit-or-miss about Conestoga. It is an all-aces golf experience.

Like much of Mesquite, Nevada, there are numerous elevation changes at Conestoga, and the club meanders through canyons and rock outcrops. There are 51 bunkers that are more than just cosmetic; virtually all of them come into play. And, don't think because you're in the desert that there is no water. There is one lake that comes into play on two holes. Abbott Wash and Pulsipher Wash come into play on five holes. And, this is no mirage.

Vision, or lack of it, is a key element to No. 7 at Conestoga. The 324-yard seventh is a blind par 4 that is reachable in the high Nevada elevation. So, if you get a proper line and you have the nerve, a grip-and-rip can get you home.

All you can see from the tee are three cavernous bunkers far off in the distance. That's your aiming point, but you can't see the green. They are short of the green, but they still are intimidating. Clear the bunkers, hope for a roll, and you just might be putting for an eagle on a green that you couldn't even see. And, that is a gamble you can live with. **JB**

**Course:** Morfontaine Golf Club

**Location:** Senlis, France

**Hole:** No. 7

**Length:** 430 yards

**Par:** 4

**Designer:** Tom Simpson

**Course Comment:** Simpson was commissioned in 1910 to build a nine-hole course at Morfontaine by the Duc de Gramont. Seventeen years later, after World War I, Simpson drew up the club's 18-hole layout.

# No. ❼  MORFONTAINE GOLF CLUB

It's a shame the vast majority of golfers aren't able to play this classic course that provides its members with the ultimate retreat in the peaceful beauty of the French countryside. Morfontaine was designed by Tom Simpson, a British aristocrat who is also renowned for his work at nearby Chantilly, as well as Ballybunion in Ireland, Cruden Bay in Scotland, and Royal Antwerp in Belgium. The only French layout consistently ranking among the world's top 100 golf courses, Morfontaine is one of Europe's most exclusive private clubs, although it does open its doors to an occasional top amateur event. Simpson's masterpiece, which contains narrow fairways, thick forests and heather, has undergone virtually no alterations since its creation in 1927.

The seventh hole, a dogleg left, requires a partially blind tee shot to be hit over a hill that slopes from left to right, making it tough to keep your drive in the uneven fairway. Even if you do, plenty of work remains. The approach shot must carry a sneaky false front with an uphill slope that sends many balls rolling back down into the fairway. The putting surface is relatively large, but contains plenty of contours and is protected by a bunker on its left side. **KA**

| |
|---|
| **Course:** Rio Secco Golf Club |
| **Location:** Henderson, Nevada, USA |
| **Hole:** No. 7 |
| **Length:** 417 yards |
| **Par:** 4 |
| **Designer:** Rees Jones |
| **Course Comment:** The 18-hole, championship course is designed primarily for the guests of the Rio All-Suite Hotel & Casino in Las Vegas and is located just 12 minutes south of the award-winning resort. |

# No. ❼ RIO SECCO GOLF CLUB

Rio Secco Golf Club lies at the foothills of the Black Mountain Range in Nevada, about 15 minutes southeast of the Las Vegas Strip, and can play to over 7,400 difficult yards. But it also offers four teeing grounds to allow golfers of any skill level a memorable time. Rio Secco also features six holes through steep canyons, six holes on a plateau overlooking the city, and six holes in a broad desert wash.

The signature hole is the 417-yard, par-4 seventh hole. This slight dogleg right is one of the more scenic holes on a course known for scenery. And like many of the slots at the casino, the odds of success on this hole are stacked against you. From the tee, you need to rip it about 260 to 270 yards. And you might need every yard because the second shot is the key, so get it as far up the fairway as possible. A 40-foot vertical caliche wall serves as the backdrop for the green, which sits inside a cavern. Three bunkers and a challenging green make this hole even more difficult. Hopefully, you have saved some of that good luck for the golf course. **TJ**

**Course:** Tong Hwa Golf &
Country Club

**Location:** Lin Kou, Taipei, Taiwan

**Hole:** No. 7

**Length:** 444 yards

**Par:** 4

**Designer:** Sato Takeshi

**Course Comment:** Tong Hwa played
host to the Asian PGA Tour's Taiwan
PGA Championship in 2000.

## No. ❼ TONG HWA GOLF & COUNTRY CLUB

Golf began in Taiwan during the Japanese Colonial period with the opening of the Tamsui Golf Course (today known as Taiwan Golf & Country Club's Tamsui Course), which was built as a three-hole layout in 1914. The course was expanded to nine holes in 1919, then to 18 holes in 1929.

Since then, golf on this island has come a long way, as evidenced by modern clubs such as Tong Hwa Golf & Country Club, set in the hills along Taiwan's northern coast. Tong Hwa is best known for its tough par-4 seventh, a hole those early golfers in Taiwan probably could have never envisioned the likes of.

The tee shot requires a downhill drive to the left side of a sloping, mounded fairway in order to stay away from bunkers and woods on the right side. But that's easy compared to what you'll face on your second shot, which more than likely won't be from an even lie. The green is fiercely protected on the left and front by a pond and a long, winding bunker, requiring a precise approach with a long to mid-iron to the right half of the putting surface. **KA**

**Course:** Mill River Golf Course

**Location:** Prince Edward Island,
Canada

**Hole:** No. 7

**Length:** 419 yards

**Par:** 4

**Designer:** Robbie Robinson

**Course Comment:** One of Prince
Edward Island's most popular and
affordable playgrounds, Mill River
features wide rolling fairways, well-
bunkered greens, subtle elevation
changes, and numerous lakes
and streams.

## No. ❼ MILL RIVER GOLF COURSE

Rodd Mill River Resort on Prince Edward Island is a true golf destination with the acclaimed Mill River Golf Course, always rated as one of Canada's best places to play. You won't soon forget the resort. You will never forget the seventh hole on the Mill River Golf Course. And if you have trouble hitting straight, you will love this hole.

From tee to green, the 419-yard par 4 features a series of ponds right down the middle of the fairway. You can go right. You can go left. But you can't go straight. Trees line both sides of the fairway, so don't think that if you avoid the water you have avoided all the trouble. The left side is a little narrower than the right.

A good tee shot leaves you about 150 yards and a slight dogleg left to an elevated green. And we do mean elevated. It's a good 50 feet above the fairway, so take this into consideration when choosing a club. The green is surrounded on three sides by woods.

Mill River was built in 1969 and has gone through some tweaks over the years. But No. 7 is almost the same layout that Robbie Robinson first put down all those years ago. **TJ**

**Course:** Sotogrande Golf Club
(Old Course)

**Location:** Cadiz, Spain

**Hole:** No. 7

**Length:** 422 yards

**Par:** 4

**Designer:** Robert Trent Jones Sr.

**Course Comment:** This was Jones'
first work in continental Europe,
completed in 1964, and it plays
host annually to the Spanish Open.

No. **❼** **SOTOGRANDE GOLF CLUB**
**(OLD COURSE)**

Sotogrande Golf Club's Old Course is often referred to as Valderrama's older
brother. Not a bad family of siblings, to be sure.

Sotogrande has become known as one of the finest golf courses in
Europe, and along with famed neighbor Valderrama, it is generally regarded
as the best in Spain. Located next to one of the Mediterranean's finest
beaches adjacent to the Guadiaro River, the course predated Valderrama,
but there is nothing outdated about Sotogrande's Old.

The seventh hole, like the rest of the Sotogrande layout, has very little
rough. But, as with the first, 12th, 13th, 14th, 16th, 17th, and 18th holes,
where water comes into play, it is on the right side of the fairway. The left
side is water-free, but there is *agua* on the right.

The left side of the hole is not without its own danger, however. Players
must avoid the line of pines, oaks, palms, eucalyptus, and cork trees. If you
find the fairway off the tee, you are faced with an approach into a thin strip

of green, protected by four bunkers all around. The bunkers actually can serve as a saving grace for errant shots, because they could keep a ball from traveling into the small pond on the right side of the green. It doesn't help matters that the green slopes toward the water, so sand obviously is the better option if you don't land on the putting surface.

The course actually is flatter than the topography of the surrounding area, which is filled with cliffs and rolling foothills. But Sotogrande Golf Club has salt marshes and it is filled with native colors — purples, reds, and soft, rusty browns. The climate of the area is exquisite for golf as well, with an average of 300 days of sunshine per year.

Sotogrande Old is a special golf course that would perhaps have greater fame if it didn't live in the shadow of Valderrama. It is advised you play both courses to see which you enjoy most. But whichever sibling you prefer, it is a family gathering you won't forget. **JB**

**Course:** Plainfield Country Club

**Location:** Plainfield, New Jersey, USA

**Hole:** No. 7

**Length:** 458 yards

**Par:** 4

**Designer:** Donald Ross

**Course Comment:** Plainfield Country Club, located about 25 miles outside of New York City in northcentral New Jersey, was originally founded in 1890 and is listed by the USGA among the first 100 clubs established in the U.S.

## No. ❼  PLAINFIELD COUNTRY CLUB

The No. 3 handicap hole at Plainfield Country Club, this 458-yard par 4 is a challenge from tee to green. From the tee, you are hitting straightaway and over a slight dip in the fairway with trees to the right. Your first goal is to avoid the huge bunkers on the left side of the fairway. This group of big, deep bunkers have a steep face and it's very difficult to hit out of them.

About 30 yards past the bunkers is a large oak tree along the left side. So if you land in one of the bunkers, you need to pitch out back toward the center of the fairway. There will be no driving the ball from these sand traps. At around the 150-yard marker, the fairway begins to drop. There is about a 20-foot drop from this point to the green below.

Bunkers come back into play closer to the green. There is a row of bunkers about 30 yards out from the green extending along the right side. The bunkers don't go all the way to the green, but close.

There are about 10 to 15 yards of fairway between the traps and the green. Like many of the greens at Plainfield, the No. 7 putting surface is fairly flat but tricky. Don't be fooled by this green — it's not as easy as it looks. **TJ**

Course: Lakeview Hills
(North Course)

Location: Lexington, Michigan, USA

Hole: No. 7

Length: 459 yards

Par: 4

Designer: Jeff Gorney

Course Comment: This hole is reachable in two, but you better have confidence in your long iron. Landing a ball on this green from 175 yards is not an easy task. Miss just a little and you will be reaching in your bag for another ball. Then again, if you can hit it far enough to go for it in two, confidence probably isn't a problem.

## No. ❼  LAKEVIEW HILLS (NORTH COURSE)

Michigan has as many golf meccas as it does lakes. And the so-called "Thumb Area" isn't short of outstanding courses. Lakeview Hills, a chip shot from Port Huron and the shores of Lake Huron, can play with any of them. The upscale resort, which includes a hotel, bowling alley, and health club, became a real player in the Michigan golf scene when it opened the North Course in 1991. It's a true Michigan golf course — lined with big pines and native trees. Eight holes feature some kind of water and traps are perfectly placed in the "wrong" places.

The 459-yard par 4 is one of several signature-quality holes at Lakeview Hills. A good drive from the back is 270 to 280 yards and sets you up for a shot — albeit a long one — to the green. This is where it gets tricky. The peninsula green is surrounded by water on three sides. The green itself is divided by a crown and plays like two separate greens.

"This is a difficult hole," said Dennis Fabbri, the head professional and part of the family-run business that stresses the "family" touch when it comes to service and atmosphere. "If the flag is in the back, you better land it on the back. If the flag is up front, you better hit the front." There also are fairway bunkers, one about 320 yards from the tee on the right and another one 55 yards further down. With four sets of tees, those bunkers are reachable, especially from the whites (345 yards). While this is a challenging hole, you might remember it more for its natural beauty. The same way you will remember Lakeview Hills for its hospitality. **TJ**

Course: Woodlands Golf Club

Location: Mordialloc, Victoria, Australia

Hole: No. 7

Par: 4

Length: 375 yards

Designer: R.S. Banks, S. Bennett

Course Comment: Players will find this to be another gem in the famed Melbourne Sand Belt. Founded in 1913, it is noted for its short par 4s, especially No. 7, and its remarkable green-side bunkering created by former Royal Melbourne greenskeeper Mick Morcom.

## No. ❼  WOODLANDS GOLF CLUB

This dogleg left is not necessarily a hole on which you would want to hit a driver.

To be sure, there are no tricky fairway bunkers to contend with, but the landing area for tee shots is small, and all that is really needed to reach the crook is a fairway wood or long iron. All that is usually needed after that is a firm wedge to a testy green that is small in stature but subtly tough; it falls slightly from back to front, is protected by bunkers left, front, and back and has a tendency to roll very fast in summer.

Club members say that if a golfer can land his second shot onto the green, and keep it there, he is doing very well. And the general consensus at Woodlands is that a par on No. 7 is an excellent result. **JS**

**Course:** The European Club

**Location:** Brittas Bay, County Wicklow, Ireland

**Hole:** No. 7

**Length:** 470 yards

**Par:** 4

**Designer:** Pat Ruddy

**Course Comment:** The European Club was voted one of Ireland's six greatest golf courses in 1995 — two years after it opened — joining Portmarnock, Royal Portrush, Royal County Down, Ballybunion, and Waterville.

**BELOW AND OPPOSITE** *Two views of the seventh hole at The European Club.*

# No. ❼ THE EUROPEAN CLUB

The European Club, which opened for play in 1993, is a mere infant in relation to golf throughout Europe. Surrounded in its own country and throughout the continent by golf courses hundreds of years old with centuries of tradition, The European Club has ascended to must-play status in little more than a decade.

In order to climb the pecking order of a golf-rich country, a course has to make an immediate impression. And this isn't done with hype, tricks, or gimmicks. It's accomplished through quality. Cavernous bunkers, rugged dunes, sea breezes, and large undulating greens call on the golfer to display strength of character, an ability to think, and shot-making skills. This is the kind of quality that makes The European Club an eye-opener.

The rough and rugged seventh is carved through all of the elements which make The European Club so special. But, where Ruddy could have made blind shots, he opened up the fairway just enough to let players see their targets. Usually this is a good thing. But the landing areas are set among dangers that appear closer than they really are, so casting your eyes on the prize is more frightening than advantageous. There is plenty of room to land your shots, but the areas of safety appear choked by mounds and reeds and hills.

A burn runs down the right-hand side of the hole, and the left side is framed by mounds, reeds, a large marsh, and a carpet of beautiful purple heather.

The design of the seventh, as with the entirety of The European Club, modernizes the traditional values of links golf. Blind shots, deemed by many as an outdated feature of current links golf, are limited, with 14 holes offering complete tee-to-green visuals, and the other four providing a clearly visible landing area. The seventh's fast fairway, and its green that invites running shots, however, stay within the tradition of links golf. Ruddy has kept the best of links, and modernized the rest. It is a rare combination, and it has resulted in a golf course that truly is unique.

The seventh hole well exemplifies the great demand of the entire course: It is designed to command players to think as purely as they strike the ball. **JB**

**Course:** Sand Hills Golf Club

**Location:** Mullen, Nebraska, USA

**Hole:** No. 7

**Length:** 283 yards

**Par:** 4

**Designer:** Ben Crenshaw, Bill Coore

**Course Comment:** The course is hilly — including the seventh hole — but not too difficult to walk. Plenty of bunkers and natural pitfalls along the way, but no water hazards or out-of-bounds stakes on the golf course.

# No. ❼   SAND HILLS GOLF CLUB

North Central Nebraska, an isolated part of the United States five hours removed from the nearest major city (Denver, Colorado), might not be your first choice to build a golf course. But this very isolation provided a major opportunity for a splendid track. A piece of property absolutely perfect for a golf course awaited Ben Crenshaw and Bill Coore when they surveyed the site at Sand Hills. And they took full advantage of the wind-tossed dunes, heather, and rolling elevation changes to create a masterpiece.

The holes roam through the land, appearing not as an intrusion but as if they had been there forever. The seventh, very short for a par 4 at 283 yards, is a perfect example of using the natural land as its direction and not taking charge itself.

The seventh meshes wonderfully with the land, and offers a risk-reward play for big hitters who eye the green from the tee. But the ever-present Nebraska wind makes the risk far more likely than the reward. The green is

reachable, but you must come in very high because the front is protected on both sides by large mounds of knee-deep heather and scraggly bunkers. A ball in this area is going to be findable, but being able to get a club on it is another matter.

The wiser play off the tee is a lay-up, but even that takes some planning because of those bunkers placed perfectly to demand a smart first shot. The bunkers are located in spots providing a landing area either in front or in back, but placement is mandatory even with a fairway wood or an iron.

Then comes the approach to the tiny green that peeks like an emerald eye through a golden sheath of heather. It is a beautiful sight, but not so enjoyable to negotiate. The seventh is not lengthy, but you'd better not be short on smarts from tee to green. A soft approach gives you a shot at birdie, but if you get caught by any of the bunkers, mounds, or grassy hazards along the way, par becomes a task probably not performed. **JB**

## No. ❼ NANTUCKET GOLF CLUB

**Course:** Nantucket Golf Club

**Location:** Siasconset, Massachusetts, USA

**Hole:** No. 7

**Length:** 471 yards

**Par:** 4

**Designer:** Rees Jones

**Course Comment:** Heavy winds, common to Nantucket and the surrounding area, add another element of difficulty to this already challenging golf course. Look no further than No. 7 for proof. The wind has been known to blow head covers and a good score all over the seventh fairway and green.

It won't take long to understand the natural problems you will be facing on this 471-yard par-4 hole at the prestigious Nantucket Golf Club. As you look over the fairway on this dogleg left, you more than likely will be greeted with the Nantucket head wind — right in your face.

Needless to say, this hole plays a little longer than 471 yards.

Don't look for the green from the tee because you can't see it. What you can see are bunkers along the left side and thick Nantucket brush to the right. There is a depression of about 20 feet between the tee box and the landing area in the fairway.

The brush is not the place to be. And the bunkers on the left are very tough to hit out of, and are about 240 to 280 yards from the back tees.

Your second shot is one of the more difficult at Nantucket. There is about a 10-foot elevation climb to the green and you are hitting into the prevailing wind. So be sure and take this into account when reaching in the bag for a club.

The green also is tricky. It's a rectangle-shape green but is very shallow. There also is a large bunker to the left of the green. **TJ**

## No. ❼ INVERNESS CLUB

**Course:** Inverness Club

**Location:** Toledo, Ohio, USA

**Hole:** No. 7

**Length:** 456 yards

**Par:** 4

**Designer:** Donald Ross

**Course Comment:** In the 2003 U.S. Senior Open, Inverness Club's seventh hole played to a 4.516 stroke average, yielding only 20 birdies compared with 146 bogeys and 34 double bogeys.

Inverness has received several makeovers in advance of some of the many major championships it has held, with the first in 1919, when Donald Ross turned the original nine-hole track into an 18-hole championship course worthy of the 1920 U.S. Open. It was also refined in 1978 by George and Tom Fazio and in 1999 by Arthur Hills, who stretched the course to 7,255 yards.

Through it all, the seventh has remained one of Inverness' toughest tests. The added length brought the creek and mounds at the dogleg right more into play on the tee shot, as the creek is now a 240-yard carry from the tips. The real tough part of this hole, however, is almost all Ross — a contoured, raised green that can easily turn downhill birdie putts into chips for par.

Inverness has been the site of four U.S. Opens (1920, 1931, 1957, 1979) and two PGA Championships (1986, 1993). The most remembered? Probably the 1931 Open, where Billy Burke and George Von Elm battled for 144 holes (including two 36-hole playoffs) before Burke won by a single stroke, and the 1986 PGA, which Bob Tway won by holing out from a greenside bunker at No. 18 to defeat Greg Norman. **KA**

## No. ❼  WANNAMOISETT COUNTRY CLUB

**Course:** Wannamoisett Country Club

**Location:** Rumford, Rhode Island, USA

**Hole:** No. 7

**Length:** 347 yards

**Par:** 4

**Designer:** Donald Ross

**Course Comment:** Despite working with only 104 acres, Donald Ross was able to design variety and challenge into all 18 holes at Wannamoisett. He has more famous courses, but he proved here he could build a lot with a little.

Holes like this prove that length doesn't always mean difficulty. Looking at this hole on the scorecard one would think that a birdie is in order. The hole is only 347 yards away, after all. But a lot of golfers end up putting five down on the scorecard and calling Donald Ross a few names along the way.

The tee shot must avoid five sizeable fairway bunkers in order to find the beautifully rolling fairway. There is a little strategy on the tee. You can hit it 225 yards to a flat part of the plateau fairway which falls off on both sides. Or you can rip it and try to bring your ball within a wedge of the green.

The approach shot is uphill to a long but relatively narrow green that falls away on all sides. The strong contours of the green suggest that a birdie isn't in the bag after all.

Regardless of where the flag is, aim for the center of this green, which has bunkers short right, short left, and behind. This green might look large from where you are standing in the fairway, but since it rolls off on all sides, it's actually very small.

Our expert in the clubhouse said the green is what makes this hole fun — and challenging. Most of the difficulty comes on the putting surface so don't think because you are on in two you have at least a par. So much can still go wrong — and often times does. **TJ**

## No. ❼  THE GOLF CLUB KENNEDY BAY

**Course:** The Golf Club Kennedy Bay

**Location:** Longbeach Key, Port Kennedy, Western Australia

**Hole:** No. 7

**Par:** 4

**Length:** 313 yards

**Designer:** Michael Coate, Roger Mackay, Ian Baker-Finch

**Course Comment:** The "Fremantle Doctor" is the name of the wind in this area, contributing toward the Scottish Links-style atmosphere of the course.

The scorecard says it plays 313 yards from the back tees, and the immediate temptation is to discount both the difficulty of this hole — which is built in the sand hills of Port Kennedy outside Perth — and the many ways that par can elude even the very best players.

The name of No. 7 is "Temptation," and is a wonderful risk-reward play that is intended to "tempt" players to take out a driver and "go" for the green, or lay up with a long iron or fairway wood in hopes of nestling a short-iron by the hole.

It doglegs slightly to the left, with pot bunkers set on both sides of the fairway, one short and to the left and another farther out from the tee and to the right. Bomb a big drive with a slight draw, and it is possible to reach a small, raised green only 25 yards deep, or at the very least leave yourself with a very short pitch.

The more sensible approach, however, is to play a shorter tee shot to the right side of the fairway and hit a wedge in. **JS**

**Course:** Lake Nona Golf Club

**Location:** Orlando, Florida, USA

**Hole:** No. 7

**Length:** 432 yards

**Par:** 4

**Designer:** Tom Fazio

**Course Comment:** Lake Nona has served as a U.S. base to several of golf's premier international players, as Annika Sorenstam, Ernie Els, Retief Goosen, and Nick Faldo all own homes there.

# No. ❼   LAKE NONA GOLF CLUB

It didn't take long for Lake Nona Golf Club to firmly establish itself as a championship course. Only three years after its opening, the Tom Fazio design played host to the inaugural Solheim Cup in 1989, as the U.S. squad led by Beth Daniel, Betsy King, and Nancy Lopez defeated Europe 11 ½ to 4 ½. That was followed by another international team event, the 1993 World Cup of Golf, won by the American duo of Fred Couples and Davis Love III in what was the second of their record four consecutive victories.

Lake Nona's par-4 seventh hole has always been a challenge, even to the world's top professional players. The drive must carry the front portion of a lake that runs down the right side, then battle a huge ridge that splits the fairway directly down the middle, with rough and trees on the left and the water on the right. Regardless of your choice of fairways, you'll want to get as close as possible for your second shot to the narrow green, which is protected by a bunker front left and deep grass swales to the right and back left. **KA**

Course: The Harvester Golf Club

Location: Rhodes, Iowa, USA

Hole: No. 7

Length: 405 yards

Par: 4

Designer: Keith Foster

Course Comment: Harvester is actually 300 acres of converted prairie land; its designer has also created Arizona's Sun Ridge Canyon and two delicious courses in Texas — The Tradition and The Quarry.

## No. ❼ THE HARVESTER GOLF CLUB

You're coming off the tough, par-5 sixth at The Harvester and you are looking for some relief. Well, if relief is what you seek at the 405-yard seventh, you're looking in the wrong place.

Like much of The Harvester, the seventh is awash with fescue and native grasses, and water comes into play off the tee. Designer Keith Foster has a great ability to maintain a natural-is-better philosophy throughout the course, and that is true on No. 7.

The dogleg-right seventh is made more difficult after crossing the water off the tee by its uphill climb. It is a graceful, gradual uphill slope, but it cuts down on roll on every shot and adds distance to what appears to be a relatively short hole on the scorecard.

The fairway is lined with trees down the right-hand side, so if you opt to try to shorten the dogleg, be careful on the right. The safer play is left.

There is a bunker on the right-hand side near the dogleg, and two more bunkers that surround the green once you reach the putting surface.

Bent grass makes up the tees, fairways, and greens at No. 7 and throughout the rest of The Harvester. Foster called for bluegrass in the rough and the thicker, coarser grass grabs golf balls and presents a surprisingly different feel as players try to dig their way out. **JB**

Course: Ellerston Golf Course

Location: Upper Hunter Valley, New South Wales, Australia

Hole: No. 7

Length: 451 yards

Par: 4

Designer: Greg Norman, Bob Harrison

Course Comment: Kerry Packer wanted Ellerston to be tough, and the idea for the course was for it to be designed for players carrying a 12 handicap, or lower.

## No. ❼ ELLERSTON GOLF COURSE

The extreme difficulty of this long, downhill par 4 is evident from the very beginning, with a dramatic drive from an elevated tee down Pages Creek, a central feature of the track that runs along the entire right side of No. 7 and is incorporated in no less than nine Ellerston holes, to a small island of Santa Ana Couch fairway some 200 yards away.

Somehow, golfers must seemingly thread their balls between a pair of trees and over the creek to the landing area. From there, they have to play an approach shot to an elevated green of Pennlinks Bentgrass set right on the banks of the Pages and protected on both the right and left sides by bunkers and a slope that will often send balls landing on the left side of the putting surface right into the hazards.

Golf course critics rate this hole among the best par 4s in Australia, and the consensus among many of those reviewers is that it provides the finishing touches to perhaps the greatest consecutive trio of modern golf holes in the land, Nos. 5, 6, and 7. **JS**

# CASTELCONTURBIA GOLF CLUB (YELLOW COURSE)

**Course:** Castelconturbia Golf Club (Yellow Course)

**Location:** Agrate, Conturbia, Italy

**Hole:** No. 7

**Length:** 383 yards

**Par:** 4

**Designer:** Robert Trent Jones Sr.

**Course Comment:** Records show that a golf course was laid out in 1898 on the same land that Castelconturbia sits on today.

This impressive 27-hole layout by Robert Trent Jones Sr. is set on gently rolling, countryside terrain that is dotted with small lakes and ancient trees, and provides spectacular views of the Monta Rosa mountains.

The seventh, considered the signature hole of the entire 27-hole layout, is a dogleg left that provides a wide landing area off the tee, but demands an accurate approach to an island green with the Monta Rosa massif rising in the background. Hit the drive as far as you can to cut down on your chance for a second-shot error. The putting surface is shallow, so select your club wisely: too short or too long will likely lead to a lost ball and double bogey — or worse.

Castelconturbia has twice played host to the PGA European Tour's Italian Open, with vastly different results. Patrick Sjoland won there in 1998, shooting consecutive rounds of 64-65-66 for a 21-under-par total in the rain-shortened event. Compare that with Craig Parry's 9-under-par winning score in 1991, when he managed to break 70 only one day — a third-round 67. During those events, the seventh hole of the Yellow played as the 16th hole, providing a late opportunity for a crucial birdie — or a critical mistake. **KA**

**Course:** Oak Hill Country Club
(East Course)

**Location:** Rochester, New York, USA

**Hole:** No. 7

**Length:** 432 yards

**Par:** 4

**Designer:** Donald Ross, Robert Trent
Jones Sr., George, Tom Fazio

**Course Comment:** Oak Hill,
which played host to the 2003 PGA
Championship (won by long-shot
Shaun Micheel), also staged the 1949
U.S. Amateur, 1984 U.S. Senior Open,
U.S. Opens in 1956, 1968 and 1989,
the 1980 PGA Championship and
the 1995 Ryder Cup.

BELOW *Seve Ballesteros of Spain
plays his tee shot at Oak Hill,
September 1995.*

OPPOSITE *The seventh hole at
Oak Hill.*

# No. ❼  OAK HILL COUNTRY CLUB
## (EAST COURSE)

Much like the game of golf and the legend of Donald Ross — the man who created this aesthetically pleasing yet strenuously difficult hole — there is a mixture of history and great golf at Oak Hill. And this blend comes to play perfectly on the seventh hole. The club, which was formulated officially in 1901, once used an old farmhouse as its clubhouse. Yet today Oak Hill stands as one of America's finest designs by one of its great course architects. No. 7 at Oak Hill is among Ross's best, and this in a portfolio filled with greatness.

The hole isn't terribly long at 432 yards, but because of its routing, two nearly perfect shots need to be executed to have a realistic chance at par. A stream runs diagonally across the fairway (shorter on the right, longer on the left), so you must use your wits off the tee. If you opt for a long ball, you better stay left or you will find water. If you go intentionally short to the landing area on the right, you leave yourself quite a hefty approach.

There are trees guarding the green on the right, and the hole was made more difficult when Robert Trent Jones Sr. tinkered with the front of the green — adding two bunkers that all but removed the possibility of a running approach. It points to the history of Oak Hill that Jones' "new" work to the seventh actually was executed in 1995.

Also revealing the history of the place is a rundown of tournament champions who have hoisted trophies at Oak Hill. In 1941, a star-studded field arrived, led by native son Walter Hagen, Sam Snead, Ben Hogan, and Gene Sarazen. Snead shot 277 and won by seven strokes over Hogan. "This course is certainly one of the finest I have ever seen, fit for either an Open or a PGA," Snead said after his victory.

Hogan loved the course, too, and he vowed to return in 1942. He did, and he won, shooting a 64 in the first round, which remains the course record. Other winners through the years have included Lee Trevino, Jack Nicklaus, and a surprising victory by the underdog European squad in the 1995 Ryder Cup.

In 1998, 49 years after its first Amateur, the tournament returned, the first time it had been held in the state of New York since it was at Oak Hill in 1949. So, you see, Oak Hill has stood the test of time. The old farmhouse has long since been removed for a stately clubhouse, Ross's wonderful original design has been tweaked by some of the great architects, ensuring that Oak Hill, its beauty, and its great golf will remain an American fixture. **JB**

**Course:** Westin La Cantera Golf Club (Resort Course)

**Location:** San Antonio, Texas, USA

**Hole:** No. 7

**Length:** 316 yards

**Par:** 4

**Designer:** Tom Weiskopf, Jay Morrish

**Course Comment:** There are five sets of tees on this hole, starting with the tips or the blacks at 316 yards. Then you have the golds (309 yards), the copper (308), the silver (307), and the jade (252). So nine feet separate three sets of tees. Now that's unique.

## No. ❼ WESTIN LA CANTERA GOLF CLUB (RESORT COURSE)

Nestled in the beautiful Texas Hill Country just north of San Antonio, Texas, the resort provides breathtaking views of the Hill Country, Six Flags Fiesta Texas Theme Park, and downtown San Antonio from one of the highest peaks in the area.

Breathtaking is also a very fitting description of the two championship courses at La Cantera. The Resort Course at La Cantera is home to the PGA Tour's Valero Texas Open and The Palmer Course at La Cantera offers challenge and beauty side by side.

From the seventh tee you get a great view of Six Flags and all of the potential danger ahead on this 316-yard par 4. There is an 80- to 100-foot drop from the tee and the big hitters will go for it.

Don't let the scenery blind your judgement. There is a good-size landing area about 100 yards from the green. There are bunkers on both sides of the fairway and a deep pot bunker right in the middle of the fairway about 200 yards off the tee.

The green isn't easy. There are two tiers and three bunkers guarding it. The pin is often on the front of the green, which is a pretty good-size target.

If you want to go for the green but don't have enough club in your bag, there are four other tees to choose from. The shortest one is 252 yards from the green. **TJ**

**Course:** North Berwick (West Course)

**Location:** North Berwick, East Lothian, Scotland

**Hole:** No. 7

**Length:** 354 yards

**Par:** 4

**Designer:** David Strath

**Course Comment:** If "global golf" is a term to be coined, it originates here. The much-copied par-3 Redan was born at the West and remains a model for holes worldwide. Its greens were cleverly contoured ages ago for a timeless, wicked challenge.

## No. ❼ NORTH BERWICK (WEST COURSE)

The world-famous and much-copied Redan seventh hole is tougher than it looks. Hit the ball hard and steadfast because the wind blowing from the North Sea confounds many a player, and will send a scarcely errant shot tumbling into the drink. The winding Eil Burn snakes the fairway just shy of the green, making the approach more than treacherous.

This course dates back to a time when players conquered it wielding hickory clubs, targeting hardened leather balls. Think ancient, old-world charm. The West has a demanding layout dotted with unconventional and ingenious holes and unparalleled ocean vistas. It is a stunning test of skill at all levels — a marriage of conventional holes and blind tee shots that must sail over walls and dunes. With its back layout hugging the shoreline, the West is seaside Scottish golf at its scenic finest.

Many holes are within a chip shot of the beach. It's not the longest course you'll ever play, but it may be among the trickiest. Shot-making takes pure imagination here. With roots that date to 1832, North Berwick West is the 13th oldest golf club in the world. One of its original members fought at the Battle of Waterloo. **KLL**

**Course:** Grand Cypress Resort
(North Course)

**Location:** Orlando, Florida, USA

**Hole:** No. 7

**Length:** 423 yards

**Par:** 4

**Designer:** Jack Nicklaus

**Course Comment:** Grand Cypress'
North and South nines have played
host to numerous professional
tournaments over the years,
including the World Cup of Golf
(1990), Greg Norman's Shark Shoot-
Out (1986-90) and LPGA Tour events
in 1998, 1999, and 2001.

No. **7**   # GRAND CYPRESS RESORT
## (NORTH COURSE)

The seventh is the No. 1 handicap hole on Grand Cypress's North Course, which is considered to be the toughest nine of the resort's 45 Jack Nicklaus-designed holes. The North-South combination, the resort's championship layout, places a premium upon accuracy, and is marked by sharply ledged fairways, tall mounds and undulations, and plateau greens set above water and/or sand.

The seventh hole contains most of these features, and in the Nicklaus tradition, sets up well for long-hitting faders off the tee, as it bends around a huge lake that lines the right side of the hole all the way to the slightly elevated green. The water can come into play again on the second shot, as does a bunker directly in front of the wide, but shallow green. Huge mounds await behind and to the left of the putting surface, which drops off steeply at the right rear portion.

Bernhard Langer led Germany to a victory at the 1990 World Cup held at Grand Cypress. Se Ri Pak won the LPGA Tour's season-opening tournament held there in 2001, after Kelly Robbins captured back-to-back victories there to start the 1998 and 1999 seasons. **KA**

**Course:** Bay Harbor Golf Club
(Links Course)

**Location:** Bay Harbor, Michigan, USA

**Hole:** No. 7

**Length:** 500 yards

**Par:** 5

**Designer:** Arthur Hills

**Course Comment:** Bay Harbor
developers wanted Arthur Hills
to design their courses so badly
they pulled him from a sister project,
Boyne Highlands Resort, after just
nine holes so he could focus his
attention on Bay Harbor.

OPPOSITE *The seventh hole at
Bay Harbor.*

## No. ❼ BAY HARBOR GOLF CLUB
### (LINKS COURSE)

Perched some 150 feet high above Lake Michigan, the seventh hole at Bay Harbor Golf Club's Links Course has been called the prettiest anywhere, and with a cool wind blowing in off the water and a bright sun illuminating the way, it's hard to argue.

It also helps that the seventh follows the Links' most taxing hole, the monstrous 418-yard sixth. The 500-yard, par-5 seventh is the perfect combination of challenge and beauty.

From the tee, players will be drawn away from the right side of the fairway by the mass of deep-blue water that waits over the cliff's edge. However, there is more room to the right than appearances suggest and the best angle from which to lay up or go for the green in two shots is down the right-hand side.

Second shots are best played to the left of a leaf-shaped fairway bunker, which will leave a short iron to a large links-style green.

A long drive will tempt players to go for the green in two shots but avoid missing to the right. The putting surface runs toward the lake and will quickly feed shots to the cliff's edge and into oblivion. **RH**

**Course:** Desert Forest Golf Club

**Location:** Carefree, Arizona, USA

**Hole:** No. 7

**Length:** 557 yards

**Par:** 5

**Designer:** Red Lawrence

**Course Comment:** Desert Forest
Golf Club is one of a kind in Arizona.
There are around 17,000 golf courses
in the U.S., including about 350 in
Arizona. Desert Forest is the only
course in the state ranked every year
since 1966 among the top 100 in the
nation by *Golf Digest* magazine.

## No. ❼ DESERT FOREST GOLF CLUB

The seventh hole at Desert Forest has all the ingredients that make up a great golf hole. It's memorable. You aren't about to forget the dry wash that runs along the entire right side of the fairway. It's challenging: the split fairway offers you a choice from the tee. But serve up a little slice or push or hook or anything else off line, and you are looking at plenty of trouble. It's fun to play: short hitters can play it safe down the left fairway. Big hitters can crank it up and try to fly the desert floor to the right fairway. It's scenic: what hole at this course isn't?

This hole isn't too tough if you can drive the ball. If you can put 270 yards between you and your drive and nail it right over the desert, you can position yourself for an iron shot to the green. The dry wash runs the entire right-hand side and then cuts over between the second and third section of the fairway.

The green has a bunker on the left and two along the right side. The green slopes severely right to left and there is desert directly behind the putting surface. There are no fairway bunkers, water hazards, or cart paths on the entire golf course. **TJ**

**Course:** Colorado Golf Club

**Location:** Parker, Colorado, USA

**Hole:** No. 7

**Length:** 583 yards

**Par:** 5

**Designer:** Bill Coore, Ben Crenshaw

**Course Comment:** Colorado Golf Club will play host to the 2013 Solheim Cup, a biennial women's competition between the United States and Europe. And, this, just six years after Colorado Golf Club was opened in 2007.

# No. ❼ COLORADO GOLF CLUB

This 7604-yard gem of a golf course features hillsides packed with picturesque woods, it meanders through meadows, and it is loaded with streams and barrancas. It takes shot-making abilities that take you uphill, downhill, and everything in between.

The par-5 seventh presents a legitimate set of distinct strategic tests from tee to green. The decisions are forced by a set of fairway bunkers that dominate the natural line where your drive and second shot just crave to land. Were it not for the bunkers, that would be the aiming point.

You can play short of the bunkers if you choose on your drive, but this results in a blind second shot that requires a launch over the bunkers to a second tier of fairway on the other side of the bunkers. If you can make it over the bunkers on your drive, that's the play. But that takes quite a 320-yard drive from the back tees. A 285-yard drive will stop short of the sand.

The challenge and the decisions don't stop on your first or second shots. The No. 7 green is positioned above the right edge of the another set of bunkers, so it's either try to carry the bunkers and stick the green, or lay up short of the sand. **JB**

## No. ❼ AA SAINT-OMER GOLF CLUB

**Course:** Aa Saint-Omer Golf Club

**Location:** Westbecourt, Lumbres, France

**Hole:** No. 7

**Length:** 575 yards

**Par:** 5

**Designer:** Joan Dudok van Heel

**Course Comment:** Like most quality golf courses, the layout is designed to give choices to golfers of all skill levels. Give Aa Saint-Omer an A+ in this category. The seventh hole plays 575 yards from the tips. But three other tees soften the challenge a bit. The shortest tee is 418 yards.

As soon as you arrive at the clubhouse, you will be immediately impressed by the exceptional view. In fact, the Aa, that Northern river particularly familiar to crossword enthusiasts, has given its name to the magnificent valley that opens out for miles in front of you.

There are several outstanding holes at this scenic course in France. No. 7 is a perfect postcard for the entire course. In fact like many holes at Aa Saint-Omer, you will enjoy the scenery as much as the golf. This long par 5 of 575 yards runs past undergrowth, which, in the spring, is full of the blue, yellow, white, and purple of periwinkles, cowslips, violets, anemones, and hyacinths. And with any luck, you will come across a couple of stags on the fairway, toward the green.

Another great hole at Aa Saint-Omer is the 439-yard par-4 13th. A dogleg left, your drive will need to be long and accurate if you hope to approach the green with an iron. This shot will have to fly over a 20-meter deep valley, dotted with copses and a pond, in order to reach the green on the hillside. The best part is you get to play both holes — and 16 other good ones — when you sign up at Aa Saint-Omer. **TJ**

## No. ❼ HOLLYWOOD GOLF CLUB

**Course:** Hollywood Golf Club

**Location:** Deal, New Jersey, USA

**Hole:** No. 7

**Length:** 550 yards

**Par:** 5

**Designer:** Isaac Mackie, Walter Travis

**Course Comment:** Walter Travis is often called golf's "Grand Old Man" because even though he didn't take up the game until age 36, by age 42 he had won three U.S. Amateur titles (1900, 1901, 1903).

You might say Walter Travis liked sand. Best known for his heavily bunkered designs at Garden City Golf Club and Westchester Country Club in New York, Travis included 220 of the hazards in his noted Hollywood remake — including 57 on the famous "Heinz 57" 12th hole. His friend and fellow designer A.W. Tillinghast once joked that if he made a poor shot on a Walter Travis golf hole, there was no need to ask his caddie where the ball was. "I know it's in a bunker," he said.

The par-5 seventh at Hollywood certainly fits the bill, beginning with the tee shot and ending with a dangerous approach to a tricky, tiered green.

The twisting, mounded fairway has several well-placed, high-faced bunkers that can easily be found with a drive that's just slightly awry. The best play is to hit two shots down the fairway's right side to position yourself for the approach.

The slanted, diagonal putting surface is well guarded by a massive, meandering bunker at the left front, making it almost impossible to come in from there. Two more bunkers protect the right and rear portions of the green. **KA**

**Course:** The Concession Golf Club

**Location:** Bradenton, Florida, USA

**Hole:** No. 7

**Length:** 606 yards

**Par:** 5

**Designer:** Jack Nicklaus, Tony Jacklin

**Course Comment:** The Concession played host to the Big Ten Conference Championship in February 2012. The Big Ten Conference includes Ohio State University, where The Concession designer Jack Nicklaus attended and played golf from 1957 to '61.

OPPOSITE *The seventh hole at The Concession.*

## No. ❼ THE CONCESSION GOLF CLUB

Jack Nicklaus designed the Concession Golf Club in association with Tony Jacklin, and its name commemorates the sporting gesture by Nicklaus in the 1969 Ryder Cup singles match between Nicklaus and Jacklin. Nicklaus conceded a putt on the 18th hole to Jacklin rendering the two teams in a 16–16 tie. It was the first tie in Ryder Cup history, and the U.S. retained the Cup because it had won in 1967.

Ryder Cup placards are on tee boxes at The Concession and the image of Nicklaus and Jacklin walking off the 18th green arm in arm is used as the club's logo. You get the idea. Sportsmanship is the name of the game at The Concession, which opened in 2006.

The highlighted hole — the horseshoe-shaped, par-5 No. 7 — is extremely difficult and it can be downright frustrating. So watch your sportsmanship if things don't go right. Remember, you are at The Concession.

You start with a tee shot that must funnel through a thicket of trees on either side as it rockets toward a picture-perfect fairway. There is a vast sandy area on the left side of the fairway to contend with off the tee, there is a huge amount mounding all the way down the fairway, there are eight bunkers just waiting to swallow your golf ball, and the fairway just never stops turning left toward a huge and sloping putting surface. **JB**

**Course:** Ekwanok Country Club

**Location:** Manchester, Vermont, USA

**Hole:** No. 7

**Length:** 597 yards

**Par:** 5

**Designer:** Walter Travis

**Course Comment:** Ekwanok played host to the 1914 U.S. Amateur, with Francis Ouimet defeating Jerome D. Travers, 6 and 5, for the first of his two U.S. Amateur championships. It was Travers' only loss in five trips to the finals.

## No. ❼ EKWANOK COUNTRY CLUB

Ekwanok's No. 7 is one of New England's most famed holes, and deservedly so. Called "Saddleback" for obvious reasons, the tee box features a view of mist-covered mountains in the background and a smaller, but much more relevant mountain in the middle of the fairway.

The hole's dominant feature is a monstrous, rough-covered hill that bisects the fairway approximately 300 yards from the tee, forcing even longer hitters to lay up in front of it. Second shots must clear the massive mound and avoid a pair of fairway bunkers just to the left of the landing area, leaving an approach to a slightly elevated green that's protected by sand to the left and a thickly wooded slope to the rear and right. Three excellent shots are always required for par (in the course's first 100 years, not one golfer managed to reach the green in two).

Ekwanok, which opened in 1899, was the great Walter Travis' foray into architecture, and very few designers managed a finer inaugural attempt. Interestingly, the nearby Gleneagles layout at The Equinox, another legendary Vermont track, is the last course Travis designed. Fittingly, as was his desire, he was buried in a cemetery that lies between his first and final masterpieces. **KA**

## No. ❼ CAPITAL GOLF CLUB

**Course:** Capital Golf Club

**Location:** Melbourne, Victoria, Australia

**Hole:** No. 7

**Par:** 5

**Length:** 555 yards

**Designer:** Peter Thomson, Michael Wolveridge, Ross Perrett, Lloyd Williams

**Course Comment:** Capital has a much-lauded layout that is brilliantly designed and meticulously conditioned.

The ultra-exclusive Capital Golf Club is the brainchild of local businessman Lloyd Williams, and it is a sumptuous retreat with spectacular amenities.

The first thing most people think of when they play the seventh at Capital is how much it reminds them of No. 13 at the Augusta National Golf Club, the famed par 5 that finishes Amen Corner.

And the comparison is understandable, given that this par 5 is a dogleg left with water running down the left side and a green that can be reached in two by big hitters. There are bunkers on the left at the corner, water to the left of the green, and golfers can often find emus ambling through the wildlife preserve to that side of the putting surface.

Williams built back tees at Capital to make it as playable for the touring professionals who visit as it is to weekend duffers, but they have not prevented Tiger Woods from reaching the green on No. 7 in two (with a 6-iron) when he teed it up there, or Aaron Baddeley from holing a 2-iron some time ago for an albatross two. **JS**

## No. ❼ MOUNT MALARAYAT GOLF & COUNTRY CLUB (MAKULOT COURSE)

**Course:** Mount Malarayat Golf & Country Club (Makulot Course)

**Location:** Lipa City, Batangas, Philippines

**Hole:** No. 7

**Length:** 526 yards

**Par:** 5

**Designer:** Robert Moore, JMP Golf Design

**Course Comment:** Lipa City has been dubbed the "Rome of the Philippines" because of the number of seminaries, convents, monasteries, retreat houses, and a famous cathedral that are located there.

The 27-hole layout of Mount Malarayat is set on a beautiful, rolling piece of terrain at a height of almost 1,200 feet above sea level. It is a site that offers captivating views of the Malarayat mountain range and an abundance of mango trees and coconut palms.

The well-regarded seventh hole of the Makulot nine is a downhill dogleg right, with three pot bunkers set in the hillside serving as the defining target from the elevated tee box. A long, meandering bunker guards the inside corner of the dogleg and must be carried to have a shot at the green in two, making a long fade the preferred shot off the tee. Getting home for a chance at an eagle putt is possible with two perfect shots, but danger abounds, even for those who lay up on the left side of the fairway for a much shorter approach.

The peninsula green juts into a small lake and is surrounded by four deep bunkers, with a stone wall across the water and extensive ornamental plantings providing a scenic backdrop. The putting surface slopes from left to right, meaning the farther right the pin position, the more frightening the target becomes. **KA**

**Course:** Butler National Golf Club

**Location:** Oakbrook, Illinois, USA

**Hole:** No. 7

**Length:** 623 yards

**Par:** 5

**Designer:** George Fazio, Tom Fazio

**Course Comment:** Some of the world's best players have played a round or two at Butler National Golf Club. And they've been impressed. No. 7 is among the toughest Butler offers.

## No. ❼ BUTLER NATIONAL GOLF CLUB

Considered one of the best courses in a state known for excellent golf, Butler National is mostly flat with tree-lined fairways, plenty of water and magnificent scenery. It doesn't get any prettier — or tougher — than the 623-yard par 5. This is not a typo. It plays 623 yards from the back tees so get out the heavy lumber on this hole. The seventh hole is a severe dogleg right with the Salt Creek running along the right side from tee to green. It even wraps around the back of the green so keep that ball retriever at the ready.

To have a shot at bending your second shot around the dogleg, you need to hit your tee shot at least 240 yards. Try and keep it to the left side of the fairway if you can. You also want to keep your second shot left. This is the biggest shot on this hole and it's important to keep it away from a giant willow tree that sits about 130 yards from the green along the right side. Your third shot is to a green with bunkers to the right side and left side. If you can make par on this hole consider yourself lucky. And good.

Butler National was once the host course for the PGA Tour's Western Open. **TJ**

**Course:** Hazeltine National Golf Club

**Location:** Chaska, Minnesota, USA

**Hole:** No. 7

**Length:** 542 yards

**Par:** 5

**Designer:** Robert Trent Jones Sr., Rees Jones

**Course Comment:** Hazeltine was site of the 2002 PGA Championship, the 84th staging of the tournament. The seventh hole is the shortest of Hazeltine's par 5s.

## No. ❼ HAZELTINE NATIONAL GOLF CLUB

The game of golf, as it is played today, has forced an evolution of sorts. Many of the great golf courses have had to be lengthened, or at least toughened up, in order to remain challenging. Nowhere is that idea more evident than at the 542-yard, seventh hole at Hazeltine.

"If you could look at how this hole used to play, it would surprise you," said Rees Jones, who did a redesign of his father's work before the 2002 PGA Championship. "Originally, there was a 90-degree angle at the turn, and it was a far different hole."

The seventh today is a far different hole than it was for the 1970 U.S. Open. The tee has been moved to the left to make the dogleg less severe, and the hole has been lengthened by 24 yards. Although there are no fairway bunkers on the hole, there are now hollows which pose a problem.

It is crucial to be in the fairway off the tee if you want to have a chance to go for the green in two. It is possible, but your second shot needs to avoid a large pond. There are bunkers opposite the pond, so precision — and length — are needed to reach the green in two.

Rees Jones added a bunker on the left side of the green, and the putting surface is long and follows parallel to the pond. This is a hole that can be birdied, even if you land in a greenside bunker. But, despite its relatively short length, eagles are scarce. **JB**

# Hole **8**

As you step to the eighth tee, you are almost halfway home. This is where the challenge can kick up again. Many designers want to present the sternest tests on holes 8–13.

The Oxfordshire in Thame, Oxfordshire, England, is a prime example of a devilish designer trying to catch a golfer looking ahead to the turn. It is only 380 yards, but is still very difficult and deceptive because of a lake and a 90-degree dogleg to a claustrophobic green.

The halfway house might be beckoning, but this is no time to look ahead — particularly if you are playing well.

**LEFT** *Ian Poulter of England plays a shot on the eighth hole at Emirates Golf Club, Dubai, United Arab Emirates.*

**Course:** Southport & Ainsdale Golf Club

**Location:** Southport, Merseyside, England

**Hole:** No. 8

**Length:** 157 yards

**Par:** 3

**Designer:** James Braid

**Course Comment:** The 1933 Ryder Cup at Southport & Ainsdale was the last that namesake Samuel Ryder would attend. He died in 1936.

# No. ❽ SOUTHPORT & AINSDALE GOLF CLUB

Set among the sand dunes and heathland of England's northwest coastline, Southport & Ainsdale Golf Club is not an incredibly long course at 6,687 yards, but its narrow fairways require plenty of strategy and accuracy right off the tee. The club traditionally has been one of the final British Open qualifying sites when the Open Championship comes to neighboring Royal Birkdale.

As with the rest of the layout, the length of the par-3 eighth hole isn't the problem. Holding the green is, as the plateau putting surface slopes from right to left, and is protected by mounds and bunkers. If you don't find the green with your first shot, getting up and down will be a true challenge for anyone.

Southport & Ainsdale played host to the 1933 and 1937 Ryder Cup matches, and at the time, was considered by many players to be Britain's toughest course.

Great Britain edged the United States 6 ½–5 ½ in a down-to-the-wire match in 1933, but the U.S. squad, captained by Walter Hagen and led by Sam Snead, Gene Sarazen, and Byron Nelson, won the last four matches in an 8–4 triumph in 1937, marking the first American Ryder Cup victory on British soil. **KA**

## No. ❽ BENAMOR

**Course:** Benamor

**Location:** The Algarve, Portugal

**Hole:** No. 8

**Length:** 213 yards

**Par:** 3

**Designer:** Sir Henry Cotton, Stuart Woodman

**Course Comment:** Benamor was the first course in the Eastern Algarve when it opened in 2000, although Cotton had laid out the course in 1980.

Benamor's eighth hole is one of two outstanding par 3s that make up this delightful, albeit short layout just near the town of Tavira. The other is the 187-yard 17th.

The eighth calls for a long iron or even a fairway wood to be played uphill to a green that is well protected. If the wind is blowing then a bogey here may actually be a good score.

The ideal shot is one that starts on the left-hand side of the green and fades back onto the putting surface. A cork tree guards the right-hand side of the green, and has to be safely negotiated to have any chance at all of making par.

However, a bunker protects the left-hand side of the green, so that any ball pulled slightly finds the sand.

The green is stepped and it's easy to see why more bad scores are posted at this hole than any other on the golf course. Even if you miss the putting surface, such are the subtleties of the green that you will probably be left with anything but a straightforward chip.

Players who can hit high long irons should do very well on this hole. Unfortunately most who play this hole will not have that shot in their arsenal. **AT**

## No. ❽ BALLYBUNION GOLF CLUB
### (OLD COURSE)

**Course:** Ballybunion Golf Club (Old Course)

**Location:** Ballybunion, County Kerry, Ireland

**Hole:** No. 8

**Length:** 155 yards

**Par:** 3

**Designer:** Tom Simpson, Molly Gourlay

**Course Comment:** Near the first tee at Ballybunion's Old Course rests an old graveyard. The regulars will say it's a warning to golfers who breeze through the first five holes only to then encounter the difficult challenges of No. 6, No. 8, No. 11, and No. 15.

"[Ballybunion] is a course that will test your patience," explains Tom Watson, with whom the Ballybunion track is a firm favorite. "It is not a course that favors one particular style of play over another, but one that simply rewards good play and good shots. For example, the 8th is only 155 yards and plays almost straight downhill, yet you must hit your shots within a 10 to 12 yard area or face a bogey . . . or double-bogey. In a wind, it's one of the most demanding shots I've ever faced. And that's the character of the course."

You can count the number of trees, and the human element has been kept off the golf course. In other words, why mess around with perfection? The course looks intimidating, yet it's a fair test of the great game. The contoured fairways and the tiny greens give Ballybunion a unique feel.

You must be on-line here. Accuracy is the key to success, especially on approach shots to such small targets.

Although overshadowed by the Old Course, the Cashen Course at Ballybunion, designed by Robert Trent Jones Sr., is also a world-class course which has a great reputation. **TJ**

**Course:** Royal Troon Golf Club
(Old Course)

**Location:** Troon, Ayrshire, Scotland

**Hole:** No. 8

**Length:** 129 yards

**Par:** 3

**Designer:** Willie Fernie, James Braid

**Course Comment:** In 1973, 41
years after winning the British
Open Championship at Royal Troon,
Gene Sarazen, 71, struck a perfect
5-iron to ace the eighth.

# No. ❽ ROYAL TROON GOLF CLUB
## (OLD COURSE)

It carries perhaps the most famous nickname of any hole in golf — Postage Stamp. So named because of the diminutive nature of its putting surface, there has been no small amount of drama at the eighth hole at Royal Troon's Old Course. The hole is just 129 yards, but its difficulty is immense when trying to hit a green that is just 25 feet at its widest point.

Toss in the wind changes and the absolute necessity of reaching the putting surface in one, and the shortest hole in the British Open rota also is one of the most lethal.

Dramatic would perhaps be the best way to describe Royal Troon, which last hosted the British Open in 1997. When the wind blows on the Old Course, strange things can happen on this classic undulating links, which is full of bumps and hollows and rated amongst the world's best. Founded in 1878 by 24 local enthusiasts, the course consisted of only five holes, but it rapidly grew in stature and hosted the Open Championship five times between 1923 and 1989. The British Opens at Royal Troon always seem to include moments among the event's most dramatic, and one of the classic Opens came in 1997 when Justin Leonard overcame Jesper Parnevik's five-shot lead to win by three strokes.

Speaking of drama, the eighth hole features plenty of it. One of the more famous quotes about the short but deadly hole calls it "the hardest stamp in the world to lick." It is a simple hole, architecturally, with the tops of two dunes shaved tight to create the tee and the green. There is no safety in between the dunes, with deep, thick native grasses filling every yard. A large dune guards the left side of the putting surface and a huge bunker sits to the right. Five bunkers circle the green, so there really is no option: you simply must hit the green.

Players have had varied reactions after playing the Old Course at Royal Troon — from awe and wonder when witnessing the course's beauty and brilliance, to dejection and disappointment after being beaten down by its difficulty. But perhaps the best description of the challenge comes from the club motto "Tam Arte Quam Marte," which means "as much by skill as by strength." **JB**

**BELOW AND OPPOSITE** *Two views of the eighth hole at Royal Troon.*

**Course:** Waialae Country Club

**Location:** Honolulu, Oahu, Hawaii, USA

**Hole:** No. 8

**Length:** 185 yards

**Par:** 3

**Designer:** Seth Raynor

**Course Comment:** Waialae was the site of the 2004 PGA Sony Open in Hawaii won by Ernie Els. You better know someone if you want to play here. The private club only allows guests to play if accompanied by a club member.

## No. ❽ WAIALAE COUNTRY CLUB

As you might expect in Hawaii, the views at Waialae Country Club are spectacular. That's simply a given, and the reason why there are so many memorable golf courses — and golf holes — in the Pacific playground.

Still, there are special places that are highlights. And Waialae Country Club is one of them. There also are special holes that stand out. And No. 8 is one of them.

Standing on the tee at No. 8 is something you will not soon forget. You might lose your ball on this 185-yard par 3 but you won't lose the memory of looking out over the mighty Pacific.

Look to the right and see the mountains. Look left and watch the swimmers and fisherman enjoying the ocean. Look straight ahead and see the challenge of landing your tee shot on the green.

There is a little mountain stream that intersects the fairway about 100 yards out — it shouldn't come into play but certainly adds to the view. The green has one big sand trap on the left side, another trap on the right, and a few others that circle around the back.

On normal days, the wind comes off the mountains moving right to left and actually is an advantage to the golfer. **TJ**

## No. 8  KILSPINDIE GOLF CLUB

**Course:** Kilspindie Golf Club

**Location:** East Lothian, Scotland

**Hole:** No. 8

**Length:** 162 yards

**Par:** 3

**Designer:** Willie Park

**Course Comment:** The land on which Kilspindie is built is virtually void of any landmarks other than the Firth of Forth and Gullane Hill, which makes No. 8 such a vivid contrast to its sister hole, the 17th at Cabo del Sol in Mexico which is situated between towering mountains and the deep blue waters of the Sea of Cortez.

It is an astounding age in which we live when 300-yard drives are shrugged off as the norm and conventional wisdom dictates that length is par's primary defender.

Consider the 2005 PGA Championship at Baltusrol and its cross-country par-5 17th that will play to an extended 647 yards. And, of course, New York's Bethpage Black proved to be a brutish test at 7,214 yards for the 2002 U.S. Open, even for the game's most prodigious hitters.

Lost somewhere in this distance dementia is the subtle simplicity of short. Simply put, less is more and few layouts in the world prove this like Kilspindie Golf Club.

As clever a layout as one could concoct, Kilspindie plays to a curt 5,500 yards and features seven par 4s that weigh in under 300 yards. Five of these holes play predominantly downwind.

To master Kilspindie a player needs skill and strategy, not strength.

The par-3 eighth, for example, requires little more than an 8-iron for most players at 160 yards, yet a par on this hole is akin to winning a long drive contest.

The tee shot is across Gosford Bay to a putting surface devilishly circled by bunkers and thick rough. The prevailing right-to-left wind demands a daring tee shot over the water, and bailing out to the left leaves little chance for a par save. **RH**

## No. 8  HORIZONS GOLF RESORT

**Course:** Horizons Golf Resort

**Location:** Port Stephens, New South Wales, Australia

**Hole:** No.8

**Length:** 168 yards

**Par:** 3

**Designer:** Graham Marsh, Ross Watson

**Course Comment:** Horizons has hosted three of Australia's most prestigious golfing tournaments: the 2002 NSW Open, the 2002 and 2003 ALPG Players' Championship, and the 2004 ANZ Championship.

Laid out near the popular vacation town of Port Stephens, this parklands course features man-made lakes, stretches of marshland, and fairways lined with tea trees, with most holes separated from each other by different vegetation and hazards. The idea, according to the architects, is to give Horizons a feel of memorable, individual holes, and the sort of experience resort guests expect and want. Horizons counts its par-3 eighth as perhaps the most popular hole on the course.

The smallish, two-tiered green is surrounded by wetlands, which grow thickly and also run along the right side of the putting surface, posing an intimidating lateral hazard to anyone pushing his ball in that direction.

Come up short with your tee shot, and your ball will likely be engulfed by the sinister bunkering in front, and there is out-of-bounds on the left for anyone who comes over the top a bit too strongly. **JS**

**Course:** Pronghorn Club & Resort (Fazio Course)

**Location:** Bend, Oregon, USA

**Hole:** No. 8

**Length:** 187 yards

**Par:** 3

**Designer:** Tom Fazio

**Course Comment:** When the Tom Fazio design was added to Pronghorn in 2006, which already offered a Jack Nicklaus course (2004), Pronghorn became the second club in the world to have a Nicklaus and Fazio course at the same location. Carlton Woods, located north of Houston, Texas, is the other.

# No. ❽ PRONGHORN CLUB & RESORT
## (FAZIO COURSE)

Pronghorn's lava tube — one of the most intriguing architectural features you will see in golf and the personality of the entire eighth hole — was discovered accidentally after the desert between the tee and the green was dynamited to create a tunnel through which to play — some might say, an example of explosive good luck.

Fazio took brilliant advantage of the lava rock walls that form the tube. He used them to create the frame beneath the eighth green. Toss in a 45-foot canyon on the hole and 25-foot walls surrounding the green, and the result is an unforgettable sight. It creates one of the best par-3 settings ever.

Pronghorn is the first Fazio course in Oregon, and he created a very challenging test in the 7,456-yard gem that brings out the best of the inherent beauty that comes with a central Oregon setting. We have already spoken of the lava rock outcroppings. And where did that lava come from, you ask? Just look into the distance at Pronghorn.

Those brilliant views include Mount Bachelor, Broken Top, and Three Sisters volcanoes — just a few more examples of explosive good fortune. **JB**

**Course:** Bandon Dunes (Old Macdonald Course)

**Location:** Bandon, Oregon, USA

**Hole:** No. 8

**Length:** 181 yards

**Par:** 3

**Designer:** Tom Doak, Jim Urbina

**Course Comment:** Doak and Urbina drew a touch of design inspiration for Old Macdonald No. 8 from the ninth hole at The Course at Yale and from No. 9 at Piping Rock Golf Club.

# No. ❽ BANDON DUNES
## (OLD MACDONALD COURSE)

Perhaps the best way to understand the challenge that awaits at No. 8 at Bandon Dunes' Old Macdonald Course is to examine the name of the hole. The 2010-designed No. 8 is known on the scorecard as Biarritz.

A Biarritz green features a deep gully bisecting its middle, and the name comes from La Phare Course in France, where the original Biarritz green was constructed (as an aside, that green no longer exists).

When standing on the tee at Macdonald's splendor-filled No. 8, soaking in the scenery and contemplating strategy are foremost in the consciousness, but don't forget that the gully awaits 181 yards away. The hole plays from an elevated tee that offers a wonderful view of several parts of the course as well as the ocean, and it also gives plenty for the eye to take in as far as the green is concerned. The best shots will be played on a low trajectory, landing short of the gully and going through to the back of the green.

Then, of course, comes the need for a two-putt. The flat stick and the gully must go head to head. And more often than not, the putter, unfortunately, has a very difficult task winning the battle. **JB**

**Course:** Moon Palace Golf & Spa Resort (Lakes Course)

**Location:** Cancun, Quintana Roo, Mexico

**Hole:** No. 8

**Length:** 150 yards

**Par:** 3

**Designer:** Jack Nicklaus

**Course Comment:** This 27-hole facility is played mostly by tourists, but it can be beefed up for tournament play. It has been host to the Mexican Open on more than one occasion.

## No. ❽ MOON PALACE GOLF & SPA RESORT (LAKES COURSE)

Jack Nicklaus recognized the natural beauty that surrounds the property he had to work with, and he wanted to come up with something special for the golf course. He did, for both tourists and low handicappers alike.

Yes, it's a tourist course, and yes, the Lakes Course is shorter and more forgiving than the Jungle and Dunes courses at Moon Palace. But No. 3 is the signature hole of the property, and the staff got it absolutely right.

The tee shot is definitely beautiful and challenging in that it plays to an island green. A rock wall surrounds the putting surface, which elevates it some 30 feet from the man-made lake. The green is plenty large at more than 6,500 square feet, so a pure tee shot can find home with little problem. But something about an island green can strike some shaky nerves, even in a shot that is just 150 yards.

No. 8 is a microcosm of the rest of Moon Palace. It is a beautifully manicured hole that is fun to play. The fairways are friendly and the front tees make for an enjoyable round while the back tees can make it a tougher round for low handicappers.

This way, the high amount of tourists who play the course can be accommodated, regardless of their handicap. **JB**

**Course:** Capital Golf Club

**Location:** Melbourne, Victoria, Australia

**Hole:** No. 8

**Length:** 208 yards

**Par:** 3

**Designer:** Peter Thomson, Michael Wolveridge, Ross Perrett, Lloyd Williams

**Course Comment:** Watch the water carry on the tee shot for this hole, which has undergone a significant facelift since its opening, with a handful of small bunkers bordering the peninsula green being converted into a sandy wasteland.

## No. ❽ CAPITAL GOLF CLUB

Hailed by Michael Wolveridge as "the best kept secret in Australian golf," Capital Golf Club is a sight to behold, for the select few privileged enough to witness it. Opened in 1997, the club boasts the most luxurious amenities in the whole country, and to say that the tees, fairways, and greens are smooth as velvet would be an understatement.

The view from the tee of this hole at Capital Golf Club, which is built on a 300-acre site, is both pleasing and terrifying.

Stretching beyond the water hazard is a waste area that is framed by stands of kangaroo grass, with the green behind (put your drive in there, and you have a brutal recovery shot and an almost certain bogey). The pin is often placed behind the green-side bunkers on the right, making birdies under these conditions exceedingly difficult. Wind can create enormous problems for players as well, and clubbing becomes a crucial consideration.

Shots that come up short usually fall into the waste area, and if they are long, they will fly the green and tumble down the slope beyond the putting surface and into the water that cuts behind. **JS**

**Course:** Chateau Whistler

**Location:** Whistler, British Columbia, Canada

**Hole:** No. 8

**Length:** 212 yards

**Par:** 3

**Designer:** Robert Trent Jones Jr.

**Course Comment:** Located at the base of Blackcomb and Whistler mountains, two of the more popular ski hills in Canada, Chateau Whistler is a unique layout with many glacier-fed springs and especially rugged mountain terrain.

# No. ❽  CHATEAU WHISTLER

With all due respect to Robert Trent Jones Jr., he didn't design this golf course. A much higher power moved the earth at Chateau Whistler. Jones might have provided the fairways and putting surfaces, but the beauty of this upscale resort was around long before anyone started moving dirt.

Opened in 1993, the par-72, 18-hole course features elevation changes of more than 400 feet.

The signature hole is the 212-yard, par-3 eighth. Before teeing off on this hole where challenge and beauty play a duet, see what the course pros say: "Take pride in any pars or birdies here. Safe bet is to play to the middle of the green. Good luck."

When the hosts wish you luck, you know you are in for a challenge. This hole requires an elevated tee shot with rocks on the right and behind, and a large pond that runs from the left side all the way around to the front. Just in case you barely clear the pond, there is a bunker between the left front and the water.

If you can land the green, you are in good shape. Jones showed some mercy by creating a relatively flat green. **TJ**

**Course:** Uplands Golf Club

**Location:** Thornhill, Ontario, Canada

**Hole:** No. 8

**Length:** 232 yards

**Par:** 3

**Designer:** Stanley Thompson

**Course Comment:** Uplands first opened in 1922 as an 18-hole private course, but became a nine-hole gem in 1989, when nine of its holes were lost to urban development.

## No. ❽  UPLANDS GOLF CLUB

You don't hear much talk of fairways on par-3 holes, but many players will need it on the eighth hole at Uplands Golf Club, long considered one of the most challenging holes in Canada. This marvelous test requires both length and precision off the tee, which sits 60 feet above the narrow chute of a fairway that is set in a valley surrounded by thick woods and a stream that runs along the entire left side. The green sits 15 feet above the fairway, and shots coming up just short will find a difficult chip from the steep hill leading to the putting surface.

If you're confident in your ability to reach the green, hit a long draw to the hill on the right side and let the ball funnel to the middle of the flat putting surface. But beware: There's little margin for error.

Otherwise, the smart play is to a slightly wider landing area in front of the steep slope to the green, offering at least a chance to get up and down. And if not, take solace: on this hole, there are worse scores than a 4. **KA**

## No. **8**  THE HEATHERS CLUB

**Course:** The Heathers Club

**Location:** Bloomfield Hills, Michigan, USA

**Hole:** No. 8

**Length:** 350 yards

**Par:** 4

**Designer:** Bill Newcomb

**Course Comment:** From the eighth hole you can see some old trees that have fallen in the lake over the years. Turtles have made these trees their home. The pro shop host says you can see as many as 30 turtles at one time all lined up on the trees.

This is a private nine-hole course in the wealthy community of Bloomfield Hills, a suburb of Detroit in Oakland County. Don't be fooled by the lack of a back nine. These nine can play with anybody.

And No. 8 is at the top of the list.

Standing on the tee you're looking at what they like to call a reverse pyramid. The further you hit the ball the more of the fairway you will find. So this hole certainly rewards the bigger hitters. It's about 210 yards to the middle of the pyramid.

On the left side of the pyramid is a berm. To the right of this very scenic hole is a large lake, and golfers can usually see a large variety of birdlife.

There are two ways to reach the green in two shots. One is to play the cart path on your second shot. The more advisable way is to hit your second shot and nail the green. But watch out.

There is a pot bunker in front of the green. And a sand trap behind the green. So you better be accurate or you might be sitting with the turtles. **TJ**

## No. **8**  RATTLE RUN GOLF COURSE

**Course:** Rattle Run Golf Course

**Location:** St. Clair, Michigan, USA

**Hole:** No. 8

**Par:** 4

**Length:** 360 yards

**Designer:** Lou Powers

**Course Comment:** Opened in 1977, Rattle Run will leave you with two lasting impressions. The first is that the course plays more like a northern Michigan course than one in southeastern Michigan. Second, there are no gimmies here. Every hole is tough.

Rattle Run has earned a reputation as being one of the toughest courses in Southeastern Michigan. If you want a challenge, make a tee time here and you will be in for the round of your life.

The first mistake you can make is to believe what those in the know say about this 360-yard par 4. For example, here is the advice from the course pros: "avoid the trees on the right side and this hole plays easy." Nothing comes easy at Rattle Run.

From the back tees, you need a drive of about 253 yards to give yourself a good shot at the green of this very sharp dogleg right. Of course, if you are playing from the back tees you should be able to hit a drive 253 yards. But you better hit it straight.

If you go too far, you can drive it right through the fairway. Too short, though, and forget the green in two.

The fairway is pretty narrow with trees lining both sides. The pros are right in that you don't want to go right. Playing out of those trees is certain to cause trouble.

If you don't think this is a tough course, check out the stat book. Rattle Run has 78 bunkers, tight tree-lined fairways, and water on 15 of the 18 holes. **TJ**

# No. ❽ THE OXFORDSHIRE GOLF CLUB

The Oxfordshire Golf Club is set in the rolling English countryside near the historic university town of Oxford. The American-style parkland course, designed by Rees Jones, opened in 1993.

The unique par-4 eighth hole, a dogleg right around a huge lake, requires both finesse and accuracy. The tee shot must avoid the water on the right and find a fairway that narrows considerably at the preferred landing area. There's not much bail-out room on the left either, as a group of mounds and bunkers wait just to the left of the fairway at the outside corner of the hole's dogleg, which makes a sharp turn to the peninsula green that juts out into the lake.

The putting surface slopes from back to front, so make sure to keep your second shot below the hole in order to have any chance at birdie. Come up short, long, or right and your ball could find the water.

In its four years at The Oxfordshire, the PGA European Tour's Benson and Hedges International Open produced a most worthy group of champions, including greats such as Bernhard Langer (1997), Darren Clarke (1998), and Colin Montgomerie (1999). **KA**

## No. ⑧ CLUSTERED SPIRES GOLF COURSE

**Course:** Clustered Spires Golf Course

**Location:** Frederick, Maryland, USA

**Hole:** No. 8

**Par:** 4

**Length:** 414 yards

**Designer:** Ault, Clark & Associates

**Course Comment:** The course, laid out upon 200 acres of rolling hillsides, was built by the City of Frederick for its residents. But everyone is welcome and it won't take long to discover how lucky golfers in Frederick are.

Officials at Clustered Spires are very proud of their golf course. And they should be. But while the land, design, and execution are first rate, it's the extra touches that really add a little zip to their game.

Take No. 8 for example. There used to be a time when you had a great view of the Monocacy River from the tee box. But overgrowth changed that. Get your camera out. The good people at Clustered Spires have done a little clearing out to once again give you a view of the scenic river.

Okay, back to golf.

The fairway on this 414-yard par 4 is lined with trees (and out-of-bounds) to the right. There is a fairway bunker along the left side that acts as a perfect target. No, you don't want to hit in there. You want to clear it — and that will require about 250 yards off the back tees. It's 225 yards to the front of the bunker.

The fairway slopes left to right so your tee shot should filter down to the middle of the green if you can fly the bunkers.

Your second shot is to a two-tiered green well protected by a green-side bunker on the right. The most difficult pin placement would be back right because of the slope of the green. **TJ**

## No. ⑧ SHENANDOAH GOLF COURSE

**Course:** Shenandoah Golf Course

**Location:** West Bloomfield, Michigan, USA

**Hole:** No. 8

**Length:** 335 yards

**Par:** 4

**Designer:** Bruce Matthews

**Course Comment:** This beautiful public course in the upscale Detroit suburb of West Bloomfield was built on rolling hills, so you should expect plenty of uneven lies. Large and old maple and oak trees line many of the fairways.

Shenandoah has plenty of tough holes and plenty of scenic holes. This 335-yard eighth hole is more scenic than tough, but you better hit a good tee shot or all of that could change.

A half dogleg to the right, No. 8 has water to worry about on the right and trees on the left. Let's first worry about the water.

At about 180 yards out from the back tees, there is water that comes into play along the right side. The water will continue all the way up to the green so get used to seeing it.

On the left, there is a hillside with plenty of trees and underbrush. Your ideal tee shot is on the left side, but not too far left or you will be swinging from those trees.

The tee shot sets everything up on this hole. Hit a good one, and you are more than halfway home.

The green does have some problems. There are deep bunkers on both sides of the green, which also features a severe slope. So three-putts are certainly possible.

Play this smart and you should at least earn a par. But remember, trouble lurks. And enjoy the view. **TJ**

**Course:** Noordwijkse Golf Club

**Location:** Noordwijk, Holland

**Hole:** No. 8

**Length:** 406 yards

**Par:** 4

**Designer:** Frank Pennink

**Course Comment:** Noordwijkse is one of three magnificent links courses — resting in between Royal The Hague and Kennemer — located along Holland's North Sea coast between Amsterdam and The Hague.

BELOW *The eighth hole at Noordwijkse.*

OPPOSITE *Padraig Harrington of Ireland plays a shot on the eighth hole at Noordwijkse, July 2001.*

The Noordwijkse Golf Club was founded in 1915, but its original nine-hole course was given up for development in 1971 as the seaside resort of Noordwijk was expanded. The club moved to another site located a few miles away along the North Sea coast, and the dramatic Frank Pennink-designed layout opened in 1972. The move was a good one for members, as portions of the course wind through high sand dunes alongside the North Sea, and the layout is considered one of the best in Continental Europe.

The par-4 eighth hole brings golfers back to the coastal links land after a stretch of several holes through an inland forest, and it features a tee shot to a narrow, heather-lined fairway that twists through the undulating dunes. That leaves a tricky approach to a putting surface that is protected by mounds and several deep pot bunkers, with stiff ocean breezes almost always a factor.

Noordwijkse played host to the PGA European Tour's Dutch Open on nine occasions from 1978 to 2001, producing a Who's Who of golf greats as champions, including Graham Marsh (1979, 1985), Seve Ballesteros (1986), Payne Stewart (1991), Bernhard Langer (1992, 2001), and Colin Montgomerie (1993). **KA**

**Course:** Pebble Beach Golf Links

**Location:** Pebble Beach, California, USA

**Hole:** No. 8

**Length:** 416 yards

**Par:** 4

**Designer:** Jack Neville, Douglas Grant

**Course Comment:** Golf course designers often talk about "shot value" in their design. This is the degree of difficulty of the execution one faces standing at the tee. No. 8 at Pebble Beach is as good as it gets when designers talk of "shot value."

**BELOW** *The eighth hole at Pebble Beach.*

**OPPOSITE** *Jack Nicklaus hits a shot on the eighth hole at Pebble Beach, February 1993.*

# No. ❽ PEBBLE BEACH GOLF LINKS

The eighth at Pebble Beach is a lot of things. Famous. Dangerous. Beautiful. And those are just the beginning.

The 416-yard par 4 features a second shot played off a 100-foot cliff over the Pacific Ocean. With a tee shot up a small hill and a mid- to long-iron second with a carry over fairway, cliff, sea, and sand, there are few golf holes in the world more picturesquely difficult than right here.

The pros, who usually aim at one of two chimneys on a mansion on the hill, often take a 3-wood off the tee. Players lay up in front of the chasm where the ocean cuts into the fairway, then launch over the gorgeous blue water on what Jack Nicklaus calls his "favorite second shot in golf."

Nicklaus learned early in his career that the first shot is also important. In the fourth round of the 1961 U.S. Amateur, Nicklaus played his 3-wood, and even that was too much club. Since it was match play, all he lost were his ball and the hole — although he ended up winning both the match and the whole tournament.

The greens at Pebble Beach Links are typically small, and this one is no exception. It's 20 yards deep through on the left and only 23 yards through on the back right. This is a classic hole so don't be concerned about your scorecard. Worry more about your camera. **TJ**

## No. ❽ AGILE GOLF & COUNTRY CLUB (SOUTH COURSE)

**Course:** Agile Golf & Country Club (South Course)

**Location:** Zhuhai, Guangdong, China

**Hole:** No. 8

**Length:** 472 yards

**Par:** 4

**Designer:** JMP Design Group

**Course Comment:** This is a hole with plenty of choices. Risk-reward (not to mention a split fairway) awaits one of the best holes in China.

There is a tendency to think of the eighth hole on Agile's South Course as a touch schizophrenic. Off the tee, it can offer either a nice, comfortable shot to the right, or a narrow, risky endeavor to the left. Okay, maybe the label of split personality is a little harsh. But that split fairway sure raises an eyebrow or two.

Whichever way you elect to play the hole, whether it be to safety or tucked between a river along the left and a group of trees that splits the fairway, the view from the elevated tees overlooking the fairway and into the mountains is spectacular.

The eighth hole is built on rolling and sometimes rugged mountain terrain, and this influences bounces on the fairway. No. 8 isn't quite as severe as the slope on other holes, where there are massive swings to left or right. The terrain poses an immense challenge to even the best players, and it isn't made any easier by the tricky and sometimes tight fairways. Such is the case on No. 8: tight on the left, tricky in the middle, and safe on the right (providing you can get there).

The eighth is among the more entertaining on the course. No matter which route you take off the tee, you are left with an elevated look at your approach. It is one of the many opportunities for vista watching. And the green on No. 8 is in excellent shape, as are all of the putting surfaces.

The South Course is also adjacent to the Chang Jiang reservoir, one of the most scenic locations in Zongshan. **JB**

## No. ❽ LESLIE PARK

**Course:** Leslie Park

**Location:** Ann Arbor, Michigan, USA

**Hole:** No. 8

**Length:** 355 yards

**Par:** 4

**Designer:** Edward Lawrence Packer

**Course Comment:** This scenic course has many beautiful mature Austrian pine trees lining the fairways. The course was built on hilly terrain and is one of two city-owned courses.

The course opened in 1968 and is one of the hidden gems in a crowded area of great golf courses. In 1995, Arthur Hills was brought in to make some improvements, including making changes on No. 8.

You better keep your tee shot well on the fairway. To the right is a pear orchard. Not a great place to be unless you are making a fruit salad. There is a wooded out-of-bounds area on the other side of the fairway.

From a slightly elevated tee you are hitting downward to a fairway that slants to the left toward the pond. Oh, forgot to mention the pond. The pond is on the left about 230 yards from the back tees.

The water extends to the green. Just thought you should know that, too.

The green doesn't have as much slope as others on the course, but the eighth is certainly one of the prettier holes at Leslie Park.

The signature hole at Leslie Park is actually the par-5 11th hole. No. 11 is tough and very popular, so it's worth knowing that you get two outstanding holes at Leslie Park. **TJ**

**Course:** Prairie Dunes Country Club

**Location:** Hutchinson, Kansas, USA

**Hole:** No. 8

**Length:** 430 yards

**Par:** 4

**Designer:** Perry Maxwell

**Course Comment:** Prairie Dunes plays host to the 2006 U.S. Senior Open. It also has staged the U.S. Women's Amateur, the Curtis Cup matches, the U.S. Mid-Amateur, and the U.S. Women's Open.

# No. ❽  PRAIRIE DUNES COUNTRY CLUB

Perry Maxwell, the legendary American course architect, believed that the land makes the golf course. As he was in the preparation stages at Prairie Dunes Country Club, he was quoted as saying "the golf course should be there, not brought there." In 1936, Maxwell walked the 480-acre site for weeks before deciding where and how to begin the construction. After his first look at the land, he said, "there are 118 golf holes here . . . and all I have to do is eliminate 100."

Thankfully, the eighth hole made the cut at this linksland-style golf course in the middle of the prairie. Not that there was ever any doubt that No. 8 was a keeper. It is the most publicized hole at Prairie Dunes, and the dogleg right that weaves in and around a handful of dunes is a microcosm of the rest of the course. It is an uphill climb from tee to green, each dune taller and more perilous than the last, and by the time a player reaches the putting surface he most certainly feels like he's walked far more than 430 yards.

Prairie Dunes' eighth hole also contains a feature that became a staple at many of the 70-plus courses designed by Maxwell — two-tiered, undulating greens. The undulations are obvious from far back on the fairway, but it behoves a player not to get ahead of himself. In order to reach the slope-laden surface, the approach must steer clear of five bunkers around the green. And, lest a player be too brave, there is grass behind the green as thick as it is penal.

No. 8 is the signature at Prairie Dunes, and that's saying something because the layout is filled with gems. Here is what some of the greats of the game of golf have said about the Kansas track:

"A touch of Scotland in the land of Oz" — the words of Tom Watson, a native of Kansas.

"This is golf of the first order" — PGA Tour player Ben Crenshaw.

"You'd have to get to heaven to play on a course this fine" — Judy Bell, the only woman ever to have served as president of the U.S. Golf Association.

The land of Oz . . . A mention of heaven . . . You get the idea. This is a paradise of a golf course, and the eighth is an other-worldly hole. **JB**

**Course:** Emirates Golf Club (Majlis Course)

**Location:** Dubai, United Arab Emirates

**Hole:** No. 8

**Length:** 434 yards

**Par:** 4

**Designer:** Karl Litten

**Course Comment:** Emirates Golf Club was the first all-grass championship golf course in the Gulf region, way back in 1988.

BELOW *Ian Poulter of England plays out of the scrub on the eighth hole at Emirates, March 2004.*

OPPOSITE *Gary Evans of England plays a shot on the eighth hole at Emirates, March 2004.*

# No. ❽ EMIRATES GOLF CLUB
## (MAJLIS COURSE)

The first grass course in the Middle East and a favorite venue of the PGA European Tour event, The Dubai Desert Classic, Emirates has become one of the popular places to play for the world's top players. Especially Ernie Els, who holds the course record with a 61.

Opened in 1988, one of the most prominent features on the course is the Majlis building itself, positioned between the eighth and ninth holes.

And one of the most prominent, attractive, and certainly memorable holes on the golf course is No. 8. This 434-yard par 4 retains much of the character of the desert and is a true test of one's golf game.

The third toughest hole on the course according to the scorecard, the fairway of the eighth bends to the right, setting up a nice shot for those who like a little slice off the tee. The fairway also heads uphill quickly with the big desert acting like a giant sand trap catching those hitters trying to cut a little too much off their dogleg. From the fairway, only the very front section of the green is visible. And the green is protected so accuracy is key. The slope and wind further make club selection very important. **TJ**

## No. ⑧   CHERRY CREEK

**Course:** Cherry Creek

**Location:** Shelby Township, Michigan, USA

**Hole:** No. 8

**Length:** 318 yards

**Par:** 4

**Designer:** Lanny Wadkins, Mike Bylen

**Course Comment:** This is a challenging course to all players with four sets of tees measuring from 5,012 to 6,784 yards with gentle rolling terrain, and a variety of oak, ash, and cherry trees.

Cherry Creek is another of many outstanding golf courses in southeastern Michigan. And No. 8 is one great view and challenge all rolled into one.

The 318-yard par 4 is a dogleg left with thick dense trees lining the fairway. There is some room on the fairway, so take your best shot. The tee box is set behind one of two marshes you are going to have to carry. You want to hit it off the tee about 210 yards to clear the marshes.

About 80 to 100 yards from the green is a set of bunkers on the right side. There also are bunkers on the left side of the fairway.

If you want to make this hole a little less challenging, you can play the green tees which require you to clear just one marsh. Of course challenges are why many people play the game.

Once you've cleared the marshes, you haven't cleared all the trouble. The green is tucked back in the corner with two bunkers, one along the right side and one closer to the front. The green is a two-tiered design with a ridge running through it.

This is a scenic and difficult hole on a first-rate golf course. **TJ**

# No. ❽ GARY PLAYER COUNTRY CLUB

Continually ranked the best golf course in South Africa, the Gary Player Golf Course didn't raise the bar for golf in South Africa, but set the standard.

Talk about your challenges. This course has that and then some. Don't be fooled by the amazing scenery or the excellent conditions or the first-class resort. This par-72 layout has often been rated the best in South Africa. That could be debated.

What's difficult to argue is that the Gary Player Country Club is one of the most demanding tests of golf to be found anywhere — in South Africa or the world.

The par-4 eighth, in particular, is a perfect example of how tough the course plays. The 431-yard hole has come under criticism in the past. Some professionals dislike the semi-blind tee shot. They also aren't thrilled with the clover-leafed green, which makes a second shot, which can range from a 4-iron to a 7-iron depending on the wind, a tough shot to say the least.

At over 7,000 yards from the back tees and with the harsh African sun beating down on you, a good long game and plenty of patience is required.

It is arguably the most famous course in South Africa and has hosted the Nedbank Million Dollar Golf Challenge. Past champions include inaugural winner Johnny Miller, Seve Ballesteros, Bernhard Langer, Ian Woosnam, David Frost, Nick Price, Nick Faldo, Colin Montgomerie, Ernie Els and Sergio Garcia.

The fairways are kikuyu grass. In 1996, U.S. Open champion Steve Jones said the fairways were the best he'd ever played on. **TJ**

**No. ❽  CARNEGIE CLUB AT SKIBO CASTLE**

**Course:** Carnegie Club at Skibo Castle

**Location:** Dornoch, Sutherland, Scotland

**Hole:** No. 8

**Length:** 450 yards

**Par:** 4

**Designer:** Donald Steel

**Course Comment:** Although Andrew Carnegie commissioned John Sutherland to build the original links at Skibo Castle in 1883 he played most of his golf at nearby Royal Dornoch. In 1991, Donald Steel rebuilt Carnegie Club on the site of the original course.

Compared to its aged brethren, Carnegie Club is a babe in an old-growth forest. An infant mingling in an elderly crowd.

Located just four miles from venerable Royal Dornoch Golf Club there is nothing easy about being the new kid on this block.

The mistake, of course, is to dismiss the Donald Steel design as novel or even contrived. Without a century's worth of play what could a newcomer bring to the cradle of golf?

The answer is a wonderful and varied layout. A course that weaves its way through marsh and along Dornoch Firth and includes an inspiring mix of long and short, dramatic and subtle.

Like every Scottish links, at its core Carnegie Club is about the wind. Depending on the breeze's direction and strength, the par-4 eighth may play as a gambling, go-for-broke hole that tempts the player to cut across Loch Evelix. Into the wind and low, boring shots are the staple, and par is something to be savored.

The hole bends to the right around the Loch with the best line to the green from the right side of the fairway. Although more conservative, tee shots to far left bring bunkers on the left of the green into play. The putting surface was designed to receive a low, running shot under the wind. **RH**

**Course:** Tangle Ridge Golf Club

**Location:** Grand Prairie, Texas, USA

**Hole:** No. 8

**Length:** 575 yards

**Par:** 5

**Designer:** Jeff Brauer

**Course Comment:** This course was built on rolling terrain and is highlighted by several changes in elevation. Even though the fairways are lined with thick brush and trees, they still afford generous landing areas.

OPPOSITE *The eighth hole at Tangle Ridge.*

## No. ❽ TANGLE RIDGE GOLF CLUB

Considered one of the top public courses in the U.S., the layout has the feel of the Texas hill country with dramatic elevation changes, gently rolling hills and sand bunkers standing guard on every hole.

The 575-yard eighth hole is one of the toughest on the golf course and that's not taking into account the wind — which you almost always will have to take into account. A creek, which crosses the fairway right in the middle, can't be reached on the downhill tee shot without a big north wind at your back. The same creek comes into play on your uphill second shot. So don't go left.

There is also trouble on the right, including the driving range. Don't play the ball with the stripe if you hit it over there.

Your landing area is pretty small for the important second shot, but don't leave yourself too short. You are going to need — not want — to get as close as possible for your shot to the uphill green. A steep bank which falls into a pond guards the front of the green, while a group of trees sits to the right. Severe slopes behind the green could bring a long shot back onto the green, which is built atop two large mounds. **TJ**

**Course:** The Links at Challedon

**Location:** Mount Airy, Maryland, USA

**Hole:** No. 8

**Length:** 537 yards

**Par:** 5

**Designer:** Brian Ault

**Course Comment:** Opened in June 1996, this link-style course with native fescue grass surrounding Challedon hosts more than 175 charity and corporate events.

## No. ❽ THE LINKS AT CHALLEDON

It's a nice look standing on the eighth tee at the Links at Challedon. There are houses along the right side of the fairway and some in the background. This also is a fun hole to play — and as the fourth handicap, a difficult hole to play indeed.

The green is off to the right side and you have a somewhat blind tee shot. Your best play is straight. The fairway slopes left to right, so keep that in mind. Also keep in mind that you can reach this hole in two shots, but you have to have plenty of confidence in your game.

On the right side of the fairway is a mound with tall, natural fescue. You will find plenty of that along your travels at Challedon. On the left side is the cart path and an incline leading to more natural fescue about four yards from the cart path. The fescue is much better to look at than to hit out of.

If you hit a good tee shot, take a good look at going for the green in two. But take a closer look at all the water you have to carry. There isn't much room for error. If you are short, there is a bunker ready for you between green and the pond.

There is also a landing area about 100 yards from the green to aim for if you decide to lay up.

The green is tough. There are two different levels with a two-foot high ridge to the back level. **TJ**

**Course:** Crystal Downs Country Club

**Location:** Frankfort, Michigan, USA

**Hole:** No. 8

**Length:** 550 yards

**Par:** 5

**Designer:** Alister MacKenzie, Perry Maxwell

**Course Comment:** A small pond at No. 8 is the only water hazard that comes into play at Crystal Downs.

# No. ❽ CRYSTAL DOWNS COUNTRY CLUB

When talking about Crystal Downs, the discussion begins with the greens. Their speed, their slope, and their challenge. The eighth green proves that the sloping, glassy surfaces are troublesome even while your putter remains in your bag.

The green at No. 8, if approached from the left side, offers a terrible angle that threatens to feed weak approaches right back toward the golfer. This can be avoided when approaching from the right.

But, we're getting ahead of ourselves. There are 550 yards of hole to consider before you make it to the undulating green. This par 5 tumbles and doglegs right up a hill to a green placed on a ledge. Its roller-coaster fairway is difficult from start to finish, and every contour must be considered when deciding where to place both your first and second shot. Even when landing the ball in the proper spot, you are virtually assured of an uneven lie.

If the golfer can place his second shot long down the right side of the fairway, he is rewarded with an approach more on the same level as the green. From the left side, the approach shot is both distinctively more uphill and from a worse angle. Any weak approach shot to this green is guaranteed to roll 10 to 20 yards back toward the golfer.

The green's challenges become even more distinct if a player's approach goes beyond the hole. Then there is the very real possibility of the first putt traveling right off the putting surface. If your approach is too weak, then you might roll down the slope. If it is too strong, you might roll off the slope on your putt. There is no easy way to negotiate the green at No. 8.

The greens are what grab all the attention at Crystal Downs, but there is much more to talk about at this inspiring locale — the view of Lake Michigan from the bluff, the English-style clubhouse, distinctive bunkers, and tricky rough. All are Crystal Downs trademarks, and the eighth hole incorporates many of the characteristics into its lumpy ride to a stunning conclusion.

When Crystal Downs was completed and opened in 1933, many considered the eighth hole to be the best par 5 created by either the famed Perry Maxwell or Alister MacKenzie, who collaborated on this Michigan project. To this day, that still might be true. **JB**

**Course:** Predator Ridge Golf Resort (Peregrine Course)

**Location:** Vernon, British Columbia, Canada

**Hole:** No. 8

**Length:** 510 yards

**Par:** 5

**Designer:** Les Furber

**Course Comment:** Predator Ridge resort features three first-rate and very different nine-hole courses: The Opsrey, The Peregrine, and The Red Tail. Each nine ranges in length some 2,600 yards to over 3,500 yards so you can pick the tees to match your game.

# No. ❽ PREDATOR RIDGE GOLF RESORT (PEREGRINE COURSE)

Visiting the Okanagan Valley is like visiting another planet. It's a safe bet you've never seen anything like Predator Ridge before. And it's also a safe bet you will return to see it again.

Without sounding like the resort's marketing department, Predator Ridge tees up 27 spectacular golf holes and countless spectacular views.

You don't need an overzealous marketing spokesperson to explain what a great hole the eighth is. All you need is a picture. So let's try and paint you one close to the original.

"This is our inland Pebble Beach 18th with water from tee to green on the left side," say the course pros. Comparing yourself to Pebble Beach is quite a statement. But in this case, it's not an overstatement.

Your target off the tee on this dogleg left is the lone tree on the right side of the fairway. The water along the left is unforgiving. There is little, if any, rough between the fairway and the water. There are bunkers along the left side of a narrow fairway.

The risk-reward factor on this hole is very high. How much of the water do you want to cut over? This is one of those holes where you should play it smart, but you just can't resist the temptation.

Good luck — there is a possibility you'll need it. **TJ**

# No. ❽ LAS BRISAS GOLF CLUB

Las Brisas Golf Club features ten lakes fed by two streams stationed throughout the property, and somehow half of them touch the par-5 eighth. The hole's length, at 507 yards, isn't daunting on the scorecard, but its challenge is multiplied when water is factored in.

One of the lakes on No. 8 actually sits behind the tee and serves as a hazard for the seventh green. However, the other four bodies of water on the eighth are dangers that make the right side of the fairway and the back left of the green areas to avoid.

The water is more than cosmetic. It must be considered on all three shots to this par 5. First, off the tee, you hit over a stream that cascades down the right side of the fairway. Then on your second shot, you have to stay close enough to the lake on the right to afford yourself an angle into the green, but far enough away to stay dry.

On the approach to the putting surface, the shot must be struck back over the lake. There is the option of going for the green in two, of course. But to make this work, a player must make a long carry over the water, and avoid a collection of trees to the front of the lake. Then, he must be accurate enough to seek a small opening to the putting surface just to the left of a protective bunker.

Wiser, safer, and dryer is the three-shot approach, leaving the second shot short of the water and adjacent to the group of trees. This still leaves a tricky pitch to a green protected on both sides by bunkers, but it's a far easier effort with a wedge in your hands. **JB**

# No. ❽ PENINSULA COUNTRY GOLF CLUB (SOUTH COURSE)

Members say the eighth on the South Course, a par-72 track measuring over 6,600 yards, is a true "three-shot" hole, a tight par 5 playing 576 yards from the tips over beautifully undulating and sandy terrain.

The drive is a slightly uphill shot that must avoid a deep bunker on the left, and the second shot, generally a fairway wood, is played over the crest of a hill to a valley. That's where most players will then hit their third shot back up a small hill to a two-tiered green fronted by a pair of bunkers.

It is important to be on the correct tier on this hole, or the likely outcome is a dreaded three-putt. **JS**

**Course:** Scioto Country Club

**Location:** Columbus, Ohio

**Hole:** No. 8

**Length:** 505 yards

**Par:** 5

**Designer:** Donald Ross

**Course Comment:** Opened in 1916, Scioto has staged the 1926 U.S. Open, the 1931 Ryder Cup, the 1950 PGA Championship, the 1968 U.S. Amateur, the 1986 Senior Open, and the 1994 Ohio Amateur Open.

# No. ⑧  SCIOTO COUNTRY CLUB

When Columbus, Ohio, and golf are mentioned in the same breath, many make the tie between Ohio State graduate Jack Nicklaus and the city in which he matriculated. However, long before the Golden Bear made his mark, a lesson in golf architecture was being given by one of the game's true professors of design — the great Donald Ross. It was in 1916 that Ross declared his work finished at Scioto Country Club in Columbus, and a course that has since been the site of countless nationally prominent events was opened for play.

Ross was one of the original members of the American Society of Golf Course Architects, and his courses tend to require strategy and deceptive simplicity. Between 1912 and 1948, Ross was constantly in demand, walking sites and designing courses throughout the eastern United States.

Scioto Country Club, one of between 400 and 600 courses said to be laid out by Ross, is a primary example of his straightforward yet challenging philosophy. It takes a discipline to play Scioto, and the eighth is a challenge of character and will as much as strength. It is Ross at his finest.

If you hit a solid drive and find the fairway at No. 8, there is an inviting landing area for the second shot, which leaves a casual approach and a decent shot at birdie. However, the hole is short enough to reach in two and this is where the mental part of Ross' genius comes into play.

Golfers who are able to contain their bravado, and play the hole as a three-shotter often are rewarded. Going for the green in two requires either running the shot between two protective bunkers, or going over them and still landing the ball softly enough to hold. Neither option is easily achieved. Playing this hole in three shots is much the more intelligent play.

Ross was one of the first American architects to detail the design and strategy of a golf hole rather than just stake out tees, bunkers and greens. And he liked to keep his work personal. Most of his courses were built by hand even after bulldozers began to be used. **JB**

**Course:** Breckenridge Golf Course (Beaver Course)

**Location:** Breckenridge, Colorado, USA

**Hole:** No. 8

**Length:** 580 yards

**Par:** 5

**Designer:** Jack Nicklaus

**Course Comment:** The town of Breckenridge in scenic Colorado can boast that it is the only municipality in the world to own a Jack Nicklaus-designed, 27-hole golf course. The course opened for play in 1985.

BELOW *A general view of Breckenridge.*

## No. ❽ BRECKENRIDGE GOLF COURSE
### (BEAVER COURSE)

The Breckenridge Golf Course is situated in a beautiful mountain valley where the clubhouse sits at an elevation of 9,324 feet — where the golf ball flies further and straighter than at lower elevations because of less air resistance. The air not only allows you to hit the ball further, but also offers temperatures that make you forget about the heat of the summer (typical daytime summer temperatures range from 65 degrees to 80 degrees).

The 580-yard par 5 is pictured on the course's scorecard, beating out some impressive competition. The tee shot is straight but very tight with a hazard on the left that crosses the fairway and ends up on the right side.

You don't have to worry about the crossing hazard until your second shot. The hazard — which is actually a creek that turns into Beaver Pond — crosses over about 345 yards from the back tees.

Forget about the green in two. From the back, it plays the full 580 yards and there is too much risk involved trying to reach the green in two.

Your approach shot must carry Beaver Pond. This is a tough hole on a tough golf course.

From the back tees on the Beaver/Bear rotation, the course plays 7,276 yards and has a course rating of 73.3 with a slope of 150. This set of tees has the second most difficult course rating in the state. **TJ**

# OCEAN EDGE

**Course:** Ocean Edge

**Location:** Brewster, Massachusetts, USA

**Hole:** No. 8

**Length:** 601 yards

**Par:** 5

**Designer:** Geoffrey Cornish, Brian Silva

**Course Comment:** Ocean Edge is a grand Massachusetts New England hotel on 400 acres from the Cape Cod Golf Course to the sea in Brewster, near Chatham, Cape Cod. The course was recently named one of the state's top 10 golf courses by *Boston Magazine*.

Here's the warning from the pro shop at Ocean Edge: the eighth hole is one you will play much better the second time round. Why? Because you will (hopefully) play it the right way. You see, the wrong way means trouble.

The signature hole at Ocean Edge, No. 8 is a 601-yard par-5 dogleg left you won't soon forget. From an elevated tee, there is out-of-bounds to the right and a hazard on the left. Remember the hazard because you can't see it from the tee and it's about 230 yards out.

But you sink or swim on your second shot.

It's important to know your yardage and not just grip and rip it. Many players grab their 3-wood for their second shot and that's where the trouble begins.

Play this shot like a long par 3. Try and hit the fairway at around the 150-yard marker. The fairway slopes from right to left between 150 and 50 yards from the green, so trying to pick up some extra yardage will only cause you more grief.

There are some tough shots on this hole. But you can reduce the risk by playing smart. And remember, know your yardage. **TJ**

**Course:** Royal Liverpool Golf Club (Hoylake)

**Location:** Hoylake, Merseyside, England

**Hole:** No. 8

**Length:** 519 yards

**Par:** 5

**Designer:** Robert Chambers Jr., George Morris

**Course Comment:** Bobby Jones won the British Open here in 1930 as part of his Grand Slam season, despite taking an eight on this relatively straightforward par 5. Jones lay third on the fringe of the green, yet took five more strokes to hole out.

# No. ❽ ROYAL LIVERPOOL GOLF CLUB (HOYLAKE)

The Royal and Ancient Golf Club has announced that Royal Liverpool Golf Club will host the 2006 British Open Championship, the first time the Open Championship will be played at Hoylake since 1967 when Roberto de Vicenzo of Argentina won his first and only major title.

The British Open returns to Royal Liverpool in 2006 after a 39-year absence, but the course has never been considered unworthy. In the years since de Vicenzo's victory, the demands of the Open in terms of space, infrastructure, and traffic management ruled Royal Liverpool out as an Open venue. Now, however, with plans in place as a result of the three-way agreement signed by The Royal and Ancient Golf Club, Royal Liverpool Golf Club, and the Metropolitan Borough of Wirral, the Open will make a welcome and long-overdue return.

Peter Dawson, Secretary of the R&A said: "Royal Liverpool is a club with a long and distinguished history and we are delighted that we are now able to bring the Open back to this wonderful course at Hoylake."

Joe Pinnington, captain of Royal Liverpool added: "We are delighted that the greatest golfing event in the world is to come back to Hoylake."

The eighth hole does not look imposing, but it certainly humbled Jones before he turned matters around to win the Open Championship more than 50 years ago (see course comment). Nicknamed "Far," because it represents the most distant point from the clubhouse of any hole, the eighth's biggest defense is the shoulder-high bunker in the right front of the green.

Also adding to the difficulty are the rough and swales that will make themselves known at the upcoming British Open.

Despite its somewhat flat and benign appearance, the eight hole is deceptively tough because of the aforementioned protection, not to mention the near-constant gales at Royal Liverpool. The Links at Hoylake is among the toughest and most demanding of the great seaside championship links of Britain.

Hoylake is the very essence of golf history in Britain. Built in 1869 on what was then the racecourse of the Liverpool Hunt Club, Hoylake is nearly the oldest of the English coastal courses — with the exception of Westward Ho! in Devon, which predates it by just a few years. **JB**

BELOW *The eighth hole at Royal Liverpool.*

## No. ❽  KING'S CHALLENGE

**Course:** King's Challenge

**Location:** Cedar, Michigan, USA

**Hole:** No. 8

**Length:** 548 yards

**Par:** 5

**Designer:** Arnold Palmer

**Course Comment:** The key to No. 8 at King's Challenge is quite the challenge. "You really need to hit three good shots in a row. There are no gimmies on this hole," says head professional Chuck Olson.

This hole features many elevation changes and there is a 100-foot drop from the tee with spectacular views of Leelanau County.

This slight dogleg to the right has a number of valleys and plateaus, and your second shot is a lay-up unless you can get down the hill — which is not easy to do. Water certainly comes into play on your second and third shots on one of the toughest holes on King's Challenge.

Trees line both sides of the fairway, and be prepared to hit at least one downhill lie. There are five sets of tees.

The green is kidney shaped and bends around the lake with water along the front right. There are traps on the left, front and back sides of the green.

Your approach shot to the green is usually a wedge from between 100 and 150 yards out, with an abundance of danger between your ball and the putting surface.

This 6,593-yard, par-71 course was designed by Arnold Palmer and takes full advantage of the lush rolling land and its hilly vistas. And No. 8 is the perfect example. **TJ**

## No. ❽  FOOTHILLS GOLF CLUB

**Course:** Foothills Golf Club

**Location:** Phoenix, Arizona, USA

**Hole:** No. 8

**Length:** 510 yards

**Par:** 5

**Designer:** Tom Weiskopf, Jay Morrish

**Course Comment:** This is not your typical desert links-style golf course. Many courses that cut through the desert are considered target golf, but Foothills offers plenty of wide fairways — although the desert is never out of the picture.

With wide, rolling fairways of lush green, Foothills Golf Club is a beautiful facility tucked away in the ridges and buttes of South Mountain. Grab a scorecard at Foothills and you can see a wonderful photo of where No. 7 and No. 8 come together.

It doesn't get much better than this.

No. 8 is a 510-yard, par-5 dogleg right. Despite the length of the hole, it is reachable in two shots. Of course, that would be two very good and very long shots.

You must drive the ball off the tee and carry a bunker on the right side. If you can do this, you will be rewarded with a little extra roll, setting up nicely for your second shot.

Our expert in the pro shop notes that there is usually a good crosswind on your approach shot, so take an extra second and make double sure you have the right club. The golf course is not responsible for you choosing the wrong club.

The green is difficult and actually is back-to-back with the No. 1 green, so while you are there, make sure you get a good look at No. 8. There are bunkers on the left and a pond on the right, and the green slopes back to front, so make sure you are ready.

A tough pin placement is in the back left part of the green. **TJ**

# Hole 9

You have reached the midway point of your round, which can mean one of two things, depending on when the course you are playing was built.

If you are playing a relatively modern course (post-1960), after you've finished the ninth, chances are you are at the clubhouse and have a brief moment for refreshment before the 10th. But, if you are playing a classic gem, you still could be halfway through a long, looping route that doesn't return to the clubhouse until the 18th.

Because the ninth is so visible from the clubhouse on a modern course, and if it truly is laid out as the outward "finisher," architects often want to make it the most memorable on the front nine.

It might not get the same attention as No. 18s, but more and more, No. 9 is becoming a hole to remember.

**LEFT** *The ninth hole at The Gary Player Country Club, Sun City, South Africa.*

**MOOSE RIDGE GOLF COURSE**

**Course:** Moose Ridge Golf Course

**Location:** South Lyon, Michigan, USA

**Hole:** No. 9

**Length:** 193 yards

**Par:** 3

**Designer:** Raymond Hearn

**Course Comment:** Like many Raymond Hearn designs, target golf is an ultimate aim here. And Hearn doesn't leave a lot of room for error, creating tight fairways with rolling hills often resulting in uneven lies.

Don't call the pro shop at Moose Ridge and ask for the signature hole. The answer will be "all of them." And no, they aren't kidding.

Moose Ridge has plenty of company when it comes to first-rate golf courses in southeastern Michigan, but no sentence in the "best of the best" category is complete without a mention of this 18-hole masterpiece.

If you had to pick one hole as the best of the best of the best, the par-3 ninth would certainly stand up as a serious contender. Standing at the tips, you face 193 yards of trouble between you and the flag. The trouble begins — but doesn't end, by any means — with the marsh or wetlands or whatever you want to call it.

From those back tees, the green looks tiny. And that's because it is. Mr. Hearn didn't leave you a very big target at which to shoot. The green features trees to the right and a severe slope on the left that will require another ball if you happen to end up over there.

But there is hope on this hole.

If your shot is right, it has a good chance of banking off the hill and rolling onto the green. Hitting long on this hole also is a safe shot. There is a large bail-out area in the back of the green. **TJ**

**Course:** Arcadia Bluffs

**Location:** Arcadia, Michigan, USA

**Hole:** No. 9

**Length:** 203 yards

**Par:** 3

**Designer:** Warren Henderson, Rick Smith

**Course Comment:** One of Michigan's most scenic courses, Arcadia Bluffs is a links-style course set on a bluff, teeing up breathtaking views of Lake Michigan from every hole.

# No. ❾ ARCADIA BLUFFS

Hopefully, by the time you reach No. 9 at Arcadia Bluffs, the views will have stopped being such a distraction so you can concentrate on golf. And if you aren't focused on the task ahead of you, this course will turn your scorecard into recycled paper.

The expert in the pro shop does have some suggestions on how to play this difficult ninth hole, a 203-yard par 3: trust your yardage and don't be afraid to be aggressive.

In other words, have faith in your tee shot and take aim at the green. There is no place to lay up, and trouble lurks if you miss.

And don't be fooled by the front of the green. It might look like the green from up on the tee, but the front portion of the green draws short shots back into the approach area, leaving a difficult pitch.

The green is shaped like a giant foot with the wider part to the right side. There is a bunker in front of the green and a large tree hovering along the right side — but it shouldn't come into play.

Built in 1999, the course drops 225 feet from its highest point down to the bluff, 180 feet above sea level, and has 3,100 feet of Lake Michigan shore frontage. So bring a lot of golf balls. **TJ**

**Course:** Yale University Golf Course

**Location:** New Haven, Connecticut, USA

**Hole:** No. 9

**Length:** 211 yards

**Par:** 3

**Designer:** Charles Blair Macdonald, Seth Raynor

**Course Comment:** David Duval, when he was a college player at Georgia Tech during the 1991 NCAA Eastern Regional, made a double-bogey 5 on No. 9. But he still finished with a tournament-low round of 65 to capture the regional's individual championship.

# No. ❾   YALE UNIVERSITY GOLF COURSE

What are the first thoughts that pop into your mind when thinking of Yale University? Let's see . . . academia, serene campus setting conducive for study, and a thoughtful site capable of housing some of the world's most intelligent students and future brilliant contributors to society? This is what most people think when they think of Yale. However, when thinking of the university's golf course, other adjectives ought to come to mind: tough, arduous, and grueling. And the ninth hole, the second-toughest hole on an incredibly difficult golf course, is as big a golf test as you'll find.

The grueling Yale course has been the site of every significant state championship: two U.S. Golf Association Junior National events, several NCAA Eastern Regional championships (including 2004), the ECAC Men's Championship, and the ECAC Women's Championship. During the last NCAA tournament held here, only 21 subpar rounds were recorded of the 360 played during the three days. The course has also been the home of the Connecticut Open.

You get the idea. Take off your horn-rimmed glasses and get ready to roll your sleeves up. Particularly at No. 9, which is considered by many to be the finest Biarritz hole in the world. The name Biarritz comes from Willie Dunn's creation of the third hole at the Golf de Biarritz golf course in France. It refers to a deep trench that runs right through the center of the green. At Yale the gully is five feet deep, and as you might imagine, pin placement can make an incredible difference in your score here. If you have to putt through the trench, getting it anywhere close to the hole is next to impossible.

The ninth green at Yale is actually a fairly large target. It is 60 feet long, which is ample enough for quality players to find. But, landing on the putting surface becomes much more difficult when you consider that your tee shot comes from 60 feet above Greist Pond.

Charles Blair Macdonald came out of retirement to consult with his protégé, Seth Raynor — a Princeton grad — on the Yale course. In 1926, when the Yale course opened, it was just the second major university in the world, besides St. Andrews in Scotland, that had a world-class golf course. And the Biarritz at the ninth was its signature hole. **JB**

OPPOSITE *The ninth hole at Yale University.*

**Course:** Jupiter Hills Club
(Hills Course)

**Location:** Tequesta, Florida, USA

**Hole:** No. 9

**Length:** 192 yards

**Par:** 3

**Designer:** George Fazio

**Course Comment:** Soon-to-be PGA
Tour player Billy Mayfair won the
1987 U.S. Amateur at Jupiter Hills,
defeating Eric Rebmann, 4 and 3,
in the 36-hole final.

## No. ⑨ JUPITER HILLS CLUB (HILLS COURSE)

Standing on the tee at Jupiter Hills's ninth hole, golfers face a challenge
that's fairly unique to South Florida golf: an uphill par 3, and a scary one at
that. The hole rises approximately 40 feet from the tee box to the green,
which is set at the top of a sand dune. What's really challenging, however,
is what you'll have to go over to get there — a ravine that's filled with sandy
waste areas and thick native vegetation that has claimed many a golf ball.
As if more difficulty was needed, the swirling breezes from the nearby
Atlantic can also dramatically affect your shot.

Although there's a slight landing area just right of the green, the rest of
the putting surface is surrounded by jungle, with the left side of the green
sharply falling off into more sand. Your best bet is to aim for the right side
of the putting surface, then cross your fingers and hope for the best.

Mayfair's victory at the 1987 U.S. Amateur at Jupiter Hills made him the
first player to triumph in both the Amateur and the U.S. Amateur Public
Links Championship. He had won the latter in 1986. **KA**

**Course:** Royal Dar-Es-Salaam
(Red Course)

**Location:** Rabat, Morocco

**Hole:** No. 9

**Length:** 199 yards

**Par:** 3

**Designer:** Robert Trent Jones Sr.

**Course Comment:** Site of the annual
Hassan II Trophy, a tournament that
has become increasingly popular
since its inception in 1971. Robert
Trent Jones Sr. designed the course
for King Hassan II.

# No. 🄮 ROYAL DAR-ES-SALAAM
## (RED COURSE)

When a country has just 14 golf courses, it is rather surprising that one of
the great golf holes in the world should reside there. But the Red Course at
Royal Dar-Es-Salaam Golf Club is one of the most spectacular courses in the
world, and the ninth hole is the most brilliant on the property.

The Red's ninth is an island green, which is daunting enough, but when
you consider that at 199 yards it is extremely long for an island hole, it
becomes even more frightening. The ninth exemplifies the difficulty of
island-hole golf, but it also brings to light the natural possibilities. Geese,
flamingos, ducks, and other wildlife add to the atmosphere at the ninth,
and this is a small collection of what awaits on the rest of the course.

Caddies are the norm at Royal Dar-Es-Salaam, and they are particularly
useful at No. 9, being good judges of conditions that might affect club
selection when aiming at the all-or-nothing target. And, if you are
fortunate enough to strike the green off the tee, the caddies are helpful in
reading the undulations on No. 9. There are other, more famous island
greens in the world — No. 17 at the TPC at Sawgrass comes to mind, or the
Golden Horseshoe in Williamsburg, Virginia (said to be the first island hole)
— but neither can match Royal Dar-Es-Salaam Red's No. 9 for natural
beauty or difficulty.

The ninth hole is part of a magnificent 7,372-yard, par-73 layout. A sub-
70 round is quite an accomplishment, even for the pros who visit each
November for the Hassan II Trophy. The tournament consists of three days
of pro-am play, with about 40 pros and 100 amateurs from around the
world. Then there is a final two days of competition for pros only, with the
player posting the lowest 72-hole score taking home the title, and the
much-coveted jewel-encrusted gold dagger that
goes with it.

Over the years, the Moroccans have lured
some of golf's biggest names to the Hassan II,
including Nick Faldo, Vijay Singh, Payne Stewart,
Gary Player, Billy Casper, Colin Montgomerie, and
Nick Price — mostly by paying tens of thousands
of dollars in appearance money.

The maintenance budget at Royal Dar-Es-
Salaam is seemingly unlimited, and the course
conditions are truly exceptional. Cork trees are all
over the course — including around the island
green at No. 9 — and the majority of these have
been stripped of their bark for use in making
corks for wine bottles. **JB**

**BELOW AND OPPOSITE** *Two views of the
ninth hole at Royal Dar-Es-Salaam.*

**Course:** Myopia Hunt Club

**Location:** South Hamilton, Massachusetts, USA

**Hole:** No. 9

**Length:** 136 yards

**Par:** 3

**Designer:** Herbert C. Leeds

**Course Comment:** Built in 1894, Myopia has been listed by the USGA as being one of the first 100 clubs established in the United States.

This famous club was the brainchild of Delano Sanborn, a one-time pitcher on the Harvard baseball team and one of four sons of then-Boston mayor Frederick Prince. Originally, the club's main activity was lawn tennis, but not any more.

Myopia is now a beautiful old golf course featuring wooded hills and distinctive green undulations, giving the overall impression of a classic.

No. 9, along with No. 4, are two memorable holes at Myopia. In fact, No. 9 is more than memorable. Our source in the pro shop said he'd played many of the top 100 golf courses in the country, and No. 9 at Myopia was easily in his top five favorite holes.

Don't be fooled by the 136 yards because if you miss the green, you are in big trouble. And the green is easily missed, even from that distance. One of the more unusual greens you will ever play, No. 9 is 40 paces deep but only seven paces wide.

The green is surrounded by seven pot bunkers — there are over 100 on this golf course. All seven of the bunkers have ladders to help you reach your golf ball. Try not to spend all day in there if you can help it. Once in though, it's difficult to negotiate your way out.

There is water right off the tee, but it shouldn't come into play. Hit the green and the bunkers won't come into play either.

It's a safe bet that whatever you write down on the scorecard, you won't soon forget this neat little hole. **TJ**

## No. ⑨ CLEARWATER

**Course:** Clearwater

**Location:** Christchurch, New Zealand

**Hole:** No. 9

**Length:** 187 yards

**Par:** 3

**Designer:** John Darby

**Course Comment:** The par-72 championship layout already is turning heads. Designed by John Darby in consultation with New Zealand golf legend, Sir Bob Charles.

Clearwater combines elements of classic links golf inspired by the great Scottish courses with parkland golf, more reminiscent of Florida.

Bring plenty of confidence, because water comes into play on 14 holes, and if those lakes don't catch errant balls, then the acres of tussocks and marram grasses will.

It's obvious why Clearwater has been awarded the highest rating of any course in the country by the New Zealand Golf Association. At 76.8 off the black or championship tees, it ranks as the toughest in the country.

All this brings us to No. 9.

Here is a perfect example of water and trouble. All down the right side of this awesome par-3 is water. And more water.

They didn't name this hole "Challenge" for nothing. You have to carry water to reach the green from all the tees. No gimmies here.

Bunkers guard the front and middle left of the green.

Remember to take a little more club if the flag is in the back. And try and avoid the water. **TJ**

## No. ⑨ OCEAN DUNES GOLF CLUB

**Course:** Ocean Dunes Golf Club

**Location:** Phan Thiet, Vietnam

**Hole:** No. 9

**Length:** 148 yards

**Par:** 3

**Designer:** Nick Faldo

**Course Comment:** Phan Thiet is a traditional Vietnamese fishing village where cyclos and wooden baskets are still a main mode of transportation.

Ocean Dunes Golf Club is a Nick Faldo design sculpted out of the dunes along Vietnam's southeast coast, approximately 125 miles northeast of Ho Chi Minh City. The area is full of interesting sites, including an ancient temple built in the 15th century by the Cham, and the Kega Lighthouse, the first lighthouse in South-east Asia, which was built by the French in 1899 with stone taken from the beachside cliffs.

For golfers, however, the par-3 ninth hole at Ocean Dunes will be the obvious highlight. Faldo allowed the dunes landscape to determine much of the routing and look of the links-style course, and that's evident on this hole. The shallow green is partially hidden by two large dunes at the left front and right front, with a bunker set in the right dune offering another obstacle. To add even more difficulty, the hole is slightly uphill from tee to green, and the putting surface has a fairly steep slope from back to front. Views of the Eastern Sea are visible through the trees on the right, adding beauty to the hole but also offering a reminder that the ocean breezes could dramatically affect the tee shot. **KA**

**Course:** Point O' Woods
Country Club

**Location:** Benton Harbor, Michigan,
USA

**Hole:** No. 9

**Length:** 192 yards

**Par:** 3

**Designer:** Robert Trent Jones Sr.

**Course Comment:** Point O' Woods
is the annual site of the Western
Amateur Championship, one of the
country's most prestigious amateur
tournaments.

# No. ❾ POINT O' WOODS COUNTRY CLUB

Point O' Woods is pleasantly flat and walkable, but don't mistake that for an easy test by any means. Deep bunkers and narrow landing areas off the tees make up for lack of swales. This course is an example of beautifully scenic design with ponds coming into play on most of its holes.

It's a tricky business to make par on many of this course's holes, the ninth in particular. Tree-lined fairways force golfers to think their way to hole nine, and once there, to think about their strategy even more. It's not the longest par 3 at Point O' Woods, but it's the toughest. Trees flank its left side, opposite its wide, shallow green, so if you're going to miss the green you better miss right. Five bunkers protect the green, but a short shooter is in luck — the front bunker saves shorter shots from hitting water.

The ninth helps make Point O' Woods worthy of the terrific amateur competition it attracts — its configuration is a test of accuracy for even the best of the best. In spite of its prestige, it isn't nearly as expensive as you might think. The green fees are reasonable, and the scenery and layout are excellent — a bargain at a much higher price.

The rolling terrain and beautiful vistas leading to No. 9 are legendary. The last hole on the outward nine is another Jones classic in a career that spawned many. **KLL**

## No. ❾  STEWART CREEK

**Course:** Stewart Creek

**Location:** Canmore, Alberta, Canada

**Hole:** No. 9

**Length:** 417 yards

**Par:** 4

**Designer:** Gary Browning

**Course Comment:** Stewart Creek incorporates several old mine entranceways, which really gives the course an historical feel. Golfers can enter no further than 15 feet into the mines so don't expect to find any gold in these mountains. But you might find a few golf balls.

Stewart Creek Golf Club is located on the Three Sisters Mountain Village, a 2,300-acre development in Canmore, Canada. This spectacular par-72, 18-hole mountain golf course promises seclusion, scenery, and splendor. Not to mention some excellent golf.

Stewart Creek has quickly become one of Canada's favorite golf courses. When it first opened, *Golf Digest* ranked it the second-best new layout in the country.

And No. 9 is simply one of the best holes here.

At about 230 yards from the tee, the fairway vanishes. Gone. So, either lay up or bring a lot of golf balls. You could hike down to get your ball but you would be holding up a lot of people.

From the fairway, there's another eye-catching vista and another tough mid-iron shot to a green protected by two massive water features — both guarding the two sides of a difficult green.

There is nothing easy about this hole. But it is loaded with scenery that is tough to forget.

It's not a bad idea to stuff a camera in your bag — along with a lot of golf balls. You might lose the balls, but the photograph will be with you forever. **TJ**

## No. ❾  KINGSTON HEATH GOLF CLUB

**Course:** Kingston Heath Golf Club

**Location:** Cheltenham, Victoria, Australia

**Hole:** No. 9

**Length:** 363 yards

**Par:** 4

**Designer:** D.G. Soutar, Alister Mackenzie

**Course Comment:** This Sand Belt classic is regularly ranked among the top two or three courses Down Under and has played host to six Australian Open Championships over the years, the last in 1995, when native son Greg Norman was the winner.

No. 9 is one of those classic short par 4s, full of risk-reward possibilities, and a real pleasure to play. So long as you make the right choices off the tee, that is.

Some players like to bomb a driver off the tee, turning the ball over so that they have only a wedge into a fairly spacious green. But that play is fraught with danger, mostly in the form of the thick tea trees that run along the right side of the fairway, and bunkers short and on the left as well as long right. To say that accuracy is at a premium with that shot is an understatement, and many golfers are apt to keep the big stick in their bag and use a fairway wood or long iron.

Then there is the second shot, which must be precise in its own right, as a gruesome bunker complex looms short and to the right, and a gaping one stands guard back and to the left.

The green itself is rather spacious, allowing for intriguing and varied pin placements that often make frustratingly great use of the many undulations the putting surface features. **JS**

**Course:** Turnberry Golf Club (Ailsa Course)

**Location:** Turnberry, Ayrshire, Scotland

**Hole:** No. 9

**Length:** 455 yards

**Par:** 4

**Designer:** Mackenzie Ross

**Course Comment:** One of the great duals in the history of golf took place here, when in 1977 Tom Watson beat Jack Nicklaus by one stroke in the British Open Championship. Their one-on-one battle prompted Hubert Green, who finished 10 strokes behind Nicklaus in third place, to quip: "I won the Open — those guys were playing a different tournament."

## No. ❾  TURNBERRY GOLF CLUB (AILSA COURSE)

There are two courses at Turnberry Golf Club, and while the par-69 Arran Course is a quaint place to play and worth a visit, there is little doubt that the true gem at Turnberry is the Ailsa.

This stretch of coastal land was owned by a railway company at the turn of the century and was then used as a wartime airfield. The damage of industry and war placed the property on the verge of ruin by 1946. But the intervention of course architect Mackenzie Ross not only saved the land, but transformed it into what has now become one of the world's finest golf courses.

More finely manicured than many Scottish courses, this coastal stretch of holes, intermingling turbulent dunes and rocky crags, represents links golf at its best. Named after the landmark rock "Ailsa Craig", holes No. 4 through No. 11 on the Ailsa Course, which play alongside the sea, are among the most beautiful and demanding as anywhere in the world.

One of those lovely seaside holes is the 455-yard ninth, Bruce's Castle. It is a postcard of a golf hole, whose mere sighting creates ambience.

The back tees sit on a slim finger of land that nearly departs the ground for the sea. A rocky elevation proves a perfect spot for a nearly perfect hole. From the back tees, a nearly 200-yard carry is required to a fairway that slopes both right and left. Rough and rocks await those who either don't make the carry or whose ball falls victim to the hogback.

As the fairway becomes narrower near the green, so does your chance of success if you happen to miss the putting surface. The green is huge and hilly, but like the rest of the hole and course, it is kept immaculate.

The ninth is framed by sand dunes and flanked by craggy rocks, and the picturesque Turnberry lighthouse stands stoically bearing witness to the many seafarers who have come to a watery grave off the rugged coastline. That the weather often changes by the hour only serves to augment the challenge of this superb hole.

In order to play at Turnberry, you must stay at the Turnberry Hotel, located in over 800 acres of beautiful countryside and offering spectacular views over the Firth of Clyde to Arran, the Mull of Kintyre, and Ailsa Craig. Among the sites visible from the hotel is the par-4 ninth. **JB**

OPPOSITE *The ninth hole at Turnberry.*

## No. ❾ LAUREL VALLEY GOLF CLUB

**Course:** Laurel Valley Golf Club

**Location:** Ligonier, Pennsylvania, USA

**Hole:** No. 9

**Length:** 485 yards

**Par:** 4

**Designer:** Dick Wilson

**Course Comment:** Built in 1960 by Dick Wilson, Laurel Valley has seen plenty of changes over the years. The course was redesigned by Paul Erath in 1965, and again in 1988 by Arnold Palmer and Ed Seay.

This par-4 ninth hole is one of those you pull up to in the cart. Get out. Grab your club. Start walking to the tee and then pause, and take in the view. This is one beautiful hole.

It is a hole worth the pause.

This is a fairly straight hole except for some big pine trees by the green which make it a slight dogleg right. The good news is you have a pretty clear and open fairway to let her fly on this slightly uphill tee shot.

Don't bother looking for the green. Because of the elevation, it's very difficult to see the putting surface.

Your second shot won't be as easy as the first. About 100 yards out from the green is a small stream that easily can come into play.

The stream runs along the right side but unless you really slice the ball off the tee, it's nothing to worry about until your second shot.

And don't forget about the trees on the right.

The green has two tiers so it's important to know where the flag is and use the right club to land on the same level as the pin. Otherwise, you could be looking at three putts to get you home. **TJ**

**Course:** Newport Country Club

**Location:** Newport, Rhode Island, USA

**Hole:** No. 9

**Length:** 448 yards

**Par:** 4

**Designer:** William Davis

**Course Comment:** One of the interesting aspects of the ninth hole is the elevated green. Many golfers mistakenly forget to take this into account when selecting a club. The green is 32 yards deep with a severe right-to-left slope.

## No. ❾   NEWPORT COUNTRY CLUB

Some history. Newport Country Club is one of the original five founding member clubs of the USGA. William Davis is the original architect of the club, but the course was remodeled in 1924 by A.W. Tillinghast. Tiger Woods won the U.S. Amateur at Newport in 1995.

As for the future, Newport Country Club will play host to the 2006 U.S. Women's Open.

Now, let's play some golf.

Considered the toughest par-4 on the golf course, this slight dogleg right requires a difficult tee shot. There is a cross bunker about 217 yards out. Your ideal shot is to hit your tee shot about 230 yards and carry the cross bunker on the right.

You can miss the cross bunker by going left. But this will make for an even longer second shot. There also is a bunker about 250 yards out on the left side.

If you can carry the cross bunker, you are looking at a 6- or 7-iron to the green. Remember to take the wind into account on both your tee shot and approach shot. The wind makes a big difference on this hole.

And try to avoid all those bunkers around the green. **TJ**

## No. ❾ EASTWARD HO! GOLF CLUB

**Course:** Eastward Ho! Golf Club

**Location:** Chatham, Massachusetts, USA

**Hole:** No. 9

**Par:** 4

**Length:** 395 yards

**Designer:** Herbert Fowler

**Course Comment:** This club was called Chatham Country Club when it was first built, but was changed to Eastward Ho! in 1926 as a tribute to Fowler, who had designed the revered Westward Ho! Golf Club in England.

Similar to Fowler's beloved Westward Ho! in Devon, England, Eastward Ho! Golf Club on Cape Cod requires golfers to invent shots from uneven, hilly lies and awkward positions, all the while as they are battling the winds off Pleasant Bay and the Atlantic Ocean beyond, testing almost all facets of a golfer's game. No wonder such noted players as Francis Ouimet and Bobby Jones spent so much time here.

Because of its location along the Atlantic, Eastward Ho! is links golf, no doubt, but is unique in its rolling, rocky terrain that was created from an ancient receding glacier. Eastward Ho!'s ninth hole, which begins at the highest spot on the course, is certainly prime evidence of that. Situated upon a huge ridge, its spine provides the location for the second half of the fairway and green.

The downhill tee shot should be hit to the right side of the plateau fairway to gain a level lie for the second shot, another downhiller that usually must be hit into the wind. Any approach that is made to the left or the right will end up below the green, as the fairway slopes off severely on both sides, leaving a difficult chip and tricky up-and-down opportunity to save par. **KA**

## No. ❾ FOREST HIGHLANDS GOLF CLUB (CANYON COURSE)

**Course:** Forest Highlands Golf Club (Canyon Course)

**Location:** Flagstaff, Arizona, USA

**Hole:** No. 9

**Length:** 478 yards

**Par:** 4

**Designer:** Tom Weiskopf, Jay Morrish

**Course Comment:** Forest Highlands' Canyon Course has been selected to host the 2006 U.S. Mid-Amateur Championship.

The scenic Canyon Course, a highly regarded Weiskopf/Morrish design that's considered one of the best in the golf-rich state of Arizona, is nestled among the mountain wilderness of the Arizona high country, located at the foothills of the San Francisco Peaks and in the midst of one of the largest stands of Ponderosa pines in the world. It features tree-lined fairways, and ponds and creeks that come into play on many of its holes.

A perfect example is the long par-4 ninth. The downhill tee shot must be hit over a lone pine tree located in the right side of the fairway, which slopes from right to left. It's a play that allows you to stay away from a creek and fairway bunker on the left, funnels your ball to the center and sets up a preferred angle for the second shot, as the hole bends ever so slightly to the left at the landing area.

The approach to the double green, which is shared with No. 18, must carry the edge of a small lake and avoid a pair of bunkers at the right front and left rear of the putting surface, which also slopes from right to left. **KA**

**Course:** Royal County Down

**Location:** Newcastle, County Down, Northern Ireland

**Hole:** No. 9

**Length:** 485 yards

**Par:** 4

**Designer:** Old Tom Morris, Harry Vardon

**Course Comment:** The Walker Cup Matches between the United States and Great Britain and Ireland will be held at Royal County Down, September 8–9, 2007. It is the second time the matches pitting the great amateurs of the participating nations have been held in Ireland, following Portmarnock in 1991 (the United States won those matches, 14–10).

**BELOW** *Jack Nicklaus looks out of the rough on the ninth hole at Royal County Down, July 2001.*

**OPPOSITE** *The ninth hole at Royal County Down.*

# No. ❾ ROYAL COUNTY DOWN

The fact that the Walker Cup matches have been played in Ireland just once, and the Royal and Ancient Golf Club of St. Andrews chose to return the amateur competition to the country in 2007 at Royal County Down, is a testament to the quality and splendor of the Northern Irish links. When the matches are contested over the testing Newcastle layout around the curve of Dundrum Bay and within sight of Slieve Donard and the mountains of Mourne, players will find out what Tom Watson did the many times he played Royal County Down.

"Royal County Down is a pure links, in the truest sense of the word," Watson said. "My advice to anyone playing this great course is to keep it very straight off the tee — stray from the fairways at your peril. It is a tremendous test of golf and the outward half especially is as fine a nine holes as I have ever played."

Players would be well advised to listen to the words of Watson, a man who knows a thing or two about links golf, having won the British Open Championship five times in his storied career.

Watson speaks of the inward nine as being particularly illustrious, but the set-up for the final nine — the long, par-4 ninth hole — serves as both a great finisher for the outward nine and a shining precursor to the excellence that awaits.

A blind tee shot on No. 9 needs to stay close to the large dune on the left of the fairway to set up the best approach to the green. There is no room for error in the left as any shot drifting too far will be lost in a dense gorse-covered dune. There's more room to the right for the shorter hitter, although it's not the best line for the second shot.

There are two well-placed bunkers some 50 yards short of the green, level with a large mound on the right of the green. Look out for a green-side bunker and two deep pots on the left. This is one of the more undulating greens.

Officials at Royal County Down call the ninth "one of the most photographed holes in the world." Certainly that is a claim made by many clubs about a number of holes, and it's verification is impossible, but after seeing the ninth, it is difficult not to reach for a camera if you have one handy. The ninth hole will be a highlight for competitors at the Walker Cup, just like it is for every player who steps up to its tee. **JB**

# No. ❾ PABLO CREEK

**Course:** Pablo Creek

**Location:** Jacksonville, Florida, USA

**Hole:** No. 9

**Length:** 448 yards

**Par:** 4

**Designer:** Tom Fazio

**Course Comment:** If you call and ask the pro shop if Pablo Creek is public or private, you're likely to get this response: "It's very private." And don't expect to see the course on television in the near future. Pablo Creek does not allow outside tournaments.

Even though only members and their guests can play Pablo Creek, the golf course is certainly worth a look. So grab your clubs and let's head out to the ninth tee — remember, this is just pretend.

Wow. This is one picturesque-looking hole. It's really a shame not many people get to see this. Considered one of the best holes at Pablo Creek, the 448-yard par 4 begins here at this elevated tee. Our guide (I mean, our pretend guide) says it's about 150 feet above the fairway.

To the right is a marsh which leads right into that river which leads right up to the green. In other words, don't go right.

On the left is another water hazard and two bunkers which sit out there about 270 to 280 yards off the tee. In other words, don't go left.

So where can you go? "Right down the middle," says our guide.

A good tee shot will leave you about 180 yards from the green. The river shouldn't come into play on your second shot unless you slice it over the bunkers. And there is no chance you would ever do that.

In all, there are four bunkers around this elevated green which our guide calls "subtle." In other words, it's not too tough.

You can now open your eyes. We're done pretending. **TJ**

**Course:** St. Andrews Links (The Castle Course)

**Location:** Fife, Scotland

**Hole:** No. 9 (No. 18)

**Par:** No. 9: Par 4 (No. 18: Par 5)

**Length:** No. 9: 381 yards (No. 18: 555 yards)

**Designer:** David McLay Kidd

**Course Comment:** The only "dual hole" that is named in the book, it seemed impossible to differentiate between No. 9 and No. 18, because their combined green make their personality as one.

# No. ❾ ST. ANDREWS
## (THE CASTLE COURSE)

David McLay Kidd was given quite an assignment when he was contracted by the St. Andrews Links Trust to design course No. 7: Give us something new, but make sure it fits right in. He had already worked wonders at Bandon Dunes on the Pacific Coast in Oregon, so the challenge was within reach.

With the world of golf watching closely, Kidd has worked his magic to the approval of all. It's just two miles from the center of the town of St. Andrews, and there already was a brilliant landscape, but Kidd was sure to work within the framework of the birthplace of golf. Playing more than 7,000 feet from the back tees, the course is already attracting visitors from around the globe to try out St. Andrews' newest test. And at the Castle Course, they will not be disappointed.

Particularly at No. 9. Well, let's say No. 9 and No. 18, because it is one of St. Andrews' charming double greens that makes The Castle Course finish so memorable. Kidd turned somewhat nondescript and rugged farmland into pure linksland. The closing stretch of holes is among the best in Scotland, and none exemplifies this better than this enormous double green.

Making the green even more magnificent is the fact that it overlooks the splendid, award-winning Castle Course Clubhouse, which offers unparalleled views over St. Andrews Bay and the town of St. Andrews. It is a hole (and a green) that just keeps on giving. **JB**

## No. ❾ SWINLEY FOREST

**Course:** Swinley Forest

**Location:** Ascot, Berkshire, England

**Hole:** No. 9

**Length:** 435 yards

**Par:** 4

**Designer:** Harry S. Colt

**Course Comment:** Swinley Forest, while without a major tournament, is consistently rated among England's best courses. Logistics preclude parking, galleries and the rest, but the course itself is a favorite among European Tour players on their "off" weeks who are looking for a venue that calls for a variety of shots.

Swinley Forest is without question one of the finest courses on the British Isles. And, while some point to the excellent diversity of the course's par-3 holes, the par 4s — particularly the ninth — offer a brilliant challenge. The sixth, the 12th, and the 15th are all excellent par 4s, but many say the 435-yard ninth is the best par 4 on the course.

The tee on this hole is elevated some 60 feet above the fairway, and provides a wonderful view of this stunning heathland hole. The fairway turns grandly from right to left, and there is protection from trying to cut the corner. Gorse and fescue greet any ball too far left, so the idea is to play as far to the left side of the fairway as you can, without trickling into the junk that awaits off the fairway.

If you go to the right side of the fairway, you avoid all trouble, but you also leave a hugely long shot into the green. Perhaps you could reach the green in two from the right, but you have forfeited the precision necessary to give yourself a reasonable putt. The green is small, but it has no bunkers. So if you afford yourself a proper angle, it is a hole that can be birdied. **JB**

## No. ❾ TRYALL CLUB

**Course:** Tryall Club

**Location:** Montego Bay, Jamaica

**Hole:** No. 9

**Length:** 404 yards

**Par:** 4

**Designer:** Ralph Plummer

**Course Comment:** Tryall once played host to the LPGA and also staged the 1995 Johnnie Walker World Championship, which was won by Fred Couples.

If you visited Jamaica in past years and happened upon Tryall Club, you might not be impressed. There were times in its history when it had fallen into less-than-top condition. However, much money and effort has been pumped into the club and it is now in pristine shape. It features holes that kiss the Caribbean Sea, and No. 9 — with vistas so beautiful as to be distracting — is among Tryall's most distinctive holes.

Without question, Tryall is worth a visit. In fact, it's worth more than one stop.

The hillside ninth tee offers a panoramic view of ocean, mountains, and the Tryall Great House, which dates back to 1834 and is the centerpiece of the 2,200-acre resort. There is a ditch to the left, but if you overcompensate trying to avoid it, you probably won't be able to reach the green in regulation from the right rough. The putting surface is long and narrow and slopes back to front.

The Great House, plainly visible from several holes, offers guests one- and two-bedroom villas in which to stay. There are also larger villas throughout the property, all with personal staff. Beside the sea and great golf, Tryall is famous for its caddies. They are personable, experienced, and dedicated — with an uncanny ability to track down wayward shots and to read the breaks on even the trickiest greens. **JB**

## No. ❾   **MAIDSTONE GOLF CLUB**

**Course:** Maidstone Golf Club

**Location:** East Hampton, New York, USA

**Hole:** No. 9

**Length:** 400 yards

**Par:** 4

**Designer:** Willie Park

**Course Comment:** Willie Park is somewhat overlooked in the world of architecture. Much of his work was done before the so-called "Golden Age" of golf-course architecture, including Sunningdale Old in 1899 and Huntercombe in 1901. But his influence was still prominent during the Golden Age of the 1920s, and nowhere was it felt more than at The Maidstone Club, which opened in 1922.

It appears to be man versus golf course in its purest form — golfer staring into the teeth of a haggard, yet beautiful piece of real estate. There is no backing away from this challenge if there is to be any hope of success. A thin strip of opportunity lies crouched amid topsy-turvy rumblings of horror to the right and left. Mounded earth dares you to miss the fairway. The green ribbon between seems so desirable, yet a touch beyond reach.

This is not hyperbole.

It is Maidstone's mighty ninth.

The sight of this island fairway surrounded by sand and slope, the view of the Atlantic Ocean to your right, or the gale from which relief is so rare as to be laughable, all are indicators that even the best players in the world are oh-so-close to coming unhinged. Often, elevated tees are a welcome opportunity to enjoy a vista. But at this gnarly par 4, vision might be best put to rest.

Quite simply, there is no escape for anything less than perfection. To the left is a dune covered with vegetation so dense that finding an errant shot should be considered success. But the thought of playing a ball from here is an idea not worth entertaining. The heather-filled dunes on the right are not quite as thick, but playing from this golden fluff — while possible — offers the ball too many questionable options on its way out.

A cross-bunker 85 yards short of the green is merely esthetic following a purely struck effort from the tee. If you are attempting to escape from a first-shot mistake though, it reminds that a humble return to the fairway is in order.

Even a perfect drive leaves yet another call for the best in the bag. There is hope for a mistake if you happen to miss left. Birdie might be gone, but par remains a hope. However, miss to the right and you've found yourself in "Yale Bowl," a bunker dug by the finger of God.

The green is uplifted, not only by its topography, but by the relief it offers upon arrival. Its barely discernable slopes, steady cant to the rear, and exposure to the wind are no bargain. But at least you've reached it.

Be happy. **JB**

**Course:** Chart Hills Golf Club

**Location:** Biddenden, Kent, England

**Hole:** No. 9

**Length:** 365 yards

**Par:** 4

**Designer:** Nick Faldo, Steve Smyers

**Course Comment:** Chart Hills is the first British design work of six-time major championship winner Nick Faldo. When it was named to Golf World's top-100 courses in 2011, it was the only inland course in Kent to be so honored.

# No. ❾ CHART HILLS GOLF CLUB

When there was a fire at Chart Hills in 2005, many feared that the club, which opened in 2003, would suffer. There was severe damage to the clubhouse (now up and running once again), but those who play the course will tell you quite bluntly: The golf is still first-rate. That has been the case straight through.

Perhaps top of the list of prideful spots is the signature ninth hole, whose distance at 365 yards would suggest a reachable par 4. But, anyone going for this hole on the drive would be feeling extremely lucky.

There are eight bunkers blanketing the area around the green, and there is virtually no way to reach the putting surface on the drive, which is narrow and sits perpendicular to the tee box and fairway.

The smarter play is to hit about 260 yards off the tee, which clears five bunkers and some water to the right, and leaves you with just over a 100-yard pitching wedge to the well-protected green. Any closer than that, and the mounded fairway gets ultra-narrow, and brings into play those bunkers on the left and nasty gorse on the right. Play it safe, hope for a close chip, and a two-putt just might bring you birdie. Forget about ego, and never mind driving the green. **JB**

**Course:** Philadelphia Cricket Club

**Location:** Flourtown, Pennsylvania, USA

**Hole:** No. 9

**Length:** 459 yards

**Par:** 4

**Designer:** A.W. Tillinghast

**Course Comment:** Founded in 1901, this private cricket and golf club has been listed by the USGA as one of the first 100 clubs established in the U.S., and *Golf Magazine* recognized it in their 1995 list of "The First 100 Clubs in America."

## No. ❾ PHILADELPHIA CRICKET CLUB

This 459-yard par 4 is the No. 1 handicap hole on the golf course. So if you are not a good golfer, don't expect to score well here. And if all else fails, there is always cricket.

But since we are standing on the tee, let's take a swing at this. How difficult can it really be?

The slightly elevated tee allows you to see the entire challenge in front of you. The railroad tracks that run the length of the hole on the right are out-of-bounds.

There is a fairway bunker on the left about 275 yards out and a bunker more in the middle, roughly 240 yards from the back tees. The goal is to carry the middle bunker and avoid the left bunker — and the railroad tracks.

The second shot (or third depending on your skill level) is very difficult. The biggest part of the three-tier green is the back shelf and that's usually where the flag is. So this shot is uphill, to a flag on the back of the green with a strong wind usually into your face.

And you're still 185 to 205 yards away from the target. Just deciding what club to use is difficult enough. Laying up is not a bad idea, but watch out for the bunker in the middle about 70 yards from the green.

Tough enough for you?

Where do they play cricket? **TJ**

**Course:** Metrowest Golf Club

**Location:** Orlando, Florida, USA

**Hole:** No. 9

**Length:** 405 yards

**Par:** 4

**Designer:** Robert Trent Jones Sr.

**Course Comment:** Public course has hosted over 2,500 Orlando golf tournaments since 1987, including Champions Tour and U.S. Open qualifying. Located less than five miles from Universal Studios and International Drive, this well-manicured layout is popular among tourists and Florida residents alike.

# No. ❾ METROWEST GOLF CLUB

Like a schoolyard dare, Metrowest urges players to take the "John Daly Challenge" on its ninth hole. The Lion's roar still resonates from the gold tee box, where a plaque informs players that the popular PGA Tour professional drove the green on this signature par 4 — a 328-yard carry over the water.

From the tee, players can accept the challenge and aim for the pin with nothing but water standing in their way. Mere mortals, however, attack the hole in the manner Robert Trent Jones Sr. intended, making their way around the demanding dogleg left.

A solitary oak through the fairway is the ideal target line, calling for a softly drawn driver into the fairway. A more conservative approach is knocking a long iron or fairway wood down the right side of the fairway. Accuracy off the tee is imperative as a smattering of trees down the right rough can impede an approach shot. On the other hand, anything moving too far left will be exaggerated by a fairway that slopes toward the lake.

Water guards the front and left portions of the green, setting up a difficult second shot. A pair of greenside bunkers penalizes players who bail out right, while a well-placed pot bunker through the green punishes those who take too much club. Feeling up to the challenge? **BB**

**Course:** Pebble Beach Golf Links

**Location:** Pebble Beach, California, USA

**Hole:** No. 9

**Length:** 462 yards

**Par:** 4

**Designer:** Jack Neville, Douglas Grant, H. Chandler Egan

**Course Comment:** Is there a more difficult, more famous stretch of golf than Nos. 8, 9, and 10 at Pebble Beach. Actually, go back a little further. How about Nos. 4 through 10. Like Augusta and St. Andrews, just the name Pebble Beach gets the blood flowing and the golf clubs swinging.

BELOW *Jack Nicklaus plays a shot on the ninth at Pebble Beach, June 2000.*

OPPOSITE *Players putt out on the ninth hole at Pebble Beach.*

# No. ❾ PEBBLE BEACH GOLF LINKS

The eighth hole might be one of the most dramatic in the world of golf, but No. 9 is simply a great golf hole. The locals like to say the ninth is as good as the eighth is dramatic.

Let's get one thing straight. To say that No. 8 is better than No. 9 or No. 10 is better than No. 7 or No. 17 is as good as No. 18 is like saying Elvis was as good as the Beatles or Ted Williams was better than Ty Cobb or . . . you get the picture.

"The best" hole is very subjective, and it doesn't get more subjective (or debated) than at Pebble Beach. Everyone is right, yet everyone is wrong.

Speaking of right, that's where the Pacific Ocean is on this long par 4. The ninth hole would be the signature hole on almost any other golf course in the United States. At Pebble Beach, it's one of many magical holes.

From the tee, there is 245 yards between you and the bunker on the left. Aim your tee shot just inside the bunker on the left. The fairway slopes severely to the right in the landing area and it won't take much for your ball to roll into the rough.

You often have a downhill second shot into a narrow right front opening guarded by the deep bunker in the front left of the green, and the ocean to the right. The 9th green is only 24 yards deep and slopes from left back to right front and down toward the ocean. **TJ**

**Course:** Siena Golf Club

**Location:** Las Vegas, Nevada, USA

**Hole:** No. 9

**Length:** 420 yards

**Par:** 4

**Designer:** Lee E. Schmidt, Brian Curley

**Course Comment:** The "Crown Jewel" of the Siena active adult community, Siena Golf Club features elevated terrain that provides panoramic views of the nearby mountains and Las Vegas city lights.

# No. ❾  SIENA GOLF CLUB

Back in the day, gambling and Elvis were both kings in Las Vegas. Gambling is certainly still rolling along as strong as ever both on and off the strip, but golf has replaced Mr. Heartbreak Hotel as the Bright Light City's other king.

When you're in the casinos, you're pretty much on your own. The casino employees aren't exactly there to give you tips on how to win. But the golf course is a different story. Here is some advice from the good people at Siena Golf Club:

"This long par 4 demands an accurate tee shot. Water lines the left side of the fairway through the green."

"A safe play to the right side of the fairway may encounter the deep, cavernous bunkers protecting the right side. This finishing hole of the outward nine will challenge everyone."

Siena Golf Club has 97 pot bunkers and massive three-tiered greens. It is also one of the best-maintained courses in all of Nevada.

And then there are the views.

Some holes tee up views of the Strip. Then there are spectacular views of Red Rock Mountain, while with others you get great looks at Spring Mountain. **TJ**

---

**Course:** Honors Course

**Location:** Ooltewah, Tennessee, USA

**Hole:** No. 9

**Length:** 370 yards

**Par:** 4

**Designer:** Pete Dye

**Course Comment:** This 370-yard par 4 is not as tough as several others on the Honors Course and isn't the type of hole that will ruin your scorecard. But it's considered the signature hole because of its tremendous view as it plays back toward the glamorous clubhouse.

# No. ❾  HONORS COURSE

It's decision time as you stand on the tee looking out at this picturesque hole on one of Tennessee's best golf courses.

One decision, of course, is to let her rip and try to land your tee shot on a fairway that gets narrower as it gets closer to the green. There is plenty of room out there at about 235 yards off the tee. From there, it begins to narrow, making for a tough tee shot.

The so-called smart play is to take aim at the 235-yard section. It's a big target and sets you up nicely for your approach shot. Picking up another 20 to 30 yards really isn't worth it — but that decision is left up to you. Also consider that fairway bunker on the left.

If you do lay up, you are left with about 140 to 150 yards to a very small green. There also is water to the front and left of the green — and of course we have railroad ties around the water, a Pete Dye trademark.

The green is usually firm and slopes back to front. And we've been told that if you are short, your ball can easily spin back right off the green and into the water. **TJ**

## No. ⑨ ROYAL ABERDEEN

Royal Aberdeen essentially runs out and back along the North Sea shore. The outward nine (which is arguably acknowledged as one of the finest in links golf anywhere in the world) cuts its way through some wonderful dune formation and the inland nine on the plateau.

A traditional old Scottish links design, the course is well bunkered with undulating fairways. It is an excellent balance of holes, including strong par 4s, tricky par 3s, and two classic par 5s.

The 8th hole is the signature hole at Royal Aberdeen. The tiny green is protected by 10 bunkers and is an amazing sight. With all due respect to No. 8, we selected No. 9. Why?

Well, Tom Watson is on record as saying it's his favorite hole on the course. So, we will go with his recommendation.

A classic dogleg right, this par-4 has plenty of warning signs for those interested in pulling out the driver. The fairway is rather narrow and there are bunkers all along the left side. The green is further around the bend and tucked up into the sand dunes.

Play this smartly and be happy with par. **TJ**

## No. ❾ ROYAL BIRKDALE

**Course:** Royal Birkdale

**Location:** Southport, England

**Hole:** No. 9

**Length:** 395 yards

**Par:** 4

**Designer:** George Lowe, F.F. Hawtree, F.W. Hawtree

**Course Comment:** It's back. The British Open will return to Royal Birkdale for the ninth time in 2008. There have been plenty of famous moments on the Lancashire course, including Arnold Palmer's victory in 1961.

OPPOSITE *The ninth hole at Royal Birkdale.*

This scenic par 4 is another of Royal Birkdale's outstanding holes.

This dogleg right has a blind tee shot requiring you to have your swing and game in order. After eight holes, let's hope you do.

With plenty of trouble on the left, you might be thinking of favoring the right side. Big mistake. That pot bunker on the right is very deep indeed. As in deep trouble.

A good tee shot is only half the challenge. The second shot is even more important because missing the plateau green will add unwanted strokes to your day.

And don't be long — there are plenty of problems behind the green.

The keys to success here are simple. You need an accurate drive to the landing area. Again, it's a blind shot so it will be a little easier the second time you play the course.

Another key is selecting the right club on approach. With the elevated green, distance becomes a problem. So you can't see where you're going on one shot. And you don't know how far on your second shot.

No one said golf was easy. And playing the historic Royal Birkdale won't be easy to forget. **TJ**

## No. ❾ MILWAUKEE COUNTRY CLUB

**Course:** Milwaukee Country Club

**Location:** River Hills, Wisconsin, USA

**Hole:** No. 9

**Length:** 332 yards

**Par:** 4

**Designer:** Harry S. Colt, Charles Hugh Alison, Robert Trent Jones Sr.

**Course Comment:** Charles Hugh Allison was Colt's design partner and handled much of their work in the United States, including Milwaukee Country Club and the Country Club of Detroit.

Milwaukee Country Club, founded in 1894, is credited as being one of the first 100 clubs of America. Its revered Harry S. Colt and Charles Hugh Alison layout, however, wasn't built until 1929, then was given a makeover by Robert Trent Jones Sr. in preparation for the 1969 Walker Cup. Located in suburban River Hills, the course is situated in rolling, wooded terrain, and features an abundance of wildlife and fast, sloping greens.

No. 9 is a deceptively short par 4, and if you take it for granted, this slight dogleg right can jump up and bite you, sending you into the inward nine on a not-so-pleasant note. A group of trees and a trio of fairway bunkers on the right encroach on the narrow landing area for the tee shot, and the short uphill approach is complicated by a deep bunker that looms right and short of the putting surface, an obstacle that also causes trouble for those who may attempt to reach the green with their drives.

The U.S. squad, led by future PGA Tour players Lanny Wadkins, Bruce Fleisher, Steve Melnyk, and Joe Inman, edged out Great Britain and Ireland 10–8 in the 1969 Walker Cup held at Milwaukee. **KA**

401

**Course:** St. Eurach Golf &
Country Club

**Location:** Iffeldorf, Bavaria, Germany

**Hole:** No. 9

**Length:** 434 yards

**Par:** 4

**Designer:** Donald Harradine

**Course Comment:** The PGA
European Tour's BMW International
Open was held at St. Eurach for
three years, with Mark McNulty
(1994), Frank Nobilo (1995), and
Mark Farry (1996) the champions.

# No. ❾ ST. EURACH GOLF & COUNTRY CLUB

This course is set in picturesque pre-Alps countryside in upper Bavaria, approximately 30 miles south of Munich, and features slightly hilly terrain, forests, meadows, and moorland basins. St. Eurach offers marvelous views of the Karwendel mountain range and is located in the Osterteen lakes region, an environmentally protected group of 19 unique and ecologically rich kettle lakes.

The ninth hole at St. Eurach is such a stern test that it was played as the 18th when the BMW International Open was held here. The view of the Alps in the distance is marvelous from both tee and green, but golfers would be wise to keep their focus on the task at hand. The tee shot must be hit to the left side of the narrow fairway on this slight dogleg right. If not, a group of trees on the right-hand side will block a clear approach to the uphill green, which is guarded by bunkers on the front left and right.

Native son Bernhard Langer finished tied for second place at the 1995 BMW, two shots behind New Zealand's Frank Nobilo. The BMW remains the only major PGA European Tour event that Langer has not won in his own country. **KA**

## No. ❾ SHADOW CREEK GOLF CLUB

**Course:** Shadow Creek Golf Club

**Location:** North Las Vegas, Nevada, USA

**Hole:** No. 9

**Length:** 409 yards

**Par:** 4

**Designer:** Tom Fazio, Andy Banfield

**Course Comment:** Getting to Shadow Creek is part of the fun. Your entrée to Shadow Creek begins when you register as a guest at one of the MGM Mirage properties. A limousine will transport you to and from your appointment and upon arrival, your personal caddie will greet and guide you through your round. First class all the way.

The course is located just 20 minutes from the Vegas Strip, so it is no surprise that Shadow Creek has attracted big names such as Michael Jordan, Joe Pesci, Matt Damon, George Clooney, and Michael Douglas.

This very scenic and challenging hole is one of the signature holes on the course — let's see what the pros at the club have to say about it:

"At the ninth hole, the course runs parallel to Shadow Creek and plays from south to north with an orientation of the fairway to the mountains. Alternate tees on the left and right provide variety, and from the tee, the fairway appears to be rather tight, but there is plenty of room to play."

Well, that's good to know. But don't think it gets any easier. No matter where the pin is located on the green, the approach shot is a difficult one. If the pin is rear-placed, the angle of the green is a problem; if the pin is front-placed, a carry-up shot is required to overcome the tricky contours.

The description in this book is just the beginning, however. A first-hand experience of Shadow Creek's ninth is the only way to go. With its immaculate fairways running up to a finely manicured green guarded by dense woodland on one side and a crystal-clear lake to the other, it is beauty and splendor in true Las Vegas style. **TJ**

## No. ❾ ARABELLA GOLF COURSE

**Course:** Arabella Golf Course

**Location:** Kleinmond, South Africa

**Hole:** No. 9

**Length:** 297 yards

**Par:** 4

**Designer:** Peter Matkovich

**Course Comment:** The theme at Arabella is balance. It's challenging enough to bring you back for more, yet enjoyable enough to make you not want to leave.

Peter Matkovich has created a course that complements the environment without disappointing the golfer, whether expert or amateur.

The scenery alone makes this course worth the walk. Even without a club in your hands, it's almost worth it to pay the green fees and take a ride or stroll through the 18 holes of this Kleinmond magic. But we strongly recommend playing.

The course was built on the gently undulating foothills of the Kogelberg Nature Reserve, nestled between sandy plains and fertile, verdant hills. The Bot River, the country's largest lagoon, offers a breathtaking panorama in resplendent surroundings of unsurpassed natural beauty.

And how scenic is No. 9? For that, let's ask one of the hometown heroes.

Ernie Els, one of the best players in the world, describes the ninth hole of the golf course as the most beautiful par 4 in his homeland.

Also watch out for sudden gusts of wind that have been known to adversely affect the flight of a ball.

Arabella Golf Course is always listed among the top 10 golf courses in South Africa. There are plans for a second 18-hole course with Jack Nicklaus as the head designer. **TJ**

**Course:** PGA West (Stadium Course)

**Location:** La Quinta, California, USA

**Hole:** No. 9

**Length:** 452 yards

**Par:** 4

**Designer:** Pete Dye

**Course Comment:** Inspired by the Scottish seaside courses, the PGA West Stadium Course has few equals when it comes to spectacular beauty. Its design is as awesome as it is beautiful, and belongs early in the conversation of the best courses in the world.

**BELOW AND OPPOSITE** *The ninth hole at PGA West.*

# No. ❾ PGA WEST (STADIUM COURSE)

Named "Reflection," this 452-yard par 4 is the No. 1 handicap on an 18-hole test of golf considered by many as the toughest golf course in the United States. It's safe to assume that the toughest hole on the toughest course will be . . . well, tough.

Standing on the tee from the tips, it's clear to see the danger on the right side. First sand, then water will escort you down the entire right side of the fairway. Just knowing it's there is intimidating as you pull the driver out of the bag.

Why the driver? Why not lay up?

You didn't think Pete Dye was going to make this easy, did you? Remember the part about being the toughest? Well, if you don't hit it far enough on this slight dogleg, you don't have a chance at the green on your second shot.

There is plenty of trouble around the green — so laying up might not be a bad idea after all. Deep rough, bunkers, and water surround the green. This is one of those holes where a par will feel like a birdie.

Holes five through 10 are as difficult a stretch of golf you will find anywhere. And the rest of the back nine don't let up much. No wonder it's considered one of the toughest. **TJ**

**Course:** Silver Tip Golf Resort

**Location:** Canmore, Alberta, Canada

**Hole:** No. 9

**Length:** 464 yards

**Par:** 4

**Designer:** Les Furber

**Course Comment:** Carved from the natural beauty of the Canadian Rockies, Silver Tip is a world-class, 7,200-yard championship course.

# No. ❾ SILVER TIP GOLF RESORT

Picture this. You are surrounded by some of the world's most spectacular scenery, including tremendous mountain ranges and untouched wilderness. The warm southern Alberta sunshine is all around you. And moments of solitude are broken by the voices of nature.

Heaven here on earth in Alberta, Canada. Enough, already. Grab your clubs and let's play some golf.

No. 9, along with No. 4 and No. 11, is one of the more scenic holes on the spectacular Bow Valley corridor, deep in the heart of the breathtaking Rocky Mountain wilderness.

It's also a pretty tough golf hole.

This dogleg left is extremely downhill with water on the left side of the green and trees on the right side.

Off the tee, big hitters will be rewarded. If you can hit your drive about 250 to 260 yards you can catch the start of where the fairway takes a nosedive. The roll alone will take your breath away.

But this tee shot is very intimidating indeed. And there is a bunker about 260 yards from the tee on the right side of the fairway.

The green has three tiers and slopes from back to front. **TJ**

**Course:** Buenos Aires Golf Club
(Yellow Course)

**Location:** Buenos Aires, Argentina

**Hole:** No. 9

**Length:** 456 yards

**Par:** 4

**Designer:** Kelly Blake Moran

**Course Comment:** Buenos Aires
was the site of the last U.S. victory
at the World Golf Championship/
World Cup in 2000. Tiger Woods
and David Duval combined for a 254
total and a three-stroke victory over
local favorites Angel Cabrera and
Eduardo Romero.

# No. ❾  BUENOS AIRES GOLF CLUB
## (YELLOW COURSE)

In 1987 a group of influential Argentine businessmen decided it was time Buenos Aires had a world-class golf course. The result of that decision is 27 holes weaved through a collection of lakes, ponds, and streams, which has become one of the region's top designs.

At the heart of Buenos Aires' Yellow Course lies the ninth, a 456-yard par 4 that plays into the prevailing wind. The dogleg right plays around a large lake with out-of-bounds waiting down the left side of the fairway.

Even if players can avoid the water and out-of-bounds, there are deep fescue grasses that run along the left side of the hole making a missed drive particularly penalizing. For the 2000 World Golf Championship/ World Cup a new set of tees was built further back, making the hazards even more punishing than they already were.

The approach shot is usually a long iron across the water to a long, but narrow green set at an angle. Wayward second shots run the risk of finding a green-side bunker on the left. A mound waits at the back of the green to stop long shots. Players must also avoid another bunker that runs along the right side near the stream that flows into the lake. **RH**

## No. ❾ ST. EUGENE MISSION

**Course:** St. Eugene Mission

**Location:** Cranbrook, British Columbia, Canada

**Hole:** No. 9

**Length:** 556 yards

**Par:** 5

**Designer:** Les Furber

**Course Comment:** Many of the greens at St. Eugene Mission are more than 30 yards in depth placing a premium on club selection for your shorter approach shots.

St. Eugene Mission is home to a first-rate golf course and a casino, giving an exciting dimension to a golf vacation in the British Columbia Rockies. The $42.1 million facility features a 19,000-square-foot casino and a 125-room Delta Hotel.

It's the best of both worlds. You can gamble at night and play golf during day. Or you can gamble during the day while out on the golf course. Of course, there is plenty of reward out there for the aggressive player. But plenty of danger as well.

Let's see if it's worth the gamble on the ninth, which runs right along the St. Mary River.

Considered by many as one of the best holes on the course, No. 9 has plenty of personality and uniqueness. The river cuts into the landing area and will wash away any ball you hit left.

However, with a long drive you can carry a big part of the water and set yourself up for a "gambling" second shot at the green.

The wise play on your second shot is with a mid-iron aimed over the 150-yard marker leaving you a short-iron approach.

There is plenty of trouble greenside, so keep that in mind. The green is very small and narrow with sand and a pond guarding it. Don't miss the green or you're in big trouble. **TJ**

## No. ❾ YARRA YARRA GOLF CLUB

**Course:** Yarra Yarra Golf Club

**Location:** Bentleigh East, Victoria, Australia

**Hole:** No. 9

**Length:** 529 yards

**Par:** 5

**Designer:** Alex Russell

**Course Comment:** This fabulous club in the famed Sand Belt region of the Victoria capital opened in 1928 and gets its name from the nearby Yarra river, which means "flowing-flowing" in the Aboriginal language.

Architect Alex Russell was trained by the great Alister MacKenzie, and it is not hard to feel the influences of the master designer himself at Yarra Yarra, especially on No. 9. The meaty par 5 is a dogleg left, and the best play off the tee is a drive to the right center of the fairway, avoiding the four fairway bunker at the turn on the left.

As for their second shots, golfers would be wise to lay up and keep again to the right side of the fairway; the fairway slopes to the left, and there is always the chance of a well-hit ball ending up in the first of a series of bunkers on the left that run all the way to the green.

And the green is no easy matter for even the shortest of approach shots. Yes, it is massive in size, and there is room on the right to run up your balls. But as is the case with many of the holes at Yarra Yarra, the slopes and undulations of that surface can make even the simplest putts exceedingly difficult. **JS**

## No. ❾ LAKE NONA GOLF CLUB

**Course:** Lake Nona Golf Club

**Location:** Orlando, Florida, USA

**Hole:** No. 9

**Length:** 532 yards

**Par:** 5

**Designer:** Tom Fazio, Andy Banfield

**Course Comment:** In an area where there are as many golf courses as grocery stores, Lake Nona is considered by some to be among the best places to play in Orlando. The course has a reputation for always being in excellent condition and it is one of the tougher tests of golf around.

There have been many discussions over the years about the best hole at Lake Nona. No. 7 and No. 15 always get brought up — and you can read about them in this book. Some also like the challenging finishing hole. But the 532-yard par-5 No. 9 also justly deserves consideration as one of Lake Nona's finest.

The ninth hole is one of those par 5s where you have a real good shot at reaching it in two. The fairway is pretty wide open for your tee shot and the big hitters can take advantage of a slope at about 300 yards where your ball can get a nice roll.

On the right from the tee are trees and then the No. 1 fairway off in the distance. There is a fairway bunker that runs along the left side of the fairway but doesn't come into play for most people.

The toughest shot is your second — especially when you are going for the green. There are fairway bunkers on the left you have to clear with your second shot. You can lay up and have a nice wedge to the green from about 100 yards.

The green also is tricky. There is a severe ridge that runs off to the right, and it is possible to putt right off the green. And watch out for the cluster of trees on the right of the green as well as the left bunker. **TJ**

## No. ❾ ELLERSTON GOLF COURSE

**Course:** Ellerston Golf Course

**Location:** Upper Hunter Valley, New South Wales, Australia

**Hole:** No. 9

**Length:** 557 yards

**Par:** 5

**Designer:** Greg Norman, Bob Harrison

**Course Comment:** Conditioning is a marvel at Ellerston, which may well be the most highly acclaimed of all Greg Norman's golf courses, as well as the hardest to get on.

The hole at this ultra-private retreat begins with a spectacular tee shot, played across a deep valley to a landing area on a hill. There are four bunkers in diagonal ridges along the left side of the fairway, and the more of those you can carry with your tee shot, the better your chances of putting your second shot onto the green.

But getting on that green is no easy matter, as there is a ditch about 20 yards before it. And the green itself runs downhill from front to back, with large trees rising on the left short of the putting surface, as yet another impediment to those trying to launch a fairway wood or long iron onto the elusive green.

Any miss to that side will result in you being blocked out, and you will have a very tough time getting down in two (or even three). So, the best play at No. 9 is coming in from the right, preferably with a low runner. **JS**

**Course:** Muirfield Golf Links

**Location:** Gullane, East Lothian, Scotland

**Hole:** No. 9

**Length:** 504 yards

**Par:** 5

**Designer:** Old Tom Morris, Harry S. Colt, Tom Simpson

**Course Comment:** Muirfield is home to the Honourable Company of Edinburgh Golfers who held their first meeting on Leith Links in 1744.

**BELOW** *The ninth hole at Muirfield.*

**OPPOSITE** *Robert Allenby of Australia plays a shot on the ninth hole at Muirfield, July 2002.*

# No. ❾ MUIRFIELD GOLF LINKS

You know a course had a good future when a legend such as Old Tom Morris couldn't wait to open the place. In May of 1891, 16 holes had been finished by hand and horse, with two more to go. Morris, however, insisted the course be opened, and the final two holes were completed as players made their way around the links. Nos. 17 and 18 were completed by December 1891, and Morris's eagerness proved to be justified.

Many consider Muirfield to be the finest course in all of Scotland, and some say its pre-eminent status extends beyond the borders of its country and might include the entire European continent. The debate over which course is best is always a subjective exercise, but Muirfield's trailblazing design at the time of its construction more than 100 years ago, proves what a visionary Old Tom undeniably was.

Muirfield was the first course designed in two loops of nine holes — the first nine going round the perimeter of the property in a clockwise direction, the second nine contained inside the first, running counter-clockwise. This is particularly brilliant at Muirfield because no more than three consecutive holes go in the same direction, and the always-tricky wind gets even trickier because the player keeps shifting his aim. The course would be tough enough on its own, but this devilish use of Scotland's natural gales makes Muirfield a sometimes torturous test.

No hole toys with a player's mind more than the ninth, because regardless of wind direction, it is difficult. Usually the wind at a golfer's back is welcome, but not at Muirfield's ninth because the further the ball travels down the fairway, the more claustrophobic the landing area. And against the wind, the hole's length is considered monstrous. Regardless of the direction of the breezes, if you find the rough at Muirfield you can almost toss away a possibility at birdie . . . and hope like heck for par.

Even on the fairway, an approach must carry five bunkers front and right and land softly on a smallish green. It doesn't pay to get cocky at Muirfield, particularly at the ninth. Caution not only is advised; it is mandatory. **JB**

**Course:** North Berwick Golf Club
(West Course)

**Location:** East Lothian, Scotland

**Hole:** No. 9

**Length:** 510 yards

**Par:** 5

**Designer:** David Strath

**Course Comment:** A match between
Willie and Mungo Park and Young
and Old Tom Morris in 1875 at North
Berwick was abruptly halted when
a telegram arrived informing Young
Tom that his wife was seriously ill
after the birth of their son. Both
mother and son died. Three months
later, a grief-stricken Young Tom
Morris also died.

## No. ❾ NORTH BERWICK GOLF CLUB
### (WEST COURSE)

Golf has been played at North Berwick since 1832, making it the second-oldest club, behind St. Andrews, to host continuous play. Among the club's original members was a soldier who fought in the Battle of Waterloo, and the West Course's greatest hole, the original Redan 15th, has been copied more times than the reality television genre.

History is something this quiet edge of the Firth of Forth has plenty of. Yet lost in the club's vast venerable past is a nondescript gem that more times than not is often overlooked and underrated.

The West Course's ninth has been dubbed mundane, a brief respite before embarking on North Berwick's classic closing stretch. However, to miss the ninth's unpretentious character would be a mistake.

Much of the ninth hole's public perception problem may be its order in a peculiar line-up. The short par 5 (510 yards) follows an even shorter par 5 (495 yards). Although the ninth is short by modern standards, depending on the wind there is nothing easy about the hole nicknamed "Mizzentop."

The tee shot must be perfectly positioned in a rolling fairway to give a player any chance of reaching the green in two shots. As is the case on almost all of North Berwick's putting surfaces, the real challenge awaits on the well-contoured green. **RH**

**Course:** BlackHorse Golf Club
(South Course)

**Location:** Cypress, Texas, USA

**Hole:** No. 9

**Length:** 518 yards

**Par:** 5

**Designer:** Jacobsen Hardy
Golf Design

**Course Comment:** BlackHorse Golf
Club, which features two 18-hole
courses (the South and the North)
is located just a chip shot northwest
of Houston.

## No. ❾ BLACKHORSE GOLF CLUB
### (SOUTH COURSE)

The old saying is that everything is bigger in Texas. Well, you can certainly say that about BlackHorse Golf Club when it comes to the number of tees. Bigger as in the quantity. Believe it or not, they have eight sets of tees.

The back tees are called "Big Jake." And these are certainly designed for the "big" hitters. The championship and combo tees both play this par 5 from 500 yards and the shortest tees measure in at 343 yards.

Now that's a big difference in length.

But let's take a trip to the tips. Keep your driver in the bag.

The pressure is really on your first two shots on this shorter par 5. According to the scorecard, accuracy is the key to success here. A 3-wood off the tee should do just fine. The fairway gets pretty narrow in the landing area you are shooting for. There is a creek that cuts through the fairway but shouldn't come into play. Unless of course, you hit a bad shot.

The second shot is another tough go. Not a bad idea to lay up and have a short approach shot. The green has a bunker short left and side left. The scorecard suggests avoiding these. As if you needed their advice on the subject. **TJ**

## No. ⑨ MONTEREY PENINSULA COUNTRY CLUB (DUNES COURSE)

**Course:** Monterey Peninsula Country Club (Dunes Course)

**Location:** Pebble Beach, California, USA

**Hole:** No. 9

**Length:** 479 yards

**Par:** 5

**Designer:** Seth Raynor, Charles Banks, Robert Hunter, Rees Jones

**Course Comment:** Architect Seth Raynor died of pneumonia at age 51 while the Dunes Course was still under construction, and his assistant Charles Banks and local architect Robert Hunter finished the work on the original layout.

Monterey Peninsula Country Club's Dunes Course is set in the midst of some of the most famous golfing land in the world, and thanks to a Rees Jones renovation in the late 1990s, manages to more than hold its own.

The ninth hole's lack of length makes it a fairly simple three-shotter. The temptation for most golfers, though — perhaps inspired by their first glimpse of the ocean and the sounds of crashing waves behind the green — is to go for it in two, and that can bring all sorts of problems into play.

The approach shot must carry a natural sand ridge that crosses most of the fairway, approximately 30 yards short of the putting surface, and also must manage to avoid bunkers at the left front and right front of the green, as well as a small water hazard further left. The ridge of sand partially obscures the green from most angles, leading many to the wiser choice of playing it safe by laying up in front of the dune. Hit a tight approach on your third shot and you've still got an excellent chance at birdie. **KA**

## No. ⑨ LOCHINVAR GOLF CLUB

**Course:** Lochinvar Golf Club

**Location:** Houston, Texas, USA

**Hole:** No. 9

**Length:** 551 yards

**Par:** 5

**Designer:** Jack Nicklaus

**Course Comment:** Nicklaus designed this course in 1980 but there have been some changes along the way. The order of the holes was changed to allow the golfers to finish up in front of the clubhouse — giving the patrons a nice view. The changes also made the front nine more difficult than the back.

The original so-called signature hole at Lochinvar was the old No. 12. That hole is now the current No. 3. But No. 9 is as memorable and challenging a golf hole as there is at Lochinvar — and that's saying something.

This is a straight-up hole, or as our expert in the pro shop described, "what you see is what you get." There are no surprises here but plenty of potential danger.

Standing on an elevated tee you see that the water goes all along the left side of the fairway before cutting out a little bit in front of the green. You don't have to worry about that on your tee shot.

On the right side of the fairway are 15- to 16-year-old pine trees. You should be worrying about them. There are plenty of pine needles in there so you could easily find your ball, but playing it out is another story.

There is also a trap on the left side. At 255 yards from the back tees, it's very reachable.

Once you get to your approach shot, remember the water. The green is elevated about five to eight feet and has a "casual" back-to-front slope, according to our expert.

There is a front left bunker and grass pot bunkers behind the green. **TJ**

Course: Victoria Golf Club

Location: Cheltenham, Melbourne, Australia

Hole: No. 9

Length: 585 yards

Par: 5

Designer: Alister MacKenzie, William Meader, Oscar Damman

Course Comment: In the 1961 Australian Open, Arnold Palmer hit a ball that became hung up in one of the imposing gum trees just off the fairway. Palmer simply climbed the tree, hit the ball to safety and saved par.

# No. ❾ VICTORIA GOLF CLUB

Victoria Golf Club, with its history dating back to when the 20th century was in its infancy, is undoubtedly a club laden with tradition. And with just one look at the golf course, it is plain to see that the course is in wonderful shape. But members at Victoria are equally proud of a detail that might be missed by the casual observer. "We enjoy superb playing conditions and a wonderfully warm environment in our grand old clubhouse . . . " are the words that surprise in Victoria's archives. This club is about more than just golf holes, although the layout is splendid. It also is filled with history, and most importantly of all, a warm atmosphere.

"We all should be thankful to Billy Meader for giving us such a wonderful place . . . " reads another passage from the club's archives. You get the idea. Members are thrilled with their club.

On the inspired initiative of Meader, a group of influential Melbourne businessmen gathered one evening in 1903 at Fisherman's Bend to discuss forming a good golf club to play over leased links land at Port Melbourne. Meader, a stocky, sometimes dour sort, is the "father of Victorian golf" and members today are constantly reminded to whom they should be thankful by plaques and a portrait as they walk through the clubhouse.

Since the 1903 meeting and the forming of the club in 1906, Victoria Golf Club's fame has spread throughout the world. It has produced players of a quality that has brought fame to their native Australia and to the club they represent in the heart of Melbourne's rolling Sand-Belt country in the suburb of Cheltenham.

The glory days of Victoria Golf Club members started way back in 1909 when the great Claude Felstead captured the Australian Open title at Royal Melbourne. In subsequent years, Peter Thomson, a member at Victoria and winner of five British Open Championships, three Australian Opens, and two World, brought glory to the club.

There is great history at Victoria, but there still is plenty to be enjoyed today. To say that the course is wonderful is an understatement, and one of its best holes is the 585-yard ninth.

This is a legitimate three-shot hole because of the dramatic rise in elevation off the tee. A well-struck first shot can carry the hill, but that's the key: it must be well struck. If you are unfortunate enough not to get up the hill in one, this three-shot hole suddenly becomes four. Then, amazingly, another hill awaits. If you've carried the first hill, and get over crest No. 2 with your second shot, you have a huge advantage on this hole.

There are severe fairway bunkers, but the tricky elevation changes are your biggest challenge on the ninth. It is a fantastic hole and a fantastic club. **JB**

**Course:** Congressional Golf Club
(Blue Course)

**Location:** Bethesda, Maryland, USA

**Hole:** No. 9

**Length:** 607 yards

**Par:** 5

**Designer:** Devereux Emmet

**Course Comment:** Congressional
is home to two outstanding 18-hole
courses (the Blue and Gold). The club
played host to the U.S. Open in 1964
and 1997 as well as the U.S. Senior
Open in 1995.

# No. ❾ CONGRESSIONAL GOLF CLUB
## (BLUE COURSE)

There have been plenty of changes over the years at Congressional. The Blue Course has been redesigned several times, most recently by Rees Jones in 1989. Robert Trent Jones Sr. added nine new holes on the Blue Course in 1957, and the back nine on the Gold Course was designed by George and Tom Fazio in 1977.

But one thing that never changes is the quality of the golf. Congressional is one of the best. And that will never change.

The ninth hole is the perfect example. It's both scenic and tough. Throw enjoyable and memorable into the mix also, and you have a can't-miss foursome. When you're done buying shirts and hats in the pro shop, grab a yardage book and see what it says about No. 9.

Right after the sentence that says it is one of the most demanding holes in U.S. Open history, read their suggestion on how to play it. Yes, the part that says it is unwise to attempt this green in two.

If players in the U.S. Open have trouble, what chance do you have? So when you walk to tee, remember it's three to reach the green.

No. 9 features a fairly straight and flat fairway with bunkers on both the right and left side. You need about 280 yards to carry the bunkers. This will put you in good shape for a second shot to the end of the fairway, which is about 80 yards to a three-tier demanding green with five bunkers. **TJ**

**Course:** The Gallery at Dove Mountain (North Course)

**Location:** Marana, Arizona, USA

**Hole:** No. 9

**Length:** 725 yards

**Par:** 5

**Designer:** Tom Lehman, John Fought

**Course Comment:** Co-host (with Omni Tucson National Resort) of the 2001 Touchstone Energy Tucson Open, which was won by Garrett Willis. The Tucson Open is now held only at the Omni Tucson National Resort. Perhaps players didn't like the idea of having a 725-yard monster like No. 9 thrown at them.

## No. ❾ THE GALLERY AT DOVE MOUNTAIN (NORTH COURSE)

Here are a few statistics to consider when regarding the ninth hole at The Gallery at Dove Mountain's North Course: It is the No. 1 handicap hole on the course, there is a downhill elevation change of about 80 feet, and the green measures 7,900 square feet. Interesting numbers, to be sure, but here is the statistic to remember:

Seven-hundred and twenty-five yards.

No misprint. One of the longest holes in the world, and co-designed by PGA Tour player Tom Lehman and partner John Fought. When asked about the golf course, Lehman answered: "What I like most about this golf course is that each hole has its own distinct personality." More specifically, when commenting on the bear he helped create to end the outgoing nine, Lehman commented: "I wanted to make a legitimate three-shot hole."

Ya think?

The length at the ninth is amazing enough, and there are other factors to consider, as well. Thin desert air makes the ball travel farther than you might be used to, and the elevation change from tee to green also needs to be considered when gauging distance. But, mostly, it's all about length.

The gargantuan ninth requires three, long, well-placed shots to have any hope of birdie or par. This hole begins with a downhill tee shot to a generous landing area, which is devoid of trouble, except for two fairway bunkers on the left.

The second shot, which is decidedly downhill, offers several options because there is a bunker left, two bunkers center, two bunkers right, and a large lake bisecting the right half of the fairway. If a player chooses to play safe down the right center of the fairway, he leaves a long third shot. If he chooses to play closer to the green, he must negotiate a shot near the lake and around the bunkers on the left.

The green is protected jealously by five randomly placed bunkers and a small wash, which bisects the fairway 40 yards short of the putting surface.

In promotional material for The Gallery at Dove Mountain, there is the following line: "This hole is sure to be considered one of the most interesting three-shot par 5s in North America." This could be one of the biggest understatements in golf. They think this is only interesting? Try tantalizing, overwhelming, challenging, and awesome. **JB**

## No. ❾ GARY PLAYER COUNTRY CLUB

**Course:** Gary Player Country Club

**Location:** Sun City, South Africa

**Hole:** No. 9

**Length:** 596 yards

**Par:** 5

**Designer:** Gary Player

**Course Comment:** Through 2003, native sons David Frost, Nick Price, and Ernie Els shared the record of three Nedbank Golf Challenge titles.

BELOW *The ninth hole at Gary Player.*

OPPOSITE *Lee Westwood of England plays his second shot on the ninth hole at Gary Player, November 2000.*

There are not many par 5s that offer more risk-reward shots than this one, which offers thrilling theater for the galleries at the annual Nedbank Golf Challenge, golf's richest tournament.

The hole, which Player calls "a truly heroic par 5," is so long that even the world's best professionals rarely play from the 596-yard back tees, offering players the chance to go for the island green in two. To get there, a player must first hit a long tee shot to the right side of a narrow, tree-lined fairway, then carry a beautiful two-tiered lake with a rocky shoreline that goes right to the edge of the elevated putting surface.

It's a risk that requires a rare combination of power and finesse, one that even Ernie Els admits "can be intimidating" with a wood or long iron in hand, especially when a shot that's long will find the water back of the green. Even laying up can be difficult, especially when the pin is placed at the back left or back right of the putting surface. Go for broke, and you could be putting for eagle. Hit it less than perfectly, however, and you're staring a bogey or worse in the face. **KA**

## No. ❾ BADLANDS GOLF CLUB (DESPERADO COURSE)

**Course:** Badlands Golf Club (Desperado Course)

**Location:** Las Vegas, Nevada, USA

**Hole:** No. 9

**Length:** 541 yards

**Par:** 5

**Designer:** Johnny Miller

**Course Comment:** All three nine-hole layouts were designed by Johnny Miller, but he did have some help. Mother Nature played a hand, as did Chi Chi Rodriguez, who was a consultant on the project. Not a bad team.

This popular Las Vegas golf club is the epitome of a target desert golf course. With four sets of tees from which to choose, the Badlands features spectacular terrain and breathtaking views.

Badlands starts to get really good at No. 6. And then it takes off. The four finishing holes on the Desperado nine are spectacular. No. 8, a challenging and scenic par 3, is a favorite among many. But No. 9 is just as memorable — it's very hard to pick a signature hole at Badlands. Everyone has their favorite. This 541-yard par 5 is not soon forgotten.

Getting to the green is certainly a challenge, but once you arrive you will see it was worth the wait. The green sits atop the edge of a dramatic cliff. The waste area in front of this huge green is around 30 feet deep and 30 yards wide. In other words, you better hit your target.

Many people like this hole because it's true desert golf. Others like it for the simple beauty of the cliffside green. Luckily, if you play it you can experience both. **TJ**

Course: Black Mountain Golf and
Country Club (Desert Course)

Location: Henderson, Nevada, USA

Hole: No. 9

Length: 530 yards

Par: 5

Designer: Bob E. Baldock

Course Comment: Built in 1959,
Black Mountain received a redesign
in 1990. The course hosts both the
Las Vegas qualifier and the USGA
Regulation Tournament every year.

OPPOSITE *The ninth hole
at Black Mountain.*

No. ❾ **BLACK MOUNTAIN GOLF &
COUNTRY CLUB** (DESERT COURSE)

A member-owned facility, Black Mountain is proud to boast one of the largest and most active golf memberships in the Las Vegas valley. Set in the shadows of the panoramic Black Mountains and amidst the flora of the Mojave Desert, Black Mountain Golf and Country Club is a most unique and affordable 27 holes of golf.

And selecting just one hole off these 27 is not easy. The best we could do is No. 9 on the Desert Course. In fact, you can't go wrong here. It's simply one of the best holes in the Las Vegas area.

There is a little ravine in the middle of the fairway about 280 yards out. The success or failure on this hole will most likely come on your second shot. Big hitters can reach the green in two but it's not an easy shot – even for the good, big hitters.

You have to fly the water that is in front of the green and to the left. There is a parking lot behind the green and out-of-bounds to the right. There are two sections to the relatively small green. So trying to land it on the right section from over 200 yards out is no easy task.

You can lay up, giving yourself a much easier shot to the green. But you're in Vegas, so feel free to gamble. **TJ**

Course: Royal Dornoch

Location: Dornoch, Sutherland,
Scotland

Hole: No. 9

Length: 496 yards

Par: 5

Designer: George Duncan,
John Sutherland

Course Comment: This is from
the secretary/manager's welcome
on the course's Web site: "Dornoch
is considered the finest northerly
course in the world, and no
other course offers as delicious
a feeling of getting away from
it all or better provides the
pieces of natural seaside beauty,
challenge and enjoyment and shot
values." Delicious Dornoch. Has
a certain ring.

No. ❾ **ROYAL DORNOCH**

The North Sea breaks on the shore to the right with majestic mountains straight ahead and rolling hills along the left. If this is your picture, then Royal Dornoch must be your location.

With 18 incredible golf holes to play, choosing one over the other is not an easy task. It's as tough as some of the shots on this course.

But let's head out to No. 9. And stick that camera in your pocket. You will want it when we reach the tee.

Named "Craiglaith," this par 5 reminds you that you are near the sea as the beach rolls along with you along the left side from tee to green. But this is no day at the beach, so keep your ball on grass.

And that would be bent grass, not long grass, which you can reach from the tee if you hit your drive too far or too off the mark. The long grass is almost as bad as the beach. Almost.

An even more difficult challenge is trying to land your approach shot on the plateau green. There are bunkers, two of them in fact, on the right and another one along the left side of the green.

Here's some history for you. The first three golf links in Scotland of which there is a written record are St. Andrews in 1552, Leith in 1593, and Dornoch in 1616. Remember, you are on sacred ground. **TJ**

**Course:** San Francisco Golf Club

**Location:** San Francisco, California, USA

**Hole:** No. 9

**Length:** 570 yards

**Par:** 5

**Designer:** A.W. Tillinghast

**Course Comment:** When Tiger Woods was playing for Stanford University, he hit driver off the tee, then driver off the deck, and still came up about 15 yards short of the green.

# No. ❾   SAN FRANCISCO GOLF CLUB

You want to know how old the San Francisco Golf Club is? The site of the seventh hole is said to be where California's last official duel was held between Senator David S. Broderick and California Supreme Court Justice David S. Terry in 1859. Knowing that someone actually paid the ultimate price at the site might contribute toward making you feel a little less helpless two holes later, when you run into the treacherous ninth.

Golf purists love the San Francisco Golf Club (established in 1895) for its tradition, and another bonus for the old school: it's strictly a walkers' course. The only reason members are allowed to ride golf cars is if they have a medical problem. This philosophy works well for noted golf-course architecture expert Bradley S. Klein, who once wrote: "If someone tells you a course is unwalkable, you should consider it a euphemism for unbearable and head the other way as fast as possible."

The ninth hole is definitely walkable, but some might deem it close to unplayable if looking to reach the green in two. The length is enough of a barrier to the brutish approach, but toss in some edgy-lipped bunkers that protect the right side from 50 yards out all the way to the green, and the lay-up on the left is virtually the only play. If Tiger Woods goes driver-driver (see course comment), and still can't get home in two, suffice to say you're looking at a legitimate three-shot hole.

Even the lay-up needs to be played smartly. If you stray too far to the left to avoid the nasty bunkers to the right, there are some bunkers waiting on that side, albeit closer to the green. There is reasonable area to land the third shot, but it should be considered carefully as well.

The ninth at the San Francisco Golf Club is a beautiful hole, and a wonderful place to test your mettle. But good luck getting on the course. The club is extremely exclusive and is shared only by a handful of members and their guests.

Another one of architect A.W. Tillinghast's gems, the course features extremely fast greens that border on the ridiculous if you're on the wrong side of the hole. Caddies are mandatory and their advice will prove quite helpful — especially on the putting surfaces. **JB**

**Course:** Interlachen Country Club

**Location:** Edina, Minnesota, USA

**Hole:** No. 9

**Length:** 530 yards

**Par:** 5

**Designer:** Willie Watson, Donald Ross

**Course Comment:** This classic Donald Ross course (he redesigned it in 1919) is famous for being the site of the 1930 U.S. Open. This was the last major tournament during the year Bobby Jones won the Grand Slam.

BELOW *Paula Marti of Spain celebrates a birdie putt on the ninth hole at Interlachen, September 2002.*

# No. ❾ INTERLACHEN COUNTRY CLUB

There is plenty of history here. For the historians among you, here's a little nugget. During the 1930 U.S. Open, Bobby Jones skipped his ball over the lake and made the famous birdie that would assure his Grand Slam victory. The locals like to call it the "lillypad" shot.

The signature hole at Interlachen is the 530-yard, par-5 ninth, with a dogleg right fairway and a lake on the inside bend near the green.

The key here is your second shot but it all depends on your first shot.

From the tee, you have bunkers on the left side and big trees to the right. You can cut the dogleg a little bit, and you need to if you have plans to go for this in two shots. But don't just let her fly because if you go too far you can end up in the water.

There is a large pond from about 200 yards out from the green. Your second shot is going to have to fly this in order to find the green. The fairway does run along the left side but even laying up is a tricky shot.

The green isn't too difficult although it does slope toward the water. Don't worry about the green though until you are actually there. **TJ**

# Hole ⑩

Other than the first hole, the 10th tee box is probably the one place on the golf course where optimistic attitudes prevail most. Whether that optimism is justified or not can often be determined with one swing of the club.

A purely struck drive on No. 10 can sometimes wash away a whole front nine of misery. And if you've put together a solid first nine, a solid tee ball on the 10th immediately reinforces the belief that you just might be on the way to a decent round.

Of course, that optimism can be squelched in short order with an errant drive on No. 10. But, in the interest of positive swing thoughts, we'll put that notion away.

**LEFT** *The 10th hole at Turnberry, Turnberry, Ayrshire, Scotland.*

## No. ⑩ SOUTH HEAD GOLF COURSE

**Course:** South Head Golf Course

**Location:** Kaipara Harbour, New Zealand

**Hole:** No. 10

**Length:** 174 yards

**Par:** 3

**Designer:** Jack Eccles

**Course Comment:** The course was designed in 1969 by Jack Eccles, a prominent figure in New Zealand golf at the time.

Built on rolling land on the spectacular South Kaipara peninsula, South Head Golf Course provides a fair test for all grades of golfer. The course has stood the test of time and just keeps getting better.

With well-drained fairways of tightly groomed kykyuyu grass, the course is playable virtually the whole year round. The greens are quite large, with excellent putting surfaces that accept a well-struck approach shot.

The 10th hole at South Head is the 174-yard par 3 that challenges greatly. From the championship tee, you have to carry about 120 yards of a scenic lily-covered pond. The green is well-protected by bunkers to the left, right, front and back. In other words, all the way around.

You either need to hit the green — a short to mid-iron should do the trick — or get a lucky bounce from the fringe. As you might expect, we suggest hitting the green. Everything kicks to the left and if you miss the front bunker your ball will end up down a steep bank.

This is not considered a difficult hole, but the peace and serenity of the surroundings and the beauty of the hole could distract you from the task at hand. So stay focused and hit that green. **TJ**

## No. ⑩ TÖREBODA GOLF CLUB

**Course:** Töreboda Golf Club

**Location:** Töreboda, Sweden

**Hole:** No. 10

**Length:** 132 yards

**Par:** 3

**Designer:** Club members

**Course Comment:** Töreboda is home to Sweden's smallest ferry, which crosses the Göta Canal in less than 20 seconds.

Töreboda is a Swedish city that's all about the water. The legendary Göta Canal, a 300-mile system of rivers, lakes, and canals that links Göteborg in the west and Stockholm in the east, winds through the center of Töreboda. The waterway, which opened in 1832 and includes 58 locks — several of them in the Töreboda area, including one of the canal's only two remaining manually operated locks — is essential to the town's atmosphere, with inns, guest cottages, cafés, museums, and other historical attractions all located along the water. The canal's oldest lock was built in 1607 and the highest lock is 300 feet above sea level.

Water also plays a big part at Töreboda Golf Club, where many holes play over and around scenic Lake Mansarudssjön. Among them is the short but treacherous par-3 10th, where golfers shouldn't let the lack of distance fool them. Wise club selection is a necessity on this tee shot, which must carry the lake and often contend with winds that can affect the ball's flight. The horseshoe-shaped peninsula green juts out into the water and is guarded in front by a long, shallow bunker and by trees in the back. **KA**

## No. ❿ HILLSIDE GOLF CLUB

**Course:** Hillside Golf Club

**Location:** Southport, Merseyside, England

**Hole:** No. 10

**Length:** 147 yards

**Par:** 3

**Designer:** Martin Hawtree

**Course Comment:** In the late 1970s both the British Ladies Championship (1977) and the Amateur Championship (1979) were held at Hillside. In 1982, the European Tour's PGA Championship was staged here.

Hillside lies almost side by side with the Royal Birkdale course, amid a stretch of sandhills near Southport. Typical of the links courses on the northwest coastline, Hillside is open to the wind coming in from the Irish Sea and laid out in a truly stunning setting.

This short par 3 kicks off a back nine you won't forget soon. The front nine is special, but the back is spectacular. Both nines are known for being in excellent playing conditions.

The distance on this hole won't leave you running in fear for the clubhouse bar, but it's a much tougher green to hit than most. A series of cavernous bunkers guards the green.

Greg Norman, a two-time winner of the British Open, once sent the club a letter stating that the back nine holes are the best in Britain. High praise indeed from a man who has seen a few good courses.

The course plays 6,850 yards from the back tees.

The course is a highly regarded qualifying venue for the British Open, but has never hosted the event. Some around the club say it's one of the best links courses never to have hosted the Open. **TJ**

**Course:** Pine Valley Golf Club

**Location:** Clementon, New Jersey, USA

**Hole:** No. 10

**Length:** 146 yards

**Par:** 3

**Designer:** George Crump, Harry S. Colt

**Course Comment:** Despite never designing a golf course before, Crump hired Colt as a consultant in 1912 and created what some call the best course in the United States. Crump died in 1918 when only 14 of Pine Valley's holes were open for play. The final four were opened the following year.

Pine Valley is a golf course that makes no apologies for its difficulty. In fact, with one of the highest course ratings and slopes in North America (74.1/153), it revels in its severity. And nowhere on the course is this danger more present than on Pine Valley's shortest hole — No. 10.

The hole is nicknamed after a part of Satan's anatomy that is perhaps best left unprinted, but suffice to say it speaks of a place you do not want to be. How can a hole be so difficult when all it requires is a 7- or 8-iron to safety? The explanation lies in the areas that aren't so safe. And even the alleged safe area — the putting surface — slopes outward to all sides, so hitting its edges lead straight into the perilous surroundings.

And, what of the danger? The hole is surrounded by a craggy sand pit that is man-made but looks so natural you can't believe it wasn't there long before Pine Valley was created. The most severe of the penalties around the putting surface is the nasty pot bunker that allows only a backward escape. In other words, if you land in the pot bunker off the tee (from which the hole gets its nickname), you cannot reach the green in two.

Pine Valley opened in 1919 and was immediately praised by architects throughout the world, even though it was more difficult and more drastically designed than almost any previous course. In addition to being a great challenge of the game, Pine Valley has a great history. When the property was acquired in 1912 during the Golden Age of golf course design in the United States, it became a spot for some of the great course architects of the world to gather, discuss, and contribute. Names such as Hugh Wilson, Charles Blair Macdonald, Walter Travis, Alister MacKenzie, Donald Ross, and many others were part of the great Pine Valley gatherings. Tom Fazio redesigned two holes in 1989, but if players were hoping for a relaxation of the challenge, forget it. Pine Valley remains a bear.

And the 10th is one of Pine Valley's trickiest tests, even though it is less than 150 yards long. It isn't unusual for shorter holes to offer a difficult challenge at windy locations such as Pebble Beach or Royal Troon, but rarely do short holes on inland courses present such a severe test. The 10th at Pine Valley, however, is an exception. **JB**

# No. ⑩  CHICAGO GOLF CLUB

**Course:** Chicago Golf Club

**Location:** Wheaton, Illinois, USA

**Hole:** No. 10

**Length:** 139 yards

**Par:** 3

**Designer:** Charles Blair Macdonald

**Course Comment:** Founded in 1893, this links-style course hosted the 1897, 1900, and 1911 U.S. Opens, won by Joe Lloyd, Harry Vardon, and John McDermott.

The Chicago Golf Club is famous for its past, present, and future. Its past is highlighted by the four U.S. Opens and other tournaments it has hosted over the years. Its present is reflected in the reputation the course has earned for outstanding golf and unequal playing conditions, which has resulted in the 2005 Walker Cup coming to visit. And the future, no doubt, includes many other prestigious events.

Chicago is famous for many things, the great Chicago Golf Club being one of them.

The 10th hole is a short par 3. But the hole is not short on character. This is one of only two holes on the course with water. No. 9, a par 4, shares the same pond.

Your tee shot must carry a small pond to a green guarded on both sides by bunkers. There is also a bunker behind the green and one to the front left side. You have just five paces between the front of the green and the water, so don't be short.

The tricky part is the green. It is very undulating with a back-to-front slope and features plenty of hills and valleys. "Difficult to negotiate" is how our expert in the pro shop described it. Be careful, because it isn't unthinkable to putt your ball right off the green. **TJ**

**Course:** Winged Foot Golf Club
(West Course)

**Location:** Mamaroneck, New York,
USA

**Hole:** No. 10

**Length:** 190 yards

**Par:** 3

**Designer:** A.W. Tillinghast

**Course Comment:** Claude Harmon
holds the course record with a 61.
Legend has it that he set the record
while listening to the World Series
on the radio.

# No. ⑩ WINGED FOOT GOLF CLUB
## (WEST COURSE)

Just like the other 17 holes on Winged Foot's famed West Course, there isn't one drop of water that comes into play on the par-3 10th. But the hole doesn't stand defenseless. Far from it; it relies on the classic Redan defense, drawn from North Berwick's original Redan hole, which was designed before the turn of the century by David Strath.

The Redan is a military term that refers to a type of guarding procedure which involves two faces or two lines of works pointing away from the fortification and reduces the enemy's points of assault. Unlike the Redan at North Berwick, however, the 10th at Winged Foot West employs defenses that are plainly visible from the tee. However, that doesn't make them any easier to deal with.

The green is plenty wide and deep, but it slopes forward and to the right. There are bunkers surrounding the green — two on the right that feed on balls falling off the green's slope, and one in front that creates an optical illusion and confounds players trying to properly gauge distance.

Even after overcoming the Redan defense, it is no guarantee that the difficult green can be negotiated in two putts. The frontward slope is so severe that a mis-struck downhill putt could end up in one of the bunkers, or at the very least leave a difficult putt back up the hill to finish.

The 10th requires power and accuracy, much like the rest of the West. The exclusive club's West Course features narrow fairways, long and thick rough, and contours on every green. It is important to hit most tee shots long, but as straight as humanly possible. The West is not quite as tight as its sister course to the east, but it still requires accuracy off the tee — not to mention a little more length. Even with long tee shots on the West, players will make use of their middle irons more frequently than they might be accustomed. They will also need to do some creative work on and around the greens.

Winged Foot West is laid out over a rather ordinary piece of land, although it is superbly maintained. The course is an exception to the rule that says an exquisite piece of land is a prerequisite for having a great course. A gifted architect working with an acceptable piece of land may well produce a far superior course to an average architect who fails to take advantage of a great site. Such is the case at Winged Foot West, and the 10th hole is a prime example. **JB**

**Course:** Kasumigaseki Golf Club
(East Course)

**Location:** Saitama, Japan

**Hole:** No. 10

**Length:** 177 yards

**Par:** 3

**Designer:** Kinya Fujnta, Charles Alison

**Course Comment:** Toshi Izawa won the 1995 Japan Open played at Kasumigaseki.

## No. ⑩ KASUMIGASEKI GOLF CLUB
### (EAST COURSE)

First opened in 1929, this venerable layout only 80 minutes from Tokyo is perhaps the most renowned golf course in Japan. It was designed by Japan's Kinya Fujnta and later renovated by Englishman Charles Alison, a design partner of Harry Shapland Colt who was one of the most respected golf course architects of his day.

The 10th is Kasumigaseki's signature hole and, like many courses originally designed by Japanese architects, it contains two greens — one with korai grass for the summer and the other with bent grass for the winter. The two-green system was considered necessary to keep golf clubs open during all of Japan's four unique seasons. Tee shots to both greens, which are separated by a line of tall trees, must clear a lake and avoid Alison's namesake deep bunkers in front.

Kasumigaseki's East Course was host to the 1957 Canada Cup (renamed the World Cup in 1967), which was won by the Japanese duo of Torakichi Nakamura and Koichi Ono over American stars Sam Snead and Jimmy Demaret. The pair's surprise victory in their home country is often credited with beginning a golf explosion in Japan that lasted more than three decades. **KA**

**Course:** La Boulie Golf Club
(La Vallée Course)

**Location:** Versailles, France

**Hole:** No. 10

**Length:** 213 yards

**Par:** 3

**Designer:** Wilfrid Reid, Seymour Dunn, Willie Park Jr.

**Course Comment:** Golf is but one of 17 sports offered to the 20,000 members of the Racing Club de France, which was the first European omnisports club.

## No. ⑩ LA BOULIE GOLF CLUB
### (LA VALLEE COURSE)

La Boulie was originally formed as Paris Golf Club near the turn of the century and played host to the inaugural French Open in 1906. The two 18-hole courses (La Vallée and La Forêt) were purchased by the Racing Club de France in 1951.

The 10th hole of the La Vallée course is a long par 3 with an elevated tee box featuring a pleasant view of forests and the open French countryside. The tee shot must be hit to a relatively large green that slopes from back to front and is well-protected on the front and sides by a complex of bunkers.

After winning the first French Open at La Boulie in 1906, Frenchman Arnoud Massy became the first non-British player to win the British Open in 1907. The next week, he successfully defended his title at La Boulie, which played host to the French Open for the first seven years and has served as host site 20 times, more than any other course. Other French Open champions at La Boulie include John H. Taylor (1908–09), James Braid (1910), Walter Hagen (1920), Bobby Locke (1953), Byron Nelson (1955), Nick Faldo (1983), and Seve Ballesteros (1986). **KA**

**Course:** Brudenell River Golf Course

**Location:** Charlottetown, Prince Edward Island, Canada

**Hole:** No. 10

**Length:** 135 yards

**Par:** 3

**Designer:** Robbie Robinson

**Course Comment:** The course and the Rodd Brudenell River Resort complex are noted for staging some of the finest professional matches, notably the Lorie Kane Island Challenge of 2000 — Canada's first women's "skins" game and numerous Canadian Tour events.

## No. ❿ BRUDENELL RIVER GOLF COURSE

Long recognized as the most popular golf course on scenic Prince Edward Island, this picturesque course has been named one of the top 50 golf courses in Canada.

The signature hole at Brudenell River is the 135-yard, par-3 No. 10. Take a look to the left and you will see the Atlantic Ocean. Look right and you will see a large pond you are going to have to clear to reach the green.

And there is no way around going over the pond. Just be thankful you don't have to clear the Atlantic Ocean to reach the green — now that would be a golf hole.

The center of the green is elevated with the surface rolling off to all sides. But the green does hold well even with the slope.

There also are two large bunkers in the front.

Your big decision here will be deciding what club to use on the tee. There is always a lot of wind on this course and it can make club selection a little tricky.

Bordered by the scenic Brudenell River, the course is set on 1,500 acres of rolling hills, and features beautifully maintained and tricky greens. **TJ**

**WENTWORTH CLUB** (WEST COURSE)

**Course:** Wentworth Club (West Course)

**Location:** Virginia Water, Surrey, England

**Hole:** No. 10

**Length:** 184 yards

**Par:** 3

**Designer:** Harry S. Colt

**Course Comment:** During World War II, the West Course became known as the Burma Road course after German prisoners of war were brought in to clear vegetation that had overgrown the last six holes.

BELOW *The 10th hole at Wentworth.*

OPPOSITE *Gary Player of South Africa plays a shot on the 10th hole at Wentworth, October 1974.*

How good is Wentworth. Let one of golf's great personalities explain:

"I rate Wentworth at the very top of my list of favorite places alongside Augusta. The club is warm and friendly and has always treated me well. I might add, the West Course is, for me, the ultimate examination," said Spain's Seve Ballesteros.

The 184-yard 10th hole is one of the prettiest on the golf course. From the tee, you must carry a ravine and do your best to avoid a group of trees guarding the right side of the green.

The green, with bunkers front and back, has some tricky reads. Take your time here and make sure you are on line with your line.

On a historical note, the Ryder Cup grew out of an informal match between Americans and Britons that was played in 1926 at Wentworth.

Wentworth boasts far more facilities than the golf course. Visitors can enjoy the full-service spa, swimming pools, a health and fitness center, and world-class tennis.

Wentworth is only 15 minutes from Heathrow Airport and about an hour from Gatwick Airport. **TJ**

**Course:** Carnoustie Golf Links

**Location:** Carnoustie, Angus, Scotland

**Hole:** No. 10

**Length:** 466 yards

**Par:** 4

**Designer:** Allan Robertson, Old Tom Morris

**Course Comment:** Talk about a tough neighborhood. Carnoustie is located within a pitching wedge of some of the greatest golf courses in the world. But Carnoustie, which hosted the British Open first in 1931 and more recently in 1999, can play with any of them.

At 466 yards from the back tees, the par-4 10th is one of the most testing holes on the course. The 10th also reintroduces you to the infamous Barry Burn which you met, hopefully, in passing, on the first hole.

At No. 10, however, the burn is far more menacing, curving almost completely around the green.

There are ways to play this hole and there are ways to survive this hole. You can decide which best fits your game.

The tee area offers a break from the winds, but not a break from the challenges. With a wall of bunkers along the right side of the fairway, lean your driver a little to the left. Anything right off the tee is trouble.

Now, when we say lean a little left, that's what we mean. Too far left leaves you in some thick and unpleasant rough. There is also a bunker that is not clearly seen from the tee. Consider yourself warned.

If you manage a good drive, consider your options. Play it short of the burn and go for an up-and-down par. Or you can take your chances by going for the green. Sometimes, like here, the risk isn't worth the rewards.

Enjoy. **TJ**

## No. ⑩ SAN FRANCISCO GOLF CLUB

**Course:** San Francisco Golf Club

**Location:** San Francisco, California, USA

**Hole:** No. 10

**Length:** 410 yards

**Par:** 4

**Designer:** A.W. Tillinghast

**Course Comment:** Built in 1915, San Francisco Golf Club is one of the oldest courses in California and has been listed by the USGA as one of the first 100 clubs established in the U.S.

Almost everything about this hole is difficult. There isn't an easy shot from tee to green. But this is why we tee it up. For the challenge. And it doesn't get much more challenging than this hole on this historic golf course in this magnificent city by the bay.

The adventure begins on the tee. Our guide in the pro shop says the tee shot is the key here. "A good drive puts you in pretty good shape for the rest of the hole, but a bad drive leaves you with limited options."

The bunker on the right is very difficult to carry from the tee and there is little chance of reaching the green if you land in it. There also is a bunker on the left side — hit it in there and you have to chip out because there is a tree between you and the green.

The fairway is very narrow off the tee, but the ideal shot is center or right of center.

The green is a tough target to hit with bunkers short left and short right. There also is a bunker 40 yards short of the green in the center of the fairway that can come into play and is not easy to hit out of.

The very testing green has a big slope on the left side where you can roll right off into a tough chipping area. **TJ**

## No. ⑩ GLENDOWER COUNTRY CLUB

**Course:** Glendower Country Club

**Location:** Edenvale, South Africa

**Hole:** No. 10

**Length:** 450 yards

**Par:** 4

**Designer:** Charles Alison

**Course Comment:** In winning the 1939 Transvaal Open, played just two years after Glendower's opening, South African Bobby Locke set a then world-record score of 265 with rounds of 66-69-66-64.

Glendower Golf Club has a natural beauty highlighted by the fact that it was declared a nature reserve in 1973 in order to protect its lush vegetation and an abundant number of bird species that frequent the course. Water hazards are located on 11 of the 18 holes, and the course as a whole has 85 bunkers.

Both of these obstacles are featured extensively on Glendower's tough par-4 10th. The tee shot must be hit to a narrowing fairway that is lined by trees and has bunkers on the left and right sides. But the really tough shot is the second one, which must carry a pond and narrow stream located to the left and front of the green. Adding to the difficulty of the approach are bunkers at the front left and front right of the putting surface. If you're not sure you can make it in two, lay up in front of the stream. You'll be very glad you did.

Fiji's Vijay Singh shot four rounds in the 60s (69-66-66-69) to win by one shot over Zimbabwe's Nick Price at the 1997 South African Open held at Glendower. The course also played host to South Africa's top professional event in 1989 and 1993. **KA**

**Course:** Shelter Harbor Golf Club

**Location:** Charleston, Rhode Island, USA

**Hole:** No. 10

**Length:** 495 yards

**Par:** 4

**Designer:** Michael Hurdzan and Dana Fry

**Course Comment:** Unlike many modern golf clubs, real estate is not part of the plan at Shelter Harbor. With the exception of two visitors' cottages between the 10th and 18th fairways, the club's 400 acres does not contain houses.

# No. ❿   SHELTER HARBOR GOLF CLUB

When Shelter Harbor opened in 2004, it was the first new private club in Rhode Island's Washington County in more than a century. And, even with an initiation fee that has reached as high as $175,000, new members continue to join Shelter Harbor. With a golf course as first-rate as Shelter Harbor, members are getting their money's worth.

Shelter Harbor boasts one of the best views in all of Rhode Island golf — in all of Rhode Island, period, for that matter — from the top step of the staircase of its clubhouse, just a short distance from Long Island Sound. From there, you can see the entire 400-acre club, and among the splendor is the 495-yard 10th, the best of a fine collection of 18 golf holes that make up a challenging parkland layout.

Like the rest of the golf course, the 10th includes large trees, glacial boulders, and wetlands that outline the hole. And, even though the course is less than a decade old, because of the meticulous care given by architects Michael Hurdzan and Dana Fry, it appears the holes have been carved in the landscape for ages.

Another element of the 10th is elevation change. There is 100 feet of elevation change throughout Shelter Harbor, and there is a 50-foot downhill play from tee to green on No. 10. This offers two advantages: it gives extra distance on the near-500-yard hole, and it allows for better view of the natural beauty of the property.

The hole is actually straightforward, but forces accuracy as it meanders through the aforementioned boundaries with bunkers dotting here and there on the semi-narrow fairway. The green offers challenge because it is a punchbowl variety that does not forgive errant approach shots. **JB**

## No. ⑩ MAIDSTONE GOLF CLUB

**Course:** Maidstone Golf Club

**Location:** East Hampton, New York, USA

**Hole:** No. 10

**Length:** 382 yards

**Par:** 4

**Designer:** Willie Park Jr., John Park, William H. Tucker

**Course Comment:** The Maidstone Club, founded in 1891, is listed by the U.S. Golf Association as one of the first 100 clubs established in the United States.

Historic Maidstone Golf Club, with most of its holes set along Long Island's Gardiner Peninsula, has some of the most dramatically scenic ocean-front golf property on the Atlantic coast, complete with unspoiled stretches of dunes, marshes, ponds, coastal grasses, and sandy soil that form the perfect setting for links-style golf.

Maidstone's ninth and 10th holes — a pair of par 4s that are almost always affected by the winds blowing off the Atlantic — together form one of the great coastal tandems of American golf; back-to-back gems that invigorate the golfer and challenge his or her game to the utmost.

Although No. 9 is probably better known, No. 10 more than holds its own, featuring a tee shot to a fairway that ends suddenly at a huge hill covered with thick coastal vegetation. The second shot must be strong enough to carry the huge rise but still possess enough finesse to hold a green that has little margin for error. The putting surface has a huge undulation at its center, slopes hard from back to front and is protected by steep drops on the right and rear and some fearsome bunkers on the left.

Invigorating indeed. **KA**

## No. ⑩ SANKATY HEAD GOLF CLUB

**Course:** Sankaty Head Golf Club

**Location:** Nantucket, Massachusetts, USA

**Hole:** No. 10

**Length:** 431 yards

**Par:** 4

**Designer:** Phil Wogan

**Course Comment:** First some good news. This beautiful course offers views of the Atlantic Ocean from an amazing 14 holes. The bad news is that the course features plenty of rolling hills that often means plenty of uneven lies.

There are very few trees at Sankaty. You could probably count them on one hand. But you can't count the number of spectacular views on this golf course. Or the memorable shots you will be asked to hit.

Deep fescue and the wind make up the course's defense system. And they will prove to be admirable foes. No. 10 is a slight dogleg right with an elevated tee and a terrific view of the ocean.

There are bunkers on the right side of the fairway just at the landing area so keep it straight. The fairway then bends a little to the right before going back up to an elevated green, which slopes severely from right to left.

You want to hit your second shot to the right side of the green and let it feed down to the center.

There is deep fescue all over this terrific golf course, including plenty around the green at No. 10. There also is a bunker to the left and back right of the green.

You won't play many courses where every hole stands out. Consider this one of them. **TJ**

**Course: :** Turnberry Golf Club
(Ailsa Course)

**Location:** Turnberry, Scotland

**Hole:** No. 10

**Length:** 452 yards

**Par:** 4

**Designer:** MacKenzie Ross

**Course Comment:** Long regarded
as one of the finest courses
in the world, the Ailsa came to
international prominence with
the famous duel between Jack
Nicklaus and Tom Watson over
the four days of the 1977 Open.

BELOW *The 10th hole at Turnberry.*

OPPOSITE *Carl Mason of England
plays his second shot on the 10th hole
at Turnberry, July 2003.*

# No. ❿ TURNBERRY GOLF CLUB
## (AILSA COURSE)

From No. 4 to No. 11, the Ailsa Course at Turnberry plays along the spectacular shoreline. The 10th hole may be the best of the bunch.

Named Dinna Fouter, No. 10 is a long par 4 with a slight dogleg left. There is a large bunker about 60 yards in front of the green right in the middle of the narrow fairway. But what a tremendous view from the fairway to the ocean on the left.

Even if you can hit your drive 300 yards and straight, you are still looking at 150 yards on your second shot to a small green. For most golfers, that second shot will be even longer — and more difficult.

Going for the green requires two things: confidence and talent. One without the other won't get you there. The water on the left shouldn't come into play but you need to be straight on this hole.

The Ailsa Course is beautiful, so enjoy the scenery on this hole.

There is history on this golf course that must be recognized and honored. Take a bow to the golf legends who have passed this way then take a crack at doing what so few have been able to do — beat Turnberry at its own game. **TJ**

**Course:** Loch Lomond Golf Club

**Location:** Luss, Dunbartonshire, Scotland

**Hole:** No. 10

**Length:** 455 yards

**Par:** 4

**Designer:** Tom Weiskopf, Jay Morrish

**Course Comment:** Loch Lomond is the first golf course in Scotland designed by an American architect. Weiskopf has said he considers Loch Lomond to be his "lasting memorial to golf," and has called No. 10 "one of the most scenic and demanding par 4s anywhere . . . "

**BELOW** *Sergio Garcia of Spain crosses a stream on the 10th hole at Loch Lomond, July 1999.*

# No. ⑩  LOCH LOMOND GOLF CLUB

This hole, Arn Burn, is trouble from the start.

From the tee, there is wicked rough both left and right, so hitting the fairway is a must. Driving down from the elevated tee looking toward Glen Fruin, the ball seems suspended against the mountain backdrop.

Missing the short grass off the tee virtually assures that birdie opportunity has gone awry. Par is still possible, but an errant tee shot leaves a good lie iffy. And if you don't get lucky, you might end up just hacking away to try to get back into the fairway. A 3-wood might be a smart play off the tee, not only to keep it straight, but also because if you hit your drive too purely, you run the risk of trickling into Arn Burn, for which the hole is named.

The burn runs diagonally across the fairway, so both direction and distance must be considered. If you hit your ball the right distance, yet send it a part of the fairway other than intended, you might find the burn anyway. It is a vexing, yet lovely tee shot.

The pond on the left does not really threaten the second shot as it is much further from the big, receptive green than it looks. A solid tee shot leaves a mid-iron into the green, which slopes from front right to back left.

The 10th hole exemplifies the parkland treasure that is Loch Lomond Golf Club, which is nestled alongside the beautiful banks of the Loch.

The club sits on the historic Clan Colquhoun estate, which is steeped in Scottish tradition dating back to the 12th century. Loch Lomond enjoys the history and tradition associated with golf in the homeland, yet the club provides an experience uniquely its own. Loch Lomond's clubhouse, Rossdhu, is a Georgian manor home constructed in 1773, exactly 200 years before Tom Weiskopf won the British Open Championship at Troon and 221 years before Weiskopf teamed with Jay Morrish to design Loch Lomond.

Weiskopf considers Loch Lomond "my finest work ever" and insists the piece of property with which he had to work was the finest in the world. After seeing Loch Lomond Golf Club, let alone playing it, few could argue. **JB**

**Course:** Manila Southwoods Golf & Country Club (Masters Course)

**Location:** Carmona, Cavite, Philippines

**Hole:** No. 10

**Length:** 429 yards

**Par:** 4

**Designer:** Jack Nicklaus

**Course Comment:** Manila Southwoods was the first course in Asia — and only the third outside North America — to become a fully certified Audobon Cooperative Sanctuary because of its emphasis on environmental stewardship.

No. ⑩ **MANILA SOUTHWOODS GOLF & COUNTRY CLUB (MASTERS COURSE)**

As a designer, Jack Nicklaus is known for his difficult par 4s, and No. 10 at Manila Southwoods Golf and Country Club, a slight dogleg left, is certainly no exception. The No. 2 handicap hole on the Masters Course contains no bunkers, but there are plenty of other obstacles to prevent par here, beginning with a shallow stream that snakes down the left side then crosses the center of the fairway before forming a pond to the right and front of the green. Also affecting play are the prevailing winds off Laguna de Bay. Players should attempt to keep their tee shots as close to the creek as possible for the best line of approach into the slightly elevated green, which is set at a diagonal angle from the fairway.

Manila Southwoods has hosted several international tournaments, including the World Amateur Team Championships (won by Australia) in 1996 and several Philippine Opens. The Masters layout, which has water on 15 of its 18 holes, is considered one of the finest in Asia, and was named "Venue of the Year" by pros on the Asian PGA Tour in 1999 and 2000. **KA**

**Course:** Shinnecock Hills Golf Club

**Location:** Southampton, New York, USA

**Hole:** No. 10

**Length:** 410 yards

**Par:** 4

**Designer:** Willie Dunn, Jr.

**Course Comment:** Shinnecock Hills is one of five clubs that founded the USGA and has the first clubhouse ever built in the U.S. It opened in 1892. It also was the first club to allow women as members.

**BELOW** *The 10th hole at Shinnecock Hills Golf Club.*

**OPPOSITE** *Retief Goosen of South Africa plays his tee shot on the 10th hole at Shinnecock Hills, June 2004.*

# No. ⑩ SHINNECOCK HILLS GOLF CLUB

The course comment to the left speaks of old history. Here is some recent history. Welcome to the 2004 U.S. Open at Shinnecock Hills. This is the fourth U.S. Open and the eighth USGA competition held at the club.

There have been plenty of tests and memorable moments for U.S. Open competitors. And there are plenty of memorable tests for any golfers on this classic jewel — including the 410-yard, par-4 10th.

No. 10 is a unique hole at Shinnecock, situated across the most undulating part of the layout.

This is one rollercoaster ride and one that many approach differently. There is no blueprint on how to play No. 10 at Shinnecock.

Many players lay back off the tee for the purpose of gaining a level lie for their approach shot — usually about 160 to 175 yards into the green. Still, others take a chance with the driver in hopes of reaching the bottom of the hill, leaving them with a short pitch.

The elevated green has bunkers to the right. There also are bunkers along the left side of the fairway. **TJ**

## No. ⑩   QUINTA DA RIA

**Course:** Quinta da Ria

**Location:** Tavira, The Algarve, Portugal

**Hole:** No. 10

**Length:** 465 yards

**Par:** 4

**Designer:** Rocky Roquemore

**Course Comment:** Roquemore has made a name for himself in The Algarve. This course has only served to enhance that reputation.

The 10th is the toughest hole on the Quinta da Ria course by a long shot. If ever a course called out for course management and the ability to shape the ball, then this is it.

Ideally the drive from an elevated tee needs to find the left-hand side of the fairway to offer the best route into the green. That line takes most of the water that fronts the green out of play.

The major problem with the left-hand route is a bunker on the left-hand side of the fairway. Find this bunker and par almost becomes an impossibility. Trees on this side of the fairway can also present an obstacle for any pulled tee shot.

Most players will favor the wider, right-hand side of fairway. However, that means the second shot has to be played over the full length of the water. A precise iron shot then has to be played to find the putting surface. Anything short will end up in the water, while anything hit long can run through this narrow green. **AT**

## No. ⑩   GARDEN CITY GOLF CLUB

**Course:** Garden City Golf Club

**Location:** Garden City, New York, USA

**Hole:** No. 10

**Length:** 414 yards

**Par:** 4

**Designer:** Devereux Emmet

**Course Comment:** There have been a couple of famous and notable changes to Garden City since it first opened in 1896. In 1926, Walter Travis reworked the course and Robert Trent Jones Sr. put his stamp on it in 1958. It is now regarded as one of the top 50 courses in the world.

There are designers, experts, and yes, authors, who call the 10th at Garden City their favorite hole in golf. And everyday players no doubt also remember the 10th at Garden City, a club that hosted the U.S. Open in 1902.

Garden City is known as one of the most unique courses in the United States. Experts struggle to come up with a comparison or a label for these majestic 18 holes.

It's not a true links-style course. And it's unfair to call it just a heathland course in the tradition of England — Garden City, first of all, doesn't have any heath.

No. 10, a 414-yard par 4, is the perfect example of why this course is just a little "off course" from others in the United States.

The hole seems like everything is tilted from right to left. The fairway bunkers are tilted in that direction and the green also is canted that way. The green, as an added danger, also slants from front to back.

You must first attempt to position your ball on the left side of the fairway, which brings you dangerously near the fairway bunkers. But the slope of the green makes it necessary to play the approach shot from here.

In particularly arid conditions, it is advisable to land your approach about 60 feet short of the green and allow it to gently roll toward the hole.

But you must make sure the ball makes the green, because you don't want to leave it short. It's best to miss this green long, if you're going to miss at all. **TJ**

## No. ⑩ ENNISCRONE

**Course:** Enniscrone

**Location:** Sligo, Ireland

**Hole:** No. 10

**Length:** 359 yards

**Par:** 4

**Designer:** Eddie Hackett

**Course Comment:** When you step on the first tee you will know right away that this course has the right to be included among such exalted company as Ballybunion, Connemara, Lahinch, Waterville and Bantry Bay as the premier links on the Western seaboard.

If you want to step back in time take a ride out to Enniscrone. This famous Irish bit of history paints a rugged picture with scenic dunes, seemingly untouched over time, the most beautiful beach in Ireland, the Moy Estuary, and then there is the Atlantic Ocean. These are just some of the elements that make up this stunning picture.

A favorite hole among the loyal players is the 359-yard 10th. It's not a long hole, and standing on the picturesque elevated tee can give you a boost of confidence. But reality quickly takes over. The drive might look rather easy, but you better hit it straight — or your confidence will fall to the wayside.

There are mounds on both sides of the fairway that you want to split from the tee. Nice and straight does the trick. It also sets up a nice second shot. You will need every bit of a good drive because the two-tiered green is guarded by two very deep bunkers.

When Eddie Hackett was invited to design an extension to the modest nine-hole course that existed up to 1974, the terrain prompted his observation: "A pleasing feature is the variety. As well as holes in the open flatland there will be those ranging through the sand dunes with the occasional dog-leg adding to the attraction." **TJ**

## No. ⑩ ROYAL MELBOURNE GOLF CLUB (WEST COURSE)

**Course:** Royal Melbourne Golf Club, (West Course)

**Location:** Black Rock, Victoria, Australia

**Hole:** No. 10

**Length:** 307 yards

**Par:** 4

**Designer:** Alister MacKenzie

**Course Comment:** The greens at this fine club are renowned to be among the truest and best-conditioned in the world; generally large in size and magnificently contoured, they can be set up to challenge the touring pro as sternly as the weekend Joe.

It is hard not to get fired up on the tee of this short par 4 at one of Alister MacKenzie's true masterpieces, especially when the wind is at your back and you know you can work the ball right to left. For it is entirely possible to drive this green, or at the very least hit a ball long enough that you leave yourself a little bump-and-run to the pin that should ensure par and may even produce a birdie.

But it is also very possible that a big swing with the driver will only produce heartbreak and distress, because there is not a lot of margin for error here. First off, it is critical to play to the center-right of the fairway, clearing a ridge at roughly 220 yards and avoiding the bunker at the turn of the dogleg. And what a bunker it is, Augustaesque in look and feel, and said by some to be the largest and deepest sand hazard in the country.

Then there is the matter of the green, which is Royal-Melbourne smooth and guarded by a pair of bunkers to the right. Anything leaking in that direction often disappears into the sand, and anything long will fall down steep slopes in the back and quickly put double bogey — or worse — into play. **JS**

**Course:** Bel-Air Country Club

**Location:** Los Angeles, California, USA

**Hole:** No. 10

**Length:** 200 yards

**Par:** 4

**Designer:** George C. Thomas, Jack Neville

**Course Comment:** Bel-Air was built during the "Golden Age" of golf-course architecture and construction in Southern California in the 1920s. In 1919, the Southern California Golf Association included 18 clubs and 1,371 members. By 1925, there were 45 clubs and more than 20,000 members. Bel-Air Country Club was one of the big draws during the Golden Age and the 10th hole was its main attraction.

# No. ⑩  BEL-AIR COUNTRY CLUB

Several prominent designers have performed renovations and updates on Bel-Air Country Club, modernizing an American beauty that opened post-World War I. But, for the most part, the additions made by Robert Trent Jones Jr., George Fazio and others have been tweaks, because Bel-Air is consistently rated among the best courses in the United States, and it is difficult to improve upon a legend.

Part of the reason for Bel-Air's status among America's elite is No. 10, which has some features not ordinarily found when playing a round. The 10th includes a suspension bridge to get players across the deep canyon which lies between tee and green. Now, a suspension bridge is somewhat unusual but not unheard of. However, when you toss in four underground tunnels and an elevator which helps players traverse the clubhouse at the 10th's tee, it becomes a bit out of the ordinary.

Also unique is the beauty of Bel-Air's 10th. It forces a 150-yard carry across the canyon, then the walk across the suspension bridge to a large green loaded with slopes and guarded by four bunkers of varying shapes and sizes. Depending on the greenkeeper's mood, this hole can be either very difficult, or nearly impossible. Pin placement can be downright treacherous because of all the elevation differences on the green. The green exemplifies the rest of the course — beautiful and loaded with trees, but difficult and hilly.

The course is consistently rated in the top 100 in America by *Golfweek* magazine, and also has been rated highly by other publications, but numbers don't begin to tell the story. The course is one of George C. Thomas' jewels in a stellar design career — a career that produced a portfolio that included Ojai Valley, Riviera, Stanford, and Los Angeles North.

Thomas was a rich man from Philadelphia who moved to Los Angeles with the idea that he would become involved in landscaping and gardening. But that interest evolved into golf-course design, and the world of golf should be eternally grateful. Thomas has created some beauties, and the 10th hole at Bel-Air is one of his signature holes. **JB**

OPPOSITE *The 10th hole at Bel Air.*

**Course:** Pine Knob

**Location:** Clarkston, Michigan, USA

**Hole:** No. 10

**Length:** 351 yards

**Par:** 4

**Designer:** Leo Bishop, Lorrie Viola, Dan Pohl

**Course Comment:** Pine Knob is three nine-hole courses built into one. The Eagle Course is tight due to homes lining many fairways. The Falcon is more open, yet longer. And the newer Hawk Course features plenty of wetlands.

# No. ⑩  PINE KNOB

The 10th hole at Pine Knob is actually No. 1 on the Eagle Course at this 27-hole golf club. But when you play 18 holes, this is your first hole as you make the turn — so, we will still call it No. 10.

We will also still call it a wonderful golf hole with a tremendous view. Unless you are in an airplane, you can't get much higher than on the tee at No. 10. It's the highest natural point in Southeastern Michigan and you can see about 30 miles, at least that's what our expert in the pro shop told us.

As you would suspect, it's also a long way down to the green. So when you are done enjoying the view, grab a club and go for the green if you like. It is very reachable from the tee, but watch out for the million-dollar homes on the right.

The fairway drops maybe 100 feet from tee to green.

The green is huge, over 9,000 square feet. It slopes front to back and is not too severely sloped. But it can trick you, so be careful.

Behind the tee box is the "mansion," where the club hosts banquets and weddings. **TJ**

**Course:** Royal St. George's Golf Club

**Location:** Sandwich, Kent, England

**Hole:** No. 10

**Length:** 413 yards

**Par:** 4

**Designer:** Laidlaw Purves, Alister MacKenzie, J.J.F. Pennink

**Course Comment:** Royal St Georges' nickname — or at least what the locals like to call it — is simply "Sandwich," after the neighboring small town.

**BELOW** *Davis Love of the USA plays out of a bunker on the 10th hole at Royal St. George's, July 2003.*

**OPPOSITE** *Tiger Woods of the USA walks on to the 10th green at Royal St. George's, July 2003.*

# No. ❿ ROYAL ST. GEORGE'S GOLF CLUB

Royal St. George's, which was host to the 2003 British Open, is one of the most famous and most difficult golf courses in the world. It's also one of the most debated.

Some golfers simply don't like it. Jack Nicklaus doesn't seem to be a big fan of the place. But others love it for its openness and solitude. The debate could be around for as long as the golf course stands.

And St. George certainly stands the test of time.

The par-4 10th isn't going to grab your attention right away. The fairway is straight and not too exciting. But the green is where the 10th begins to take off — literally. The green — like at No. 4 — is perched atop a dune and is an impressive sight.

There are some troublesome bunkers on both sides. It's advisable to attempt to keep your ball on the fairway or this nice-looking hole will turn ugly very fast.

The 10th hole at Royal St. George's is thought by many to be one of the most dangerous par 4s in England. And it ruined any chance Tom Kite had of winning the 1981 British Open. **TJ**

**Course:** Naruo Golf Club

**Location:** Hyogo, Japan

**Hole:** No. 10

**Length:** 480 yards

**Par:** 4

**Designer:** H.C. Crane

**Course Comment:** This is a hole that does not receive the worldwide recognition it deserves. Many golfers, even those who consider themselves aficionados, may not have heard of Naruo. But it is consistently rated among the top 100 in the world, and the long par-4 10th is the course's signature hole.

## No. ⑩ NARUO GOLF CLUB

Because the 10th hole at Naruo plays downhill from tee to green, the 480 yards on the scorecard may somewhat overstate its challenge. It isn't so much the length on this hole that makes it difficult, but the precision necessary to reach the green in regulation.

It is necessary to be middle fairway or left fairway off the tee, because anything to the right side runs the risk of running into the bunker waiting on top of a hill. And if your ball rolls there, forget about reaching the green in two. You are left with no alternative but to lay up short of the deep trench in front of the green. A par might still be possible, but it would take getting up and down.

The green, which is protected in front by the aforementioned gulley up front and four treacherous bunkers all around, must be hit softly and held. If your approach is short, the deep gulley, filled with sand, gorse, and other unmentionables, leaves an unpredictable yet certainly horrific third shot. There is danger in every direction if you don't hit the green.

This is a lovely hole when played with precision, but quite a nasty consequence awaits for anything less exact. **JB**

**Course:** St. Andrews (New Course)

**Location:** St. Andrews, Fife, Scotland

**Hole:** No. 10

**Length:** 464 yards

**Par:** 4

**Designer:** Old Tom Morris

**Course Comment:** To let you know just how much tradition is at St. Andrews, the "New" course was built because of an increasing demand for golf and the Old Course wasn't enough to keep up with the demand. So how new is the New Course? It was built in 1895, right after the new railway brought golfers to St. Andrews' door.

# No. ❿  ST. ANDREWS (NEW COURSE)

When the Royal and Ancient Golf Club of St. Andrews, Scotland, saw the venerable Old Course wasn't able to handle the new flood of golfers heading to St. Andrews just before the turn of the 20th century, it engaged W. Hall Blyth, an Edinburgh civil engineer, to design the New Course, and entrusted the layout to Old Tom Morris and his assistant David Honeyman.

The result was a classic links course which uses the natural features of the land to create a top-drawer challenge. The course has the traditional out and back layout, with the 18th green just to the right of the first tee. It also has, in the great St. Andrews' tradition, shared fairways and even a double green at the third and 15th holes. Other similarities include deep pot bunkers, a perilous rough of wild grass, gorse, and brush and generously large, rolling greens.

But while the Old Course has it over the New in terms of tradition, most give the nod to the New Course in terms of toughness, a call for precision, and variety of shot-making. Located in the shadow of its illustrious neighbor, the New Course is said by locals to be one of St Andrews' best-kept secrets.

Even more secret still is the unassuming par-4 10th. It isn't even listed among the "highlight" holes in the New Course's promotional materials, but after playing the hole, you will definitely think someone missed the boat on that call.

The length is stern at 464 yards, and it is made more difficult still considering that the hole almost always plays into a forceful prevailing wind blowing in from The North Sea. The breeze poses an in-air challenge, but most of the tests on the 10th come from the rugged land.

The fairway cannot be seen from the tee because of a mound about 100 yards out; the fairway is even tougher to hit because it also snakes into an S-shape — making local knowledge paramount to success. There are no hazards the rest of the way — no bunkers, no water — but the approach requires a soft fade in order to hold the green.

The 10th hole at the New Course is a challenge and — despite the course's name — is laden with more than 100 years of tradition. The hole, like the course upon which it sits, is a hidden gem. **JB**

## No. ⑩ BANDON DUNES

**Course:** Bandon Dunes

**Location:** Bandon, Oregon, USA

**Hole:** No. 10

**Length:** 362 yards

**Par:** 4

**Designer:** David McLay Kidd

**Course Comment:** Here is a quote from the course's designer that says it all: "It thrills me now to watch the public playing the game as it was originally meant to be played, on the finest linksland I've seen outside the British Isles."

The sand dunes and indigenous vegetation give Bandon Dunes a natural feel. It's as if the golf course was already here when the first settlers pulled in on horseback with their clubs in the back hitch."

The natural feeling takes you to Great Britain. But the course conditions and amenities offered are straight out of an American textbook. And while there are tougher holes here, and even a few you might consider more memorable, No. 10 is worth a look back as you walk off the green. This would be a signature hole on most other courses. But Bandon Dunes isn't most other courses.

The par 4 is a sharp dogleg right with a couple of options at the tee. You can drive your tee shot along the right side of the fairway to give you the shortest approach shot to the green. Or you can go left and give yourself a better angle into the putting surface.

Your second shot is usually a blind shot, but don't worry. Trust not only your yardage, but your game. This shot is not for the timid, so flash a little confidence and then a little smile if you land on the green. **TJ**

## No. ⑩ DEERHURST (HIGHLANDS COURSE)

**Course:** Deerhurst (Highlands Course)

**Location:** Huntsville, Ontario, Canada

**Hole:** No. 10

**Length:** 464 yards

**Par:** 4

**Designer:** Bob Cupp, Thomas McBroom

**Course Comment:** The resort's original course, the Deerhurst Lakeside, was initially designed by C.E. Robinson in 1966, and then reconfigured by Thomas McBroom in 1990 to offer a gentle but surprisingly challenging round for all skill levels.

There are a lot of reasons to remember golf holes. Maybe it was very difficult. Maybe you eagled the hole. Maybe the scenery just knocked you over. Memorable means a lot of things to a lot of people.

But a lot of people remember No. 10 on Deerhurst's Highlands Course. How can you easily forget an 80-foot high rock face which runs along the right side of the fairway all the way up to the corner of the dogleg right?

Talk about unique.

This par 4 isn't only memorable, but it's one of the more difficult holes at Deerhurst. And it's certainly fun to play with dangers lurking around every corner.

You have the rock face on your right and a pond on your left that really doesn't come into play as you stand on this elevated tee. Don't bother looking for the green because you can't see it. You need to be aggressive here and hit it about 280 yards to reach the turn and have a shot at the green in two.

If you can get to the bend, you will be looking at about 150 yards to the putting surface, which is both massive and undulating.

There is one bunker about 80 yards out from the green on the left and three bunkers about 50 yards out on the right. **TJ**

# BETHPAGE STATE PARK (BLACK COURSE)

**Course:** Bethpage State Park (Black Course)

**Location:** Farmingdale, New York, USA

**Hole:** No. 10

**Length:** 492 yards

**Par:** 4

**Designer:** A.W. Tillinghast

**Course Comment:** The 492-yard 10th hole was the second longest in U.S. Open history, behind the 499-yard 12th hole. Bethpage Black was the longest par 70 in U.S. Open history at 7,214 yards.

Only walking is permitted, slow players are not welcome, and large signs warn golfers at every turn to beware. Built to challenge the best players of the time and rival Pine Valley as a true test of golf, the Black Course at Bethpage State Park continues to live up to every bit of its original billing.

The world was formally introduced to Bethpage Black during the 2002 U.S. Open, the third time in the championship's history it was played at a truly public golf course, and the par-4 10th was center stage of a grand play.

For the week, the 10th played to a 4.499 average, third toughest behind the 15th and 12th. There were more double bogeys (31) at No. 10 than birdies (22) and after 72 holes there had been a staggering 187 bogeys recorded at the 492-yard hole.

The 10th doglegs slightly to the left and its narrow fairway is protected by deep bunkers left and right, and shin-high rough. From a new tee built for the U.S. Open, players must carry their drives nearly 250 yards to the narrow fairway.

The elevated green is protected front left and right by deep bunkers and a recovery shot from an errant approach to the 10th green is typical Bethpage Black — a long sand shot that requires both length and height. **TJ**

**Course:** Riviera Country Club

**Location:** Pacific Palisades, California, USA

**Hole:** No. 10

**Length:** 311 yards

**Par:** 4

**Designer:** George C. Thomas Jr.

**Course Comment:** Ben Hogan won the first two of his four U.S. Open championships here, and also made his return to competition at Riviera after nearly being killed in an automobile accident.

# No. ⑩ RIVIERA COUNTRY CLUB

George C. Thomas Jr., nicknamed "the Captain," was one of the most significant figures in the history of golf course design, but he probably isn't among the first most would think of when it comes to big-time architects. Design students may know the creations of Thomas, but beyond purists, he may be anonymous. That's because Thomas created golf courses just because he could — not for the fame — and he loved it to the core. Proof of his devotion to his craft is furthered when you consider he never once charged a fee for his work.

Following a stint as a pilot in World War I, Thomas began dabbling in course design for wealthy friends on the East Coast. In 1920, he moved to California. There, he designed several of the most important and visually unique golf courses in the country, including Los Angeles Country Club, Bel-Air Country Club, Stanford University Golf Club, and, of course, Riviera Country Club.

Thomas was among the select geniuses who produced golf's "Golden Age of Architecture" in the 1920s.

And the 10th at Riviera is one of his most strategically tantalizing challenges — short at 311 yards, but devilish the entire way. It offers robust players a shot at the green, but if the wind isn't at your back, it isn't very realistic. Even if you can make the green, the trajectory on your shot is such that it's doubtful it would hold. Perhaps with the wind, you could give it a try, but other than that, safety is probably wiser.

Not that there is much safe ground on Thomas' 10th. Two bunkers bisect the fairway — at 215 yards off the tee on the right and 260 yards on the left. A 240-yard lay up is the ideal shot off the tee, then the second shot must carry five bunkers circling the front of a green that cants severely from left to right.

Thomas loved the strategy of golf, and No. 10 is a shining example. The hole was built in an era when the only earth-moving possible was with mules and hand labor. Instead of bulldozing a site, the architect had to rely upon the routing to optimize use of the land. And Thomas was working before course design was a profession for which you trained. Thomas' first love was gardening, and roses were his specialty. He wrote many books on roses, and also authored one of the most interesting books ever on golf course design, *Golf Architecture in America* (1927).

George C. Thomas Jr. was one of the best at his craft. And No. 10 at Riviera is lasting legacy of his genius. **JB**

## No. ⑩ COPPER CREEK GOLF CLUB

**Course:** Copper Creek Golf Club

**Location:** Copper Mountain, Colorado, USA

**Hole:** No. 10

**Length:** 396 yards

**Par:** 4

**Designer:** Pete and Perry Dye

**Course Comment:** In 1987, the back nine holes were added and the original holes redesigned by Perry Dye. Yes, railroad ties are par for the course at this Dye layout.

Here is a greeting you are likely to run into at Copper Creek: "We're not overly burdened by a bunch of rules. Except maybe one. You're required to have a good time. Mandatory."

That isn't very difficult to do at this upscale resort. Located at the base of Copper Mountain Resort, Copper Creek Golf Club is North America's highest championship golf club (elevation 9,700 feet).

Even though there are four sets of tees, there is no way to avoid the difficulty that awaits you on No. 10, a tricky 396-yard par 4. Tee off from wherever you'd like (they range from 396 yards to 293), but you have to clear that large lake if you want to reach the green — the fairway does wrap around the right side, but what fun would that be?

The fairway is pretty generous so hit out there somewhere in the middle. The closer to the water, the easier your approach shot will be. Bunkers guard the front right and left of the green. **TJ**

## No. ⑩ CAVES VALLEY GOLF CLUB

**Course:** Caves Valley Golf Club

**Location:** Owings Mills, Maryland, USA

**Hole:** No. 10

**Length:** 360 yards

**Par:** 4

**Designer:** Tom Fazio

**Course Comment:** Don Pooley set the U.S. Senior Open record for the lowest 18-hole score at Caves Valley, shooting a third-round 63 on his way to a playoff victory.

From its nondescript entrance on Park Heights Avenue to its welcoming clubhouse, everything about Caves Valley Golf Course is wonderfully understated. However, there is nothing understated about the course itself.

The idea, when the club's founders commissioned Tom Fazio to build Caves Valley amid the rolling hills of Maryland's estate and hunt country, was to create something of a Pine Valley Central. Unlike its high-profile cousin to the north, however, Caves Valley has opened its fairways to the nation's best players on a regular basis since opening in 1991.

In 1995 the club hosted the U.S Mid-Amateur, and seven years later one of the most dramatic U.S. Senior Opens was played at Caves Valley. In each event, the par-4 10th played a crucial role in the outcome. In 2002, champion Don Pooley played the short 10th in 1 under on his way to a playoff victory over Tom Watson.

From the 10th tee, the hole unfolds in grand fashion to a large hill and across a valley to the green. Most play a mid-iron from the tee to avoid the first of two fairway bunkers on the right. Players will be left with a short-iron approach shot to an elevated green guarded by a large, gaping bunker along the front left portion of the putting surface. **RH**

**Course:** Augusta National Golf Club

**Location:** Augusta, Georgia, USA

**Hole:** No. 10

**Length:** 495 yards

**Par:** 4

**Designer:** Robert Tyre Jones, Alister MacKenzie

**Course Comment:** Perhaps the most arduous hole on the most well-maintained golf course in the world. It leads into the famous Amen Corner at Augusta, the 11th, 12th, and 13th.

BELOW AND OPPOSITE *Two views of the 10th hole at Augusta.*

# No. ❿ AUGUSTA NATIONAL GOLF CLUB

It is nicknamed Camellia, but do not be fooled by the gentle sound of its moniker. The 10th hole at Augusta National Golf Club is one of the toughest holes on the course, and among the fiercest you will find.

The downhill, dogleg left 10th, which serves as the first playoff hole if the Masters needs to go to sudden death to be settled, has historically set a stern challenge to the world's finest players each April. In the 2003 Masters, for example, the par-4 hole ranked third in terms of difficulty, with a stroke average of 4.33, giving up just 21 birdies while forcing 84 bogeys.

Augusta National is all about tradition, but No. 10 has undergone changes over the years. The 10th hole used to be the first hole before the nines were reversed in 1935, and along with the rest of the putting surfaces at Augusta, No. 10's green was changed to bent grass in 1981.

The 10th hole serves as a rude welcome to the back nine, and it became even more abrasive in 2002 when Augusta National Chairman Hootie Johnson led a movement to lengthen the course by 300 yards. The 10th hole was among those given some added meat in an effort to fend off the advancements in equipment technology. It was just an extra 10 yards to reach its current distance of 495, but it gave even more claws to what was already one bear of a hole. **JB**

## No. ⑩ THE GRAND GOLF CLUB

**Course:** The Grand Golf Club

**Location:** Gilston, Queensland, Australia

**Hole:** No. 10

**Length:** 336 yards

**Par:** 4

**Designer:** Greg Norman, Bob Harrison

**Course Comment:** Originally built by Norman and Harrison for a Japanese client and ready to be played in 1991, this course took a name — Gilston Golf Club — but never opened when the owner took a bogey in his business life and fell upon hard times. It lay fallow for five years until a consortium of local golfers asked the architects to bring it back to life. They did, and then some, renaming it The Grand Golf Club and reopening in 1997.

When it finally opened, The Grand featured fierce undulations on both fairways and greens that utilized the natural contours of the Queensland countryside and sometimes drove players crazy with their maddening breaks and bounces.

The landing areas were made tight, the bunkers, for the most part, deep, and it was all surrounded by thick, subtropical vegetation. The initial reviews were strong, so much so that the Australian Golf Union decided to host the Australian Open there in 2001. But there were plenty of complaints after that tournament as well, mostly about the difficulty of three specific golf holes on the back side, beginning with No. 10.

You wouldn't think there would be a whole lot to whine about with 10, especially given its modest length and fairly straightforward layout. It sensibly demands an accurate drive off the tee that has to thread a narrow corridor between trees. Following that, players are left with only a short iron to the green.

But it is a brutal green, and the aspect of the hole that stirred all the controversy, due to its smallish size and wicked undulations. The bunkering also poses its shares of problems, with two deep ones in back and a pair short and to the left. Many of the pros found it difficult to post par on that hole, and while amateurs no doubt experience those same difficulties each time they play No. 10, it does not stop many from putting it on their list of favorites. **JS**

## No. ⑩ INDIANWOOD GOLF & COUNTRY CLUB (OLD COURSE)

**Course:** Indianwood Golf & Country Club (Old Course)

**Location:** Lake Orion, Michigan, USA

**Hole:** No. 10

**Length:** 351 yards

**Par:** 4

**Designer:** Wilfrid Reid, William Connellan

**Course Comment:** The New Course has a different feel to it than the Old Course, despite both being Scottish-link styles. The New Course is more target golf with plenty of uneven lies, tall heather rough, and water hazards on 14 holes.

"Old Course" should not be misunderstood. There is some history here, but this classic beauty defies her age.

The Old Course is truly a classic, best known for its magnificent fescue rough and countless pot bunkers. The terrain of this track differs greatly from most American courses and challenges the best golfers.

Here is what Indianwood Golf and Country Club expert Marvin Stahl had to say about the 351-yard par 4: "One of the most beautiful holes on the course, it is also one of the most exciting."

About 240 yards from the elevated tee, the landing area is narrowed from 46 to less than 25 yards in width by a water hazard on the left. Players may elect to use a long iron off the tee to keep short of the water.

Some pin placements can result in large breaking putts once the golfer negotiates the mounds and bunkers protecting the green.

The club hosted the U.S. Ladies' Open on the Old Course in 1994 and is a longtime host of the Michigan PGA Championship. **TJ**

## No. ❿  CASTLE PINES GOLF CLUB

**Course:** Castle Pines Golf Club

**Location:** Castle Rock, Colorado, USA

**Hole:** No. 10

**Length:** 485 yards

**Par:** 4

**Designer:** Jack Nicklaus

**Course Comment:** Castle Pines has played host to the PGA Tour's Sprint International since 1986. The International is a unique event in that a modified Stableford scoring sytem is used.

Castle Pines offers a number of spectacular Rocky Mountain views from its 6,400 foot perch in northern Colorado. The private course is located in the Crowfoot Valley where residents enjoy over 250 days of sunshine a year with an average high temperature of 85 degrees in the summer and 44 degrees in the winter.

Narrow fairways are lined with pine, and elevated greens demand precision. Ernie Els, winner of the 2000 International, praises the Nicklaus design and counts Castle Pines as one of the most well-conditioned courses on the Tour's schedule.

The most demanding hole of the hilly track is the par-4 10th. From an elevated tee, players must execute a long, accurate drive as this lengthy hole could easily pose as a par 5. A prominent target from the tee is the rock in Castle Rock, the mini mountain the city is named after.

A solid 250-yard drive, however, still leaves a skilled player with a 235-yard downhill approach. A long iron or fairway wood will be required to reach an undulated green closely guarded by an unforgiving pond and two bunkers. A rather small bail-out area is available short and left of the green. **BB**

## No. ❿  LAKEWOOD SHORES RESORT (GAILES COURSE)

**Course:** Lakewood Shores Resort (Gailes Course)

**Location:** Oscoda, Michigan, USA

**Hole:** No. 10

**Length:** 348 yards

**Par:** 4

**Designer:** Kevin Aldridge

**Course Comment:** Lakewood Shores Resort is one of the most popular and first-rate golf destinations in northern Michigan. Despite awesome competition, the Gailes Course was rated the No. 1 resort course in Michigan by *The Detroit News* in 1997.

Michigan isn't exactly the Scottish countryside, but this course in Northeast Michigan is a little bit of Scotland in the Midwest USA. The Gailes, one of three 18-hole championship courses at Lakewood Shores Resort, was designed with the look and feel of those famous seaside courses in Scotland.

The 10th hole at The Gailes, a relatively short and seemingly simple 348-yard par 4, captures the true essence of links golf. There are deep sod-faced bunkers ready to pounce on less than perfectly placed shots to the fairway or green, as well as gnarled mounds of knee-high fescue that stand ready to swallow your golf ball.

Play this one smart, like the great Scottish players would. Keep your driver in the bag because accuracy counts much more than distance here.

Because of bunkers on the left side of a partially hidden green, take aim at the center. Don't get too concerned with hitting the flagstick. Continue to play smart target golf and this hole won't ruin your round.

Those winds off Lake Huron and this spectacular golf course will make you believe you are somewhere other than Michigan. **TJ**

## No. ❿ CATTAILS GOLF CLUB

**Course:** Cattails Golf Club

**Location:** South Lyon, Michigan, USA

**Hole:** No. 10

**Length:** 499 yards

**Par:** 5

**Designer:** John Williams

**Course Comment:** Opened in 1991, Cattails joined a number of outstanding golf courses within a wedge shot of one another. The South Lyon course didn't mind the competition and quickly earned a reputation as one of the better courses in the area — and that's saying something.

Michigan seems to have plenty of the two-in-one style golf courses where the front nine is different from the back nine. The front side at Cattails is wide open, but the back is pretty tight with a lot more trees.

The good thing is if you pay for 18 holes you get to play "both" courses. Cattails doesn't waste any time introducing you to the second nine. No. 10 is easily the most memorable hole at the course. And that's not saying there aren't other good holes. All it means is you won't soon forget this one in a hurry. The dogleg-right par 5 is one of the more tempting holes you will ever play. It almost dares you, then it beats you down.

But first, the tee shot. To get your ball past the wall of trees on the right and into view of the green, you need a good 230 yards off the tee from the back. If you don't get past the trees, you have no choice to play around the fairway, which runs around the left side of a huge marsh.

If you get past the trees, you are left with a tough decision. It might be a difficult call, but almost everyone chooses the same route — right over the marsh to a very tough green.

It's about 200 to 210 yards over the cattails to the green. But there is very little room for error. The front and left side of the green slope right into the marsh and there is a bunker on the left side. **TJ**

## No. ❿ WHITE WITCH

**Course:** White Witch

**Location:** Rose Hall, Montego Bay, Jamaica

**Hole:** No. 10

**Length:** 621 yards

**Par:** 5

**Designer:** Robert Von Hagge, Rick Baril

**Course Comment:** The first event at this Caribbean wonder was a "Shell's Wonderful World of Golf" made-for-television match between Hal Sutton and Notah Begay in 2000. Sutton and Begay each shot even-par 71 in their duel.

Robert von Hagge lists the White Witch, operated by the Ritz-Carlton Golf and Spa Resort, as among his greatest challenges as an architect. The course was literally blown into the mountainside, blasted into rock to create a majestic seaside track that belies its origin. It was built into, on to, and around solid rock. Von Hagge said:

"There was no topsoil. This is a beautiful piece of property to be sure, but it's hard to explain what it took to turn it into a golf course."

It is also hard to explain the beauty of White Witch, which is blessed with elevation changes, ocean views, and holes that wind their way along the mountains.

The 10th hole, which originally was the first before the nines were reversed in 2001, is a monster on the scorecard at 621 yards, but that is somewhat deceptive. The tee box is elevated some 100 feet, so it cuts down considerably on how long the hole actually plays. No. 10 doglegs around bunkers on the edge of a ravine, and cutting the corner — while certainly not without risk — offers a real reward and a genuine shot at the putting surface. It's hard to believe that you could reach a 621-yard hole in two, but it is possible because of the huge elevation of the tee box and the possibility of cutting the dogleg. **JB**

**THE RENAISSANCE CLUB**

**Course:** The Renaissance Club

**Location:** Dirleton, East Lothian, Scotland

**Hole:** No. 10

**Length:** 593 yards

**Par:** 5

**Designer:** Tom Doak

**Course Comment:** Doak long has been a fan of British golf, particularly links-style golf, as much of his U.S. work shows. But the Renaissance Club, was his first work in the UK.

The Renaissance Club has to go a bit to "keep up with the Joneses" in the neighborhood. It is within a few miles of North Berwick, Gullane, and Luffness, and it sits right next to Muirfield. So when Tom Doak picked this property to work on, he knew he had to be up to the task.

The former estate of the Dukes of Hamilton was covered in pine trees, but Doak took care of that in short order, and has turned the Renaissance Club into a first-class traditional Scottish Links, with the perilous pot bunkers, undulating fairways, and fescue surfaces. And, by all accounts, Doak's first work in the UK has been a roaring success.

The 593-yard 10th hole has a unique green indeed. A large mound blocks off the right side, creating an ominous punchbowl on that side. If the hole location happens to be on that side, it will be nearly impossible to get close to, so do the best you can and hope for two putt.

No. 10 has a high-shouldered approach shot that is a tad treacherous. Going for the green in two is possible, but not probable if the wind is in your face. The risk-reward is a perfect par-5 decision for those deciding whether they want to lay up in the mounding or go ahead and rip away at the putting surface. Either way, you have quite a hole. Not a bad UK debut for a legend in golf-course design. **JB**

**Course:** Pinehurst (No. 2 Course)

**Location:** Pinehurst, North Carolina, USA

**Hole:** No. 10

**Length:** 615 yards

**Par:** 5

**Designer:** Donald Ross

**Course Comment:** Not one single player reached the 10th green in two during the 1999 U.S. Open.

## No. ❿ PINEHURST (NO. 2 COURSE)

As of 2004, Pinehurst Resort, with eight beautiful golf courses, had the most golf holes on site of any locale in the world. But the 144-hole North Carolina golf haven, founded in 1894, is known for far more than quantity. Each course has defined cuts of rough along tree-lined fairways, a plethora of bunkers, and stately trees that make you think on virtually every hole. It was the opening of the Centennial Course in 1996 that gave Pinehurst the distinction of having more golf holes than any other resort in the world.

There is a picturesque quality about each of the courses, but when searching for the best of the best, there is no question: It's Pinehurst No. 2, created by Donald Ross in 1907. Of No. 2, Ross said, "it is the fairest test of championship golf I have ever designed."

No. 2 is a challenge not because of its curvaceous routing, length, land forms, water hazards, or green size and slickness — but because of the combination of factors that have both frustrated and enthralled the players fortunate enough to have trodden the hallowed ground.

It has undulating greens. Carefully placed bunkers. A strategic layout that tests both the long and the short game. It is the site of more championships than any other course in the United States, including the 1999 and 2005 U.S. Opens.

And the 10th hole, like the rest of No. 2, is a stern test. Its length produces a rare phenomenon for the best players in the world — a par-5 hole that actually takes three shots to get there.

The length is prodigious, and uphill to boot, but the hole requires more than brute strength. It's all about angles here — angles that almost guarantee that you won't be thinking about making the green in two shots. The hole doglegs left, and cutting the corner is so perilous — and the chance of reward so slim — that it turns the hole into a legitimate three-shotter. It is a true par 5, lending truth to Ross's statement about Pinehurst being a fair test.

The 10th is a great hole, as Pinehurst is a splendid resort. Listen to what Tommy Armour said of the place: "The man who doesn't feel emotionally stirred when he plays golf at Pinehurst beneath those clear blue skies and with the pine fragrance in his nostrils is one who should be ruled out of golf for life. It's the kind of course that gets into the blood of an old trooper." **JB**

**Course:** Royal Melbourne Golf Club, (East Course)

**Location:** Black Rock, Victoria, Australia

**Hole:** No. 10

**Length:** 500 yards

**Par:** 5

**Designer:** Alex Russell

**Course Comment:** Though Russell is credited with designing the highly acclaimed East, it was head greenkeeper Mick Morcom who actually built the course that opened for play in 1932 and to date has hosted two Australian Open championships.

## No. ❿ ROYAL MELBOURNE GOLF CLUB (EAST COURSE)

Located deep in the heart of Victoria's famed Sand Belt region, which is to Australian golf what Reno, Nevada is to wedding chapels, the often-overlooked East Course at the Royal Melbourne Golf Club is a must-play for the golfing aficionado.

And one of the better holes at that track is the par-5 10th. It is a fabulous dogleg — or would that be wallaby-leg? — bending to the right, with a pair of fairway bunkers at the turn that almost force golfers to play their drives out to the left. That really is not a problem, for there is plenty of room on that portion of the fairway for those who want to stay out of the sand, and away from the out-of-bounds hazard that runs down the entire right side of the hole.

Yes, it is possible for longer hitters to reach the green in two, but a steady second shot will usually bring more favorable results in the form of a simple chip to get onto the two-tiered putting surface in regulation.

Beware the bunkers short and to the right of this green; it is also important to leave approaches under the hole in order to avoid those sinister downhill putts that can run right past the hole when it is tournament quick. **JS**

---

**Course:** Newcastle Golf Club

**Location:** Fern Bay, New South Wales, Australia

**Hole:** No. 10

**Length:** 525 yards

**Par:** 5

**Designer:** Eric Apperly

**Course Comment:** This layout is something of a sleeper among Oz's golf-course collection, often overlooked by outsiders but regularly — and rightfully — regarded as one of the country's classic gems.

## No. ❿ NEWCASTLE GOLF CLUB

There is nothing quite as enjoyable at the beginning of a back nine than to find a risk-reward par 5, providing golfers the possibility of a great start to a second side and the option either to go for it or to keep things in check.

And the 10th at Newcastle offers just that, a sort of rollercoaster hole with a pair of sand dunes that create three distinct dips in the terrain and a wildly undulating fairway. Hit a perfect drive, and it is entirely possible that a good player can put his, or her, second shot onto the green.

But the thing is, each shot on this hole can be blind, or at least partially blind, depending on your position. And the green, onto which a player can run up shots, is set behind the second dune and usually out of sight.

Regulars say the best play on this track, which is carved out of a forest of gum trees and populated by kookaburras and kangaroos, is to lay up with both the first and second shots, and then hit a wedge to the green that is modest in size and never easy to hit and hold. **JS**

**Course:** Country Club of Detroit

**Location:** Grosse Pointe Shores, Michigan, USA

**Hole:** No. 10

**Length:** 581 yards

**Par:** 5

**Designer:** Harry S. Colt and C.H. Alison

**Course Comment:** On August 28, 1954, Arnold Palmer won the U.S. Amateur Championship at the Country Club of Detroit in dramatic, come-from-behind fashion where he rallied for a 1-up victory over Robert Sweeny. Palmer refers to that victory as "my turning point in golf." In August 2004, Palmer returned to the site of his first glory, hosting a charity event that drew 30 former U.S. Amateur champions and raised a record $5 million.

# No. ⑩  COUNTRY CLUB OF DETROIT

This is your first hole after the turn, so make sure you take time after your outward nine to grab a sandwich and a beverage. No. 10 is a monster, and you'll need plenty of energy on this 581-yard par 5.

Off the tee you need both a solid and straight tee shot to be safe. A 240-yard carry will get you safely in the fairway and away from the three big church-pew bunkers. Stay to the right center because if your ball leaks to the left you may go out-of-bounds, which runs down the left side. If you can hit a 280-yard drive, the second shot's distance will be just under 300 yards, and if you can't hit it that far it is a traditional three-shot par-5.

There are nine traps on this hole and most line the right side, so stay in the middle. In front of the green you will find a traditional bunker on both the right and left side. The green is big, fair, and the center is your optimum location. Because this hole is so long the green is fairly easy, but speed will still be a factor.

Very few people hit this hole in two, and it isn't advised to try it. Take three shots to get on the green, give your birdie putt a try, and move on. **GE**

**Course:** Ellerston Golf Course

**Location:** Upper Hunter Valley, New South Wales, Australia

**Hole:** No. 10

**Length:** 549 yards

**Par:** 5

**Designer:** Greg Norman, Bob Harrison

**Course Comment:** No one has ever reached this monstrous, uphill par 5 in two, not even the lead designer himself.

# No. ⑩  ELLERSTON GOLF COURSE

Working with what the stunning land at Ellerston gave them, Norman and Harrison thought nothing about building back-to-back par 5s at the turn.

The second of those, No. 10, is laid out in the most mountainous region of this retreat, and it requires a big hit with the Big Dog that is best worked from left to right, playing off a large eucalyptus tree in the left center of the fairway. The smart move from there is a lay-up down the middle of the fairway with a long iron.

Then, it is time for the approach, generally a precise pitch to a testy, undulating green that rises to the back left. A gully runs up the left side of the fairway around the spot where the second shot lands and then crosses in front of the putting surface, which is one of three greens on the course without bunkers.

A pin placement on the right makes the third shot exceedingly tight, while one to the left can be thrown a bit long, allowing the ball to roll gently back toward the flag. **JS**

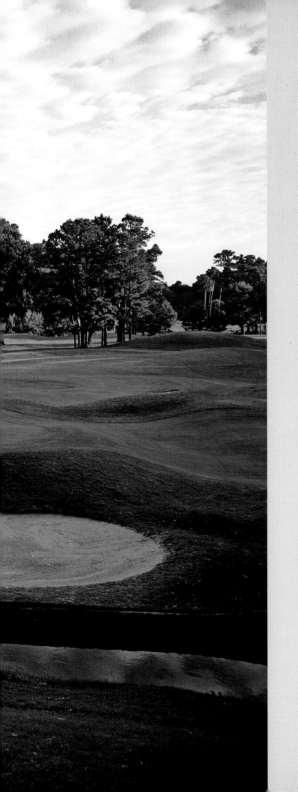

# Hole **11**

The round is more than halfway finished as you approach the 11th hole, which means you've been on the course for roughly 2 ½ hours. No time to let down your defenses, however, as the 11th hole looms. It is a hole to firmly establish yourself on the back nine, as you make the trek farther from the clubhouse.

Ballybunion's Old Course in the rolling Irish hills, and Shinnecock in Southampton, New York, are a couple of venues throughout the world where the 11th hole stands out. It may seem like an early time in the round for drama, but No. 11 — particularly in tournament play — can establish a player as a front-runner that is uncatchable, or one that might just be vulnerable.

**LEFT** *The 11th hole at TPC at Sawgrass, Ponte Vedra Beach, Florida, USA.*

**Course:** Yarra Yarra Golf Club

**Location:** Bentleigh East, Victoria, Australia

**Hole:** No. 11

**Length:** 181 yards

**Par:** 3

**Designer:** Alex Russell

**Course Comment:** PGA Tour players Robert Allenby and Stuart Appleby were members of Yarra Yarra before they turned professional.

## No. ⑪  YARRA YARRA GOLF CLUB

Yarra Yarra is a wonderful Alex Russell design that feels a great deal like the work of the man who taught him all about golf-course architecture — Alister MacKenzie.

And this par 3, with its triple-tiered green guarded by deep bunkers front, right, and back, is considered its signature hole. Australian great Peter Thomson, he of five British Open championships, has described No. 11 as a "national treasure" and rates it as one of the top 18 holes in Australia.

Critics of considerably less note and knowledge simply say it is one of their favorites anywhere, though they do lament the way apparent pars on No. 11 quickly turn into bogeys. The key to carding a three, in their view, is to hit a straightforward iron to the correct shelf of a green renowned for its fierce undulations and unforgiving speed when the course superintendent cuts it close.

Then, it is only a matter of getting the first putt close, and the second one into the hole. That may sound easy enough, to be sure, but regulars at Yarra Yarra readily admit that two putts here are usually much easier said than done. **JS**

**Course:** Fishers Island Club

**Location:** Fishers Island, New York, USA

**Hole:** No. 11

**Length:** 164 yards

**Par:** 3

**Designer:** Seth Raynor

**Course Comment:** How good are the short holes at Fishers Island? This amazing par 3 isn't even the trademark hole on the golf course. That honor belongs to No. 5, another par 3.

# No. ⑪ FISHERS ISLAND CLUB

Fishers Island is a private country club. And it's no secret that the private, up-scale courses redefine special. Fishers Island is special in a lot of ways. Many ways you would expect at a country club of this magnitude.

The course is always in impeccable condition. The holes are challenging, yet playable. But Fishers Island is one memorable hole after another — and the perfect example is No. 11.

The 164-yard par 3 is, well, special.

With water, which is part of Fishers Island Sound, on the right side and a cove behind the hole, this par 3 is as scenic as it gets.

There is an elevated tee box with a big dip in the middle of the fairway. About six feet below the green is a bunker on the right side. And about 13 feet below the green are bunkers on the left side and behind the green.

The hole has fescue in front of the tee that extends all the way to about 30 yards before the green.

The green isn't easy and requires a good eye and a good stroke.

Completed in 1927, after Seth Raynor's death, the 18-hole true seaside links golf course seems to come directly from the Atlantic Ocean that it calls its neighbor. **TJ**

**Course:** Christchurch Golf Club

**Location:** Shirley, Canterbury, New Zealand

**Hole:** No. 11

**Length:** 141 yards

**Par:** 3

**Designer:** Bob Charles

**Course Comment:** In 1990, Christchurch hosted the Eisenhower Trophy, which was won by the Swedish group of Mathias Gronberg, Klas Eriksson, and Gabriel Hjertstedt. The U.S. squad of Phil Mickelson, David Duval, and Allen Doyle finished in second place.

## No. ⑪ CHRISTCHURCH GOLF CLUB

In 1973 Christchurch Golf Club celebrated its centennial. One hundred years of gorse and golf, and the short yet exacting layout proved to be as challenging as ever. A quarter of a century later, the links-style track remains a subtle study in golf-course design. The lesson at Christchurch — less is almost always more.

The original nine-hole design took advantage of the area's natural topography. The use of small bumps and holes framed by pine, gorse, and broom trees provided a dramatic test. Prior to the 1990 Eisenhower Trophy, the club commissioned Peter Thomson to refine the layout and the results were remarkable.

Expansive, lush green fairways are complemented by impressively flat greens and an assortment of deep, foreboding bunkers.

A drop of a golf hole at 141 yards, the par-3 11th appears to be little more than a temporary diversion at first glance. A fleeting stopover between the demanding 12th and 13th holes. But this small hole carries a big bite.

Depending on the wind, players will need little more than an 8-iron into the small, well-guarded green but tee shots must be played perfectly if it's to have any chance to give a player a birdie attempt. **RH**

**Course:** Trickle Creek

**Location:** Kimberly, British Columbia, Canada

**Hole:** No. 11

**Length:** 171 yards

**Par:** 3

**Designer:** Les Furber

**Course Comment:** Furber, who designed several other outstanding courses in the region, is known for his undulating greens. No. 11 at Trickle Creek has his signature all over it. Instead of sloping side-to-side, the two-tiered green slopes front-to-back.

## No. ⑪ TRICKLE CREEK

There is spectacular, there is awesome, there is dramatic. And there is No. 11 at Trickle Creek.

You won't remember your score on this hole — unless you get a hole-in-one — and you probably won't remember much about the hole itself. But you will never forget the view.

The tee on this 171-yard par 3 overlooks A Valley of a Thousand Peaks and the view is wide, long, and inspiring. There are those who say you can see two provinces and three states on a clear day, and you can see some mountains across the border as well. The view carries for hundreds of miles up there.

The states would be Montana, Idaho and Washington.

There is some serious elevation change at Trickle Creek, with about 150 feet from the highest tee to the lowest green. On No. 11, you have an 80-foot drop and bunkers on both sides.

The tough choice here is what club to use. If you use a 7-iron to hit 150 yards at sea level, you will need an 8-iron at 3,800 feet because of the thin air. Then, with the 80 feet of elevation change on No. 11 you would use either a 9-iron or pitching wedge. **TJ**

**Course:** Alwoodley Golf Club

**Location:** Leeds, West Yorkshire, England

**Hole:** No. 11

**Length:** 175 yards

**Par:** 3

**Designer:** Alister Mackenzie

**Course Comment:** Alwoodley is the first course designed by Mackenzie, who designed many masterpieces, among them Augusta National in the United States, home of the Masters.

# No. ⑪ ALWOODLEY GOLF CLUB

Ben Crenshaw, a major-championship winner, and a course architect himself, has been quoted as saying No. 11 is one of his favorite holes at Alwoodley, so that is the hole we will study today. After all, it is hard to argue with an expert such as Crenshaw.

The 11th is fairly short from even the back tee, but the green slopes severely from back to front, and it also sucks golf balls from right to left. So, in order for the ball to be in any kind of shape on the putting surface, it must hit the right side of the green to slope to the center. This is true regardless of where the pin placement might be on any given day.

And, taking into account the aforementioned slopes, putting can be long and treacherous.

The walk to the green is a nice, brisk walk with lots to view. There are plenty of bunkers on both sides, particularly the closer you get to the green. There is a blanket of trees surrounding the fairway, and the fairway also is protected by thick stands of trees.

Sometimes par 3s are not the choice when picking a favorite hole, but the 11th is different in Crenshaw's eyes. And, after playing the hole, many others seem to agree. **JB**

**Course:** St. Andrews (Old Course)

**Location:** St. Andrews, Fife, Scotland

**Hole:** No. 11

**Length:** 172 yards

**Par:** 3

**Designer:** Old Tom Morris

**Course Comment:** In the 1933 British Open Championship, Gene Sarazen took three shots from the bunker, finished with a 6 on the hole and missed a playoff by one stroke.

# No. ⓫ ST. ANDREWS (OLD COURSE)

There are seven double greens on the Old Course at St. Andrews, but when discussing which course in the world receives the moniker "birthplace of golf," there is no sharing to be done. That honor goes to the Old Course.

The 11th is one of the holes that uses a double green, sharing its putting surface with No. 7. Historians say the track on which the Old Course was laid out was so narrow that golfers played to the same holes going out and coming in. As more people started to play the game, this caused so much congestion that it was decided that two holes would be cut on each green — red flags for the outward nine, white flags for the inward, a tradition that still continues.

Old Tom Morris broke from another tradition, however, when he created a separate green for the first hole and laid out the 18th. For the first time, it became possible to play the course in a counter-clockwise direction, after centuries of playing strictly clockwise. For many years, the course was played clockwise one week and counter clockwise the next.

The Old Course's 11th hole is one of the most celebrated par 3s in golf. But it has also been the site of some great frustration. When the great Bobby Jones first visited the Old Course in 1919, he landed in the head-high Hill bunker adjacent to the 11th green and took three shots to get out. Facing a short putt for a triple-bogey 6, Jones picked up his ball in frustration and withdrew from the event. Jones often spoke of the incident as "childish."

He wrote, "And often I have wished I could in some way offer a general apology . . . " Such is the challenge at No. 11, which brought one of the game's all-time greats to his knees.

Besides the deep and steep Hill bunker to the left, the Eden River lies behind the green, and the putting surface is canted so as to be nearly unreadable. Avoiding the hazards is no guarantee of par, because a downhill putt can be disastrous. **JB**

**BELOW** *The 11th hole at St. Andrews.*

**OPPOSITE** *Payne Stewart of the USA plays out of a bunker on the 11th hole at St. Andrews, October 1999.*

**Course:** Atlantic Golf Club

**Location:** Bridgehampton, New York, USA

**Hole:** No. 11

**Length:** 128 yards

**Par:** 3

**Designer:** Rees Jones

**Course Comment:** Despite some excellent golf courses in the Hamptons — including the revered triumvirate Shinnecock Hills, Maidstone, and National — Atlantic Golf Club was built because of the growing demand for more great places to play.

## No. ⓫ ATLANTIC GOLF CLUB

First some background on this spectacular golf course:

This Rees Jones design features a linksy personality, but isn't pure links. Most of the holes are framed by mounds and moguls that look as if they had been crafted over time by the hands of nature.

The land rises and falls, rolls and ripples like the swells at sea, with tall fescue rough swaying and shimmering in the ever-constant breezes and ever-changing lighting.

Now that we have established the background and the overall picture, let's move on to No. 11.

The 128-yard par 3 is one of the more scenic holes on this very picturesque golf course. It's also one of the least difficult.

"It's the easiest hole on the golf course, but it's anything but easy," said our pro shop guide for the day. "It's easy to make a 2 or 3, but just as easy to make a 5."

There is out-of-bounds on the left and the green is guarded by a large bunker that begins some 50 yards from the green. There are four deep bunkers around a green that is narrow and slopes right to left. **TJ**

**Course:** The National Golf Club, (Ocean Course)

**Location:** Cape Schanck, Victoria, Australia

**Hole:** No. 11

**Length:** 186 yards

**Par:** 3

**Designer:** Peter Thomson, Michael Wolveridge, Ross Perrett

**Course Comment:** This championship course winds through the Mornington sand hills and boasts the soothing feel of a wild Scottish links.

# No. ⑪ THE NATIONAL GOLF CLUB
## (OCEAN COURSE)

To many traditionalists, the best part of the 11th hole on the Ocean Course is the one thing they want to avoid at all costs when they play it — the gaping bunker that sits in the center front of the narrow green.

That's because the hazard is inspired by the one protecting the original Redan hole (No. 15) at North Berwick in Scotland and gives a nice historical context to a rather young layout (opened in 2000).

It also instills a fair amount of fear in golfers as they step to the elevated tee here, located on top of a ridge that also happens to offer spectacular views. Obviously, club selection is key for this par 3, but deciding what to hit is no easy feat due to the mercurial winds of the Mornington Peninsula; locals will tell you they have played as little as a 9-iron, and as much as 3-iron, depending on the volume of the blow that particular day.

And once they have figured out the proper stick, they then need to position carefully on a putting surface that is some 50 yards in width and famous for its devilish pin placements. **JS**

**Course:** Southern Dunes Golf &
Country Club

**Location:** Haines City, Florida, USA

**Hole:** No. 11

**Length:** 216 yards

**Par:** 3

**Designer:** Steve Smyers

**Course Comment:** This challenging
track is positioned on the second-
highest elevation in central Florida.
There are 186 bunkers on the course,
and 18 on No. 11.

# No. ⑪ SOUTHERN DUNES GOLF & COUNTRY CLUB

Feeling trapped in the Mouse's house? Southern Dunes is located a mere 15 miles from Disney World, offering tourists and residents alike an attractive alternative to resort golf. Architect Steve Smyers' other Florida designs include greats such as Tampa's Old Memorial, Tarpon Springs' Crescent Oak, and a complete renovation of Orlando's Isleworth Country Club, home to PGA Tour heavyweights such as Tiger Woods, Lee Janzen, and Mark O'Meara.

Drawing from the area's sandy soil and warm climate, Smyers intended Southern Dunes' hilly design to play firm and fast. Southern Dunes was built on the site of an old orange grove, and orange trees require a sandy soil to thrive. There is plenty of sand at Southern Dunes. In fact, Smyers and his crew had to haul sand out of the site, and were still left with enough sand to build nearly 200 bunkers.

On the par-3 11th, skilled players can attack the downhill hole in a number of ways depending on the day's pin placement. Bunkers on either side of the fairway shouldn't come into play as they are positioned well before the green.

If the pin is tucked left, land the ball short and left of the green and watch as it feeds toward the hole. To reach a right pin placement, an aeriel shot over the hollow is required, while a back hole location calls for a bump and run.

Beware of taking too much club as the green falls off sharply in the back, leaving players with a difficult chip. Those looking for the easy route should aim well away from the pin, taking the demanding up-and-down out of the equation. **BB**

**Course:** Las Brisas Golf Club

**Location:** Málaga, Nueva Andalucia, Spain

**Hole:** No. 11

**Length:** 210 yards

**Par:** 3

**Designer:** Robert Trent Jones Sr.

**Course Comment:** Las Brisas originally was called Nueva Andalucia Golf Club before its name was changed in the early 1970s.

# No. ⑪  LAS BRISAS GOLF CLUB

Part of Spain's Costa del Sol region, Málaga is a port city on the Mediterranean Sea. The aptly named Las Brisas Golf Club (translation: Golf Club of The Breezes) is located in the shadow of the La Concha mountain peak, and shots are often affected by winds that run through the valley. The course contains many unique species of tree, including at least one species that represents every continent, as well as numerous palms and native Mediterranean plants.

The tee shot on No. 11 must carry water in front and on the entire left side of the green, which slopes from front to back and is further protected by bunkers at the front left and front right and a group of trees on the right.

It didn't take long for Las Brisas to establish itself as a host to top professional events. Soon after its inauguration, the course was site of the 1970 Spanish Open, won by native son Angel Gallardo. The course also hosted Spanish Opens in 1983 (Eamon Darcy) and 1987 (Nick Faldo), and it served as the venue for two World Cups of Golf: the United States team of Jack Nicklaus and Johnny Miller won in 1973, and the Australian pair of Peter Fowler and Wayne Grady triumphed in 1989. **KA**

**Course:** Cordova Bay

**Location:** Victoria, British Columbia, Canada

**Hole:** No. 11

**Length:** 174 yards

**Par:** 3

**Designer:** Bill Robinson

**Course Comment:** A frequent stop on the Canadian Tour (including the 2005 Victoria Open), Cordova Bay's No. 11 was once rated the most difficult par 3 on the tour.

# No. ⑪  CORDOVA BAY

Cordova Bay is one of the busiest and most popular golf courses in Western Canada. Yet despite all the play, the course is always in excellent shape.

And No. 11 is simply an excellent hole. One of the most aesthetically pleasing holes at Cordova Bay, it's also been rated as one of the toughest (see course comment to the left).

Your target is an hourglass-shaped green that is just seven yards wide in the middle of the hourglass and 46 yards deep. The first five or six paces of the green are false — meaning your ball won't stay on the green if you land it there.

The back of the green has two tiers, an upper tier on the left and a slightly lower tier on the right. The pin placement isn't often in the middle of the hourglass but it's trouble when they do decide to place it there.

There is plenty of trouble around the green. A very large pond is on the right side and cuts into the hourglass green. So don't go right.

There are two pot bunkers on the left. They are both tough to hit out of, especially the front-left bunker. There also are three pot bunkers behind, but they aren't as severe. **TJ**

## No. ⑪  FALSTERBO GOLF CLUB

**Course:** Falsterbo Golf Club

**Location:** Falsterbo, Sweden

**Hole:** No. 11

**Length:** 160 yards

**Par:** 3

**Designer:** Gunnar Bauer

**Course Comment:** Adding to Falsterbo's challenge is a collection of natural water hazards called "Flommen" and a completely reworked collection of putting surfaces. The club completed a six-year project to restore all of its greens in 2001.

From the moment you arrive at Falsterbo Golf Club signs of what awaits you abound, from the low-slung clubhouse, which seems to hug the earth in an attempt to brace against the wind, to the flowing flag high atop a pole which seems to dance with the almost non-stop gale.

Falsterbo — about 30 kilometers southwest of Malmo — is a links-style course in every sense of the word. In fact, it is as close to the Scottish links as a player will get in Sweden.

The Gunnar Bauer design is located within the confines of a nature reserve at the tip of Sweden's southwest peninsula, where the waters of the sound and the Baltic Sea meet. The erratic winds from the Baltic combined with Falsterbo's treeless, rolling topography give the layout its best defense.

The 11th, for example, is a shortish par 3 that plays just 160 yards from the back tees, but into the prevailing wind players could be forced to hit two, even three clubs more than they ordinarily would.

Any tee shot on the putting surface is a triumph of sorts, yet on the 11th's demanding green a two-putt is no guarantee. **RH**

*OPPOSITE An aerial view of Falsterbo.*

## No. ⑪  LOS ANGELES COUNTRY CLUB (NORTH COURSE)

**Course:** Los Angeles Country Club (North Course)

**Location:** Los Angeles, California, USA

**Hole:** No. 11

**Length:** 244 yards

**Par:** 3

**Designer:** Herbert Fowler, George C. Thomas Jr., William P. Bell

**Course Comment:** In true Hollywood fashion, Hugh Hefner's longtime playpen, The Playboy Mansion, backs up to the 13th green of Los Angeles Country Club's North Course.

Located off well-known Wilshire Boulevard in the midst of Beverly Hills, the ultra-exclusive Los Angeles Country Club long has boasted a roster of famous members, including former president Ronald Reagan, former L.A. mayor Richard Riordan, sports broadcaster Keith Jackson, and PGA Tour golfer Fred Couples.

The North Course contains some of the longest, toughest par 3s anywhere, with three of them coming in a five-hole stretch from holes 7–11.

The finale of this one-shot trio is the 244-yard 11th, a reverse Redan with an elevated tee that offers magnificent views of the L.A. skyline in the distance. The downhill tee shot, which usually requires a fairway wood or long iron, is hit over a valley to a push-up green that is protected by a pair of huge diagonal cross bunkers which meander in front of the putting surface. The one on the left actually forms a false front, as the green sits 30 yards behind it. The design allows crafty players to carry the bunker short and left, and bounce their shots onto the green, which slopes from back to front. That's assuming, of course, that they can get it there. **KA**

**Course:** Shinnecock Hills Golf Club

**Location:** Southampton, New York, USA

**Hole:** No. 11

**Length:** 158 yards

**Par:** 3

**Designer:** Willie Dunn, William S. Flynn, Howard Toomey

**Course Comment:** At the 1995 U.S. Open, No. 11 played to a 3.188 stroke average, giving up only 56 birdies compared with 107 bogeys and 17 double bogeys or worse.

# No. ⑪ SHINNECOCK HILLS GOLF CLUB

This uphill gem requires unerring precision to earn either birdie or par. From the three deep bunkers that sit diagonally on the right side of the green and the intimidating bunker on the front left, to the wickedly steep slope at the left rear, this hole contains plenty of trouble.

The tee shot is relatively short and often golfers have the prevailing wind behind them, but that just adds to the trickery. Aim for the right center of the green and hope for the best, because your options are limited. Come up short or leave it ever so slightly left or right and you'll likely find one of the bunkers, with a sand save next to impossible.

Go long, and you'll find your ball resting in a swale that could lead to double bogey or worse because of the green's severe back to front slope. Come up short on a chip from here and the ball will return to your feet. Punch it too hard and you'll be chipping again from in front of the green.

In the final round of the 1995 U.S. Open, Greg Norman somehow managed to save par from this position on his way to a second-place finish, two strokes behind winner Corey Pavin. **KA**

Course: Monterey Peninsula Country
Club (Shore Course)

Location: Pebble Beach, California,
USA

Hole: No. 11

Length: 181 yards

Par: 3

Designers: Michael Strantz, Robert
Baldock, Jack Neville

Course Comment: The Crosby golf
tournament, which is now called the
AT&T Pebble Beach National Pro-Am,
was held at the Shore Course in 1965,
1966, and 1977. In 2010, it was
brought back into the rotation,
replacing Poppy Hills Golf Course.

# No. ⑪ MONTEREY PENINSULA COUNTRY CLUB (SHORE COURSE)

The Monterey Peninsula Country Club's Shore Course was originally built in 1961 by Jack Neville and Robert Baldock, but it was Michael Strantz' 2005 redesign that revitalized the layout. Unfortunately, Strantz died less than a year after the project's completion. But his legacy lives on in grand fashion.

It is extremely difficult to pick just one hole to exemplify the beauty and challenge of the Shore Course, but the par-3 11th is a good place to start. The elevated tee is situated on a granite rock outcropping. Natural granite, of course. This is Pebble Beach, after all.

The visuals from the tee are breathtaking. You look out over the pristine green and past the emerald putting surface to the coastal beauty beyond. The course is kept in splendid condition, so it seems as if it is a natural part of the landscape. There are no spike marks visible. Ball marks are kept to a minimum and are certainly not visible from 181 yards away. It is beautiful, and with the winds whipping in off the water, it also presents a challenge.

Depending on the wind, club selection can be treacherous. But, regardless of score, the experience is one to remember. **JB**

## No. ⑪ ROYAL ADELAIDE GOLF CLUB

**Course:** Royal Adelaide Golf Club

**Location:** Seaton, South Australia, Australia

**Hole:** No. 11

**Length:** 388 yards

**Par:** 4

**Designer:** H.L. Rymill, C.I. Gardiner, Alister MacKenzie

**Course Comment:** Club members Rymill and Gardiner designed the first course at Royal Adelaide's present site, and then MacKenzie developed a plan to reconfigure the 18 holes during a visit in 1926.

They fondly term this beauty "The Crater." It is a mid-range par 4 that requires a drive played from a tee built against the club's western boundary between a pair of bunkers and in the direction of a rising fairway to the top of a ridge.

From there, players have to hit their balls over a vast, sandy crater to a small green set in front of a lovely sand hill covered with pines and two bunkers out front. If you end up in the crater, then you are in trouble. The fairway runs out at roughly 280 yards, so the bigger hitters are much better off taking a 3-wood or long iron with their first shots.

In fact, the perfect play may be to check your ego before smacking a 200-yard shot, landing the drive well before the end of the fairway, and just before the bunkers. At that point, it is only 150 yards to the pin and a green that seems to invite three-putts if you are not careful. **JS**

## No. ⑪ OJAI VALLEY INN AND SPA

**Course:** Ojai Valley Inn and Spa

**Location:** Ojai, California, USA

**Hole:** No. 11

**Par:** 4

**Length:** 297 yards

**Designer:** George C. Thomas Jr., William P. Bell

**Course Comment:** Ojai Valley is an area filled with natural beauty and the perfect setting for a championship golf course. Built in 1923, this historic trek is a par-70 course that plays at 6,305 yards from the back tees.

Before you tee off on No. 11, here are a few tips. First, leave your driver in the golf bag. You will have plenty of chances to let the shaft out on this golf course, but this 297-yard par 4 isn't one of them.

You don't need the distance. You need the accuracy. So play the tee shot with some thought. And your first thought should be, forget the driver.

The second tip is to check the flag while standing on the tee because you won't get a chance on your second shot. And you will need to know the pin location when setting up that approach shot. How else will you get the proper yardage?

Since we are passing out tips, here's another. Don't take this for granted. It might say No. 14 handicap on the scorecard, but this is a challenging hole.

Your tee shot must clear a large marsh, but a drive of about 210 yards should do the trick. The fairway begins at about 136 yards from the green.

A good drive with some accuracy should leave you about 99 yards to the green. The second shot will make or break this hole. **TJ**

# OAKLAND HILLS COUNTRY CLUB (SOUTH COURSE)

**Course:** Oakland Hills Country Club (South Course)

**Location:** Bloomfield Hills, Michigan, USA

**Hole:** No. 11

**Length:** 423 yards

**Par:** 4

**Designer:** Donald Ross, Robert Trent Jones

**Course Comment:** Did you know? It was at the 1951 U.S. Open that Oakland Hills received its nickname, "The Monster." Only two players that year had rounds under par. Ben Hogan's 287 total won the Open and caused him to exclaim his joy at having "brought this course, this monster, to its knees."

Oakland Hills has plenty of outstanding holes and a number of excellent par 4s. The 11th is a prime example.

Playing 423 yards from the back, No. 11 has plenty of trouble along the way. The landing area is located in a saddle. If you hit your drive well, the ball should end up just over a ridge and end up on the left side of the fairway. This is where you want to be. The green is perched atop a ridge with four bunkers protecting the front side.

There is a series of small mounds along the right side of the fairway leading up to the green. There also are a few trees in this area including one just off to the right of the right-front bunker.

Oakland Hills staged the 2004 Ryder Cup and has played host to six U.S. Opens, the last being in 1996. It has also hosted two PGA championships.

There is plenty of history at Oakland Hills. Here are two quick hitters:

Robert Trent Jones Sr. redesigned Oakland Hill's South Course before the 1952 U.S. Open and again in 1972 and 1984.

The clubhouse's design is based on George Washington's home in Mt. Vernon and is the second-largest wooden structure in Michigan. **TJ**

**Course:** Royal Troon Golf Club (Old Course)

**Location:** Troon, Ayrshire, Scotland

**Hole:** No. 11

**Length:** 488 yards

**Par:** 4

**Designer:** Willie Fernie, James Braid

**Course Comment:** The lengthy 11th is dubbed "The Railway," after the railway line that runs parallel to the fairway. The first time Jack Nicklaus played the 11th hole, he made an 11.

**BELOW AND OPPOSITE** *Two views of the 11th hole at Royal Troon.*

# No. ⑪ ROYAL TROON GOLF CLUB
## (OLD COURSE)

If you're going to score at Royal Troon's Old Course, you'd better make hay on the outward nine, because the prevailing north-westerly wind that awaits on the way back to the clubhouse makes the nine-hole trip tough.

The wind at No. 11 — not to mention that it's a par-4 hole measuring nearly 500 yards — is the most severe test on the golf course. It is the No. 1 handicap hole, and it takes two purely struck shots to have a chance at par. In fact, members play this hole as a par 5. However, when tournaments are played here, it rapidly becomes one of the most difficult par 4s in the world. In fact, the 11th was rated the most difficult hole in the 1997 British Open.

Walking to the 11th tee you have time to ponder over the difficulties of this long and dangerous hole. It is a monstrous view, beautiful and classic to be sure, but it spreads out before you to present a frightening challenge. There is no mystery here; no blind shots. Most times that is a blessing, but seeing what lies before you on No. 11 is no bargain.

The railway runs parallel to the hole on the right for its entire length, and the trains run against the flow of play — an intimidating sight and sound when getting ready to strike. If you go right, you've got the railway line, and your ball might end up somewhere in southern Scotland. If you go

left, your ball might as well be in another part of the country because the gorse on that side is so thick it is almost certainly lost for good. Even if you happen to spot the ball in the gorse, the chances of being able to play it are virtually nil.

A long second shot waits, with the railway just a few yards off the green to the right. The green is ample enough, but the railway can be daunting. It is a somewhat frightening finish to a hugely intimidating hole. No. 11 is the second hole in a series of three that ranks as the toughest in the world. There is no shame in going three over par on Nos. 10–12. In fact, most players would walk away happy with that result. **JB**

## No. ⓫ GLEN ABBEY GOLF CLUB

**Course:** Glen Abbey Golf Club

**Location:** Oakville, Ontario, Canada

**Hole:** No. 11

**Length:** 452 yards

**Par:** 4

**Designer:** Jack Nicklaus

**Course Comment:** This golf course is famous for a number of reasons, including the fact that this was Jack Nicklaus' first solo design. A pretty solid debut.

What an opening tee shot Jack Nicklaus hit with his first solo design. It's like winning the Masters your first time out.

Glen Abbey is one of Canada's most celebrated and popular golf courses. One reason is the 452-yard, par-4 11th, the second-hardest hole on the golf course and one of its best.

This green was rebuilt recently by Jack Nicklaus and tends to be a little firm and very fast. This is never more true than when putting toward the creek. No. 11 is the first of the spectacular "Valley Holes" and is recognized as one of the most beautiful holes in Canada.

Check the tree tops for wind direction before you tee off and do your best to split the fairway. There are bunkers out there on the right side, starting at about 174 yards from the green.

On your approach shot, be sure to remember that the distance to the flag is all carry. An extra club is recommended, and if the pin is at the back, you'd better add another.

And watch out for that big bunker on the right side of the green. **TJ**

## No. ⓫ LAUREL SPRINGS

**Course:** Laurel Springs

**Location:** Suwanee, Georgia, USA

**Hole:** No. 11

**Length:** 418 yards

**Par:** 4

**Designer:** Jack Nicklaus

**Course Comment:** Big hitters need to watch out on this hole. Put the driver back in the bag and take out a 3-wood or even an iron. If you hit your tee shot too well, a group of trees will prevent you from going for the green.

Jack Nicklaus, like he so often does in his golf-course design, has perfectly combined beauty and difficulty on this 418-yard, par-4 hole here at the spectacular Laurel Springs.

And it's a bear of a hole.

The perfect tee shot is a long and perfectly placed shot that carries the fairway bunkers and lands on the left side of the fairway. This gives you the best approach to a difficult green.

But hold on. There is a lot of water over on that side. An L-shaped lake runs along the left side and then in front of the green. That perfect tee shot is also a dangerous tee shot because you are challenging the water.

It's important to take note of that giant pine tree sitting in the middle — and we mean middle — of the fairway. The pine is about 200 yards from the green and can cause problems on your second shot. Your approach shot must also carry the creek and land on a long, yet narrow green.

The green has a tricky ridge, or hump, in the middle. The up-front pin placement is the easiest and the back is the most difficult on this excellent signature hole.

No. 11 is one of the prettiest holes on a golf course full of pretty holes. **TJ**

**Course:** Bethpage State Park
(Black Course)

**Location:** Farmingdale, New York,
USA

**Hole:** No. 11

**Par:** 4

**Length:** 435 yards

**Designer:** A.W. Tillinghast

**Course Comment:** Tiger Woods
marched to victory here in the 2002
U.S. Open and he will get a chance
to defend his Bethpage title when
the U.S. Open returns in 2009. The
Black Course, built in 1936, is one of
five courses at Bethpage State Park.

No. ⓫   # BETHPAGE STATE PARK
## (BLACK COURSE)

The key to this hole, like almost every hole at Bethpage, is keeping your drive in the fairway. When you step up to the tee at No. 11, there is usually a downwind in play on this somewhat deceiving hole. While it might look like an airport runway from the tee, don't be fooled by the line. From the green, you can see that the entire fairway is not straight, but is actually lined up to the left from the flag back to the tee.

Those playing this hole for a second time have a true advantage over the first-timers. Experience counts at Bethpage.

The fairway plays narrower than it appears, with a series of bunkers on both sides that start from about 200 yards off the tee and extend almost all the way to the green. The green itself has a false front, so take an extra club if you need to in order to land in the middle.

While not considered the most difficult on the course, this is the kind of hole that can jump up and really cause problems. Don't take it for granted, especially with the very tough No. 12 and No. 15 lurking around the bend. **TJ**

Course: The National Golf Club
(Moonah Course)

Location: Cape Schanck, Victoria,
Australia

Hole: No. 11

Length: 394 yards

Par: 4

Designer: Greg Norman,
Bob Harrison

Course Comment: Bass Strait can be
viewed behind the punchbowl green
here, and the rolling waters of the
sea easily heard in the distance.

## No. ⑪ THE NATIONAL GOLF CLUB
### (MOONAH COURSE)

The dogleg-right No. 11 on the Moonah is regarded by many players as the most unique on a unique course often praised for its natural grasses, rugged sand dunes, and, on occasion, very strong winds.

Located in the remote, northwest corner of the property, the hole begins with a tee shot that from the back tees has to clear a series of ridges in order to reach a plateau fairway surrounded by sand. At roughly 285 yards, the terrain drops down to a hollow before rising to another ridge.

What's left after a good drive for most golfers is a mid- to short-iron (depending on wind and positioning) to a partially hidden green carved out of yet another hollow and backed by two bunkers to the right.

There is also out-of-bounds that seems only too happy to swallow up any balls flying beyond the putting surface to that side, and plenty of misery for those who miss the green in that direction. JS

ourse: Merion Golf Club
(East Course)

Location: Ardmore, Pennsylvania,
USA

Hole: No. 11

Length: 369 yards

Par: 4

Designer: Hugh Wilson

Course Comment: Merion is home
to two 18-hole courses, both of
which were built on gently rolling
terrain and feature fast greens and
narrow fairways. There aren't many
trees along the fairways but plenty
of nasty rough.

## No. ⑪ MERION GOLF CLUB
### (EAST COURSE)

It's difficult to play this 369-yard par 4 without reflection. You are walking on historic ground — and why would you not want to think about what happened on the very spot you now stand?

In 1930, Bobby Jones completed his legendary grand slam at Merion.

So when you place your ball on the tee, imagine Mr. Jones doing the same thing some 74 years ago. His ball ended up in the record books. Hopefully, yours will eventually land on the green.

The key to this hole is your approach shot, but first you must hit your tee shot. Because of Cobbs Creek, you want to lay up a bit on the drive. A good 200 to 220 yards should suffice.

From there, you are looking at about a 125-yard approach shot, which calls for perfection.

The small green is guarded by Cobbs Creek, which follows along the right side of the green and wraps around to the back. There is also a bunker on the left side.

In addition, this hole is known for its thick rough around the green. And because the green is usually quite firm, it's tough to keep your ball on the putting surface from that rough.

No. 11 is one of Merion's trademark holes and one of the prettiest on the golf course. TJ

# BALLYBUNION GOLF CLUB (OLD COURSE)

**Course:** Ballybunion Golf Club (Old Course)

**Location:** Ballybunion, County Kerry, Ireland

**Hole:** No. 11

**Length:** 446 yards

**Par:** 4

**Designer:** Tom Simpson, Molly Gourlay

**Course Comment:** Watson says: "Having played the Old Course many times since my first visit in 1981, I am now of the opinion it is one of the best and most beautiful tests of links golf anywhere in the world."

Tom Watson, a five-time winner of the British Open, has made the Old Course at Ballybunion his "home course" away from home. In fact, Watson was millennium captain at Ballybunion and he called his 1995 renovation of the Old Course a "labor of love." Few can blame Watson for his admiration of Ballybunion's Old Course, and no hole exemplifies the venue's beauty, ruggedness, and seaside power more than No. 11, a 446-yard par 4 perilously perched on seaside cliffs.

There is nary room for a safe step between the sea and the green, which is protected on the left by enormous mounding that makes an approach to the green virtually impossible if your drive happens to stray left. The only option off the tee is to be on the right side of the fairway, and even that's no bargain. A perfect drive still leaves a very narrow approach into a green where two sandhills squeeze the avenue to an elevated surface.

There isn't a bunker on this hole, which is a bit strange because the Old Course is a traditional links course set among the purest sand dunes nature has to offer. But, even without sand, never has there been a more perilous approach.

This hole, like the rest of the Old Course, hugs the Atlantic, and offers golfers a feel of the sea as they play the hole. It's a wonderful golf hole on a special Irish venue.

But one word of advice: watch your step. **JB**

**Course:** Shoreacres Golf Club

**Location:** Lake Bluff, Illinois, USA

**Hole:** No. 11

**Length:** 352 yards

**Par:** 4

**Designer:** Seth Raynor

**Course Comment:** Shoreacres is a fine golf course all summer long, but if you get a chance to play when the colors are changing in autumn, it is an experience you won't forget. The 11th hole, with its tree-lined fairways and ravines, is among the most beautiful holes on the course.

# No. ⑪ SHOREACRES GOLF CLUB

Both the famous and the infamous have called Chicago home. There was gangster Al Capone and mayor Richard Daly, baseball Hall-of-Famer Ernie Banks and football legend Mike Ditka. But there is one character who was making his way around Chicago just before Scarface made his mark: Seth Raynor, while not much of a celebrity, made an impact on the Chicago area that is still felt today. His renovation of Chicago Golf Club turned it into a nationally respected golf course, and this came right after his 1917 creation of an American gem — Shoreacres Golf Club.

Raynor's ability to make the land work in his favor when designing a course is never more evident than at Shoreacres, where he takes the natural ravines and turns them into hazards with which to be reckoned. Cutting narrow fairways through existing trees also gives Shoreacres a wonderfully natural feel.

Nowhere on the course is Raynor's use of ravines more obvious than at the 11th — a short par 4 at 352 yards, but made far more difficult than length would indicate because of the pair of gulleys that slither through the fairway.

Off the 11th tee, there is a carry over a snaking ravine. A solid tee shot renders the first ravine irrelevant, but the shot must be well struck. This is where the dilemma unfolds, because you must hit a good shot to clear the first ravine and land safely in the fairway, but you can't strike it too purely or else you will roll into ravine No. 2. Big hitters usually take a fairway wood or a long iron out of the bag on the tee.

The first ravine is an inconvenience, but it is the second gulley that creates havoc. It rests directly against the front side of the smallish green, and it proves an unrelenting guard to any shot that comes up short. And you can't just blast away to avoid the ravine because the small green doesn't welcome shots that don't come in softly.

The 11th at Shoreacres is a great example of the genius of Raynor, a man who worked with fellow architects such as Charles Blair Macdonald and Charles Banks. Raynor had an influence on all with whom he worked, and his mark — particularly in the Windy City — has stood the test of time. **JB**

## No. ⑪   GOLF CLUB OF OKLAHOMA

**Course:** Golf Club of Oklahoma

**Location:** Broken Arrow, Oklahoma, USA

**Hole:** No. 11

**Length:** 451 yards

**Par:** 4

**Designer:** Tom Fazio

**Course Comment:** The wetland area on this hole looks more like something you'd find in a Florida swamp rather than the middle of Oklahoma. Members often joke that they expect to see an alligator crawl out any day now.

This hole is the No. 1 handicap at this well-respected 1983 Tom Fazio design in the Tulsa suburbs, and for good reason. It's long, uphill, and has plenty of hazards to frustrate golfers along the way.

The tee shot should be hit to the right side of the fairway, as the hole bends just slightly to the left. But beware: hit it too far right, and a large fairway bunker and wetlands await. Hit it in either the bunker or the wetlands and your chance at par is probably gone. Hit it too far left, though, and the path to the green will be blocked by a group of oak and elm trees that lines the left side, forcing a lay-up on the second shot.

A good angle on the ball is most definitely needed for the mid- to long-iron approach to this green, which is protected by a false front and a deep, difficult bunker on the left. The putting surface is fairly narrow but deep, and slopes from right to left with a number of undulations. Land your approach on the right side of the green, then hope for the best. **KA**

## No. ⑪   STONEBRIDGE GOLF CLUB

**Course:** Stonebridge Golf Club

**Location:** Ann Arbor, Michigan, USA

**Hole:** No. 11

**Length:** 387 yards

**Par:** 4

**Designer:** Arthur Hills

**Course Comment:** Stonebridge Golf Club offers innovative packages such as a reduced all-you-can-play twilight rate during the Fall, beginning at 3 pm.

Stonebridge Golf Club is an Arthur Hills classic — and he has plenty of classic courses in south-eastern Michigan. Stonebridge is a links layout that winds through an exclusive housing development.

Complete with fieldstone bridges, the course covers 6,932 yards from its tournament blue tees and cuts through rolling hills, woods, and wetlands. Water, in the form of creeks and ponds, comes into play on at least 11 holes.

Like many Arthur Hills courses, there are a few holes that really stand out. The one that really jumps to mind is No. 11, a 387-yard, par-4 dogleg right. And we mean dogleg right. It's a 90-degree turn and there is nothing easy about this hole, the No. 6 handicap.

A tee shot to about 180 yards at the windmill is a safe shot. Anything more than this will be risky. There is water all along the right side of the fairway that you eventually have to cross because it cuts right in front of the green.

There are trees along the left side of the fairway.

From the back tees you need to hit the ball 260 yards to reach the back of where the fairway breaks. Another good shot is about 226 yards off the back tees to just before a marsh area. Your second shot can fly the marsh and water to the green, but it's a tough shot.

Actually, your second shot is tough from anywhere. There is water to the front and right of the green, which has some trees to the left and is pretty narrow. **TJ**

**Course:** Augusta National Golf Club

**Location:** Augusta, Georgia, USA

**Hole:** No. 11

**Length:** 455 yards

**Par:** 4

**Designer:** Robert Tyre Jones, Alister MacKenzie

**Course Comment:** Prior to 1950, Masters competitors had to contend with Rae's Creek, which fronted the 11th green, on their approach shots. Now they face a larger pond.

**BELOW** *David Duval of the USA plays a shot on the 11th hole at Augusta, April 1999.*

**OPPOSITE** *Tom Watson of the USA in the water on the 11th hole at Augusta, April 2001.*

# No. ⑪ AUGUSTA NATIONAL GOLF CLUB

Tradition is a hallmark at Augusta National, but change has always been in the air here, as well. Many famous designers, including Perry Maxwell and Robert Trent Jones Sr., have taken turns making alterations on the course.

No. 11 has been the focus of some of that change.

The tee was moved back 30 to 35 yards in 2002 and some new trees were added down the right side in the landing area for the 2004 tournament.

Named "White Dogwood," this par 4 is part of Amen Corner, and wind is often a factor. A pond guards the green to the left and a bunker is placed right center.

This hole has decided all but two Masters sudden-death playoffs, including Larry Mize's stunning triumph in 1987.

We will leave you with this from Larry Mize: "Everyone remembers the 140-foot chip I holed on No. 11 from off the right side of the green to win the title in a playoff in 1987. But what they fail to remember is that I made a clutch 20-footer on exactly the same line to save par about two hours earlier. That putt was a must. I had bogeyed No. 10 and another would have really hurt my chances." **TJ**

**Course:** Garden City Golf Club

**Location:** Garden City, New York, USA

**Hole:** No. 11

**Length:** 416 yards

**Par:** 4

**Designers:** Devereux Emmet, Walter Travis, Robert Trent Jones Sr.

**Course Comment:** Home to the 1902 U.S. Open, this classic links course is more than a century old. Simple, squared teeing areas, wide fairways, and heavy rough define its character. Garden City Golf Club is dotted with pot bunkers, and water comes into play on just two of these vintage 18 holes.

# No. ⑪ GARDEN CITY GOLF CLUB

Angles. The 11th hole at Garden City Golf Club is all about angles. Stepping onto the green from the fairway's right side is the preferred way to shoot the visually stunning 11th. Negotiating this prime position is no small task, though, with a row of diagonal bunkers guarding the area. A careful shot to the left, carrying the ball precariously over broken ground and one bunker, is the only path to the prize.

Golf was simpler when No. 11 was designed, but don't be overconfident approaching the challenge no matter what brand of technology you happen to be carrying. The fast greens make this course seem younger than it is, and this prime example of minimalist golf-course architecture can fool the savviest player.

Careful — lots of unseen traps are tucked into this course, so it plays tougher than it looks. The 11th hole is a prime illustration of how perfectly an unpretentious and low-key design harmonizes with nature, rather than competes against it, to present players with surprise after hidden surprise.

Sweeping wind and heavy cut rough lend it a delightfully English feel. The 11th is pure golf and pure tradition — a tricky hole on an absolutely timeless golf course. **KLL**

---

**Course:** Timber Trace

**Location:** Pinckney, Michigan, USA

**Hole:** No. 11

**Length:** 298 yards

**Par:** 4

**Designer:** Conroy-Dewling Associates, Inc.

**Course Comment:** The signature hole at Timber Trace is the par-5 16th. It's another one of Timber Trace's excellent holes on a course known for its excellent conditions. No. 11, however, isn't easily forgotten.

# No. ⑪ TIMBER TRACE

Even the bravest of the brave should consider a little temperance here.

Pulling out the driver, are you? What's your reasoning?

It's only 298 yards to the green? So, you think you can get it there. I know you can sometimes hit it 298 yards, but you really have to give it a ride. And you don't always hit it straight.

Now where are you going? What's that? A 3-iron? I see. Playing it smart.

This scenario plays out a few times a day on this hole. But Mr. Big Hitter probably goes for it more times than not. And this 298-yard par 4 is certainly reachable.

But you better hit it straight. If you don't, you've turned a fairly easy hole into big trouble.

There is out-of-bounds on the right and some nasty heather on the left. And there are also five bunkers along the way, including a particularly dangerous one in front of the green.

Speaking of the green, the left side slopes from right to left and the right side slopes from left to right. There are a few pot bunkers and more heather behind the green.

The smart play is a 3- or 4-iron to about 80 yards out and then a nice wedge to the green. Unless, of course, you are a big hitter with a lot of accuracy off the tee. **TJ**

**Course:** Royal Johannesburg
(East Course)

**Location:** Johannesburg,
South Africa

**Hole:** No. 11

**Length:** 500 yards

**Par:** 4

**Designer:** Robert Grimsdell

**Course Comment:** Essentially,
the improvements to the
clubhouse and the two courses at
Royal Johannesburg were funded
from the sale of the Kensington
property. The result is a superb
facility, with two outstanding
parkland golf courses ideally suited
to preserve the value of both clubs.

## No. ⑪ ROYAL JOHANNESBURG (EAST COURSE)

Some historical perspective if you will.

"Founded on 6 November 1890, members of the Johannesburg Golf Club first began playing 'behind Hospital Hill,' in the area that later became known as Clarendon Circle and Empire Road. The search for more suitable land, and the rapid development of the city, caused the club to move no less than four times, before finally being established in 1909 on the land it still occupies today."

The signature hole of the East Course is the 11th. The hole features gigantic poplars that make the lower holes on the East Course stunning and dramatic. There are five sets of tees, which not only alter how you are going to play this hole but change in length from a monstrous 500 yards to a rather easy 418 yards. Your approach shot should be a nice easy mid-iron but you better have enough stick to clear the water.

Famously or infamously, the 10th and 11th holes are reputed to be the two longest back-to-back par 4s in the world. The course was revamped in 1998 by Mark Muller. Certain holes were altered but mostly it was the greens that, while keeping their original feel, were vastly improved. **TJ**

Course: Predator Ridge Golf Resort (Peregrine Course)

Location: Vernon, British Columbia, Canada

Hole: No. 11

Length: 481 yards

Par: 4

Designer: Les Furber

Course Comment: Voted the No. 1 Favorite Golf Course by *Vancouver Province* readers in 2004, this upscale resort is located in the heart of the Okanagan Valley and features a 27-hole championship trek.

OPPOSITE *A view from above of the 11th hole at Predator Ridge.*

# No. ⑪ PREDATOR RIDGE GOLF RESORT
## (PERIGRINE COURSE)

It's difficult to decide which nine is the most popular but you can't argue against the Peregrine Course. Since it gets the nod, we will play this nine last, making No. 2 the 11th hole on our 18-hole course.

And you can argue all day over the nines, but this par 4 gets plenty of votes for the best hole not only at Predator Ridge but in British Columbia.

After spending time on the links-style holes, this 481-yard challenge introduces you to the back nine, as in the backwoods nine.

This hole drops 40 yards from tee to green and begins a thrilling five-hole journey into Predator Ridge's unforgiving forest. It's similar to Augusta National's No. 10.

Predator Ridge is two courses in one, and you get the feeling you have crossed over to an entire different course when you walk out on the tee at the impressive No. 11.

The fairway is very narrow as it winds its way through the huge trees, which are much nicer to look at from the fairway than they are standing under them.

The three courses each range in length from 2,600 yards to over 3,500 yards, and each course has its own style and beauty. The No. 4 hole on the Peregrine Course offers a tremendous view of Okanagan Lake. **TJ**

Course: The Vines Golf & Country Club (Lakes Course)

Location: The Vines, Western Australia

Hole: No. 11

Length: 431 yards

Par: 4

Designer: Graham Marsh, Ross Watson

Course Comment: The Vines Resort is located in the foothills of the Darling Ranges — and the heart of the acclaimed Swan Valley wine country — some 35 miles outside central Perth.

# No. ⑪ THE VINES GOLF &
## COUNTRY CLUB (LAKES COURSE)

Western Australia golf professional Wayne Smith rates the 11th here as the best of the bunch on the Lakes Course, one of two 18-hole layouts that make up this retreat in the glorious wine country of Western Australia and rambles through gently undulating grassland.

It is a favorite among Australian and European touring pros who played it during the years that the Vines hosted the Heineken Classic. And though that event moved to Royal Melbourne after 2001, the rave reviews for the inspiring design features of the Lakes did not.

The best way to play your first shot here is with a driver, heading over the water that Smith says puts a flutter in his heart every time he steps to the tee.

Next, players have to hit a longish approach shot to a green — the greens here are known for their huge size and heavy contours — with three bunkers providing all the trouble potential a weekend hacker needs. **JS**

**Course:** Singapore Island Country Club (Bukit Course)

**Location:** Sime Road, Singapore

**Hole:** No. 11

**Length:** 425 yards

**Par:** 4

**Designer:** James Braid, J.J.F. Pennink

**Course Comment:** There are three courses to choose from — the Bukit, the Sime, and the Island — all par 71.

# No. ⑪ SINGAPORE ISLAND COUNTRY CLUB (BUKIT COURSE)

There might be three layouts at Singapore Island Country Club, but unless you are very well connected, forget about playing two of them on this ultra-exclusive property. The Bukit and Sime Courses are private — very private. Guests have to be accompanied by a member if they wish to play at either of those two courses, and members are allowed to bring only one guest on any day. The Island Course is public, and is a decent enough track. But we're here to talk about the Bukit Course — more specifically, the par-4 11th.

The Bukit is built around two large reservoirs, which provide a refreshing effect, but the breezes the two bodies of water bring with them can be a little baffling — particularly if you are playing the Bukit Course for the first time. And, because of the exclusivity of the place, unless you are a member, you are probably not privy to local knowledge. Chalk one up for your host.

The 11th would be a difficult enough test even on the calmest of days, but a day without wind at Singapore Island Country Club is fairly rare. You throw in the sometimes tricky breezes, and the 425-yard 11th becomes even more testing.

The tee box is encased in a collection of stately trees, but the feeling of protection is strictly temporary. You are on your own the rest of the way, starting with the tee shot, which is straightforward enough. The hole starts to get trickier from there, however, turning gradually to the right.

Ideally, you want to land your tee shot on the left half of the fairway so you can get around the corner, but beware of straying too far left, because of a row of trees on that side backed by a dirt road further left. The fairway slopes from right to left, so the play is to aim for the middle of the fairway with a slight draw, ideally catching the slope and ending up on the left side of the fairway.

The green is fairly inviting from that position. It's large, but also hard and fast — particularly when it's dry. And because of all the wind, it is dry most of the time. A kidney-shaped bunker protects the left side, so a pin placement on the left half of the green is very difficult, because the only way to get to the green is from the left side of the fairway. You are forced to carry the bunker and stop the ball on a dime. **JB**

**Course:** Quaker Ridge Golf Club

**Location:** Scarsdale, New York, USA

**Hole:** No. 11

**Length:** 387 yards

**Par:** 4

**Designer:** A.W. Tillinghast

**Course Comment:** Quaker Ridge has 18 great golf holes, but three very special ones. No. 6, a dogleg-right, uphill par 4, is the toughest on the golf course. No. 12 is another highly rated hole. And then there is No. 11, simply one of the best holes on any golf course.

# No. ⑪ QUAKER RIDGE GOLF CLUB

Your success or failure on this hole is all set up on your tee shot. The dogleg left isn't long, and you don't have to crush it off the tee to reach the bend. If you can hit it straight about 230 yards, you will set yourself up in a very fine position.

There is a fairway bunker about 150 yards from the tee. Avoiding that sand trap is highly advisable. And try to place your shot on the right side of the fairway.

Why?

Because there is a very large 100-year-old tree that will hinder your approach shot from the left. And they have no plans on cutting it down.

You will want to pause for a moment before hitting your second shot. Take a second and admire the view. It doesn't get much better than standing out in the middle of the fairway on No. 11 at Quaker Ridge. It's one of the prettiest spots on the course.

You better hit because here comes the marshal.

Your target is a fairly good-size green which slopes from left to right with a bunker on the left. There also are bunkers in the back — just in case you are a little strong on your approach. **TJ**

## No. ⑪ THE OTAGO GOLF CLUB

**Course:** The Otago Golf Club

**Location:** Dunedin, New Zealand

**Hole:** No. 11

**Length:** 394 yards

**Par:** 4

**Designer:** J. Somerville

**Course Comment:** In an exhibition match in 1966, Arnold Palmer ripped his drive 375 yards to the center of the green. His two-putt earned him a birdie, only good enough to halve the hole with Bob Charles, his opponent that day.

Named the "Glen," this hole is often considered among not only the best holes in New Zealand, but the world. Even if it's not the great challenge it was in earlier times, it's still a spectacular golf hole. And there is still nothing easy about it.

As the legend goes, "the gorse forest proved a bottomless maw." These days that bottomless maw is nothing more than rough. Still, not a great place to find yourself.

The landing area is, as they say, "generous." The ideal drive off the tee is about 215 yards on this dogleg right. You want to favor the left side of the fairway, if you can. From here you would have about a 100-yard drive to the putting surface.

The green is long, but narrow and well protected. There are two bunkers flanking the left side of the green and a large one along the right side.

In 1935 Gene Sarazen took three swings at the green from the tee box. Unlike Arnold Palmer, he never got there, finally playing short with a long iron. But he had to use a wooden driver, so don't let this horror story stop you from trying. **TJ**

## No. ⑪ BALD MOUNTAIN

**Course:** Bald Mountain

**Location:** Lake Orion, Michigan, USA

**Hole:** No. 11

**Par:** 4

**Length:** 319 yards

**Designer:** Wilfrid Reid, William Connellan

**Course Comment:** This golf course is located just a chip shot from a palace — The Palace of Auburn Hills arena. Designed in 1929, Bald Mountain is one of Metro Detroit's more classic and traditional layouts.

Bald Mountain won't ever be confused with one of the more challenging golf courses in the Midwest. For the most part, the fairways offer ample landing areas but are lined with plenty of mature trees.

There are level landing areas at which to take aim, but also plenty of rolling hills and elevation changes.

Welcome to No. 11. A memorable par 4 that is reachable from the tee, especially if the wind is behind you. If you play from the white tees, it's only a 278-yard drive to reach the green, so there is no excuse not to go for it from the whites.

Pull out the driver and go for it, because that's why you are here. Take note though, that the fairway ends about 40 yards short of the green.

Your tee shot is over a valley, which drops a good 30 feet. The green is on the other side of the valley.

The green is well-protected on both sides by bunkers, so if you are off just a little bit, get your sand wedge out. The right side of the green is severely sloped and then flattens out. Check the pin placement. **TJ**

## No. ⑪ TROON NORTH GOLF CLUB (MONUMENT COURSE)

**Course:** Troon North Golf Club (Monument Course)

**Location:** Scottsdale, Arizona, USA

**Hole:** No. 11

**Length:** 539 yards

**Par:** 5

**Designer:** Tom Weiskopf, Jay Morrish

**Course Comment:** The Monument features wide fairways that wind through lush desert vegetation, natural washes, and towering saguaro cacti.

Home to two outstanding courses, the Monument and the Pinnacle, Troon North Golf Club is one of the pinnacle courses in Arizona. And while the two courses wind through an upscale subdivision with some homes in the $400,000 range, Troon North maintains a distinct feeling that you are in the middle of the desert.

When attempting to select a memorable hole on this course, you feel like a child in the candy store — the holes are all so great, it is almost impossible.

Nicknamed the "Saddle," this hole is no easy ride, but it's a fun ride. And that's the point when you saddle up to this first-class resort. At one time named the best golf hole in the state by the Arizona Republic, this par-5 beauty is a dogleg left with a very generous fairway cut between spectacular granite formations.

Think you can do this hole in two? Think again.

A desert wash about 70 yards in front of the putting surface gives Mr. Big Hitter reason to rethink his aggressiveness. **TJ**

## No. ⑪ BALTUSROL GOLF CLUB (UPPER COURSE)

**Course:** Baltusrol Golf Club (Upper Course)

**Location:** Springfield, New Jersey, USA

**Hole:** No. 11

**Length:** 596 yards

**Par:** 5

**Designer:** A.W. Tillinghast

**Course Comment:** Baltusrol has hosted 15 U.S. Golf Association championships, second only to Merion Golf Club's (Ardmore, Pennsylvania) 16, but few were as dramatic as the 1954 U.S. Open. During that championship, Ed Furgol played the Lower Course's 18th hole via the fairway of the Upper Course's 18th hole to secure victory.

Sometimes overshadowed by the Lower Course, Baltusrol's Upper layout has a persona that in many ways eclipses that of its high-profile neighbor.

Grouped along the foothills of what the locals call "Baltusrol Mountain," the Upper Course takes advantage of the area's natural hazards (lakes, streams, and woodlands) to present an exacting test.

The sharp contours of the Upper's terrain requires a tactician's resolve as well as a sound swing and plenty of fortitude.

The 596-yard 11th is the Upper Course at its trying best. Tee shots at the 11th must be played down the right side of the fairway, away from the 100-yard stretch of bunkers which guard the left side.

Only the longest hitters will have a chance to reach this green in two shots, and they must avoid a slight swale in front of the green, which is framed by a pair of sand sprawls.

Deep bunkers also guard the back right and left of the green. Yet, as is typically the case on either of Baltusrol's venerable layouts, the real challenge awaits on the greens. No. 11's putting surface has a lateral terrace sloping toward the left front. Any legitimate birdie opportunity must come from below the hole. **RH**

**Course:** Worplesdon Golf Club

**Location:** Woking, Surrey, England

**Hole:** No. 11

**Length:** 520 yards

**Par:** 5

**Designer:** J.F. Abercromby, Willie Park Jr., Harry S. Colt

**Course Comment:** The 11th is across a busy road (it is surprising how often a car will stop for you) and is a wide open and inviting par 5.

# No. ⑪ WORPLESDON GOLF CLUB

The 11th at Worplesdon is indeed a wonderful golf hole, but as you stand on the tee, enveloped in the soothing heathland, you can't help but wonder how it played in its infancy. At 520 yards, it is easily reachable in two with today's technology, yet even though it has been reduced to a two-shotter, it retains its charm.

An expansive bunker on the right side — that obviously caused problems when the hole was originally designed — can be carried by players of today. A dip in the fairway offers mild protection for the 11th's challenge, because the downhill lie affects a player's rip into the green, but it isn't enough to make big hitters consider laying up.

There are bunkers to avoid, but they are avoidable. Don't get the idea that this hole is an automatic birdie, however. The green cants from front to back left, so a run-up is ideal and bunkers must be considered. But, all in all, this is a wonderfully strategic hole that was a three-shotter in its day, but has changed drastically since its design. Willie Park Jr. would undoubtedly have been shocked by the way it plays today.

And Willie Park Jr. knew golf from every angle.

Born in Musselburgh in 1864, Willie Park Jr. was the son of "Auld" Willie, winner of four British Open championships. Willie Jr. was raised in the golf business and its culture. He not only designed golf courses, but he won two British Open championships and was one of the best-known clubmakers of his day. His first job as an architect was arranged by his Uncle Mungo — who, incidentally, won the 1874 British Open — and was to lay out the club in Ryton, Northumberland, England. He also served as the club's first ever golf professional.

Park Jr.'s British Open victories in 1887 and 1889 opened the door for the introduction of four clubs he invented, including the deep-face mashie cleek (for hitting out of long grass), a patent compressed driver with a splice head and a leather-face insert, and a smooth-face lofter for the shorter game.

Junior lived and breathed golf. He wrote an instruction book entitled *The Game of Golf* (1896). The book was widely read at the time, as it represented the first such book on golf. But his first love was club making and course design. His influence carried across the Atlantic and his signature American course is the Olympia Fields North Course, Illinois, which has hosted the U.S. Open, the PGA Championship, and the U.S. Senior Open.

Golf was Willie Park Jr.'s life, and Worplesdon's 11th — while changed by today's big hitters — remains a lasting testament to his vision. **JB**

**Course:** TPC at Sawgrass
(Stadium Course)

**Location:** Ponte Vedra Beach, Florida,
USA

**Hole:** No. 11

**Length:** 529 yards

**Par:** 5

**Designer:** Pete Dye

**Course Comment:** TPC at Sawgrass
features two outstanding 18-hole
courses. The Valley Course is a
bit milder than its more famous
sister course, but it has more
undulation in the fairways than
the Stadium Course.

BELOW  *The 11th hole at TPC at
Sawgrass.*

OPPOSITE  *Fred Couples of the USA
plays his approach shot on the 11th
hole at TPC at Sawgrass, March 2003.*

# No. ⓫ TPC AT SAWGRASS
## (STADIUM COURSE)

The TPC at Sawgrass may be more known for its famous short hole (the
par-3 17th with the island green), but this course is long on great par 5s. And
No. 11 is both long and great.

This hole is a middle-length par 5 and is one of those famous make or
break holes. There is a chance for eagle here, but don't count out an eight
or nine. Yeah, one of those.

To have a shot at the green in two, you need to hit your drive down the
right side of the fairway. There is a large bunker to the left of the landing
area that stops anything in that area. You need to be right of the big trap
and have plenty of distance in your swing.

If you hit your drive straight, you could even end up in the big trap if you
go through the fairway. That's not to say the right side is hazard free. There
are some overhanging trees over there that can cause significant trouble.

The fairway is split by a lateral water hazard and two enormous sand
traps. You can go right on your second shot and come in from that angle, or
try for the much more demanding left side. The harder shot needs to fly
another oak tree and the bunker. Get used to that bunker on the left. It runs
from your second shot to the putting surface. **TJ**

## No. ⓫ SKOKIE COUNTRY CLUB

**Course:** Skokie Country Club

**Location:** Glencoe, Illinois, USA

**Hole:** No. 11

**Length:** 560 yards

**Par:** 5

**Designer:** Tom Bendelow, Donald Ross, William Langford, Ted Moreau, Ron Prichard

**Course Comment:** Skokie Country Club played host to the 1922 U.S. Open, with Gene Sarazen edging amateurs Bobby Jones and John Black by a stroke. It was the first U.S. Open at which tickets were sold.

Few courses have undergone as many changes as Skokie Country Club, which began in 1897 with nine holes designed by members, was expanded to 18 holes by Tom Bendelow in 1905, and was then redesigned by Donald Ross in 1914.

In the mid-1930s, the club lost several Ross holes because of a housing concern, and in 1938, local architects William Langford and Ted Moreau replaced the Ross holes with seven new ones (today's Nos. 3–6 and Nos. 11–13).

In the ensuing 60 years, however, the course underwent numerous renovations. Bunkers were removed and softened, mounds were added and putting surfaces shrank. Finally, in 1999, Ron Prichard was hired to restore Skokie to its glory days, and the results were stunning.

On No. 11, a Langford and Moreau hole, Prichard restored the fairway bunkers and added a Ross-like collection area at the back left of the green. The double dogleg — which turns left, then right — includes a fairway bunker 240 yards from the tee on the left side, then two more bunkers on the right about 140 yards before the green.

The hole is lined on the right side by a brook that juts out into a small pond just before the green on the right. Adding further difficulty, the putting surface slopes from front to back and is guarded by bunkers on both sides. **KA**

## No. ⓫ PLENEUF-VAL-ANDRE GOLF CLUB

**Course:** Pleneuf-Val-Andre Golf Club

**Location:** Pleneuf-Val-Andre, Brittany, France

**Hole:** No. 11

**Length:** 535 yards

**Par:** 5

**Designer:** Alain Prat

**Course Comment:** The Brittany coast has only approximately a dozen frost days annually, no more than the French Riviera, allowing for golf year-round.

Pleneuf-Val-Andre Golf Club is set amid the cliffs, beaches, and bays of Brittany's rugged Armor coast. (Armor is Breton for "Country of the Sea.") Thanks to its location in Brittany, which is bordered on the north by the English Channel and on the south by the Bay of Biscay, Pleneuf-Val-Andre features spectacular, stunning views, said to be comparable to the great links courses of the British Isles. Nowhere is the scenery more magnificent than on Pleneuf-Val-Andre's back-to-back signature holes, the cliff-hugging Nos. 10 and 11.

The par-5 11th begins from an elevated tee box set into a cliffside overlooking the sea to the left. A lone stone house and a single tree grace the left side of the hole, but there is plenty of landing area to the right for both the drive and the second shot.

That is most definitely the preferred side of the fairway, for a long dune ridge — complete with rough, gorse, and treacherous mounds — runs down the left side from just beyond the stone house all the way to the green. The putting surface is protected by a trio of bunkers but can be reached in two with a pair of long, accurate shots. **KA**

**Course:** Sporting Club Berlin
(Faldo Course)

**Location:** Bad Saarow, Brandenburg,
Germany

**Hole:** No. 11

**Length:** 538 yards

**Par:** 5

**Designer:** Nick Faldo

**Course Comment:** In addition
to 63 holes of golf, the Sporting
Club Berlin also offers equestrian
sports, yachting, tennis, biking,
and swimming.

No. ⑪ **SPORTING CLUB BERLIN**
**(FALDO COURSE)**

The Faldo Course at the Sporting Club Berlin is set in a vast clearing in the midst of otherwise wooded terrain, offering Faldo the opportunity to create a links-style layout reminiscent of his native England. The course contains more than 130 bunkers and contoured greens.

The 11th hole features a fairway lined by tall heather grass — which can be tricky — and an intimidating array of mounds, undulations, and steep sod bunkers that run virtually from tee to green. Finding a level spot from which to hit your second and third shots is no small feat. The relatively large green is guarded by a sand bunker on the front right.

Because of holes such as No. 11, the Faldo Course quickly established itself as one of the best in Germany and continental Europe. Two years after its 1996 opening, the Faldo track played host to the final two editions of the PGA European Tour's German Open (won by Stephen Allan in 1998 and Jarmo Sandelin in 1999). It has also served as host site for European Senior Tour and Ladies' European Tour events, as well as the 2000 World Amateur Team Championship, won by the United States, which finished 16 shots ahead of Great Britain and Ireland. **KA**

RIGHT *Steve Webster of England plays on the 11th hole at the Sporting Club Berlin, August 1998.*

**Course:** Hillside Golf Club

**Location:** Southport, Merseyside, England

**Hole:** No. 11

**Length:** 493 yards

**Par:** 5

**Designer:** Frederick William Hawtree

**Course Comment:** Hillside played host to the 1982 Volvo PGA Championship, where native son Tony Jacklin captured his last significant professional victory.

# No. ⑪   HILLSIDE GOLF CLUB

Thanks to holes like the 11th, Hillside is considered by many to be the best links course never to have hosted the British Open. That is why this magnificent layout is not as well known internationally as some of its neighbors on England's north-west coast. The course does often serve as a site for final Open qualifying, however.

Hillside is adjacent to the revered Royal Birkdale, and thanks to its setting amid large coastal dunes, offers stunning views of the ocean, several Birkdale holes and the surrounding countryside. As spectacular as Royal Birkdale is, many golfers have commented that Hillside is every bit as good, if not better. That's especially true of Hillside's inward nine, which was designed by Fred Hawtree in 1967 and has been called the best back nine in Britain by no less authorities than Greg Norman and Jack Nicklaus.

The climb to the 11th tee is well worth it, as the par 5 offers marvelous views of the Irish Sea. The drive is hit downhill to a mounded fairway that runs through a dune-lined valley some 100 feet below. Although the hole is relatively short, plenty of obstacles await, including gorse and heather lining the fairway and a deep bunker at the right front of the green. **KA**

## No. ⑪   **LINKS AT CROWBUSH COVE**

**Course:** Links at Crowbush Cove

**Location:** Morell, Prince Edward Island, Canada

**Hole:** No. 11

**Length:** 565 yards

**Par:** 5

**Designer:** Thomas Broom

**Course Comment:** Canada doesn't get as much publicity as it should on the international stage. Links at Crowbush Cove is among the courses that prove Canada is a serious player.

The 11th at the Links at Crowbush Cove is a Canadian postcard of a hole. This golf course has five holes that run along the ocean but none more spectacular or scenic than No. 11. From the "Crow" tees, this par 5 plays 565 yards and a bunch of steps.

You see, you need to take the stairs to get up to the tee box, which is elevated 60 feet from the green. And check out the amazing view once you get up there.

There isn't a beach on one side, but a beach on both sides. And they stretch as far as you can see. When you finally return to playing golf, you want to hit your tee shot straight down the middle.

The big variable here is the wind. There is a large marsh about 350 yards off the tee. If the wind is behind you, you can clear the marsh on your second shot and have a chip to the green. If the wind is in your face, then forget about it.

Once you clear the marsh you have a short pitch from the landing area to a slightly elevated green. This is considered by many to be one of the prettiest holes in Canada. **TJ**

## No. ⑪   **ROSSLARE** (OLD COURSE)

**Course:** Rosslare (Old Course)

**Location:** Rosslare, County Wexford, Ireland

**Hole:** No. 11

**Length:** 469 yards

**Par:** 5

**Designer:** F. W. Hawtree, J.H. Taylor

**Course Comment:** First opened for play in 1905, the Old Course makes its way out by the Irish Sea and is a classic championship links golf course designed by Hawtree and Taylor.

Situated in the sunniest part of Ireland, Rosslare, with recent changes to seven holes, has never been better. It has long been considered one of Ireland's hidden gems, but the word is getting out that this is an outstanding golf course.

Rosslare's links offer two excellent nines, with the homeward nine probably the better of the two halves. Two of the finest holes on the outward journey include the par-4 5th and the par-5 7th. A three-hole stretch starting at 15 is also first rate.

But the finest or most memorable hole on the course according to many is the 469-yard 11th, which is an extremely challenging par 5. The hole usually plays into the prevailing wind, while the second shot must be played blind over a hill marked by a red and white post.

And hence its name the "Barber's Pole."

This hole is certainly a cut above the rest.

The prevailing southwesterly winds make the links both a challenging and an enjoyable test for golfers. The links at Rosslare is what you would expect with wind-swept hills and plenty of burrows.

The potential for golf on this spot was realized by the famous architect James Farrell, who founded the club in 1905. His mark remains on the course to this day. **TJ**

**Course:** The Lakes

**Location:** Rosebury, Sydney, Australia

**Hole:** No. 11

**Length:** 575 yards

**Par:** 5

**Designer:** Robert Von Hagge, Bruce Devlin

**Course Comment:** This hole is shaped like a boomerang, which seems only fitting for an Australian highlight. Presumably, however, a wayward shot won't come back to you.

# No. 11    THE LAKES

The lengthy par-5 11th wraps itself neatly around one of the many lakes on this course, which might give you a clue as to where The Lakes draws its name. The lake is, of course, the primary source of concern on No. 11.

There are a few fairway bunkers with which to contend — mainly one to the left off the tee and a couple more on each side on the second shot — but the lake is what causes some players' rounds to go walkabout.

The large lake faces you on your third shot, forcing a carry over one of its fingers to a smallish green that directly abuts the water. In an effort to avoid the water in front, countless shots go over the green in three, forcing a player to go up and down just to make par.

It is the kind of deception and difficulty that Bruce Devlin and Robert Von Hagge had in mind when they designed the hole. The pair used to be a design team until Von Hagge broke out on his own to design golf courses throughout the world.

There are names that conjure up magical images in the world of modern golf course design: Rees Jones, Pete Dye, Tom Fazio, and, perhaps as much by legend as accomplishment, Jack Nicklaus. But Von Hagge, despite creating more than 200 courses from raw land and rock around the world, just doesn't seem to get the ink he deserves. Perhaps it's his easy-going style, or his stay-in-the-background approach to golf-course design. However, a more likely reason is that, while other architects are at PR functions, Von Hagge is out walking in the dirt: "It really is an art form if you do it right," said Von Hagge. "I love getting out of bed every morning, knowing I'll be going to a site and putting an idea into motion." And now that the idea of the boomerang 11th at The Lakes has been set in motion, it's a great place to play. **JB**

**Course:** Royal Lytham & St. Annes

**Location:** St. Annes-on-Sea, Lancashire, England

**Hole:** No. 11

**Length:** 540 yards

**Par:** 5

**Designer:** Harry S. Colt

**Course Comment:** Like most British links courses, accuracy is a must. But it's even more so here at Royal Lytham and St. Annes. There are 197 bunkers on the golf course, which is a big number even for this part of the world.

# No. ⑪  ROYAL LYTHAM & ST. ANNES

This 540-yard par 5 means decision time for the big hitters as to whether they take the left-hand route to clear the cross bunkers for a shorter and more direct line to the green.

It would certainly make a nice second shot to the green. And there is nothing better than being on the green in two, especially on a long par 5. But the risks are huge, because the rough can send you scrambling and the landing area is not an easy target.

The bunkers one would be trying to fly on the left cut well into the fairway, as do two others earlier in the fairway on the right. End up in either bunker and this hole gets much longer.

There are more fairway bunkers closer to the green and several green-side bunkers along the front right and front left.

Royal Lytham & St. Annes Golf Club is one of the premier links courses in the world, host to 10 Open championships, two Ryder Cups and numerous other major tournaments including the Women's and Seniors Open championships. **TJ**

BELOW AND OPPOSITE *Two views of the 11th hole at Waterville.*

# No. ⑪  WATERVILLE GOLF LINKS

Ireland is laden with much tradition and history, but Waterville and the surrounding area have taken it to another level. According to the *Book of Invasions* written about AD 1000, Cessair, the granddaughter of Noah, landed in Ballinskelligs Bay near Waterville after the Great Flood. And it is said that the Milesians settled in 1700 BC and left behind many of the archeological sites found in the area. These rich legends form the kind of history unknown to many regions of the world.

Waterville Golf Links may not go back that far, but its history runs pretty deep.

The earliest structured golf at Waterville has been traced to 1889 and it was a formalized part of village life by 1900, when Waterville became one of the first clubs to be affiliated to the Golfing Union of Ireland.

Waterville's past is well-documented, but its current state is what we are fortunate enough to enjoy today. It is one of the finest links golf courses in the world. Located on the Ring of Kerry, the surrounding scenery and quality of golf holes are striking.

One of these quality holes is "Tranquility," the par-5 11th that runs 500 yards through a narrow passage of huge dunes. Gary Player described the 11th as "the most beautiful and satisfying par 5 of them all."

There is competition all around Waterville, but the Links stacks up. The south-west coast of Ireland has a love affair with golf, with such famous courses as Ballybunion, Tralee, Old Head, Kinsale, and Killarney. Waterville is regarded by many as the best of the bunch.

Around World War II, Waterville Golf Club had a tremendous reputation, but the links lay virtually dormant through the latter part of the 1960s until the arrival of John A. Mulcahy, an Irish-born American who came with the vision of building the most testing golf links in the world. Mulcahy teamed up with Irish architect Hackett and most would say they succeeded in their challenging quest.

Since re-opening in 1973, Waterville has recovered its former place of prominence among the best venues in the world. In 1994, Mulcahy died and his ashes were buried on "Mulcahy's Peak," the par-3 17th at Waterville. **JB**

**Course:** Walden on Lake Conroe Golf & Country Club

**Location:** Montgomerey, Texas, USA

**Hole:** No. 11

**Length:** 589 yards

**Par:** 5

**Designer:** Bruce Devlin, Robert Von Hagge

**Course Comment:** This hole is wicked because it is a double dogleg, and the green is virtually an island.

## No. ⑪ WALDEN ON LAKE CONROE GOLF & COUNTRY CLUB

Everyone knows about the famed island green at TPC Sawgrass's 17th hole, but at least it takes just one shot to get there. At Walden on Lake Conroe's 11th, you get two shots to prepare yourself for an approach to a green that isn't quite a pure island, but is pretty close. And all this finishes up a par-5 hole that is nearly 600 yards long.

Bruce Devlin and Robert Von Hagge must have been in bad moods when they designed this hole. For it is nasty from start to finish.

There is no chance to reach this green in two. The length would make it challenge enough, although the longest of the long hitters could make a 589-yard green in two shots if the wind were right.

But there's no shot at this green in two, regardless of wind. First, because of the double dogleg — both times to the right, first around trees and then around Lake Conroe — and second, because of the peninsula green, which juts into water and is surrounded on three sides by water.

There is no water in the slim entry to the front of the green, but there is a bunker there that makes a run-up impossible.

Treacherous, from tee to green.

Large and plentiful pines, nine bunkers, and suffocating water creeping in on the fairway create a hole that would leave you craving the arrival of the 12th if it weren't so much fun to play.

It is just as enjoyable to observe.

"It is important for a course to play well, for the holes to be interesting, and for there to be a variety," said Von Hagge. "But, you have to remember, while one person is playing a shot, three others are standing and observing.

"I don't want that to be idle time. I want to give them something worth looking at."

Von Hagge, 6' 5" tall and always sartorially splendid when he isn't out in the dirt, strikes an imposing presence when he walks into a room. And that natural flair for style seems to carry over into his work.

That is certainly the case with the brutal yet beautiful 11th winding around Lake Conroe. **JB**

**Course:** Golf Club of Georgia
(Lakeside Course)

**Location:** Alpharetta, Georgia, USA

**Hole:** No. 11

**Length:** 607 yards

**Par:** 5

**Designer:** Arthur Hills

**Course Comment:** The Golf
Club of Georgia played host to
the Senior PGA Tour's Nationwide
Championship from 1995 to 2000.

No. **⓫**   # GOLF CLUB OF GEORGIA
## (LAKESIDE COURSE)

From the second shot on, golfers are drawn to the sparkling, shimmering waters that spectacularly fill the horizon behind the small target of the green. Hopefully, at the end, their golf balls won't be.

But we're getting ahead of ourselves, because concentration is key from the very beginning of this monstrous par 5, from a tee shot that should be placed on the right side of the slight dogleg left fairway to a second shot that must split a trio of bunkers on the right and a group of trees on the left. Get as close as you can on the first two shots, because you want as short a shot as is possible for the important downhill approach to a putting surface that juts out into Lake Windward and is protected by a huge three-bunker complex at the front left and another bunker at the rear, just in front of the lake. Those who land in the back bunker ought to count their blessings. It beats the alternative.

After finishing second by a shot in both 1997 (to Graham Marsh) and 1998 (to John Jacobs), Hale Irwin went on to win the final two Nationwide Championships, capturing back-to-back crowns in 1999 and 2000. **KA**

# Hole 12

One should look no further than one of golf's cathedrals, Augusta National Golf Club, to understand the importance of the 12th hole of a round. No. 12 at Augusta, a 155-yard par 3 and the middle entry in a three-hole stretch known as Amen Corner, is often instrumental in determining the winner of the Masters tournament.

Amen Corner encompasses three distinct tests, and its three-hole challenge is rather a microcosm of what designers attempt to execute at the great golf courses of the world. Holes Nos. 8–13, as a general rule, compose the toughest stretch on the golf course. Obviously, there are exceptions to this, but if the land allows, architects would like to put the most rugged challenges at Nos. 8–13.

No. 12, as exhibited not only at Augusta, but also at Barsebäck in Sweden and Sotogrande in Spain, is often a highlight hole in the middle third of your round.

**LEFT** *Sven Struver of Germany tees off on the 12th hole at Barsebäck Golf and Country Club, Landskrona, Sweden.*

**Course:** Whistling Straits

**Location:** Kohler, Wisconsin, USA

**Hole:** No. 12

**Length:** 166 yards

**Par:** 3

**Designer:** Pete Dye

**Course Comment:** Only six years after its opening, Whistling Straits played host to its first major championship, the 2004 PGA Championship.

# No. ⑫ **WHISTLING STRAITS**

Visit Whistling Straits today and you would never know that Pete Dye's masterpiece along a two-mile stretch of Lake Michigan was created from what was fairly flat, uninspired land that formerly contained an airfield.

For what is there today is truly inspiring, an 18-hole gem crafted by Dye as a tribute to the traditional seaside links of the British Isles. The traditional influences also carry over in other areas: Whistling Straits is a walking course only and requires caddies for most tee times.

The par-3 12th hole features a downhill tee shot to a long, undulating, angled green that is surrounded by the course's treacherous trademark sand-dune bunkers and provides the opportunity for plenty of interesting pin placements.

Even many tee shots that land on the green will kick into deep bunkers, and if your shot is left, short, or right, there's little hope of recovery, as there is a plunge of 40 feet to grassy dunes, fearsome bunkers, and the waters of Lake Michigan.

And that's not even taking into account the often-present winds, which can affect club selection dramatically. Play to the left side of the green and hope for the best. **KA**

**Course:** Ko Olina

**Location:** Kapolei, Oahu, Hawaii, USA

**Hole:** No. 12

**Length:** 183 yards

**Par:** 3

**Designer:** Ted Robinson

**Course Comment:** One of Ted Robinson's masterpieces, Ko Olina played host to the LPGA Orix Hawaiian Ladies' Open from 1990 until 1995 and also hosted a Senior Tour event in 1992.

# No. ⑫ KO OLINA

It's not easy to stand out when there are golf courses built on cliffs and beaches and lava fields. Almost every golf course in Hawaii has spectacular views, unique holes, and well-maintained playing surfaces. It's easy to throw around words such as spectacular, breathtaking, and magnificent.

Welcome to Ko Olina. Spectacular. Breathtaking. Magnificent.

Ko Olina has many holes that stand out. No. 8 is a picturesque par 3. No. 18 is a watery and challenging finishing hole. But No. 12 stands alone because it's as memorable a golf hole as any on the islands.

On how many holes do you drive through (or at least under) a waterfall to get to the tee box? Probably very few, which makes your drive to the No. 12 tee on this hole a ride you will never forget.

This cascading waterfall is just below the tee box and is the only road to No. 12. Enjoy the ride. Then enjoy the challenge.

All of the greens at Ko Olina are split-level and multitiered, plus there are several dozen pot bunkers strategically placed throughout the course. No. 12 is no exception.

There is a pot bunker left and a large sand bunker on the right side of this two-tiered green. Putting is key on this hole, as it is on many at Ko Olina. Just because you reach the green, don't think your work is done. Often times, it's just getting started. **TJ**

**Course:** Muirfield Village Golf Club

**Location:** Dublin, Ohio, USA

**Hole:** No. 12

**Length:** 166 yards

**Par:** 3

**Designer:** Jack Nicklaus, Desmond Muirhead

**Course Comment:** This hole played as the second toughest in the 2003 Memorial with a stroke average of 3.259. Players marked down only 43 birdies compared with 74 bogeys and 25 double bogeys or worse.

Muirfield Village was Jack Nicklaus's dream project, set in the rolling hills of Ohio, the Golden Bear's beloved native state. The course has been enjoyed and respected since its 1972 debut, and it remains Nicklaus's most highly regarded and well-known design.

No. 12 is Muirfield's most photographed hole, with a tee shot played from a wooded hillside across the course's largest lake to a green that is set diagonally from the tee. Although the hole isn't long, the putting surface is a difficult one to hit. Bunkers protect the right front and rear left of the two-tiered green, which slopes from back to front toward the lake. A shot that isn't struck perfectly will likely find either sand or water.

Because of the Nicklaus name and the quality of the design, Muirfield has attracted a host of top events, including the PGA Tour's Memorial Tournament, which annually boasts one of the season's top fields. Muirfield has also played host to the 1987 Ryder Cup (Europe defeated the United States 15–13 for Europe's first victory on American soil), the 1992 U.S. Amateur (won by Justin Leonard), and the 1998 Solheim Cup (the United States defeated Europe 16–12). **KA**

## No. ⓬    THE CHALLENGE AT MANELE

**Course:** The Challenge at Manele

**Location:** Lanai, Hawaii, USA

**Hole:** No. 12

**Length:** 202 yards

**Par:** 3

**Designer:** Jack Nicklaus

**Course Comment:** In 1994, billionaire Bill Gates got married on the tee box of this signature par 3.

Built on natural lava outcroppings and overlooking scenic Hulopo'e Bay and the Pacific Ocean, the Jack Nicklaus-designed layout at the Challenge at Manele is rich with native Hawaiian trees and rolling hills and includes several preserved archeological sites.

From the back tee box spectacularly set atop a cliff, this intimidating tee shot is scary enough simply because of how high you are above the green and the crashing waters of the Pacific 150 feet below. It's even more frightening because of the challenge it presents to golfers, who must carry a "fairway" of ocean, then finally a rocky ravine filled with thick native vegetation to reach the green, leaving little margin for error. Even though the tradewinds often help, players would be advised to take a little extra club, as it's much better to be long than short here.

Although this hole is a monster from the tips, five sets of tees offer plenty of playing options for the less adventurous, ranging from 185 yards from the golds to 153 from the middle and a mere 65 yards from the forward tees. None, however, provide quite the thrill — and terror — that the aptly named Nicklaus tees do. **KA**

## No. ⓬    WATERVILLE GOLF LINKS

**Course:** Waterville Golf Links

**Location:** Waterville, County Kerry, Ireland

**Hole:** No. 12

**Length:** 200 yards

**Par:** 3

**Designer:** Eddie Hackett

**Course Comment:** Architect Tom Fazio was commissioned by Waterville Golf Links to update the memorable Hackett masterpiece.

This 200-yard par 3, nicknamed the "Mass Hole," is a wonderful short hole with plenty of tradition. When you line up your tee shot, forget the history for a moment and focus more on the wind direction. You are teeing off out of the dunes to a green that is wide open to the mighty breeze, so adjust your club selection accordingly.

The green is elevated with a sharp drop off the front. It's better to be long than short to this almost perfectly circular green. There is one bunker, to the right front.

Now for a few quotes. First, from Tom Fazio, who helped with the design improvements: "Everything about Waterville is truly spectacular. The setting is one of the best I have seen for golf."

And another from golf pro and designer Raymond Floyd: "This is one of the most beautiful places I have ever seen. It has some of the finest links holes I have ever played."

Founded in 1889, Waterville is one of the oldest Irish clubs and is a truly magical place to play golf. The course eases you in with some wonderful holes you're sure to remember and admire, but as the game progresses, the course becomes more and more spectacular. The stretch run at Waterville is links beauty at its best. It doesn't get any better than right here. **TJ**

**Course:** Royal Birkdale

**Location:** Southport, Merseyside, England

**Hole:** No. 12

**Length:** 183 yards

**Par:** 3

**Designer:** George Lowe, F.W. Hawtree, J.H. Taylor

**Course Comment:** Royal Birkdale has played host to scores of prestigious tournaments, including eight British Opens, two Ryder Cups, the Walker Cup, and the Curtis Cup. The 2005 British Amateur Championship is the latest addition to the list of events held at Royal Birkdale.

**BELOW AND OPPOSITE** *Two views of the 12th hole at Royal Birkdale.*

# No. ⑫  ROYAL BIRKDALE

When searching for a site on which to hold the 100th British Open championship, Royal Birkdale was a natural selection. Natural is a perfect word to describe the great Royal Birkdale, which stretches along the Lancashire coast, one of the most famous stretches of golf property in the world. Among the natural beauties of Royal Birkdale is the 12th hole, which features colorful rough, dunes, bunkers, and Scottish heather.

With world-famous courses such as West Lancashire, Hillside, Royal Liverpool, and others nearby, it takes quite a course to leap to the top of the list. Royal Birkdale, without question, is the area's leader. Not only does it lead amid illustrious company, but it also stands out.

The course is made up of towering sand dunes and unexpectedly wide and inviting fairways that include flat landing areas, valleys, and blind spots. Trouble awaits, and it is severe if you land in mound or dune areas. It is avoidable trouble, but if you find it, the penalty is drastic. Although there are dunes throughout the course, they are by no means overly obtrusive. If you find trouble here, it is of your own doing. Royal Birkdale demands accuracy with elevated tees, set into trees and bushes and plateau greens surrounded by deep bunkers.

The 12th hole is no exception. Penal trouble is on hand if you aren't careful. The shot off the tee must carry a narrow valley to a plateau green

that sits among a gathering of hills. It is a narrow green, and appears half-hidden amid the mounding. Adding to the protection are four deep bunkers on either side of the green, and a collection of sand hills covered in scrub tower over either side that add to the beauty but also to the need for accuracy. It is a very attractive short hole, and plenty long enough to make the small green look downright tiny from the tee.

New greens were installed before the last British Open held at Royal Birkdale in 1998, and many feel they are the best in Britain. Mark O'Meara beat Brian Watts in a three-hole playoff in that British Open. Peter Thompson, Arnold Palmer, Lee Trevino, Johnny Miller, and Tom Watson are among the other pros who have won here. **JB**

**Course:** Champions Golf Club
(Cypress Course)

**Location:** Houston, Texas, USA

**Hole:** No. 12

**Length:** 232 yards

**Par:** 3

**Designer:** Ralph Plummer

**Course Comment:** For the 2003
Tour Championship, the fifth time
the PGA Tour's season finale was
played at the Ralph Plummer-
designed layout, Chad Campbell
forged his way to victory with
a steady performance at No. 12.
Campbell played the hole in one
under for the week with three
pars and a birdie (round 3).

# No. ⑫ CHAMPIONS GOLF CLUB
## (CYPRESS COURSE)

When Jack Burke and Jimmy Demaret decided nearly five decades ago to build Champions Golf Club they had a single driving theme — combine form and function to create a unique golf atmosphere.

The two legends, with help from architect Ralph Plummer, were successful on both fronts. Champions' grounds were arranged to maximize a player's experience, with the clubhouse set back from the road and the first and 10th tees placed far enough apart to create dramatic vistas of the on-course action from the comfort of the dining area.

That same detail was used to create the Cypress Course, a 7,301-yard layout that is as challenging to today's prodigious pros as it was in 1967 when it hosted the Ryder Cup. Out-of-bounds looms far and wide, and over 70,000 trees test players' skill as well as their mettle.

As is usually the case in Texas, wind is the single most important factor at Champions and few of Cypress's holes are affected by the breeze as much as the par-3 12th. Most players will hit long irons or fairways woods to a sprawling green. With warm, swirling winds, however, the lake left of the green and large bunker at right frames what may be the most demanding tee shot on the course. **RH**

**Course:** Shoreacres Club

**Location:** Lake Bluff, Illinois, USA

**Hole:** No. 12

**Length:** 127 yards

**Par:** 3

**Designer:** Seth J. Raynor

**Course Comment:** Solidly
bunkered, rapid greens make
Shoreacres a challenge and
a pleasure. Narrow tree-lined
fairways test the straightest
shooters, and several ravines
are creatively routed into play.

# No. ⑫ SHOREACRES CLUB

After slicing through treacherous terrain where deep gulleys loom and tough shots prevail, it's a golfer's pleasure to arrive at No. 12, especially those playing a crackerjack short game.

This short hole is a tough nut to crack on a demanding course — tricky and well-suited to the land. It is a steep shot, 40 feet downhill to an oversized green that is bunkered in front. The 12th is a dramatic target where up-and-downs for par are nearly impossible. The rough surrounding its green are treacherous, so if you miss it on your tee shot, you're almost certainly out of luck.

Raynor's strategic use of the bubbling ravines that twist through the course make it a wonderful juxtaposition of first-class design and peaceful nature. A weekend golfer might consider this hole a punishment, but a player with a solid short game is in heaven on No. 12, where bunkers are aggressive protection for the green and competition is fierce.

Old-fashioned golf culture defines this course; tradition has reigned supreme at Shoreacres for nearly 90 years. It's an ultra-private test of expertise with the 12th as its showcase. No. 12 is 127 yards of pure iron-wielding skill. And the other 17 holes don't disappoint, either. **KLL**

**Course:** Fairmont Algonquin

**Location:** St. Andrews by-the-Sea, New Brunswick, Canada

**Hole:** No. 12

**Length:** 154 yards

**Par:** 3

**Designer:** Thomas McBroom

**Course Comment:** There aren't many places where you can stand on a tee and see another country, but the 12th at Fairmont Algonquin is one of them. That's Maine you can see across the St. Clair River.

# No. ⓬ FAIRMONT ALGONQUIN

Nos. 11, 12, and 13 are an amazing stretch of holes at this highly rated and very scenic golf course. The elevation drop of No. 12 is more than 80 feet, and this hole is often called the Pebble Beach No. 7 of the north.

Here is what you are looking at from the tee: water to the right and behind, bushes, brush and bad news to the left. If you hit the ball right or back right, you will hit a wall and end up in the water.

The best place is on the green. Actually, the only place is on the green.

Selecting the right club will be one of the more difficult choices you will make all day — right up there with LaBatts or Molson.

Before selecting your club of choice, check the flag for an accurate wind report. On the tee the trees will block much of the wind, but the green is wide open so it swirls quite a bit. Our club expert said he's used everything from a wedge to a 3-iron on this hole.

The green is tough. The kidney-shaped putting surface has a hump that pushes everything to the right.

But take some time on this hole. Spend a few minutes enjoying the spectacular view — if you are lucky you will see one of those giant ocean liners heading for port.

And then spend another couple of minutes picking the right club. Just don't go right. **TJ**

**Course:** Augusta National Golf Club

**Location:** Augusta, Georgia, USA

**Hole:** No. 12

**Length:** 155 yards

**Par:** 3

**Designer:** Alister MacKenzie, Robert Tyre Jones

**Course Comment:** No. 12 is the middle hole in the treacherous three-hole stretch known as Amen Corner, and is home to the famed Ben Hogan bridge.

## No. ⑫  AUGUSTA NATIONAL GOLF CLUB

You can almost feel the tension and drama as you stand on the tee at Augusta's 12th, the central hole in the world-famous trio of Amen Corner. It has been the site of many a tense moment at the Masters, and it is one of the rare places on the course where both the hole in front and the one just played are visible. Taking in three holes at Augusta is enjoyable enough, just based on the finely manicured beauty, but when standing on the tee and conjuring images of tradition and tension, it is a golf experience to be remembered.

The hole, named "Golden Bell," is protected by Rae's Creek and one bunker in the front, and behind the narrow green are two bunkers side by side. It calls for a precise judge of distance, and precision is difficult when the breezes are blowing. The picturesque pines which surround the hole add beauty, but they offer little defense to the wind.

Golden Bell's green is much like the others at Augusta National — it follows the natural contour of the land, which means there is plenty of slope. There are enough flat spots for plenty of pin positions, but there are also treacherous areas. The 12th fits in nicely with the rest of the course, appearing to be part of a vast park with meandering grounds. The slopes and hills on the 12th don't come into play because it is a par-3 hole, but it still reminds players of their long and sometimes arduous walk on the mound-laden layout.

The 12th isn't overly long, and doesn't appear a strenuous test, but the unpredictable breeze is what makes this hole daunting. Club selection, as on any par 3, is crucial, and choosing the right short iron becomes difficult because the wind is apt to change in the time it takes to walk from bag to tee box.

Obviously, at 155 yards, distance isn't what makes No. 12 difficult. In fact, before the 2002 Masters, Tom Fazio was brought in to add teeth to the course and he left No. 12 alone. Length was added on half of Augusta National's holes, including the 12th's two partners in Amen Corner, but Fazio figured that No. 12 was best left untouched. **JB**

**BELOW** The 12th hole at Augusta.

**OPPOSITE** Arnold Palmer of the USA plays his tee shot on the 12th hole at Augusta, April 2004.

**Course:** Somerset Hills Country Club

**Location:** Bernardsville, New Jersey, USA

**Hole:** No. 12

**Length:** 144 yards

**Par:** 3

**Designer:** A.W. Tillinghast

**Course Comment:** The back nine at Somerset Hills, natural and densely wooded, is like a split personality from the open, links-style front nines, which are laid out around an old racetrack. It's as near to playing two different courses as one 18-hole round can be, with the front being flat and the back rollercoaster hilly — but both are characterized by difficult uphill or downhill approaches.

## No. ⑫ SOMERSET HILLS COUNTRY CLUB

The beauty of this course is eye-catching, but aesthetics can be deceiving — with greens and fairways bordered by very thick rough and fringe, making Somerset Hills simultaneously tough and fair on creatively contoured greens. A.W. Tillinghast used the natural layout of the land (and water) in 1917, and he used it to the benefit of the green's defense on this short par 3. The hole is short, but precision is a must.

Play it with strategic caution. A tee shot over the green sends it splashing into a large pond in the back. A lake to the green's left and the right-to-left sharp slope of the putting surface work together to guard the 12th, but use the slope to feed your ball left and you might get close, depending on pin placement. Stay left, stay close to the water, and the prize is within reach on this tricky water-filled par 3.

Somerset Hills is with filled with variety. Sloping greens, with par 3s, 4s, and 5s of varying lengths, and difficult approach shots, make Somerset Hills a distinct, testing round of golf. The complete spectrum of shots, will be required to score here.

There are 109 bunkers on this course and water throughout. Your patience and your aim will be tested in particular on hole No. 12. **KLL**

## No. ⑫  WANNAMOISETT COUNTRY CLUB

**Course:** Wannamoisett Country Club

**Location:** Rumford, Rhode Island, USA

**Hole:** No. 12

**Length:** 215 yards

**Par:** 3

**Designer:** Donald Ross

**Course Comment:** This club offers famous and popular holes. No. 12 ranks right up there with the best. And check out that apple tree near the tee box. It's left over from an old orchard that used to dominate the property until about 1850.

Welcome to the Sahara Desert — or the bunker on No. 12 at Wannamoisett. Yes, the Sahara Desert does extend to Rumford, Rhode Island. And the best way to see it is from the outside, looking in.

This enormous bunker is located on the front right of the green and what's even more amazing is that you can barely see it from the tee box. But it's there.

The bunker is 40 yards in diameter and 30 yards front to back. And it's big enough to house a small village in it — all right, perhaps that's a stretch.

There is also a bunker on the left side.

You can roll up your shot between the two bunkers but the best way to avoid both of them is to land your tee shot on the green, which is elevated from the bunkers.

The bowl-shaped green will funnel anything long back to the center, but hitting over the green will mean a tough shot coming back because the green is running away from you. **TJ**

## No. ⑫  GOLF CLUB AT CINCO RANCH

**Course:** Golf Club at Cinco Ranch

**Location:** Katy, Texas, USA

**Hole:** No. 12

**Length:** 191 yards

**Par:** 3

**Designer:** Carlton Gipson

**Course Comment:** The Golf Club at Cinco Ranch is located within the 5,000-acre Cinco Ranch master-planned community on Houston's fast-growing west side. But this isn't your typical golf course winding through an American subdivision. This place is special.

Carlton Gipson's design features a surprising (and pleasing) amount of roll, with several holes featuring elevation changes of as much as 15 feet. The elevation changes help ensure an interesting round of golf — so do 50 bunkers and water hazards that come into play on 16 holes.

Water and bunkers certainly come into play on the 191-yard, par-3 12th hole. And so does the elevation change. So this one par-3 hole gives you a little bit of everything the Golf Club at Cinco Ranch has to offer, including some stunning scenery.

Your tee shot is over water to a well-bunkered and elevated green. And you have to carry all the water. The water should look familiar because you had to clear the same pond on No. 11. Now you have to carry it again.

There is no room for error short of the green. You are either putting or hitting again if you are short of the stick. There is a slight bail-out area to the right of the hole.

The hole is on an open area on the golf course, which means that right to left Southland wind will play tricks with your Titleist.

Then there is the three-tier green to worry about, but just be thankful you are on the green. **TJ**

**Course:** Thirteenth Beach Golf Links

**Location:** Barwon Heads, Victoria, Australia

**Hole:** No. 12

**Length:** 171 yards

**Par:** 3

**Designer:** Tony Cashmore

**Course Comment:** The collaboration between architect Cashmore and entrepreneur Duncan Andrews, who also built the Dunes on the other side of Melbourne's Port Phillip Bay, once again produced a superior golf course with the highly rated Thirteenth Beach.

Beautiful is the first adjective that comes to most golfers' minds when they play No. 12 at Thirteenth Beach Golf Links, and there is no doubt this downhill par 3 deserves such an accolade, for it is a challenging, seaside hole built within gorgeous sand dunes.

Wind and pin placements make club selection particularly tough here, and it is not at all surprising to find players openly fretting over their tee shots, unsure of whether or not they have reached into their bags for the right sticks.

Locals say the key to success at this hole is to take half a club more than they might normally think is sufficient, and then aim squarely for the center of the green.

Golfers have no real reason to worry if they go a little long, for there is a sand dune behind the putting surface that can be used as a sort of backstop for strong tee shots. But the rugged green-side bunkering can present more than its fair share of difficulty should the mid-range irons usually required to reach the pin here go slightly astray. **JS**

Course: Chicago Golf Club

Location: Wheaton, Illinois, USA

Hole: No. 12

Length: 405 yards

Par: 4

Designer: Charles Blair Macdonald, Seth Raynor

Course Comment: At the first Walker Cup held at Chicago Golf Club, captain Bobby Jones went undefeated to lead the United States to an 11–1 rout over Great Britain and Ireland.

BELOW  *The 12th hole at Chicago Golf Club.*

# No. ⑫  CHICAGO GOLF CLUB

Chicago Golf Club's "Punchbowl" 12th hole is a sturdy par 4 that offers a test for all players, no matter from which tees they hit. That's because a series of fairway bunkers are scattered on both sides all the way to the green, where more trouble awaits.

The "Punchbowl" green is surrounded by ridges on three sides, with the opening to the front guarded by a deep-faced bunker at the right front of the green. Another problematic bunker is located several yards back and to the left, providing something of a false front and affecting many players' depth perception.

Chicago will play host to the 2005 Walker Cup, returning the ultra-exclusive private club to its prestigious roots as the site of some of golf's top professional and amateur events.

The U.S. Open was held here in 1897 (won by Joe Lloyd), 1900 (Harry Vardon), and 1911 (John McDermott), with McDermott's victory marking the first time an American-born player had captured the championship.

The club also played host to the U.S. Amateur — considered at the time to be just as big an event as the Open, if not even bigger — in 1897, 1905, 1909, and 1912. **KA**

## No. ⑫ TROON GOLF & COUNTRY CLUB

**Course:** Troon Golf & Country Club

**Location:** Scottsdale, Arizona, USA

**Hole:** No. 12

**Length:** 400 yards

**Par:** 4

**Designer:** Tom Weiskopf, Jay Morrish

**Course Comment:** At an elevation of 2,400 feet above sea level, Troon is slightly higher than Royal Troon, its namesake in Scotland.

Troon Golf & Country Club was named after designer Tom Weiskopf's great 1973 British Open victory at Royal Troon in Scotland, and the two clubs maintain a warm relationship even today.

Of course, Weiskopf's layout in the rolling Arizona desert shares few characteristics with its counterpart on the Scottish coast, with mountains and cactus replacing sand dunes and the ocean.

The 12th hole requires a strong and precise tee shot to carry a rise in the fairway, which is lined on both sides by treacherous desert landscape. Getting to the top of the hill allows golfers to avoid a blind second shot to a wide but shallow green with small mountains in the background.

Many golfers hit their tee shots with a fairway wood or long iron, though, because if they land their drives too far past the rise, their second shot must be hit off a downhill lie.

Adding to the difficulty of the approach: the green is protected by a trio of deep bunkers — one right, one left, and one directly in front — and this tricky putting surface is separated into two sections by a severe slope in the middle. **KA**

## No. ⑫ PELICAN WATERS GOLF CLUB

**Course:** Pelican Waters Golf Club

**Location:** Golden Beach, Queensland, Australia

**Hole:** No. 12

**Par:** 4

**Length:** 334 yards

**Designer:** Greg Norman, Bob Harrison

**Course Comment:** Architect Bob Harrison says the 12th is among the best of the dozens of par 4s he and Greg Norman have ever built.

Wind can make golfers do goofy things, to be sure, and the temptation for big hitters playing this par 4 is that a little breeze at their backs often makes them think they can reach the green with their drives.

If they hit a good ball, they will usually be rewarded. Under normal circumstances, however, No. 12 is best played as a two-shot hole, with a tee shot placed down the left side of a spacious fairway, which slopes from left to right.

True to form, Norman and Harrison have given golfers a lot of choice off the tee, and lots of room to land their drives. But then they demand a very precise approach to an intensely contoured green guarded by a huge bunker short right and another behind the putting surface.

Shots to that putting surface have a habit of ending up in that first hazard, and getting up and down from that spot can be a daunting proposition, especially considering that the bunker is so deep that you cannot see the green once you set your feet in the sand. **JS**

**Course:** The Grove

**Location:** Watford, Hertfordshire, England

**Hole:** No. 12

**Length:** 462 yards

**Par:** 4

**Designer:** Kyle Phillips

**Course Comment:** It did not take long for the world to take note of the truly spectacular course Phillips had created. Three years after it opened, Tiger Woods won the 2006 WGC American Express Match Play Championship at The Grove (see below).

# No. ⓬ THE GROVE

Somehow, The Grove — a 7,152-yard tester of a layout that was created by Kyle Phillips in 2003 — combines the warm accommodation of public golf with the immaculate conditioning of a private club.

There is but a ribbon of landing area at which to aim off the tee on the 462-yard par-4 12th. There is a frightening bunker on the right side of the fairway that is slightly hidden by a tree line, and there is an even more menacing pot bunker farther down the fairway on the left side.

Should you escape the bunkers on your tee shot, there is no bargain the rest of the way home. There is a tricky punchbowl in front of the green that will suck anything short of the green into its depths. The choices are either stick the green or forget about it (Woods is pictured chipping out of it below). There is no chance to roll the ball onto the green on the tough 12th.

The green is long and inviting, but there is a bunker guarding its entire right side. This hole is long, cunning, and it commands your attention from start to finish. If you happen to strike par, pick up your ball and stride proudly to the 13th. **JB**

**Course:** ChampionsGate
(International Course)

**Location:** Davenport, Florida, USA

**Hole:** No. 12

**Length:** 344 yards

**Par:** 4

**Designer:** Greg Norman

**Course Comment:** Surrounded by waste bunkers and featuring fast greens, ChampionsGate is a little bit of Europe with Florida weather. The international 18 holes are constructed in the traditional links style of Scotland and Ireland.

# No. ⑫ CHAMPIONSGATE
## (INTERNATIONAL COURSE)

With Greg Norman working the blueprints, ChampionsGate rapidly became a major player in Florida golf soon after opening its gates. With some pretty stiff competition in the neighborhood, ChampionsGate offered excellent playing conditions and a unique golf course.

One of the unique holes at ChampionsGate is the par-4 12th.

When Norman and his team laid out No. 12, they must have been busy. There was a green to create, bunkers to place, and plenty of thought was required to pull off such a spectacular dogleg left.

But Norman and his fellow designers forgot all about a tree in the middle of the fairway. Someone must have forgotten to notify the tree removal company to take it down before the grand opening. Imagine Norman's face when the first group pulled up to the tee and saw a big tree in the middle of the fairway, right at the break in the dogleg.

Norman simply regrouped and convinced everyone that it belonged there. Whether or not that's how it happened, the tree is there and must be avoided. It's 238 yards from the back tees, but trying to drive past it is risky. If you do and try to cut the dogleg, you have a large bunker short (along the left side of the fairway), a series of bunkers, and unfriendly rough waiting on the other side of the fairway. The bunkers on the far right are 274 yards from the back tees. Don't rule out the bunkers on the right closer to the tee yet. The green has a ridge in the middle and slopes back to front. **TJ**

**Course:** The Golf Club Kennedy Bay

**Location:** Longbeach Key, Port Kennedy, Western Australia

**Hole:** No. 12

**Par:** 4

**Length:** 363 yards

**Designer:** Michael Coate, Roger Mackay, Ian Baker-Finch

**Course Comment:** Dubbed "Finchy's Folly," the 12th here is named after Australian golfing great — and architectural team member — Ian Baker-Finch.

# No. ⑫ THE GOLF CLUB KENNEDY BAY

This hole is actually less folly than it is anomaly, for the 12th is a modest par 4 that boasts a two-tiered fairway, with the left side being about eight yards shallower than the one on the right.

The side you play depends primarily on where the pin is placed on the raised green that runs front to back and features two bunkers on the right side and one front left, as well as run-off areas that make players pay for their misses. Regulars at links-style Kennedy Bay, which has 115 pot-style bunkers, typically play a mid-iron off the tee at No. 12, oftentimes a 5-iron, and then hit a short iron to the green.

It's a position hole, made much more difficult than its length might indicate by the accuracy and maturity required to score a par, and also by the so-called Freemantle Doctor, the southwesterly wind that blows incessantly across the Western Australia golf course and wreaks havoc on even the best-hit shots. **JS**

**Course:** Quaker Ridge Golf Club

**Location:** Scarsdale, New York, USA

**Hole:** No. 12

**Length:** 437 yards

**Par:** 4

**Designer:** A.W. Tillinghast

**Course Comment:** Chad, the assistant pro and our tour guide for Quaker Ridge, says looks may be deceiving at No. 12. "In the summer, when the trees fill in, it looks like you are hitting into a narrow tunnel off the tee. It looks tighter than it really is. You have some room out there."

# No. ⑫ QUAKER RIDGE GOLF CLUB

Standing on the tee at No. 12, you have a full picture of the hole. What you see is what you get. This hole is straight uphill and everything is right there in front of you.

And you may not like what you see.

It just looks like an incredibly hard hole. The view can be intimidating, and justifiably so. Hitting out of a chute of trees uphill is no bargain. And you have to hit two very pure shots and two very difficult shots to reach this green in regulation.

You do have some fairway to work with on your tee shot, but as you get closer to the green, the fairway narrows. There is a creek on the right side near the tee box but it doesn't come into play. It does, however, add to the ambience of this scenic hole.

There are two fairway bunkers about 170 to 190 yards from the green along the right side that are reachable from any of the four sets of tees (the reds play the shortest at 350 yards).

Your second shot is usually with a long iron and here is where this hole begins to really bite. The green slopes back to front and is one of the faster greens at Quaker Ridge. There are bunkers middle left and middle right, just in case you are slightly off target. And behind the green are little mounds which make for a tough chipping area, particularly when the green slopes away from you. **TJ**

**Course:** Southern Hills Country Club

**Location:** Tulsa, Oklahoma, USA

**Hole:** No. 12

**Length:** 458 yards

**Par:** 4

**Designer:** Perry Maxwell

**Course Comment:** This storied club has played host to four U.S. Opens, three PGA Championships, two PGA Tour Championships, as well as five major USGA amateur championships since 1946. Among the major championship winners here are Babe Zaharias, Tommy Bolt, Ray Floyd, Nick Price, Billy Mayfair, Tom Lehman and Retief Goosen.

**BELOW AND OPPOSITE** *Two views of the 12th hole at Southern Hills.*

# No. ⑫ SOUTHERN HILLS COUNTRY CLUB

The prodigious 12th hole at the great Southern Hills plays at 458 yards for major championships, but members get a "break" — they face a challenge 32 yards shorter, but it still remains a fierce and fine golf hole.

Ben Hogan and Arnold Palmer both called No. 12 one of America's greatest par-4 holes, even though neither player ever won a tournament here — a testament to its memorability and difficulty. The 12th, a slight dogleg left, calls for a precision long drive to a blind landing area to take full advantage of the right-to-left slope of the fairway. Long hitters can cut the corner, but they must carry a bunker that sits in the elbow of the left turn 261 yards out. If they carry it, the ball will run a good distance on the manicured fairway, leaving an achievable approach shot.

However, even those players who have drilled their drive face a second shot that must be even more precise than their tee shot. The approach shot, a long- to middle-iron, must be extremely accurate because there is simply no safety other than the putting surface.

The approach must come in high and soft — opportunity for a runner is precluded by small streams front left and from front to back on the right side. Three treacherous bunkers add to the claustrophobic peril up front and left, and the green is banked so even the most accurate approaches can face tricky putts.

Like virtually every hole at Southern Hills, there are also trees. And trees and trees. Trees protect the dogleg on the left, and they also line the rides side of the fairway from tee to green. Thick stands of pines on the left side of the green turn this hole into a chute through forest, with sand and streams to boot.

The 12th is a beautiful golf hole — one of Perry Maxwell's finest. Maxwell designed brilliant golf courses throughout the world, but he seemed especially fond of Southern Hills. The course was built during the bleakest economic time ever in U.S. history, and the fact that Maxwell was a native of Oklahoma working to improve his home state during the Great Depression no doubt added to his dedication to Southern Hills. **JB**

539

Course: Camargo Club

Location: Indian Hill, Ohio, USA

Hole: No. 12

Length: 415 yards

Par: 4

Designer: Seth Raynor

Course Comment: Although the overall design of the course was firmly in place, the death of Seth Raynor in 1926 left some of the final details in the hands of the club's early leaders. William Jackson was the original superintendent and golf professional and was responsible for many of these last-minute additions, including the construction of bridges over ravines on Nos. 3, 5, 9, 12, and 18. By 1940, however, all the bridges had been replaced by ramps.

## No. ⑫ CAMARGO CLUB

Since 1927, when the back nine opened for play, Camargo Club has been in an almost constant state of flux. Seth Raynor's original design was a wonderful collection of long and short, subtle and severe holes. As the years have passed, however, Camargo has evolved like few other clubs.

Few of Raynor's original 18 have changed as much as the par-4 12th. The original 12th had two fairways, reached from two widely separate tees. The design was modeled on Raynor and Charles Blair Macdonald's "Channel" hole at the Lido Club.

Initially, No. 12 had a small, island fairway that required a 200-yard carry over a ravine and an extremely accurate shot to hold the sloping landing area. The second fairway was to the right of the current hole and was much more forgiving but eliminated any chance to reach the green in two shots. The hole was later redesigned using the riskier island fairway.

Adding to the hole's risk is a diagonal row of fairway bunkers about 100 yards short of a green which is elevated. Short approach shots leave a decent chance to save par, while anything long is doomed to run down a steep slope and leave little chance for a recovery. **RH**

Course: Pittsburgh Field Golf Club

Location: Pittsburgh, Pennsylvania, USA

Hole: No. 12

Length: 469 yards

Par: 4

Designer: Alex Finley

Course Comment: Finley may have been the first designer at Pittsburgh Field Club, but he wasn't the last. A total of nine designers have had their influence on this great golf course, including the likes of A.W. Tillinghast and Donald Ross.

## No. ⑫ PITTSBURGH FIELD GOLF CLUB

This 469-yard par 4 sets up directly in front of you: a very straight hole with a large fairway bunker on the right. This trap cuts well into the fairway at about 285 yards, so big hitters be careful.

A bunker on the left is positioned at about 265 yards and is another possibility from the tee. The fairway, which slopes right to left, is very small with a tough landing area for those who can hit the ball a long way.

Another way to picture the fairway is in the shape of an "S," with a shorter bunker left, then the fairway cutting behind it and in front of a bunker on the right before winding behind that one.

The best tee shot is anything short of 265 yards and on the right center of the fairway.

The green is on a large plateau which drops off to the left and behind. There is a bunker to the right and a large one on the left side.

Pittsburgh Field Golf Club is a parkland course with a lot of trees, tight fairways and little water. The key to success on this old trek is shot making. You have to position your ball well if you are going to score. **TJ**

**Course:** Royal Liverpool Golf Club

**Location:** Hoylake, Merseyside, England

**Hole:** No. 12

**Length:** 412 yards

**Par:** 4

**Designer:** Cameron Sinclair

**Course Comment:** If you haven't played the Royal Liverpool Golf Club recently, you may notice a new pond on the left side of the 12th green. It was created not only to help penalize a poor shot but also to establish a natural habitat for the Natterjack toad, which is native to Hoylake. It is also reputed to be Europe's noisiest amphibian, audible over several miles.

# No. ⑫   ROYAL LIVERPOOL GOLF CLUB

The par-4 12th is called "Hilbre" and it's arguably the finest hole on the links — and that's a pretty bold statement. This hole, which plays 412 yards from the championship tees, is a significant dogleg left with plenty of danger for those trying to cut a little off the corner.

There are three bunkers right at the corner and only a big hitter with plenty of stick in his bag should even attempt to carry them.

It's more than 300 yards from the back tees to clear the bunkers and land with a clear, straight approach shot to the green.

Playing this hole in three is a much safer route. Remember, par or even bogey are good scores on this hole. A nice drive to about 250 yards straight down the middle off the tee leaves you an easy second shot to about 80 yards and then a straight look at the green.

To the left of the green is a recently constructed pond — which should be avoided at all costs.

Hoylake lies at the very heart of the history and development of golf in Britain. Built in 1869, on what was then the racecourse of the Liverpool Hunt Club, Hoylake is the oldest of all the English seaside courses, with the exception of Westward Ho! in Devon. **TJ**

**Course:** Monterey Peninsula Country Club (Dunes Course)

**Location:** Pebble Beach, California, USA

**Hole:** No. 12

**Length:** 415 yards

**Par:** 4

**Designer:** Seth Rayner, Charles Banks, Rees Jones

**Course Comment:** This course plays fast and firm, with several holes going uphill and away from the water. Waves batter the nearby shore for a spectacular aesthetic effect; ferocious winds render this a course where the ability to play the game close to the ground is simply crucial.

# No. ⑫   MONTEREY PENINSULA COUNTRY CLUB (DUNES COURSE)

The 12th at Monterey's Dunes Course is both visually stunning and a tough nut to crack. Rees Jones moved the tee back and constructed three fairway bunkers to the left of No. 12 when he revamped it, and removed some trees to expose players to the sparkling Pacific waters. This facelift, combined with an uphill approach, makes this hole play quite a bit longer and tougher than the 1926 original. Its contoured green sports a sharp right fall-off and is marked by two deep, protective bunkers.

Jones put his indelible stamp on the Dunes Course by roughing up its flat, cupped fairways and adding mounding to sharpen already distinct Seth Raynor course lines. The result is tricky greens in a stunning setting.

This course is 18 holes of unparalleled beauty bordered by pine trees and sand dunes. It's a sparkling gem on the Monterey Peninsula — a classic dating back to 1926. **KLL**

**Course:** Bald Mountain

**Location:** Lake Orion, Michigan, USA

**Hole:** No. 12

**Length:** 420 yards

**Par:** 4

**Designer:** Wilfrid Reid, William Connellan

**Course Comment:** Bald Mountain rolls over hilly terrain with tight fairways and an abundance of dogleg holes. The short holes are impressive, including the back-to-back 13th and 14th, both par 3s.

## No. ⑫  BALD MOUNTAIN

No. 6 at Bald Mountain is the hardest hole on the course. No. 15 is the prettiest hole. But No. 12 is the hole people most remember. And with two consecutive par 3s next, it's good practice for the short game.

At 420 yards from the back tees, this dogleg-left par 4 isn't the longest hole at Bald Mountain, but you have to hit your ball straight and long off the tee to have a good shot at the green in two.

There are woods on the left and some trees to the right. The play off the tee should be straight, or you will get a closer look at those trees than you would prefer.

To get to the break in the dogleg, you are going to have to hit it about 260 yards from those back tees.

The green, like most of the greens at Bald Mountain, is undulating. And there are some deep grass bunkers protecting the No. 12 green. There is no true signature hole at Bald Mountain, but there are plenty of memorable holes. And you won't soon forget No. 12. **TJ**

**Course:** Orange County National Golf Center (Crooked Cat Course)

**Location:** Orlando, Florida, USA

**Hole:** No. 12

**Length:** 461 yards

**Par:** 4

**Designer:** Phil Ritson, Dave Harman, Isao Aoki

**Course Comment:** Designed with a distinct links flavor, Crooked Cat's open and flowing design features few trees, and native heather grass in the rough. This design gives the player an experience reminiscent of that found about 3,000 miles to the east in the Scottish Highlands.

## No. ⑫  ORANGE COUNTY NATIONAL GOLF CENTER (CROOKED CAT COURSE)

This course needs to be handicapped again because it's difficult to believe there is a tougher hole in Florida, let alone on this golf course. Many golfers, even the good ones, are going to have to scratch and claw their way around this Crooked Cat beauty.

The No. 2 handicap hole has four sets of tees and the word "easy" doesn't apply to any of them. This hole is hard no matter how far back you hit your driver from.

The hole is named the "Sweep" and it can brush away a good round in a hurry. The idea is to play your first two shots down the left center of the fairway. It's not just good enough to be in the center.

The reasoning is that you want to avoid the water that runs along the right side of the fairway from tee to green. You actually have a nice landing area off the tee, but you need to get some length behind it if you are going to have a good shot to the green. But be careful because the fairway almost disappears — it turns into marsh.

The green rests off to the right side with water right and even in front, depending on the angle you are coming in from. This is a tough shot and you'd better be accurate.

Once on the green, you are far from done. The two-tier green can cause great difficulty. **TJ**

**Course:** Torrey Pines (South Course)

**Location:** La Jolla, California, USA

**Hole:** No. 12

**Length:** 504 yards

**Par:** 4

**Designer:** William F. Bell, Rees Jones

**Course Comment:** No. 12 is the toughest hole at Torrey Pines South Course, which holds the PGA Tour's Buick Invitational each year, and will be the host of the 2008 U.S. Open championship.

# No. 12 **TORREY PINES** (SOUTH COURSE)

This hole is scarily long and a true monster among par 4s — a massive 504 yards from the back tees. Not only does a player have to deal with length on this hole, but there is also a drop of 25 feet from tee to green and it usually plays into the wind.

Off the tee a long, straight drive is required because there are two bunkers on the left side of the fairway, which are in play, and on the right side there are also two bunkers, but unless you really rip it they should not be in play. Also on the left is the beach, which is out of bounds and a really bad shot needs to take place to get there.

The second shot requires a long iron or a fairway wood, so a second consecutive straight shot is needed. The fairway is pretty level, but the approach shot will be to a semi-elevated green, which is protected by bunkers on both the left and right side.

The green has some very high points around the center and back left. The severe slope is on the left and it tends to run to the right, then turn hard to the front. Another slope is found in the center left and it is very slick and runs to the front right side. The green is always fast and a two putt is wonderful at No. 12.

Remember that this is the toughest hole on the course, so a bogey 5 is not a bad score. **GE**

**RIGHT** *Marco Dawson of the USA plays a shot on the 12th hole at Torrey Pines, February 2003.*

**Course:** The Homestead (Cascades Course)

**Location:** Hot Springs, Virginia, USA

**Hole:** No. 12

**Length:** 476 yards

**Par:** 4

**Designer:** William S. Flynn

**Course Comment:** The Homestead's Cascades Course played host to the 2004 NCAA Division I Men's Championship, won by the University of California with a 14-over-par total.

## No. ⑫  THE HOMESTEAD
### (CASCADES COURSE)

No less an authority than the legendary Sam Snead, the first head golf professional at the Cascades Course, said of this William S. Flynn mountain gem: "If you can play here, you can play anywhere." And many of the world's top amateurs and professional golfers have gotten the chance to find out. The Cascades has been the host for numerous top events, including seven U.S. Golf Association championships.

Often called the finest mountain course in the country, the Cascades was built on land so rocky and rolling that at least two architects, including the legendary A.W. Tillinghast, said the land was not suited for golf.

Flynn begged to differ, and in 1923, thanks to the help of 20 tons of dynamite and crews that moved boulders weighing as much as 20 tons, one of Flynn's finest works had been produced amid the splendor of Virginia's Allegheny Mountains.

No. 12 is considered by many to be the best hole in the state of Virginia. The long, narrow par 4 is guarded by a tree-lined ridge on the right and a stream that snakes down the hole's left side. The approach is also difficult, thanks to cross bunkers approximately 90 yards in front of the green and a long, narrow putting surface protected by bunkers on each side. **KA**

## No. ⑫  THE NATURAL

**Course:** The Natural

**Location:** Gaylord, Michigan, USA

**Hole:** No. 12

**Length:** 335 yards

**Par:** 4

**Designer:** Jerry Mathews

**Course Comment:** Pulling into the town of Gaylord with your golf clubs in the back seat is like opening a menu at a world-class restaurant. So many choices. You can have more than one entrée in Gaylord. The Natural doesn't get the attention of Treetops or Garland (a little further down the road), but the Natural is one of the area's most enjoyable tracks to play.

Gaylord, located in northern Michigan, is a golf smorgasbord filled with golf courses. But these aren't your typical golf courses. Each one is special and each one is outstanding. The Natural is just a natural piece of the Gaylord puzzle.

By the time you reach No. 12, you have already discovered that this is indeed a special course. This 335-yard par 4 will only confirm your opinion. You will discover not only a challenging hole but also a fun hole to play. That's why you're here in the mecca of the north in the first place.

Standing on the tee you are on the top of the world facing a 70-foot deep valley that you must carry on your first shot. The target is a severely winding fairway on this dogleg-right hole.

The valley shouldn't come into play unless you hit a really bad shot, but it adds to the beauty of the hole. Hopefully, the fairway comes into play for you, or this hole gets even tougher.

As the green is completely surrounded by trees, cutting the corner leaves you no shot to the putting surface. In other words, play it straight — it's the natural thing to do. **TJ**

## No. ⑫  PUMPKIN RIDGE
### (GHOST CREEK COURSE)

**Course:** Pumpkin Ridge (Ghost Creek Course)

**Location:** North Plains, Oregon, USA

**Hole:** No. 12

**Length:** 444 yards

**Par:** 4

**Designer:** Bob Cupp

**Course Comment:** Ghost Creek has 18 unique holes, each with its own characteristics, making the course fun to play. The five par 3s all have some challenge to them, either in distance, water hazards to carry, and uphill or downhill tee shots.

You can see the proper line from the tee here on No. 12 at this popular and famous Oregon golf course. But what happens if you cut the corner? That's the question raised many times during a summer's day up on the tee box of this 444-yard par 4. Taking the gamble, however, is simply not a high percentage shot. And the reward isn't worth the risk — which is pretty high.

Take a mid-iron and drop a shot down near — but not in — the set of bunkers on the left side of the fairway. This usually works well. Don't forget about the bunkers on the left because there is a bunch of them, and they extend from the break of the dogleg all the way to the green.

And what of the putting surface? A bunker and mound cut into the green, creating a back and front putting surface. Take note of where the flag is and aim for the right level.

Another important reminder here on No. 12: those bunkers and mounds around the green make for a very difficult up-and-down, not to mention what can happen to your score if you knock the ball into the tall grass outside of the bunkers.

Taking aim at par with a safe approach on this hole won't hurt your score or your pride. **TJ**

## No. ⑫ COYOTE GOLF CLUB

**Course:** Coyote Golf Club

**Location:** New Hudson, Michigan, USA

**Hole:** No. 12

**Length:** 494 yards

**Par:** 4

**Designer:** Scott Thackher

**Course Comment:** Like many courses in Michigan and around the United States, Coyote Golf Club has an excellent Web site, which includes discounts and directions to the course.

There are many great holes at this course, located just north of Ann Arbor in southeast Michigan. Many of the club members like No. 18, an excellent finishing hole.

But No. 12, the No. 2 handicap, could be the most impressive hole on the golf course. It's memorable because it never seems to end.

The 494-yard par 4 plays extremely long. Only the few big hitters can take a crack at reaching this hole in two — especially when it's windy, which is quite often on this open hole.

There are some trees along the left side, but they are there to help separate the 12th and 13th fairways. In other words, it's not a thick forest by any means.

There is some water on this hole. It starts to come into play about 100 yards from the green, so be careful with your second shot.

A two-tier green has bunkers behind.

The distance alone gets people on this hole. At 494 yards, it's already a long par 4, but when the wind kicks in, it's even longer. **TJ**

## No. ⑫ RIO FORMOSA GOLF CLUB

**Course:** Rio Formosa Golf Club

**Location:** The Algarve, Portugal

**Hole:** No. 12

**Length:** 395 yards

**Par:** 4

**Designer:** William Mitchell, Joe Lee, Rocky Roquemore

**Course Comment:** Although the course is named after the nearby nature reserve, the course is not actually near the coastal wetland and has only two holes with water hazards.

The 12th is the most visually memorable hole on the Rio Formosa course, the one that will stick in your mind for a long time afterwards. The hole's main feature is a large lake around which the hole sharply doglegs left at a 90-degree angle. The temptation on the tee is to pull out the driver and try to hit a long shot over the water to leave a shorter approach into the green. Of course, that brings the water into play, and many balls end up there.

The conservative play is to hit a long iron off the tee to find the fairway. However, that means having to hit an iron over the full extent of the water. Thankfully the green is quite generous and an accurate approach shot should find the putting surface. Of course the water plays more on your mind since for the previous 11 holes water has not featured, unlike most other courses on the Algarve. Those who do miss the green can end up in one of three bunkers surrounding the putting surface.

The key on this hole is to put the ego on hold and play safely rather than try to blast the ball over the water. The former should reap rewards while the latter can end up resulting in a double bogey. **AT**

## No. ⑫ THE DUNES GOLF LINKS

**Course:** The Dunes Golf Links

**Location:** Rye, Victoria, Australia

**Hole:** No. 12

**Length:** 591 yards

**Par:** 5

**Designer:** Tony Cashmore

**Course Comment:** The Dunes lies on 240 acres of land that was once home to the Limestone Valley Golf Club. The new owners bought it through a liquidation sale in 1994 and then hired Cashmore to redesign the course completely. It opened for play three years later.

Designer Tony Cashmore has said that the 12th at the Dunes is his favorite, and as was the case with several other holes on the course, it required a fair amount of earthmoving to create something special from what was relatively flat and uninspiring terrain.

But you wouldn't know it from looking at it, as the par 5 appears to be as natural as the rest of the links-style layout set in the sand hills of the Mornington Peninsula.

Players must hit a long drive down the center of this lengthy, dogleg right if they want to open up an approach to the hidden green, which lies beyond a sandy expanse reminiscent of the wonderful wastelands of the great Pine Valley in the United States.

From there, the better golfers will need to carry a shot perhaps 150 yards over that stretch, and then hit a short iron to a tough green made of Cobra bentgrass. **JS**

## No. ⑫ WAIKOLOA BEACH (BEACH COURSE)

**Course:** Waikoloa Beach (Beach Course)

**Location:** Waikoloa, Hawaii, USA

**Hole:** No. 12

**Length:** 502 yards

**Par:** 5

**Designer:** Robert Trent Jones Jr.

**Course Comment:** This resort is home to two uniquely different golf courses. While both are set among lava fields and oceanfront, the Beach is more of a resort course while the Kings' Course is more of a links-style design.

Known as "Hemolele," this 502-yard par 5 is one of the more difficult challenges at a place where other "difficult challenges" include getting out of bed after an all-night luau.

It's also a hole loaded with character.

This scenic hole has lava throughout and runs along the Pacific Ocean to a point where views of breaching whales and vistas of the other Hawaiian islands are not uncommon.

The tee box faces the ocean and extends about 250 yards before turning left. From here, you are looking at about 220 yards to a very large green that actually sits a little bit to the right of the fairway.

As you can imagine, there are nice views from several spots on this hole. There is also a traditional Hawaiian fishing spot between the fairway and the ocean — a marker on the fairway tells golfers all about it.

Your second shot requires plenty of length and even more accuracy. The fairway is a little downhill, then comes back up a bit and cuts a little right to the green, which is protected by four bunkers.

That breeze in your face on the tee is nice and warm, but it also means more club.

Opened in 1981 by Robert Trent Jones Jr., the Beach Course was literally carved from the lava flow along the picturesque Anaeho'omalu Bay. **TJ**

## No. 🅬 MACHRIHANISH GOLF CLUB

**Course:** Machrihanish Golf Club

**Location:** Campbelltown, Argyll, Scotland

**Hole:** No. 12

**Length:** 513 yards

**Par:** 5

**Designer:** Old Tom Morris

**Course Comment:** Because of Machrihanish's isolation along the south-west Scottish coast, a U.S. Navy Seals team often trains near here, jumping from helicopters into the chilly waters of Campbelltown Loch for a three-mile, early morning swim.

The Kintyre Golf Club was founded in 1876, but some members felt that name was simply too mundane for such a spectacular layout. So a move was made to change the club's name in 1888 "in consequence of some members preferring the sonorousness of the word Machrihanish."

Golfers fortunate enough to set foot on this isolated Scottish links gem along Scotland's remote south-west shores can certainly understand their reasoning. But in the end, no words are adequate for describing this romantic, exhilarating course.

Machrihanish is a little quirky, no doubt. Its par of 70 is arrived at by an outward nine that includes eight par 4s and only one par 3, and an inward nine that consists of three par 3s and two par 5s (No. 10 and No. 12), which are separated by only one hole.

The par-5 12th, appropriately called "Long Hole," is Machrihanish's longest, and plays to its full length because of a pair of deep, steep-faced bunkers just short of an elevated green that slopes from front to back.

The first two shots are nothing out of the ordinary, but long hitters must be certain they can get home in two. Otherwise, they would be better off laying up and trying for birdie the more conventional way. **KA**

## No. 🅬 INTERLACHEN COUNTRY CLUB

**Course:** Interlachen Country Club

**Location:** Edina, Minnesota, USA

**Hole:** No. 12

**Length:** 541 yards

**Par:** 5

**Designer:** Willie Watson, Donald Ross

**Course Comment:** Bobby Jones won the third leg of his Grand Slam in the 1930 U.S. Open played at Interlachen.

Interlachen's 12th hole is a testy par 5 that requires a perfect combination of power and finesse. The No. 2 handicap hole, No. 12 is a right-to-left challenge that requires a strong drive to reach the turn and avoid woods on the right.

The landing area for the second shot is protected by a fairway bunker on the right, although that side provides the best angle to a tricky, elevated green that slopes severely from back to front and is guarded by bunkers front left.

In the 2002 Solheim Cup at Interlachen, the United States won 8 ½ of a possible 12 points in singles matches to overcome a two-point deficit on the final day and earn a 15½ to 12½ victory over Europe.

Interlachen has also played host to a number of other top professional and amateur events, including the 1930 U.S. Open, won by legendary amateur Bobby Jones, and the 1993 Walker Cup, in which the United States triumphed over Great Britain and Ireland by a 19–5 margin.

This venerable layout will also serve as host site for the 2008 U.S. Women's Open. **KA**

**Course:** Royal Melbourne Golf Club (West Course)

**Location:** Black Rock, Victoria, Australia

**Hole:** No. 12

**Length:** 478 yards

**Par:** 5

**Designer:** Alister MacKenzie

**Course Comment:** In reflecting on the magnificent layout that is Royal Melbourne, perhaps it was Gene Sarazen who said it best when he allowed that with the billions of dollars spent on course construction over the past 50 years, all the architects in the world have not been able to build another Royal Melbourne.

# ROYAL MELBOURNE GOLF CLUB (WEST COURSE)

The members of Royal Melbourne have been very careful over the years about maintaining the integrity of MacKenzie's original design, and there have been only two significant changes in seven-plus decades. One of those came in the late 1940s, when the green on No. 12 was moved back and to the left, adding 33 yards of distance to the par 5.

Change to such a classic may seem anathema to traditionalists, but the consensus has long been that the alteration only added to the quality of this slight dogleg left, which measures 478 yards from the back markers and can be reached in two.

Drives should be hit over the center of the right fairway bunker that can be seen from the tee, and toward a second hazard lying some 300 yards from the tee. The distance, and position, of the tee shot determines what players will do next, but however they approach the green, they must beware of a bunker short and to the left of the putting surface as well as some very difficult rough on that same side of the green.

Anything pushed to the right may well find its way into the only other bunker protecting the pin, a gaping morass of sand that sits center right. Avoid at all costs. **JS**

**Course:** Barsebäck Golf
& Country Club (New Course)

**Location:** Landskrona,
Loddekopinge, Sweden

**Hole:** No. 12

**Length:** 561 yards

**Par:** 5

**Designer:** Ture Bruce

**Course Comment:** Nick Faldo, Colin
Montgomerie and Jesper Parnevik
have all won Scandinavian Masters
at Barsebäck.

**BELOW** *Lee Westwood of England
plays a shot from the rough on the
12th hole at Barsebäck, August 2001.*

**OPPOSITE** *Sven Struver of Germany
tees off on the 12th hole at Barsebäck,
August 2003.*

# No. ⑫ BARSEBÄCK GOLF & COUNTRY CLUB (NEW COURSE)

For some time Barsebäck Golf & Country Club's New Course was a well-known commodity within the European golfing community. The 2004 Scandinavian Masters marked the PGA European Tour's seventh trip to the seaside layout that is located about 20 miles north of Malmo.

Yet few outside Scandinavia knew the course was such a superb stage for high-profile dramatics before the 2003 Solheim Cup. The transatlantic event marked the first time the biennial matches were held in Sweden and the 7,365-yard layout didn't disappoint.

Barsebäck also made for a fitting finale to Annika Sorenstam's historic season. In 2003, she became the first Swedish player since 1945 to play a PGA Tour event, qualified for the LPGA Hall of Fame, and topped her season with a dramatic victory over the U.S. team in her home country.

Barsebäck's par-5 12th was a perfect fit for match play. At 561 yards most players could reach the green in two shots, but the narrow landing area that is guarded on both sides by deep poa annua rough magnified the slightest mistake. Players discovered, however, that reaching the wildly pitched green in two shots was no guarantee of a birdie. **RH**

# No. ⑫  PLAINFIELD COUNTRY CLUB

**Course:** Plainfield Country Club

**Location:** Plainfield, New Jersey, USA

**Hole:** No. 12

**Length:** 585 yards

**Par:** 5

**Designer:** Donald Ross

**Course Comment:** There is more than a touch of history at Plainfield. It was among the first 100 clubs registered with the U.S. Golf Association, and Plainfield's Leighton Calkins created the first handicap method that is still the basis of today's USGA handicapping system.

From the tee, this hole seems pretty straightforward. Yes, it is lined with trees and there is a stream that snakes through the fairway right where you might want to land your second shot. But as far as difficult holes go, this one does not appear to be so.

However, by the time you are finished with the 12th — or, if you're not careful, it is finished with you — you will understand how deceiving first appearances can be.

Club members call No. 12 the "Big One," and it takes two very lengthy shots, accuracy, and a whole lot of luck to reach the green in two. The safe and smart play is to approach it as a three-shot hole. This is not a place to get greedy. The first two shots are important, but if you play this as a three-shotter and throttle back a bit on your first two, you can make this hole playable. Not easy, but playable.

The second shot must land to the left of the creek, which sets up a Donald Ross staple — a green complex that makes or breaks the hole. Even if you've played two good shots, you are still required to hit basically a perfect approach.

Players need local knowledge of this hole in order to succeed, because the approach shot is almost completely blind. You can glimpse a sliver of green, but you cannot see the dangers surrounding it. The green is small, protected by a treacherous ditch on the left and a line of tricky bunkers on the right. Throw in a ridge in the center of the putting surface, and the green keeper can have some fun with pin placements, especially on U.S. Open Sunday.

It is a most wonderful hole on a difficult golf course, which is a most cherished piece of American golf history. To the regulars, Plainfield is known simply as "The Club," and the course is, simply, "The Course." Nothing else needs to be said.

Always pristine in condition and challenging to the end, players rarely tire of playing this gem because it can play differently depending on pin placements, weather conditions, and how your game is going on a certain day. It is at once rewarding, yet penal. Beautiful, yet brutal. **JB**

<table>
<tr><td>

**Course:** Sotogrande Golf Club (Old Course)

**Location:** San Roque, Cadiz, Spain

**Hole:** No. 12

**Length:** 572 yards

**Par:** 5

**Designer:** Robert Trent Jones Sr.

**Course Comment:** Nearby Valderrama was built by the owners of Sotogrande in 1975, and originally was called Sotogrande New before being sold in 1985, redesigned and renamed.

</td></tr>
</table>

## No. ⑫ SOTOGRANDE GOLF CLUB (OLD COURSE)

Sotogrande is part of the so-called Golden Triangle of golf — made up of Sotogrande, San Roque and Valderrama — in the scenic Costa del Sol region along the southern coast of Spain.

Sotogrande, which opened in 1964, was the first European course designed by Robert Trent Jones Sr., and is still considered one of the continent's top layouts. Though it is a private club, visitors are thankfully allotted a few tee times each day, and golfers touring this region would be well-advised to take advantage.

No. 12, Sotogrande's longest hole, begins a fierce finishing stretch that includes water in play on six of the final seven holes — and always on the right-hand side.

Although out-of-bounds looms to the left and a stream to the right, the fairway is relatively generous, allowing long hitters to blast away. A good drive will tempt better players to go for the green in two, but beware. The fairway takes a sharp right just before the green, and the stream widens into a pond in front of the putting surface. Try to blast it too far, and your ball may find an out-of-bounds area beyond the green. **KA**

<table>
<tr><td>

**Course:** Gallagher's Canyon

**Location:** Kelowna, British Columbia, Canada

**Hole:** No. 12

**Length:** 551 yards

**Par:** 5

**Designer:** Billy Robinson, Les Furber

**Course Comment:** Gallagher's Canyon is known internationally as an impressive test of golf, and *SCORE Golf* magazine, a Canadian publication, has ranked Gallagher's Canyon among the best in Canada.

</td></tr>
</table>

## No. ⑫ GALLAGHER'S CANYON

The 18 holes range from quiet woodland glades to absolute cliffhangers on a superb golf course that overlooks Gallagher's Canyon and provides awesome views of Kelowna.

When it comes to choosing top holes on this course, it's tough to top No. 12. It's also tough to make par, let alone birdie.

It might not look like it standing on the hill, but this long par 5 (551 yards from the back tees) slowly heads uphill. The hole starts straight before it takes a slight dogleg left and then doglegs back again to the right.

And forget about any ideas of reaching the green in two shots. It can't be done, so realize that going in.

The best way to play this hole is with a 3-wood off the tee. If you hit that straight, you should be in fine shape for a 4- or 5-iron second shot. This should set you up for an approach shot of around 100 yards.

Now it gets tough.

Your approach shot needs to favor the right side of the green. The green severely slopes from back to front and left to right. It's important to know the pin location.

There is one bunker on the right side of the fairway about 50 yards from the green and two short pot bunkers short right of the green.

Despite being long and tough, this is a pretty golf hole. Enjoy. **TJ**

# Hole ⑬

Thirteen. Superstition aside, this number would seem to have no significance to your round. It does, however, signify that when you step to the 13th hole, you have completed exactly two-thirds of your round of 18.

After No. 12, you truly are in the final leg of your day. A solid score on the 13th often sets you up for a sprint through the finish line.

The wonderful, par-3, 182-yard 13th at Crooked Stick Golf Club in Carmel, Indiana, and the 595-yard monster at The European Club in Brittas Bay, Ireland, point to the diversity of No. 13s. The yardages, pars and challenges may be different at No. 13s throughout the world, but one fact is constant: after the 13th, you are in the homestretch, on the way to the house.

**LEFT** *The 13th hole at Oak Hill Country Club, Rochester, New York, USA.*

**Course:** Pelican Hill
(Ocean South Course)

**Location:** Newport Coast, California, USA

**Hole:** No. 13

**Length:** 121 yards

**Par:** 3

**Designer:** Tom Fazio

**Course Comment:** There are five sets of tees on this par-3 hole and none of them is very long. The championship tees or golds are at 121 yards. The forward tees are at 98 yards.

# No. ⓭ PELICAN HILL
## (OCEAN SOUTH COURSE)

Built across the cliffs of the Pacific Ocean, the Ocean South Course features gently rolling terrain, dramatic, canyon-crossing tee shots, breathtaking views and a series of holes built right along the coast.

Best doesn't necessarily mean long. Remember the old saying that good things often come in small packages. Well, No. 13 at Pelican Hill is small when it comes to yardage but huge when it comes to memorability.

The 13th features two small greens divided by a large bunker and fronted by another. In fact, there is probably more sand than fairway and green combined. The big bunker runs almost the entire way from tee to green.

Although very short, the size of the greens and the diversity of tees create interesting playing angles, which make this a very dangerous hole when played to either green.

From the tees you have the perfect position to view the rocky cliff down to the beach. The green is framed in the background by Newport Harbor and in the foreground by the coastline.

If you are hitting for the left green, avoid going left. Those cliffs are nice to look at but difficult to chip out of. The "right" green does have a little fairway in the front but both of these greens are surrounded by sand. **TJ**

**Course:** The Grove

**Location:** Watford, Hertfordshire, England

**Hole:** No. 13

**Length:** 244 yards

**Par:** 3

**Designer:** Kyle Phillips

**Course Comment:** When playing on a corporate outing at The Grove in 2010, European Ryder Cup captain Colin Montgomerie said it was the "best conditioned course he had played in Europe this year." That should be enough to make a believer out of anyone.

# No. ⓭  THE GROVE

The 13th hole at The Grove is nicknamed Praeneste, from the ancient Greek. Praenestine graves have been found in Greece: they contain stone coffins with rich bronze, ivory, and gold ornaments beside the skeleton. As you might it expect, it is a treasure to play No. 13 at The Grove.

It is a deceptive hole, in that it plays much longer than it appears. Perhaps it is the trees, but whatever the reason, many players find themselves short of the putting surface on their second shot. And that is not ideal when you are supposed to be pulling out the flat stick on shot No. 2.

Of course, when you are playing from the back tees on No. 13, it is a whopping 244 yards, so you have to really have both length and accuracy to be putting for birdie.

There is a landing area to the right front of the green if you cannot make it to the putting surface, but bunkers to the left and to the right protect it. And the fairway, from tee to green, is lined by majestic trees, so don't miss the short grass.

Four bunkers encircle the putting surface, so it is important to stick the green. Fortunately, there is an opening in the front so you can roll your ball up to the green. **JB**

**Course:** Muirfield Links

**Location:** Gullane, East Lothian, Scotland

**Hole:** No. 13

**Length:** 191 yards

**Par:** 3

**Designer:** Old Tom Morris, Harry S. Colt, Tom Simpson

**Course Comment:** When Jack Nicklaus won the British Open here in 1966, he joined Gene Sarazen, Ben Hogan, and Gary Player as the only players to have won all four major championships. Tom Watson won the third of his five British titles here in 1980. In 2002, the most recent of the 15 times the Open Championship has been held at Muirfield, Ernie Els won the Claret Jug.

BELOW *Colin Montgomerie of Scotland putts on the 13th green at Muirfield Links, July 2002.*

OPPOSITE *Ernie Els of South Africa blasts his way out of a bunker onto the 13th green at Muirfield Links, July 2002.*

# No. ⑬  MUIRFIELD LINKS

Muirfield departs from the typical links-style golf course, relying more on rough and bunkers for its defense, but the frequent site of the British Open does not stray from the concept of outstanding Scottish golf.

That's not to say the layout is completely bereft of dunes. A particular example of this is the 13th, which is Muirfield's jewel. The hole is enveloped in dunes, and it makes for a feeling of submersion. Another interesting twist, quite literally, is that the 13th takes a perpendicular turn from the rest of the course. The front nine flows clockwise, and the back counterclockwise, but the 13th seemingly marches to its own drummer, connecting the 12th and 14th with a 180-degree departure from the norm. This change requires more than a simple turn. It also forces the player to alter his perception of conditions, and if the wind is kicking at Muirfield, the conditions are no small consideration.

After the 13th hole, however, the course continues counterclockwise back to the clubhouse. If this doesn't have a dizzying effect on players, then the putting surface just might.

After playing 191 yards uphill and dodging three severe bunkers adjacent to the green, the long, narrow putting surface itself awaits. The green is enormous and fast, and depending on where the pin is placed, can make for some absolutely devious putts. While the bunkers are certainly no bargain, they sometimes present a more welcome shot than being on the green yet facing a downhill putt.

Muirfield is home to the Honourable Company of Edinburgh Golfers, which is regarded as the oldest golf club in the world, having been founded in 1744. The course in its current form opened in 1891 and is consistently rated as one of the finest in the world. It plays 6,801 yards — relatively short by today's standards — but it still presents even the finest players in the world with all they can handle.

Access to Muirfield is either by membership or through petitioning in writing. It is difficult to get on the course, and it is difficult to play. But, in terms of golf tradition, Muirfield — and its gem of a 13th hole — might offer more history of the sport than anywhere on earth. **JB**

**Course:** Oak Tree Golf Club

**Location:** Edmond, Oklahoma, USA

**Hole:** No. 13

**Length:** 171 yards

**Par:** 3

**Designer:** Pete Dye

**Course Comment:** The fairways are nice and spacious but on many holes hitting the fairway isn't enough. With plenty of slopes and rolling hills, you better hit the correct side of the fairway or be faced with a tough lie.

# No. ⑬  OAK TREE GOLF CLUB

There are quite a few scenic holes at Oak Tree, including some stunning par 3s. But No. 13 is at the top of the list when it comes to short holes at one of Oklahoma's premier golf courses.

It's also Oak Tree's shortest. But it's not short on character. It's not short on difficulty. And it's not short on scenery. The 171-yard hole, called "Postage Stamp," is considered one of the "birdie" holes at Oak Tree, but there is nothing easy here. It takes a good iron shot to reach the green and then some eye-on-the-cup putting.

Standing on the tee can be a little scary. On the left side of the green is a creek. Some call it a beautiful creek. Others call it a water hazard, one which offers no room for error because it hugs the left side of the green. There is no fairway or rough or anything to save you if you should go left.

On the right is a deep pot bunker, which can come into play especially when the flag is up front. The green is a little unusual in that it features a very narrow front. And they like to put the flag up there at times.

On a course full of fun shots and spectacular views, No. 13 is as good as it gets. And that's saying something at Oak Tree. **TJ**

---

**Course:** Le Meridien Penina Golf & Resort

**Location:** Penina, Portimão, Algarve, Portugal

**Hole:** No. 13

**Length:** 202 yards

**Par:** 3

**Designer:** Sir Henry Cotton

**Course Comment:** Cotton designed Le Meridien Penina's unique back nine with four par 5s and a par of 38.

# No. ⑬  LE MERIDIEN PENINA GOLF & RESORT

Sir Henry Cotton was the first to see the potential of Portugal's Algarve region as a golf destination, and European golfers — indeed, golfers from around the world — are glad he did. Cotton's foresight in building Le Meridien Penina in 1966 opened the golf floodgates along the Portugese coast, and today it is one of Europe's hottest golfing destinations.

The demanding par-3 13th, which features a green protected by water and a tee set diagonally from the putting surface, was said to be Cotton's favorite hole. Recent renovations added more water around the green, turning it into a small island and making a tough hole even tougher.

The course has played host to nine Portugese Opens, the most recent in 2004, when Miguel Angel Jimenez won by two strokes at 16-under-par 272 despite a three-putt bogey on No. 13 in the final round, the Spaniard's lone bogey in the last 54 holes. Overall, No. 13 had a stroke average of 3.1876 in the PGA European Tour event, yielding only 44 birdies compared with 79 bogeys and 24 double bogeys or worse.

Le Meridien Penina also served as host for the 1976 World Amateur Team Championship, won by Great Britain and Ireland. **KA**

**Course:** Wild Coast Sun Country Club

**Location:** Port Edward, KwaZulu-Natal, South Africa

**Hole:** No. 13

**Length:** 183 yards

**Par:** 3

**Designer:** Robert Trent Jones Jr.

**Course Comment:** Wild Coast serves as host course for the Nashua South African Masters, one of three majors on South Africa's Sunshine Tour.

# No. ⑬ WILD COAST SUN COUNTRY CLUB

One of six par 3s on this American-style layout sculpted out of wild and undulating terrain along the Indian Ocean, Wild Coast Sun's 13th hole, provides little margin for error.

The tee shot must be hit over a ravine that features a spectacular waterfall in the midst of an intimidating gorge filled with jungle-like vegetation. The green is relatively large, but you'd better hit it. Come up short or right, and your ball will be in the ravine, or bouncing down the falls. Hit it long and a back bunker and more thick bushes await. There is a slight bail-out area to the left, with the emphasis on "slight." Making matters worse is that the prevailing wind is in golfers' faces, making judging the ocean breezes and club selection key.

Though the course is only a par 70 and measures only 6,350 yards from the tips, don't be fooled. Native son Hennie Otto captured the title at the 2003 SA Masters, played in windy and wet conditions, with a 1-under 279 total. Roger Wessels led for most of the final round and stood on the 13th tee with a one-shot lead over Otto. But he double bogeyed the hole to hand Otto the lead. **KA**

**Course:** Colonial Country Club

**Location:** Fort Worth, Texas, USA

**Hole:** No. 13

**Length:** 178 yards

**Par:** 3

**Designer:** Perry Maxwell

**Course Comment:** One of the top courses in Texas, Colonial has hosted a PGA Tour event since 1938. The club hosted the 1941 U.S. Open, which was won by Craig Wood.

## No. 🕐 COLONIAL COUNTRY CLUB

Golf fans around the world know this golf course pretty well. Any course that is on television every year, challenging the greatest players in the world, is well-known. But it's one of those courses that a TV screen just doesn't justify.

You can't feel that warm Texas wind sitting in your living room. You need to grab the clubs and play it for yourself. Then you will know what it's like to feel how strong the wind is and understand just how challenging a course like this can be.

No. 13, a par 3, plays 178 yards from the back. And it's all carry. As in all carry over water. The pond can be a little intimidating standing on the tee but shots like these are why we play golf.

It's important to remember that wind, which averages about 15 to 18 mph throughout the course of the year. The wind is usually a factor on every hole at every time of the season, and No. 13 is no different.

What's different is the green. There are two well-defined sections and it's important to land your tee shot on the one hosting the flag stick. The right side is a little larger and a little easier target — so if it's over there, you've caught a little break.

The green is very narrow, only about 25 paces deep and 50 paces wide. There also is a bunker behind the green and two bunkers on the left side.

This is a pretty golf hole and fits in very well with the rest of this spectacular golf course. **TJ**

**BELOW** *Kenny Perry of the USA hits his tee shot on the 13th hole at Colonial Country Club, May 2003.*

## No. ⑬ DEVIL'S PAINTBRUSH

**Course:** Devil's Paintbrush

**Location:** Caledon, Ontario, Canada

**Hole:** No. 13

**Length:** 226 yards

**Par:** 3

**Designer:** Dana Fry

**Course Comment:** Although architect Dana Fry did little earth moving to build Devil's Paintbrush there are plenty of hazards awaiting wayward shots. Players must avoid the stone ruins of a barn in the middle of the eighth fairway while a large mound fronting the par-3 16th obscures nearly every hole location.

Being treeless and swept by an almost incessant barrage of wind, Devil's Paintbrush is just 35 miles from downtown Toronto — but from a golfer's point of view it may as well be clinging to a seaside cliff in Scotland.

The Dana Fry design is fixed upon a Niagara escarpment and has everything a links-style course demands. Hard, fast fairways are framed by fescue-covered hills which turn various shades of brown depending on the season and contrast dramatically with the bright green of the playing areas.

Devil's Paintbrush rounds out its links resumé with an assortment of obligatory blind shots, such as from the fifth tee, and an almost haphazard collection of wooden-banked bunkers.

The par-3 13th hole has been called one of the most intimidating tee shots in golf. Most players will fret over the approach, a 226-yard blast that is demanding even without the ever-present wind. The hole plays along the course's property and out-of-bounds looms right while a deep chasm awaits anything that falls short.

The real challenge, however, may come when the player reaches the green. The two-tiered putting surface is vast and extremely contoured. Only the most accurately placed tee shots assure a two putt. **RH**

**Course:** Harbour Town Golf Links (Sea Marsh Course)

**Location:** Hilton Head Island, South Carolina, USA

**Hole:** No. 13

**Length:** 163 yards

**Par:** 3

**Designer:** George Cobb

**Course Comment:** There are three great courses at The Sea Pines Resort on Hilton Head Island, each with a different feel and flavor. You can't go wrong with any of them, but the best way to make the right choice is to simply play all three.

BELOW  *Hal Sutton of the USA hits out of the pine needles on the 13th hole at Harbour Town, April 2003.*

# No. ⑬  HARBOUR TOWN GOLF LINKS
## (SEA MARSH COURSE)

The Sea Marsh Course is what they like to call "the best of the Lowcountry." Designed in 1967 by George Cobb and revitalized by Clyde Johnston in 1990, the course winds through lush forest and alongside tidal marshes.

At 6,515 yards from the back tees, the course is not considered long, but the fairways are tree-lined and the greens are well bunkered.

While the Harbour Town course gets plenty of attention around the resort and around the world, it's hard to believe there is a better hole on the entire island than No. 13 on the Sea Marsh Course. Standing on the tee, it's as good a golf postcard shot as any you will ever see. There are many memorable holes on the Sea Marsh Course, but you won't forget not only the hole but the moment you first walked on to the tee.

The scorecard calls this a "dramatic par 3" and they aren't kidding. Let's take that postcard for you. There is a large lagoon that cuts into the fairway and rests between you on the tee and the green. The hole seems to have been cut right out of a thick forest as large trees surround the hole and make for a scenic backdrop. Simply a very pretty and, yes, "dramatic-" looking hole.

Forget the small bail-out fairway to the right because to find any success here you are going to have to clear water. It's pretty to look at —

until you have to grab a club. There is a dangerous bunker to the front left between the green and the water. There is another bunker along the right side of the green and another way to the back.

Because of the changing winds and numerous pin placements, you could be going up or down a few club lengths from day to day on this hole. Take note of the wind. The green depth is 33 yards and there are three sets of tees. **TJ**

## No. ⑬ CROOKED STICK GOLF CLUB

**Course:** Crooked Stick Golf Club

**Location:** Carmel, Indiana, USA

**Hole:** No. 13

**Length:** 182 yards

**Par:** 3

**Designer:** Pete Dye

**Course Comment:** John Daly's thrilling major breakthrough at the 1991 PGA Championship is considered Crooked Stick's greatest tournament, but for pure dramatics Lauri Merten's one-shot victory over Donna Andrews and Helen Alfredsson at the 1993 U.S. Women's Open may be the layout's true legacy.

Pete Dye created Crooked Stick Golf Club with a weary eye toward the future. The legendary architect lamented the day even average PGA Tour players were swatting drives well over 300 yards, and most people's idea of a three-shot par 5 was a historical footnote.

To combat this, Dye designed open, inviting fairways but with tee shots that played into steep slopes. The result, at least for the 1993 U.S. Women's Open and 1991 PGA Championship, was a championship course in every sense of the word.

Although long-hitting John Daly won the 1991 PGA, most observers agree it was his touch around the greens, not his grip-it-and-rip-it persona, that proved crucial at Crooked Stick.

The par-3 13th is another example of how Dye endeavored to negate yardage gains. The 13th plays a meager 182 yards but the tee shot is played uphill to a large green and often into the prevailing wind.

Tee shots must carry a hazard to a green that is framed by towering trees left and right and a steep hill behind. Beware a back-right pin placement as the putting surface slopes dramatically toward the back and a long tee shot leaves a player little chance to save for par. **RH**

**Course:** Medinah Country Club
(No. 3 Course)

**Location:** Medinah, Illinois, USA

**Hole:** No. 13

**Length:** 219 yards

**Par:** 3

**Designer:** Tom Bendelow

**Course Comment:** The 1949,
1975, and 1990 U.S. Opens were
held at Medinah and won by Cary
Middlecoff, Lou Graham, and Hale
Irwin, respectively.

## No. ⓭ MEDINAH COUNTRY CLUB
### (NO. 3 COURSE)

The green is very small. You have to carry water. There are bunkers guarding the putting surface. Sound like fun?

Welcome to Medinah's 13th hole on the famous No. 3 Course. At 219 yards from the back tees, you better be able to get it there. If not, move up to one of the other tees (there is one at 173 yards and another at 148) or expect to use a lot of golf balls.

But just getting length behind your drive isn't your only concern on this stunning-looking hole. You need to be aware of the pin placement and the wind direction before selecting your club of choice. All of these factors lead to the basic understanding of "don't be short."

There is a fairly severe slope to the left front of the green which will kick your ball into the water. To the right front is a sand bunker. There are three bunkers in all around the green — one to the back left and one directly behind the green. There also are some trees behind the green to cause problems if you are long.

The two-tiered green slopes steeply from back to front — in other words, toward the water.

Roger Packard (1986) and Bob Lohmann (1986) have done redesigns on Course No. 3. **TJ**

**RIGHT** Hale Irwin of the USA plays on the 13th hole of the No. 3 Course at Medinah, August 1999.

## No. ⑬ HIGHLANDS LINKS

**Course:** Highlands Links

**Location:** Ingonish Beach, Nova Scotia, Canada

**Hole:** No. 13

**Length:** 435 yards

**Par:** 4

**Designer:** Stanley Thompson

**Course Comment:** In signature Thompson style, the 13th green was originally built down into a hollow. However, this punchbowl-like putting surface drained poorly and collected ice during the long Cape Breton winters. The putting surface was rebuilt in the 1960s and is the layout's only non-Thompson green.

Perched on the eastern edge of Nova Scotia, Cape Breton Highlands National Park is a 367-square-mile oasis of hiking trails, ski runs, and fishing coves. The park's primary point of interest, however, is the towering Headland Cliff which rises from the chilly Atlantic waters.

The park's dramatic elevation changes draw thousands of visitors each year. This same topographical signature also inspired Stanley Thompson when he was commissioned to build the park's Highlands Links layout.

Although Thompson took full advantage of Cape Breton's tumbling terrain throughout the layout, few holes on the Highlands Links course feature as much roll and pitch as the 435-yard 13th hole, known as "Laird."

Following a tee shot that must weave its way short of a stand of trees down the right while avoiding more hazards on the left, a player will face a difficult second from an uneven lie. In fact, there's hardly a flat lie to be found on the 13th.

Tee shots are best played to the right-center of the fairway. This sets the stage for an approach over a large mound guarding the front right of the green that will feed shots onto the putting surface. Approach shots short and left will leave a demanding uphill chip to a well-contoured green. **RH**

## No. ⑬ FALCON'S FIRE GOLF CLUB

**Course:** Falcon's Fire Golf Club

**Location:** Kissimmee, Florida, USA

**Hole:** No. 13

**Length:** 394 yards

**Par:** 4

**Designer:** Rees Jones

**Course Comment:** Central Florida vacationers on a budget can save $5-10 by booking tee times online at www.falconsfire.com.

Hazeltine, Atlantic, Ocean Forest, Torrey Pines, Congressional, Bethpage Black . . . championship courses with one thing in common — Rees Jones. Whether it's nurturing an original design or touching up a classic, the talented architect has left his award-winning mark from coast to coast.

Falcon's Fire, a Jones original located a mere three miles outside the gates of Disney World, is a challenging public resort course that typifies the veteran's desire to reward the skilled player without punishing the novice.

Nowhere is the Jones risk-reward philosophy more apparent on this links-style course than the par-4 13th. For long-hitting low handicappers, a solid drive over the water cuts the dogleg right considerably, leaving a wedge shot into the medium-sized green.

Average players who choose to play away from the water, however, must contend with Bunker Hill, a large collection of bunkers that begins near the 150-yard marker on the left side of the fairway and extends to the green.

When avoiding the water beware of playing too much draw on the approach shot as a vast greenside bunker with an intimidating 4-foot ledge awaits. Since all incoming shots will funnel to the front right portion of the green, this downhill bunker shot is all the more intimidating with a hazard as the backdrop. **BB**

## No. ⓭ APACHE STRONGHOLD GOLF CLUB

According to legend, the Apache Stronghold was created by the Indian god Usen as a region abundant with everything the Apache people would need to survive. Guarded by mountains, the Stronghold was a mystical haven in which the Apaches could walk invisibly among their enemies. When this previously uninhabited desert wilderness was made available for a Tom Doak golf course owned and operated by the San Carlos Apache tribe as part of its Apache Gold Casino Resort, its natural beauty and historic treasures were preserved.

Conveniently located 90 miles northeast of Phoenix and 100 miles north of Tucson, this Doak masterpiece fits seamlessly into the desert terrain and is a rare example of golf minimalism in an Arizona desert layout that reaches 3,200 feet above sea level and features rocky valleys, ridges covered by sage and mesquite trees, and majestic views of the distant mountain ranges.

Apache Stronghold's 13th hole is a dogleg right that dares players to knock their tee shots over the bunkers at the corner of the dogleg. An accurate drive will reward you with a wide landing area that offers the chance for a successful second shot.

The tricky approach must carry a valley to a sloping green that's guarded by a bunker at the front right and a ridge at the rear. **KA**

## No. ⓭ THIRTEENTH BEACH GOLF LINKS

It is a good idea for golfers to pause for a moment on the narrow, elevated tee of No. 12 after they have walked through the dunes from the 12th green to that spot, and take in the wonderful vista through the driving chute of this shortish par 4.

And then they need to get serious about the shot they have to hit from that box, for precision is key if they want to get their par. The best play for most is a 3-wood or long iron down the right side of the fairway.

Yes, there is plenty of trouble there, mostly in the form of bunkers that appear some 220 yards from the tee and run the rest of the way down that side to the green. But a well-hit drive to that area can also put people in the best position to approach the tricky three-tiered green, which slopes left to right.

Plus, a drive to that part of the hole all but eliminates the problems on the left, including tussocks and a sandy waste area. **JS**

# No. ⓭ ROYAL OAKS COUNTRY CLUB

**Course:** Royal Oaks Country Club

**Location:** Dallas, Texas, USA

**Hole:** No. 13

**Length:** 475 yards

**Par:** 4

**Designer:** Billy Martindale

**Course Comment:** In February 2004, the *Dallas Morning News* listed the best 18 holes in the state of Texas. Royal Oaks' No. 13 was among the holes listed.

Everyone in Texas who has played Royal Oaks Country Club knows all about No. 13. It's tough and pretty and memorable — although a lot of people who play it would probably like to forget it or at least forget it on the scorecard.

This is a dogleg right that demands a long, faded drive. Not only do you want to be on the fairway, but the best spot to be is on the left side of the fairway. This will give you a much easier — wait, that's a bad word because nothing is easy on this hole — approach shot.

The fairway is lined with trees on both sides so you better keep it straight. At 475 yards from the back tees, this hole is long enough without having to hit out of trees or take a penalty stroke for a lost ball.

Getting some distance off the tee is important because you are going to have a tough approach shot. Your shot to the green must carry White Rock Creek, which runs from 30 to 100 yards out from the green. If you are going to lay up, you still have about 110 yards to the green — and over the creek.

Just beyond the creek is a hill that can easily kick your ball right back into the water, so make sure you get it over the hill as well.

The green is narrow and elevated and tricky, and not an easy target when you are hitting a long iron from 220 yards. There are no bunkers to the front but there is one to the back right. **TJ**

# No. ⑬  PINE VALLEY GOLF CLUB

Pine Valley is often called the most difficult golf course on earth, and it is with morbid fascination that one notes its creator died before Pine Valley was completed. Many quality golfers have been slain by Pine Valley. Certainly it is a coincidence that George Crump died suddenly and unexpectedly in 1918 before the course was finished.

And, triskaidekaphobia aside, one should read nothing into the fact that No. 13 — unlucky 13 — is one of the most demonic holes of all. The 13th offers as stern a test as can be found not only at Pine Valley, but anywhere in golf. Because of its difficulty, however, there can be few more satisfying golf holes in the world on which to succeed.

On the scorecard, this reads as a par 4. But, only the most courageous, the straightest, and the most fortunate of players should think of it as such. Five is a good score here; four is off the charts. The green is invisible from the tee, and requires an uphill drive that must carry a cavernous rut to a plateau of a fairway. You simply must be in the right spot off the tee. If you don't land on the crown, par is virtually unachievable.

The 13th hole, like Pine Valley itself, is a wonderful test of golf from start to finish. However, when discussing No. 13, the conversation centers on the approach shot. This is where the fun begins. It is the ultimate in decision-making. A golfer's ego is bruised if he thinks about laying up on a par-4 hole, but unless you are feeling extremely confident, the lay-up on the safe right side — hoping for a pitch and one-putt for par — is the play. Otherwise, you are forced with an enormous carry shot over ground that can only be described as moonscape — brush, gouged earth, mashed twigs — an unthinkable place to find a golf ball.

Whichever way you decide to play the unforgettable second shot, the green then awaits. It is quasi-Redan — protection up front, sloping to the rear. Because of the surrounding hazards, it is turned into a peninsula of peril. Safety is a welcome, if unlikely, companion. Birdie is rarer still. **JB**

**Course:** Mount Juliet Golf Club

**Location:** Thomastown, County Kilkenny, Ireland

**Hole:** No. 13

**Length:** 433 yards

**Par:** 4

**Designer:** Jack Nicklaus

**Course Comment:** Since the course opened in 1991, there have been several high-profile events played, including three Irish Opens (won by Nick Faldo, Bernhard Langer, and Sam Torrance, respectively).

# No. ⓭  MOUNT JULIET GOLF CLUB

Jack Nicklaus, after playing an exhibition match at Royal Dublin against Seve Ballesteros, was approached by Tim Mahony, chairman of Toyota Ireland, which sponsored the exhibition. Mahony asked Nicklaus if he was interested in designing a new course in Kilkenny. Nicklaus said he might well be, and out of that meeting sprang the existence of Mount Juliet.

Along with the K Club, the opening of Mount Juliet in 1991 is credited with being the start of a modern resurgence of quality golf in Ireland. Among the top courses that followed shortly thereafter were Mount Wolseley, Glasson, Adare, and Esker Hills.

"Mount Juliet is such a magnificent setting for a golf course," Nicklaus said. "I feel proud of the layout and my work here."

The golf course is a fair challenge, and the most challenging on the course is No. 13. Many consider the 10th hole the "signature hole" on the course, but that might be because they are shying away from No. 13, which is the No. 1 handicap hole on the course.

Water is in play on seven holes, including the 13th. The water hazard surrounding the elevated green at No. 13 is beautiful. The green is built up and framed by rough brick, and the hazard below acts as a horseshoe nearly surrounding the putting surface.

A tough hole, a tough course, but a trailblazer in modern Irish golf. **JB**

# NORTH BERWICK GOLF CLUB
## (WEST COURSE)

**Course:** North Berwick Golf Club (West Course)

**Location:** North Berwick, East Lothian, Scotland

**Hole:** No. 13

**Length:** 365 yards

**Par:** 4

**Designer:** David Strath

**Course Comment:** The North Berwick Golf Club is the world's 13th-oldest golf club, second only to St. Andrews for continuous play over the same course.

North Berwick Golf Club's West Course is a unique golf experience, with a variety of holes and obstacles that no club can replicate, although many have tried. Blind shots, stone walls, burns, deep bunkers, contoured greens, and magnificent views of the Firth of Forth and Bass Rock all are found on the West layout, making for a delightful combination of quirks.

The 13th, called "Pit," begins one of the most invigorating and inspiring finishing stretches in all of golf, and can certainly be counted among the innovative challenges unique to North Berwick.

Playing along the beach and the sea, the fairway is innocent enough, but golfers will want to put all they have into their drives to prepare themselves for a delicate approach that will require plenty of finesse.

The narrow green is indeed a pit, protected by a sand dune on the left, mounds on the back right, and — most impressively — by a 3-foot-high stone wall that runs completely across the front and right sides, preventing players from running the ball onto the green and demanding a high shot that lands softly on the putting surface. It's difficult, yes, but even more than that, it's downright fun. **KA**

**Course:** Druids Glen

**Location:** Newtownmountkennedy, County Wicklow, Ireland

**Hole:** No. 13

**Length:** 471 yards

**Par:** 4

**Designer:** Pat Ruddy, Tom Craddock

**Course Comment:** Druids Glen Golf Club opened in 1995 and hosted the Murphy's Irish Open, Ireland's premier golf event and one of the richest on the European PGA Tour from 1996 to 1999. It also was the scene of Sergio Garcia's first professional victory.

OPPOSITE *The 13th hole at Druids Glen.*

BELOW *Colin Montgomerie of Scotland and his caddie cross the bridge on the 13th hole at Druids Glen, April 2002.*

Even though Druids Glen is just a baby, it's already been called the Augusta of Europe. That's a pretty bold statement, but Druids Glen is a pretty bold golf course.

Speaking of bold, take a walk out to No. 13. This is a very unique golf hole with a fairway that is set at an angle. Like hitting a fairway wasn't hard enough in the first place.

Make sure you have your drive on line before teeing off on this 471-yard dogleg left. If you hit it too far to the left, you could run out of real estate. The other side is even worse. Go right off your mark and there is water. Most players will more than likely end up with a lengthy approach across water to a very narrow green.

Draped in the shadow of Mt. Rainier, the 7,100 yard, upscale public course is carved out of 230 acres of second-growth forest and features sculpted, bentgrass tee boxes, fairways, and greens.

With over 60 strategically placed sand bunkers and nine lakes, Druids Glen challenges golfers of all skill levels.

The greens at Druids Glen are near perfect, perhaps the best in Ireland. The layout follows the contours of the natural land. There was no need to move a lot of earth on this course. **TJ**

**Course:** The Homestead
(Cascades Course)

**Location:** Hot Springs, Virginia, USA

**Hole:** No. 13

**Length:** 440 yards

**Par:** 4

**Designer:** William Flynn

**Course Comment:** The Cascades
Course is one of three courses
connected to The Homestead, the
oldest resort in North America.

BELOW *A bunker guards the approach
to the 13th hole at The Homestead.*

OPPOSITE *An aerial view of the 13th
at The Homestead.*

# No. ⓭ THE HOMESTEAD (CASCADES COURSE)

The Cascades Course is a rare gem that was surprisingly almost left uncultivated. According to historians, two designers, Peter W. Lees and A.W. Tillinghast, declared the property unfit for a golf course in the early 1900s. Luckily for The Homestead, it was third time lucky. William Flynn not only claimed a course could be built, but a championship course at that.

After tackling a bear of a par 4 in the 476-yard 12th hole, the Cascades's lucky 13 seems more like a cub. Continuing down a Virginia mountainside the 13th fairway follows the contour of a gurgling stream, gently bending from right to left. Players who favor a draw find this setup appealing to the eye as the fairway's right side is peppered with trees.

Club selection on the approach shot is key as first-time players may be remiss when factoring in the hole's deceptive downhill slope. A collection of bunkers leads up to the green, penalizing mishit shots. On the other hand, players who select too much club will quickly discover that the hole's decline carries through to the back of the green, setting up a difficult uphill return putt.

The 13th may not be a bear, but it still has plenty of bite. **BB**

**Course:** Kawana Hotel Golf Club
(Fuji Course)

**Location:** Ito, Minamitsuru,
Yamonashi, Japan

**Hole:** No. 13

**Length:** 395 yards

**Par:** 4

**Designer:** C.H. Allison

**Course Comment:** The Fuji Course
annually hosts the Japan Golf Tour's
Fuji-Sankei Classic and often
produces the circuit's most low-
scoring finishes. In 2003, Todd
Hamilton took the title with a 17
under total, and Paul Sheehan won
with the same tally a year later
thanks to a third-round 62.

## No. ⑬ KAWANA HOTEL GOLF CLUB (FUJI COURSE)

Imagine Pebble Beach Golf Links' 18th hole. Now picture the venerable par 5 without the sweeping vistas of Carmel Bay. Or what of St. Andrews's "Road Hole" without the St. Andrews Hotel guarding the corner?

Both are sound holes made unforgettable by their history and, to a greater degree, locale.

It is a truth of real estate that rings true in golf architecture as well — location, location, location. And few courses in the world can claim a more appealing address than Kawana Golf Club's Fuji Course.

From the opening tee shot, Mt. Fuji looms ever-present and the player is treated to views of Hatsushima Island, the Pacific Ocean, and a host of ponds, valleys, and woodlands.

Center stage on the Fuji course is the par-4 13th. Although at 395 yards the hole is short by today's standards — only three of the course's other par 4s are shorter — it is a stern test that sports equally impressive scenery.

The tee shot on No. 13 is exacting and also demands almost perfect placement to set up the most forgiving angle to the green. Although well protected by a host of deep bunkers and swales, the 13th's green has one of the course's most accessible putting surfaces and will, if played correctly, yield a birdie. **RH**

---

**Course:** Humewood Golf Club

**Location:** Port Elizabeth,
South Africa

**Hole:** No. 13

**Length:** 446 yards

**Par:** 4

**Designer:** Colonel S.V. Hotchkin,
Donald Steel

**Course Comment:** Humewood
features an abundance of plovers,
otherwise known as "kiewietjies,"
so many of them that one is
featured on the club's emblem.

## No. ⑬ HUMEWOOD GOLF CLUB

Humewood Golf Club, a windswept links layout in the coastal city of Port Elizabeth, plays along Algoa Bay and features undulating fairways, fast greens, and thick coastal bush. It has played host to the South African Open four times and the South African Amateur on numerous occasions. Both tournaments were held there in 1934, only three years after the course was opened for play.

Considered to be one of the most demanding par 4s in South Africa, Humewood's 13th hole is a beast that has been tamed by few. The slight dogleg right must often be tackled by playing directly into a stiff wind, making the hole play even longer, and the fairway is rife with undulations, meaning only a small amount of drives find a level lie from which to hit an all-important approach that has virtually no margin for error. The elevated green has a narrow entrance and is hidden behind a sand dune and further guarded by a waste area on the right, a steep bunker on the left, and thick gorse in the rear.

No wonder South African professional Hendrik Buhrmann is on record as requiring 14 strokes on this hole during a tournament at Humewood. **KA**

Course: Princeville Resort Golf Club
(Prince Course)

Location: Princeville, Kauai, Hawaii,
USA

Hole: No. 13

Length: 418 yards

Par: 4

Designer: Robert Trent Jones Jr.

Course Comment: The Prince is one
of Hawaii's most challenging golf
courses, with a USGA course rating
of 75.3 and a 145 slope. It's also one
of Hawaii's best. *Golf Digest* has
named The Prince Course the No. 1
course in the state.

# No. ⑬ PRINCEVILLE RESORT GOLF CLUB (PRINCE COURSE)

Golf courses on this grand island are what you would expect they would be. Stunning comes to mind. But spectacular is even better.

Princeville Makai Golf Course can play with any on the island. There are three nine-hole layouts here and each one offers some challenging and scenic golf holes. There really isn't a bad hole on the course so just picking off a few notable ones is tough. But No. 13 on the Prince nine stands out. More because it's a little different than many holes on the island.

This demanding 418-yard, par 4 is cut right out of the jungle. You are in the valley of trees and mountains and pure Hawaii beauty on this hole.

A lay-up tee shot is required because of a perfectly placed stream cutting through the fairway about 195 yards out from the white tees or 240 yards from the back tees.

Only a well-placed tee shot will set up the possibility for one of the most difficult and beautiful approach shots of your life. The elusive green is tucked into the corner of a stream created by the cascading waterfall immediately behind.

This will always be one of your favorite holes no matter what your score is. But if you keep it straight and play smart, a 4 on the scorecard will make it even more enjoyable. **TJ**

Course: Elie Golf House Club

Location: Elie, Fife, Scotland

Hole: No. 13

Length: 380 yards

Par: 4

Designer: Old Tom Morris

Course Comment: No. 13 once
was called "the finest hole in
the country" by noted player
and architect James Braid.

# No. ⑬ ELIE GOLF HOUSE CLUB

Sixteen excellent par 4s, only two par 3s and nary a par 5. That is the Elie Golf House Club, a slightly quirky layout along the Firth of Forth, which has remained much the same since Old Tom Morris expanded the layout to 18 holes in 1896.

Unlike many links courses in the United Kingdom, Elie contains few sand dunes and instead is routed on a broad piece of land that slopes to the sea. No. 13 is played along the sandy shoreline to the left, and requires an accurate drive to a twisting fairway lined by thick rough on both sides. That's followed by a delicate approach to the narrow but deep green, which is slightly elevated and set diagonally from the fairway. How strongly the wind is blowing off the sea, of course, can mean a difference of several clubs when selecting what to hit for the second shot.

Elie's eccentricity is exemplified by the opening drive, a blind shot that must be hit over a huge hill approximately 50 yards in front of the tee box. To see if all is clear, golfers must peek through a periscope adjacent to the first tee. **KA**

**Course:** Paraparaumu Beach
Golf Club

**Location:** Paraparaumu Beach,
Wellington, New Zealand

**Hole:** No. 13

**Length:** 408 yards

**Par:** 4

**Designer:** Alec Russell

**Course Comment:** Russell, a
famed Australian architect, first
visited Paraparaumu in 1949 and
commented at the time that this
site could become one of the best
golf courses in the world.

## No. ⑬ PARAPARAUMU BEACH GOLF CLUB

The 13th hole at Paraparaumu Beach Golf Club is like many others on this golf course. It's a classic. But No. 13 is special for several reasons and stands out among 18 standout golf holes.

A good drive on this tough par 4 is essential because your second shot will be the most testing hit of your round. Your drive needs to land safely on the plateau fairway leaving you with the most challenging second shot at Paraparaumu. This is a shot — good or bad — you aren't likely to forget.

The approach shot must carry water to a long, narrow, and elevated green. And don't be a club-length short or your ball will roll right back down to the fairway.

There also is trouble behind and to both sides of the green.

Since this is such an important shot, we offer some advice. Get a good reading on the wind, both direction and speed. It will come into play here and you need to be aware of that.

Paraparaumu Beach Golf Club is a test for any golfer. Even the great ones have found the course challenging. And No. 13 — along with the first five holes, among others — will test your game. **TJ**

**Course:** Salem Country Club

**Location:** Peabody, Massachusetts,
USA

**Hole:** No. 13

**Length:** 342 yards

**Par:** 4

**Designer:** Donald Ross

**Course Comment:** This club was
originally founded in 1895 and has
been listed by the USGA as one of
the first 100 clubs established in the
United States.

## No. ⑬ SALEM COUNTRY CLUB

Before we tee off, let's pay homage to one of the greatest golf course designers the world has ever known, Donald Ross. Why? Because Ross drew up the Salem layout when he was in his prime, and the results are still stunning to this day.

Ross went as far as to say Salem was "one of my purest designs." He was particularly proud of his bunkering, especially on the par-4 13th hole. If you happen to land in one of them, proud might not be the word you use to describe them.

Just how good is this hole? It is estimated that Ross designed more than 7,000 golf holes in his illustrious career. This par 4 is in his top five. This is more of a fact than an exaggeration.

Standing on the tee, you know you are on sacred land. There are plenty of rolling hills and sand traps to avoid, but a friendly bowl-shaped fairway straight ahead. If you miss your target, expect an uneven lie or a sandy lie. There also are plenty of thick woods that can come into play.

The highlight of this hole though is the green. The front part of this green is the only easy hole location. Anywhere else, expect to do some work to earn a par. Ben Crenshaw has called this green one of his favorite in the world. **TJ**

## No. 🔞 **THE FORTRESS**

**Course:** The Fortress

**Location:** Frankenmuth, Michigan, USA

**Hole:** No. 13

**Length:** 443 yards

**Par:** 4

**Designer:** Dick Nugent

**Course Comment:** Nugent threw in a little nugget or curveball on this tough par-4 hole. While it might not be obvious from the tee, the fairway does bend slightly to the left and big hitters should take note because you can drive the ball through the fairway if you're not careful.

The Fortress was designed in 1992, but it reflects characteristics of golf's early Scottish origins. Bentgrass tees, greens, and fairways surround 75 bunkers. Each of the huge greens averages 7,500 square feet.

The par-4 13th hole is a great example of all the holes at The Fortress, with one exception. This hole is tougher. A par here is far more satisfying than elsewhere.

Beware of the prevailing winds here. Normal southwest winds result in a tricky tee shot. And forget your high fade. Hit one of those here and you will end up in the water, which lines both sides of the fairway.

Speaking of the fairway, there isn't much of it. The water hugs both sides with very little rough to save you. This hole is tough because you need to get some good distance off the tee to give you a safer second shot. But you have to hit straight. There is little room for error.

The green is like many at The Fortress. It's big, but doesn't have a lot of undulation to it. However, there are two tiers and plenty of trouble around it. There are bunkers at each corner, including two big ones at the front.

To make things even tougher, there is some long grass near the bunkers. The only real safe places on this hole are the fairway and the green. Everywhere else is trouble. Big trouble. **TJ**

**Course:** Fox Hills (Golden Fox Course)

**Location:** Plymouth, Michigan, USA

**Hole:** No. 13

**Length:** 357 yards

**Par:** 4

**Designer:** Arthur Hills

**Course Comment:** Fox Hills features three 18-hole courses including the Strategic Fox, an 18-hole par-3 championship course opened in 2001 and designed by Ray Hearn. The course is known for its incredible playing conditions.

# No. ⑬ FOX HILLS
## (GOLDEN FOX COURSE)

Arthur Hills has created plenty of memorable masterpieces in Michigan and the Golden Fox can play with any of them. This very popular course just outside of Detroit is as challenging as it is fun to play.

No. 13 is just a terrific hole and a good example of the other 17 holes on the Golden Fox Course. You can see by the yardage (357 yards from the back tees) that this is not a long hole, but it's still a good test of golf.

Your tee shot is straight off the tee and there is some room in the fairway. But don't go left. A large bunker runs almost the entire length of the landing area for your drive, no matter what tees you hit from. That bunker is your No. 1 priority off the tee. Avoid it, and you are in pretty good shape. There is out-of-bounds to the right side of the fairway. Straight is the way to go.

Two sand traps help protect a good-size green. The potential problem here is the large ridge in the green. It makes putting challenging to say the least if you end up on the wrong side. This is one of those holes you can birdie one day and bogey the next. There are no gimmies at the Golden Fox. But if you keep it straight and play smart, you will be rewarded. **TJ**

## No. ⓭ BALTUSROL (LOWER COURSE)

**Course:** Baltusrol (Lower Course)

**Location:** Springfield, New Jersey, USA

**Hole:** No. 13

**Length:** 401 yards

**Par:** 4

**Designer:** A.W. Tillinghast

**Course Comment:** What began as a basic nine-hole layout at Baltusrol, now is two 18-hole championship golf courses, the Upper and Lower courses.

A diagonal creek on the par-4 13th makes this hole a very good and very challenging dogleg. This is no gimmie par, even when the pros tee it up here. Although, nothing is easy at Baltusrol. That's why it's Baltusrol. No. 13 was first an unlucky hole for the great Bobby Jones.

Golf history buffs will remember this hole as the one in which the great Bobby Jones tried for too strong a carry and splashed into the creek, a shot that would end up costing him first place in the 1926 U.S. Amateur.

Then, No. 13 became a lucky hole for him. Jones, despite his setback, admired the layout and respected the challenge. He liked the hole so much that when it came time for him to design Augusta National, he used this No. 13 as his model for Augusta's No. 13.

Long sand traps wrap around both sides of the green, with the fairway running up between them to the green. Speaking of the green, it's almost a perfect circle but has plenty of breaks.

Don't get there in two and three-putt. You will feel like you wasted a golden opportunity. You might even feel unlucky on No. 13. **TJ**

## No. ⑬  ST. LOUIS COUNTRY CLUB

**Course:** St. Louis Country Club

**Location:** St. Louis, Missouri, USA

**Hole:** No. 13

**Length:** 570 yards

**Par:** 5

**Designer:** Charles Blair Macdonald

**Course Comment:** One of the best courses in the state, St. Louis Country Club was founded in 1892 and has been listed by the USGA as one of the first 100 clubs established in the United States.

After playing the unique and memorable No. 12, a par 3 with plenty of challenge, you move on to a memorable and challenging par 5. The 13th hole at the St. Louis Country Club is said to be among Macdonald's best par 5s. And he designed plenty of memorable long holes in his day.

Standing on the tee here, admire the layout before you as the fairway rolls along the tranquil Missouri countryside. It's really how a golf hole was meant to be played.

Then, grab your driver and think left. The last place you want to be on this hole is right. But that's where many end up as the fairway slopes heavily to the right side.

Your second shot must deal with bunkers, which cut into the fairway — and seem to interrupt that so-called tranquil feeling you felt on the tee. Tranquil will not be an adjective you choose to use if you land in one of these bunkers.

And watch out for snakes. As in the snake bunkers that sit between the 13th and fifth fairways.

The green is a challenge and has a false front that easily can return you to the fairway. **TJ**

## No. ⑬  TPC AT THE WOODLANDS

**Course:** TPC at The Woodlands

**Location:** The Woodlands, Texas, USA

**Hole:** No. 13

**Length:** 533 yards

**Par:** 5

**Designer:** Bruce Devlin, Robert Von Hagge

**Course Comment:** This outstanding public golf course in southwest Texas is part of the multi-course complex at The Woodlands Resort, Conference Center and Country Club.

What's striking about this hole, and the other 17 at TPC at The Woodlands, is just how well-maintained they keep this course. And unlike many other TPC courses, this is open to the public and gets a tremendous amount of play.

TPC may really stand for Tournament Players Club, but in this case, it also could stand for Totally Perfect Conditions.

Fred Couples described TPC at the Woodlands as having fairways as good as Augusta National and greens as good as the TPC at Sawgrass.

Before we tee off here on No. 13 it's important to take a look at the green — when you get closer because you can't see the flag from the tee. Note where the flag is on this long and narrow green. The pin placement could mean a difference of two club lengths on your approach shot.

This 533-yard par 5 is a dogleg right with trouble exactly where you would expect it. There is an enormous bunker — remember, everything is bigger in Texas — on the right side of the fairway just at the break. There are also peaks and valleys as the fairway rolls toward the green.

You can reach this green in two if you are able to cut a good part of the dogleg. But there is plenty of trouble around the green if you go off target.

The right side of the green is well guarded and there also is a bunker to the left front of the green. If the pin is in the back right keep the approach shot to the left side. **TJ**

**Course:** Desert Forest Golf Club

**Location:** Carefree, Arizona, USA

**Hole:** No. 13

**Length:** 446 yards

**Par:** 5

**Designer:** Robert "Red" Lawrence

**Course Comment:** Desert Forest is so exclusive, membership is limited to 250 with an estimated waiting period of four years.

## No. ⑬ DESERT FOREST GOLF CLUB

Check your problems at the door when entering Desert Forest Golf Club. All roads leading to Carefree, Arizona, deliver solid drives and a deft putting stroke. At least that's what Desert Forest's 250 members and their guests need to believe to tackle this demanding "Red" Lawrence design.

Carefree, its population close to 3,000, is situated just north of Phoenix where higher elevations offer a tinge of relief from the desert heat.

When Lawrence drew up plans for Desert Forest in 1962, he made a conscious decision to retain the natural peaks and valleys of his desert canvas — a stark contrast to the popular flat courses in the southwest at the time.

Two prominent features missing from this 7,011-yard track are cart paths and out-of-bounds stakes. Players simply make their way along the bentgrass fairways and find the natural desert brush and rock to be penalty enough for wayward hitters.

Nowhere is accuracy more ardently tested than the par-5 13th. Often considered Desert Forest's most difficult hole, this 446-yard layout has a fairway that narrows to 15 yards around the 150-yard marker.

On the second shot, players can scarcely locate the green's front edge as the hole ascends 45 feet to a putting surface protected by three greenside bunkers. **BB**

**Course:** Augusta National Golf Club

**Location:** Augusta, Georgia, USA

**Hole:** No. 13

**Length:** 510 yards

**Par:** 5

**Designer:** Alister MacKenzie, Robert Tyre Jones

**Course Comment:** In the 1937 Masters, No. 13 was a pivotal hole. Byron Nelson had just birdied No. 12, but he still trailed Ralph Guldahl by one shot. Nelson piped his drive, hit a fairway wood to eight feet, sank the eagle putt and went on to win his first Green Jacket. In the years since, a bridge at the tee has been named the Byron Nelson Bridge.

**BELOW** _The tree-lined 13th hole at Augusta._

**OPPOSITE** _Rich Beem of the USA plays an approach shot on the 13th hole at Augusta, April 2003._

# No. ⑬  AUGUSTA NATIONAL GOLF CLUB

Nicknamed "Azalea," after Augusta's most famous flower, the 13th hole represents all that is Augusta National. It is meticulously manicured, laden with approximately 1,600 of the blooms for which it is named, and fair if played properly.

Since 1942, when statistics began being kept, the 13th has played to a cumulative 4.74 stroke average during the Masters. It is considered to be a birdie hole by today's standards. Although, when Phil Mickelson won his first major championship here in 2003, the hole played to 4.9 — so birdies weren't too plentiful.

"Back in my day, you were faced with a decision," said Byron Nelson, winner of the 1937 and 1942 Masters Tournament. "Players of today often hit this green with an iron on their second shot, but in my day even with a good drive you had to decide whether to go for the green or lay up."

The tee shot must be accurate to allow an unimpeded attempt to reach the putting surface in two. The hole doglegs left, so the tee shot must be long enough and to the right portion of the fairway to get around the bend. But if it is struck too purely, or too far right or left, you will be in vegetation. The azaleas may be scenic, but they don't look too beautiful should they envelop your golf ball.

A tributary to Rae's Creek winds in front of the green and four bunkers encase the back side. For years, Rae's Creek was a trickle at best, sometimes even dry. This afforded players unfortunate enough to find the hazard at

least a chance to hit out. For a few years however, the Masters officials decided that the creek should be filled with water, driving up the scoring average and swallowing errant balls.

Lord Byron, for one, was glad when Rae's Creek was transformed to its original form.

"When it was filled with water, it prevented players from going down in there and taking a whack at the ball," Nelson said. "I think that option is part of the charm of the hole, and I'm glad the club changed it."

Little else has ever needed to be changed. Robert Trent Jones Sr., one of the many who have lauded the 13th, called it the best short par 5 ever built. **JB**

**Course:** Oak Hill Country Club (East Course)

**Location:** Rochester, New York, USA

**Hole:** No. 13

**Length:** 594 yards

**Par:** 5

**Designer:** Donald Ross, Robert Trent Jones Sr., George Fazio, Tom Fazio

**Course Comment:** Ernie Els was so taken after playing Oak Hill for the first time, he said, "I'd have to say that Oak Hill is the best, fairest, and toughest championship golf course I've ever played in all my years as a tour professional. It's totally awesome." It was at Oak Hill that Jack Nicklaus won his fifth PGA in 1980 and Curtis Strange successfully defended his U.S. Open title in 1989.

BELOW *Phil Mickelson of the USA hits out of the bunker on the 13th at Oak Hill Country Club, August 2003.*

# No. ⓭ OAK HILL COUNTRY CLUB
## (EAST COURSE)

Since Oak Hill was formally incorporated in 1901, it has drawn superlatives for its challenge and fairness, its beauty, and elegance. From start to finish it is one of America's best, staging countless internationally prominent championships. From PGA Championships to Ryder Cups, Oak Hill is a justifiable host.

When you look at the team of designers who have taken turns tweaking and reworking the course, it isn't difficult to see why the plaudits continue. Donald Ross's original layout was superb, so it wasn't a drastic need for change. Rather, Jones and the Fazios each improved, updated, and added their own personal touches. The result is magnificent.

And nowhere on this hallowed course is there a more challenging setting than on No. 13.

Playing at nearly 600 yards, a brutish approach would seem the call from the tee. However, even the need for length must be tempered. Allen's Creek crosses your path at about 300 yards, so the longest of the long must be careful. As you can see, this is a three-shot hole — a rarity as technology alters a storied game.

The play off the tee is to get as close to the creek as possible without trickling into its penalty. If achieved, a fairway wood is drawn from the bag as more power and precision are called for. The second shot should land on the right half of the fairway to properly set up the third, but the bunkers on that side allow no error.

Approaching the 13th green is no bargain; there are eight bunkers placed to protect it, huge oaks all around, and a back-to-front slope that appears inviting but plays havoc not only with shots that land short of the hole but also with putts that must play downhill.

The well-known Hill of Fame, to the left of the 13th green, gives the best view of the green, as well as of the rest of the course. There is room for thousands of people, and it is a popular place from which to watch tournaments. During breaks in play, fans can peruse the many plaques affixed to trees on the famous hill, honoring prominent members in Oak Hill's history. **JB**

## No. ⓭ TOBACCO ROAD GOLF CLUB

**Course:** Tobacco Road Golf Club

**Location:** Sanford, North Carolina, USA

**Hole:** No. 13

**Length:** 573 yards

**Par:** 5

**Designer:** Mike Strantz

**Course Comment:** Tobacco Road's back tees are called "The Ripper," named not for long hitters but for a tool used by tobacco farmers to till hard soil and break it up for cultivation.

Set in the midst of North Carolina's Sand Hills, a region seemingly created for glorious golf, Tobacco Road Golf Club is a breathtaking property carved out of an abandoned sand quarry and once described as "Pine Valley on steroids." And don't let its lack of length fool you. Though it measures only 6,554 yards from the tips, the slope is an amazing 150, which is one of the country's highest.

Tobacco Road's lack of distance comes mostly from its array of short par-3 and par-4 holes, and certainly not from the par-5 13th, the course's No. 2 handicap hole. The twisting, dogleg-right fairway is lined on both sides with sandy scruff — at some spots wide and deep, at other spots narrow and shallow — requiring accuracy with both the drive and the second shot. It is the partially blind approach to the green, however, that makes this hole.

Approximately three-quarters of the green is hidden behind a natural sand ridge, broken only by one tiny opening to the shallow putting surface, which is only 16 yards deep and has a swale in the middle. The key? Don't place your second shot too close to the huge mound. Instead, leave yourself a full wedge or 9-iron approach so you can fully trust your yardage. **KA**

## No. ⓭ STONEWATER GOLF CLUB

**Course:** Stonewater Golf Club

**Location:** Highland Heights, Ohio, USA

**Hole:** No. 13

**Length:** 625 yards

**Par:** 5

**Designer:** Michael Hurdzan, Dana Fry

**Course Comment:** This great golf course takes great pride in wreaking havoc on the golfer. The course cuts through 178 acres of wooded wetlands, with water on 16 of the 18 holes (and 23 wooden bridges). There are also 70 sand bunkers, including some of the largest and most dramatic imaginable.

This very long par 5 is the No. 2 handicap on a course known for challenges. This is a striking hole and you better be able to strike it. Strike it well. Strike it long. But most importantly, strike it accurately. There is just no room for error here.

The back tees on this hole may as well be in another county. After you come through the tree-lined tee boxes it opens up just a bit to a landing area. It's 324 yards from the back tees to hit it through the fairway and into the marsh.

Your second shot is another challenge. You want to keep it left about 100 yards short of the green. There are two bunkers toward the right side of the fairway about 100 yards and 60 yards short of the green.

You can forget par on this hole if you miss the fairway on either of your first two shots.

Closer to the green, there are two front-side bunkers guarding a small green and a bunker to the back. It's an especially small green when you consider the length of the hole.

A great feature at Stonewater is the number of tee selections. You have five sets of tees to choose from, starting at 456 yards on this par 5. But this hole is challenging from no matter where you tee it up. **TJ**

**Course:** The Dunes Golf & Beach Club

**Location:** Myrtle Beach, South Carolina, USA

**Hole:** No. 13

**Length:** 590 yards

**Par:** 5

**Designer:** Robert Trent Jones Sr.

**Course Comment:** The Dunes Club has staged PGA Tour Q-School Finals, six Champions Tour Championships and the Women's U.S. Open. Among the tournament winners at The Dunes are Ray Floyd, Ben Crenshaw, Hale Irwin, Jay Sigel, Gil Morgan, and Gary McCord.

## No. ⓭ THE DUNES GOLF & BEACH CLUB

In an area stocked (some would say overstocked) with golf courses, The Dunes, with its Southern charm and elegance, is considered among Myrtle Beach's best. The world's finest players have walked the fairways at The Dunes, and have braved its most difficult hole — the majestic 13th.

Robert Trent Jones Sr., was at his visionary best when he designed this masterpiece. The year was 1948, yet somehow Jones was able to see into the future. He made the hole playable for the day, but he also allowed enough area behind the original tees to afford for future adjustment. So a hole that began as a legitimate three-shot effort remains so even today. Technology aside, brute strength considered, it is still near folly to attempt this green in two.

Jones created the Dunes Club in the wake of the Great Depression and World War II. Events of the day had stalled his design work, so he was more than eager to get a shot at plying his craft at the Dunes — an Oceanside property loaded with beautiful oaks and natural undulations.

"Dad loved the place," said Rees Jones, who restored his fathers' greens some 50 years after they were built. "It was one of the great opportunities of his career, and it came at just the right time."

Jones's eagerness to create was evident at The Dunes Club, no more so then at No. 13. The severe dogleg right, which turns sharply around water, tempts the best and toys with others. "Waterloo" is the signature hole at The Dunes Club.

Singleton Lake is a consideration on both the tee shot and the second, and was one of America's earliest use of water as a hazard. There are various ways to get to the green — two or three, at least — and it is the variety that spikes a player's interest. Risk-reward comes into play no matter what route you take to the putting surface, a trait that would become a Jones trademark as post-war business picked up.

The elevated 13th green, which is protected by deep bunkers, is separated into four distinct quadrants, making it essential to be on the same plane as the pin placement of the day. **JB**

No. **13**

**Course:** Fairmont Algonquin

**Location:** St. Andrews-by-the-Sea, New Brunswick, Canada

**Hole:** No. 13

**Length:** 483 yards

**Par:** 5

**Designer:** Thomas McBroom

**Course Comment:** There has been plenty of debate regarding this hole among staff and regulars at this classic golf course by the sea. In 2004, this 483-yard hole became a par 5, changing from a very difficult par 4.

# No. **13** FAIRMONT ALGONQUIN

This dogleg left at one of Canada's jewel courses is a crowning example of risk-reward. It's also one of the more stunningly beautiful holes you will ever play. It's hard to believe after you play the par-3 12th that this course can get any better. But it's only a few steps until you see that it can.

What a view from the tee. Try and play this hole late in the day and take advantage of the amazing sunsets. You can see the lighthouse, the resort's hotel, and the bay as this par 5 makes its way along the waterfront.

From an elevated tee, you have a downhill tee shot that must avoid fescue on the left and water along the right side.

Your second shot is usually a mid-to-long iron with plenty of wind to take into consideration. Your target is not easy to hit. The green is pushed to the right side and if you miss even slightly, your ball can end up in the water. One important factor on your approach shot is to take into account a 20-yard gap between the bunkers and the green. This gap can easily change your perception of how far you need to hit the ball.

There is also a series of three bunkers on the right-hand side that push out from the water. The green itself slopes toward the water and so doesn't offer much in the way of forgiveness.

By all means, enjoy the spectacular views on the 13th hole at the Fairmont Algonquin, but don't forget to keep an eye on your ball. **TJ**

---

**Course:** Champions Golf Club (Cypress Course)

**Location:** Houston, Texas, USA

**Hole:** No. 13

**Length:** 530 yards

**Par:** 5

**Designer:** Ralph Plummer

**Course Comment:** Founded in 1958 by Jack Burke Jr. and the late Jimmy Demaret, Champions has hosted a variety of championship golf events. This course has hosted everything from the Ryder Cup (1967) to the U.S. Open (1969) to the U.S. Amateur (1993) and most recently the 2003 Tour Championship.

# No. **13** CHAMPIONS GOLF CLUB (CYPRESS COURSE)

The 13th at Champions Golf Club is a very fair par 5. An eagle is attainable for skilled players on this hole with two great shots, and a birdie is certainly in play for most players. The tee shot is fairly easy for most and the fairway is wide open. Cypress Creek runs the length of this hole on the right, but only a truly badly played ball will find the creek.

The second shot is where most will have a decision to make: do I go for it or not? If you choose to go for the green, a long, straight shot is required, because if you mis-hit it you will find either the water on the right or one of the four bunkers protecting the green. But if you decided to lay up, be mindful of the bunker on the right of the fairway, about 80 yards from the green. Most players will opt to lay up to give themselves a short wedge in.

The green is very large, very quick, and very fair. There is not a lot of severe break in this green, which allows players the chance to read putts and score well.

The 13th is one of the least-testing, yet most enjoyable par 5s on the course, so bring your best to this hole because it will be a rare chance to get a stroke back from par. **GE**

**Course:** The European Club

**Location:** Brittas Bay, County Wicklow, Ireland

**Hole:** No. 13

**Length:** 595 yards

**Par:** 5

**Designer:** Pat Ruddy

**Course Comment:** According to which Irish publication you read, The European Club has been ranked somewhere between No. 6 and No. 10 in the country.

## No. ⓭  THE EUROPEAN CLUB

When searching for a safe place to be at The European Club's 13th, the answer is at once simplistic yet vexing. There is only one spot where danger does not lurk at every turn. The fairway is your only option. There simply is nowhere to miss.

A simple theory perhaps, but its execution is a bit more complex.

Pat Ruddy, a golf writer-turned-designer who makes Irish projects a passion, put together a stunning combination of panorama and challenge at The European Club. In a country filled with ancient tradition and places to play, it is rather startling that The European Club has achieved such fame since opening in 1992. The course rolls through nearly 200 acres of dunes, cascading along Ireland's east coast about an hour south of Dublin. It is long, narrow, and arduous, but at the same time fair because there are landing areas to be found exactly where they should be. Finding them, sometimes, is another matter.

The course has no blind shots, which ordinarily is an advantage. But when standing on the tee at No. 13, what lies before you might just be better unseen.

The Irish Sea roars to the right, and a series of craggy bunkers await on the left. Gorse and dunes and heather and headache face all who stray from this hole's intended path. Staying the proper course, as essential as it may be, is made extremely difficult by the Irish Sea. It is not only fearsome for balls that come its way, but the wind it provides with such agitating consistency must be contemplated on every shot.

The 13th is the second half of a two-hole sequence that certainly must be considered the highlight of the European Club. Preceded by the par-4 12th, these two holes are the only ones on the course where the beach comes into play.

Sea views are nearly constant throughout the course, but sea play is restricted to Nos. 12 and 13. Players unfortunate enough to find the beach can actually play the ball where it lies, and are even allowed to ground the club in the sand. A concession by the local rule makers, perhaps, but if you're on the beach, grounding the club will not make par much easier to achieve. **JB**

**BELOW AND OPPOSITE** *The 13th hole at The European Club.*

# Hole ⑭

Much like the sixth hole on the front side, the 14th often allows for a slight "let-up," if designers have their way. Architects have put you through a rough stretch on Nos. 8-13, but more importantly, there is a sadistic need, apparently, to loosen you up a touch before the final grind.

Unlike the sixth, however, when you step to the 14th, you are nearing the end of your round. But the urge to point toward the vital finishing holes must be avoided, because even holes not deemed to be among the most challenging on the course must be afforded proper respect, or a round can be ruined at a place that might otherwise offer a chance to thrive.

**LEFT** *Cruden Bay Golf Club, Cruden Bay, Aberdeenshire, Scotland.*

**Course:** Maidstone Golf Club

**Location:** East Hampton, New York, USA

**Hole:** No. 14

**Length:** 140 yards

**Par:** 3

**Designer:** Willie Park Jr., John Park, William H. Tucker

**Course Comment:** Maidstone designer Willie Park Jr. won the British Open twice — in 1887 and 1889 — following in the footsteps of his father, a four-time Open winner.

# No. ⑭ MAIDSTONE GOLF CLUB

Willie Dunn designed a basic course of seven holes for the members at the Maidstone Club in 1894, but it was another Scotsman, Willie Park Jr., who is given credit for Maidstone's majestic back nine, which he laid out in 1922 on a stretch of pristine coastline along the Atlantic Ocean.

The premier one-shot hole in this magnificent group is No. 14, a short par 3 that is both fraught with danger and filled with thrills. It also features one of the best oceanfront golf views on the American side of the Atlantic.

From the tee box, the green sits serenely amid the sandy dunes and thick coastal scrub, an island oasis beckoning golfers' shots to land on its safe surface. Getting there, however, is a supreme test of skill, nerves, and perhaps most of all, club selection, thanks to the ocean winds that often blow hard off the water. Not helping matters are the several tiny bunkers strategically scattered around the green and the small putting surface that slopes slightly from back to front.

Regardless of where your shot lands, however, the brilliant ocean backdrop serves to remind you that you're in one of the game's most spectacular spots, and that this is a moment to be treasured. **KA**

**Course:** Newport Country Club

**Location:** Newport, Rhode Island, USA

**Hole:** No. 14

**Length:** 212 yards

**Par:** 3

**Designer:** William Davis, Donald Ross, A.W. Tillinghast

**Course Comment:** This timeless seaside links course comprises swelling short holes and gently sloped long holes on narrow fairways that make razor-sharp accuracy an absolute necessity for a birdie or par. Not much water comes into play here, but it's dotted with deep bunkers so it's no cakewalk. Newport Country Club was the site of the very first U.S. Amateur Championship and also the first U.S. Open in 1895.

# No. ⑭  NEWPORT COUNTRY CLUB

The 14th at Newport is all about wind.

If you stray left or right, large deep bunkers will suck you in and render par a pipedream — and with the Atlantic breeze at hand, you most certainly will stray. It's one course in the morning, but might be entirely another in the late day when the wind shifts.

It's up to a crackerjack shooter to figure out which way the howling wind will attack while strategizing each shot, and the 14th is possibly the trickiest of all 18 holes — a ball rolling down the open, treeless stretch toward No. 14 can easily fall prey to the 20 mph ocean current.

The hole is heavily protected and viciously slanted. A bunker guards the green's front left and several more protect the back left. This putting surface is severely tilted right-to-left, so approaching from the proper angle holds the utmost importance.

The 14th is one of a handful of hazardous holes on a par-72 course that is known for time-honored tradition and character. Newport Country Club was one of the first golf clubs established in the country and its lavish clubhouse reveals its origin as a retreat for old-money families summering on nearby Bellevue Avenue in Newport, Rhode Island.

Newport Country Club is a century-old tribute to the game's classic American roots. **KLL**

**Course:** Bearwood Lakes Golf Club

**Location:** Wokingham, Berkshire, England

**Hole:** No. 14

**Length:** 176 yards

**Par:** 3

**Designers:** Guy Hockley and Martin Hawtree

**Course Comment:** Bearwood Lakes opened in 1996 and remains a very private golf club. However, subject to limited availability, non-members can enjoy the wonderful surroundings via the club's unique Day Membership program.

# No. ⑭ BEARWOOD LAKES GOLF CLUB

All the holes at Bearwood Lakes provide memories in their own ways, but you could probably narrow the most interesting down to the seven that are situated around 50 acres of natural lakes. Narrowing it down further to the par-4 13th and the par-3 No. 14, which each force carries of a lake, is another task, and deciding finally on No. 14 as the signature hole is this rater's final determination. So, for the sake of argument, let us examine No. 14.

The 14th is a tough, one-shotter that demands carry of a lake to get to the green. Truth be told, the scorecard calls it carrying "the tip of the lake," but it is much more than that. It is more like a good chunk of the lake that must be carried in order to reach the green.

The play is definitely to the left side of the green because there is some room there if you miss, but you can't hug the right side of the green or else you face falling into reeds and other vegetation that grow close to the edge of the scenic water's edge.

Bearwood Lakes winds through stately trees that include oaks, beech, and pines, and there also is a stunning Jacobean-style mansion on the property. So, even if you are not playing well, you can imagine what it might be like to live in such a well-appointed home on a magnificent 18-hole piece of land. **JB**

**Course:** Machrihanish Dunes

**Location:** Machrihanish, Argyll, Scotland

**Hole:** No. 14

**Length:** 167 yards

**Par:** 3

**Designer:** David McLay Kidd

**Course Comment:** Machrihanish Dunes has received Golf Environmental Organization Certification for creating and maintaining a sustainable golf agenda, while fulfilling GEO's required assessments for maintenance and management practices at the most comprehensive eco-levels. Machrihanish Dunes is the first 18-hole golf course in the UK to achieve this prestigious certification.

# No. ⑭ MACHRIHANISH DUNES

Of the 259 acres on which this course sits, only seven acres were disturbed during its construction. Only the tees and greens were shaped. The fairways are just as they were found, only mown shorter. And if you see any black sheep, they are there to help keep the rough at a reasonable height.

As if to accentuate that this golf course is about far more than difficulty and challenge, and rather the setting itself, one of the chosen "signature" holes is no more than the No. 16 index hole on the course.

The par-3 is the third-easiest hole to play, if you are to believe the scorecard, but it is natural wonder of the hole itself, that makes it one of 1001 Holes You Must Play Before You Die. Quite frankly, there are more complex holes. But there may not be too many more "stunningly picturesque, ocean-front par-3s," as the scorecard describes this beauty that sprawls out on a naturally occurring dune.

The dune actually serves as protection from water in the back, and a deep pot bunker is the danger in the front of the expansive, slope-filled green. Water all around, and wind and natural grass make this hole one to remember. Take a par here and you should be proud. And, if you can do so without holding up the group behind you, don't forget to snap a photo or two. **JB**

**Course:** The Carrick

**Location:** Loch Lomond, Argyll, Scotland

**Hole:** No. 14

**Length:** 199 yards

**Par:** 3

**Designer:** Doug Carrick

**Course Comment:** Named after its designer, The Carrick is part of the De Vere Deluxe Resort at Cameron House, a stunning 18th-century lodge on the southwest shores of Loch Lomond.

BELOW *The 14th hole at The Carrick.*

OPPOSITE *A view of the 15th (foreground) and 16th (background) holes at The Carrick, taken from the elevated 14th tee.*

# No. ⑭  THE CARRICK

When a designer has the nerve to allow a course to be named after him, he knows he better come up with a spectacular effort. By all accounts, Doug Carrick did the name proud.

Golfers are taken on a wonderful journey filled with emerald greens and dramatic highland backgrounds, and it all is filled with bunkers and surrounded by one of the world's great water hazards — Loch Lomond itself.

In Carrick's first effort in Scotland, he may have created the country's most memorable round of golf on this 7,086-yard vision of splendor.

And, none of the holes are more postcard-worthy than the par-3 14th, a 199-yard gem that will leave golfers sighing in its wake.

The falling-off-the-cliff No. 14 will undoubtedly become one of Carrick's most talked-about holes. It quite frankly is a photo opportunity beyond any other you will find on the course. The tee is at least 50 feet above the 14th, which the scorecard calls "Tappet Don" on the northernmost point of the property.

Club selection will prove daunting from the tee, depending on the wind, since it can be a guessing game from such an elevation with the winds gusting. Getting anything close to the hole should be considered an accomplishment, and if you should walk away with par on this hole, you should get ready to buy a round at the pub. And don't forget to enjoy a beverage for yourself. You've earned it. **JB**

**Course:** Monterey Peninsula Country Club (Dunes Course)

**Location:** Pebble Beach, California, USA

**Hole:** No. 14

**Length:** 177 yards

**Par:** 3

**Designer:** Seth Raynor, Charles Banks, Robert Hunter, Rees Jones

**Course Comment:** Golfers playing Monterey Peninsula's 14th often have a gallery: visitors tend to congregate at a nearby coastal lookout point off 17-Mile Drive.

No. **⑭** **MONTEREY PENINSULA COUNTRY CLUB (DUNES COURSE)**

Frankly, a decade ago, the 14th hole on Monterey Peninsula Country Club's Dunes Course would not have qualified at all for an appearance in this publication. But a 1998 Rees Jones redesign has maximized its magnificent location on the Pacific Ocean and moved both the green and a new elevated tee box as close as possible to the rocky shoreline and crashing waves. That's something Seth Raynor was prohibited from doing when the course was built in the mid-1920s, because the equipment to drill through rock was not available.

Instead of being a fairly straightforward hole with a marvelous view, the transformation has made this a challenging test, especially from the tips, as golfers are required to carry the rocks and the ocean with their tee shots to a well-protected green.

The putting surface slopes from back to front, and is guarded by a bunker on the front right and another bunker complex further to the left, effectively preventing bail-outs.

Jones's renovation of the 14th has many calling it one of the most spectacular one-shot holes not only on this storied golf peninsula, but anywhere, ranking it right there with the famous No. 7 at Pebble Beach and the scenic 16th at nearby Cypress Point. **KA**

# THE JOCKEY CLUB KAU SAI CHAU GOLF COURSE (NORTH COURSE)

**Course:** The Jockey Club Kau Sai Chau Golf Course (North Course)

**Location:** Sai Kung, New Territories, Hong Kong

**Hole:** No. 14

**Length:** 205 yards

**Par:** 3

**Designer:** Gary Player

**Course Comment:** Kau Sai Chau is on an island that was formerly the site of a large graveyard, and headstones still remain scattered about the course. According to the local rules, players whose golf balls land next to a gravesite are awarded a free drop.

Hong Kong's lone public golf facility, which opened in 1995, has 36 holes located on the northern shores of the island of Kau Sai Chau, in an area that was formerly used by the British Army for shelling practice.

It isn't easy to reach, and must be accessed by boat from the small, scenic fishing village of Sai Kung. The trip, however, is well worth it for golfers. The layout, one of Gary Player's best works, offers challenging holes and amazing views of Sai Kung harbor and the majestic hills on the mainland. In fact, some have even called Kau Sai Chau the second-best public golf course in the world behind St. Andrews' Old Course.

Certainly adding to its reputation is the North Course's 205-yard 14th hole, a spectacular par 3 set on a peninsula that offers splendid vistas of the harbor in the background.

The downhill tee shot must carry almost 200 yards over a rock- and vegetation-filled ravine to a green approximately 40 feet below. The green rises sharply from the ravine, is protected by a large bunker on its left side, and slopes from right to left. Although there is a slight bail-out area to the right, an up-and-down from there is next to impossible. **KA**

**Course:** Gleneagles (Queen's Course)

**Location:** Auchterarder, Perthshire, Scotland

**Hole:** No. 14

**Length:** 215 yards

**Par:** 3

**Designer:** James Braid

**Course Comment:** Gleneagles is host to three fine golf courses, including the PGA Centenary Course designed by Jack Nicklaus. But the King's and Queen's, opened in 1919, represent the finest "classical" golf course design. The Queen's Course has spectacular scenery as well as a challenging layout.

**BELOW AND OPPOSITE** *The 14th hole at Gleneagles.*

# No. ⑭ GLENEAGLES (QUEEN'S COURSE)

Where do you start? The 14th hole is amazing on its own, but as good as it is, it's one of three great par-3 holes on the back nine of the Queen's Course. The 13th and 14th are back-to-back par 3s and the idea works exceptionally well here. They wrap around Loch an Eerie — a scenic loch and islet tucked into a nook of the hills.

Let's start here on No. 14, a 215-yard hole named "Witches' Bowster." The view of the surrounding area from both the tee and green is frighteningly spectacular. The loch, located on the right side of the hole, can be tough to judge. Going up a club length is not a bad idea.

This long par 3 has a two-tier green with a very obvious step in it (a five-foot difference in levels).

The 13th, a 140-yard par 3, again has the loch on the right and a bunker that should not be ignored. The green is large and flat, but can be tricky.

The 204-yard par-3 17th is another hole with sizzling scenery. But don't miss the green here. The fairway scarcely exists, and the ground slopes steeply to the right. Aim your tee shot to the left side of the green. And unlike No. 13, the putting on 17 is difficult, with hills and hollows all over the putting surface. The Queen's Course, in its long history, has played host to some of the world's golfing greats. **TJ**

**Course:** Peachtree Golf Club

**Location:** Atlanta, Georgia, USA

**Hole:** No. 14

**Length:** 179 yards

**Par:** 3

**Designer:** Robert Trent Jones Sr.

**Course Comment:** The greens here at this upscale private golf course are usually fast with plenty of break in them. They are also well protected by our sandy friends, the bunkers.

# No. ⑭  PEACHTREE GOLF CLUB

The golf club might say that No. 4 is the so-called signature hole (a term so subjective that golf courses should consider banning it from the scorecard), but let's face it, any hole with a peninsula green is the one you are going to remember most.

The good news is that it's not very long at all. The back tees come in at 179 yards with two other options: the blue tees (165 yards) and the whites (153 yards). But you might want to bring two balls to the tee just in case.

This course, which opened in 1947 and has long been considered one of the best places to play in the United States, has a little bit of something for everyone. As many as 10 greens are multi-tiered, which provides plenty of challenges on the putting surface.

With 11 ponds and a creek, water can come into play on 14 holes so if you don't hit it straight, bring plenty of balls.

At the risk of sounding silly, this really is one peach of a golf course. **TJ**

**Course:** Kauri Cliffs

**Location:** Bay of Islands, New Zealand

**Hole:** No. 14

**Length:** 230 yards

**Par:** 3

**Designer:** David Harmon

**Course Comment:** Harmon's design philosophy uses the natural features of a site to their maximum potential. He believes in a more traditional architectural style and his designs avoid the gimmicks and passing fads seen in many of today's newer courses.

Perched high above a jagged coastline, you won't find many golf courses as difficult to find or get to than Kauri Cliffs.

And it's not a coincidence that this course stands by itself — all alone, if you will — as a very special and unique place to play this great game.

Try picking out one or two special holes and you could be in for a lifetime of debate. There truly are 18 signature holes on this golf course. Take some of these numbers into account. Six holes are played alongside cliffs which plunge to the sea. Altogether there are 15 holes with views of the Pacific Ocean that span from the Cavalli Islands south to Cape Brett.

The fourth hole is a very risky par-5 that Michael Campbell, the resort's touring pro, calls among the five best par 5s in the world.

There also is No. 15, where the green seems to edge up along the end of the world.

But crossing the crest of the ridge to number 14, the glory of Kauri Cliffs really begins. So you won't soon forget No. 14 as the starting point to golf magic. This is a 230-yard par 3, with 20-knot winds coming in from the right and Waiaua Bay 500 feet below to the left.

It might be the best hole on the course until you get to the next hole. It's all based on perspective. **TJ**

No. **14**    # PINEHURST (NO. 4 COURSE)

**Course:** Pinehurst (No. 4 Course)

**Location:** Pinehurst, North Carolina, USA

**Hole:** No. 14

**Length:** 229 yards

**Par:** 3

**Designer:** Donald Ross, Tom Fazio

**Course Comment:** With its 2000 redesign by Tom Fazio, Pinehurst No. 4 now has the third-highest slope (74.5) and second-highest rating (136) from the tips of the resort's eight courses.

Pinehurst Resort has remained at the pinnacle of American golf not simply because of its vast selection of fine courses — eight and counting — but also its self-imposed mandate to continually update and freshen its remarkable rota. In the last decade, Pinehurst has added the marvelous No. 8 Course by Tom Fazio and had significant remakes to Nos. 2, 4, 6, and 7.

Pinehurst No. 4, originally designed by Pinehurst icon Donald Ross in 1919, was reopened in 2000 by Fazio as a brand new course. Although much of Ross's routing was kept intact, there are several dramatically remade holes, more than 140 new pot bunkers, and an expanded lake that comes into play on the 13th and 14th holes.

No. 14 is something of a rare feature on any of Pinehurst's eight courses: a long par 3 with a forced carry. The water crosses directly in front of the tee box, then continues down the left side and to the rear of the green. Anything left or long is disastrous, with several small bunkers on the right side of the putting surface offering a stiff penalty for those players who attempt to bail out. **KA**

No. **14**    # KAITAIA GOLF CLUB

**Course:** Kaitaia Golf Club

**Location:** Ahipara, Northland, New Zealand

**Hole:** No. 14

**Length:** 180 yards

**Par:** 3

**Designer:** Goldie Wardell

**Course Comment:** 90 Mile Beach Links is the home of the Kaitaia Golf Club located in Ahipara at the bottom of 90 Mile Beach in Northland. The 18-hole course is 40 years old and one of the more popular places to play in New Zealand.

The 14th hole, ranked No. 10 on the course, is an uphill par 3 that plays into the predominantly southerly wind that can make club selection vary as much as four club lengths. That's some big difference, especially when it comes to a par 3 because there is little room for error.

A large green sits on the side of the hill over a deep bunker with a drop-off down to a hazard (actually, a drain), if you manage to select the correct club for the conditions that day and hit the green. The slope and borrow still make this a tricky two-putt. Your reward after this hole is a wonderful view of 90 Mile Beach on the next tee.

This 18-hole course is cut right out of the sand hills adjacent to 90 Mile Beach. Its high rating makes it a favorite with golfers of all levels. There are also two sets of tees for both men and women. But while the course is outstanding it's the views and scenery you won't ever forget. **TJ**

**Course:** Royal Dornoch

**Location:** Dornoch, Sutherland, Scotland

**Hole:** No. 14

**Length:** 460 yards

**Par:** 4

**Designer:** Old Tom Morris, John Sutherland, George Duncan

**Course Comment:** Royal Dornoch is the third-oldest course in the world, behind the Old Course at St. Andrews and Leith.

# No. ⑭  ROYAL DORNOCH

Golf, in its purest sense, is God's game.

The design of Royal Dornoch's 14th hole may be credited to Old Tom Morris and friends but there is a sense, when gazing past the heather, over the dunes and into the 17th century, that Old Tom left the 14th pretty much to its own devices.

Certainly, the legendary Scot decided where to place the green. The tee box was his idea, as well. But to credit an earthly presence with the design of No. 14 is to exhibit a presumption whose inaccuracy would be as great as this hole is natural. The golf club was formed in 1877, but they say golf was played on these grounds as far back as 1616.

"Foxy," aptly named for it crafty requirements, is the only hole at Royal Dornoch without a bunker. Morris seemed to understand that this would be an unwelcome intrusion upon the land. It's as if he backed away, because what was there provided challenge enough. Left of the fairway is a wide expanse of mounds with patches of bent grass and moss. On the right are several grassy promontories jutting out toward the fairway and guarding the right of the green.

It is a double dogleg created by natural dunes. First you go left, and then you go right. Draw, then fade, is the only formula to get you home.

The fairway at No. 14 seems inviting enough, welcoming unknowing players to take a rip and let the ball land anywhere in the short grass. But simply hitting the fairway is not good enough. If your ball rests on the right side of the fairway on "Foxy," you can't see the green. It's hidden behind a sand hill that cuts into the fairway. It is more advisable to cut back on your swing, put a premium on accuracy, and find the left side of the fairway. This way, there is better opportunity to find the green, which is set on a precipice at nearly 90 degrees to the fairway.

Foxy is natural golf at its finest. Yet it requires an unnatural skill to earn par and move on. **JB**

**RIGHT AND OPPOSITE** *The 14th hole at Royal Dornoch.*

**Course:** Celtic Manor (Twenty Ten Course)

**Location:** Newport, South Wales

**Hole:** No. 14

**Length:** 413 yards

**Par:** 4

**Designer:** Ross McMurray

**Course Comment:** The course opened in 2007 and was built specifically for the 2010 Ryder Cup Matches, hence the name "Twenty Ten Course."

# No. ⑭ CELTIC MANOR
## (TWENTY TEN COURSE)

You know that a golf course built specifically to play host to a Ryder Cup Match is something special. Such is the case at Celtic Manor's Twenty Ten Course, where Graeme McDowell bested Hunter Mahan on the final hole in 2010 to give the Europeans a thrilling, 14 ½ to 13 ½ victory. To be able to play on the same course is a thrill indeed.

And to be able to play on what some call the very best hole on the Twenty Ten Course is a thrill of thrills. The course's scorecard says there are "six signature holes," but you can't go wrong with No. 14.

After all, water is in play on the first two shots of the short par 4. If you feel like busting a drive, you can carry all of the water to leave a short wedge to the green. But if you want to be conservative, be safe and lay up between the water hazards for a mid-range shot to the green.

The safe shot off the tee produces a more awkward angle to the green, and makes you go across water again. So, it is risk-reward in its purest form. Rip it off the green and you should have a decent shot at birdie — if you clear the water off the tee. But you had better make the play the way you designed it, or your plan for birdie will soon turn into bogey or more. **JB**

## No. ⑭ CHAMBERS BAY GOLF CLUB

**Course:** Chambers Bay Golf Club

**Location:** University Place, Washington, USA

**Hole:** No. 14

**Length:** 521 yards

**Par:** 4

**Designer:** Robert Trent Jones Jr.

**Course Comment:** Rarely has a course made such a splash so soon. No sooner had it opened in 2007, than it was announced that Chambers Bay would stage the 2010 U.S. Amateur Championship. And, soon after that came the news that it would play host to the 2015 U.S. Open.

Chambers Bay Golf Club is owned by Pierce County. And, get this. Residents of the county get a discount rate. Not a bad perk if you are buying a house inside the county line.

The golf course is situated on an old gravel mine along the Puget Sound, and Robert Trent Jones Jr. worked magic to carve the rock into a links-style layout. Of course, the fact that there is fescue grass from tee to green didn't hurt the cause.

The course, which plays at more than 7,500 yards from the back tees, can strike fear into golfers who don't have their best game at hand. Nowhere is that more evident than at the 521-yard 14th hole. In fact, the par-4 monster goes by the name of "Cape Fear."

First comes the daunting tee shot. From the elevated tees, the player faces an ultra-long downhill dogleg left. The beautiful backdrop does not disguise the two options: safety to the right, which leaves a long second shot; or a risk over a sandy pit to the left to cut the corner on the approach.

Then comes the shot to the sloping green, where a draw becomes the play because the green runs from front right to back left. A draw isn't mandatory, but it definitely makes it easier to hold the putting surface. **JB**

**Course:** TPC Four Seasons Resort &
Club at Las Colinas

**Location:** Irving, Texas, USA

**Hole:** No. 14

**Length:** 409 yards

**Par:** 4

**Designer:** Jay Morrish

**Course Comment:** Sergio Garcia of
Spain snapped a victory drought of
more than two years on the PGA
Tour with his May 2004 victory in
the Byron Nelson Championship.

## No. ⑭ TPC FOUR SEASONS RESORT & CLUB AT LAS COLINAS

PGA Tour players may not clinch victory on the 14th hole during the final round of the Byron Nelson Championship held annually at TPC Four Seasons Resort and Club at Las Colinas. But they can absolutely assure defeat on this difficult par 4 midway through the back nine.

The drive is key: because trees encroach on the right side, the preferred landing area is on the left portion of the undulating fairway, which is the only place golfers are guaranteed to have a clear sight at the green.

But be careful. Go too far left and the tee shot could find the edge of a lake which surrounds the front and left of the green. In addition to carrying the water, the second shot must navigate a few other hazards.

A cedar elm protects the front right of the putting surface, and a pair of bunkers guard the rear, thwarting many golfers who blast their shots long to ensure they make it over the water.

When it mattered most, in the final round of the 2004 EDS Byron Nelson Championship, this hole played as the second toughest with a stroke average of 4.225, giving up only eight birdies compared with 16 bogeys and five double bogeys. **KA**

**Course:** Olympia Fields Country Club
(North Course)

**Location:** Olympia Fields, Illinois,
USA

**Hole:** No. 14

**Length:** 444 yards

**Par:** 4

**Designer:** Willie Park Jr.

**Course Comment:** Opened in 1915,
Olympia Fields Country Club quickly
became the largest private country
club in America. By 1925, the club
had four golf courses, with plans for
a fifth course on the drawing board.

## No. ⑭ OLYMPIA FIELDS COUNTRY CLUB (NORTH COURSE)

Olympia Fields played host to the 2003 U.S. Open, won by Jim Furyk. Here is what Furyk said about No. 14 on the Sunday of his triumph: "I hit a 3-wood off the tee and a pitching wedge to about three feet . . . [The] first thing I said was be right, because I thought it was the perfect golf shot, and I was hoping it would be close. And that pretty much gave me the buffer I needed for the rest of the day. I played solid the rest of the way in."

Standing on the elevated tee you catch a glimpse of a creek cutting across the middle of the fairway. Don't worry. It's only 125 yards in front of you. But what you should worry about is that after the creek cuts in front of your path, it turns toward the hole and heads along the right side of the fairway. For those keeping score, don't go right off tee.

But closer to the green, about 300 yards off the tee, the creek changes its mind again and cuts back through the fairway. Then, it cuts back to the right. In other words, watch out for the snake-like creek.

The tee shot comes through a chute and huge oak trees also guard the fairway. Playing a 3-wood or even a long iron is the best play from the tee. A good tee shot will leave you with a short iron to a shallow green. The greenside bunkers may also provoke the occasional bogey or worse. **TJ**

**Course:** Bandon Dunes (Bandon Trails Course)

**Location:** Bandon, Oregon, USA

**Hole:** No. 14

**Length:** 325 yards

**Par:** 4

**Designer:** Bill Coore and Ben Crenshaw

**Course Comment:** The inland Bandon Trails Course is often overlooked at the Bandon Dunes Golf Resort because of the majesty of its oceanside sisters at the resort, Bandon Dunes and Pacific Dunes. But, that is a mistake because Bandon Trails is still a premier golf course.

No. ⑭  **BANDON DUNES**
**(BANDON TRAILS COURSE)**

Those who think it is wise to visit Bandon Dunes Golf Resort, play the Bandon Dunes and Pacific Dunes courses, and skip Bandon Trails might also think there is wisdom in missing out on some of the most magnificently rugged parkland golf in the world.

Coastal winds are shielded from tall pines on most holes, and the course was seeded with tee-to-green fescue to promote a low-trajectory ground game. Some tee shots land in blind landing areas, and there are sneaky pot bunkers that feed on tee shots and engorge scorecards.

Sounds diabolical, doesn't it? And Bandon Trails' most dastardly locale is the par-14. The views are great from the tee box, and the fairways are wide, so at first, the hole appears to be a cakewalk. But the green has an enormous bunker on the right that makes a 10-paces-wide opening the only way into the putting surface. Unless of course, you can stick the green, and that is not easy with the low-trajectory strategy employed at Bandon Trails. Some call it gimmickry. Others say it is genius. Either way, it takes pure finesse to pull off a par, and you just can't fake it or get lucky. It has to be an A-game skill play, or else you're cooked. **JB**

**Course:** Muirfield Village Golf Club

**Location:** Dublin, Ohio, USA

**Hole:** No. 14

**Length:** 365 yards

**Par:** 4

**Designer:** Jack Nicklaus, Desmond Muirhead

**Course Comment:** The course that Jack built is most famous for playing host each year to the PGA Tour's Memorial Tournament, but it also staged the 1992 U.S. Amateur Championship. Justin Leonard was the 1992 U.S. Amateur champion, thrashing Tom Scherrer 8 and 7 in the final.

# No. ⑭ MUIRFIELD VILLAGE GOLF CLUB

Jack Nicklaus has designed hundreds of golf courses at all corners of the globe. He has been afforded more glorious pieces of property since the land for Muirfield Village Golf Club was acquired in 1966. He has built more magnificent courses. But some stages of his design career have been marked by attempts to accomplish the grandly difficult, and these efforts are sometimes characterized by tricks of the trade that would have been best left in the bag.

But Muirfield Village, among Nicklaus' earliest work, remains among his best. Not tricky, not quirky. Just straightforward tough, beautiful, and challenging golf. Construction on the course didn't begin until six years after the land was acquired and the club wasn't opened until two years after that. But when the official dedication took place with an exhibition between Nicklaus and Tom Weiskoph on May 27, 1974, almost everyone agreed: it was worth the wait.

There are few gimmicks to be found at Muirfield. But that doesn't mean there are not hazards to deal with. Water is an issue on 11 holes, and 69 bunkers are strategically sprinkled throughout. Both sand and water are present on the 14th — a crafty hole that is the shortest par 4 on the course.

The driver should stay in the bag at No. 14. A fairway wood or even a long iron is the play, thus avoiding the concern of dabbling with the danger of a fairway stream. A hole that starts out with such a simple tee shot would hardly seem noteworthy. However, the strategy and delicate nature of this hole start to be revealed when standing over the approach.

The stream that forces temperance off the tee curls around the entire right side of the green. Two lengthy bunkers protect both the front and left. There is but one tiny area behind the extreme back left of the putting surface where a miss isn't penal, but thick grass there complicates matters a bit.

The hazards that suffocate safety on the approach are compounded by the fact that the green is so narrow. It also is long, exaggerating the thin visual. Both the hazards and the economical size of the green make this hole a place where even the best can come unglued. **JB**

**BELOW AND OPPOSITE** *Two views of the crafty 14th hole at Muirfield Village.*

**Course:** Shooting Star Golf Club

**Location:** Jackson Hole, Wyoming, USA

**Hole:** No. 14

**Length:** 523 yards

**Par:** 4

**Designer:** Tom Fazio

**Course Comment:** When the course opened in 2009, Shooting Star was the fifth golf course in Teton County, Wyoming. The area is notable for its elevation, and Shooting Star has perhaps more elevation changes than any of the previous four.

# No. ⓮ SHOOTING STAR GOLF CLUB

You have 50 paces. From one side of the fairway to the other, you have 50 paces. That is the challenge from the championship tee box, which is 523 yards from the green at Shooting Star Golf Club's 14th hole.

Hit that fairway, and you are off to a pretty good start. Miss it, however, and you're bound for sagebrush, bunkers, and some other nastiness that will eat a golf ball and bloat a scorecard. And, Tom Fazio makes sure it's plenty visually intimidating off the tee, leaving all kinds of the sagebrush and snarl between the drive and the landing area.

A good drive on No. 14 will land in a concave area that will attract your ball and hold it in good shape in the middle of the fairway. A solid drive is imperative, and it can set you up for a good shot at the green.

But, if you land in the rough, the tufts of native grass are so thick that it is almost impossible to get a good shot from there unless you are extremely lucky. And there is sand everywhere on No. 14. Everywhere except the fairway, that is. A couple of the many bunkers' fingers extend slightly into the fairway, but for the most part, they are restricted to the rough.

So, stay straight, enjoy the view, and remember those 50 paces. **JB**

## No. ⑭ NEW SOUTH WALES GOLF CLUB

Golfers may well need oxygen tanks in addition to drivers and balls when they step to the tee of No. 14, so breathtaking is the view down the fairway of this short par 4 to the green and Cruwee Cove beyond.

The ideal play is a slight draw that clears the second of two ridges running diagonally across the fairway and uses the hill to run right-to-left on the fairway, setting up a short approach shot to the bunkerless green that slopes significantly from back right to front left. Anything yanked left off the tee — and those closet hookers with fast-beating hearts often find that an issue — will disappear into gnarls of bushes, while drives that are left too far out to the right will make the second shot, to a green that doglegs slightly to the right from that position, considerably tougher.

Shorter is better on the approaches here, as the back of the green falls off markedly, with balls that land long running down the grassy slope and into thick vegetation below.

The tee at No. 14 boasts so compelling a vista that former greenskeeper Peter "Sparrow" Lee frequently came there to sit on the bench and take in the seaside vista. In fact, it was such a favorite spot that the seat is now called "Sparrow's Perch." **JS**

**Course:** Royal Adelaide Golf Club

**Location:** Seaton, Adelaide, Australia

**Hole:** No. 14

**Length:** 446 yards

**Par:** 4

**Designer:** Alister MacKenzie

**Course Comment:** Nine Australian Opens have been held at Royal Adelaide – the first in 1910, the most recent in 1998. Carnegie Clarke, a young Scotsman, won the tournament in 1910. Greg Chalmers shot an even-par 288 to win the 1998 Australian Open, followed by runners-up Stuart Appleby and Peter Senior at 289.

# No. ⑭  ROYAL ADELAIDE GOLF CLUB

Australia is a continent laden with golf history, where the lore of the game is of utmost importance. Tradition, however, was forsaken just a bit when a new championship tee was added to the par-4 14th hole at Royal Adelaide Golf Club.

Standard hazards such as bunkers and rough are prevalent at No. 14, but there also is a hazard that strays more than a tad from the norm. A set of railroad tracks, previously behind the tee box before the hole was lengthened, now cross between tee and fairway. Certainly, the tracks don't come into play, but technically, they are now part of the course.

Making the tracks that bisect No. 14 even more unusual is the fact that Alister MacKenzie was called in for a redesign in 1926 specifically to take the tracks out of play. He did so, but golf technology forced the hole to be lengthened in order to maintain its challenge, so the tracks are back in.

Supposing you don't strike your tee shot off the side of a passing train car, there are more standard hazards waiting. A 248-yard drive is necessary to carry a cluster of seven bunkers on the right — the first four are small and steep, followed by a grouping of three cavernous, large craters.

Another problem encountered not only on the slight dogleg-right 14th, but throughout the layout at Royal Adelaide, is the thick rough made of gnarly grass. Depending on the length, this grass can make returns to the fairway harrowing and almost eliminate full swings to the green.

Bunkers are again a problem on the second shot at No. 14, which must be played through a small gap in a group of pines. The green is elevated, and three bunkers provide protection — two on the right and one on the left. A large swale to the front of the green, and a smaller one on the left squeeze your opportunity for safety.

The 14th is a microcosm of Royal Adelaide's challenge — in the words of MacKenzie, "a delightful combination of sand dunes and fir trees, a most unusual combination even at the best seaside courses." **JB**

## No. ⑭ WALNUT LANE GOLF CLUB

**Course:** Walnut Lane Golf Club

**Location:** Philadelphia, Pennsylvania, USA

**Hole:** No. 14

**Length:** 337 yards

**Par:** 4

**Designer:** Alex Findlay

**Course Comment:** Walnut Lane features 10 par-3 holes, has no par 5s, and its longest par-4 test is a mere 370 yards. It measures just 4,509 yards from the tips.

Great golf holes aren't necessarily limited to top-ranked courses. Walnut Lane Golf Club, a quirky municipal layout in Philadelphia, is a perfect example. The par-62 layout was designed by Alex Findlay in 1940 and has changed little since.

Despite the course being jammed into a small plot of greenery in the city's Wissahickon Valley Park — where it resides amid football and soccer fields as well as walking, dirt-bike, and horse trails — Findlay was able to come up with several clever holes that he tucked away amid the rolling hills and valleys.

In addition to the uneven lies, golfers often find themselves hitting from hazards on the eight par-4 holes, as undulating greens and deep bunkers provide further challenges.

An example of Findlay's trickery at Walnut Lane is No. 14, a 337-yarder which swings hard left and soars up a hill to a green perched on a ledge.

The twisting, turning fairway is lined by trees on the right and slopes from right to left toward a chasm filled with more trees. Many golfers are tempted to hit a driver and cut off as much of the dogleg as they can, but beware: a hook can — and often does — lead to a high number. **KA**

## No. ⑭ PASATIEMPO GOLF CLUB

**Course:** Pasatiempo Golf Club

**Location:** Santa Cruz, California, USA

**Hole:** No. 14

**Length:** 426 yards

**Par:** 4

**Designer:** Alister MacKenzie

**Course Comment:** Opened in 1929, this Santa Cruz landmark was one of the last courses MacKenzie designed before dying at age 63. This difficult course is a natural wonderland featuring steep barranca, especially on the back nine.

As you stand on the tee of this 426-yard par 4, it doesn't look too difficult. Then you see your ball disappear into a grassy swell that wanders down the left side of the fairway. Don't go left on this hole. Unless of course you don't want to see the green on your second shot. It always helps to have a target you can see.

Your second shot will be difficult enough. And often from an uneven lie. The key here is to get the ball in the air because you are going to have to carry some large oak trees which extend into the fairway from the right side. Take aim at the left side of the green, not only to avoid the trees, but also to stay out of a large sand trap hugging the right of the open, flat putting surface.

The tip of the day on this hole comes on the approach shot. The best shot to this green is often a fade as that takes the bunkers on the right out of play.

This green is slightly downhill front to back, which can help those trying to run up your approach shot.

Alister MacKenzie used to live just off this golf course. **TJ**

**Course:** Portmarnock Golf Club

**Location:** Portmarnock, County Dublin, Ireland

**Hole:** No. 14

**Length:** 385 yards

**Par:** 4

**Designer:** G. Ross, W. Pickerman

**Course Comment:** The celebrated golf writer, Bernard Darwin, was prompted to comment: "I know of no greater finish in the world than that of the last five holes at Portmarnock."

**BELOW AND OPPOSITE** *Two views of the 14th at Portmarnock.*

## No. ⓮  PORTMARNOCK GOLF CLUB

Portmarnock Golf Club is located on a small peninsula which extends itself just briefly southward into the Irish Sea. This unique course is surrounded by water on three sides and laid out in a "serpentine" fashion.

Why is this course unique? No two successive holes play in the same direction so you can forget about up and down golf.

No. 14 is a slight dogleg left that requires a good tee shot in order to have a good angle at the green on your approach shot. There is a small bunker along the left side of the fairway, and you need to hit the ball about 247 yards to set up in a good spot for a go at the green.

There are two bunkers short of the green in the fairway, so don't be short on your approach shot. And while we are on the subject of bunkers at Portmarnock, it's a good idea to avoid them at all cost on all of the holes, not just No. 14.

The green is rather long and narrow with one of these bunkers guarding the right side.

Enjoy the great views of Ireland's Eye and Lambay Island — but do not allow yourself to be distracted. **TJ**

## No. ⑭   **METACOMET COUNTRY CLUB**

**Course:** Metacomet Country Club

**Location:** East Providence, Rhode Island, USA

**Hole:** No. 14

**Length:** 448 yards

**Par:** 4

**Designer:** Donald Ross

**Course Comment:** At the time Metacomet was founded in 1901, it was fashionable for New England golf clubs to select Native American names. Metacomet was a great Indian Chief of the Wampanoag tribe, a friend of the Pilgrim settlers of the 17th century.

Metacomet's original course was made up of just six holes, and when the club was first founded it had no plans for a clubhouse. Members simply met under an old grape arbor and hung their clothes on a nearby hickory branch before it was determined that more suitable accommodations were needed. The layout was eventually expanded to nine holes, then moved to its current location next to Narragansett Bay in 1919.

The first course there was designed by Leonard Byles, but Metacomet's members soon hired Donald Ross to redesign its 18 holes in 1924. The new course opened in 1926, and its layout remains much the same today.

No. 14 is Metacomet's No. 2 handicap hole and is the longest hole on Metacomet's back nine, which plays to a par 34 and contains no par 5s. A pair of hills plays a key role in golfers' chances for success on this hole.

A strong tee shot will make it past a huge crest in the fairway to a flat valley behind another large mound. That leaves golfers with a blind approach to an undulating green that is protected by a pair of bunkers on the front left, and steep slopes on the right and rear. **KA**

# No. ⑭    TROON GOLF & COUNTRY CLUB

**Course:** Troon Golf & Country Club

**Location:** Scottsdale, Arizona, USA

**Hole:** No. 14

**Length:** 440 yards

**Par:** 4

**Designer:** Tom Weiskopf, Jay Morrish

**Course Comment:** Because this course is located in the hills around Scottsdale, watch out for some serious elevation changes. This course is as challenging as it is beautiful.

There are great shots, and fun shots. Your tee shot on this 440-yard par 4 at the Troon Golf and Country Club is a great, fun shot.

Most above-average golfers will have no trouble hitting the landing area, but if you do miss it, say goodbye to your golf ball. Your tee shot must carry a canyon that sits between the tee and the landing area. It's only a 130-yard carry to find the grass, but you have to do more that simply pull out a driver and rip it.

The canyon is also on the other side of the landing area. Anything over 250 yards and your ball is gone. So you have to use a club that gets you close to 250 yards, but not over.

Named "Cliff" — for obvious reasons — No. 14 forces you to hit a good second shot as well as a tee shot. The approach shot is downhill to a well-protected green. There is a large bunker along the right side and another bunker to the front right of the putting surface. **TJ**

# No. ⑭    DRUIDS GLEN

**Course:** Druids Glen

**Location:** Newtownmountkennedy, County Wicklow, Ireland

**Hole:** No. 14

**Par:** 4

**Length:** 399 yards

**Designer:** Pat Ruddy, Tom Craddock

**Course Comment:** The 400-acre Druids Glen Estate and Woodstock House date back to the early 1600s and have had a number of prominent owners, including the Wentworth and Tottenham families. Woodstock House now serves as an elegant clubhouse for the course.

Situated a half hour south of Dublin in the heart of County Wicklow, Druids Glen Golf Club is nestled between the Irish Sea and the magnificent Wicklow mountains, and is considered by many to be one of Ireland's finest parkland courses. The course is steeped in Irish history, and the 12th hole features an ancient Druid's altar.

The 14th hole is a dogleg left that requires a tee shot over water to a narrow fairway protected by trees on both sides of the landing area, with fairway bunkers on the left and right coming into play for long hitters who hit a driver off the tee. There is little advantage in flirting with the bunkers, so choose a club off the tee that will allow you to make it over the water but lay up short of the sand. That leaves an uphill approach to a sloping green guarded by a pair of bunkers at the front.

Druids Glen, which opened in 1995, played host to the PGA European Tour's Irish Open from 1996 to 1999, with Colin Montgomerie capturing back-to-back crowns in 1996–97 and Sergio Garcia earning his first tour victory in 1999 at the age of 19. Druids Glen also served as host to the Seve Trophy in 2002. **KA**

**Course:** Fancourt Country Club
(Links Course)

**Location:** George, South Africa

**Hole:** 14

**Length:** 361 yards

**Par:** 4

**Designer:** Gary Player

**Course Comment:** Andre and Helene
Pieterse became the owners and
in 1987 they decided to transform
their country house into a hotel
and golf estate; the Fancourt Hotel
opened in grand style in March 1989.

BELOW *Tiger Woods of the USA
putting on the 14th green at the
Links at Fancourt, November 2003.*

# No. ⑭ FANCOURT COUNTRY CLUB
## (LINKS COURSE)

The Links Course is one of four golf courses at Fancourt Hotel and Country
Club Estates and played host to the President's Cup in 2003.

Designed by Gary Player, the Links at Fancourt presents undulating
windswept terrain, and dune-style landscape, and is the only such course in
South Africa. Player took a previously flat piece of land and transformed it
into a traditional links course by moving in 916,000 cubic yards of dirt.

Named "Wee Wrecker," this 361-yard par 4 is a terrific golf hole. There is
some drama off the tee. You need a good shot with your driver if you are
going to par this hole. If you can knock it out on the fairway with a little
distance in your swing, you will be rewarded with a short pitch into a very
small green surrounded by dunes.

This is one of the most picturesque holes on the golf course.

Here's what Gary Player says about the course: "It looks as if it's always
been here. I could swear I was in Scotland at times, because the holes
themselves are like holes in Scotland." **TJ**

**Location:** Saint-Germain-En-Laye, France

**Hole:** No. 14

**Length:** 445 yards

**Par:** 4

**Designer:** Harry S. Colt, Charles Alison

**Course Comment:** Its proximity to Paris makes St. Germain a wonderful place to play golf during the day and experience the finest in French culture after the sun sets.

# No. ⑭  ST. GERMAIN GOLF CLUB

What can you say about a man who convinced someone with a medical degree to abandon medicine and go into golf-course design? An unusual scenario, to be sure, but such was the case when Harry S. Colt managed to persuade a young Alister MacKenzie to lay his hands on the land.

As the world of golf quickly found out, MacKenzie was a genius. And certainly the same universe that appreciated MacKenzie owes a debt of gratitude to Colt. He was a British legend, much revered by the time he brought his craft to France. Saint Germain Golf Club is yet another example of Colt at his best. And the par-4 14th is the pinnacle of a course that was a real showcase for his art.

When it was designed, back in the 1920s, this hole had a linksy feel. But many, many years of unchecked tree growth have transformed the hole into something it was not meant to be.

It remains a solid golf hole, but you wonder what Colt and his partner Charles Alison would think if they could see it today. What was once a wide open hole now has become smothering. The trees are indeed lovely, but their intrusion is unintentional. Yes, the hole is much more difficult than it used to be, but the seven fairway bunkers on either side now seem like an afterthought. You can hit out of sand; but those trees, those intruding trees.

The fairway is shaped by mounds on either side and given urgency by the thick fescue in the rough. If you hit the fairway off the tee, it is fairly straightforward the rest of the way. There are no bunkers around the green, so you can either play a runner into the hole or hit a soft approach. **JB**

**Course:** Shoal Creek Golf Club

**Location:** Birmingham, Alabama, USA

**Hole:** No. 14

**Length:** 379 yards

**Par:** 4

**Designer:** Jack Nicklaus

**Course Comment:** This is a scenic golf course, and one of the best views of the area comes at the elevated tee on this par 4. Pull out your driver and a camera when you reach the tee.

## No. ⑭ SHOAL CREEK GOLF CLUB

When you're as good as Jack Nicklaus, it's easy to design a golf course up to your very high standards of difficulty. But Nicklaus does realize that not everyone — well, almost no one — can play the game the way he once did.

The perfect example of this is No. 14 at Shoal Creek, one of his legendary designs. This 379-yard, dogleg-right par 4 gives you that elevated feeling. The tee is a good 50 yards above the fairway and offers stunning views of Double Oak Mountain.

The fairway in front of you is also a nice postcard. The tees are set back in the trees with a nice view to look at. Mr. Nicklaus makes you hit a tough tee shot, although the reward will be a fairly easy finish. It's not an easy fairway to hit, with a big lake to the left side and bunkers on both sides. Keeping it straight — and dry — is the goal here.

Considered one of the few "birdie" holes at Shoal Creek, No. 14 features a testing green, which has a 30-degree angle from right to left.

There are much tougher holes here, but there are few that offer such a scenic view of one of the state's prettiest locales. **TJ**

---

**Course:** Klub Golf Rimba Irian

**Location:** Irian Jaya, Indonesia

**Hole:** No. 14

**Length:** 383 yards

**Par:** 4

**Designer:** Ben Crenshaw, Bill Coore, Rod Whitman

**Course Comment:** Klub Golf Rimba Irian was the first golf course outside the United States designed by the noted design team of Ben Crenshaw and Bill Coore.

## No. ⑭ KLUB GOLF RIMBA IRIAN

With its unique and spectacular location in Indonesia's easternmost province of Irian Jaya, which is part of New Guinea, Klub Golf Rimba Irian is set in the midst of jungle-like terrain which originally was an Amungme tribal lowland swamp.

The course itself, a Ben Crenshaw and Bill Coore design that opened in 1996, has been cut out of a lush rainforest that is home to countless species of birds, reptiles, snakes, and exotic plant life, much of which golfers will observe during their rounds.

The par-4 14th hole, aptly given the moniker of "Boelen's Python," winds through the rainforest like a snake that is about to catch its prey — in this case, the unsuspecting golfer.

The sharp dogleg-left hole features a stream with steep banks that curves down its entire left side, as well as a large bunker that rests in the middle of the landing area for most tee shots.

A drive that lands just to the right of the bunker is most ideal, as it sets up the preferred angle to the green, which is well guarded by trees on the left, the stream on the left and rear, and bunkers on the right. **KA**

**Course:** Clearwater Bay Golf & Country Club

**Location:** Clearwater Bay, Hong Kong

**Hole:** No. 14

**Length:** 345 yards

**Par:** 4

**Designer:** T. Sawai, A. Furukawa

**Course Comment:** Clearwater Bay Golf & Country Club played host to the Omega PGA Championship, the season-ending Asian PGA Tour event, from 1995 to 1998.

BELOW AND OPPOSITE *The 14th hole at Clearwater Bay.*

## No. ⓮ CLEARWATER BAY GOLF & COUNTRY CLUB

Located on the breathtaking Clearwater Bay peninsula and surrounded by the waters of the South China Sea, Clearwater Bay Golf Club — one of Hong Kong's most exclusive — offers splendid views of the eastern approach to Hong Kong Harbor.

Clearwater Bay, which was designed by a pair of Japanese architects and opened in 1982, measures little more than 6,100 yards from the tips, so length is usually not the issue here, although precision and accuracy most definitely are.

One example of this is the signature 14th hole, a short dogleg right that bends around a rocky cliff that slopes to the sea. The tee shot offers an enticing gamble to golfers, daring them to take their drives out over the rocks and leave nothing but a short chip onto the green. Adding to their dilemma are potentially stiff ocean winds, as well as fairway bunkers on the left side that can frustrate players who aren't careful when they choose to take the longer, more conventional route. Even if the drive lands safely, the short approach offers no guarantees as the green is guarded on the left by bunkers, and its right side juts perilously close to the cliff's edge. **KA**

**Course:** Cape Kidnappers

**Location:** Hawke's Bay, New Zealand

**Hole:** No. 14

**Length:** 348 yards

**Par:** 4

**Designer:** Tom Doak

**Course Comment:** If you haven't heard of Cape Kidnappers, you haven't been paying attention. This is simply one of the best. It's one of the must beautiful places not only in New Zealand, but on earth.

# No. ⑭ CAPE KIDNAPPERS

Don't be fooled by the distance. When you see 348 yards on the scorecard, it's easy to start thinking birdie. You can keep the big driver in the bag and still have a short approach shot to the green. How tough can a 348-yard hole be? You are about to find out.

Despite the shortcomings, ie. the length, this could be the toughest par 4 on the course. A par here isn't often par for the course. Take great caution with your tee shot. Tom Doak's suggestion is to "pick a safe line off the tee and aim 10 yards to the left of it, because any hint of a fade will not carry to the fairway."

And he's not kidding.

It doesn't get any easier at the green. There is a deep pot bunker to the front left of the putting surface and a steep, steep drop right off the back. Your ideal approach shot is to the far left. Just make sure you have enough club or you could be in the pot bunker.

The surface, both the green and fairway, is very firm, and, like all of the holes at Cape Kidnappers, wind is a big factor.

Let's go back to Doak for one last tip.

"Be especially careful around the green, as the pot bunker has a gravitational pull far greater than its size," he said. **TJ**

## No. ⑭ VAIL GOLF COURSE

**Course:** Vail Golf Course

**Location:** Vail, Colorado, USA

**Hole:** No. 14

**Length:** 416 yards

**Par:** 4

**Designer:** Ben Krueger

**Course Comment:** You have to love a golf course that plays well with all levels of golfers. Take hole No. 14. There are five sets of tees ranging from the black diamonds (416 yards) to the red juniors (284 yards).

Opened in 1963, this course has more scenery worth recording than a digital camera's memory can handle. Let's face it, all the courses in this area have spectacular views, but the Vail Golf Course can play with anyone in the landscaping business.

The mountain-style course offers spectacular views of Gore Creek; you'll need to avoid hitting your ball into any of the beaver ponds.

Also avoid hitting your ball left of the fairway on No. 14 — you could be all wet or in the trees. This somewhat dogleg left is as good as it gets here and equally as challenging.

You need to get some length behind your tee shot in order to have an easier time with your approach shot — but keep it straight. The green is elevated so take that into account when selecting a club. But don't be short because you have to clear Gore Creek in order to hit green.

A shot left of the green will normally find the green because of an embankment that often kicks the ball onto the putting surface. But there aren't many other breaks on this hole. **TJ**

## No. ⑭ CHAMPIONS GOLF CLUB (CYPRESS COURSE)

**Course:** Champions Golf Club (Cypress Course)

**Location:** Houston, Texas, USA

**Hole:** No. 14

**Length:** 437 yards

**Par:** 4

**Designer:** Ralph Plummer

**Course Comment:** The Cypress Course has hosted numerous PGA Tour events and is known for its enormous greens. While the average size of greens on Tour is 6,000 square feet, putting surfaces at the Champions Club are around 10,000 square feet.

To fully appreciate the legacy of this Texas track, one must become familiar with the pair of "Champions" who made it possible. Champions Golf Club is the brainchild of two prominent PGA Tour professionals, Jack Burke Jr. and the late Jimmy Demaret.

Demaret became the first man to slip on three green jackets when he won the Masters in 1950. Six years later Burke triumphed at Augusta and the PGA Championship to earn "Player of the Year" honors.

So it's no accident that these two accomplished players would design a course suited to host some of golf's most revered championships. Since opening in 1959, the club has held the Ryder Cup (1967), U.S. Open (1969), U.S. Amateur (1993), and multiple PGA Tour Championships.

Massive greens, generous fairways, and over 70,000 trees highlight this 7,200-yard, par-71 layout, and the par-4 14th is no exception. From the back tees, players drive through a shoot of trees. Overhanging limbs on the left side of the fairway encourage players to aim middle right off the tee.

The second shot is made difficult by a pond that guards the left side of a green that's 57 yards deep. A trio of bunkers surrounds the remainder of the putting surface which slopes toward the water. **BB**

**Course:** Congressional Country Club
(Blue Course)

**Location:** Bethesda, Maryland, USA

**Hole:** No. 14

**Length:** 439 yards

**Par:** 4

**Designer:** Devereux Emmet,
Robert Trent Jones Sr., George
Cobb, Rees Jones

**Course Comment:** Tom Lehman's
bid to overcome Ernie Els at the 1997
U.S. Open was derailed with a bogey
on Congressional's tough 14th hole.

# No. ⓮ CONGRESSIONAL COUNTRY CLUB (BLUE COURSE)

Congressional Country Club has long been a spot for Washington's elite to hobnob. It has also served as a gathering place for the world's elite golfers, and has always seemed to produce worthy champions in some of the game's most prestigious events.

Congressional's Blue Course has been the site of two U.S. Opens (1964 and 1997, won by Ken Venturi and Ernie Els), a PGA Championship (1976, Dave Stockton), and a Senior U.S. Open (1995, Tom Weiskopf), and it also played host to the PGA Tour's Kemper Open for seven years (1980–86, with Greg Norman and Craig Stadler taking two victories apiece and Fred Couples winning once).

That history is thanks in part to a strong contingent of par-4 holes such as No. 14. Although the landing area for drives is relatively generous off the tee when compared with the rest of the course, the right side is guarded by a group of fairway bunkers. The second shot must then be played uphill to a well-protected green with trees and a trio of bunkers on the front right, and another bunker back left.

It's no wonder Venturi bogeyed Congressional's 14th hole three times in four rounds in the 1964 U.S. Open. **KA**

**Course:** Shinnecock Hills Golf Club

**Location:** Southampton, New York, USA

**Hole:** No. 14

**Length:** 447 yards

**Par:** 4

**Designer:** William Davis, William Flynn, Howard Toomey

**Course Comment:** The 2004 U.S. Open was the most recent of four of which have been held at Shinnecock Hills. The others were in 1896, 1986, and 1995. The American national championship was also held here in 1986 and 1985.

**BELOW AND OPPOSITE** *Retief Goosen of South Africa plays a bunker shot on the 14th hole at Shinnecock Hills Golf Club, June 2004.*

# No. 🄭  SHINNECOCK HILLS GOLF CLUB

The 14th at Shinnecock has been called the perfectly routed golf hole. It follows a natural valley and rolls upward to a green that is not hindered by man-made mounding. Cleanliness, crispness. It is a pristine hole if there ever was one.

That doesn't mean it's without nastiness along the way. The fairway is absurdly tight at points, yet that's where you must be if there's any hope for success. To the left is a collection of bunkers seemingly placed at random all the way down the rough, yet somehow situated in spots that your golf ball seems destined to find. If you stray left and happen to avoid the bunkers, you might get lucky enough to have a shot to the green, but luck would have to play an enormous role. If you miss the fairway right, there isn't enough good fortune in the world to secure rescue. It's ugly, it's deep, it's thick, and it's brown. Don't go there, or bogey is your best.

The wind makes the narrow fairway seem nearly impossible to find. This truly is a hole that takes luck. Hit the perfect golf shot off the tee, and if you get an unexpected gale, your hopes at par virtually vanish. And this is if you hit it pure.

The 14th is an original — unfettered by the need to update or redesign. How much fun it must have been for William Davis and William Flynn. Can you imagine the two designers' reaction upon first glance of a valley so perfect for a golf hole that it seemed to be the intent of its creator? "Thom's Elbow," it is called, after Charlie Thom, who came to Southampton in 1906 when he was 25 and worked as pro here for more than 50 years.

There is no shortage of history here. It weaves in among the fabric of the holes at Shinnecock, as does the rough, the wind, and the danger.

The 14th green is slim, but its depth offers an inviting target. You must be straight on this hole. At 447 yards, it is meaty for a par 4, but not unreasonable. So accuracy is your ticket. If you leave it at home, par is a fantasy. **JB**

## No. ⓮ **OLD WARSON COUNTRY CLUB**

**Course:** Old Warson Country Club

**Location:** St. Louis, Missouri, USA

**Hole:** No. 14

**Length:** 360 yards

**Par:** 4

**Designer:** Robert Trent Jones Sr.

**Course Comment:** Opened in 1954, this classic American golf course is one of the best places to play in Missouri. The fairways are tree-lined and many of the greens are big targets, but with plenty of undulation.

The words Robert Trent Jones and masterpiece go together like Lennon and McCartney. The Old Warson Country Club is *Hey Jude* — copies of this classic will never sound quite as good as the original.

No. 14 is a hole that hits the high notes. This is one of those holes where it is easy to make a three but just as easy to make a six.

The key is not to take this for granted.

The short par-4 begins from an elevated tee with a challenging shot. It all comes down to your drive on this hole. Hit your tee shot well and you're on your way to a three. Mess it up and a six becomes a real possibility.

That big lake in front of you is the problem. It's 230 yards to clear it off the tee. That's a big hit for some people. You can bail out a little to the right but trees will block your second shot. There also is water down the left side and bunkers on both sides of the fairway.

The green is long and narrow with a bi-level on the back two-thirds. Make sure you have your line before you stroke the putter. Three-putts are possible here. **TJ**

## No. ⓮ **THE BALTRAY**

**Course:** The Baltray

**Location:** Baltray, Drogheda, County Louth, Ireland

**Hole:** No. 14

**Length:** 332 yards

**Par:** 4

**Designer:** Tom Simpson

**Course Comment:** Also known as County Louth Golf Club, Baltray is situated four miles from the historic town of Drogheda at the mouth of the River Boyne with the river to the south and the Irish Sea to the east.

Named "The Cup," this 332-yard par 4 is considered short no matter what country you play golf in. But whatever language you speak, memorable is the word you need to use in describing this gem.

Considered the best hole on the course, No. 14 is known for tempting the big hitters. And more often than not, tempting them into a six instead of a four. It's a hole the big hitters can reach from the tee. But it's also a hole where you can find plenty of trouble.

In 1985 the numerical order in which the holes were laid out was slightly altered to accommodate a new starting position. Other than that, little has changed from 1938 when Tom Simpson laid out this terrific track.

In 1993, the firm of Donald Steel and Company undertook a course upgrade under the guidance of Tom MacKenzie, himself a fan of Simpson's work. The changes, although minimal, have had a significant impact on the course, and with the addition of some new tees Baltray now measures over 7,000 yards, thus bringing it in line with the modern game. **TJ**

**Course:** Yeamans Hall Club

**Location:** Hanahan, South Carolina, USA

**Hole:** No. 14

**Length:** 430 yards

**Par:** 4

**Designer:** Seth Raynor

**Course Comment:** Often regarded as one of the better courses in South Carolina, this throwback golf course is known for deep bunkers and tree-lined fairways.

# No. ⑭  YEAMANS HALL CLUB

There are times when a golf club changes the golf course for the sake of change. Or because members complain. Or because they think it's the right thing to do. Many times it's a mistake. Look at some Donald Ross classics that have been destroyed by poor judgment.

But few courses have gone through as dramatic a redesign as Yeamans Hall. The good news is that the change wasn't only good, it was also necessary. In May 1998, the club hired Tom Doak to bring the course up to par. In just five months, Doak tore up the Yeamans Hall greens and had the course back open.

Take a poll of the members on which hole is their favorite and No. 14 is certain to garner some votes. It's also one of the most demanding — who says members like their course soft?

Your approach shot is the key. In fact, this could be the most difficult shot you hit all day. Because of a ridge in the landing area, you are often required to hit from an uneven stance. The green is perched up on a shelf with a 12-foot bunker on the left side.

Putting here can also be nerve-racking — like most of the greens, nothing is a gimmie.

Although change has been good for the course as a whole, No. 14 is one of the original holes dating back to the course's opening in 1925. **TJ**

**Course:** Oakland Hills Country Club (South Course)

**Location:** Bloomfield Hills, Michigan, USA

**Hole:** No. 14

**Length:** 473 yards

**Par:** 4

**Designer:** Donald Ross, Robert Trent Jones Sr.

**Course Comment:** Ben Hogan won the 1951 U.S. Open by shooting a final round of 67, after which he was quoted as saying "I am glad I brought this course, this monster, to its knees." The name, "The Monster" has been with the course ever since.

OPPOSITE *Sergio Garcia of Spain hits his tee shot on the 14th hole at Oakland Hills, September 2004.*

# No. ⑭ OAKLAND HILLS COUNTRY CLUB
## (SOUTH COURSE)

You want an example of a "Monster" hole, look no further than this 473-yard par-4. Let's face it, there isn't an easy hole on this golf course for most average or even above-average players. But if you can get past No. 14 without a six or seven ending up on the scorecard, consider yourself lucky.

At 473 yards, this is a wonderful and testing downhill par 4. It's also the No. 2 handicap hole.

The landing area is located just past a slight rise in the fairway. The green surface is attractive and challenging, running away from the hole. It is protected in front by three bunkers, two left and one on the right.

There are four sets of tees at Oakland Hills. From the closest tees, the reds at 422 yards, the hole becomes a par 5 and the No. 8 handicap.

No. 14 is considered one of the "Magnificent Seven" holes at Oakland Hills which the *Detroit News* said could determine the outcome of the 2004 Ryder Cup. In the event it was the European team who managed to tame "The Monster," beating the American team by 18½ to 9½ in the 35th Ryder Cup. According to his son, Robert Jr., the masterful course designer Robert Trent Jones, who was hired to toughen the course for the 1951 U.S. Open, would have been well pleased with his work. **TJ**

**Course:** Long Cove Club

**Location:** Hilton Head, South Carolina, USA

**Hole:** No. 14

**Length:** 417 yards

**Par:** 4

**Designer:** Pete Dye

**Course Comment:** What a memorable golf course Long Cove Club is. Water and swamp come into play on almost every hole and it's difficult to pick one that stands out — because they all stand out.

# No. ⑭ LONG COVE CLUB

This spectacular par 4 is guarded down its entire length on the left by the marsh. By the time you reach No. 14 you will know all about the marsh. Who knows, you may have lost a ball or 10 in the marsh by this point in your round.

There is more room to the right than appears off the tee on this rather severe dogleg left, but a bail-out lengthens the second shot considerably. And if you are in the rough, hitting the green on two becomes a very, very tough challenge.

There is a little ridge in the middle of the fairway. Your ideal shot is to get past the ridge and find the middle or left side of the fairway. But hitting anything left is a little risky or marshy.

Bunkers protect the green both short and long on this No. 2 handicap hole. This is one of those "be happy with par" holes. Some might consider themselves lucky if they have the same ball by the time they're done.

There is a magnificent view from the No. 14 green, which makes it all worthwhile. **TJ**

## No. ⑭   CHERRY HILLS COUNTRY CLUB

**Course:** Cherry Hills Country Club

**Location:** Englewood, Colorado, USA

**Hole:** No. 14

**Length:** 480 yards

**Par:** 4

**Designer:** William Flynn

**Course Comment:** Jack Nicklaus won his second U.S. Senior Open title at Cherry Hills in 1993 by edging Tom Weiskopf, a fellow Ohio State alum.

When Cherry Hills was selected to host the 2005 U.S. Women's Open, it only added to the club's long list of highlights. When the best women in the world gather in Englewood, Colorado, to compete next July, it will mark the first time an 18-hole layout has hosted the United States Golf Association's foursome of high-profile events: U.S. Open (1960), U.S. Women's Open (2005), U.S. Senior Open (1993) and U.S. Amateur (1990).

Arnold Palmer's comeback at the 1960 Open is probably the most revered moment in Cherry Hills's history. Palmer drove the green on the opening par 4 to set up a final-round charge that would see him triumph over Ben Hogan and Jack Nicklaus.

Of course, watching Phil Mickelson become the first left-hander ever to win the U.S. Amateur couldn't be seen far behind this event on a Cherry Hills highlight reel.

What William Flynn's course lacks in distance (due to the high altitude), it makes up for in accuracy. The course's small, fast greens place a premium on accuracy and control.

Still, don't expect to pull a Palmer on every par 4 at Cherry Hills.

At 480 yards, the 14th hole is the longest par 4 on the course with trees lining both sides of the fairway. The second shot, however, shortens the hole as the fairway runs downhill to a medium-sized green. Water lines the left portion of the green and runs a quarter of the way behind the putting surface, while two greenside bunkers sit on the right side. **BB**

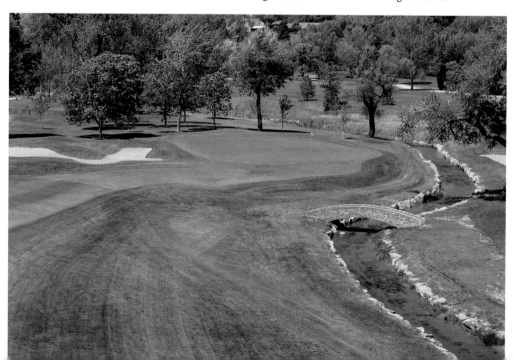

**Course:** Forest Highlands Golf Club (Meadow Course)

**Location:** Flagstaff, Arizona, USA

**Hole:** No. 14

**Length:** 603 yards

**Par:** 5

**Designer:** Tom Weiskopf, Jay Morrish

**Course Comment:** In the 2003 Golfers Choice Awards, Highlands Links retained its gold ranking as "Best Course" with *SCORE Golf*'s readers. In the interim year 2002, Highlands Links was ranked by *SCORE Golf*'s panel of Canadian golf experts as the best public course in the country.

# No. ⑭ FOREST HIGHLANDS GOLF CLUB (MEADOW COURSE)

Forest Highlands is home to two outstanding golf courses, the Canyon Course and the Meadow Course.

The Meadow Course is the newer of the two layouts and typically has smaller greens than its sister course. And there is also more water on the Meadow Course. However, the trade-off comes at the tee, where the Meadow is considered to be a little bit more forgiving.

Speaking of water, welcome to No. 14. This dogleg left has water along the left side leading up to the green and then more water to the right when you reach the putting surface. It's a tough shot trying to reach this in two. From the back tees, you can almost forget about it.

At 603 yards, it's no surprise the par 5 is the longest hole on the golf course. But it's not only the longest, it's the longest by a long shot. The next closest is the 557-yard No. 3 hole.

No. 14 also is one of the more difficult on the golf course. It's rated the second hardest of the 18 Meadow Course holes. But if length is a problem, five sets of tees offer different yardages that may be more to your liking. The closest is 484 yards (red tees). **TJ**

**Course:** The Golf Club

**Location:** New Albany, Ohio, USA

**Hole:** No. 14

**Length:** 618 yards

**Par:** 5

**Designer:** Pete Dye

**Course Comment:** Dye, who has designed some of the most famous holes in the world, seemed like he was grousing about this monster of a par 5 when he said, "It takes up more damn land than any hole I've ever seen."

# No. ⑭ THE GOLF CLUB

How long will it be before holes have to be 800 yards long to make them legitimate three-shot par 5s? With weight training, advances in ball and club technology, and improved agronomy that allows balls to run down immaculate fairways, that day might not be far off. For now, though, 618 yards of Pete Dye mega-hole is enough to make this a true three-shotter.

Dye had a rare moment of sympathy for golfers, making the landing area off the tee nearly 100 yards wide, which gives players a wonderful opportunity to grab their driver, grip it, and rip it. You can almost hear Dye saying, "they'll need the distance, let's give 'em a shot."

Dye was less magnanimous on the second shot, offering absolutely no forgiveness if players miss, either right or left. To have a decent chance to shoot at the pin on your third shot, you must hit your second down the right side, but if you stray too far right there is a sandy pit the size of a fairly large back yard. Playing safe in the middle of the fairway forfeits any angle that might afford a birdie chance. You can get it to the green from the middle, but it takes a runner because an enormous oak tree guards the middle and left of the green. And, if you miss left, forget it — a lake awaits.

The second shot is crucial — if you execute it properly, you can take aim at the pin on your third, but watch out for pot bunkers which encircle the putting surface. **JB**

**Course:** Links at Spanish Bay

**Location:** Pebble Beach, California, USA

**Hole:** No. 14

**Length:** 576 yards

**Par:** 5

**Designer:** Robert Trent Jones Jr., Tom Watson, Sandy Tatum

**Course Comment:** Says Tom Watson: "Spanish Bay is so much like Scotland, you can almost hear the bagpipes." And as dusk approaches along the Monterey Peninsula, you actually can, as the wailing of bagpipes signal the end of each day's play.

OPPOSITE *The 14th hole at Links at Spanish Bay.*

## No. ⑭ LINKS AT SPANISH BAY

The trio of designers selected to build The Links at Spanish Bay in the mid-1980s all had a special interest in the unique aspects of Scottish links golf, none more so than five-time British Open winner Tom Watson.

Their collaboration — along with the damp, cool and breezy climate of California's Monterey Peninsula — resulted in a layout that perhaps comes closer than any other American links-style course in replicating year-round the conditions found on the famous courses of the Scottish coast.

Spanish Bay measures only slightly more than 6,800 yards from the back tees, but because of the constant stiff ocean breezes, plays much longer than that. No. 14, the longest par 5 on the course, is a good example.

From a tee box that offers a magnificent view of the Pacific Ocean on the horizon, the fairway offers a generous landing area for drives, but becomes much more treacherous at the landing area for the second shot, with four well-placed bunkers — including one in the center of the fairway — causing havoc. The green, protected by another bunker several yards in front and to the right, slopes toward the sea. Hit it to the front edge, and let it roll to the flag. **KA**

**Course:** Baltimore Country Club (East Course)

**Location:** Lutherville, Maryland, USA

**Hole:** No. 14

**Length:** 603 yards

**Par:** 5

**Designer:** A.W. Tillinghast

**Course Comment:** The layout has hosted four major tournaments, including the 1928 PGA Championship when Leo Diegel routed Al Espinosa, 6 and 5, in the 36-hole final.

## No. ⑭ BALTIMORE COUNTRY CLUB (EAST COURSE)

Originally built in 1898, Baltimore Country Club was relocated in 1922 to a rolling slice of farmland northwest of downtown. As disruptive as the move must have been to club members, the replacement parcel along with A.W. Tillinghast's guiding hand more than tempered any inconveniences.

Baltimore's East Course ambles through hilly terrain with plenty of fairway contouring and steeply pitched greens. It is also one of the few mid-Atlantic courses to use bent grass almost exclusively from tee to green.

The land swap afforded the club a wonderfully organic canvas to create a new course and the result was holes like the 14th, a winding par 5 dubbed "Hell's Half Acre."

From the tee, the hole slopes dramatically down some 90 feet to the fairway and then back up about 40 feet to the putting surface. A group of fairway bunkers loom about 230 yards from the tee and 190 yards short of the putting surface, making even the most routine lay-up a daunting task. The fairway of the slight dogleg left slopes gently to the right and the green, due in large part to the elevation changes, can be reached in two.

The expansive putting surface lists sharply from back left to front right and is guarded by a bunker on the left. The most demanding pin position is front left but most contend there's no easy hole location to be found on "Hell's Half Acre." **RH**

**Course:** St. Andrews (Old Course)

**Location:** St. Andrews, Fife, Scotland

**Hole:** No. 14

**Length:** 567 yards

**Par:** 5

**Designer:** Old Tom Morris

**Course Comment:** The appropriately named Hell bunker measures more than 1,950 square feet and is almost 10 feet deep at its lowest point.

# No. 🄮 ST. ANDREWS (OLD COURSE)

This is the standard by which all other par 5s are judged. St. Andrews's 14th hole is a monster, replete with a bunker known as "Hell" and a host of accompanying demons with the monikers "Beardies," "Benty," "Kitchen," and "Grieve."

Called the best long hole in the world by Bernard Darwin, No. 14 requires three perfect shots to reach a green that's just as fearsome as the rest of the hole. The drive must be placed precisely in the midst of the Elysian Fields, to the right of the Beardies bunkers — one large and deep, the others small — and to the left of the wickedly twisting wall that marks out of bounds right. The second shot should be played to the left of the infamous Hell bunker, a vast pit which cannot be seen from the fairway but still looms ever large in the minds of players.

Landing left of Hell will give the best angle to the green, allowing the best opportunity to avoid the pair of pot bunkers front left, a larger bunker at the rear, and the famous hump in the green, which slopes front to back.

A shot that lands past the pin is most preferable, leading to an uphill putt — and perhaps to a par well-earned. **KA**

**RIGHT** *David Duval of the USA on the 14th hole at St. Andrew's Golf Club, July 2000.*

**OPPOSITE** *The 14th hole at St. Andrews.*

## No. ⑭ KINGSTON HEATH GOLF CLUB

**Course:** Kingston Heath Golf Club

**Location:** Cheltenham, Victoria, Australia

**Hole:** No. 14

**Length:** 550 yards

**Par:** 5

**Designer:** D.G. Soutar, Alister MacKenzie

**Course Comment:** Australian golfing legend Peter Thomson, winner of five British Open championships, says this is one of the best par 5s in all Australia.

This long, straightforward hole shares an enormous — and intimidating — bunker complex with the 15th, guarding the right side of both the fairway of the 14th and the green of the acclaimed par 3 that follows.

Not many players can reach the 14th green in two, and that's one of the things that makes it such a classic hole in the minds of many golf-course critics. It demands three good shots to get on the putting surface in regulation, and then two strong putts for par.

A solid drive will leave golfers with a blind, uphill second shot that must be placed precisely; there is plenty of trouble on both sides of the fairway in the form of those fabulously-designed MacKenzie bunkers as well as trees on the left (and out-of-bounds beyond them).

Hollows at the front and back of the roomy green present serious problems for players not particularly adept with their wedges, and so do its testy and subtle undulations. **JS**

**Course:** Los Angeles Country Club (North Course)

**Location:** Los Angeles, California, USA

**Hole:** No. 14

**Length:** 564 yards

**Par:** 5

**Designer:** George C. Thomas Jr.

**Course Comment:** Like everything in the City of Beverly Hills, this golf club is world famous and as good as it gets. Up-scale is a way of life in this town and it's the same deal on the local golf course.

## No. ⑭ LOS ANGELES COUNTRY CLUB (NORTH COURSE)

Just imagine how popular this hole could be. It already is a terrific hole with great scenery. But the scenery could be even better if that view of the Playboy Mansion was a little less blocked. You can see the very top of it, but just think if you could see into the back yard or the swimming pool. Tee times would be booked for the next 50 years — and the backup at No. 14 would be quite long, not that anyone would care.

We can all dream.

Still, this 564-yard par 5 is a beauty. The dogleg right has trouble all down the right side. A large slope falls off into trees, brush, and junk. You might be able to find your ball, but it will be unplayable.

The key shot here is off the tee. There is a bunker about 210 to 220 yards along the right side that cuts a good 30 yards into the fairway. The ideal shot is right over this bunker. If you can't fly the bunker here you have no chance at reaching the green in two.

The green, which is well surrounded by bunkers, is very wide but not too deep. The back slopes down right into some difficult rough. This is a tough green to hit from a long way out. The safe approach is the best approach.

And try not to think about what's going on across the way. **TJ**

---

**Course:** Bel-Air Country Club

**Location:** Los Angeles, California, USA

**Hole:** No. 14

**Length:** 590 yards

**Par:** 5

**Designer:** Billy Bell Sr., George Thomas, Jack Neville

**Course Comment:** Bel-Air was the site of one of the more lopsided victories in U.S. Amateur history. In 1976, the U.S. Golf Association's first and only visit to the layout, Bill Sander cruised to the title with an 8-and-6 triumph over Parker Moore Jr.

## No. ⑭ BEL-AIR COUNTRY CLUB

At first blush, Tinseltown would not top most player's list for must-see golf architecture. Big-screen heroes and green rooms, not heroic carries and green complexes, come to mind when the topic turns to golf here. Yet Los Angeles has no shortage of quality golf courses and Bel-Air Country Club has been a prominent fixture of that landscape since it opened in 1927.

Short by today's standards, just 6,482 yards from the back tees, Bel-Air is an intoxicating blend of sweeping vistas and tight, tree-lined fairways that require pure ball-striking and a little local knowledge. Luckily, Bel-Air's is a masterly crafted routing which allows for a wonderful walk and, even more importantly, an enlightened caddie.

Advice will be in high demand by the time a player reaches the 14th hole. The only par 5 on the back nine, Billy Bell Sr., George Thomas, and Jack Neville intended No. 14 to be a scoring opportunity, but, as is the case throughout the layout, they didn't want anything to come easy.

The 14th is long and straight with a steep hill to the right of the fairway and a stream guarding the left side of the landing area. Longer hitters will be tempted to try and reach this green in two shots, but beware an abundance of bunkers guarding the putting surface that can quickly sour any thoughts for a Hollywood ending. **RH**

**WE-KO-PA GOLF CLUB**
### (SAGUARO COURSE)

**Course:** We-Ko-Pa Golf Club
(Saguaro Course)

**Location:** Fountain Hills,
Arizona, USA

**Hole:** No. 14

**Length:** 538 yards

**Par:** 5

**Designers:** Bill Coore and Ben
Crenshaw

**Course Comment:** We-Ko-Pa sits
in the center of the Yavapai Nation
near Scottsdale, Arizona, and the
name translates into the Yavapai
"Four Peaks Mountain."

When trying to picture the 14th at We-Ko-Pa's Saguaro Course, it is important to have a grasp of pure desert golf. First, imagine the barren, cactus- and brush-filled desert. Then imagine watching designers Bill Coore and Ben Crenshaw dictate the placement of emerald-green turfgrass to create golf holes in strips and doglegs, ovals and other geometric shapes, as they did when creating the Saguaro Course in 2006.

But, the dynamic designing duo put a twist on the concept at Saguaro's pretty and pleasingly perilous par-5 14th. They created an alternate landing area off the tee. There is the tee box, and the "regular" fairway that goes to the left and is wide and inviting. But, for those feeling brave, there is an "island" of turfgrass to the right, separated from the more conventional fairway by a strip of desert. If you land your tee shot on this island, you effectively cut the corner and take considerable distance off your second shot and give yourself a legitimate chance to reach the green in two.

Missing the island means landing among the natural desert vegetation, taking a stroke, and inflating your score, but if you should hit the island, the rest of the way is pretty straightforward, save for a couple of traps guarding the horseshoe-shaped green. **JB**

**Course:** Pumpkin Ridge (Witch Hollow Course)

**Location:** North Plains, Oregon, USA

**Hole:** No. 14

**Length:** 470 yards

**Par:** 5

**Designer:** Bob Cupp, John Fought

**Course Comment:** Tiger Woods eagled this hole in the 1996 U.S. Amateur in his match with Joel Kribel.

# No. ⓮ PUMPKIN RIDGE
## (WITCH HOLLOW COURSE)

Situated in the foothills of the Tualatin Mountains and surrounded by dense groupings of maple, oak, fir, and ash, this challenging track is among the most natural America has to offer. And, observers in the know compare the 14th hole at Pumpkin Ridge to company even more elite.

This Oregonian 14th is much like Nos. 13 and 15 at Augusta National. They call it a par 4½. You can make birdie here. In fact, you should. But that doesn't make this hole any less enjoyable to play.

It is an eminently reachable hole for the best of the best, and eagle putts are the norm when the pros come to play. So when mere mortals step to the tee, they have a legitimate chance at birdie. There's nothing wrong with "Annika and I both birdied this hole."

The hole doglegs left, but it doesn't take a gargantuan drive to make the corner. And if your tee shot reaches the elbow, a long hitter has nothing more than a middle iron to the green. Well, maybe that's a stretch for mere mortals. A mid-range handicapper probably has a long iron left if he or she gets to the corner. But bombers might have a 7- or 8-iron.

This hole is beautiful to play, yet it obviously is not the toughest you're ever going to see. There is water, sand, and wetlands, but they are more cosmetic than perilous. The approach to the green is gorgeous, forcing a left turn because of a kidney-shaped bunker up front. Massive trees surround the back, but they shouldn't come into play unless you drastically misjudge distance.

Pumpkin Ridge's Witch Hollow Course played host to the 1997 and the 2003 U.S. Women's Open and is consistently rated among the top 50 courses in America. And when the best come to play, they feel cheated if they don't walk away from No. 14 with at least a birdie. **JB**

**Course:** World Woods
(Pine Barrens Course)

**Location:** Brooksville, Florida, USA

**Hole:** No. 14

**Length:** 547 yards

**Par:** 5

**Designer:** Tom Fazio

**Course Comment:** The Pine Barrens Course is the jewel of four courses at World Woods, yet it still must fight for "resort highlight" honors. That's because the resort's practice facility has been rated best in the world by *Sports Illustrated*, and is considered state-of-the-art by any measure.

# No. ⓙ WORLD WOODS
## (PINE BARRENS COURSE)

The 14th hole of World Woods's Pine Barrens Course might have players thinking they're seeing double. As if playing a par 5 through a stunning blend of native terrain and challenging design weren't enough, No. 14 also presents a challenge that includes both a two-tiered fairway and a two-tiered green.

There are two ways (of course) to look at this situation: it can be viewed either as double trouble from start to finish, or the more optimistic viewpoint, a world of different opportunities. Either way, get ready to play.

The hole is not overly lengthy at 547 yards, but whichever fairway you take — right or left — going for the green is an unlikely option because the second portion of the hole plays drastically uphill. But even a lay-up provides no certainty. That's because of the aforementioned tiered green.

The putting surface is flanked by huge, deep bunkers. There, a tree growing out of a large bunker on the left, and steep-faced traps circling around the right, make the word "protection" an understatement. Combine the tiers and the bunkers and Fazio has forced placement concerns on virtually every shot in order to avoid the trouble and get close to the pin.

Players want to lay up as far right as possible, because that's the best angle from which to approach the green. However, no coincidence, the right is where the most dangerous bunkers lie. If you choose to avoid the bunker trouble and lay up on the left, you then create an approach where the green appears a sliver. Take your pick, and hope you land your ball on the same tier as the pin. Otherwise, you face a tormenting lag.

No. 14 at World Woods' Pine Barrens is laden with the pines from which it draws its name. It is sculpted from an expansive pine forest and the elevation changes throughout the layout contrast greatly with many tracks in Florida.

The pines provide a mandate to stay on course, and Fazio has littered the course with waste bunkers to put even more premium on accuracy. The golfer who challenges Pine Barrens will find the course to test both the physical and mental aspects of the game. Pine Barrens offers many intimidating, yet, enjoyable holes — and the 14th fits right in. **JB**

**Course:** Spyglass Hill Golf Club

**Location:** Pebble Beach, California, USA

**Hole:** No. 14

**Length:** 560 yards

**Par:** 5

**Designer:** Robert Trent Jones Sr.

**Course Comment:** In 1996, one of the best golf courses in the world underwent some minor surgery. One of the biggest changes came on No. 16. The green on No. 16 was expanded, making it one of the largest on the course at approximately 2,200 square feet.

# No. ⑭  SPYGLASS HILL GOLF CLUB

The first five holes at Spyglass roll through seaside dunes challenging the golfer to carefully pick the safe route. But the following 13 holes — including No. 14 — are cut through majestic pines, with elevated greens and strategically placed bunkers and lakes, putting a premium on accuracy.

This is not only a long hole. But a challenging hole. And most of all, a fun hole. Named "Long John Silver," the 560-yard par 5 is a double dogleg swinging right, then left.

The fairway is fairly tight and this is a difficult par 5 to reach in two. Play target golf here and leave yourself with a nice, short third shot to the green.

A pond protects the right side of this shallow, but very wide green. There is also a bunker just right of the pond and another one on the left-front side of the green.

A difficult chip back to the green awaits those who play this hole too aggressively or choose the wrong club and end up overshooting the putting surface. **TJ**

**Course:** Western Gailes Golf Club

**Location:** Gailes, Ayrshire, Scotland

**Hole:** No. 14

**Length:** 562 yards

**Par:** 5

**Designer:** Willie Park, F.W. Hawtree

**Course Comment:** The course has played host to the Curtis Cup, and the prestigious Scottish Amateur Championship. It is also one of the final qualifying courses when The British Open is played at Turnberry or Royal Troon.

# No. ⑭ WESTERN GAILES GOLF CLUB

Western Gailes used to be Scotland's secret, which was a bit surprising, considering it has staged world-famous events for better than 100 years, going back to 1903 when the great Harry Vardon won his first major championship at the club. Twenty years later, Gene Sarazen played the course for the first time, and heaped praises on the place, calling it "one of the finest tests I've ever taken on."

But the reputation of Western Gailes as one of the game's finest and more exacting courses has spread. Visitors from throughout the world now show up at Western's first tee, anxious to take on the challenge Sarazen judged so stern.

The 14th hole at Western Gailes, like the rest of the course, is situated between the railway and the sea. And, like so many holes, both features come into play on No. 14. Because the course is never more than two holes wide on the thin tract of land, the sea is either a hazard or visible on every hole, as is the train track.

When you come to the 14th tee, you can take some comfort in the fact that the sea isn't an issue for the rest of the round. No. 13 is the last seaside hole on the course, and No. 14 begins your inland journey to the clubhouse. However, just because the sea doesn't come into play, don't breathe too easily. There is still trouble here.

The wind is almost always at your back on No. 14, and at 562 yards, this hole proves very tempting for lengthy players. However, this is just as much hazard as opportunity. There are many bunkers on the hole, and they are situated so that virtually every landing area for long hitters is an exercise in precise location. The bunkers prove particularly troublesome as you get closer to the green. There are 10 of them spread in strategic spots, so if you are to make an attempt at the green in two, you need to be exact. Anything short of the surface means dealing with deep, steep bunkers.

The green is spacious, and relatively flat by Scotland's standards, so it is receptive if you go for it in two shots. However, the smarter play is to lay up, get your approach close and take a shot at birdie. Greed on your second shot often leads to bigger scores. **JB**

**Course:** Royal St. George's Golf Club

**Location:** Sandwich, Kent, England

**Hole:** No. 14

**Length:** 551 yards

**Par:** 5

**Designer:** Laidlaw Purves, Alister MacKenzie, J.J.F. Pennink

**Course Comment:** The second most difficult hole at Royal St. George's, the 14th is rated second on the stroke index behind only the par-4, 455-yard eighth.

Before Royal St. George's played host to its 13th British Open Championship in 2003, officials at the ancient St. Andrews, Scotland, thought the 14th hole had become just a bit too reachable in two. It carried some bite at 508 yards, but by the time the R&A was through adding 43 yards for the Open, the 14th had all the teeth necessary to stand up to the best in the world.

Out of bounds is a worry down the right side from tee to green, leaving virtually nowhere to go right of the fairway off the tee. It does loosen just a touch as you make your way to the green, but not much.

The hole is dubbed "Suez Canal" for the burn that snakes across the fairway at 328 yards. It is a distance that doesn't come into play for mere mortals off the tee, but the pros have to worry about the burn, particularly when Royal St. George's is running fast. The play is to carry the bunkers in the middle of the fairway at 268 yards, yet stopping your ball in time to avoid the burn.

Then, it's decision time. If you decide to make a stab at the green in two, it is reachable. But it is advisable to carry a collection of bunkers in the fairway about 68 yards from the green, and run the ball onto the putting surface. This is achievable, but avoid the bunkers because they are an ugly penalty to face. There are eight bunkers or swales to consider in the fairway, and then several more surrounding the green.

The safe play is to hit your second shot to about 126 yards, leaving you with a fairly comfortable shot that can be played high and soft into the green. A runner is still an option, but from 126 yards it isn't necessary.

The 14th hole has changed quite a bit since Royal St. George's first hosted the British Open in 1894. But, fortunately, the updating and lengthening necessary to retain the challenge of the hole, has not detracted from its charm or strategy. **JB**

**BLACK DIAMOND RANCH & COUNTRY CLUB** (QUARRY COURSE)

**Course:** Black Diamond Ranch & Country Club (Quarry Course)

**Location:** Lecanto, Florida, USA

**Hole:** No. 14

**Length:** 529 yards

**Par:** 5

**Designer:** Tom Fazio

**Course Comment:** Because of the Quarry Course's elevation changes it is not considered a prototypical Florida course. Fueling that theory is a complete dearth of water hazards on the entire layout.

Strewn across the edges of a long-abandoned mine, Black Diamond's Quarry Course combines a rare excess of elevation changes with Florida's natural rugged beauty. It is this unusual marriage that gives the relatively young layout a classic appeal hardly matched by other area courses.

Tom Fazio took full advantage of the topographical variety the quarry provided, routing most of the layout in and around the gaping hollow. Yet few of Fazio's holes are as interconnected to the quarry as the par-5 14th.

The slight dogleg left bends gently around the edges of the quarry and, in quintessential Fazio style, offers driving options for the untamed as well as the timid.

The fairway to the left affords longer hitters the best chance to reach the green in two shots but requires a 260-yard carry over the gorge to make it worth the effort. Anything short or left of the intended target is doomed to the depths of the quarry.

The safe route to the right fairway, however, will present players with a difficult lay-up to a small landing area that is cornered in by a large hill on the right.

Once on the green, players must negotiate a ridge that runs through the axis of the putting surface from right to left and makes any putts from the back edge to the front an adventure. **RH**

# Hole ⓯

Mentally, the 15th hole may be as important a part of a round as there is in competitive golf. Some would point to the first hole, or perhaps the 18th, but No. 15 is a crucial "transition" hole. You've been through the majority of your round, yet you are not quite to the finishing holes. No. 15 provides that bridge.

Architects are so intent on making the final three holes memorable (which usually brings with it great difficulty) that No. 15 is often a chance to make hay before the pressure really starts to mount on Nos. 16–18. Take advantage on the 15th — it is your last opportunity before the challenge mounts even further.

**LEFT** *The 15th hole at Desert Mountain Golf Club, Scottsdale, Arizona, USA.*

**Course:** Troon Golf & Country Club

**Location:** Scottsdale, Arizona, USA

**Hole:** No. 15

**Length:** 139 yards

**Par:** 3

**Designer:** Tom Weiskopf, Jay Morrish

**Course Comment:** No. 15 is a nice change of pace after Troon's other three one-shotters, which measure 215, 207, and 189 yards respectively.

# No. ⑮  TROON GOLF & COUNTRY CLUB

Much like a body of water that suddenly and unexpectedly appears to a thirsty desert wanderer, the green on Troon Golf & Country Club's signature 15th hole calls to golfers who have been in search of a par or a birdie on this testy Tom Weiskopf and Jay Morrish design at one of the Phoenix area's premier private clubs.

Called "Troon Mountain" because of the rocky hills that can be seen beyond the putting surface, at first glance this hole appears to be simply an oasis of green in the midst of a stark desert landscape, an inviting target that's full of promise and tantalizingly close (measuring less than 140 yards from the tips). When they take a closer look, however, golfers will see a deceivingly short hole that's fraught with desert danger.

The distance is often hard to judge because of the mountains in the background and the fact that the entire green is surrounded by sand, rocks, cacti, and other desert fauna. Then there's the several bunkers scattered to the front, left, and right, and a three-tiered putting surface that makes every stroke an adventure.

Miss the green, and par — much less birdie — might just be a cruel mirage. **KA**

**Course:** Malone Golf Club

**Location:** Belfast, Ireland

**Hole:** No. 15

**Length:** 144 yards

**Par:** 3

**Designer:** Cotton & Associates

**Course Comment:** Malone Golf Club is one of Northern Ireland's finest championship golf courses, 5 miles from Belfast city center and set in 330 acres of beautiful wooded parkland.

## No. ⓯ MALONE GOLF CLUB

The original layout at Malone Golf Club made little or no use of the lake, and the course was redesigned.

The lake now comes into play, first for the tee shot at the 13th; then the tee shot at the 15th is over water all the way to a tricky, undulating green; and at the last hole the lake makes its presence very much felt off the tee.

No. 15 is what many would call the perfect par 3. It's a very short hole, but the penalty for even slightly missing your target is severe. From the tee you are going to have to carry a portion of the lake if you want to reach the green, so don't miss left or you will require another ball.

But don't miss right either. There are two bunkers on that side, with one wrapping around to the front of the green.

The tip here is to block out the water and just hit your target. Again, it's not too far. The problems begin when you start worrying about the water, overcompensate, and land in the trap.

We will leave you with a quote from John Redmond, who wrote that wonderful book *Great Courses in Ireland*: "In any 19th-hole discussion attempting to determine the accolade of supreme inland course in Ireland, it is perfectly understandable that there will be a case for the claims of Malone Golf Club." **TJ**

**Course:** Kingsbarns Golf Links

**Location:** Kingsbarns, Fife, Scotland

**Hole:** No. 15

**Length:** 212 yards

**Par:** 3

**Designer:** Kyle Phillips

**Course Comment:** Kingsbarns Golf Links is a tribute to its rich Scottish links heritage. The site has long been known for its intimate connection with the sea, and the fact that its golf origins date to 1793 is testimony to the attributes of the site.

BELOW *Philip Price of Wales on the 15th hole at Kingsbarns Golf Links, October 2002.*

OPPOSITE *Niclas Fasth of Sweden hits his tee shot on the 15th hole at Kingsbarns Golf Links, October 2002.*

# No. ⓯  KINGSBARNS GOLF LINKS

Just six miles down the coast from the most revered links in the world — the Old Course at St. Andrews — lies Kingsbarns Golf Links. Despite the fact that the course just opened in July 2000, Kingsbarns has been heralded as the last great links property available for development in Scotland.

As you might imagine, there are plenty of holes that stand out at Kingsbarns. You are unlikely to forget Nos 3, 12, 17, or 18. They are all special holes, but No. 15 can play with any of them and even beat them when it comes to most memorable.

The 212-yard 15th is not only one of the best par 3s in Scotland, but also one of the best short holes in the world.

The green perches high atop a narrow ridge of jagged shoreline. There is no bail-out left, and your only hope if you drift right is a miraculous bounce back out of the rocks.

This doesn't happen very often, but when it does, it's pretty dramatic. Just tell your playing partners that's exactly how you planned it.

The green is more or less a peninsula green with water surrounding it on three sides. The water cuts a little bit into the fairway but you should be airborne by then. **TJ**

## No. ⑮  THE KINLOCH CLUB

The Kinloch Club is Jack Nicklaus' first signature course in New Zealand, a country he first saw when he played an exhibition in the 1970s. He began planning the design of The Kinloch Club in 2003, and it opened to rave reviews in 2007. The course has the advantage of sitting on rugged and undulating volcanic terrain, and alongside lovely Lake Taupo.

The fairways, as Bob Charles said in his comments praising the place, are conditioned for ground play, making it a true links-style course. Adding to this feeling is the enormous amount of native grasses, mounding, and bunkers throughout the property.

One of the most stunning holes on this 7,363-yard gem is No. 15, a 224-yard monster of a par 3. As if the distance were not daunting enough, the hole faces the lake, so the wind is often driving straight into your face.

The hole is virtually all carry over native grass and mounds, although there is a small landing area to the front right of the putting surface. But, you most definitely do not want to finish short-left off the tee. That puts you in serious difficulty and par would be a near-miracle from there.

And, of course, once you get to the green, mounds and more mounds make putting an adventure. And depending on how devilish the superintendent was feeling that day, a two-putt can be something of an impossibility. **JB**

**Course:** Mauna Lani Resort
(South Course)

**Location:** Kohala Coast, Hawaii, USA

**Hole:** No. 15

**Length:** 196 yards

**Par:** 3

**Designer:** Francis H. Brown

**Course Comment:** Mauna Lani is 27 acres of vivid, color-splashed paradise, postcard hole after postcard hole snaking through carefully preserved Hawaiian history. Where else can you hit balls around archaic lava flows and lava tube dwellings with primitive carvings, an ancient Hawaiian fishing village, and exotic fish ponds? This course is the birthplace of the PGA Senior Skins Tournament.

# No. ⑮ MAUNA LANI RESORT
## (SOUTH COURSE)

Fairways on the route to the famed 15th at Mauna Lani South are friendly enough, and fairly flat greens yield speeds of nice variance, but most are lined by natural rough and treacherous black lava rock. Steer clear of it, because your ball is toast if it lands there.

Talk about a memorable par 3. Hole 15 is like stepping into a painting with your clubs in tow. Modeled after No. 3 at Mauna Kea, which sits a little further north up the Kohala Coast, it's one of the most photographed over-the-water golf holes on earth.

Do your best not to be distracted by a fiery orange orb sinking into the Pacific while you shoot your tee shot over the crashing turquoise surf to the two-tiered green at No. 15. Ocean crosswinds make this hole even more fun to tackle — its large green is surrounded by sand, and carrying your ball almost 200 yards over water is quite a test.

The challenge of this striking course changes with each stroke; it's a pleasant mixture of skill levels that's dramatically picturesque — studded with bunkers and framed on one side by the sparkling ocean. If you're lucky enough to find yourself on the sunny Kohala Coast of the Big Island, Mauna Lani South's 15th is resort golf at its scenic finest. **KLL**

## No. ⑮ VALDERRAMA GOLF CLUB

Before Valderrama's two nines were reversed in the late 1980s, today's 15th hole was the sixth. It is much more effective today, as the longest of Valderrama's one-shot holes begins a spectacular four-hole finishing stretch to one of continental Europe's best-known courses.

No. 15 has always been a favorite spot for galleries, offering magnificent vantage points during such notable events as the 1997 Ryder Cup, the World Golf Championships-American Express Championship in 1999 and 2000, and the PGA European Tour's season-ending Volvo Masters Andalucia.

The diagonally placed green is long and narrow, and is well guarded by a line of trees that pinch in on the right and three huge, sprawling bunkers. The back right pin placement is the toughest, as it requires a tee shot to carry the bunker, land on the back center of the putting surface, and roll with the slope of the green to the pin.

During the '97 Ryder Cup, American Jim Furyk thwarted Nick Faldo's comeback attempt at this hole. After Faldo struck his tee shot to 3 feet, Furyk holed out from a bunker for birdie to earn an unexpected half. Stuck by that dagger, Faldo succumbed on the next hole, giving Furyk a 3-and-2 singles victory. **KA**

RIGHT *The 15th hole at Valderrama Golf Club.*

660

**Course:** Cinnamon Hill Ocean Course

**Location:** Montego Bay, Jamaica

**Hole:** No. 15

**Length:** 172 yards

**Par:** 3

**Designer:** Robert Von Hagge

**Course Comment:** The James Bond movie, *Golden Eye* was filmed on location at Cinnamon Hill, and the waterfall behind the 15th hole is visible in a few scenes.

# No. ⑮ CINNAMON HILL OCEAN COURSE

If you'd like to add a bit of spice to your golf, then the Cinnamon Hill Ocean Course in Montego Bay, Jamaica, fits the bill. This 6,637-yard, par-71 layout has striking views of the Caribbean Sea and the Blue Mountains of Jamaica.

The course snakes through the historic ruins of Cinnamon Hill — an 18th-century English sugar plantation — and offers views of the Cinnamon Hill Great House, which was the getaway home of the late Johnny Cash.

The 15th hole is a par 3 with a tee box adjacent to the Caribbean Sea, but pointing away from the ocean. However, it heads down toward a natural waterfall to make a wonderfully scenic setting in which to putt.

The waterfall behind the 15th green is natural, but it was hidden behind brush so thick that, before a complete restoration in 2001, even Robert Von Hagge's design team didn't know it was there. Once it was discovered, however, it was quickly incorporated into the hole's design.

If you want more golf while in Jamaica, three of Montego Bay's most celebrated resorts have joined forces to create the Rose Hall, Montego Bay Golf Association. The golf courses are the Cinnamon Hill Ocean Course, the White Witch, and the Half Moon Golf Course. Reciprocal rates are available at all three golf courses. **JB**

**Course:** Turnberry Golf Club (Ailsa Course)

**Location:** Turnberry, Ayrshire, Scotland

**Hole:** No. 15

**Length:** 209 yards

**Par:** 3

**Designer:** Mackenzie Ross

**Course Comment:** Turnberry's Ailsa Course gets its name from Ailsa Craig, a huge island made of volcanic rock approximately 10 miles off the Ayrshire coast. The granite formation is about 1,300 yards long, 900 yards across, and 370 yards high.

No. ⑮ **TURNBERRY GOLF CLUB (AILSA COURSE)**

The famous "Duel in the Sun" between Tom Watson and Jack Nicklaus at the 1977 British Open brought Turnberry to international prominence, and the 15th hole had plenty to do with the outcome in that famous final round.

Watson sunk a long birdie putt of approximately 60 feet from the fringe to tie with Nicklaus and begin his march toward victory in one of the great down-the-stretch battles in major championship history. In 2003, Tom Watson returned to Turnberry and won the Senior British Open, making birdie on No. 15 in the first round.

This hole, called "Ca' Canny," a Scottish saying that means "take care" or "be cautious," is considered the best of Turnberry's strong quartet of par 3s. The advice in the hole's moniker should be heeded. Because the wind is often blowing directly into players' faces, many are forced to use long woods or even drivers to reach the green. It is best to take whatever you need to get there, because tee shots that come up short will land in a devilish valley of thick rough below the elevated putting surface, a purgatory from which salvaging par is nearly impossible.

Making matters even more difficult are three deep bunkers at the left and rear of the green. **KA**

**Course:** Sunningdale Golf Club (Old Course)

**Location:** Sunningdale, Surrey, England

**Hole:** No. 15

**Length:** 213 yards

**Par:** 3

**Designer:** Willie Park Jr.

**Course Comment:** Sunningdale was the site of the 1987 Walker Cup, the first time the event had not been held on a links course when Great Britain & Ireland was the host. The United States won, 16½ to 7½.

# No. ⑮ SUNNINGDALE GOLF CLUB
## (OLD COURSE)

Sunningdale's Old Course, considered the finest heathland layout in England, opened for play in 1901. Twenty-five years later, it was the site of Bobby Jones's legendary 66 during a British Open qualifier. Often called "the perfect round," it featured 33 shots, 33 putts, and a score of 33 on each side by the 24-year-old Jones, who hit a 2-iron or wood into 10 of the 18 holes. Afterward, Jones proclaimed his love for the course. Boosted by this performance, he went on to win the Open at Lytham and St. Annes.

The 15th, a long one-shotter, is protected by large bunkers on both the left and right sides, and a prevailing crosswind often pushes tee shots to the sand on the left, making for a difficult save.

The Old Course has played host to several top professional and amateur events, and the winners have included some of the top names in golf. Karrie Webb (1997) and Se Ri Pak (2001) won Women's British Open titles there, and Nick Faldo (1992), Ian Woosnam (1988), Greg Norman (1986), and Bernhard Langer (1985) were among those winning European Open titles when the event was held at Sunningdale eight times in a span of 10 years (1982–92). **KA**

**Course:** Vale do Lobo (Ocean Course)

**Location:** The Algarve, Portugal

**Hole:** No. 15

**Length:** 210 yards

**Par:** 3

**Designer:** Sir Henry Cotton, Rocky Roquemore

**Course Comment:** Vale do Lobo is Portuguese for "Valley of the Wolf." The back nine of the Ocean is the original Orange nine.

# No. ⑮ VALE DO LOBO (OCEAN COURSE)

The Ocean's 15th hole would receive a lot more attention if not for the fact that it is overshadowed by the 16th on the Royal. The 16th may be the most memorable because of its topography, but the Ocean's 15th presents its own unique challenge.

This is a par 3 with a big green that is fairly straightforward off visitor tees and with no breeze. Play it at its full yardage in any sort of wind and suddenly the green seems to shrink. Hitting the putting surface in regulation becomes more than a formality. It's in such times that the large bunker fronting the green gets a lot of play.

The 15th has the Atlantic Ocean as a natural hazard on the left, and is as near a genuine links hole as you are likely to find in Portugal. The beach is out of bounds, but seems to attract a lot of balls since golfers naturally aim right and then produce the hook that such a stance encourages.

Those who can find the right-hand side of the green will have a hard time just two-putting when the pin is on the left, for they will have a lot of land to negotiate. A good way to play this hole for those of a conservative nature is to land the ball short and slightly to the right of center of the green, and rely on a chip and a putt for par. **AT**

**RIGHT** *Graeme Storm of England putts on the 15th green at Vale do Lobo, April 2002.*

# FAIRMONT JASPER PARK LODGE GOLF COURSE

**Course:** Fairmont Jasper Park Lodge Golf Course

**Location:** Jasper, Alberta, Canada

**Hole:** No. 15

**Length:** 138 yards

**Par:** 3

**Designer:** Stanley Thompson

**Course Comment:** Like most resort golf courses, the design is generous here at Jasper Park. The scenery is spectacular, with a mountain backdrop at every hole.

The Fairmont Jasper Park Lodge, deep in the heart of the Canadian Rockies, is the setting of unforgettable memories for thousands of golfers since the course opening in 1925.

Highly acclaimed for its challenging layout and spectacular beauty, the Jasper Park Lodge Golf Club is rated by *SCORE Golf* magazine as the No. 1 Best Golf Resort in Canada.

Termed the "Bad Baby" for good reason, this 138-yard par 3 will put your short game to the test. Ignore the flag and aim for the center of the green. Anywhere on the green will leave you a relatively short putt and a good chance for birdie, but missing the green to any side will make getting up and down very difficult. And you can forget the birdie.

There are trees along the left side and a bunker in the middle of the fairway, but none of this should come into play.

But you should watch out for the bunkers on the right and left sides of the green. They very well could come into play.

The green slopes from back to front, and generally moves from left to right. Take two putts and be content with a par. **TJ**

**Course:** North Berwick Golf Club
(West Course)

**Location:** North Berwick,
East Lothian, Scotland

**Hole:** No. 15

**Length:** 192 yards

**Par:** 3

**Designer:** David Strath

**Course Comment:** Winston Churchill
was said to be on this hole in 1911
when he received a summons
informing him he was to become the
First Lord of Admiralty . . . or so the
story goes.

The world of golf is full of "mosts." Most photographed hole. Most famous hole. Most difficult hole. Most scenic hole. All of these superlatives are subject to opinion and speculation, and many stray into hyperbole, but the 15th hole at North Berwick Golf Links almost certainly lives up to its billing as the most copied golf hole in the world.

The 15th is North Berwick's "Redan," the first hole in the world that followed a specific formula. This template to protect against par follows a military strategy whereby two faces pointing away from the protected area are built to lessen the enemy's line of attack. This was the first Redan hole in the world, and there are now Redans in hundreds, if not thousands, of locations around the globe. Clearly, they all owe their origins to North Berwick — a most-deserving "most."

Despite its originality, North Berwick's Redan probably isn't the most interesting hole on the back nine. This distinction more than likely belongs to the following hole, the 16th. However, as far as innovation goes, nothing touches No. 15.

The first element of the Redan defense is the green being set at a 45-degree angle behind a deep bunker. You can see the bunker, but the other defenses are difficult to spot. The second element of the Redan is all but invisible from the tee — the green falls away to the rear, and it is hidden by a ridge about 35 yards short of the green.

Distance is critical in order to clear the bunker in the front of the green, yet you have to stop the ball on a green that slopes away. This can require a number of shots depending on the wind. A fade one day may be impossible

the next. A draw that worked in the morning may be ludicrous by noon.

North Berwick is laden with other traditions beyond the Redan. In 1899, for instance, Harry Vardon and Willie Park played a legendary match that was originally scheduled for 36 holes each at Ganton and Musselburgh. But, Vardon had heard that the locals at Park's home course of Musselburgh had a reputation for interfering with play and refused to play there, so the match moved to North Berwick. The strategy worked. Vardon went home a winner, as will visitors to North Berwick today. Tradition and excellent golf will be their rewards. **JB**

## No. ⑮ KINGSTON HEATH GOLF CLUB

**Course:** Kingston Heath Golf Club

**Location:** Cheltenham, Victoria, Australia

**Hole:** No. 15

**Length:** 156 yards

**Par:** 3

**Designer:** D.G. Soutar, Alister MacKenzie

**Course Comment:** While MacKenzie took care of all the bunkering at this fine Sand Belt layout, he is only credited with designing one hole there, No. 15, which he revamped in 1926 just three years after Soutar created the original.

What a brilliant bit of revamping MacKenzie did on this hole, because a challenge that was once a blind par 4 became a fabulous par 3 that is now regarded as the best of that ilk in the Melbourne area, if not Australia in general. It is the start of a very tough quartet of closers.

The 15th begins with a slightly uphill tee shot that is often susceptible to the tricky breezes that so often blow in the region and must negotiate a treacherous bunker complex that seems to hold more sand than the entire Outback. There are two gaping hazards short and left of the green and a cluster of five to the right.

A strong shot may seem the safest play as a result, but anything going too far will run into a deep hollow behind the putting surface, which slopes from back to front and is often brutally hard and fast. Locals say the hole can give up a birdie or two, but anyone making par at 15 is happy to mark three on his card because it doesn't take much for things there to get decidedly worse. **JS**

**Course:** Cypress Point Club

**Location:** Pebble Beach, California, USA

**Hole:** No. 15

**Length:** 139 yards

**Par:** 3

**Designer:** Alister MacKenzie

**Course Comment:** Robert Hunter, a friend and business partner of MacKenzie, said of No. 15: "It is the most spectacular hole in the world . . . over wild sea and rocky coast."

## No. ⑮  CYPRESS POINT CLUB

How does a diminutive hole of not even 140 yards make it into the category of "one of the world's best?" Here's how: it was designed by Alister MacKenzie, it is situated on perhaps the most immaculate golf property on the planet, and it begins what many call the most beautiful three-hole stretch in golf.

The following quote from George Fuller of travelgolf.com sums it up pretty well: "Cypress's sandy, forest-lined hills leading out to the Pacific's edge, the famous par-three 15th and 16th holes, and the precarious 17th — all set along a Pacific cliff — make Augusta look dull except in the colorful Masters springtime."

The first of the magnificent threesome at Cypress Point is No. 15, a tiny par 3, perhaps, but behemoth in its beauty and challenge.

The tee offers vision of what lies ahead, not only on the 15th. Its elevation of 65 feet provides a view of No. 15 and beyond, including golf, cliffs, and the Pacific. A finger of the ocean separates tee from green, and it is accented by three large rock formations — one to the right of the tee, one in front of the green, and one to the right of the putting surface. There are places to land if your ball is pushed from its target by the ocean winds, but these areas are mostly filled with straggly grass and bunkers.

There is a tiny area of safety behind the green, but too bold an effort leads to ocean. To the left of the green is a thick drapery of trees — cypress, of course — that are beautiful, yet perilous. The pin-placement options are many on No. 15, and perhaps the most difficult is up front, where the flag sits on a narrow slit of green, sandwiched between two cavernous bunkers.

It is difficult to imagine that MacKenzie could pack so much golf hole into 139 yards, but he was a golf sculptor with few peers. However, it might not be fair to the sculptors of the world to compare their works with the art of MacKenzie. Generic sculptors start out with a lump of clay that must be molded from the mind. MacKenzie's raw material at Cypress Point — which is some of the the most majestic land in the world — gave him a pretty good head start on a golf hole. **JB**

**BELOW** *The 15th hole at Cypress Point, photographed in 1940.*

**Course:** Friar's Head

**Location:** Riverhead, New York, USA

**Hole:** No. 15

**Length:** 460 yards

**Par:** 4

**Designer:** Bill Coore and Ben Crenshaw

**Course Comment:** The term "Friar's Head" is derived from a large sand formation that early sailors thought looked like a Friar's head when approaching this part of the North Shore from the water.

Most times, it takes actually seeing a hole to realize that you are in for something special. But, at No. 15 at Friar's Head, all you have to do is make the walk to the tee. In fact, before you even see the tee box, you realize a treat awaits.

When you leave the 14th green, you walk up a staircase that leads to the heavens, surrounded by white sand. The staircase seemingly goes forever, and it is a while before you can even see where it leads. Like everything else at Friar's Head, the staircase fits in perfectly with its surroundings.

And, then when you make it to the top of your ascension, you realize that it might just be heaven after all. Golf heaven, that is.

The tee shot plays down a steep hill into a cavernous valley, and must carry a large bunker on the left side. This is no easy task because the fairway slopes from left to right and funnels shots into the bunker if they are not long enough to carry.

Whereas the downhill play on the tee shot gives you some extra yardage, the payback comes on the dogleg-left approach shot.

The second shot plays uphill, which adds distance to the challenge. Not only that, but like many of the greens at this 2003 design, Coore and Crenshaw have deceived the player with a false front, so even more distance is required. **JB**

**Course:** Bethpage State Park (Black Course)

**Location:** Farmingdale, New York, USA

**Hole:** No. 15

**Length:** 438 yards

**Par:** 4

**Designer:** Joseph Burbeck, A.W. Tillinghast

**Course Comment:** The hole before this is a short par 3 and one of the easier holes on the golf course. No. 15 is the opposite. This is the No. 1 handicap hole on the course.

# No. ⓯ BETHPAGE STATE PARK
## (BLACK COURSE)

No. 15 is one of the picture holes at Bethpage State Park. It's a great view standing on the tee.

This dogleg left goes straight uphill. The green is about 40 feet above the tee. In order to have a good look at your second shot, you need to get length off the tee. Your driver better get you 260 to 270 yards if you hope to set up for an easy approach shot.

If your tee shot hits the rough, you can forget about the green in two. In fact, you can't reach any green in two at Bethpage from the rough. It's a rough place to be. Speaking of your approach shot, there is no lay up here. Bunkers in the front see to that.

The undulating green is a bit tricky with plenty of break. The middle part of the green breaks left to right and the front part goes back to front. So three-putts are not uncommon here.

Get some distance on your tee shot, clear the bunkers in front of the green — and don't three-putt. Then run for your life and consider yourself lucky — and pretty good, too. **TJ**

**Course:** Gozzer Ranch Golf Club

**Location:** Coeur d'Alene, Idaho, USA

**Hole:** No. 15

**Length:** 431 yards

**Par:** 4

**Designer:** Tom Fazio

**Course Comment:** No. 15 was used as four-time PGA Tour-winner Andrew Magee's backdrop while participating in the Golf Channel's *The Approach* show.

## No. ⓯  GOZZER RANCH GOLF CLUB

Sometimes Mother Nature just smiles on a golf-course designer. Such was the case in 2007 when the Discovery Land Company asked Tom Fazio to create a golf course adjacent to Lake Coeur d'Alene. You see, the lake, which is highlighted several times throughout Gozzer Ranch Golf Club, has been named by *National Geographic* magazine as one of the top five most beautiful lakes in the world.

And, nowhere is the lake, nor the scenic Idaho mountainous backdrop more evident or more stunning than at No. 15. There is a generous fairway, and a spectacular emerald jewel of a green that offers some of the best lake views imaginable.

"This is one of the strongest, most special and unique golf holes there is," Tom Fazio told SpokesmanReview.com shortly after the course opened. "We're not just talking Coeur d'Alene, northern Idaho, the Pacific Northwest or even the Western Hemisphere — we're talking the world. You can't find anything better anywhere."

Much of the golf course winds through pine trees, but, ironically, that is not the case on the most beautiful hole on the course. There is one iconic pine on the left side of the green that really doesn't come into play behind a rough bunker, but other than that, the fairway is open.

It isn't so much the challenge on this hole; it's the splendor. There is a rough that can be left deep if the superintendent so desires, but much of the time a player can reach the green in two even if he or she misses the fairway. The fairway does narrow in front of the putting surface, and you don't want to miss the green to the right because of the numerous massive and deep bunkers, but other than that the hole is pretty straightforward. And pretty is the operative word. **JB**

| | |
|---|---|
| **Course:** Mowbray Golf Club | |
| **Location:** Cape Town, South Africa | |
| **Hole:** No. 15 | |
| **Length:** 422 yards | |
| **Par:** 4 | |
| **Designer:** S.V. Hotchkin, Robert Grimsdell | |

**Course Comment:** Whereas most coastal courses feature holes that must often be played into the wind, Mowbray is unique in that it was laid out so golfers would seldom find breezes directly in their faces or behind their backs, making judging the crosswinds a key factor to a good round here.

# No. ⑮  MOWBRAY GOLF CLUB

Mowbray Golf Club was established in 1910 by a group of Cape Golf Club members after the Cape's course on Rondebosch Common was closed. Anything, they must have figured, had to be better than the layout on the common, which among other hazards featured rugby matches that played across the first hole each Saturday, a cemetery on No. 2, and, perhaps worst of all, a municipal garbage dump on No. 4.

You might say the change in location was an improvement. Today, Mowbray's members play on one of South Africa's best tracks, a course that has played host to seven South African Opens and all of the country's major amateur championships.

Perhaps foremost among Mowbray's holes is the signature par-4 15th, the No. 2 handicap hole.

The smart play off the tee is a strong drive down the right side of the undulating, tree-lined fairway, avoiding a pond to the left of the landing area. That leaves golfers with a semi-blind approach to a large green protected by a deep bunker on the left. The approach is beautifully framed by several tall, indigenous trees and the majestic Devil's Peak and Table Mountain in the background. **KA**

**Course:** Sonnenalp at Singletree

**Location:** Edwards, Colorado, USA

**Hole:** No. 15

**Length:** 385 yards

**Par:** 4

**Designer:** Bob Cupp

**Course Comment:** Located in Singletree about 5 minutes west of Beaver Creek, this outstanding golf course is semi-private. However it's certainly worth the membership dues.

## No. ⑮ SONNENALP AT SINGLETREE

Sonnenalp at Singletree has some pretty good company, so in order to compete they must tee up a great product — which, by the way, they do.

Case in point is No. 15, a 385-yard par 4 that breaks slightly to the right but isn't really a dogleg. What it is is very tempting. The big hitters can reach this green from the tee but the risk is very high.

One member told us that "it's crazy to go for the green. Far too much risk and I don't know many people who can pull it off."

The best play here is a nice 5-iron and then a wedge. Getting within 100 yards of the green gives a nice shot into a very guarded green. It's also important to watch out for a rock ditch that can come into play on the left side of the fairway.

There isn't a lot of room for error, so the closer the better.

There are bunkers to the right of the green and behind. Two ponds guard the left side, one next to the green and the other a little before it.

The kidney-shaped green wraps around the water. The green is fairly flat and straightforward. It's getting there that's the problem. **TJ**

---

**Course:** Villa d'Este Golf Club

**Location:** Montorfano, Como, Italy

**Hole:** No. 15

**Length:** 464 yards

**Par:** 4

**Designer:** Peter Gannon

**Course Comment:** Villa d'Este contains six par 3s, three par 5s, and nine par 4s for a total par of 69.

## No. ⑮ VILLA D'ESTE GOLF CLUB

Villa d'Este, one of the most historic courses in Italy, has been one of the gems of Italian golf since it first opened its doors in 1926.

It is set 1,200 feet above sea level among forests of chestnut, birch, ash, and pine trees on hilly terrain near Lake Montofano in the scenic Lombardia region of northern Italy. It has served as the host course for the Italian Open 12 times, most recently in 1972.

No. 15, by far the longest of Villa d'Este's par 4s, has length that's rare for a par-69 layout, but distance isn't the only challenge that the club's No. 1 handicap hole presents. The fairway slopes quite hard from right to left, ensuring that most will have an uneven lie for their long second shots, which many golfers tend to hook.

So, of course, Villa d'Este designer Robert Gannon put most of the trouble on the left side of the relatively small, contoured green, including a deep bunker at the front left portion and a line of trees farther left for those who really pull their approaches.

And for players who try to overcompensate for the lie, another deep bunker awaits at the front right. **KA**

**Course:** Galloway National Golf Club

**Location:** Galloway Township, New Jersey, USA

**Hole:** No. 15

**Length:** 409 yards

**Par:** 4

**Designer:** Tom Fazio

**Course Comment:** Tom Fazio's original design for this hole did not include the massive sandy waste area in the middle of the fairway, but he thought the hole was missing a little something extra. He found it.

## No. ⑮ GALLOWAY NATIONAL GOLF CLUB

Set on a stretch of coastal woodland and marshy wetlands along Reeds Bay just outside Atlantic City, Galloway National is a marvelous Tom Fazio layout that was born out of frustration. Vernon Hill, one of Galloway National's owners, had just suffered through a five-hour round at a neighboring course, and swore he would never do it again, vowing to build a top private club where slow play would not be a problem. Members of Galloway are glad he followed through.

The course both begins and ends along the marshes and the bay, with glimpses of the Atlantic City skyline, but it also features some compelling parkland-style holes in between, including No. 15, an uphill par 4.

The tee shot will require long hitters to lay up because of the gigantic sand pit that crosses the fairway at approximately the 275-yard mark. Although there is a slight bail-out area to the right of the sand, hitting it there is not recommended because a lone tree stands guard right and short of the green, effectively blocking the approach from that angle. The elevated putting surface is also protected by a back-to-front slope and a large bunker on the left side. **KA**

## No. ⑮ HONORS COURSE

**Course:** Honors Course

**Location:** Ooltewah, Tennessee, USA

**Hole:** No. 15

**Length:** 445 yards

**Par:** 4

**Designer:** P.B. Dye, Pete Dye

**Course Comment:** This course has hosted a number of top events, including the 1996 NCAA Championships, won by Tiger Woods, the 1991 U.S. Amateur, and the 1994 Curtis Cup Match. The 2005 U.S. Mid-Amateur Championship also comes to the Honors Course.

The Honors Course is known for its natural setting and the 15th hole says it all. The 445-yard test is a true joy for any player, regardless of skill. Pete Dye and son P.B. created perfect harmony for all types of player with this hole.

Off the tee, a straight tee shot is essential. Longer hitters have to think about the second shot when standing on the tee. A big drive will leave you a short iron into the green. But don't think just because you hit it a long way that you are in the clear; a perfect second shot is necessary to hold this green. The skilled player will love the challenge of working the ball to this putting surface and if you miss the green you will be staring at a demanding up-and-down.

More conservative players may hit a long iron or fairway wood off the tee, but this safe approach does not always pan out and and may leave a player in a predicament. This hole has a bail-out area to the right of the green, which conforms nicely to a bouncing approach and is a great risk-reward opportunity.

The green is engaging and has some break to it. Many players over-read putts here, so pick a line and stay with it. **GE**

## No. ⑮ THE GOLF CLUB KENNEDY BAY

**Course:** The Golf Club Kennedy Bay

**Location:** Longbeach Key, Port Kennedy, Western Australia

**Hole:** No. 15

**Length:** 382 yards

**Par:** 4

**Designer:** Michael Coate, Roger MacKay, Ian Baker-Finch

**Course Comment:** Its location outside Perth in the far western reaches of Australia has, in the mind of many golf-course aficionados, kept Kennedy Bay from becoming the national sensation they believe it is.

The name of this hole is "Judgment," and the reason for that is quite simple: players have to use their good sense — and judgment — when they step to the tee of this classic risk-reward par 4.

Basically, there are two options with the drive. One, they can hit their tee shot through a chute down the right side and try to land their balls between some tough mounding on the far side of the fairway and a pair of pot bunkers in the middle. Or they can bail out to a much wider landing area. That is an easier play off the tee, to be sure, but it makes for a much more difficult approach to the green, because it demands a blind approach shot to a long and undulating putting surface that is surrounded by scrubby brush and protected by one bunker short and to the left.

Everything funnels to the green itself, which means a run-up shot is possible from the right side, another reason why a tee shot hit to that part of the hole is preferable. **JS**

**Course:** Le Golf National
(Albatross Course)

**Location:** Guyancourt, France

**Hole:** No. 15

**Length:** 399 yards

**Par:** 4

**Designer:** Hubert Chesneau, Robert
Von Hagge, Pierre Thevenin

**Course Comment:** During the 2003
Open de France, the 15th hole played
to a stroke average of 4.128, with 25
scores of double bogey or worse.

BELOW *The 15th hole at Le Golf
National, Guyancourt, France.*

OPPOSITE *Robert Allenby of Australia
plays his second shot on the 15th hole
at Le Golf National, June 2004.*

## No. ⑮ LE GOLF NATIONAL
### (ALBATROSS COURSE)

Le Golf National's par-4 15th hole marks the beginning of what the French call their own little version of Amen Corner. The course's No. 1 handicap hole is visually impressive and more than a little intimidating from the tee box, as it doglegs right around a huge lake all the way from tee to green.

Golfers would be wise to hit their tee shots as far as they can down the left side of the fairway, allowing them to stay away from the water and shorten the tricky approach as much as possible.

The second shot requires a carry over a stream to a relatively small but three-tiered green. Whatever you do, especially when the pin is in front, don't dare leave the approach short, something that will make a big number a strong possibility. It's far better to make a safe play for the center tier, and be satisfied with a well-earned par.

Le Golf National has played host to the PGA European Tour's Open de France each year since 1991, and some of the world's top players have been crowned champions in recent years, including Retief Goosen (1997, 1999), Colin Montgomerie (2000), and Jose Maria Olazabal (2001). **KA**

## No. ⓯ CASA DE CAMPO (TEETH OF THE DOG)

**Course:** Casa de Campo (Teeth of the Dog)

**Location:** La Romana, Dominican Republic

**Hole:** No. 15

**Length:** 384 yards

**Par:** 4

**Designer:** Pete Dye

**Course Comment:** Teeth of the Dog is the regular host of an NCAA Division I women's tournament, as well as the site of the 1974 World Amateur Team Championship, which was won by the United States.

Long before the first hapless hacker deposited his inaugural balata into the Caribbean Sea's clear, cool waters that define the edges of the aptly named Teeth of the Dog course at Casa de Campo, the Dominican laborers had already assigned the track its foreboding moniker.

The land on which Pete Dye molded the 6,989-yard track was dubbed Dientes del Perro (Teeth of the Dog) by locals because of the area's sharp coral rock, and when the seaside masterpiece was eventually completed the name remained.

In total, Teeth of the Dog has eight holes that hug the edge of the Caribbean Sea, but none is as dramatic as the par-4 15th.

The 15th begins a trio of backside ocean holes and sets the stage for a dramatic finish. The 384-yard hole bends gently to the right with a drive from a slightly elevated tee box to a narrow landing area that slopes toward the right.

A waste bunker looms down the right side with the beach and clear blue waters of the Caribbean beyond running the length of the hole. Most players will have little more than a pitching wedge approach shot to a well-bunkered green that appears perched on the edge of a peninsula. **RH**

## No. ⓯ METROPOLITAN GOLF CLUB

**Course:** Metropolitan Golf Club

**Location:** South Oakleigh, Melbourne, Australia

**Hole:** No. 15

**Length:** 467 yards

**Par:** 4

**Designer:** J.B. MacKenzie, Alister MacKenzie, Dick Wilson

**Course Comment:** The 1997 Australian Open at Metropolitan Golf Club was one of the most exciting ever, with England's Lee Westwood needing four holes to edge native son Greg Norman in a sudden-death playoff.

Amazingly, despite having almost half of its course taken away in 1960 because of the need to build a local school, Metropolitan Golf Club remains one of the finest courses "down under." One of the holes lost was the celebrated par-4 14th, which Gene Sarazen proclaimed "one of golf's best" after winning the 1936 Australian Open.

Metropolitan's original layout had been built in 1908 by member J.B. MacKenzie, and the front nine, along with holes 17 and 18, remain much the same today.

Holes 10–16, however, had to be rebuilt on an adjacent parcel of land, and American architect Dick Wilson made the best of a bad situation, crafting seven new holes that blended in nicely.

The most difficult of those new additions is the 15th, a long slight dogleg left that features a bunker to the left of the landing area. It's that side, however, that offers the best angle to a green that slopes from front left to back right and is protected by a huge bunker at the right front.

Metropolitan has played host to numerous Victoria Opens, seven Australian Opens, five Australian PGAs, and five Australian Amateurs. It was also the site of the 2001 World Golf Championships-Match Play Championship, won by Steve Stricker. **KA**

**Course:** Black Diamond Ranch & Country Club (Quarry Course)

**Location:** Lecanto, Florida, USA

**Hole:** No. 15

**Length:** 371 yards

**Par:** 4

**Designer:** Tom Fazio

**Course Comment:** *Golfweek* named Quarry Course 14th among "America's 100 Best Modern Courses" for 1997 and 17th for 1999. Black Diamond is situated in Florida's rolling "horse country," with thoroughbred farms dotting the landscape and wonderfully uncharacteristic elevation changes.

## No. ⑮ BLACK DIAMOND RANCH & COUNTRY CLUB (QUARRY COURSE)

Legendary American golf writer Dan Jenkins calls Nos. 13–17 on Black Diamond Ranch's Quarry Course "the five best consecutive holes of golf in the world." Jenkins's estimation is hard to debate.

The entire batch skirts the edges of the layout's namesake dolomite mine and, while Nos. 13–17 are the heart of the Quarry Course, the par-4 15th may be the track's soul.

Considered the course's signature hole, the tee box sits high atop the rim of the quarry and looks down on a split fairway that is guarded by an expansive bunker down the left. Beyond the fairway bunker is a lake that runs the entire length of the hole.

The right fairway is about 30 feet higher than the left landing area and allows for a safe play away from the predominant hazards. The left landing area, however, affords an easier approach shot.

Although relatively flat, the green is well protected. A pair of bunkers guards the front of the putting surface. Anything long is also doomed to a sandy demise with a large bunker looming behind the green. Most pin positions are accessible, but beware anything cut in the back left, which brings the water into play.

Despite the assortment of hazards, the 15th is considered a birdie hole and is arguably the best of what some count as an unrivaled assortment of golf holes. **RH**

**Course:** Royal St. George's Golf Club

**Location:** Sandwich, Kent, England

**Hole:** No. 15

**Length:** 478 yards

**Par:** 4

**Designer:** Laidlaw Purves, Alister MacKenzie, J.J.F. Pennink

**Course Comment:** Through an immense spread of sand dunes, all lined up along the North Sea coast of Kent, are three outstanding and historic golf courses, Royal St. George's, Royal Cinque Ports, and Prince's Golf Club.

BELOW AND OPPOSITE *The 15th hole at Royal St. George's Golf Club.*

# No. ⓲ ROYAL ST. GEORGE'S GOLF CLUB

Looking at this hole on the scorecard doesn't do it justice. In fact, it looks pretty easy on the scorecard or according to the course pros. But they haven't been able to design a scorecard that copies the wind on each hole.

Until you stand on the tee and feel that wind, you won't ever understand how challenging this hole — in fact, most holes at St. George — can play.

Into the prevailing wind, this hole will play much longer and place a greater premium on the approach shot.

There are two bunkers along the left side at about 230 yards out, and two smaller ones along the right side. The best drive is about 260 yards right down the middle. This leaves about 200 yards to a dangerous green with plenty of trouble.

It will require a long iron to a green protected by three cross bunkers that run right up to the edge of the green and fall away on both sides.

And don't forget the wind. It can blow up your scorecard in a hurry. **TJ**

## No. ⑮ BANFF SPRINGS

**Course:** Banff Springs

**Location:** Banff, Alberta, Canada

**Hole:** No. 15

**Length:** 411 yards

**Par:** 4

**Designer:** Stanley Thompson

**Course Comment:** The century-old Banff Springs resort with its 800 rooms features 17 restaurants, a 35,000 square-foot spa, and glorious elegance. And a first-class, 27-hole, links-style course.

"Masterpiece" is the best word to describe Banff Springs. This is truly a resort in the grand tradition. The setting along the Bow River, presided over by three massive mountains, is glorious.

With 27 great holes, picking one isn't easy. As a guest, though, you can play them all, but the hole you will most likely remember is No. 15.

Your tee shot must clear a creek, which isn't very hard to do. But it also should be hit from right to left to the target area, center fairway, a good 250 yards from the tee. This will leave you with an open second shot to an undulating green guarded by traps right, left, and back.

There is also a large trap along the right side of the fairway.

The green slopes upward at the back and has many other undulations. Watch for putts that break two and even three times.

This is a scenic hole, but they all are when you get into the mountains. However, none of them is as special as No. 15. **TJ**

Location: Harlech, Gwynedd, Wales

Hole: No. 15

Length: 435 yards

Par: 4

Designer: Harold Finch-Hatton, F.W. Hawtree

Course Comment: Cecil Leitch won the last of her British Championships at Royal St. David's in 1926. Nationally prominent events held at Royal St. David's include the Home Internationals, the University Match, the British Ladies, the Welsh Ladies, the British Youths, the Welsh Amateur, the Club Professionals Championship, the British Boys, and the Ladies Home Internationals.

# No. ⑮ ROYAL ST. DAVID'S GOLF CLUB

A sense of history along with a feel for the natural lay of the land are the trademarks at Royal St. David's Golf Club. Mountains and sea, orchids and castles are just some of the highlights on the course that have nothing at all to do with golf. However, as you might imagine, the golf is very good, as well.

You can see Harlech Castle from many holes on the course, and you have to go some way to find a more historical landmark on a golf course. The castle was built in 1299 by Edward I and nearly 650 years later one of his descendants, King Edward VII, became captain of Royal St. David's Golf Club when he was but a prince.

Just as Royal Portcawl is regarded as the finest course in South Wales, Royal St David's is without peer in the North. The scenery at Royal St. David's is as compelling as anywhere in Britain.

The course's most famous hole may be No. 16, which features the Lleyn peninsula across Tremadog Bay, but the 15th is the second in a finishing five-hole stretch that forms a loop through dunes between Harlech Castle and the sea. No. 15 is a stern test adjacent to the Snowdon Mountains.

The 15th, like the rest of the course, doesn't offer much in the way of daunting length. No. 15 is just 435 yards on a course that measures just 6,495 yards overall. But each offers challenges that length cannot define. Yes, the course is under 6,500 yards, but it plays as a par 69 for competitive events. It has five fairly short holes with large greens, but it is also noted for a succession of long-testing par-4 holes. The difficulty of the 15th (one of the short par 4s) is increased by a wind that often blasts in your face and a fairway that flows to the right. Two precise shots are called for, and if you don't achieve your aim, the penalties almost certainly preclude par.

There are no bunkers on the hole, but rugged hills featuring brush and sand dot the landscape on either side, all the way down the fairway. It is difficult to get to the green, because a high shot must negotiate the prevailing wind, and a runner faces a hollow area in front of the green. **JB**

## No. ⑮ RATTLEWOOD GOLF COURSE

**Course:** Rattlewood Golf Course

**Location:** Mount Airy, Maryland, USA

**Hole:** No. 15

**Length:** 301 yards

**Par:** 4

**Designer:** Brian Ault

**Course Comment:** This course is known for many things, but the large greens really stand out. No. 15 is a perfect example of one of Rattlewood's large putting surfaces.

Maryland isn't the largest state in the USA but it comes up big when it comes to golf courses. Maryland boasts some excellent private and public places to play a round.

Rattlewood Golf Course is one of those great places everyone can play. No membership required here. But you wouldn't know that from the quality of the golf course. A public country club is a fair description.

The 15th hole, a 301-yard par 4, is a perfect example of why this course is special. You don't need a cart to see this gem. You get a perfect view of this scenic hole from the pro shop.

Don't be fooled by the length. From the back tees, you are looking to clear a shot over 175 yards of water, so be prepared to lose a few balls.

But if you can clear the water and avoid the two bunkers on the left side next to each other and the other bunker on the right, you should be in very good shape for at least a par.

Watch out for the two bunkers on the front side of the green on your approach shot.

The green is a pretty good size and slopes a little left to right, but it's a very difficult place to knock in a birdie putt. **TJ**

## No. ⑮ SHADOW CREEK GOLF COURSE

**Course:** Shadow Creek Golf Course

**Location:** North Las Vegas, Nevada, USA

**Hole:** No. 15

**Length:** 438 yards

**Par:** 4

**Designer:** Tom Fazio, Andy Banfield

**Course Comment:** Keep the camera in the car. While there is plenty of wildlife around and some scenic views, photography is not allowed. You are here to play golf, not take pictures.

The 438-yard 15th plays back to the north alongside Shadow Creek, which winds along the left side of the fairway. The creek then cuts right through the fairway in front of the green before wrapping around the right side of the green.

With the creek coming between the fairway and the green, you must fly the creek to find the putting surface. And beware of a good size bunker on the right side of the fairway.

The green is cut into four different sections, each with a drastic change in elevation. The perfect tee shot is down the right side — watch out for the bunker just off the fairway — which will give you a nice look at the green.

Once a very private course, Shadow Creek is now open to guests of MGM properties. And everything is first class all the way. A private limousine will transport you to and from your tee time. Not a bad way to travel.

Their promise is: "Your personal caddie will greet and guide you through a golfing experience you will never forget." They usually keep to their word, and the golf is great. **TJ**

**Course:** Highlands Links

**Location:** Ingonish Beach, Nova Scotia, Canada

**Hole:** No. 15

**Length:** 540 yards

**Par:** 4

**Designer:** Stanley Thompson

**Course Comment:** In the 2003 Golfers Choice Awards, Highlands Links retained its gold ranking as "Best Course" with *SCORE Golf*'s readers. In 2002, Highlands Links was ranked by *SCORE Golf*'s panel of Canadian golf experts as the best public course in the country.

In 1939 internationally renowned golf-course designer Stanley Thompson was invited by Canada's National Park Service to create a golf course in a magnificent coastal setting within Cape Breton Highlands National Park.

So how did he do? How about masterful.

Thompson designed and built what he called his "mountains and ocean" course, an inspired piece of golf architecture that has proved to be one of his finest achievements.

Each hole bears a colorful Scottish name designated with signposts in both Gaelic and English. The No. 15 hole is named "Tattie Bogle." This unusual name refers to potato pits, where potatoes are placed in hillocks and covered with thatch.

This 540-yard par 5 is a tremendous golf hole. And if you play to the right you are rewarded with a most stunning view of Ingonish Island in the background. So you get the view regardless of your score.

It's a fairly straight hole with little trouble until you get closer to the green — unless you count the dips in the fairway and the trees that line up along the entire route.

There are six bunkers along the left side of the putting surface which start about 160 yards out. There also are two bunkers to the right side. **TJ**

## No. ⑮ WHISTLER GOLF CLUB

**Course:** Whistler Golf Club

**Location:** Whistler, British Columbia, Canada

**Hole:** No. 15

**Length:** 361 yards

**Par:** 4

**Designer:** Arnold Palmer

**Course Comment:** In 2000 the Whistler Golf Club received an extensive $2.2 million renovation to ensure this 6,676-yard course continues its legacy of excellence.

The Whistler Golf Club is a par-72, 18-hole golf course winding past gentle mountain streams and nine lakes, which easily exceeds the expectations of the most discriminating golfer. This was Arnold Palmer's first Canadian design, and still one of his best.

This is a dogleg left where accuracy can bring you a birdie or at least a par. This is placement golf where length can stay in the bag.

You want to aim left center here, but don't go too far left and catch either the bunker or water. There is a creek on the right side of the cart path so you slicers, watch out!

A drive of about 220 yards straight up the middle puts you in a good position to go for the green. You will only be about 150 yards out.

As with the rest of this great golf course, wind will be a factor here. On No. 15 the wind is usually in your face.

There is a tier that runs right across the middle of the green, so check the flag position before hitting that approach shot.

There is a bunker to the right front of the green and that creek shows up again behind the putting surface. **TJ**

## No. ⑮ OAKMONT COUNTRY CLUB

**Course:** Oakmont Country Club

**Location:** Oakmont, Pennsylvania, USA

**Hole:** No. 15

**Length:** 502 yards

**Par:** 4

**Designer:** Henry Fownes

**Course Comment:** Oakmont deserves high praise for turning back the clock. In 1999, the course completed a program to clear out trees in order to restore the course to its more original open-space design.

Like many outstanding golf courses, Oakmont Country Club has 18 holes of memorable and challenging golf. Picking out a few as special is therefore no easy task. At courses like these, you can have four different favorite holes in one foursome.

Oakmont is one of America's top classic courses. With 18 classic holes. No. 15 is one of those that often stands out from the elite crowd. It's a pretty straight hole with a slight curve to the right. The green is off to the right just a bit from the fairway.

The key here is length. Any par 4 that tops 500 yards is one that requires you to hit it with a lot of power. This hole comes down to your tee shot. If you don't hit your tee shot a good 280 yards from the back tees, you can forget about birdie — and probably par.

A long second shot is not what you want to be looking at here. The green is tricky and it's not easy to hold it, so the closer your second shot the better.

There are bunkers on the right side of the fairway that you can't see from the tee, and bunkers on the left that you can see.

The fairway slopes from left to right so take that into account when teeing off with the big driver. **TJ**

**Course:** Somerset Hills Country Club

**Location:** Bernardsville, New Jersey, USA

**Hole:** No. 15

**Length:** 394 yards

**Par:** 4

**Designer:** A.W. Tillinghast

**Course Comment:** You might say Somerset Hills is for the birds, but members at the ultra-exclusive club that has hosted many major championships wouldn't take it as an insult. It would be a compliment because in 1999, Somerset Hills became the 162nd course worldwide to be recognized by the Audubon Cooperative System as a Certified Audubon Cooperative Sanctuary.

Variety is the key word at Somerset Hills. The front nine is open and flat and the back half is tree-lined and hilly. Length, terrain, different kinds of greens, and many unique approaches and strategies form a collection of seemingly haphazard characteristics that blend perfectly as a golf course.

Variety is a staple of many of the designs of A.W. Tillinghast, whose trademark, ironically enough, was that he didn't have a trademark. He didn't lay claim to the Redan, and certainly railroad ties weren't his thing. Tillinghast didn't feel the need to put his stamp on a piece of property. Rather, he let the piece of property become the trademark. He only supplied the touches necessary to turn land into golf hole.

Some critics of Tillinghast say he lacked a design philosophy, but his admirers say he let the course come to him, rather then vice versa. But, however you view his work, the result is some wonderful variety at many Tillinghast designs — not only from course to course or from front to back; sometimes the contrast is stark from hole to hole.

At Somerset's 15th hole, considered by many to be the most memorable hole on the golf course, the variety and choices are taken even further. They change from shot to shot. The choices off the tee can make a big difference in how the approach shot will be played. A player can play it safe, hit a 2-iron or fairway wood down the center of the 394-yard hole and have a short iron left. Or, if a player is a big hitter seeking a half wedge into the green, he can take out the big stick and let her rip over the top of the dogleg right.

Whichever route you choose at No. 15, you have a legitimate chance at birdie with a solid approach shot. Obviously, if you cut the dogleg, you have

a real chance, although nothing is automatic. The tight tree line offers a feeling of intimacy on this short hole, but it also forces accuracy, even though the 15th green is the most spacious at Somerset Hills. There are several bunkers around the green, and there is a creek and a diminutive yet appealing waterfall just two paces from the green.

All of this is hidden from the tee, but becomes pleasantly visible as the player ambles around the dogleg. This hole is scenic and short (on distance, not choices). **JB**

**NEFYN & DISTRICT GOLF CLUB**
**(NEW COURSE)**

**Course:** Nefyn & District Golf Club
(New Course)

**Location:** Pwllheli, Gwynedd, Wales

**Hole:** No. 15

**Length:** 441 yards

**Par:** 4

**Designer:** James Braid, J. H. Taylor

**Course Comment:** "Golf on the precipice of the planet" might seem like an exaggeration, but what else can you say about Nefyn & District Golf Club? It is perched on cliff tops on a narrow peninsula that protrudes out into the Irish Sea.

Where else can you find a pub right on the course and a 26-hole layout that requests that you find enough time to play them all? The answer to that may be nowhere else but Nefyn & District Golf Club, a 1907 oceanside beauty with mountain views. Of course, it is not mandatory that you play all 26 — the layout is broken down into Old and New courses.

The beautiful 15th on the New Course is a long, curvaceous dogleg with protective and cavernous bunkers throughout. Left-handers with a fade and right-handers with a draw had better keep their shots under control. There is trouble down the left side, and anything errant in that direction will make a decent score nearly impossible. Tall grass, mounding, and bunkering making right-handed hooks and left-handed slices a near-suicidal shot for your scorecard. But if you stay in the middle of the fairway, you'll be fine.

You'll find a walking path to the Ty Coch Inn, where you are encouraged to stop for a beverage next to the sea. So even if you are having trouble on your round, somehow afterward, things seem just a bit more palatable. **JB**

**NEW SOUTH WALES GOLF CLUB**

**Course:** New South Wales Golf Club

**Location:** La Perouse, New South Wales, Australia

**Hole:** No. 15

**Length:** 409 yards

**Par:** 4

**Designer:** Alister MacKenzie

**Course Comment:** Four times the Australian PGA Championship was held at New South Wales in the 1990s, and four times the 15th ranked as the hardest hole on the Tour in those years.

The tee shot on this testy par 4 is blind, with players shooting toward a ridge that runs across the fairway and gives the hole, which doglegs gently from left to right, its famous personality.

A strong, straight drive through a narrow chute of dunes to the saddle of land at the fairway's crest will leave you the best opportunity for par — or birdie — here, but it must be a straight and true shot, as trouble awaits anyone veering off the fairway.

It is best to be on the right side to approach the green, which slopes from back to front and seems long and quite narrow from that position. It is guarded by a pair of bunkers to the right and one to the left, and there is definite trouble with any balls that go too far, as up-and-downs from behind the putting surface are few and far between.

And there is no telling what havoc the wind can wreak with any shot here when it blows off the ocean with its usual ferocity. **JS**

---

No. ⓯ **SHAN-SHUI GOLF & COUNTRY CLUB**

**Course:** Shan-Shui Golf & Country Club

**Location:** Sabah, Tawau, Malaysia

**Hole:** No. 15

**Length:** 418 yards

**Par:** 4

**Designer:** Robin Nelson, Neil Haworth

**Course Comment:** Three-quarters of Shan-Shui borders a national park, yet despite its remoteness the layout has hosted the Asian Tour's Sabah Masters since 1998.

Shan-Shui Golf & Country Club is what one would expect from a golf course carved from 350 acres of tropical rainforest — rugged, wild, and entirely unforgettable.

The par-4 17th, for example, cuts a swath through heavy jungle vegetation to a green cradled on three sides by wilderness, while the par-5 seventh seems to cling to the side of a mountain.

Throughout the property, architects Nelson and Haworth were allowed to maximize Shan-Shui's considerable natural terrain and few holes demonstrate this better than the par-4 15th.

The 418-yard hole plays downhill into a rolling fairway that subtly flows to the left.

Tee shots should favor the right side to avoid a small creek that bisects the fairway and weaves its way to the green. But, drives too far right run the risk of finding the jungle and also create the most difficult approach to the elevated green.

The right side of the putting surface drops off dramatically to the creek some 15 feet below, while the left side of the green is protected by a single, deep bunker.

Players are lured into missing the green short and left and will find a recovery from this position difficult. The green cants to the right and requires a bold approach to the right of most pin positions to set up a legitimate birdie opportunity. **RH**

**Course:** PGA West (Nicklaus Tournament Course)

**Location:** La Quinta, California, USA

**Hole:** No. 15

**Length:** 572 yards

**Par:** 5

**Designer:** Jack Nicklaus

**Course Comment:** This is simply a magnificent golf course and it's only fitting that a round on the Tournament Course ends with a dramatic water-crossing shot to the 9th and 18th double green. But No. 15 could be the most demanding on this golf course.

No. **⓯**  # PGA WEST
## (NICKLAUS TOURNAMENT COURSE)

Every hole on this challenging course requires its own unique strategy, especially the 572-yard, par-5 15th, which culminates in a shallow and well-bunkered island green.

There is a reason this hole is nicknamed "Long Island." This hole is long. But with five sets of tees, it can play much shorter. The so-called "regular" tees are at 472 yards while the red tees are the shortest at 417 yards.

Going for this green in two is not advisable. You know what they say about par 5s: it's a bonus shot. Use your bonus shot wisely.

Your second shot should go down the right side and right of where the water begins to come out into the fairway. This will give you your best approach coming into this difficult green.

You need two good shots to get into position for hopefully a great shot. PGA West is home to six world-famous golf courses but few holes are as memorable as Jack Nicklaus' No. 15. A wonderful par 5 with a great payoff at the end. **TJ**

**Course:** Royal Birkdale

**Location:** Southport, Merseyside, England

**Hole:** No. 15

**Length:** 543 yards

**Par:** 5

**Designer:** George Lowe, F.W. Hawtree, J.H. Taylor

**Course Comment:** Should any competitive event at Royal Birkdale go to a playoff, No. 15 is where it begins. It then continues through No. 18, then back to No. 15 again if necessary.

**BELOW AND OPPOSITE** *Views of the 15th hole at Royal Birkdale.*

## No. ⑮  ROYAL BIRKDALE

This golf hole is a challenge of the highest order, both in the categories of length and placement. At 543 yards, Royal Birkdale's 15th is the longest hole on the golf course and also one of the most difficult to attack. There are 13 bunkers to be negotiated on this long and narrow hole.

Although long and arduous, it appears the designers decided to let players get a false sense of comfort. Off the tee, it is a shot that allows you to swing away. The landing area is fairly ample, and the tee shot must be long because the hole gets progressively more difficult as you move along.

The second shot must be placed on the extreme left side of the fairway in order to ensure a clear shot to the green on the third. This is no easy task, however, because any shot too far left disappears into gorse. Also lost from view will be any chance at birdie. It is a very tricky challenge, because you simply must be as left as possible because anything in the center of the fairway has an extremely difficult shot into the green.

If you don't find yourself in proper position for the third shot, there are bunkers blocking your path to the green. This forces a high lofting shot into a green that slopes, rolls, and winds. The putting surface is large, but in this case that is no blessing. Pin placement can be devilish with all the elevation changes, so just being on the putting surface doesn't guarantee a two-putt. In fact, many players would rather face a short chip than a long putt at Royal Birkdale's 15th hole.

No. 15 is Royal Birkdale's toughest, and that's saying something on a course that is as well respected as this one. The course is a common host of major championships in Britain. It stages the Women's British Open in 2005 and the men come to the course to play the British Open in 2008. This will mark the ninth time that the British Open will have been held at Royal Birkdale and the third visit for the women. **JB**

**Course:** Princeville Resort Golf Club (Prince Course)

**Location:** Princeville, Kauai, Hawaii, USA

**Hole:** No. 15

**Length:** 576 yards

**Par:** 5

**Designer:** Robert Trent Jones Jr.

**Course Comment:** The Prince Course accompanies the Makai at Princeville, both designed by Robert Trent Jones Jr.

## No. ⑮ PRINCEVILLE RESORT GOLF CLUB (PRINCE COURSE)

Exaggeration often is far too easy for both marketing departments and golf course designers to employ. The "best of this" and the "greatest of that" are thrown about so frequently that the hyperbolic phrases have been rendered nearly meaningless. However, this is a golf course and, more specifically, a golf hole that deserves the acclaim it receives — both from its creator, Robert Trent Jones Jr., and from the staffers at Princeville Resort who are paid to expound its glory.

The golf course is Princeville Resort's Prince layout, which blends the perfection and serenity of nature with the creativity of humans. Here you are surrounded by beauty, no matter where you are on the course. The vistas include green bluffs that skirt mountains and the Pacific Ocean, offering stunning views everywhere you look. Considered one of the best, if not the best course in Hawaii, it almost certainly is among the most challenging. It has a course rating of 75.3 and a slope of 145. Named after Prince Albert, the only son of King Kamehameha IV and Queen Emma, the Prince Course goes uphill, crosses ravines, and then goes back downhill.

Jones Jr. called the 15th "one of the finest par 5s I've ever built." Designers are famous for couching their creations with "one of the finest," but in this case Jones can hardly be accused of exaggeration.

The beauty is unparalleled, and the strategy is almost as striking. Jones Jr., like his father, tries to employ risk-reward on all of his golf holes, particularly the par 5s. The 15th at the Prince is a perfect example, with ravines virtually encircling the landing areas from tee to green. There are no bunkers until you reach the putting surface, but a ball that finds one of the ravines is in more trouble than any bunker could offer.

The first bunker you encounter on the green is a real doozy. A menacing pot bunker protects the front of the green, eliminating the possibility of a running approach for anyone courageous enough to give the green a go in two shots. If there is one hole you could play on the Prince that would exemplify the personality of the entire layout, it would be No. 15. It is beautiful, challenging, and memorable. **JB**

**Course:** Gorge Vale Golf Club

**Location:** Victoria, British Columbia, Canada

**Hole:** No. 15

**Length:** 541 yards

**Par:** 5

**Designer:** A. Vernon Macon, Norman Woods, Les Furber

**Course Comment:** Architect Les Furber oversaw a renovation in 2001–2002 that lengthened Gorge Vale from approximately 6,380 yards to 6,820 yards.

# No. ⑮ GORGE VALE GOLF CLUB

Although it is just minutes from downtown Victoria, Gorge Vale Golf Club takes players into a serene, park-like environment set amid forests and rolling terrain.

The scenic par-5 15th hole features an elevated tee that offers a splendid vista of the surrounding countryside. The tee shot must be hit to a fairway that narrows at the landing area, as groups of trees line both sides to catch drives that are hit slightly wide.

The green can be reached in two by the longest of hitters, but it is the smallest putting surface on the course, and is surrounded by bunkers at the left front, right front, and rear. For those who lay up, the left side is the preferred play, offering the best angle of approach to the green. But do so with caution, as two bunkers on the left side of the fairway will swallow errant shots.

Gorge Vale has played host to the Canadian Professional Golf Tour's Victoria Open on numerous occasions, as it is part of a four-course rotation for the annual event. Players capturing Victoria Open titles at Gorge Vale include such notables as current PGA Tour players Craig Parry (1987), Steve Stricker (1990), and Brandt Jobe (1993). **KA**

**Course:** Pevero Golf Club

**Location:** Costa Smeralda, Sardinia, Italy

**Hole:** No. 15

**Length:** 480 yards

**Par:** 5

**Designer:** Robert Trent Jones Sr.

**Course Comment:** South African golfer Dale Hayes won the PGA European Tour's 1978 Italian Open, held at Pevero.

BELOW AND OPPOSITE *Two views of the 15th hole at Pevero Golf Club.*

## No. 15   PEVERO GOLF CLUB

Part of the luxurious Costa Smeralda Resort, a favorite playground of the wealthy, Pevero Golf Club is widely considered to be one of the most beautiful places to play a round of golf in the world.

The renowned Robert Trent Jones Sr. design is set on a hilly peninsula between the gulf of Pevero and the bay of Cala di Volpe, providing sweeping views of both bodies of water as well as the emerald waters of the Mediterranean beyond ("Costa Smeralda" is Italian for "emerald coast").

Pevero is not a lengthy course, measuring only 6,205 yards from the back tees. It follows that the 15th hole is a relatively short par 5 at only 480 yards, but it plays much longer because it's almost entirely uphill, featuring magnificent views of the bay and the surrounding hillsides.

The fairway is lined on both sides by thick, impenetrable macchia bushes, a form of scrub vegetation found in the Mediterranean region. And those attempting to get home in two should beware. Shots that come up short or wide are likely to find one of the four bunkers that lie to the front left, front right, and right side of the small, crowned putting surface. **KA**

| |
|---|
| **Course:** Hirono Golf Club |
| **Location:** Kobe, Japan |
| **Hole:** No. 15 |
| **Length:** 565 yards |
| **Par:** 5 |
| **Designer:** Charles Alison |
| **Course Comment:** Jack Nicklaus, during an exhibition in 1963, became the first person to reach this green in two, using a driver/3-wood. This, of course, was long before the days of graphite and titanium. |

Hirono Golf Club is one of the top courses in Japan, winding through moderate undulations and encompassing the country's best in layout, design, and diversity. It doesn't hurt that it sits in Kobe, the birthplace of Japanese golf. It helps further that Hirono was designed by famed architect Charles Alison.

Even though Hirono was finished and opened for business in 1932, it escaped the trappings that hinder many Japanese golf courses built before 1985. Before that time, many Japanese course designs were influenced greatly by owners of individual clubs who insisted on having their own personal tastes incorporated into the layout. This often resulted in courses that lacked design philosophy and, frankly, made for some rather uninteresting golf.

Alison, however, insisted on autonomy when designing courses in Japan, so he was able to avoid the issue that plagued many courses. So, if you are looking for quality golf in Japan, there are two basic criteria: either book your tee times at a course that was built after 1985, or find a design by Charles Alison. His work at Hirono Golf Club is respected worldwide, and the par-5 15th is one of the shining reasons why.

Another reason is that the natural land terrain at Hirono bears a fairly strong resemblance to the heathlands of Britain. Alison saw this immediately and recognized a great opportunity to incorporate some of the great British design features into a hole sitting in another continent.

The dogleg left could be shortened were it not for one not-so-small detail: a 100-foot pine tree that keeps the corner from being cut. This keeps the long hitters from making an attempt to cut the dogleg on the left. Three sneaky bunkers on the right penalize players who are looking for too good an angle to get around the dogleg on the second shot.

Cross-bunkers and ravines in the fairway, and still more bunkers protecting the green, are other heathland features at No. 15. The ground is more green than might be seen at some British heathland courses such as Sunningdale or the Berkshire, but the resemblance to some of the classic holes at these venues is inescapable when standing on Hirono's 15th tee. **JB**

# No. ⑮  WOODLANDS GOLF CLUB

**Course:** Woodlands Golf Club

**Location:** Mordialloc, Victoria, Australia

**Hole:** No. 15

**Length:** 562 yards

**Par:** 5

**Designer:** R.S. Banks, S. Bennett

**Course Comment:** Both Banks and Bennett were area golf professionals, with Banks laying out a nine-hole course at this spot, originally known as the Mordialloc Golf Club, in 1913 and Bennett adding another nine four years later.

Though it rarely gets the same acclaim as the better known classics in Melbourne's famed Sand Belt, Woodlands is quite highly regarded among local players, and its 15th is said to be one of the region's finest par 5s. That's primarily because of its exceptional bunkering.

The first places that come into play are both sides of the fairway; neither can be reached with a tee shot, but they most definitely come into play with a golfer's second shot and must be cleared — and avoided — in order to set up a third shot to an elevated green that is quite small and features a bunker to the left.

The diminutive size of the putting surface — as well as its characteristic firmness — make it extremely difficult for players to hit — and hold — second shots here, and very few of them ever find themselves tapping in for eagle. Rather, they have to content themselves with getting on in three, even though shorter approaches are almost as difficult to keep on the green if they are not deftly hit. **JS**

## No. ⓲ PINE VALLEY GOLF CLUB

**Course:** Pine Valley Golf Club

**Location:** Clementon, New Jersey, USA

**Hole:** No. 15

**Length:** 591 yards

**Par:** 5

**Designer:** George Crump, Harry S. Colt, Hugh Wilson

**Course Comment:** From a width of about 60 yards at the landing area for drives, Pine Valley's 15th hole gradually narrows until it measures only about 20 paces across as it nears the green.

Pine Valley Golf Club's 15th hole is slightly out of character for what many consider the world's toughest golf course, as it features the only fairway that is not scarred by deep, ragged sand bunkers, native scrub, or scattered spots of deep, gnarly rough.

That may not have been the case had George Crump not died before this hole was completed, as sketches seem to indicate the course's owner and designer may have been considering adding a bunker complex to the fairway. This hole still has plenty of difficulty, however.

It is Pine Valley's longest, and has a multitude of obstacles, beginning with the lake that must be carried with the tee shot. The fairway makes a gradual uphill climb and slopes from left to right at the landing area, which does contain scattered pockets of sand on both sides for those who miss with their drives.

The fairway then begins to narrow as it draws closer to the green, with thick stands of pines pinching in on both the left and right, leaving only a tight opening at the entrance of the putting surface and preventing all but the most confident of players from attempting to get home in two. **KA**

## No. ⓲ NEW SEABURY RESORT (OCEAN COURSE)

**Course:** New Seabury Resort (Ocean Course)

**Location:** New Seabury, Massachusetts, USA

**Hole:** No. 15

**Length:** 540 yards

**Par:** 5

**Designer:** William F. Mitchell

**Course Comment:** The course has been lengthened and new strategically placed bunkers, waste areas, and water hazards make the Ocean Course tougher than ever.

New Seabury is home to two of New England's premier golf venues, the Ocean Course and the Dunes Course. The Ocean Course provides spectacular views of Nantucket Sound and Martha's Vineyard.

But forget the spectacular views. These are spectacular golf courses. And No. 15 on the Ocean Course is a spectacular hole.

The par-5 15th hole will make most people's "Best of" list when it comes to par-5 holes. And that's a pretty big statement. But this is a pretty big golf hole. You must go left off the tee and carry the water. The fairway then cuts back to the right side for another shot over water.

You need to hit a good 215 yards off the tee to clear the water. Another 40 to 50 yards puts you in really good shape. But the fun is just beginning.

There is some "safe" area along the left side of the fairway for your second shot, but the best shot is over the water.

Your third shot should be a short iron to a fairly good-size green.

This double dogleg — don't chew off more than you can handle — is as fun as it is challenging. **TJ**

**Course:** Treetops Resort
(Smith Signature Course)

**Location:** Gaylord, Michigan, USA

**Hole:** No. 15

**Par:** 5

**Length:** 485 yards

**Designer:** Rick Smith

**Course Comment:** There are 81 holes
at this exquisite resort in the middle
of northern Michigan's golf mecca.
While the Smith Signature Course is
a must-play, so is the par-3
Threetops Course that features
elevations of as much as 100 feet.

# No. ⓯ TREETOPS RESORT
## (SMITH SIGNATURE COURSE)

Walking up to the tee on No. 15 makes you think a simple eagle or birdie. The scorecard says 485 yards, a little short for a par 5. The fairway looks wide and inviting, giving your driver a little more confidence.

Reaching the green in two not only seems possible, it seems easy.

But hold on. There is trouble ahead. So hold off putting a birdie on your scorecard until you're finished.

There are some fairway bunkers along the left side of the fairway. To carry them it's 288 yards from the back tees. To reach them, it's 233 yards.

A good drive down the center of the fairway gives you a nice-looking approach shot. But now it gets tough.

The entire hole is uphill but the last 100 yards is an even steeper incline. It's a good 50-foot climb from 100 yards out to the green.

The putting surface is very narrow. It's 39 paces long, but only 10 paces wide. Cut into the side of a hill that is loaded with bunkers, the green has rough on both sides and slopes severely. Trying to get up-and-down in two from the side rough is not easy. So it's important to hit your target.

There is also a severe tier in the middle of the green. **TJ**

**Course:** Harbour Town Golf Links

**Location:** Hilton Head Island, South Carolina, USA

**Hole:** No. 15

**Length:** 571 yards

**Par:** 5

**Designer:** Pete Dye

**Course Comment:** In the 2004 MCI Heritage, No. 15 yielded only two eagles in four rounds, compared with a combined 24 eagles given up by Harbour Town's two other par 5s.

Pete Dye designed Harbour Town as a thinking man's golf course, placing a heavy emphasis on shot-making, and nowhere is this more true than the 15th hole.

The longest and toughest of Harbour Town's three par 5s, No. 15 is a true three-shotter, even with today's golf equipment technology, because of the tight turn to the left at the end of the hole. Because of the precision such a strategy demands, not many PGA Tour professionals attempt to reach this green in two in the annual playing of the MCI Heritage.

The tee shot must be kept in the center or right center of a fairway that's lined by trees on both sides, a long, serpentine waste bunker on the left, and a pair of bunkers on the right. The second shot should be placed on the right side of the fairway, away from a lagoon on the left that meanders all the way to the front of the green.

The putting surface, one of the smallest on the PGA Tour when Harbour Town opened in 1969, has since been enlarged, but it is as well protected as ever, with the lagoon to the left and bunkers at the front left and front right of the green. **KA**

**RIGHT** *Ted Purdy of the USA hits a shot on the 15th hole at Harbour Town Golf Links, April 2004.*

| | |
|---|---|
| **Course:** Lake Nona Golf Club | |
| **Location:** Orlando, Florida, USA | |
| **Hole:** No. 15 | |
| **Length:** 578 yards | |
| **Par:** 5 | |
| **Designer:** Tom Fazio | |

**Course Comment:** Only four years after opening, Lake Nona played host to the inaugural Solheim Cup in 1990, with the 15th playing a key late role in several matches as the United States defeated Europe 11½ to 4½.

This Tom Fazio-designed layout is a supreme test of golf, and some of the most famous international professionals have elected to make Orlando's Lake Nona Golf Club their home base in the United States — among them Annika Sorenstam, Ernie Els, Nick Faldo, Retief Goosen, Sergio Garcia, Justin Rose, and Trevor Immelman. The game's top players wouldn't settle for anything less than the best.

When those players are knocking it around their home course, they certainly can't be disappointed with Lake Nona's signature hole, the par-5 15th, which bends from right to left around Buck Lake and is a true challenge to any player's skills.

There's nothing but trouble left off the tee, so players are well-advised to take their drives down the right center of the landing area to be sure they avoid the lake and a long bunker that runs 175 yards down the left side of the fairway along the water.

That play also allows for a better look at the bunkerless green on the second shot, although most players prefer to lay up, setting up a short pitch into the kidney-shaped putting surface and an opportunity for a well-earned birdie. **KA**

**Course:** Royal Adelaide Golf Club

**Location:** Seaton, Adelaide, Australia

**Hole:** No. 15

**Length:** 499 yards

**Par:** 5

**Designer:** Alister MacKenzie

**Course Comment:** MacKenzie's layout was lengthened and toughened by Peter Thomson prior to the 1998 Australian Open, and some thought it went too far. Thomson made some areas so tight that marshals had to be stationed in order to keep the gallery moving through in single file parallel to the fairway.

# No. ⓯ ROYAL ADELAIDE GOLF CLUB

Royal Adelaide was one of a collection of courses that bear the Alister MacKenzie imprint. The famous doctor who never practiced medicine made a jaunt through Australia in 1926 and left a mark that still lives to this day. Although the course has gone through a number of renovations since MacKenzie's day (the only hole that remains exactly as MacKenzie designed it is the third), it is still pure MacKenzie. Just a little longer, and (for major championships) quite a bit tighter.

Six-time British Open champion Peter Thomson, along with partner Michael Wolveridge, have enhanced this seaside links. Bunkers and slopes were added, along with length.

It would seem that the difficulties at No. 15 were severe enough to be left alone. It is a double dogleg whose hazards are apparent right from the beginning. There isn't much mystery about the 15th hole. No hidden danger, nothing to hide. Just 500 yards of pure golf hole. It zigzags a bit, perhaps, but nothing gimmicky. It is an unnatural path to the finish that MacKenzie somehow pulls off naturally.

The tee shot is through a tunnel of trees, which at first protects it from the wind, then opens it to the whims of the breeze down the fairway. Because the tee box is protected from the wind, it is very difficult for the player to know what the ball will do once it gets into the open spaces.

The hole first turns left, and then right, and you must stay in the fairway to avoid the heathery rough that looks airy but is far thicker a lie than a controlled golf shot requires.

It is a par 5 reachable in two, but there are two large bunkers on the right side that make it a difficult shot. The green is small and undulating, as well, so the challenge continues until the ball hits the bottom of the cup.

When MacKenzie first saw the Royal Adelaide Golf Club he said, "One finds a most delightful combination of sand dunes and fir trees, a most unusual combination even at the best seaside courses. No seaside courses that I have seen possess such magnificent sand craters as those at Royal Adelaide." MacKenzie's lasting impact at Seaton was to incorporate these sand dunes into the course. **JB**

**OPPOSITE** *The 15th hole at Royal Adelaide.*

### No. ⑮   SHOREACRES GOLF CLUB

**Course:** Shoreacres Golf Club

**Location:** Lake Bluff, Illinois, USA

**Hole:** No. 15

**Length:** 521 yards

**Par:** 5

**Designer:** Seth Raynor

**Course Comment:** A few years back, Shoreacres decided to add a little bit of yardage to the scorecard. Five holes were lengthened to give bigger hitters more of a challenging shot. No. 15 went from 478 yards to 521 yards on the new back tee.

No. 15 isn't considered the toughest hole on the golf course, but you wouldn't think so standing on the tee on this very scenic golf hole at one of Illinois' elite tracks.

From the back tees you need to hit about 230 yards to carry a ravine that is about 80 yards in length. The ravine is along the left-center of the fairway and must be cleared to have a shot at reaching this par 5 in two shots.

There are also plenty of trees out there. About 80 yards from the tee on the left side, the fairway becomes tree-lined. There are also trees along the right side of the fairway.

You can play it safe along the right side and take the ravine out of play, but reaching the green in two becomes very difficult.

Your second shot isn't easy either. There are plenty of dangers out there. The fairway drops off into a ravine where a creek runs through about 180 yards from the green.

Speaking of the green, there are bunkers on both the left and right side. The green is a pretty big target and slopes from back to front. The grade is pretty steep too, so take that into account when lining up your putt. **TJ**

Course: Olivos Golf Course

Location: Buenos Aires, Argentina

Hole: No. 15

Length: 480 yards

Par: 4/5

Designer: Luther Koontz, Emilio Serra

Course Comment: This 27-hole layout is a regular host on the Argentine Open rotation and actually outranks the Jockey Club — an Argentine course with a grander reputation — in the ratings of many golf publications.

# No. 🄯 OLIVOS GOLF COURSE

Argentina may be an overlooked destination in golf, not only because many golfers are unaware of the great places to play in South America's second largest country, but also because one of the more interesting professional golf stories was born in Argentina.

Angel Cabrera grew up caddying in Cordoba, Argentina, with Eduardo Romero. Romero turned professional and enjoyed success in both Europe and the United States, and eventually he gave Cabrera enough financial backing to pursue a career on the PGA European Tour.

After making a decent living on the European Tour, yet never winning, Cabrera finally broke through in 2001 when he won the Argentine Open. Even though these two Argentines have enjoyed worldwide acclaim, they still maintain a strong presence in their home country.

Who can blame them? The country has several wonderful courses, and the 27 holes at Olivos are among the country's finest. The course is stuffed with bunkers and lined with trees, and has attracted the world's best golfers, hosting several international events. The 15th, being the Olivos Golf Course's trademark hole, is therefore one of the best of the best.

This hole plays as a long par 4 for competitive events, but remains a challenging, yet short, par 5 for members. The 15th fits into the mold of the rest at Olivos Golf Club — it doesn't require massive power, but strategy is a constant necessity. It is a dogleg right, lined tightly and thickly by massive trees that prevent the dogleg from being cut, despite its short distance from the tee. The direct path to the hole was an option in the course's infancy, but not since the forest has matured.

A pond protects the front of the green, although not completely. For those who want to try a runner to the putting surface, there is a razor-thin entryway of perhaps 5 yards — hardly enough to give it a go if you can't softly land your approach. A lay up is prudent if your approach is more than a middle iron away.

As if the pond weren't enough protection, there are bunkers on both sides, so it's either green or trouble when approaching a flat, moderately sized putting surface.

This is a hole, a course, and a country not to be overlooked when choosing places to play. **JB**

**Course:** The National Golf Club (Moonah Course)

**Location:** Cape Schanck, Victoria, Australia

**Hole:** No. 15

**Length:** 576 yards

**Par:** 5

**Designer:** Greg Norman, Bob Harrison

**Course Comment:** Golfers rave about the bunkering at Moonah and the wild, windswept look it has, as well as the subtle way it fits into the former seaside farmlands of Mornington.

## No. ⑮ THE NATIONAL GOLF CLUB
### (MOONAH COURSE)

The tee to this long par 5 sits on top of a dune behind the 14th green and offers fabulous views across the modern links designed by the prolific and talented architectural duo of Greg Norman and Bob Harrison.

It also provides one of the great challenges at Moonah, beginning with an accurate — and semi-blind — drive to a fairway with severe undulations and bordered on the left by some penal grasses.

Players will find that the key to scoring here is to keep their tee shots slightly to the right, as that helps to take the rough out of play but also sets up better for the second shot on this slight dogleg left. The fairway dips into a shallow valley before widening and running a bit uphill and to the left.

A mid- to long-iron is usually required for the second shot, and that will leave golfers with a short play to a difficult green that is well-bunkered on the left as well as the front right. **JS**

**Course:** Desert Mountain Golf Club (Cochise Course)

**Location:** Scottsdale, Arizona, USA

**Hole:** No. 15

**Length:** 548 yards

**Par:** 5

**Designer:** Jack Nicklaus

**Course Comment:** Desert Mountain is the only community in the United States with six Jack Nicklaus-designed courses.

OPPOSITE *The 15th hole at Desert Mountain.*

## No. ⓯ DESERT MOUNTAIN GOLF CLUB (COCHISE COURSE)

As the original home from 1989 to 2001 of the Champions Tour's Tradition, one of the senior circuit's major championships, Desert Mountain Golf Club's Cochise Course provided a strong par 5 late in the round, as No. 15 consistently challenged contenders' skills and tested their mettle.

Players are required to carry a huge fairway bunker with their tee shots, and the vast majority will choose to lay up with their second shots and set up a short approach. It's the smart choice because the green is almost completely encircled by water and further guarded by bunkers and several groups of boulders on both sides. Hit the rocks, and you'll likely be wet. In addition, the hourglass-shaped putting surface pinches in tight at its center, making the middle and back pin positions the most difficult.

Nicklaus certainly was a fan of the desert layout he created. He captured four Tradition titles — more than any other player — twice winning in back-to-back years (1990–91 and 1995–96). In addition to the legendary Golden Bear, the Cochise Course also produced such champions as Lee Trevino (1992), Ray Floyd (1994), Gil Morgan (1997–98), Graham Marsh (1999), and Tom Kite (2000). **KA**

**Course:** Kawana Hotel Golf Club (Fuji Course)

**Location:** Kawana, Shizuoka, Japan

**Hole:** No. 15

**Length:** 470 yards

**Par:** 5

**Designer:** Charles H. Alison

**Course Comment:** Kawana played host to the 1962 World Cup of Golf, won by the United States team, which defeated runner-up Canada by eight shots.

## No. ⓯ KAWANA HOTEL GOLF CLUB (FUJI COURSE)

Kawana Hotel Golf Club, often called the "Pebble Beach of Japan," is considered one of the most prestigious courses in the country. Charles H. Alison's layout overlooks Sagami Bay and the Pacific Ocean, features views of Mount Fuji and Hatsushima Island, and is built along dramatic shorelines that feature rocky cliffs and a Japanese pine forest.

All of these features come into play on the par-5 15th, the signature hole at Kawana. The hole plays along a cliff that drops dramatically to the ocean.

The tee shot offers a classic risk-reward option, with those who brave a carry of 230 yards over a tree-filled ravine to a narrow, twisting, uphill fairway having a chance at getting home in two. Those who choose the less perilous route to the right will likely need all three shots to reach the two-tiered green, which features magnificent views of the ocean.

Kawana is the long-time host of the Japan Golf Tour's Fujisankei Classic, which was won by American Mark O'Meara in 1985. Finishing second to O'Meara was Japan's Masashi Ozaki, who dominated the event in later years, earning Fujisankei victories in 1986, 1987, 1989, 1990, and 1993. **KA**

# Hole 🄰

Hopefully, as you approach the 16th tee, you are in the proper frame of mind. A birdie on No. 15, perhaps, or a round that has seen you in solid form throughout. Because you need to be ready on No. 16. This is when designers frequently add some teeth to their holes.

Tournaments (for top players) and side bets (for everyone else) are so often decided on the final three holes of the day, that the makers of these holes don't want them to be anything but a demanding test of skill. No. 16, being the first of the final triumvirate, can be a menacing challenge. Oakland Hills outside of Detroit, USA; Wentworth in Surrey, England; and Carnoustie in Scotland are famed 16s. And this is just the beginning of the list.

**LEFT** *The 16th hole at Sleepy Hollow Country Club, Scarborough-on-Hudson, New York, USA.*

Course: Clustered Spires Golf Course

Location: Frederick, Maryland, USA

Hole: No. 16

Length: 232 yards

Par: 3

Designer: Ault, Clark & Associates

Course Comment: Clustered Spires Golf Course was built in 1991 by the City of Frederick, providing a well-received attraction to the area.

## No. 🔟 CLUSTERED SPIRES GOLF COURSE

This golf course, which is a popular choice because of its conditions and affordability, is laid out upon 200 acres of rolling land and is adjacent to the Monocacy River. Clustered Spires is also known for its elevated greens and heavily mounded fairways.

You get a good view of the Monocacy River on this long par-3 hole. Hopefully, a view is all you will get — you don't want to have to hit a shot out of the river, which runs down the left-hand side of the 232-yard 16th.

From an elevated tee (a good 20 yards elevated), you want to miss the large bunker to the left front of the green and the group of trees. Also, try to miss the pot bunker located on the front right side of the green.

The green is not easy. It has two tiers so make sure you are aware of the pin placement when selecting a club. The green is medium sized with some undulation to it.

This is a scenic hole with some danger to it, but if you land on the green you only have to look at the river and not find your ball in it. **TJ**

Course: The Golf Club

Location: New Albany, Ohio, USA

Hole: No. 16

Length: 204 yards

Par: 3

Designer: Pete Dye

Course Comment: You've heard of two courses in one. How about three courses in one? The Golf Club has traditional fairways on the first six holes, then tight, tree-lined fairways for the next six, before finishing up with six links-style holes.

## No. 🔟 THE GOLF CLUB

This is one of those par 3s you love to hate. Sure, it's pretty to look at. The perfect golf hole. Then you have to play it and it's not so pretty. In fact, it can get ugly in a hurry.

There really is nowhere to make a bad shot on this hole and be able to recover in an easy fashion. Miss the green here and you are going to be faced with a tough second shot — if you can find the ball.

You are hitting from an elevated tee to an elevated green with a valley in between. There is a creek that runs from tee to green along the left side and some rather large oak trees which hug the right side of the fairway.

If you are short, you will be hitting out of some nasty tall grass and you most likely won't be able to see the pin. Or you will land in one of the two large bunkers in the front.

There is also a large bunker waiting behind the green in case you choose too much club.

The green is 35 paces deep, 18 paces wide, and slopes from back to front. It's a tough green to read because it doesn't always break the way you think it should. **TJ**

# KANANASKIS COUNTRY GOLF COURSE (MOUNT KIDD COURSE)

**Course:** Kananaskis Country Golf Course (Mount Kidd Course)

**Location:** Kananaskis Village, Alberta, Canada

**Hole:** No. 16

**Length:** 210 yards

**Par:** 3

**Designer:** Robert Trent Jones Sr.

**Course Comment:** The rugged surrounding peaks tower a full 9,600 feet above sea level, the two courses are at almost 5,000 feet, forming an unforgettable background, the cascading Kananaskis River being a constant and pleasant companion.

There are many vistas at Kananaskis Country Golf Course offering spectacular views. After a while they all start to look the same and the splendor begins to fade just a bit.

Then you walk onto the tee at No. 16 on the Mount Kidd Course and suddenly the "wows" take on a whole new meaning. The views suddenly jump back out at you and you realize you are standing in a special place.

As you hit your tee shot on this 210-yard par 3, you watch your ball climb Mount Kidd in the background and then fall against its beautiful slope. It's a tee shot you won't soon forget. Hopefully, the ball lands on the green.

The view from the 16th tee is a panoramic view of the entire Kananaskis Valley. You can see Mount Kidd, Mount Lorette, and Mount Fortress. It's a view worth pictures, but it is the memory that will last forever.

The hole is a 60-foot drop from tee to green. The wind is always a factor on this hole with a one- to two-club length difference hitting you in the face. Often times, the wind and elevation drop cancel each other out.

You have to hit it pure, though, or the wind will do tricks with your golf ball. **TJ**

**Course:** Cypress Point Club

**Location:** Pebble Beach, California, USA

**Hole:** No. 16

**Length:** 231 yards

**Par:** 3

**Designer:** Alister MacKenzie

**Course Comment:** Seth Raynor was slated to be the original designer of Cypress Point, but he died before completing the job. Raynor's plans called for the 16th to be a short par 4, but MacKenzie, at the urging of club founder Marion Hollins, converted it into a long par 3.

# No. 🄰 CYPRESS POINT CLUB

The climate in Pebble Beach has been called the best in the world for growing greens. All the putting surfaces at Cypress Point serve as evidence. But, there is a price to pay if you are to reach the lush green at No. 16. That toll is a 233-yard carry over the Pacific Ocean.

It is a laborious task, for there are blue Pacific waters waiting if your tee shot goes right or left. It is worth the effort if you make the green, which is adjacent to crashing waves, and features five jealously protective bunkers and jagged rock. There is a lay-up short of the green on the left side, but laying up hardly seems the route to take.

Speaking of unique routes to the 16th green, it is said that Alister MacKenzie, after designing the hole, thought it too severe for a mid- to high-handicapper to play. Legend has it though, that one of MacKenzie's friends was beaten on a bet after hitting his ball into the water while his playing partner used a putter to play left of the ocean all the way to the green, holing out in four.

No-one knows if this legend holds water (forgive the expression), but MacKenzie's concerns for players off the tee is justified. Many times on holes that force a long carry over water, there are shorter tees that either cut the total distance from tee to green or at least cut the angle so the carry is less extreme. This is not the case at Cypress Point Club's 16th, however. There is one tee. No gold/blue/white/red options here. It's 231 yards to the hole, period.

The 16th is one of three holes at Cypress Point that abut the sea, adding to the variety on a course that includes links holes and woodlands holes. A player will find a little bit of everything at Cypress Point — all of it good.

Another wonderful feature of this hole is that Cypress Point is a walking course, and there is no better stroll than up the 16th fairway at Cypress Point, between the cypress trees and the Pacific Ocean. Membership is very exclusive, however, so if ever you are afforded a chance to take that walk, you are advised to clear your schedule. **JB**

**BELOW AND OPPOSITE** *The 16th hole at Cypress Point Club.*

## No. ⑯   BROOK HOLLOW GOLF CLUB

**Course:** Brook Hollow Golf Club

**Location:** Dallas, Texas, USA

**Hole:** No. 16

**Length:** 220 yards

**Par:** 3

**Designer:** A.W. Tillinghast

**Course Comment:** In 1925, Brook Hollow became the first golf course to install a complete fairway irrigation system.

A.W. Tillinghast ambled into the Lone Star State nearly a century ago and left behind a collection of Texas treasures.

Brook Hollow, an exclusive Dallas club, was built in 1919 and played host to a number of prestigious events. In 1946, Ben Hogan pulled off the PGA Tour Texas two-step by capturing the Dallas Open, held at Brook Hollow, and Colonial in the same year.

Because only 400 members can call Brook Hollow home, the course averages approximately 20,000 rounds a year. It's not uncommon for Dallas residents to wait over a decade to receive a membership nod.

At 220 yards, the par-3 16th's most difficult feature is its taxing bunkers, located on either side of the green. These steep bunkers can be found throughout the course and are unique to the southwest area.

The long, medium-sized green slopes back to front and feeds into a bunker on the right side. Subtle undulations throughout the putting surface make virtually every pin placement a rigorous test of skill.

According to the scorecard, this demanding par 3 is No. 16 on the handicap index, but don't be fooled. Members and guests maintain that it's one of hardest holes on the course, and are reviewing its listing. **BB**

**Course:** The Golf Club at Ravenna

**Location:** Littleton, Colorado, USA

**Hole:** No. 16

**Par:** 3

**Length:** 240 yards

**Designers:** Jay Moorish

**Course Comment:** It did not take the Golf Club at Ravenna long to make a name for itself. It opened in 2007, and within two years was on several publications' "best" lists — including *Golfweek*'s 100 Best Modern Courses.

## No. ⑯ THE GOLF CLUB AT RAVENNA

The poor housing market dashed developers' dreams for a luxury real-estate development around the Golf Club at Ravenna, and they were forced to give the surrounding property back to the lenders. However, due to the golf course's viability and popularity, it remains up and running.

There are plans to reorganize the housing development with less-expensive homes, and the golf course is thriving. Regardless of what happens to the surrounding development, there are no plans to close the course.

The all-carry, signature 240-yard, par-3 16th hole is accessible only by suspension bridge, and it is truly an amazing site. The tee shot must carry a 50-foot ravine, and if you elect to play from the tips, it is a carry of 240 yards over rocky, tree-filled danger. It is truly an awesome spectacle, and walking over the bridge to the green is a memory of No. 16 you will not soon forget.

There is a landing area in front of the green on the other side of the bridge, but it isn't much. There are four bunkers protecting the green even if you do carry the ravine, so this hole is stiffer than stiff no matter how you look at it.

What can you say about a golf course that survives an economic plunge, and a golf hole that makes you walk a suspension bridge to finish playing? You want a unique experience? The 16th at the Golf Club at Ravenna has all you are looking for. **JB**

**Course:** Terrace Downs

**Location:** Rakaia Gorge, Darfield, New Zealand

**Hole:** No. 16

**Length:** 220 yards

**Par:** 3

**Designers:** David Cox, Sid Puddicombe, Noel Bain, Fin Hobbs

**Course Comment:** Terrace Downs Golf Course is one of New Zealand's top places to play. It is set in the foothills of the Southern Alps and is surrounded by stunning mountain scenery.

**OPPOSITE** *The 16th hole at Terrace Downs.*

## No. ⑯ TERRACE DOWNS

After a picturesque 50-minute drive through the Canterbury foothills from Christchurch International Airport, the gateway to the South Island of New Zealand, you discover one of the country's top golf courses.

No. 16 is one of the more interesting holes on this unique golf course.

The tee hangs over the gorge, and you look down 219 yards to the aquamarine water below with Mount Hutt towering above.

The green is just a wedge or so away but you will have to carry two ravines that drop all the way to the river through thick native bush. Your tee shot also has to carry a deep pot bunker short of the green and skirt another on the left.

Forget about being short because a short ball is an automatic reload.

The green slopes dramatically left to right and front to back, completing this exciting and challenging hole. For the faint-hearted golfer there is a bail-out area short left, but don't go pin high left as the chip across the green toward the river can be treacherous.

How good is this golf course? Here is what Jim Webster, editor of *Golf Australia*, had to say: "Terrace Downs is enrapturing, a course that one can play day in and day out." **TJ**

**Course:** Carnoustie Golf Links

**Location:** Carnoustie, Angus, Scotland

**Hole:** No. 16

**Length:** 245 yards

**Par:** 3

**Designer:** Allan Robertson, Old Tom Morris, James Braid

**Course Comment:** Playing into a northeasterly wind during the final round of the 1968 British Open, Jack Nicklaus was the only player to get his tee shot past the pin at No. 16. Nicklaus hit a driver from the tee.

## No. ⑯ CARNOUSTIE GOLF LINKS

Local lore has it that the rugged seascape that is now Carnoustie has been used for golf since long before Christopher Columbus discovered America. Officially, Carnoustie Golf Club was formed in 1839 and three years later the first clubhouse was established.

Although well-aged courses are nothing out of the ordinary for the home of golf, what surprises most is Carnoustie's tactical mastery. Although the prevailing wind is westerly, no two consecutive holes face the same direction and players are often baffled by swirling gusts and an almost incessant quandary over club selection.

Despite its architectural gifts, Carnoustie was a late-comer to the British Open rota. The course didn't host its first Open Championship until 1931. Since then, however, few courses have carved a more prolific chapter into Grand Slam history.

At the heart of Carnoustie's championship core lies what many consider the greatest closing stretch in Grand Slam golf. This harrowing run begins with the par-3 16th, named "Barry Burn." A mammoth hole even by today's standards, the 16th plays to 245 yards.

When the wind is blowing from the North Sea, some of the game's longest hitters have struggled to reach a putting surface that is sharply contoured and nearly 50 paces deep. Deep bunkers guard the left and right of the green and the landscape runs toward Barry Burn on the left. **RH**

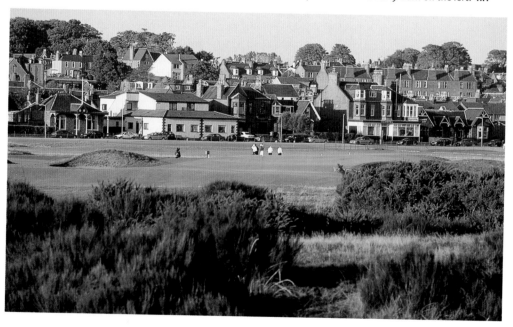

## No. ⑯ CAPITAL GOLF CLUB

**Course:** Capital Golf Club

**Location:** Melbourne, Victoria, Australia

**Hole:** No. 16

**Length:** 195 yards

**Par:** 3

**Designer:** Peter Thomson, Michael Wolveridge, Ross Perrett, Lloyd Williams

**Course Comment:** Opened in 1997, Capital has been compared to Steve Wynn's Shadow Creek outside Las Vegas, Nevada as one man's effort — in this case Melbourne businessman Lloyd Williams — to create a modern and very exclusive golfing masterpiece.

The 16th at Capital, which is considered the signature hole at this much-lauded club, is surrounded by water on three sides and protected in front by two large bunkers. A third bunker, which is not visible from the tee, guards the left side of the green, which slopes steeply from back to front.

Tee shots must carry the water in front, and the hole generally plays with a favoring wind, which makes it feel a bit shorter than the 195 yards listed on the scorecard. Once again, it is important for drives not only to land on the putting surface in order to make par, but also to be below the hole, as the green can be quite quick.

Players must be careful not to become overwhelmed by the wonderfully opulent setting at this veritable fantasy land, which includes 35 acres of man-made lakes, bountiful wildlife refuges, and some 500,000 trees that were planted during construction of the course. **JS**

## No. ⑯ THIRTEENTH BEACH GOLF LINKS

**Course:** Thirteenth Beach Golf Links

**Location:** Barwon Heads, Victoria, Australia

**Hole:** No. 16

**Length:** 129 yards

**Par:** 3

**Designer:** Tony Cashmore

**Course Comment:** It is hard not to think of the great seventh hole at Pebble Beach when considering this testy short hole, which often requires no more than a pitching wedge but is nonetheless capable of creating all sorts of problems for players.

Australian golfers say the 16th is this course's signature hole, built as it is within the sand dunes of the Bellarine Peninsula, and often buffeted by fierce winds.

The hole plays to an elevated, postage-stamp green, partially hidden by a sandy waste area, and features wicked sloping all around as well as deep rough and a small bunker in the back. In other words, accuracy is critical off the tee.

Conditions dictate club selection here, and golfers can use as much as a hard 4-iron or as little as a soft sand wedge, depending on how hard the breeze is blowing off the water and whether they want to loft, or punch, their tee shots. Even a well-hit ball can be trouble, as there is nothing easy about holding a ball on this green, especially when one has to use a mid-range iron.

Regulars say the key to success at 16 is to keep the ball below the hole or face the distinct possibility of a three-putt. **JS**

# No. ⑯ GOLDEN HORSESHOE GOLF CLUB (GOLD COURSE)

Located in one of America's most historic regions, Golden Horseshoe Golf Club's Gold Course was laid out on the site of the 18th-century John Saunders house and plantation, which encompassed 577 acres. During the building of the Gold Course, which opened in 1963, Colonial Williamsburg excavated the remains of the house's foundation.

Here's another history lesson. Before there was a No. 17 at the Pete Dye-designed TPC at Sawgrass, there was No. 16 at Golden Horseshoe. Although today, this Robert Trent Jones Sr.-designed island green isn't nearly as well known as Dye's, it is every bit as tough — maybe even tougher because of its additional 37 yards in length.

Rees Jones has renovated his father's layout, rebuilding bunkers, tees, and greens. The famed 16th was subject to this — four bunkers were added to the green alone. The green, unchanged in shape, was originally designed to be much shallower and wider than Dye's — offering the chance for more difficult pin placements — than the almost perfect circle found at TPC.

To land safely here, choosing the correct club and judging the wind accurately is key. Do both to perfection, then execute the shot, and you can cross the wooden footbridge to the green with a smile on your face. **KA**

## No. 🄰 HALMSTAD GOLF CLUB
### (NORTH COURSE)

**Course:** Halmstad Golf Club (North Course)

**Location:** Halmstad, Sweden

**Hole:** No. 16

**Length:** 180 yards

**Par:** 3

**Designer:** Rafael Sundblom, Donald Steel

**Course Comment:** The town of Halmstad, then part of Denmark, bordering on Sweden, served as a major border fortification in the early 1600s when Danish King Christian IV built a castle and ramparts around the ancient town center. The city was ceded to the Swedes in 1645 following the Torstenson War.

Halmstad Golf Club, considered one of Sweden's foremost clubs, is headquarters to the Swedish PGA and played host to the 1985 European Amateur Championship. Although Halmstad is laid out approximately 500 yards from the North Sea, it is more of a parkland-style course than a links layout, as almost every hole is lined by trees.

The 16th hole on Halmstad's North Course has been given the simple moniker of "The Brook," but it is not a simple task for golfers, who play their rounds knowing this dangerous par 3 awaits.

A creek with rocky banks winds in front of the tee box, then snakes its way down the hole and crosses back in front of the green and along its right side. And for those golfers who have the idea to attempt a bail out to the left, there are two bunkers on that side of the putting surface, which is further guarded by a thick forest in the rear. Making matters even worse is the prevailing crosswind, which blows from left to right and can send even well-struck tee shots into the creek on the right. When the wind is present, aim for the green's far left side and say a little prayer. **KA**

---

## No. 🄰 LA QUINTA RESORT
### (MOUNTAIN COURSE)

**Course:** La Quinta Resort (Mountain Course)

**Location:** La Quinta, California, USA

**Hole:** No. 16

**Length:** 168 yards

**Par:** 3

**Designer:** Pete Dye

**Course Comment:** After graduating from the University of Houston, Fred Couples worked briefly picking up range balls at La Quinta before beginning his pro career.

La Quinta Resort's Mountain Course is literally carved into the Santa Rosa Mountains, providing stunning views and requiring plenty of pinpoint precision from golfers. It also contains another signature island hole of Pete Dye's, with a slight twist. This one just happens to be surrounded by rocks and desert landscape rather than water.

Set immediately adjacent to strewn rocks at the bottom of a small desert mountain, No. 16 is one green you want to make sure to hit dead center with the downhill tee shot. To the left is a deep bunker and thick desert scrub. To the right is the mountain. Fail to hit the bunker or the putting surface, and there is no telling where your ball will end up, or what kind of crazy bounces it will take off the rocks — in some quite fortunate cases, even onto the green!

The Mountain Course has played host to some of golf's top amateur and professional events. In addition to being the site for numerous PGA Club Professional Championships, it also served as host for the 1985 World Cup of Golf (won by Canada's Dave Barr and Dan Halldorson) and the 1989 Senior Skins Game (won by Chi Chi Rodriguez). **KA**

**Course:** Port Royal Golf Course

**Location:** Southampton, Bermuda, USA

**Hole:** No. 16

**Length:** 176 yards

**Par:** 3

**Designer:** Robert Trent Jones Sr.

**Course Comment:** Dramatic oceanside cliffs provide a breathtaking vista for this 18-hole collection of loveliness on the southeast tip of the tiny, lush island of Bermuda. Bermuda feels very Caribbean, but it's just 900 miles east of North Carolina, as the seagull flies. Elevated greens and uphill shots make government-owned Port Royal pleasantly intimidating for long and short hitters alike.

BELOW *A golfer hits a shot from a bunker on the 16th at Port Royal.*

# No. ⑯ PORT ROYAL GOLF COURSE

There is a generous collection of golf balls on the floor of the Atlantic near No. 16 at Port Royal, and if you aren't careful, a watery grave could await yours as well.

The 16th's tee and green both ring a craggy cliff overlooking the surf, and, of course, the sea makes quite the formidable water hazard. Known for its marriage of visual splendor and difficulty, the par-3 16th is a stunning test of skill.

Its design is panoramic genius; sweeping wind supplements the scenic drama that renders this seaside hole both a golfer's delight and a golf photographer's fantasy. It's a favorite for golf-magazine layouts.

Depending on weather, the range of club could go from a pitching wedge or a 3-wood as your best bets off the tee. The shot goes over cliff and ocean to the reward on Port Royal's tricky 16th green. On the way there, you can enjoy the winding, well-bunkered fairways which ramble over the natural terrain of Southampton's coral cliffs. The sapphire ocean serves as a backdrop for this hole, as it does on many at Port Royal.

The 16th is near the historic, 1876 Whale Bay battery that was part of a ring of defenses protecting the Royal Navy dockyard, and it is said to be Robert Trent Jones Sr.'s inspiration for the famed third hole at Mauna Kea on the Kohala Coast on Hawaii's Big Island.

Bermuda feels like the Hamptons with a British flavor and tropical zest. This course is demanding and commanding — Jones definitely carved his legacy into the hilly landscape of Port Royal.

Its showcase 16th is both lethal and lovely. **KLL**

## No. ⑯ MOLIETS GOLF CLUB

**Course:** Moliets Golf Club

**Location:** Moliets, France

**Hole:** No. 16

**Length:** 146 yards

**Par:** 3

**Designer:** Robert Trent Jones Sr.

**Course Comment:** In addition to its 18-hole championship layout, Moliets also includes a well-regarded nine-hole short course that features six par 3s, two par 4s and one par 5.

Moliets Golf Club, considered one of continental Europe's most beautiful layouts, features numerous trademark jagged bunkers around its greens, and includes 13 holes nestled in the magnificent pine forests of Les Landes and five holes laid out along the scenic Atlantic coast.

No. 16 is the final hole of the quintet played amid the coastal sand dunes, as No. 17 and No. 18 head back to the inland forests. As such, this short par 3 can be made much longer by swirling, gusting breezes off the ocean that make club selection difficult yet all-important.

The shallow putting surface is guarded by a long, ragged bunker that curls around its entire left side, and by another, smaller bunker directly in front, making the option of a run-up shot to cut through the wind virtually impossible. Go too long, and impenetrable gorse lines the dunes rising up at the rear of the hole.

Because of the pleasant year-round climate in the region, the French Golf Federation chose Moliets as the location for its National Winter Training Center. In addition, the PGA European Tour's developmental circuit, the European Challenge Tour, frequently has played its annual qualifying tournament here. **KA**

## No. ⑯ ROYAL MELBOURNE GOLF CLUB (EAST COURSE)

**Course:** Royal Melbourne Golf Club (East Course)

**Location:** Black Rock, Victoria, Australia

**Hole:** No. 16

**Length:** 167 yards

**Par:** 3

**Designer:** Alex Russell

**Course Comment:** Morcom was in charge of building the East once architect Alex Russell, who was a former Australian Open champion and a close confidante of Alister MacKenzie, formulated his layout.

Royal Melbourne greenskeeper Mick Morcom is credited with having an extraordinary talent when it came to bunkering, something he first exhibited as he led the construction of Royal Melbourne's fabled West Course a couple of years before he began working on the East.

Nowhere is that more evident than at the 16th, considered one of the best par 3s in the Sand Belt. Set on a relatively flat site, as the very best land at Black Rock was used for the West, it relies on heavy bunkering to give it a dramatic feel and distinct character.

As is the case with all the par 3s on the East at Royal Melbourne, No. 16 plays to the north. Its smallish green features a tricky ridge running down its middle and is surrounded by a total of seven bunkers, each of which can present serious problems for the player who pulls or pushes his tee shot ever so slightly.

A well-struck mid-iron will do the trick most days, but a good wind in the face will force golfers to play longer clubs, and increase the likelihood of bogey, or worse. **JS**

**Course:** The Golf Club Kennedy Bay

**Location:** Longbeach Key, Port Kennedy, Western Australia

**Hole:** No. 16

**Length:** 151 yards

**Par:** 3

**Designer:** Michael Coate, Roger Mackay, Ian Baker-Finch

**Course Comment:** Architect Michael Coate was assisted in the creation of this links-style track by professional golfer Roger Mackay and former British Open champion Ian Baker-Finch, a collaboration that gave the routing its natural and authoritative feel.

# No. ⓰  THE GOLF CLUB KENNEDY BAY

Great architects seem to delight in putting par 3s near the end of their layouts and forcing players to test their skills with a shorter tee shot one final time before the round is over. And the 16th at Kennedy Bay is an excellent example of why that philosophy works so well.

Called "Wee Tap," it usually requires little more than a 7- or 8-iron from the back tees, but winds coming in off the water can scuttle those plans (and force a switch to a much longer club). Then there is the issue of hitting the green, which is set almost diagonally from the top left to the lower right, and features one bunker front and center, and two in the back.

The ground falls off all around the putting surface, creating some first-rate green-side chipping possibilities reminiscent of the work of the great Donald Ross. What that means, of course, is that players cannot miss their tee shots right, left, or long. And not surprisingly, that is easier said than done. **JS**

**Course:** Casa de Campo (Teeth of the Dog)

**Location:** La Romana, Dominican Republic

**Hole:** No. 16

**Length:** 185 yards

**Par:** 3

**Designer:** Pete Dye

**Course Comment:** Prior to the construction of nearby La Romana International Airport, a runway bisected two of Teeth of the Dog's holes and periodically delayed play during landings.

# No. ⓰  CASA DE CAMPO (TEETH OF THE DOG)

Everything about Casa de Campo's Teeth of the Dog is impacted by the Caribbean Sea. From the wildly pitched landscape on which the course was built, to the unpredictable winds that swoop in across its warm waters, Pete Dye's tropical masterpiece is defined by the blue-green expanse.

Even Dye's routing is a simple salute to the Caribbean. Of Teeth of the Dog's seven ocean holes, four — Nos. 5–8 — are framed by the water on the left and run from east to west, while the final three — Nos. 15–17 — are bordered by the sea on the right and head to the east. This geographic juxtaposition gives Teeth of the Dog a wonderfully diverse combination of wind conditions and scenery.

Nowhere are these directional differences more evident than on the par-3 16th. The 16th plays a lengthy 185 yards and into the prevailing wind while the fifth hole, the layout's signature, is just 153 yards and usually downwind to an inviting green.

The tee shot at No. 16 must carry the sea to an elevated green. Most players will use a long iron or fairway wood, depending on the wind, to a putting surface that slopes dramatically to the sea. Trees protect the left side of the green while bunkers await anything short. **RH**

**Course:** Eagle Ranch

**Location:** Invermere, British Columbia, Canada

**Hole:** No. 16

**Length:** 173 yards

**Par:** 3

**Designer:** Bill Robinson

**Course Comment:** In the design and construction of Eagle Ranch, the natural environment has been used to its maximum potential — the course is built in and around a network of steep cliffs and picturesque valleys.

# No. ⑯ EAGLE RANCH

There are other courses in the world that have made their reputations by challenging golfers with carries over ravines and water, but few other courses have made such brilliant use of canyon territory.

With every shot, your ball soars against the picture-perfect backdrop of the Rocky Mountains. The 6,600-yard course cuts around ravines where the panoramic views of the surrounding area are stunning.

No. 16 is a particularly spectacular hole. Not only does it have fantastic views, but the golfing challenge that it presents sets it apart from other holes on the course and in the region. This 173-yard par 3 has a good 50 to 60 foot drop down to a tough green. In addition, you are hitting over a protected ravine that only adds to the beauty of this magnificent hole. Scenery aside though, it's a "hit the green or else" kind of hole.

Around the green are what the locals call "hoodoos," or dirt formations. These are not easy to play from, so they are best avoided. The green is also surrounded by abandoned bear dens, but don't worry — the bears are long gone. Eagle Ranch is known not only for its beauty but for its course conditions, for which it often wins awards. **TJ**

**COBBLESTONE GOLF COURSE**

**Course:** Cobblestone Golf Course

**Location:** Acworth, Georgia, USA

**Hole:** No. 16

**Length:** 133 yards

**Par:** 3

**Designer:** B. Spann, K. Dye, J. Finger

**Course Comment:** This course has a reputation for devouring golf balls so bring your A (as in accuracy) Game. Designed and built in 1993, Cobblestone has earned plenty of awards for being one of the better golf courses in the state.

Considered one of the top courses in the Atlanta area, Cobblestone features undulating moguls, narrow fairways, multi-tiered greens, plenty of sand traps, and thick rough.

With all of the dangers, particularly around the green, you better hit good approach shots or that scorecard will suffer.

You won't remember this hole because of its difficulty. But you won't forget this hole because of its beauty. This is just a splendid golf hole to look at. It can also help your scorecard if you can drop it on the green.

Don't let the 133 yards from the back tees fool you. If the flag is in the back of the green, this hole plays 150 yards.

From the tee, you have to carry the lake that comes between you and the flag. You can play it short because the green is angled in a way where there is some area in the front.

There are two bunkers on the right side of this green that slopes back to front and is very narrow and small. The green is also a difficult read with three ridges on it. So just getting to the green is no automatic par. **TJ**

# No. ⑯ PLAYACAR GOLF COURSE

**Course:** Playacar Golf Course

**Location:** Mayan Riviera, Mexico

**Hole:** No. 16

**Length:** 469 yards

**Par:** 4

**Designer:** Robert Von Hagge

**Course Comment:** When visiting this resort, remember to pack some golf balls. You most likely will have some extra room in your bag on the way back because you will certainly leave some balls behind.

Playacar Club de Golf is a very difficult championship course carved out of the lush Mayan jungle — a perfect setting — and is easily one of the best places to play in Mexico.

The course features long narrow fairways and undulating greens that are protected by very large snow-white sand bunkers. And there are plenty of bunkers around these wonderful 18 holes.

Located in Mexico's beautiful Mayan Riviera about 40 miles south of Cancun on the Tulum corridor, this 18-hole course was built amongst the lush foliage of the Yucatan Peninsula, making this golf course not only beautiful, but challenging.

If you want the ultimate challenge try out the 469-yard par 4. Some say it's among the toughest holes in Mexico. And in the world, for that matter.

If the wind is blowing, you can forget birdie. This is an uphill and often into-the-wind challenge unlike any on the course. There is a jungle on the right and left side of the fairway, which is tight.

The club features a first-class practice area, complete with a spectacular driving range, and a large putting green including chipping, pitching, and greenside bunker areas.

The panoramas here are breathtaking. Mayan ruins and natural limestone sinkholes called "Cenotes" can be found around the course. **TJ**

**Course:** Fairmont Jasper Park Lodge Golf Course

**Location:** Jasper, Alberta, Canada

**Hole:** No. 16

**Length:** 380 yards

**Par:** 4

**Designer:** Stanley Thompson

**Course Comment:** In 1994, using Thompson's original course blueprints, the Fairmont Jasper Park Lodge initiated a project to restore the course to its original layout, focusing on refurbishing the bunkers and tee boxes to re-create Thompson's design from 1924.

OPPOSITE *The 16th at Fairmont Jasper Park Lodge.*

## No. ⓰ FAIRMONT JASPER PARK LODGE GOLF COURSE

From the narrow tee, this hole plays to a valley landing area, across a peninsula, and to a green semi-hidden by a group of pines. Wow. Now that we have your attention . . .

This 380-yard par 4 is named "The Bay."

The target for the tee shot is center of the fairway. Here's why you might want to consider keeping it straight — even if that means using a different club you know you can control.

Miss to the left here and you could very well end up in the water. Go too far right and you very well could be blocked by the trees. Make sure your approach is long enough as "Lac Beauvert" guards the front of the green.

Another difficult green to putt at Jasper Park Lodge, the No. 16 green slopes severely from back to front. Side hill putts are very difficult to judge. And speed is the key.

In other words, watch out for three-putts. A par here and you should thank the golf gods and move on to the two challenging finishing holes. Tell your friends, too. A par on this hole is something to be proud of and bragged about — hopefully, over a cold drink at the 19th hole. **TJ**

**Course:** Club zur Vahr (Garlstedter Heide)

**Location:** Bremen, Garlstedt, Lower Saxony, Germany

**Hole:** No. 16

**Length:** 434 yards

**Par:** 4

**Designer:** August Weyhausen, Bernhard Von Limburger

**Course Comment:** In the 1971 German Open at Club zur Vahr, Arnold Palmer shot 69 — one of only 10 under-par rounds turned in for the entire 72-hole tournament. The next day, he shot 83 to finish with a 21-over total.

## No. ⓰ CLUB ZUR VAHR (GARLSTEDTER HEIDE)

The Club zur Vahr's Garlstedter Heide championship layout is considered one of Germany's best and most difficult layouts. The course runs through heavy forests and heath, so many natural obstacles were already in place — therefore the course contains only a few artificial hazards.

The par-4 16th hole is a good example of that, as it features no bunkers, just a lone tree on the right side of the fairway that must be avoided with the tee shot.

That requires golfers to hit a long fade past the tree in order to set up the best angle of approach into the green. The second shot then requires players to carry a stream that cuts across the fairway to a large, relatively flat putting surface.

Hit two strong, perfectly placed shots, and you have a good chance at par, perhaps even a birdie. And isn't that the way it should be?

Club Zur Vahr's difficulty was proven when it played host to the German Open in 1971, when champion Neil Coles of England was the only player who managed to finish below par at 1-under 279. Peter Thomson of Australia was the runner-up with a score of 3 over. **KA**

**Course:** Cog Hill Golf Club
(Dubsdread Course)

**Location:** Lemont, Illinois, USA

**Hole:** No. 16

**Length:** 397 yards

**Par:** 4

**Designer:** Dick Wilson, Joe Lee

**Course Comment:** Tom Watson,
Western Open Champion in 1974,
1977, and 1984 regards this as one of
maybe two lay up holes on the
course, along with No. 8.

## No. ⑯ COG HILL GOLF CLUB
### (DUBSDREAD COURSE)

Despite its relative lack of length, the 16th hole usually plays as one of the toughest par 4s when the world's top professionals visit Cog Hill's Dubsdread Course for the annual playing of the PGA Tour's Western Open.

No. 16 played to a 4.116 average in the 2003 event, yielding only one eagle and 53 birdies compared with 80 bogeys and 10 double bogeys or worse.

The dogleg left has trees and a bunker to the right of the fairway, but the right side is by far the preferred landing area for tee shots because of the severe right-to-left slope of the fairway. Otherwise, your golf ball could wind up in the left rough, and that's one of the worst places you could be for the uphill approach to a well-guarded green. And if you really pull your drive, trees and a stream to the left come into play.

The approach also requires precision, as the green — although quite flat when compared with the rest of the course — is surrounded by bunkers on the front left, right left, and right rear. It also has a steep drop-off on the left side, sending pulled second shots to the stream and woods below. **KA**

**Course:** Los Angeles Country Club
(North Course)

**Location:** Los Angeles, California,
USA

**Hole:** No. 16

**Length:** 445 yards

**Par:** 4

**Designer:** George Thomas, William
P. Bell, Robert Muir Graves

**Course Comment:** Los Angeles
Country Club's North Course was
the site of five Los Angeles Opens,
the final time in 1940, but it hasn't
played host to a major amateur or
professional event since the 1954
U.S. Junior Amateur.

## No. ⑯ LOS ANGELES COUNTRY CLUB (NORTH COURSE)

Los Angeles Country Club is quite the irony. Despite its location in the midst of Beverly Hills, the club shuns publicity at all costs — indeed a rarity for Hollywood. And because it hasn't played host to a professional major championship — the membership has turned down repeated U.S. Golf Association overtures to serve as host site for the U.S. Open — the course isn't well known by golf fans of today.

But it is most definitely worthy.

Indeed, it's a shame golf fans haven't been able to witness a major championship battle on this course's tough finishing stretch of long par 4s that begins on No. 16. It is set on the top of a hill that overlooks the 10th hole on the right and the 11th hole on the left.

The tee shot must avoid a large fairway bunker on the left and a group of trees that pinch in on the right. That sets up an approach that must get by a large, steep bunker that's deceptively located about 10 yards short of the right front portion of the green. Adding to the difficulty: the putting surface slopes hard from back left to the front right. **KA**

**Course:** Big Sky Golf & Country Club

**Location:** Pemberton, British
Columbia, Canada

**Hole:** No. 16

**Length:** 405 yards

**Par:** 4

**Designer:** Bob Cupp

**Course Comment:** The golf season
in this mini-banana belt runs from
mid-April through mid-October —
downright lengthy by British
Columbia interior standards.

## No. ⑯ BIG SKY GOLF & COUNTRY CLUB

Big Sky Golf & Country Club features a golf course carved around and over seven lakes and a flowing creek at 600 feet above sea level, roughly 1,600 feet lower than the nearby ski village of Whistler.

Course designer Bob Cupp, who bulldozed 350,000 cubic yards of dirt to add movement to a site known previously for its seed potatoes, built a dyke around the course to facilitate irrigation. Cupp limited the number of tree plantings so he wouldn't block the spectacular panoramic views of the Coast Mountains, notably 8,450-foot Mount Currie.

Cupp knew to play to his strengths, and the scenery here is certainly one of those.

No. 16 is a 405-yard par 4 that sweeps to the right around a beautiful lake. This dogleg is wonderful to look at from the tee but a great challenge to play, especially from the back tees.

Named "Deep Breath," the ideal tee shot is about 260 yards and favors the left side of the fairway. This will give you an approach shot of about 115 yards to a good-size green with no bunkers around.

This is a classic risk-reward hole. **TJ**

**Course:** Bayonne Golf Club

**Location:** Bayonne, New Jersey, USA

**Hole:** No. 16

**Length:** 486 yards

**Par:** 4

**Designer:** Eric Bergstol

**Course Comment:** When you experience the architectural masterpiece that is Bayonne Golf Club, it is hard to fathom that the course was created in 2006 when more than 7 million cubic yards of sludge from the New York Harbor was spread out over 140 acres to form the base of the course.

## No. ⑯ BAYONNE GOLF CLUB

The 16th hole at Bayonne Golf Club is called "Heaven's Gate" for a reason. Its beauty and difficulty seem to be an opening into golf paradise. Offering views of New York Harbor and the skyline of New York City, it has unique scenery indeed. Toss in the challenge of the hole itself, and you have something special.

Looking down at you as you play, watching every shot you take, is the Statue of Liberty. She is visible off in the distance in the harbor, so make sure and keep your head down on your swings. You would not want to embarrass yourself in front of Lady Liberty.

Bayonne staffers say that Heaven's Gate "may be the most challenging two-shotter on the course." This seems hard to believe at first because of the generous fairway and the unusually large green, but par is a genuine feat.

Nuance is the reason. Yes, the fairway is large, but you must drive over a ravine to get to it. Failure to do so eliminates the chance of par before you get the opportunity to take your second swing.

Even if you are fortunate enough to clear the ravine, there comes the challenge of that green. It is large, but it is a peninsula, surrounded on three sides by water. Miss right, left, or in the rear and you are wet. It is large, but you better hit it, or, once again, kiss par goodbye. **JB**

| | |
|---|---|
| **Course:** Bali Golf & Country Club | |
| **Location:** Nusa Dua, Bali, Indonesia | |
| **Hole:** No. 16 | |
| **Length:** 460 yards | |
| **Par:** 4 | |
| **Designer:** Robin Nelson, Rodney Wright | |
| **Course Comment:** England's Nick Faldo set the Bali Golf & Country Club course record, a 9-under 63 during the 1994 Alfred Dunhill Masters. | |

# No. ⑯ BALI GOLF & COUNTRY CLUB

It only seems fitting that this tiny island nation with its diverse collection of towering mountains and warm sandy beaches has a golf course that weaves its way through an equally varied setting.

From Bali Golf & Country Club's first tee, players are ushered through an inland loop of dense tropical vegetation with occasional glimpses of the Indian Ocean below. After the turn, the layout works its way back toward the ocean through a mature coconut grove with palms that tower some 100 feet into the clear sky.

Bali's 16th is a hearty par 4 that plays 460 yards and sets up the course's dramatic finale on the beach adjacent to the Indian Ocean. Before this refreshing finish, however, players must negotiate the demanding 16th.

Considered Bali's toughest hole, No. 16 requires a slight draw (for a right-handed player) from the tee to cut the dogleg. A waste area runs down the left of the hole while mounds and palms guard the right side of the fairway. Anything short of the dogleg will require a lay-up that must hug the left side of the fairway.

A long iron or fairway wood approach shot will be required to a green that is 22 paces deep and protected on the front right by a bunker. Anything long will feed into a collection area directly behind the putting surface. **RH**

## No. ⑯  **BALTUSROL GOLF CLUB**
### (UPPER COURSE)

**Course:** Baltusrol Golf Club
(Upper Course)

**Location:** Springfield, New Jersey, USA

**Hole:** No. 16

**Length:** 447 yards

**Par:** 4

**Designer:** A.W. Tillinghast

**Course Comment:** The 16th hole was the climax of the 1936 U.S. Open. With three holes to play Tony Manero holed a 12-foot birdie putt at No. 16 for a commanding two-shot lead.

**BELOW** *The 16th hole at Baltusrol Golf Club.*

**OPPOSITE** *Lee Janzen of the USA celebrates chipping his shot in the 16th hole on the Upper Course at Baltusrol Golf Club, January 1993.*

As a general guide, major championship venues are often defined by the layout's level of difficulty. The reasoning: the harder the course, the more deserving it is to host a high-profile event. By this standard, few courses seem as suited for a major event as Baltusrol Golf Club.

Baltusrol's Upper and Lower courses have been the site of 15 national championships and both courses have proven themselves worthy tests. At the 2000 U.S. Amateur a score of 4-over 145 was good enough to earn players a spot in match play, and at the 1961 U.S. Women's Open Mickey Wright prevailed, or maybe preserved is closer to the truth, with a 5-over 293 total.

Few holes on either layout can match up to the challenge of the Upper Course's par-4 16th.

The right side of the 16th's relatively generous fairway is protected by a large oak tree that can block a player's approach while fairway bunkers await down the left side of the 447-yard hole.

The putting surface cants sharply away from Baltusrol Mountain and is framed in the front right and left by three deep bunkers. Players must keep approach shots right of the hole for any chance at birdie. **RH**

**Course:** Huntsman Springs

**Location:** Driggs, Idaho, USA

**Hole:** No. 16

**Length:** 424 yards

**Par:** 4

**Designer:** David McLay Kidd

**Course Comment:** Kidd, winner of *GOLF Magazine*'s "Architect of the Year," cites Huntsman Springs as his "greatest architectural achievement."

## No. 16   HUNTSMAN SPRINGS

Many times, golf-course architects would prefer to be minimalists when deciding to move earth around and disturb the natural layout of the land. However, when David McLay Kidd was given the job of designing Huntsman Springs, the property was such that he was forced to move about 4 million cubic yards of dirt to construct the course in 2009.

It created a wonderful golf course for the Huntsman family ownership, and the 16th hole may be the most shining example of its splendor.

The 16th is a short par 4 that forces a choice with a left or right fairway decision off the tee. This is risk/reward golf at its finest. The fairway is large enough, so is inviting. However, there is a meandering (yet lovely) stream directly down its center. Depending on the length of your shot, the stream could swallow your ball, even if you strike it purely.

The risk/reward is prevalent throughout the course, and as the Grand Tetons stare you in the face at No. 16, the fairway to the right of the stream is the easier shot, but the fairway to the left offers a better shot to the green. Pin placement is the key. If the hole is on the far-right side of the green, it is recommended to play the left fairway to avoid the deep bunkers in the front of the green. If the hole is in the left or the middle, the right fairway is the recommended play. **JB**

**Course:** Bandon Dunes
(Bandon Dunes Course)

**Location:** Bandon, Oregon, USA

**Hole:** No. 16

**Length:** 363 yards

**Par:** 4

**Designer:** David McLay Kidd

**Course Comment:** Forget having to pay for a cart. Bandon Dunes is a walking-only course right out of the Scottish-links design playbook about 100 miles from the California border.

Bandon Dunes was built along the Pacific Ocean bluffs on an undisturbed section of coastline, and can play with any course in the world when it comes to breathtaking beauty.

The wind, the sea, the openness, and the fog will remind many of Scotland and Ireland. And the conditions are impeccable. It's the best of both worlds.

You will find the prevailing wind at your back on this 363-yard par 4 that runs along the ocean. It is much easier to carry your drive onto the top fairway than it looks. Don't go right unless you want to see the Pacific Ocean close enough to taste the salt water.

The approach shot from the upper fairway is much shorter and provides a good look at the green.

Do not attack the right-hand hole locations, as the gorse is much closer than it appears from the fairway. The green is tucked into the right a bit with the ocean just a wave or two off the fringe.

The resort features two courses, both built on a beautiful stretch of sand dunes perched 100 feet above the ocean. Between them, the two courses feature a dozen holes that run along the bluffs overlooking 23 miles of sweeping shoreline. **TJ**

**Course:** Rock Creek Cattle Company

**Location:** Lecanto, Florida, USA

**Hole:** No. 16

**Length:** 467 yards

**Par:** 4

**Designer:** Tom Doak

**Course Comment:** When Rock Creek Cattle Company was created in 2008, many called it the finest private facility Tom Doak had ever designed. In its first year, it was rated No. 1, No. 3, and No. 4 in the "New Course" category by three separate ratings publications.

# No. ⑯ ROCK CREEK CATTLE COMPANY

We're not sure how many ranch hands out there are golfers, but if there are any, we have found a perfect place for them to play. In this magnificent Montana course, Tom Doak has found a perfect 350-acre mix of brush, mountains, rock, ranchland, fescue, and golf.

The 16th hole at Rock Creek Cattle Company is loaded with enormous pines, the mountains act as a picturesque backdrop, and the classic Doak touches along the way make No. 16 Rock Creek's most lasting memory.

At 467 yards, it isn't overly long, but it does offer enough distance to force two stout shots to get home. There is a majestic tree on the right side of the fairway that serves as the hole's defining characteristic, but the aiming point is actually a bunker on the left. The fairway slopes toward the tree, so anything hit toward the bunker will end up filtering toward the middle of the fairway.

Keeping left continues to be the story at No. 16, even as you ready for your approach shot. There are bunkers to the right, so the play is to hit toward the left side of the green. Even if you miss left, there is a good chance that you will kick onto the green because of the undulations there.

When you think of Montana, you may think big and bold. You may think rough, rocky, and mountainous. If these truly are your thoughts of Montana, then No. 16 at Rock Creek Cattle Company fits right in. **JB**

**Course:** Hazeltine National Golf Club

**Location:** Chaska, Minnesota, USA

**Hole:** No. 16

**Length:** 402 yards

**Par:** 4

**Designer:** Robert Trent Jones Sr., Rees Jones

**Course Comment:** The site of the 2016 Ryder Cup has also played host to the U.S. Open, the PGA Championship, the U.S. Women's Open, the U.S. Senior Men's Open, the U.S. Amateur Championship and the NCAA Championships.

# No. 🄰 HAZELTINE NATIONAL GOLF CLUB

The mission statement at Hazeltine National Golf Club says it all:

"The mission of the founders of Hazeltine was to build and maintain a golf course suitable for the conduct of national championships. An important part of the mission was to develop a membership that supported this concept — a membership that felt a responsibility to the game of golf and its rules and traditions. Similarly, it requires the highest standards of conduct by all members and guests as they play the game."

You get the idea. The people at Hazeltine — from pro-shop staff to members to groundskeepers — are interested in first-class golf.

"Our record of past events and championships scheduled through the Ryder Cup in 2016 attest to the fact that we hold true to our mission statement," said Bob Muschewske, president of Hazeltine National, "but Hazeltine is more than that. It is also a special place because we have developed and nurtured a culture that emphasizes a passion for the game of golf and respect for its traditions and rules.

"The only test we ask of prospective members is — do you support our Mission Statement and do you share that passion?"

The word passion is easily associated with a golf club and golf course as hallowed as Hazeltine. If by some odd chance you weren't passionate about the game going into a round at Hazeltine, you certainly would be by the time you finished. It is one of America's gems. And the 16th is its signature, which is odd because until 1970, this was a par-3 hole. But it was transformed into one of the great medium-length par 4s in championship golf when flat land was discovered on a steep hill behind the 15th green.

This flat spot at the bottom of the hill soon became the 16th tee, and the par 3 was instantly a par 4.

Further revision was carried out in 1991, when Rees Jones refined his father's work, creating a stream from a drainage ditch on the left side. Possible disaster lurks on each shot at No. 16. The tee shot must carry 220 yards of Hazeltine Lake to reach the fairway, which is flanked on both sides by water. The most skilled players would probably use a fairway wood for their tee shot, which leaves approximately 150 yards to the green.

"The green is a small peninsula out into Lake Hazeltine," Rees Jones warns. "It is an intimidating target." **JB**

*BELOW AND OPPOSITE Two views of the 16th at Hazeltine National Golf Club.*

**Course:** Royal Canberra Golf Club

**Location:** Canberra, Australian Capital Territory, Australia

**Hole:** No. 16

**Length:** 432 yards

**Par:** 4

**Designer:** John Harris, James Scott

**Course Comment:** Built in the gorgeous Westbourne Woods in Australia's capital, Royal Canberra is regularly ranked among the country's top 10 golf courses.

## No. ⑯ ROYAL CANBERRA GOLF CLUB

The course has often been called Australia's Augusta National, largely because of its diverse plant life and the fact it was laid out on land that at one time served as an arboretum for the city of Canberra — remember that the home of the Masters tournament was laid out on an old tree nursery.

But the quality of the track itself draws favorable comparisons as well, and no hole is more highly regarded than the 16th. This meaty par 4 is a modest dogleg right and begins with a drive off an elevated tee across a small glen to a fairway lined with cypress pines.

The best play for that shot is a slight fade, and then it is time for the approach, again traveling over another hollow to an elevated green that slopes from back to front and is ringed by a quartet of bunkers.

It is a rather large landing area with some 33 yards of depth, but golfers should not let the size lull them into any sort of false security, as two-putts here are by no means a given, and it makes the most sense to leave approach shots comfortably below the hole. **JS**

**Course:** Commonwealth Golf Club

**Location:** South Oakleigh, Victoria, Australia

**Hole:** No. 16

**Length:** 400 yards

**Par:** 4

**Designer:** Sam Bennett, Charles Lane, Sloan Morpeth

**Course Comment:** Commonwealth was founded in 1920, and its first golf professional, Sam Bennett, designed the initial 12 holes of the golf course, while architect Charles Lane completed the job, adding his own touch to some of the initial green and bunker work along the way.

## No. ⑯ COMMONWEALTH GOLF CLUB

In many ways, it is all about the drive on No. 16 — probably the best hole at this old line Sand Belt course — and how much a player wants to flirt with the lake that runs along this dogleg left.

You have to be careful about not hooking your tee shot into the hazard, though a drive down the left side of the fairway sets up better for the approach to the green. The green is tricky because it slopes from right to left as well as back to front.

Move your ball a little farther to the right and you can more easily avoid the lake, but you are then faced with the prospect of either going through the fairway and into the rough, or having a tougher second shot from the short grass.

That's largely because there is a bunker on the right of the green that must be cleared with any approach from that side of the hole, and the slightest mis-cue will often result in a difficult up-and-down. **JS**

**Course:** Half Moon Bay Golf Links (Ocean Course)

**Location:** Half Moon Bay, California, USA

**Hole:** No. 16

**Length:** 387 yards

**Par:** 4

**Designer:** Arthur Hills

**Course Comment:** Like many courses in this region of California, the scenery is amazing. The Ocean Course is a true links design — completely open and playing along the Pacific Ocean with stunning views.

## No. ⑯ HALF MOON BAY GOLF LINKS (OCEAN COURSE)

When a hole rides along the edge of the Pacific Ocean, you can be sure it's going to be a memorable moment. Standing on the tee, it's easy to imagine you're in a different time at a different place — Scotland, say.

The slightly doglegged right fairway has a nice open landing area — even with the wind playing games with your golf ball.

Take aim off the tee at that left bunker. Check the yardage and pick the right club. Remember, it's not too long to get yourself in good position for an approach shot. Landing a little short of that left bunker which sticks its nose out into the fairway is a good place to be — about 120 yards from the green. Where you don't want to be is left of the cart path, unless of course you're carrying a camera and not a golf club. The ocean lines the entire left side of the fairway and there is a great view of the resort up on the cliff in the near distance.

The second shot must carry the gorge onto a shallow green. If you're going to miss, miss long.

Heaven here on Earth? Oh, yeah. **TJ**

**Course:** Oakland Hills Country Club (South Course)

**Location:** Bloomfield Hills, Michigan, USA

**Hole:** No. 16

**Length:** 406 yards

**Par:** 4

**Designer:** Donald Ross, Robert Trent Jones Sr.

**Course Comment:** The 16th hole is the signature of the South Course, the site of the 2004 Ryder Cup.

**BELOW** *Luke Donald and Paul McGinley of Europe on the 16th hole during the Ryder Cup, September 2004.*

**OPPOSITE** *Darren Clarke of Europe plays a shot on the 16th hole during the Ryder Cup, September 2004.*

# No. ⓰ OAKLAND HILLS COUNTRY CLUB (SOUTH COURSE)

The pedigree at Oakland Hills is almost mind-boggling. Six U.S. Opens, for starters. Not to mention several other major national and international competitions, including the 1972 PGA Championship, in which the 16th hole played a major role when eventual champion Gary Player birdied and Gary Jamieson parred to break a tie.

The great thing about Oakland Hills is, even though its reputation has brought some of the greatest events in golf to southeastern Michigan, officials at the club haven't rested on their laurels. Robert Trent Jones Sr. redesigned the South Course before the 1952 U.S. Open and twice more in 1972 and 1984. Arthur Hills did a redesign on the South Course in 1987.

Its long legacy, the attention to detail, and a wonderful layout that has been tweaked over the years, are just a few reasons why the Oakland Hills South Course was chosen to stage the 2004 Ryder Cup Matches.

Said U.S. Ryder Cup captain Hal Sutton: "Every time I drive through the gates at Oakland Hills, I feel golf."

Nowhere on the grounds is that "feel" more present than at No. 16.

The dogleg is nearly a right angle, and is created by a bending water hazard that starts with a protrusion into the fairway and ends on the right side of the green. A beautiful yet perilous weeping willow in the right rough offers greater penalty than deep grass if players stray right off the tee.

The green at No. 16 is very small. It is protected left and back by bunkers, right and front by water. The 16th is the middle hole in a five-hole South Course sequence known as the "Fearsome Fivesome."

When you are finished with the South Course at Oakland Hills (or it is finished with you), you will be more than ready for a beverage in the clubhouse that is the second-largest wooden structure in Michigan (The Grand Hotel on Mackinac Island is the largest). The clubhouse is also an exact replica of George Washington's Mount Vernon home. We cannot tell a lie: The South Course lives up to its nickname "Monster," given to it by the immortal Ben Hogan after he brought the course to its knees. **JB**

**Course:** Pasatiempo Golf Club

**Location:** Santa Cruz, California, USA

**Hole:** No. 16

**Length:** 395 yards

**Par:** 4

**Designer:** Alister MacKenzie

**Course Comment:** MacKenzie designed some of the most beautiful golf courses in the world, but chose to make his American home at Pasatiempo. The home still stands today.

## No. ⑯ PASATIEMPO GOLF CLUB

Alister MacKenzie's American home when he wasn't traveling the globe adding golf splendor everywhere he went, was along the sixth fairway at Pasatiempo Golf Club. But it was the medium-length challenge 10 holes further along that he often called his "favorite four par in all the world."

MacKenzie must have been getting in touch with his sadistic side when he said those words, for the 16th at Pasatiempo is the most difficult hole on a most difficult golf course. Quite simply, Pasatiempo's 16th strikes fear into the hearts of nearly all who play it.

A blind tee shot over an indicator flag calls for some intelligent planning, not to mention a precise placement with a draw. It also requires a ton of local knowledge. If your playing partner hasn't played the hole, or if he chooses not to share any knowledge he might have, you better have a caddie along because there are problems if you play this unwisely. For instance, even if you somehow know you need to hit a draw, if that draw is too severe, the ball ends up in a barranca on the left. If you hit it straight right, or worse yet, fade, you're out of bounds on the right. If you are particularly accurate but don't draw the ball, you can play your drive slightly left of the aiming flag on the hill.

But even the best drive leaves a long, downhill approach to an elevated putting surface featuring three tiers, a jealous gathering of greenside bunkers, and a stream below. Even though there are three levels, the ball never stops in the lower portion.

When the pin is white and left, on that little bit of the green above the left bunker, the best approach shot is aimed at the yellow traffic sign in the background, and the shot should be past the hole onto the upper level. It is easier to putt slightly down to that pin than it is to putt up to it from the middle portion.

"You simply must be on target on this hole," said head pro Ken Woods. "If you're not, the penalties are very severe." **JB**

**Course:** Ocean Forest Golf Club

**Location:** Sea Island, Georgia, USA

**Hole:** No. 16

**Length:** 394 yards

**Par:** 4

**Designer:** Rees Jones

**Course Comment:** As you would expect, wind is a major factor on this links-style course that offers spectacular views where the ocean comes into play on the final three finishing holes.

# No. ⑯ OCEAN FOREST GOLF CLUB

This is a par-4 dogleg left and a very pretty hole — like all the rest of the holes at Ocean Forest.

The ideal drive is down the right-hand side. There are some mounds over there that you can play to your advantage. If you hit the right side of these mounds they will kick your ball into the fairway. But if you hit the wrong side of these mounds they can kick your ball into a hazard.

There are also plenty of pine trees and oak trees on the right side to be aware of. They look nice, but they aren't a lot of fun to hit out of.

Big hitters can try and cut the corner, but it's at least a 300-yard shot from the back tees.

A good shot is straight down the middle or along the right side a little over 250 yards. This gives about a 150-yard approach shot to a green with bunkers front right and front left.

There is a ridge in the center of this three-section green and plenty of marsh behind.

Because of the big marsh around the green, depth perception becomes a problem. Trust the yardage because the view from the fairway on this hole can be deceptive. **TJ**

**Course:** Wentworth Club (West Course)

**Location:** Surrey, England

**Hole:** No. 16

**Length:** 481 yards

**Par:** 4

**Designer:** Harry S. Colt

**Course Comment:** Wentworth features three 18-hole courses and one nine-hole executive course. The West Course is among the best in the world with an outstanding layout and flow to it.

**BELOW AND OPPOSITE** *The 16th hole at Wentworth.*

# No. ⑯ WENTWORTH CLUB (WEST COURSE)

The West Course, which was opened in 1926, winds through the heavily wooded estate. Once you leave the clubhouse there is no short-cut back. The West Course is also famous from an historical perspective. According to the history books, Wentworth was known as the Burma Road Course during World War II. German prisoners from a nearby camp became golf-course workers when they were brought in to clear vegetation that had become overgrown while the course was closed.

The monstrous, 481-yard, par-4 16th kicks off a very difficult finishing stretch at Wentworth. This hole could easily be a par 5, but the final two holes already are par 5s.

The key to No. 16 is on the tee. It is important to stay left because the hole doglegs slightly to the right and you don't want to pull your tee shot. Why? There are three bunkers sittting there waiting for you to do just that.

Watch out for the bunker on the right side of the green, which slopes from right to left. A birdie here is reason to celebrate. A par or even a bogey is considered a good score and something to be proud of. **TJ**

**Course:** Ganton Golf Club

**Location:** Ganton, North Yorkshire, England

**Hole:** No. 16

**Length:** 448 yards

**Par:** 4

**Designer:** Tom Chisholm

**Course Comment:** Golf was first played at Ganton in the summer of 1891 on a course laid out by Tom Chisholm of St. Andrews, who had assistance from Robert Bird, the club's first professional and head greenskeeper.

# No. ⑯  GANTON GOLF CLUB

Regarding the bunkers at Ganton, Patric Dickinson described them in his book *A Round of Golf Courses* as seeming to say, "Good morning, we hope to be introduced."

Ganton is known for its bunkers. They are big. They are well-placed. And they are very difficult to get out of. The biggest one on the golf course is on No. 16. This monster is about 180 yards off the tee and stretches across the entrance of the fairway.

Most players will clear this with little difficulty, but they won't soon forget the size of the thing.

There are trees all along the right side of the fairway. The left is pretty open but there is a bunker closer to the green that cuts into the fairway and there is another bunker on the left side of the green.

Wind is always a factor at Ganton, so keep that in mind as far as club selection goes.

The 15th and 16th here are both stiff two-shotters requiring perfectly struck shots to subtle greens. **TJ**

# GULF HARBOUR COUNTRY CLUB

**Course:** Gulf Harbour Country Club

**Location:** Whangaparoa, Auckland, New Zealand

**Hole:** 16

**Length:** 443 yards

**Par:** 4

**Designer:** Robert Trent Jones Jr.

**Course Comment:** Home of the 1998 World Cup of Golf, Gulf Harbour can challenge the best players in the world. But with five sets of tees it can play for any level player.

**BELOW** *Colin Montgomerie of Scotland putts on the 16th green at Gulf Harbour, November 1998.*

This 443-yard, par 4 stands alone at Gulf Harbour, a course with many signature holes. But No. 16, a classic risk-reward hole, is special.

This hole is not only the most dramatic hole on the golf course but the most difficult as well. A setting such as this is rarely found in the golf world and is compared with the 8th at Pebble Beach or the 17th at Cypress Point.

The tee shot plays over a rugged ravine to a rolling fairway that naturally turns to the right. The long hitter can opt to play over the rugged ocean front terrain to considerably shorten his approach. Such a tee shot is clearly risky, as any shot less than perfect will not be found.

The green rests at the point of a narrow peninsula providing 270 degrees of photographic ocean views. The hole can be frightfully long when played into the wind, and is unreachable in certain conditions. Once you have reached the green you have to deal with its severe slope back to front.

Nothing is easy here. But nothing is as pretty, either.

Enjoy. **TJ**

**COLLETON RIVER PLANTATION (NICKLAUS COURSE)**

**Course:** Colleton River Plantation (Nicklaus Course)

**Location:** Bluffton, South Carolina, USA

**Hole:** No. 16

**Length:** 437 yards

**Par:** 4

**Designer:** Jack Nicklaus

**Course Comment:** This course with native marshland on 12 holes has impressed many. Greg Norman once said this course is the best course Jack Nicklaus ever built.

Any discussion about unique golf courses would have to include Colleton River Plantation. There are two great courses here, including this one designed by Jack Nicklaus. And The Bear left his mark (or should that be tracks?) on this spectacular piece of real estate.

The beginning holes cut through oak trees and towering pines before heading out to the marshes. Then it's back into the woods and back again to the marshes. Then, on No. 14, the course begins its final journey through the wind-swept dunes bordering the Colleton River.

Welcome to one of those finales, the 437-yard No. 16, "River Bound." This par 4 drops down from an elevated tee to the river banks and then heads left around a group of fairway bunkers that *must* be avoided. This isn't the time or place to go to the beach.

Even though the dunes ride along the right side and even cut in front of the green, the ideal tee shot is to the right and beyond the bunkers on the left, giving you the green straight ahead. The westerly wind is in your face on the long second shot, making it even longer and that much more difficult. The green is set back among a series of natural dunes. **TJ**

**Course:** Kittansett Club

**Location:** Marion, Massachusetts, USA

**Hole:** No. 16

**Length:** 400 yards

**Par:** 4

**Designer:** William Flynn, Fred Hood

**Course Comment:** Often ranked among the best courses in a state with a lot of best courses, Kittansett is basically a flat course built next to Buzzard Bay.

# No. 🕧 KITTANSETT CLUB

To fully understand and appreciate the Kittansett Club, you first have to understand the region. Kittansett is one of only a few true New England seaside courses.

Situated at the end of Butler Point, which extends several miles into Buzzard's Bay, Kittansett offers a challenge to even the best golfer. The waters which surround the point provide a moist climate so that the course is seldom hard and fast. Over these waters come various wind patterns, which can cause difficult playing conditions.

There are few places you get the full picture of this gorgeous area than the par-4 16th hole. This is one of those holes where it doesn't really matter how you play it. Because, frankly, who cares what your score is?

Standing on the tee, you get a nice view of Buzzard's Bay with the tall fescue blowing in the wind along the fairway and up by the green. There are traps about 20 yards short of the green, which sits up off by itself on a small hill.

On the green, you get the full view of the bay and most of Cape Cod. It's one of the prettiest holes you will ever play. **TJ**

No. **⓰** **CHERRY HILLS COUNTRY CLUB**

**Course:** Cherry Hills Country Club

**Location:** Englewood, Colorado, USA

**Hole:** No. 16

**Length:** 433 yards

**Par:** 4

**Designer:** William Flynn

**Course Comment:** Cherry Hills has hosted seven U.S. Golf Association events, and the 2005 U.S. Women's Open makes it eight.

Cherry Hills's heyday of men's championships may be coming to a close, but that shouldn't stop scratch golfers and high handicappers alike from appreciating this historical track.

When Arnold Palmer drove the opening par 4 at the 1960 U.S. Open, he made headlines when he went on to outplay Ben Hogan and Jack Nicklaus for the title. Colorado's high altitude has always made the 7,160-yard layout shorter than it appears, but advancements in fitness and equipment technology seemingly make William Flynn's design come up short when considering sites for modern-day men's championships.

On paper, holes like No. 16 at 433 yards seem more than enough for the average Englewood resident. Skilled players, however, often leave their drivers in the bag when attacking this dogleg left, as a stream that meanders down the right side of the fairway cuts across almost 295 yards from the tee.

Using a fairway wood or long iron, players should aim down the right side as overhanging limbs on the left often interfere with approach shots. Once players do find the fairway, a mid- to short-iron is necessary to reach a medium-sized green protected by bunkers on either side.

Altitude and advancements in fitness and equipment aside, Flynn's creation still packs plenty of punch. **BB**

**Course:** Merion Golf Club (East Course)

**Location:** Ardmore, Pennsylvania, USA

**Hole:** No. 16

**Length:** 428 yards

**Par:** 4

**Designer:** Hugh Wilson

**Course Comment:** Merion Golf Club has hosted more national U.S. Golf Association championships (16) than any other club in America.

# No. 🔟 MERION GOLF CLUB (EAST COURSE)

Talk about a one-hit wonder. Hugh Wilson may be the prime example in the history of golf, or any other category for that matter.

Wilson, a Scottish immigrant who as an 18-year-old Princeton University freshman won the first club championship at Aronimink Golf Club in Philadelphia in 1897, picked up an affinity for golf-course architecture when he turned 31. His first project, Merion Golf Club's East Course, has gone on to be one of the most revered courses in America. Wilson went on to assist in the designs at Cobbs Creek and consult at Pine Valley, but before he could complete another project on his own, he died at age 46. So, Merion Golf Club East is the only design credited to Hugh Wilson.

Wilson certainly made the most of his one chance, and he also made prime use of limited land available at Merion. He crammed 18 wonderful holes into 126 acres, which is extremely tight — courses can sometimes take up to 300 acres of land. The holes are fair, they are compact, and they are challenging. Most of all though, they are fun, and none is more fun, nor more memorable than No. 16.

It begins at an elevated tee that overlooks a valley of a fairway that stops at the mouth of an old limestone quarry. Now a pit full of sand, rock, thicket, and brush, the old quarry is to be avoided at all costs. The optimum play is to aim straight at the quarry, which is on the same line as the green, and have your ball drop just short of it. However, if you don't trust your judgment, there is a safer area to the right that avoids the quarry, though it forces a more difficult angle to the green.

If you choose the straight route and are lucky enough to stop short of the quarry, it is back up a hill to the elevated green, on about the same level as the tee. You can't see the green on the approach, so some guesswork is required. The putting surface is narrow and long, and fronted by three bunkers that could actually save a player from falling back into disaster. **JB**

**Course:** Barton Creek (Fazio Foothills Course)

**Location:** Austin, Texas, USA

**Hole:** No. 16

**Length:** 420 yards

**Par:** 4

**Designer:** Tom Fazio

**Course Comment:** Although it opened in 1986, the Fazio Foothills Course already has its share of tournament history. The course is a regular stop on the Canadian Tour and hosted the 2003 USGA Senior Womens' Amateur.

ABOVE *A golfer takes his putt on the 16th green at Barton Creek.*

## No. ⑯ BARTON CREEK
### (FAZIO FOOTHILLS COURSE)

It is Barton Creek's diverse terrain that draws an unsuspecting player's first double take. Fairways lined with steep cliffs give way to natural limestone caves, waterfalls, and dramatic elevation changes.

With Barton Creek Tom Fazio was afforded an eclectic canvas, and the renowned architect used this pot pourri of natural features to create a test that is as challenging as it is scenic.

However, after the initial topographical shock, it's the Foothills's narrow landing areas that take center stage. At least for the wayward from the tee box. Foothills' par-4 16th is an example of this exacting driving philosophy.

From the tee, players face a long carry to reach the turn on this dogleg right. Anything to the left, and the second shot will be blocked by trees. Too far right and the difficulty of the approach increases exponentially.

The green is protected in the front by a waste area and one of Foothills' signature waterfalls, while anything long will leave an awkward, downhill chip to a small and slightly mounded putting surface.

Pin positions front right bring the water hazard and a small clump of bushes into play, while anything back left is likely to run off the green. **RH**

## No. ⑯ THE GLADES GOLF CLUB
### (GOLD COAST COURSE)

**Course:** The Glades Golf Club (Gold Coast Course)

**Location:** Robina, Queensland, Australia

**Hole:** No. 16

**Length:** 336 yards

**Par:** 4

**Designer:** Greg Norman, Bob Harrison

**Course Comment:** Built on an old dairy farm and opened in the year 2000, The Glades is a modern classic whose signature feature are wetlands that stretch throughout the site, providing terrific visuals as well as testy hazards for some of the holes.

The beauty of this short par 4, which doglegs to the left around a lake, is that it requires sound decision-making as soon as one steps to the tee and begins considering which club to hit.

The driver is the first thing that — quite naturally — comes to mind, and a well-hit ball will leave a player with a pitch of 50 yards or so to a small green guarded by four bunkers and angled to the left. But this is a narrow hole with not much of a bail-out area, and a long iron will easily do the job for most golfers — and give them perhaps a 100-yard approach shot. That seems the most logical choice, but it is also one of the most difficult ones on this track, largely because golfers of all ages and levels of skill tend to prefer to hit the Big Dog and, in the local vernacular, "have a go at it."

At least that's what locals say often happens at No. 16 at The Glades, and the results of those selections are frequently scores above par. **JS**

## No. ⑯ GOLF CLUB DE URUGUAY

**Course:** Golf Club de Uruguay

**Location:** Punta Carretas, Uruguay

**Hole:** No. 16

**Length:** 337 yards

**Par:** 4

**Designer:** Alister MacKenzie

**Course Comment:** Montevideo's 26-storey Palacio Salvo, which can be seen from the 16th hole, was the tallest building in South America when it was built in 1927.

Opened in 1923, the Golf Club de Uruguay is one of three layouts designed early in the 20th century by the legendary golf-course architect Alister MacKenzie, who was hired by British and American entrepreneurs in a successful effort to bring the sport to this tiny yet vibrant country, the smallest Hispanic nation in the Americas.

The club is situated along the southeastern Uruguay coast, just five minutes from the center of the country's capital city of Montevideo. Although golfers will experience magnificent views of the city skyline, they still will have the feeling that they are worlds away, as the course is set in serene wooded parkland that faces the sea.

The 16th hole is a short par 4 that plays significantly longer because of the uphill climb it makes from tee to green. The landing area is lined by trees and other vegetation on both sides, meaning accuracy is crucial on the drive.

Put it in the center of the fairway, and you'll be in much better shape for the short, tricky approach to the tiered, undulating green, which is protected by deep front bunkers and features a panoramic vista of the city in the distance. **KA**

**Course:** Fujioka Country Club

**Location:** Aichi Prefecture, Japan

**Hole:** No. 16

**Length:** 605 yards

**Par:** 5

**Designer:** Peter Thomson, M. Wolveridge

**Course Comment:** Part of the land that Fujioka was built on was formerly a tea plantation.

# No. ⓰ FUJIOKA COUNTRY CLUB

Fujioka Country Club, recognized as one of the best courses in Asia, was laid out on 180 acres of hilly terrain complete with a large lake, a winding creek, and numerous pine trees.

This private club opened in 1971, with Australian golfer Peter Thomson as the designer. At that time, Thomson was one of the few foreign-born golf-course architects doing work in Japan, where he designed more than a dozen courses. Of those, Fujioka is considered the best.

And the best of Fujioka might just be its monster of a 16th hole. It's such a long and difficult par 5 that the back tees — which are a lengthy 605 yards — are normally put into play only for professional events.

The uphill tee shot should be hit to the right side of a narrow landing area, although a steep bank on the right does help funnel even some slices back to the center.

The tree-lined fairway then twists and turns until golfers are hitting a downhill third shot to a large green that sits at an angle, slopes from right to left, and is guarded by a small pond at the front left. **KA**

## No. ⑯ DISNEY'S OSPREY RIDGE

The knock-on effect of resort-style golf courses is that sometimes they are too soft. They don't want to upset their guests by making the golf course too challenging because they want their business back.

This hole is an example of how you can please both the average golfer and the one looking for a real test of the game.

First of all, the Osprey Ridge course offers four sets of tees, ranging from 459 yards to 542 yards on this par-5 hole. Then there is your plan of attack. On No. 16, you have a chance to go for the green in two but plenty of opportunity to lay up.

Off the tee there is a sizeable landing area. But after that, the fairway narrows and multiple bunkers are positioned on both sides. The big hitters thinking of reaching the green in two will try to clear all of the bunkers and hit the fairway beyond that point.

Then, the better players will have to clear plenty of water to reach the green. The fairway curves around the water, which is on the left side. There is a bunker between the water and green that can come into play if you find yourself short.

The fairway curves around and meets up with the green. That's the safe route and often the smart route.

The green is pretty big with a huge bunker along the backside. **TJ**

## No. ⑯ EAGLE CREST GOLF CLUB

Even though this is just off the busy I-94 expressway outside of Detroit, the golf course offers plenty of seclusion from the hustle and bustle nearby. Golfers are also treated to some great views of nearby Ford Lake and the surrounding area.

There are plenty of outstanding golf holes on this course with rolling hills and some surprising elevation changes. And then there is the water. This brings us to the best hole on the golf course — also considered one of the more difficult, earning a No. 2 handicap rating.

A long and precise drive is required to carry the marsh area in front of the tee box on the 16th. Trees extending on the left side of the fairway and Ford Lake on the right present more hazards. A second lay-up shot should position a golfer in front of the water that guards the peninsula green.

This green extends a great length from left to right but has a narrow landing area from front to rear. **TJ**

## No. ⑯ LYON OAKS

**Course:** Lyon Oaks

**Location:** Wixom, Michigan, USA

**Hole:** No. 16 (also known as No. 7 East)

**Length:** 575 yards

**Par:** 5

**Designer:** Arthur Hills

**Course Comment:** Lyon Oaks is one of four courses owned and operated by Oakland County. All four of the courses end with "Oaks," but only one roars above the rest as a real masterpiece — Lyon Oaks.

One of the unwritten rules at Lyon Oaks is to leave your driver in the car — and we are not talking about the person who drove you to the course. This is a tight course where shotmaking is the key and placement is rewarded.

At 6,837 yards from the tips, the course isn't exceptionally long. But it's anything but easy.

The 575-yard par-5 16th is a lengthy exception. Not only is this the longest hole on the course, but it's also the most difficult (it's the No. 1 handicap hole). This dogleg right wraps around a marsh from tee to green, so anything to the right is either gone or in big trouble.

The fairway is narrow all the way and there is always the temptation to cut some marsh. You can do that but the advice here is to lay off a little. There is no reason to gamble on this hole. The best play is for a par or even a bogey.

There is a fairway bunker along the left side about 311 yards from the back tees. If you can't hit it 300 yards, it's a good target to shoot at. It's another 175 yards to carry the grass bunker in the middle of the fairway from the 250-yard marker.

Like most of the holes at Lyon Oaks, No. 16 is basically as tough as you want to make it. **TJ**

**Course:** Gleneagles (Centenary PGA Course)

**Location:** Auchterarder, Perthshire, Scotland

**Hole:** No. 16

**Length:** 543 yards

**Par:** 5

**Designer:** Jack Nicklaus

**Course Comment:** To play any of the courses at Gleneagles, you don't call for a tee time, you check in at the front desk.

BELOW *Søren Kjeldsen of Denmark plays from a bunker on the 16th hole at Gleneagles, June 2003.*

# No. 🅖 GLENEAGLES (CENTENARY PGA COURSE)

Jack took care of golfers of all levels at this hole. For players like himself, the back tees at No. 16 measure 543 yards, but four sets of tees provide plenty of options for the rest of us.

These 18 holes at the newest course at Gleneagles are consistently very good. But what else would you expect from the Golden Bear?

Your ideal tee shot to start this hole should be just left of the fairway bunker (like most of the bunkers here, it is not a good place to be). This gives you the best look onto the green.

The second shot should be straight and short of the loch. Play this smart and don't get carried away. Having to pitch back onto this green will add a few strokes to your scorecard. The green steps up in the back left corner so pay attention to the pin placement.

Like many of the holes here, No. 16 offers some splendid views of the surrounding countryside. But don't spend too long admiring the scenery — there is plenty of good golf to be played. **TJ**

**Course:** Pennard Golf Club

**Location:** Southgate, Swansea, Wales

**Hole:** No. 16

**Length:** 495 yards

**Par:** 5

**Designer:** James Braid

**Course Comment:** Pennard Golf Club features several historic landmarks, such as the ruins of a 12th-century Norman castle and the site of a medieval church.

## No. ⑯ PENNARD GOLF CLUB

Having been founded in 1896, Pennard Golf Club is one of Wales's oldest courses, and has one of the most spectacular settings of any golf club in the British Isles. It is a classic seaside links course that features breathtaking views across Oxwich Bay and Three Cliffs Bay, and golfers can expect to be troubled by stiff breezes that blow up the Bristol Channel.

Thanks to its clifftop setting along the Gower Peninsula, Pennard enjoys remarkable rolling — some might even say severe — topography. Its bunkers are quite basic and its greens somewhat nondescript. But the windy conditions and the natural twists and turns of the terrain provide more than enough challenge. And the scenery is simply spellbinding, especially during the magnificent final stretch of Nos. 16–18.

The 16th is a short par 5 that plays directly along the coast. The tee shot must be hit over an expanse of gorse and rough to a fairway that slopes hard from right to left, then falls over the horizon at the point of a slight dogleg turn to the right.

The green can be reached in two with a pair of strong shots, but is set on a ledge, meaning that shots which come up shy will likely roll back down to the fairway. **KA**

## Course Information (Desert Dunes)

**Course:** Desert Dunes Golf Course

**Location:** Desert Hot Springs, California, USA

**Hole:** No. 16

**Length:** 530 yards

**Par:** 5

**Designer:** Robert Trent Jones Jr.

**Course Comment:** Beginners beware. This course has everything to challenge the best golfers in the world — from elevation changes to narrow fairways, to fast and sloped greens, to water hazards.

# No. ⑯ DESERT DUNES GOLF COURSE

This is one of those great holes that can make or break a round. It's an opportunity for par or better. But it's so easy to go the other way. A sure five can turn into a seven faster than a putt rolling down a severely sloped green.

So try and stay focused. But it's tough to do with the incredible scenery all around. There are great views of Big Bear Mountain (a popular ski destination for the Los Angeles snowbirds) and Jacinto Mountain. Both tower over 10,000 feet and usually have snow at the top of them almost year-round.

There are also plenty of cactus, octillo, and other desert plants to see as you make your way around No. 16.

OK, back to the hole.

Your tee shot should be long and straight. There is a bunch of bunkers along the right side.

About 200 yards from the flag, water joins the fun along the right side of the fairway. If you are going to make the green in two, you have to carry the water. The green is narrow, but deep with a bunker on the left side.

This is a breathtaking hole that is fun to play. **TJ**

## Course Information (Canterbury)

**Course:** Canterbury Golf Club

**Location:** Beachwood, Ohio, USA

**Hole:** No. 16

**Length:** 611 yards

**Par:** 5

**Designer:** Herbert Strong

**Course Comment:** One of Ohio's best golf courses, Canterbury hosted the U.S. Open in 1940 and 1946 and is known for its narrow fairways and many blind shots on the back nine.

# No. ⑯ CANTERBURY GOLF CLUB

They have a saying here during tournaments that when you cross the road, you have survived so far. Yet, on the other side of the road is one of the best tests of golf you will find anywhere.

It's easy to see why they call the final three holes the toughest three-hole stretch anywhere. In Ohio. In the United States. In the world. It just doesn't get any more difficult.

No. 16 kicks off this challenging run, and it certainly can kick your score up a few notches. At 611 yards from the back tees, it's long. And you need three really good shots if you are going to birdie or even par this hole.

Your tee shot should be either straight or along the right side of the fairway. If you are left, you will be blocked on your second shot by trees. There is also some long rough over there.

Your second shot is a blind shot uphill. If you can really hit a 3-wood, you could reach the bottom of the plateau. The top of the plateau is about 130 yards from the green.

Your approach shot to the green is also a blind hit to a green that is about 27 yards deep and slopes back to front.

Don't be long on your approach shot. There are bunkers in the back and it's very difficult to get up-and-down in two from the backside. **TJ**

**Course:** TPC at Sawgrass
(Stadium Course)

**Location:** Ponte Vedra Beach, Florida,
USA

**Hole:** No. 16

**Length:** 497 yards

**Par:** 5

**Designer:** Pete Dye

**Course Comment:** TPC at Sawgrass
is famous for its annual staging of
the Players Championship, but it
also has held prestigious events
that didn't involve million-dollar
prizes. Tiger Woods won the 1994
U.S. Amateur Championship at TPC,
and he trailed by one at No. 15 before
evening up the match on No. 16.

# No. ⑯ TPC AT SAWGRASS
## (STADIUM COURSE)

It is said that the great golf holes of the world have a flavor all their own, a personality, if you will. If that's the case, and you carry it one step further, you can imagine the 16th hole at TPC at Sawgrass' Stadium Course is burdened with a bit of an inferiority complex. It is a tremendous hole in its own right, but the fact that it directly precedes one of the most famous holes in the world might have it feeling just a touch unworthy. During the PGA Tour's TPC, the 17th is one of the most watched holes of the tournament. But, no one is there to watch the action at No. 16. They are all on the hill across the pond to watch the famous par-3 17th. Anything they see at No. 16 is mere afterthought.

However, for those who scoff at such a concept of golf spirituality, for those who view a golf hole as just fairway, rough, and green, No. 16 at the Stadium stands on its own.

It is a rarity in tournament-quality golf today — a par-5 hole less than 500 yards that still proves a difficult challenge to reach in two. Obviously, it isn't the length that proves troublesome — 497 yards is easily manageable by top players armed with state-of-the-art alloys and solid cores.

The affectations of the hole, which at first appear cosmetic, actually have a great deal to do with the difficulty of a birdie attempt. Water lines the right side of the fairway, from tee to green, which tends to make players aim to the left. However, if they go too far left, a pair of palms next to the green block entry. And if they decide to hug the water to avoid those palms, there is a large dual-trunked tree about 90 yards short of the green on the right side. These trees are far more than visually pleasing. They force pinpoint accuracy if a player hopes for birdie, even if the hole is 497 yards.

Angle is important all the way down the fairway, and proper distance becomes imperative at the green, which juts into the pond supported by Pete Dye's trademark railroad ties. There is perhaps three feet between the back edge and the pond. It isn't length at the 16th that's most important, it's accuracy and proper gauge.

An inferior hole? Highly doubtful. **JB**

**Course:** Turnberry Golf Club (Ailsa Course)

**Location:** Turnberry, Ayrshire, Scotland

**Hole:** No. 16

**Length:** 409 yards

**Par:** 5

**Designer:** Mackenzie Ross

**Course Comment:** Turnberry provides long-handled ball retrievers for the many golfers who end up in the burn on No. 16.

**BELOW AND OPPOSITE** *The 16th hole at Turnberry Golf Club.*

Following immediately on the heels of Turnberry Golf Club's tough par-3 15th hole, No. 16 marks the second of superb back-to-back holes that can spell certain victory or imminent defeat for contending players when the British Open Championship comes to the Ayrshire coast.

Called "Wee Burn," this is the lone hole on the course where water crosses the fairway. But what a water hazard it is. The stream, which cuts immediately in front of the elevated green, isn't wide, but is intimidating — steep banks make sure that once a ball finds the burn, there is little chance of getting out clean without a penalty stroke.

The hole contains only two bunkers — one to the left of the landing area for tee shots, and one left for the green — an apt location for those who come through a little too quickly on their swings in an effort to make it over the stream. Indeed, the burn looms large in players' psyches from the very beginning of this hole, proving it's not so "Wee" after all.

No. 16 provided the turning point in the 1963 Walker Cup Match, as the Americans took control in two separate foursomes matches on Day 1. **KA**

**Course:** Southport & Ainsdale Golf Club

**Location:** Southport, Merseyside, England

**Hole:** No. 16

**Length:** 508 yards

**Par:** 5

**Designer:** James Braid

**Course Comment:** In the 1937 Ryder Cup Matches at Southport & Ainsdale, the United States captured the Cup for the first time on British soil.

# No. 🔟 SOUTHPORT & AINSDALE GOLF CLUB

In 1904, The Grosvenor Golf Club was established by approximately 50 members. This in itself was a fairly common number to start a club, but what set the club apart was that were about an equal number of men and women members. A rough nine-hole course was built, bridge was played in the primitive clubhouse, and the unique club was born.

Renamed Southport & Ainsdale in 1907, members in 1923 built a new course, designed by James Braid, a few miles south of the original location. They also constructed a new clubhouse and began a tradition that carries on proudly today. The club has been setting itself apart in the century since its inception. It has hosted numerous prominent English tournaments, even though it went through some serious difficulty during the World War II period. Existence of the club was threatened, but through perseverance, members kept the financially strapped institution alive.

Today, those who play at Southport & Ainsdale are glad they did.

The 16th hole, known as "Gumbleys," is a symbol of the unique spirit employed by the original members. It features a "sleeper-faced bunker," which is what the British call railroad ties. Using them as a feature in a bunker was not completely unheard of in Braid's day, but it was fairly unique. And, the fact that the sleeper-face still exists today speaks greatly to the S&A's independent thinking.

And you thought Pete Dye invented the railroad tie.

The hole, at 508 yards, isn't overly long for a par 5, but as on many British tracks, the yardage number on the scorecard isn't nearly as important as the direction of the wind. At Gumbley's, the breeze is almost always in your face.

The drive should be on the left side of the fairway, carrying over an immense bunker, and bisecting two smaller fairway bunkers. The second shot is the most important on this hole, and it is where the dominating sleeper-faced bunker comes into play. The wind at S&A might have eroded this perilous bunker over the years, were it not for the reinforcement of the railroad tie. So the danger of hitting into this bunker is just as ominous as it was in 1923.

The second shot is directly over huge sand mounds, and then you must avoid the sleeper-faced bunker. Also in the path are two smaller bunkers, but you wouldn't know it. They are invisible from where you play the second shot because of the sand hill.

The hole becomes straightforward after the second shot. If you survive unscathed, and are in good position for your third shot, you have a decent shot at birdie. But, avoid that bunker or it might just knock out any chance you have of a decent score on this hole. **JB**

**Course:** Paiute Resort
(Sun Mountain Course)

**Location:** Las Vegas, Nevada, USA

**Hole:** No. 16

**Length:** 527 yards

**Par:** 5

**Designer:** Pete Dye

**Course Comment:** Paiute is home
to three excellent courses cut into
the desert not far off the strip. The
Tav-ai-Kaiv Sun Mountain Course
opened in 1996 and includes four
lakes which come into play on
four holes.

# No. ⓰ PAIUTE RESORT
## (SUN MOUNTAIN COURSE)

These golf courses have earned more awards than a classic movie on Oscar night. From the general manager, to the clubhouse, to the golf instructors and, of course, the courses themselves, they have the hardware and certificates to prove they are among the best in Vegas golf.

Once you pull off the highway and catch a glimpse of the lush green fairway cut into the desert floor, you will see for yourself this is worthy of every accolade.

No. 16 on the Sun Mountain Course is what you might call a give-a-little, take-a-little golf hole. Pete Dye gives you the tee shot here. It's a wide open fairway and you can really let it rip off the tee. At 527 yards from the back, you have a long way to go.

But the second shot is where Dye takes it back. This is a challenging shot. First of all, there is a pot bunker right in the middle of the fairway. It's a good idea to avoid this.

To reach the green in two, you are going to have to carry a little desert to a green that's tucked in back left. The fairway bends slightly left to a difficult green. **TJ**

**Course:** Mullingar Golf Club

**Location:** Mullingar, West Meath, Ireland

**Hole:** No. 16

**Length:** 500 yards

**Par:** 5

**Designer:** James Braid

**Course Comment:** Established in 1884, Mullingar is a very popular course in Ireland that is located close to a lake. It was redesigned by James Braid in 1937.

# No. ⓰ MULLINGAR GOLF CLUB

Mullingar is a great test for so-called straight hitters, in a wonderful parkland setting. The course is known all over Ireland for excellent playing conditions, and the fairways are simply terrific.

Speaking of being a straight hitter, this is the perfect example of how important that is at Mullingar. A good drive is required at No. 16, a par-5 dogleg right that finishes with another elevated green — another common occurrence at Mullingar.

Off the tee, you need to avoid a large ditch that cuts across the fairway. The ditch is about 220 yards out and often catches balls in which players are attempting to lay up. Either carry it or make sure you don't hit it too far.

The ditch has been described as a magnet that sucks in balls. Par is very difficult if you land in the ditch.

If you can get some length behind this and stay straight, you can reach the green in two with another good hit from the fairway.

The approach then becomes relatively straightforward, although don't be long. The green drops right off the back and makes for an almost impossible up-and-down play to a green sloping away from you. **TJ**

## No. ⑯  WALTON HEATH (OLD COURSE)

**Course:** Walton Heath (Old Course)

**Location:** Walton on the Hill, Tadworth, Surrey, England

**Hole:** No. 16

**Length:** 510 yards

**Par:** 5

**Designer:** Herbert Fowler

**Course Comment:** The 16th hole on the Old Course is a legendary hole, with its cavernous greenside bunker gathering any shot with the merest fade.

Situated only 20 miles south of London, and close to both Heathrow and Gatwick International Airports, Walton Heath is the only club in England to have had a reigning monarch as captain. The then Prince of Wales became King Edward VIII during his captaincy between 1935 and 1936.

The perfect tee shot on the 16th of what some describe as a peaceful golf course is about 316 yards from the back tees, landing just before the fairway narrows down to practically nothing.

Hitting a tee shot 316 yards, you should be in good shape as long as you avoid the bunkers to the right side. Those bunkers are not easy to hit out of, so note their position and distance.

About 145 yards out from the green is a fairway bunker. You need to clear this area on your second shot and look for an approach shot to the green within 100 yards. **TJ**

**Course:** Sperone Golf Club

**Location:** Bonifacio, Corsica, France

**Hole:** No. 16

**Length:** 580 yards

**Par:** 5

**Designer:** Robert Trent Jones Sr.

**Course Comment:** Cliffs and sea. Sound familiar? This seaside hole is similar to Pebble Beach's 18th, even though it was built by a different designer on the other side of the globe.

# No. ⑯  SPERONE GOLF CLUB

In a collection of 1001 golf holes, obviously the concentration of just about every hole, in fact the highlights, would be the strategy, shot-making, and, well . . . golf. But there are golf courses, and golf holes, for that matter, whose serenity, beauty, and peaceful isolation render the sport itself almost secondary. Such is the ambience of Sperone Golf Club.

Of course, playing a round of golf is the reason Sperone is in business, but travel companies in the area have arranged for walking tours at twilight. Whether you are carrying a golf club or a walking stick, there are few sights more soothing than this club's grounds, perched on white cliffs overlooking the emerald sea and the Lavezzi Islands. Designed by Robert Trent Jones Sr., this 90-acre golf course is just as much landscaped park with red cedars, century-old pines, and nature trails. As one travel brochure describes the tour: "This is a mecca for the day-tripping yacht crowd."

You will find not tourist vans here. Its isolation is such that the crowd of camera-carrying gawkers is kept so minimal as to be nearly non-existent. Tourists of that ilk do not often enjoy the long journey it takes to get to Sperone. Hence, protection from their intrusion.

Okay, it's time to talk a bit of golf. More specifically, the beautiful 16th hole at Sperone.

The aforementioned white cliffs serve as a 100-foot wall between the sea and the 16th fairway. At the top of the wall is the fairway. At the bottom of the glistening border is the Strait of Bonifacio. You tee off on this 580-yard hole on a thin strip of scruffy ground next to the sea, and you have an ample landing area at which to aim. If you take the perilous approach and hug the shore, you have a shot at the green in two. However, if safety is your guide, you can aim for the middle and play this hole as a three-shotter.

Even a perfect drive raises a question: can my next shot be perfect? Can I get it over the jutting sea, past the snow-white cliffs and onto the green? These are the questions that make Robert Trent Jones Sr. famous. Somehow, overlooking the shot, you can see him smiling. **JB**

Course: Desert Forest Golf Club
(North Course)

Location: Carefree, Arizona, USA

Hole: No. 16

Length: 523 yards

Par: 5

Designer: Red Lawrence

Course Comment: Lawrence
did some of his best work in the
American Southwest later in his
career, earning the nickname
"The Desert Fox."

# No. 🟠 DESERT FOREST GOLF CLUB
## (NORTH COURSE)

Desert Forest was one of the first modern-era, target-style courses in the Arizona desert, and for that reason, golfers who have enjoyed rounds in the state owe a huge debt to architect Red Lawrence. The unfortunate thing is, not many of them know it, because Desert Forest is a strictly private club with little more than 250 members.

Located north of Phoenix, at 3,000 feet, this Lawrence gem has changed little since it opened in 1962. The cost? Approximately $275,000, including a payment of $16,000 to Lawrence. Compare that with the hefty price tag of Arizona golf courses today, with many costing $1 million or more — per hole.

Unique in many ways, Desert Forest contains no fairway bunkers, water hazards, cart paths, or out-of-bounds, meaning that golf balls landing in the desert can be played.

Long hitters intent on getting home in two on the par-5 16th hole, which features a stunning view of Black Mountain, must hit their drives to a narrow landing area lined by desert on both sides.

The long second shot must then make it past the overhanging branches of a huge Mesquite oak on the left side near the green, which also is guarded by bunkers at the front right and left. **KA**

**Course:** Mission Hills Golf Club (World Cup Course)

**Location:** Guanlan Town, Shenzhen, China

**Hole:** No. 16

**Length:** 523 yards

**Par:** 5

**Designer:** Jack Nicklaus

**Course Comment:** The 1995 World Cup of Golf at Mission Hills attracted more than 120,000 spectators, more than three times what tournament organizers had expected.

# No. ⑯ MISSION HILLS GOLF CLUB (WORLD CUP COURSE)

Mission Hills' 16th hole originally was No. 7 before the nines were switched several years after the course's opening. The move makes for a more difficult finish, as one of Asia's toughest three-shotters now begins the home stretch.

From the tee box, the hole is scenic but scary, as two large water hazards immediately grab golfers' attention. The drive must be hit over a wide creek that crosses the fairway, and golfers who want to get home in two must carry a large lake on the left on their second shots.

A ribbon of fairway extends down the right side for those who want to lay up, but the water must still be carried on the short approach to a large, undulating green protected by a pair of bunkers in the rear.

The first — and still the most highly regarded — course at what has since become the largest golf resort in the world with an amazing 10 18-hole layouts, the Jack Nicklaus-designed World Cup Course takes its name from serving as the host site of the 1995 World Cup of Golf. Won by the United States team of Davis Love III and Fred Couples, it was the first international competition of its type on mainland China. **KA**

**Course:** PGA West (Stadium Course)

**Location:** La Quinta, California, USA

**Hole:** No. 16

**Length:** 566 yards

**Par:** 5

**Designer:** Pete Dye

**Course Comment:** The San Andreas Fault bunker left even Tip O'Neill, the former U.S. Speaker of the House, speechless during the pro-am portion of the 1987 Bob Hope Chrysler Classic. After numerous unsuccessful tries at blasting out, O'Neill finally picked up his golf ball and threw it onto the green.

# No. ⑯ PGA WEST (STADIUM COURSE)

PGA West's Stadium Course is famous for its numerous water hazards, but the 16th hole doesn't have any of them. Instead, the primary obstacle here is sand — and plenty of it.

Long waste bunkers guard much of the left side of the fairway on this long dogleg left par 5, but they are but a mere prelude to the diabolically deep bunker that guards the entire left side of the putting surface.

Called "The San Andreas Fault," the long, narrow bunker comes complete with its own set of stairs and rests more than 18 feet below the level of the green. Make sure to avoid it at all costs on the approach. Because if you land in "The Fault," there's no telling how many shots it may take to get out.

If you do find yourself in those devilish depths, however, looking up the steep slope to a putting surface that seems miles away, take solace in this. The hazard has claimed some of the world's very best players, as the Stadium Course has been the site of numerous top professional events, including the Skins Game, the Bob Hope Chrysler Classic, the Champions Tour's Liberty Mutual Legends of Golf, and the PGA Grand Slam of Golf. **KA**

**Course:** Firestone Country Club
(South Course)

**Location:** Akron, Ohio, USA

**Hole:** No. 16

**Length:** 625 yards

**Par:** 5

**Designer:** Bert Way, Robert Trent
Jones Sr.

**Course Comment:** Down by five
strokes to Bruce Crampton in
the 1975 PGA Championship, Jack
Nicklaus made an unbelievable
par on the 16th hole as part of a
comeback on the way to winning
his fourth PGA.

# No. ⑯ FIRESTONE COUNTRY CLUB
## (SOUTH COURSE)

Arnold Palmer dubbed the 16th at Firestone South "The Monster," and it has
stuck to this day. No one knows for sure if the nickname has endured
because Palmer made triple bogey in the 1960 PGA Championship, or
because countless others have suffered at least as dismal a fate in the
ensuring decades.

It is a monster, all right. All 625 yards of it. But, close observers of golf at
least can say they have had a chance to see the hole, even before they have
had an opportunity to come to Akron, Ohio, to take on the challenge. That's
because Firestone is the only golf course in the world to play host to three
nationally televised events in the same year: The American Golf Classic, The
CBS Golf Classic, and The World Series of Golf. Another televised event that
you might have needed to squint to see was Tiger Woods's famous shot in
the dark to win the 2000 WGC-NEC Invitational.

But television doesn't do justice to The Monster. You must see it
yourself. Strength, finesse, and an ample helping of guile. The visual off the
tee is more than just a tad frightening, even though you might think the
downhill look offers some relief. But, still, 625 yards is 625 yards, even if the
hole falls off a cliff. Yes, it runs downhill, but it still represents a true three-
shot challenge.

The test became even tougher in 1960 when Robert Trent Jones Sr.
redesigned the hole. Jones forced length and accuracy off the tee, and
required another long shot to a split fairway on the second shot in order
to get close enough to have a decent chance of getting close to the pin on
the approach.

The green, although ample, is protected on all sides by either sand or
water. Pin placements and weather conditions can dictate the amount of
speed (and fear) you must negotiate when putting.

It is rare when par is considered a good score at a par 5. These holes are
where the best of the best generally make up strokes to par. But a par on
the monstrous 16th at Firestone's South Course is proof enough that you've
met the challenge. Take it happily and move along. **JB**

**OPPOSITE** *Darren Clarke of Northern
Ireland hits a shot to the 16th green at
Firestone Country Club, August 2003.*

Course: Oak Tree Golf Club

Location: Edmond, Oklahoma, USA

Hole: No. 16

Length: 479 yards

Par: 5

Designer: Pete Dye

Course Comment: When the PGA Championship was played at Oak Tree in 1988, the course's rating was 76.9 — the highest in the country.

## No. ⓰ OAK TREE GOLF CLUB

Hit two great shots, and this is an easy birdie — perhaps even an eagle — but miss just slightly on either, and plenty of trouble awaits.

The tee shot must avoid a winding creek on the right, with the preferred landing area just to the right of a large oak on the fairway's left side. That will leave approximately 225 yards to a three-tiered green with a left side that is well protected by the creek and a massive, deep bunker.

Sitting in the midst of the sand is a lone tree that appropriately symbolizes the fate of golfers who land their approaches in the creek — it has a noose hanging from one of its branches. As the club likes to say, "Hangman's Noose" is there for a reason.

Jack Nicklaus can attest. Although this hole gave up nine eagles in the second round of the 1988 PGA Championship (won by Jeff Sluman), Nicklaus took a 9 on the hole, blocking his tee shot into the creek, then losing his 3-wood approach in the trees to the right of the green. It was the first time in competition — professional or amateur — that Nicklaus had lost two balls on the same hole. **KA**

Course: St. Enodoc Golf Club (Church Course)

Location: Rock, Cornwall, England

Hole: No. 16

Length: 495 yards

Par: 5

Designer: James Braid

Course Comment: No. 16 is one of only two par-5 holes on St. Enodoc's Church Course, which plays to a par of 69. It has 11 par 4s and five par 3s.

## No. ⓰ ST. ENODOC GOLF CLUB
### (CHURCH COURSE)

Founded in 1890, St. Enodoc is one of those quirky British Isles' layouts that is a pure pleasure to play. The most unique feature of the aptly named Church Course is that holes 10 through 15 play around a 12th-century stone church, where John Betjeman, former Poet Laureate of England and a St. Enodoc member, is buried. His longtime love affair with the golf course is well-documented by the crafting of such poems as "By the Ninth Green" and "St Enodoc."

Laid out on some of the most inspiring land ever used for a links course, St. Enodoc is routed through and around massive sand dunes and offers splendid views of the Camel Estuary and the ocean beyond. The Church Course also comes complete with the famous 60-foot-high "Himalayas" bunker on the sixth hole, hedgerows, brick walls, and wandering livestock.

The 16th hole, a short par 5 that at times is played downwind, isn't known for its difficulty. In fact, it's rated as St. Enodoc's No. 15 handicap hole. But for pure beauty, especially late in the day when the sun is about to set over the Camel Estuary, it truly is one of golf's magical spots. **KA**

**Course:** Shinnecock Hills Golf Club

**Location:** Southampton, New York, USA

**Hole:** No. 16

**Length:** 542 yards

**Par:** 5

**Designer:** William Davis, William Flynn, Howard Toomey

**Course Comment:** Phil Mickelson finished second in the U.S. Open at Shinnecock in 1995. He played No. 16 in a combined six over par and finished four shots out of the lead.

For those who watched the 2004 U.S. Open at Shinnecock Hills Golf Club, the fearsome conditions and the fact that only two players broke par for the tournament might strike fear. It is okay to be a little intimidated, because Shinnecock Hills indeed is a test. However, once the U.S. Golf Association left town, superintendent Mark Michaud slowed down the greens, cut back the rough, and made the course playable for mere mortals.

*Golfweek* columnist Jeff Babineau said it best when he wrote of the Open conditions at Shinnecock, labeling them "a Coney Island carnival on a golf course that got away . . . " Many of the players said the course was out of control, pointing in large part to the slippery sloping seventh green. But No. 7 wasn't the only source of consternation. The par-5 16th also raised an eyebrow or two.

"The greens are looking a little thirsty," said Mark Calcavecchia after round one. "The 16th green is purple already. By 4 o'clock, it might be almost dead. But they know what they're doing out here. They want them right on the edge. If it was howling out here, it might be kind of crazy."

Crazy, indeed. But No. 16, while still tough, is now back to members' conditions. In other words, it's no longer playing on the edge of doom.

The 16th at Shinnecock isn't long by today's standards, but the wind sometimes makes this par 5 unreachable even for big hitters. The prudent player does not attempt to reach this green in two. The fairway is ultra-thin, and there are slopes and valleys in the landing areas for both the first two shots. It is more important to sacrifice a little length and put a premium on accuracy to find the flat.

The key shot is the third to a small, narrow green that slopes from back to front and is well-guarded by five bunkers. There is a chipping area in front and to the right of the green. Visible from the 16th green is the stately clubhouse, which was the first golf clubhouse in America when it was built in 1892.

You have to wonder what those members would say today, if they could sit in the clubhouse and watch the way their course played for the 2004 U.S. Open. Or, if they would even recognize the place. **JB**

# Hole **17**

There are two ways to look at the 17th hole, depending on your level of competition. If you are playing a tournament, the pressure is at its greatest, but, if you are out for a casual round, you may be feeling a touch of angst at the day being nearly over.

An often overlooked point to consider on the 17th hole,  particularly if you are finishing in the evening, is that you may have the sun in your eyes. Course architects try to avoid pointing the 18th hole into the setting sun, and the 17th is often laid out in the opposite direction to the final hole.

But sunshine aside, the 17th is often a dramatic set-up to the finale. TPC at Sawgrass, the par-3 island in Ponte Vedra, Florida, is perhaps the most famous example, but it is not the only storied 17th. Pebble Beach (USA), Waterville (Ireland), Nagoya (Japan), and the Jockey Club (Argentina) offer more proof that No. 17 is a place for architects to show their stuff.

**LEFT** *Players walk to the 17th green at Sahalee Country Club, Sammamish, Washington, USA.*

**Course:** Stonewall Golf Club

**Location:** Gainesville, Virginia, USA

**Hole:** 17

**Length:** 186 yards

**Par:** 3

**Designer:** Tom Jackson

**Course Comment:** Stonewall Golf Club is the centerpiece of the Lake Manassas master-planned community and measures 7,000 yards from the back tees.

# No. ⑰  STONEWALL GOLF CLUB

The course is named after the Confederate Brigadier General Thomas J. "Stonewall" Jackson. For those not up on their history of the American South, Jackson was a great warrior and legend in these parts.

Speaking of legends, a birdie on No. 17 and you can add that nameplate to your resumé. This 186-yard hole is pretty much what you would expect from a classic par 3 at a classic golf course. Your tee shot must clear water and there are plenty of bunkers guarding the green on all sides, leaving little room for error.

Welcome to the tee at No. 17, "Seven Pines." Bring your confidence and you might also want to bring an extra club as your tee shot must climb uphill. The green is big and because it slopes from back to front you will want to stay in front of the hole.

There are two large bunkers to the front right and left of the green. There are also bunkers behind, in case you grab too much club. Five sets of tees allow golfers to choose their level of difficulty, and the back tees offer quite a challenge. The water and scenery around the hole make this a very picturesque part of the golf course. A good score here is considered a major victory, but there many obstacles to overcome before you can celebrate. **TJ**

**Course:** Old Tabby Links

**Location:** Spring Island, South Carolina, USA

**Hole:** No. 17

**Length:** 205 yards

**Par:** 3

**Designer:** Arnold Palmer, Ed Seay

**Course Comment:** Arnold Palmer was so enamored with the natural beauty of Spring Island that he purchased a home site off the 18th hole.

# No. ⑰  OLD TABBY LINKS

Spring Island, located in the midst of South Carolina's lovely Lowcountry, has a rich history that includes habitation by members of the Yemassee Indian tribe, 16th-century Spanish and French explorers, and pre-Civil War cotton farmers. Old Tabby Links gets its name from the tabby ruins that sit adjacent to the ninth green. The portions of the sand-and-shell walls are all that remain from a mansion that served as the centerpiece of a 3,000-acre cotton plantation during the 17th and 18th centuries but was burnt by Union soldiers during the Civil War.

Today, Spring Island is an environmentally protected private community with a magnificent golf course, designed by Arnold Palmer and Ed Seay, as its centerpiece.

No. 17 is considered one of the best par-3 holes along the golf-rich South Carolina coast, even with its location near one of the game's meccas, Hilton Head Island. Located on a narrow peninsula, the putting surface is protected by a natural, spring-fed pond on the left, by a deep bunker front right, and on the right and rear by the spectacular salt marshes of the Chechessee River. This green isn't an easy one to play, but it sure is fun to try. **KA**

**Course:** Kemper Lakes Golf Club

**Location:** Hawthorn Woods, Illinois, USA

**Hole:** No. 17

**Length:** 203 yards

**Par:** 3

**Designer:** Ken Killian, Dick Nugent, Jeffrey Brauer

**Course Comment:** The late Payne Stewart changed his image at Kemper Lakes when he bagged the 1989 PGA Championship. Until then, he was a consistent second-place finisher for whom victory always seemed elusive. Kemper Lakes was the end of that.

The flat, narrow fairways of Kemper Lakes look innocent enough, but a tight tree line and a staggering number of hazards make it a must to hit the driver long and straight on this sprawling course.

Did someone say "water?" This course is a nature lover's dream carved into vast lake country — 1,500 acres of lakes, ponds, wetland, and forests. Kemper Lakes is large, but it's fair — water taunts golfers from the lion's share of its 18 holes, but on some, golfers who can't carry the water can play around it.

Signature No. 17 is all carry over water flanked on three sides by a retaining wall. Two bunkers protect the left of this stunning semi-island green. The two-tiered green is the course's longest at 53 yards, affording myriad pin positions. It plays anywhere from 203 yards from its tips to 130 yards for men and as short as 82 yards for women.

Greens are quick and the pace of play is brisk on this 18-hole Illinois nature hike. Kemper Lakes was the site of the 92nd USGA Women's Amateur Championship in 1992 and is the annual home of the Illinois PGA Section Championship since 1979. **KLL**

## No. ⑰   **NAGOYA GOLF CLUB** (WAGO COURSE)

**Course:** Nagoya Golf Club (Wago Course)

**Location:** Aichi, Japan

**Hole:** No. 17

**Length:** 171 yards

**Par:** 3

**Designer:** M. Otani

**Course Comment:** In the 2004 edition of the Chunichi Crowns, Nagoya's 17th hole played to a stroke average of 3.069, yielding 44 birdies compared with 64 bogeys and two double bogeys.

Nagoya Golf Club's 17th hole, a tough par 3 to play late in a round, can often play a key role in the outcome when some of the world's best golfers compete in the Chunichi Crowns, one of the Japan Golf Tour's most prestigious and historic events. The tee shot must be hit over a lake to an elevated green guarded by several bunkers. But golfers intent on making it over the lake and past the front bunkers must be careful not to hit it too far. Go too long and trouble awaits, as the green drops off into dense trees, making for a difficult up-and-down.

Nagoya's Wago Course, as long-time host for the Chunichi Crowns, has produced some worthy champions, including Masashi Ozaki (1987, 1992, 1995, 1996, 1997), Greg Norman (1989), Seve Ballesteros (1991), Davis Love III (1998), Darren Clarke (2001), and Justin Rose (2002). In 2001, Clarke bogeyed the hole in Round one, then birdied it each of the final two days to win by four. Japan's Shingo Katayama won the 2004 tournament by two strokes with a 16-under-par total, despite a late stretch of four bogeys in five holes that ended with a bogey at No. 17. **KA**

## No. ⑰   **WADE HAMPTON GOLF CLUB**

**Course:** Wade Hampton Golf Club

**Location:** Cashiers, North Carolina, USA

**Hole:** No. 17

**Length:** 196 yards

**Par:** 3

**Designer:** Tom Fazio

**Course Comment:** Even though this course is in the mountains there is no need to bring your hiking shoes. Surprisingly, most holes play downhill and the elevation change is only around 110 feet.

Before teeing off double-check your club selection. Remember the general rule about downgrading by one club-length for a downhill shot. This 196-yard, par-3 downhill shot certainly requires you to downgrade a club.

Just remember, downhill means downgrade.

With that in mind, don't be short here. There is a creek that runs in the front and winds around the right side of the green. There is also a bunker on the left side of the green.

Two large hemlock trees frame both sides of one of Wade Hampton's larger greens that slopes back to front. The green narrows as you move to the back so a front-pin placement isn't a bad thing.

But what you will most likely remember on this hole, is the awesome view of Chimney Top Mountain in the background. The 13th hole plays right up to the base, but at the 17th you get the full effect of the mountain.

This private course has five sets of tees with five unique names. For example on No. 17, the back tees, or the Fazio's, play at 196 yards. Other tees here include the McKees (190 yards), the Wade Hamptons (171), the Founders (140), and the Chimney Tops (134). **TJ**

**TPC AT TAMPA**

**Course:** TPC at Tampa

**Location:** Lutz, Florida, USA

**Hole:** No. 17

**Length:** 217 yards

**Par:** 3

**Designer:** Bobby Weed, Chi Chi Rodriguez

**Course Comment:** The back nine is the most challenging part of the course. Remember PGA professional golfer Isao Aoki's 45 on the back in the 1996 GTE Classic. Aoki's spectacular collapse allowed Jack Nicklaus to win the event.

First, a quote from one of the game's best players ever and someone who knows a little bit about course design: "It's a beautiful course," said 1995 U.S. Senior Open Champion and TPC of Scottsdale architect Tom Weiskopf about the TPC of Tampa Bay. "We (on the Champions Tour) just don't play courses that are in this kind of condition with this kind of challenge, for the most part. This is not a normal experience."

If you miss the green, there aren't many safe havens. There is a large bunker hugging the right side of the green and another one along the left side. Beyond the bunker on the right is water. Trees behind make long hitters pay a big price, but there is some fairway just in front of the green. Watch out for the small bunker along the front right.

The long tee shot that gets close will be rewarded on this 11,000 square foot-green, that is basically divided into three sections. Because of some subtle undulations throughout the green that make reading your putt difficult, birdies are rare so the closer you get the better.

Four sets of tees allow for players of all levels of skill to feel at home. The tees on the par-3 17th range from the reds at 102 yards to the championship tees at 217 yards. **TJ**

No. ⑰ **SCIOTO COUNTRY CLUB**

**Course:** Scioto Country Club

**Location:** Columbus, Ohio, USA

**Hole:** No. 17

**Length:** 191 yards

**Par:** 3

**Designer:** Donald Ross

**Course Comment:** Built in 1916, this historic country club has hosted many major events, including the 1926 U.S. Open, the 1950 PGA Championship, the 1968 U.S. Amateur, the 1986 Senior Open, and the 1994 Ohio Amateur Open.

This is a straightforward par 3. Donald Ross left the tricks in the bag with this one. What you see is what you get. With all that said, this is still a wonderful short hole on an Ohio classic.

Your tee shot is downhill — remember this when selecting your club — to a small green. Starting to sound a little more difficult than you thought?

In front of this tiny target is a small pond. Yes, water awaits your short tee shot. Straightforward doesn't always mean easy. Mr. Ross wasn't going to give you a pass.

There are also bunkers short and to the right side of the green.

At 191 yards, it's one of the more difficult short holes at Scioto. The green isn't going to give the better putters much trouble. It's not too difficult to read and if you can land on the green, a birdie is a definite possibility here.

Four sets of tees give golfers of all skill levels the chance to battle the golf course. At No. 17 you can play from the back tees at 191 yards or the closer tees at 130 yards. **TJ**

**Course:** Oakland Hills (South Course)

**Location:** Bloomfield Hills, Michigan, USA

**Hole:** No. 17

**Length:** 201 yards

**Par:** 3

**Designer:** Donald Ross, Robert Trent Jones Sr.

**Course Comment:** Ben Hogan first called it "The Monster," and that was during a stroke-play event some four decades ago. Oakland Hills South proved every bit as monstrous for the 2004 Ryder Cup matches. Just ask the U.S. team.

BELOW AND OPPOSITE *The 17th hole at Oakland Hills.*

# No. ⑰ OAKLAND HILLS (SOUTH COURSE)

Ben Hogan's words immortalized the South Course at Oakland Hills and slapped it with a nickname that stuck. He dubbed it "The Monster" after winning the sometimes-torturous 1951 U.S. Open with a total of 287 after shooting a final-round 67. It was a vicious track (that soon bloomed into legend), with just two sub-par rounds shot during the entire tournament.

The 1951 U.S. Open was the third of five Opens that Oakland Hills has hosted, and Robert Trent Jones Sr. dotted the course with bunkers when he toughened it up for that competition. Two PGA Championships have also been played at Oakland Hills since it opened in 1918.

No. 17 is a classic, a true great among longish par 3s. Its green is severely sloped with a ridge running from front-right to back-center. The best bet for par is to hit a 4- or 5-iron to a green that plateaus 30 feet above the tee and is completely encircled by cavernous bunkers. A hole situated on the back right makes for one of the toughest tee shots you're going to see.

The greens at Oakland Hills are sizeable and largely elevated with narrowly tapered fairways and high rough. Celebrated for its level of challenge, Oakland Hills is one of the most prestigious, stately courses ever carved into what once was rolling Michigan farmland. **KLL**

**Course:** Whistler Golf Club

**Location:** Whistler, British Columbia, Canada

**Hole:** No. 17

**Length:** 181 yards

**Par:** 3

**Designer:** Arnold Palmer

**Course Comment:** Whistler Golf Club is the first design work Palmer did in Canada. And the folks at Whistler paid a little homage to the King on his 75th birthday on September 10, 2004. Every golf cart had a birthday card commemorating Palmer's milestone, and the staff served complimentary cupcakes in the clubhouse.

In the splendid golfing destination of Whistler, where mountains provide backdrops for practically every hole in the region and winding creeks tumble down to feed the lakes, the Whistler Golf Club is a highlight. No. 17 here is both beautiful and challenging.

Whistler Mountain and Blackcomb Mountain surround the entire course, and there are nine lakes on the property to both enhance the experience and endanger golf balls. One of the lakes sits between the tee and green on No. 17, and while it would take a fairly severe mis-hit to end up in the lake, the body of water is the reason for the hole's nickname, "Birdbath."

More difficult than the small lake is the false front on the green. It appears that 165 yards will get you to the hole, but you've got to hit it every bit of 180 to land in the center of the putting surface. Don't be fooled by the optical illusion. There are bunkers on either side of the green, and majestic pine and cedar trees that run on both sides the entire length of the hole. The 17th at Whistler Golf Club, like the entire course, is bordered by a forest that is home to black bear, coyote, beaver, and other wildlife. The putting surface is spacious, but curvaceous. Birdbath is a challenge, but its majestic spectacle is what you'll remember. **JB**

**Course:** TPC at Four Seasons Resort & Club Las Colinas

**Location:** Irving, Texas, USA

**Hole:** No. 17

**Length:** 196 yards

**Par:** 3

**Designer:** Jay Morrish

**Course Comment:** The EDS Byron Nelson Classic golf tournament in May 2002, won by Shigeki Maruyama, was the first to take place on the Tournament Players Course (TPC) at Four Seasons Resort Las Colinas following a two-year renovation program.

## No. ⑰  TPC AT FOUR SEASONS RESORT & CLUB LAS COLINAS

The most scenic hole on the golf course — and there are no shortage of these on this Tournament Players Club gem — is the 196-yard par-3 17th.

You begin in the clouds on this hole with an elevated tee box that faces southeast teeing up not only a great golf hole below but a panoramic view of the resort, the grounds and No. 18 off in the distance.

When you have finished admiring the view, make sure that you take note of the small lake to the right of the green. It's a fader's nightmare but creates a real hazard when the wind is coming from the south or north. An undulating bunker that guards the left front of the green can also make this hole a bogey waiting to happen.

In the 2001 Byron Nelson Classic, Robert Damron and Scott Verplank played this hole together three times during the competition's final round. The championship went to Damron when he made a 124-foot birdie putt in an exciting four-hole playoff.

But even without the TV audience and large galleries, this hole is exciting all on its own.

And don't forget that this is a TPC course so you can expect only the very best in course conditions. **TJ**

---

**Course:** The Dunes Golf Links

**Location:** Rye, Victoria, Australia

**Hole:** No. 17

**Length:** 196 yards

**Par:** 3

**Designer:** Tony Cashmore

**Course Comment:** Marketing brochures describe this Mornington track thus: "God made it, and we just mow it."

## No. ⑰  THE DUNES GOLF LINKS

Tom Watson describes No. 17 at The Dunes as "exquisite," and there is indeed something special about the 196-yarder, which plays from an elevated tee to an elevated green on the other side of a shallow valley.

Miss to the heavily bunkered left side of the putting surface, and you are more than likely faced with a sinister sand shot to a moderately large green replete with interesting contours and a "spine" that divides it into two distinct halves. Fall short, and you will probably see your ball trickle down an apron of grass cropped to fairway length, while anything long will tumble down a steep incline to a chipping area.

The championship pin placement here is back left, which most definitely puts the bunkers on that side into play for the golfer who draws the ball. The degree of difficulty on No. 17 is enhanced by the fact that it often plays into the wind and can be a couple of clubs longer than the actual yardage indicates. **JS**

## No. ⑰ PINHEIROS ALTOS

**Course:** Pinheiros Altos

**Location:** Quinta do Lago, The Algarve, Portugal

**Hole:** No 17

**Length:** 136 yards

**Par:** 3

**Designer:** Ron Fream

**Course Comment:** Pinheiros Altos is one of three courses created in The Algarve by noted Californian designer Ron Fream.

Who would have thought there would be a little bit of Florida to be found in The Algarve, especially a little bit of Tournament Players Club at Sawgrass. The TPC's 17th hole is the first thing that springs to mind from the moment you walk onto the 17th tee at Pinheiros Altos on the Quinta do Lago estate. The hole only measures 136 yards, but it is an all-or-nothing shot from the tee. It's a case of hit the green or run up a big score that can potentially ruin a good card. The green slopes into the water in places and any ball that is too hot can run off into the water.

Like the 17th at the TPC, if you play this hole in any sort of wind then club selection can be a nightmare. In a cross-wind you might be required to hit a fade to hold the ball into the wind, especially if the wind is off the right, whereas you will have to hit a slight draw if the wind is off the left. If you can't manage either of those two shots at will then it's just a case of hit and hope. The hole features one very deep bunker which acts as a magnet for most golfers. Still, better a shot from the sand than hitting another shot from the drop zone. **AT**

## No. ⑰ THE EAGLES GLEN

**Course:** The Eagles Glen

**Location:** Charlottetown, Prince Edward Island, Canada

**Hole:** No. 17

**Length:** 175 yards

**Par:** 3

**Designer:** Graham Cooke

**Course Comment:** It's always a difficult task to pick your favorite hole. Eagles Glen has plenty of candidates for most memorable. But No. 8 and No. 17 more often than not get more votes. The good news is you get to play all 18 when you sign in.

A par 3 over water is always a memorable golf shot. Sure, it's intimidating, nerve-racking, and stressful. But that's golf. And it's why we love it.

This 175-yard par 3 at Eagles Glen is all of the above and then some. This is a great shot. One swing makes or breaks you. It's a lot of pressure. And a lot of fun.

You stand on an elevated tee and look at an elevated green. In between is a pond that reaches all the way to the green. There is also a tricky bunker between the green and the water.

Don't be too strong in your attempt to clear the water. Behind the green is no fun at all. The green is protected in the back and left with huge mounds and tall fescue.

A red-rock ledge along the green and the water helps make this a postcard hole. It's a terrific sight from the tee.

If the shot is too scary, the forward tees eliminate the water hazard and give you a nice angle into the green. If you're low on balls, this might be the place for you.

You can also play it a little safer by staying left. **TJ**

## No. ⑰ ROYAL TROON GOLF CLUB
### (OLD COURSE)

History is important here. This golf course must be appreciated and respected before you hit one shot or miss one putt. Founded in 1878 by a few enthusiasts, Troon Golf Club soon outgrew its local reputation and boundaries. The Old Course today presents one of the greatest tests of golf you will find anywhere in the world. The inward half of Royal Troon could be the most challenging back nine in Europe.

Called the "Rabbit" (members of the *Leporidae* family seem to enjoy this hole more than others on the golf course), this 222-yard par 3 has all of the ingredients that make up the word challenging.

This is the pinnacle at Royal Troon. A par here is worth a pint later. Because of the wind — which seems to pick up at No. 17 — a driver on the tee is not unusual. Some players will need everything they have in their bag and in their swing to reach the green.

The difficult plateau green, with bunkers nearby, slopes off sharply on both sides. It's 208 yards (playing longer with the wind) to the front of the green and there are plenty of sand traps to catch any wayward shots. If you can keep it straight, don't worry if you are short — this isn't a bad play. **TJ**

## No. ⑰  SHADOW CREEK GOLF CLUB

**Course:** Shadow Creek Golf Club

**Location:** North Las Vegas, Nevada, USA

**Hole:** No. 17

**Length:** 155 yards

**Par:** 3

**Designer:** Tom Fazio

**Course Comment:** To play at Shadow Creek, guests must be staying at one of the MGM Mirage properties — and also be able to plop down a green fee that can exceed $500.

Shadow Creek is perhaps the most magnificent man-made golf wonder found anywhere on earth. It is a place where lush gardens, sparkling creeks, cascading waterfalls, and exotic birds seem to have magically popped up out of the arid Nevada desert. They didn't, of course. Instead, this track was built in the late 1980s with the skill of architect Tom Fazio and the money of Vegas casino mogul Steve Wynn. Even today, more than 15 years after its opening, Shadow Creek enjoys a reputation shrouded in mystery because of its exclusive nature, the long list of celebrities that frequent it and, most of all, the fact that the course was dug deep into the desert and remains hidden behind a 10-foot-high chain-link fence.

The 17th hole certainly is one of the most dramatic at Shadow Creek. The tee shot is hit from the top of a ridge and over a lake to a tiny green that's surrounded by huge rocks and four deep bunkers — two at the right, one at the left front, and one at the rear. But the hole's most spectacular feature is the large waterfall that drops into a small pool behind the green. **KA**

## No. ⑰  WHITE COLUMNS GOLF CLUB

**Course:** White Columns Golf Club

**Location:** Alpharetta, Georgia, USA

**Hole:** No. 17

**Length:** 235 yards

**Par:** 3

**Designer:** Tom Fazio

**Course Comment:** One of the best courses in the Atlanta area (and there are quite a few of those), White Columns is known for its always-perfect conditions and requires length more than accuracy.

The most memorable and talked about hole at White Columns is the stunning and dramatic 235-yard, par-3 17th. It's not only one of the more difficult short holes on the course but a simply stunning golf hole that requires you to stand and admire before hitting. It's one of the few holes where you don't mind waiting for the group in front of you.

There is a significant and spectacular change in elevation from tee to green. It's so drastic that the employees of the club don't dare guess how big a drop it is. The change in elevation also helps provide one of the most scenic vistas on the course.

Just in front of the green is a creek that runs from one length to the other. It's very possible to end up in there, especially from the back tees. In between the creek and the green is a bunker. There is also a bunker that runs along the back left of the green.

Getting to the green is a good test, but your work isn't done. The two-tiered green is split down the middle, right, and left, and it slopes down toward the creek.

This par 3 is the most difficult on the course. **TJ**

**Course:** Cabo del Sol Golf Club
(Ocean Course)

**Location:** Los Cabos, Mexico

**Hole:** No. 17

**Length:** 178

**Par:** 3

**Designer:** Jack Nicklaus

**Course Comment:** No. 17 is part of a six-hole piece of property that has 1.5 miles of coastline, and it is the hole that brings the sea closest to the game — some would say, too close for comfort.

No. **17** **CABO DEL SOL GOLF CLUB (OCEAN COURSE)**

It is the signature hole on a Jack Nicklaus signature course. It requires a mere 178-yard shot off the tee, but it isn't the starting and landing points that crave attention, it is the grueling splendor in between.

The par-3 17th hole at Cabo del Sol's Ocean Course cozies up to the ocean, although "cozy" might not be the feeling that enters your mind when you hear the Pacific waves crashing into rocks that serve as the full-length, right-hand border to this wonderful hole. The shot off the tee goes over a sandy beach and rock outcroppings to a small green framed by bunkers on one side and a drop to the ocean on the other.

No. 17 is a prime example of why many familiar with Los Cabos golf consider the Ocean Course to be the most daunting in the area. But, that debate aside, there is no arguing against the fact that the 17th is a sampling of the Ocean Course's spectacular design and thrilling challenge.

*Pacific Golf Magazine* has called the Ocean Course "one of Nicklaus' finest creations" and the "Mexican version of Pebble Beach." But it isn't necessary to take the word of pundits. Nicklaus himself, when speaking of the 17th and the other holes that come right to the Pacific's edge, called this stretch of Los Cabos, "the best piece of golf property in the world." **JB**

**Course:** Sahalee Country Club

**Location:** Redmond, Washington, USA

**Hole:** No. 17

**Length:** 215 yards

**Par:** 3

**Designer:** Ted Robinson, Robert Muir Graves

**Course Comment:** The name Sahalee means "High Heavenly Grounds" in the language of the Chinook.

BELOW AND OPPOSITE *The 17th hole at Sahalee Country Club.*

# No. ⓱ SAHALEE COUNTRY CLUB

Sahalee Country Club was cut out of a mature forest of fir, cedar, and hemlock trees on the Sammamish Plateau outside Seattle. One of the more beautiful holes on a spectacularly scenic course, the par-3 17th hole is set amid dozens of trees, which frame the hole on both sides and the rear.

The downhill tee shot must carry a pond that wraps in front of the green and around its right side. The thin ribbon of grass between the front edge of the green and the water's edge is usually cut short, causing balls that miss short to roll back into the water. A bunker is placed perfectly to the left of the putting surface to catch bail-out shots to the left, and another bunker guards the rear.

At the 1998 PGA Championship, No. 17 played to a stroke average of 3.19, yielding 61 birdies compared with 72 bogeys and 34 double bogeys or worse. Steve Stricker finished second to Vijay Singh by two shots, and he might look back on Sahalee's 17th hole as the reason. Stricker double bogeyed the hole in Round two, then bogeyed it the final day to fall two strokes behind Singh with one hole to play. **KA**

**Course:** Woodlands Golf Club

**Location:** Mordialloc, Victoria, Australia

**Hole:** No. 17

**Length:** 169 yards

**Par:** 3

**Designer:** R.S. Banks, Sam Bennett

**Course Comment:** Built in 1913 on the old Mayfield Estate outside Melbourne, the original Woodlands golf course did not have any bunkering until the 1920s, when Royal Melbourne course superintendent Mick Morum oversaw their construction.

## No. ⓱ WOODLANDS GOLF CLUB

Length can certainly be deceiving when it comes to par 3s, and the initial reaction most players have when they see the modest yardage on the 17th hole at Woodlands is that par is going to be a veritable piece of cake.

But more often than not, they end up trudging to the next tee without their dessert, for this is a tight hole with a very small green that is perhaps the most difficult to hit on the course. In fact, it just might be the toughest 3-par in Melbourne's Sand Belt region.

A crisp 5- or 6-iron can set up a player nicely for par, but those who miss to the right or come up short will frequently find their balls in bunkers so deep they could use a set of stairs to get in and out.

And anything drifting left will likely skittle down a steep slope and settle in spots from which even a short-game specialist will find up-and-down a challenge. **JS**

**Course:** White Witch

**Location:** Montego Bay, Jamaica

**Hole:** No. 17

**Length:** 161 yards

**Par:** 3

**Designer:** Robert Von Hagge

**Course Comment:** White Witch is named after Annie Palmer, who, according to Jamaican legend, was an evil slave owner who killed three husbands and several slaves. She is said to haunt the area, and there have been Annie Palmer "sightings" for centuries.

## No. ⓱ WHITE WITCH

Robert Von Hagge, the 6' 5" designer of White Witch golf course, is an imposing presence when he walks into a room. It seems only natural that his White Witch golf course is daunting, as well.

But Von Hagge doesn't apologize.

"I think we're right where we need to be, as far as difficulty," Von Hagge said. "We want it to be tough, and we know we've got beautiful golf theater out here, too."

The signature par-3 17th hole at White Witch plays downhill, 161 yards to a green carpet of a putting surface surrounded by snow-white bunkers. The Caribbean makes for a gorgeous backdrop to the green, and a large native tree standing sentry over the green adds to the atmosphere.

The 17th is beautiful, as are the rest of the holes at White Witch. The course is indeed scenic, but at first glance it can also be daunting. Several of the holes are visible from the elevated clubhouse, and they look a bit frightening to the average golfer. But it is an illusion, much like some of the claims of passers-by who say they have seen White Witch Annie Palmer's ghost peeking out her mansion window.

Once a player gets on the course, all fears should be dispelled. Just play the shots and don't fear the beauty, revel in it. The landing areas are ample, the front and middle tees allow mid-range handicappers to make all the carries, there are just three blind shots on the entire course, and it's a very playable layout.

So the White Witch has legend. And it has illusion. The question is: do you have the nerve? **JB**

**Course:** Kiawah Island
(Ocean Course)

**Location:** Kiawah Island, South
Carolina, USA

**Hole:** No. 17

**Length:** 211 yards

**Par:** 3

**Designer:** Pete Dye

**Course Comment:** Host to the 1991
Ryder Cup, Ocean Course is made
difficult by the numerous dunes,
marshes, and bunkers spread
throughout its design.

**BELOW** *Ian Woosnam of Wales plays
out of a bunker on the 17th hole at
Kiawah Island, September 1991.*

# No. ⑰ KIAWAH ISLAND (OCEAN COURSE)

You have arrived at golf paradise. Don't expect to find many golf courses
more spectacular. Or more perfect.

This par 3 offers the challenge of keeping it straight. If you go right, you
are in the water. Go left, and you can catch a good size bunker. There is also
a smaller bunker to the front left of the green.

Before reaching into your bag it's important to check the wind. That
should play heavily into what club you decide to use.

What's different about this hole are the tee boxes. The two back tees
(211 and 197 yards) require a full swing over water. It's a much different hole
from these tee boxes. You take the boardwalk out into the water to reach
the blue tee box. The red tees drop you off on the other side of the water,
although it still lurks along the right side.

Forget the pin placement here. Aim for the middle of the green and feel
fortunate if you land a par on this challenging hole.

Considered among the best places to play golf in the world, Kiawah
Island Golf Resort is the only resort in the country that has three courses
ranked on *Golf Digest*'s list of "America's Top 75 Resort Courses." **TJ**

**Course:** Pebble Beach Golf Links

**Location:** Pebble Beach, California, USA

**Hole:** No. 17

**Length:** 178 yards

**Par:** 3

**Designer:** Jack Neville, Douglas Grant

**Course Comment:** This par 3 plays against the ocean wind and into the setting sun. It is one of the most famous and scenic golf holes in the world. No. 17 at Pebble Beach speaks for itself.

BELOW *Rocco Mediate of the USA hits a shot out of a bunker on the 17th hole at Pebble Beach Golf Links.*

# No. ⑰ PEBBLE BEACH GOLF LINKS

This world-famous golf hole is best defined by history.

During the 1972 U.S. Open, Jack Nicklaus struck one of the most famous shots ever made on this spectacular par-3 hole. Ahead by three strokes, he readied himself to hit a 1-iron. But the wind forced his club face further closed than he intended, forcing him to make a split-second adjustment on impact. The result: a shot that defied the wind, hit the flagstick, and rolled to a stop five inches from the cup. His birdie sealed a three-stroke victory.

Sometimes, the shot you don't like ends up working out just fine.

In the 1982 U.S. Open, Nicklaus was again involved in a memorable moment on 17th hole. Tom Watson was tied with Nicklaus, who was already in the clubhouse, and Watson was uphill from a fast green. It seemed he would have a tough time chipping close enough to get a par. That's what caddie Bruce Edwards was thinking, anyway, when he cautioned, "Get it close." Said Watson: "I'm not going to get it close, I'm going to make it!" Whereupon his quick runner hit the flagstick and dropped in, giving him a one-stroke lead that made 18 a relative walk in the park. **TJ**

# BLUE CANYON COUNTRY CLUB
## (CANYON COURSE)

**Course:** Blue Canyon Country Club (Canyon Course)

**Location:** Phuket, Thailand

**Hole:** No. 17

**Length:** 221 yards

**Par:** 3

**Designer:** Yoshikazu Kato

**Course Comment:** A regular stop on the Asian Tour, the Canyon Course has hosted three championships since 1988 (Johnnie Walker Classics 1994, 1995; Honda Invitational 1996).

There are images, garnered primarily from old movies, of a land stuck somewhere between the dark ages and the digital revolution. Visions of rickshaws racing around crowded streets while merchants barter loudly with one another are what comes to mind when talk turns to Thailand.

The tiny nation, however, is a land of extremes. Here, old has embraced new. What else would explain the curious naming of a small parcel of land off the southwest coast "James Bond Island." Not far inland from 007's namesake, Blue Canyon Country Club towers as a similarly peculiar addition to an ancient place.

Open in 1988, Blue Canyon is cut from the remains of a tin mine and rubber plantation. Developed and routed with a minimalist philosophy, Blue Canyon's Canyon Course is, by almost all accounts, a simple jewel. And few places at Blue Canyon demonstrate the dichotomy of this exotic place as well as the Canyon's par-3 17th.

Dubbed "one of the best par 3s anywhere in the world," by Fred Couples, the 17th exhibits an unpretentious beauty that contrasts perfectly with a demand for precision.

At 221 yards most will reach almost instinctively for a fairway wood or long iron from the tee, but the hole plays downhill to a green that slopes from front to back and demands less club than its yardage suggests.

Anything short or right all but guarantees a bogey or worse, while a tee shot that sails long and left will afford a player a modest chance to get up-and-down. **RH**

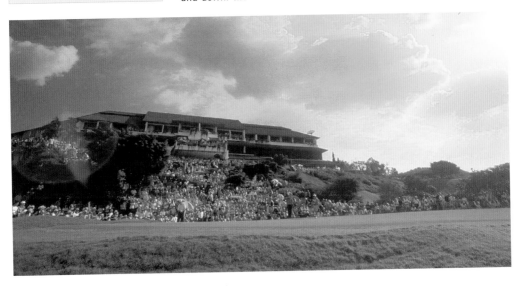

**Course:** George Golf Club

**Location:** George, South Africa

**Hole:** No. 17

**Length:** 182 yards

**Par:** 3

**Designer:** Charles Molteno Murray

**Course Comment:** George Golf Club was formed in 1906 and remained nearly unaltered until expansive renovation in 1994 that included a complete re-grassing of all 18 greens.

## No. ⓱ GEORGE GOLF CLUB

In 2003 the world was given a royal introduction to golf in South Africa. The Links Course at Fancourt Hotel and Country Club Estate was the site of the 5th Presidents Cup — and what a stage it turned out to be. What the cameras and international media missed, however, was Fancourt's little-known sister course.

George Golf Club occupies the same rolling land as Fancourt's Links layout and, if you polled the local players of this Western Cape Province town, may be favored over its high-profile neighbor.

Set in the heart of the Garden Route at the foothills of the Outeniqua Mountains, George Golf Club is a woodland layout that takes full advantage of the area's lively landscape and stark elevation changes.

The entire course is considered one of the most picturesque in the world and the par-3 17th is a central reason behind those lofty portrayals.

Yet the beauty of George is much more than ornamental. The stately trees that frame the 17th are strategically placed and put a premium on accuracy. The 17th's putting surface, although approachable, will deny anything but a truly played shot. Three-putts are common and players' only chance for birdie is to keep the ball below the hole. **RH**

---

**Course:** Puerto Azul Beach & Country Club

**Location:** Ternate, Cavite, Philippines

**Hole:** No. 17

**Length:** 234 yards

**Par:** 3

**Designer:** Gary Player, Ron Kirby

**Course Comment:** Corregidor Island, which can be seen from Puerto Azul's 17th hole, was surrendered to Japan by Allied forces on May 6, 1942. It was recaptured in March 1945.

## No. ⓱ PUERTO AZUL BEACH & COUNTRY CLUB

Puerto Azul Beach & Country Club is considered one of the Philippines' premier resort courses, featuring excellent views of the South China Sea and laid out in a hilly, forested setting along the coast. Some have even compared its scenery to that offered by Pebble Beach in the United States. Puerto Azul's 17th hole offers magnificent vistas of Corregidor Island, a small, rocky island that was courageously defended by American and Filipino forces against the Japanese in World War II.

No. 17 is so tough and intimidating a par 3 that it's sometimes played as a par 4 by members and resort guests. During major tournaments, however, it turns into a beast of a one-shotter, with a tee shot that must carry over the South China Sea coastline and a gusting wind that sometimes has even the longest of hitters pulling out their drivers. The putting surface has two tiers, slopes from front to back and right to left, and is further protected by a pair of bunkers on the right.

How tough a hole is it? Well, to give you an idea, the course's designer, the legendary Gary Player, once marked down a 7 here. **KA**

**Course:** Mid Ocean Club

**Location:** Tucker's Town, Bermuda

**Hole:** No. 17

**Length:** 220 yards

**Par:** 3

**Designer:** Charles Blair Macdonald, Robert Trent Jones Sr.

**Course Comment:** Surprisingly, the 17th hole isn't even the longest par 3 on Mid Ocean's back nine. That honor belongs to the 238-yard 13th.

# No. ⑰   MID OCEAN CLUB

At Mid Ocean Club on this island nation's scenic northeast coast, Charles Blair Macdonald had a wonderful canvas on which to work, and he didn't disappoint. Along a series of bluffs above the Atlantic Ocean, he produced a marvelous golf course that, more than 80 years after its 1921 opening, is still considered among the world's best.

No. 17 at Mid Ocean, considered by many to be the layout's best hole, is a rare Redan that plays downhill, offering players a magnificent view of the green below and the deep blue of the Atlantic off to the left. Of course, the scenery becomes a little less pleasant when golfers see the group of bunkers that encircle the severely undulating, saucer-style green, that will have to be avoided on the tee shot, which must usually be hit into the prevailing wind, making this beast of a par 3 play even longer.

Golfers fortunate enough to play a round at Mid Ocean Club can count themselves as part of an elite crowd. Among others, the private course has been graced by the presence of such notable figures as Dwight Eisenhower, Sir Winston Churchill, The Duke of Windsor, and Babe Ruth. **KA**

**Course:** TPC at Sawgrass
(Stadium Course)

**Location:** Ponte Vedra Beach, Florida,
USA

**Hole:** No. 17

**Length:** 137 yards

**Par:** 3

**Designer:** Pete Dye

**Course Comment:** The island green
at the next-to-last hole makes for a
nail-biting finish each year at the
PGA Tour's Players Championship.
Fred Couples once hit his first shot
in the water, went to the drop area,
and promptly hit a wedge into the
hole on the fly for a less-than-
routine par.

**BELOW AND RIGHT** *Two views of the
17th hole at TPC at Sawgrass.*

# No. ⓱ TPC AT SAWGRASS
## (STADIUM COURSE)

In the world of golf, a hole that is just 24 years old is a mere baby, an infant
in an arena where famed holes date back several decades. But, when
something as dramatic as No. 17 at Sawgrass comes along, even in a game
which prides itself so rightfully on tradition, the most ardent of purists
must tip their caps.

In its short but colorful history, the 137-yard island hole has become one
of the most famous in the world. Designer Pete Dye's trademark is target
golf, and this is undoubtedly the most resolute example of target golf on
the planet. The hole is short, but if you miss the green, you are virtually
assured of taking a penalty stroke . . . unless you land on a lily pad.

The putting surface at No. 17 is wide, but it narrows on the right side. There is a small bunker to the right side of the green, which actually is a blessing for those few players who can find a place other than the putting surface to stay dry. Never has sand been such a relief.

Club selection is always important in golf, but it is even more critical on No. 17 at Sawgrass. Poor club selection can be the difference between lining up a birdie putt or digging in your bag in the drop area. It can also make the difference on Sunday in The Players Championship, held annually at the PGA Tour headquarters course. And the wind, never predictable at this hole, makes club selection even more strenuous.

No hole is more memorable, more photographed, or more famous than the par-3 17th at the Stadium Course. And to think, it's just a baby. **JB**

## No. ⑰  HUALALAI GOLF CLUB

**Course:** Hualalai Golf Club

**Location:** Kailua Kona, Hawaii, USA

**Hole:** No. 17

**Length:** 164 yards

**Par:** 3

**Designer:** Jack Nicklaus

**Course Comment:** Lava is the name of the game here. This spectacular lava-lined golf course features lava areas which come into play on every hole. These are considered water hazards by the locals.

Remember, the lava is considered a lateral hazard.

Lava?

Don't worry, it's had plenty of time to cool down but it can still heat up your emotions if you hit your tee shot that way. And don't ever plan on seeing that golf ball again.

There is plenty to look at on this hole, including the lava. But the ocean off in the near distance isn't bad either. You are basically teeing off into the ocean because the green is cut right into the surf. But it's better to land on the turf, not the surf.

There is also a bunker that runs down the entire side of the fairway. The approach shot must be hit to a large, elevated green well guarded by bunkers. The green slopes back to front and left to right. Most of the greens on this course are flat, but No. 17 has some slope to it.

As you can imagine, the wind is a factor here. It usually blows left to right but the tradewinds can rise up any time and play tricks with your ball.

Winding over 7,100 yards, this carefully groomed course begins in a lush oasis contoured against the black lava. The course returns to the ocean, where the finishing holes capture the beauty of seaside golf. **TJ**

## No. ⑰  INDUSTRY HILLS
### (BABE ZAHARIAS COURSE)

**Course:** Industry Hills (Babe Zaharias Course)

**Location:** City of Industry, California, USA

**Hole:** No. 17

**Length:** 198 yards

**Par:** 3

**Designer:** William Bell

**Course Comment:** This resort is the home to two excellent golf courses that ramble over rolling terrain. The Babe Zaharias Course is considered the more difficult of the two because of its smaller greens and narrower fairways.

This is one pretty hole. It's also a pretty tough hole to play, perhaps the toughest par-3 hole on the Babe Zaharias Course.

This hole is all about size. It's a super-sized par 3 where huge is the common theme on the scorecard.

The downhill tee shot must carry a huge lake in front. Your target is a huge green, the biggest putting surface at this upscale resort that is home to two outstanding golf courses.

But watch out for those huge bunkers to the right, left, and back of the green. This hole gets much more difficult to reach par if you hit your ball into one of those.

Remember, you are up on a hill so take that into account when selecting a club. But there are a few other variables to consider. The first is the pin placement. This green is so big that it's a three- or four-club difference from the front to the back. And second, the wind can come into play. In the late afternoon, the wind blows from left to right or into your face, which makes things a bit tricky.

Another hole to note is No. 5 on the Eisenhower Course. This par 3 features a spectacular three-tiered green. **TJ**

Course: El Saler Golf Club

Location: Valencia, Spain

Hole: No. 17

Length: 215 yards

Par: 3

Designer: Javier Arana

Course Comment: Located within the confines of Albufera Nature Park, El Saler is a regular stop for the PGA European Tour's Spanish Open.

# No. 17  EL SALER GOLF CLUB

With El Saler Golf Club, renowned Spanish architect Javier Arana has created a course that combines the best of linksland and parkland. Although the final product is something short of authentic it is certainly a magical mix.

While more than half of El Saler's holes weave through a pine forest, it's the layout's closing stretches (Nos. 7–9 and 17–18) that venture toward the Mediterranean Sea that inspire visions of Scotland.

Carved from sand dunes and deep native grasses, El Saler features everything one comes to expect from a links golf course. These coastal stretches include plenty of wind along with firm, fast fairways and, as is the case at the par-3 17th, some difficult choices.

Depending on the wind, players can opt to fly tee shots 215 yards to a large green that is bordered by bunkers on either side.

Or, in true links fashion, a punch shot can be weaved between the bunkers. If the hole is playing into the wind, which is usually the case, keeping the ball low is the better option. **RH**

BELOW *Paul Casey of England holes his bunker shot on the 17th hole at El Saler Golf Club, November 2003.*

**Course:** The Jockey Club (Red Course)

**Location:** San Isidro, Argentina

**Hole:** No. 17

**Length:** 180 yards

**Par:** 3

**Designer:** Alister MacKenzie

**Course Comment:** The Jockey Club served as host for the World Cup of Golf in 1970. Australia (David Graham and Bruce Devlin) won the team title, while native son Roberto de Vicenzo thrilled local galleries by capturing the individual crown.

## No. 🔟 THE JOCKEY CLUB (RED COURSE)

The Jockey Club of Buenos Aires was founded in 1882 as an institution to organize and manage horseracing activities at a national level, as well as serve as a top social center for the country, similar to the best European clubs. It also became a center of golf in Argentina when legendary architect Alister MacKenzie designed two golf courses there in the late 1920s. Today, the two courses are still considered among the best in South America. Other facilities at the Jockey Club include swimming pools, polo fields, and tennis courts.

The par-3 17th hole on the Red Course features a long, narrow green fiercely protected by a pair of bunkers on the left that are set diagonally from the tee, making the hole especially difficult when the pin is on the left rear portion of the putting surface.

Angel Cabrera delighted the fans of his home country when he captured his first PGA European Tour title at the 2001 Open de Argentina at the Jockey Club, which was sanctioned by the tour for the first time that year. The club has played host to the event on numerous occasions, with other notable winners such as Mark Calcavecchia in 1993 and 1995, and Jim Furyk in 1997. **KA**

**Course:** Blairgowrie Golf Club
(Rosemount Course)

**Location:** Blairgowrie, Perthshire,
Scotland

**Hole:** No. 17

**Length:** 165 yards

**Par:** 3

**Designer:** James Braid

**Course Comment:** Blairgowrie's
Rosemount Course was the site of
Greg Norman's first PGA European
Tour victory, the 1977 Martini
International.

No. ⑰ **BLAIRGOWRIE GOLF CLUB**
**(ROSEMOUNT COURSE)**

Blairgowrie Golf Club's Rosemount Course is so impressive, it never ceases to motivate avid players from the far reaches of the globe to hop on a flight bound for Scotland. Located some 25 miles inland from Dundee, the club is less seaside and more seclusion. The 6,588-yard layout is not so much windblown as it is welcoming.

The James Braid design capers its way through thick wooded areas with fairways lined by pine, silver birch, and heather. The genius of Rosemount is its crafty design and an abundance of natural corridors. Each hole seems to meander away from the previous one, untouched and unaffected by other holes. The overall impact is a feeling of isolation. Players may long for some company, however, by the time they reach the par-3 17th hole.

At 165 yards it's not even Rosemount's longest par 3 but it is, without question, the layout's most intimidating. Dubbed the "Plateau," the 17th plays longer than the yardage suggests and players are always advised to take more club.

A large mound cuts a swathe through the center of this teardrop-shaped green, creating a legion of pin positions but few that will easily yield birdie opportunities. A pair of bunkers are perched on the right, while a single trap waits to the left. Long shots run the risk of feeding off the back of the elevated putting surface, while anything short leaves a tricky pitch across the mound. **RH**

**Course:** Club West Golf Club

**Location:** Phoenix, Arizona, USA

**Hole:** No. 17

**Length:** 215 yards

**Par:** 3

**Designer:** Brian Whitcomb

**Course Comment:** During this
course's first year in 1993, it was
rated as one of the top 20 courses in
the state by *The Arizona Republic*.
This desert golf course was only the
second all-sodded course in the
Western United States.

No. ⑰ **CLUB WEST GOLF CLUB**

When you pull up to the tee at No. 17, it's important to remember that this is a difficult par-3 hole. But you can't do that right away. The view is too overwhelming, so take it all in for as long as you can.

The tees are elevated nearly 100 feet above the rest of the course. Up from the perch you can see South Mountain on one side and the Estrella mountain range on another. But the best view of all is right in front of you. And you have options on this challenging and breathtaking hole, a par 3 with a double green. If you take too long admiring the breathtaking part, though, the challenging part may cause some problems on your scorecard.

You will want to be extra careful when selecting a club. Take a moment to mark off the distance from the marker on the tee after you decide which green to aim at. Then take another moment to judge the wind. Don't be afraid to go up or down a club depending on the breeze, and aim for the center of the green.

The course as a whole can play from as short as 4,985 yards in length to as much as 7,142 yards. **TJ**

# No. ⓱ WATERVILLE GOLF LINKS

Located amid rolling sand hills on a peninsula between the River Inny and Ballinskelligs Bay near a remote fishing village in southern Ireland, Waterville captures the fancy of virtually all who play it.

Golf in the Waterville area dates back to 1889, when the Waterville Athletic Club played on a rather modest nine-hole course that was laid out on the eastern section of today's Waterville Golf Links. When Irish-born American John Mulcahy returned to his homeland to build his dream course, he bought the land and together with architect Eddie Hackett expanded and refigured the original layout to form the basis for the front nine of the new Waterville Golf Links, which opened in 1973.

The 20-foot-high tee on the 17th hole, dubbed "Mulcahy's Peak," marks the highest point of the course at 250 feet above sea level, and as such, it offers magnificent views of the bay and the mountains in the distance. No wonder Mulcahy had his ashes buried here after his death in 1994. When the wind is blowing in, the hole plays much longer, making it even tougher to hit the sliver of green set between rough-covered hills in the front and thick native vegetation in the rear. **KA**

**RIGHT AND OPPOSITE** *Two views of the 17th hole at Waterville Golf Club.*

# No. ⓱ ST. ANDREWS (CASTLE COURSE)

As hard as it is to imagine, the Castle Course is not a links-style course. Just ask the golf staffers themselves.

"It's technically not linksland," said Kevin Mackay, director of operations at the Castle Course, was quoted as saying shortly after it opened in 2008. "Although we have done all we can with the grasses, it's a cliff-top course. This was all agricultural land previously."

It seems blasphemous, but it is true. And, once you have played the course, you will find there is nothing wrong with a cliff-top on this property. David McLay Kidd, who designed the famed Bandon Dunes, did himself proud, on this side of the Ocean.

The 17th hole, quite simply, is a masterpiece. It plays over a cave in the Kinkell Braes. It is advised to play toward the bunker that is stationed far left of the green because the ball will almost certainly roll toward the large valley and onto the green. If you aim toward the green on your tee shot, it will be difficult to hold. Like most shots on the par 3s at the Castle Course, it is best to take the hit-and-roll approach.

The Castle Course has great views out over the bay and the town of St. Andrews, and its views are equaled by the great challenge. And, sticking with the St. Andrews tradition, it is a walking-only course. **JB**

**Course:** Harbour Town Golf Links

**Location:** Hilton Head Island, South Carolina, USA

**Hole:** No. 17

**Length:** 185 yards

**Par:** 3

**Designer:** Pete Dye

**Course Comment:** The owl decoy perched on the wooden railroad ties at the back of the left-hand bunker on Harbour Town's 17th hole has seen more than its share of birdies and bogeys (and worse). The decoy was placed there to scare off pelicans.

# No. ⑰ HARBOUR TOWN GOLF LINKS

This one-shotter is all about club selection and correctly gauging the wind coming off Calibogue Sound. If it's in your face, it can mean as much as a three-club difference off the tee. The norm, however, is a cross-wind that blows from right to left, and left is where most of the trouble is on this hole, which has little margin for error.

The tee shot must be hit over marsh and water to a long, narrow green which is protected by a 90-yard bunker that starts in front, and then runs down the green's entire left side. The sand can actually be a golfer's best friend, saving some shots from a watery doom farther to the left. And there's virtually no bail-out room on the right, where two deep bunkers await, or long, where a steep slope leads down to the certain misery of the Calibogue marshes.

It's a shot that's not always easy to hit if you play down the stretch at the PGA Tour's MCI Heritage, fought out annually at Harbour Town. In the 2004 MCI Heritage, the hole played to a stroke average of 3.056, with the number of birdies and bogeys exactly even at 59 apiece. There were also 10 double bogeys or worse. **KA**

Course: Sand Hills Golf Club

Location: Mullen, Nebraska, USA

Hole: No. 17

Length: 168 yards

Par: 3

Designer: Ben Crenshaw, Bill Coore

Course Comment: When you make the journey to Sand Hills, you're truly in the great outdoors. The closest major city is Denver, which is approximately a five-hour drive to the west.

# No. 🕖 SAND HILLS GOLF CLUB

Sand Hills Golf Club is heaven on earth for serious golfers. No houses, no tennis courts, no swimming pools. Just marvelous golf holes set amid the magnificent rolling sand hills of north central Nebraska that stretch on and on for as far as the eye can see. Despite its isolation, it didn't take long for Sand Hills to get noticed. Only a few years after its 1995 opening, this Ben Crenshaw and Bill Coore design was being considered one of the nation's best layouts.

The visual appeal of the course is stunning. Ribbons of green wind among wavy golden-brown tall grasses and the white sand underneath, leading players through a unique golf wonderland that begins with a mile-long cart ride to reach the first tee.

By the time you reach No. 17, you know you're near the end of a visit to one of the game's meccas, and you don't want the round to end — at least not without a strong shot at this inspiring downhill par 3. Just don't let its lack of length fool you. The ever-present wind and a tiny green surrounded by bunkers and thick native grasses make for as difficult a tee shot as you'll find anywhere. **KA**

Course: Nicklaus North Golf Course

Location: Whistler, British Columbia, Canada

Hole: No. 17

Length: 226 yards

Par: 3

Designer: Jack Nicklaus

Course Comment: Although Nicklaus has designed more than 150 courses worldwide, Nicklaus North is the only one that bears his name. Golfers from all over the world have come to understand why he is proud that it does.

# No. 🕖 NICKLAUS NORTH GOLF COURSE

*Golf Digest* named Nicklaus North "best new Canadian course for 1996." "In the design, we tried to utilize Green Lake and Fitzsimmons Creek," said Nicklaus. "The idea was not to build a golf course that was going to murder everybody, but to build a course that people could enjoy."

The 17th hole is worth the wait. While the other 16 holes here are impressive, No. 17 is spectacular from the tee, the fairway, and the green. The beauty will take your breath away while at the same time recharging your game for the final two holes. While your visual eye will bounce back and forth from the water to the river rocks to the mountains, your "game eye" had better focus on its target.

This is not only one of the prettiest holes here, it's also among the hardest. You have to go after the flag to have any shot at a par. There is trouble everywhere. Starting right at the front of the green is a huge sand trap that wraps around the left side of the green all the way to the back.

This trap is the only thing between the green and the Green Lake. A pot bunker guards the front right of the green. While you don't want to aim for the pot bunker, there are worse places to fly your drive. At least you can see your ball in the sand. Other places, you can't see it or find it. **TJ**

## No. 🄰 **BAY HILL CLUB AND LODGE**

**Course:** Bay Hill Club and Lodge

**Location:** Orlando, Florida, USA

**Hole:** No. 17

**Length:** 223 yards

**Par:** 3

**Designer:** Dick Wilson

**Course Comment:** Tiger Woods seized four consecutive Bay Hill Invitational titles from 2000–2003.

In 1970 the King himself situated his palace 10 miles down the road from Cinderella's Castle, and Bay Hill Club and Lodge has never been quite the same since.

After playing in an exhibition match five years earlier, an enamored Arnold Palmer set out to acquire the 270 acres located in sunny, central Florida. Throughout Palmer's reign the semi-private club has flourished, hosting the PGA Tour's Bay Hill Invitational every spring since 1979. Palmer teamed with Ed Seay to redesign the track in 1989.

Part of Bay Hill's tournament success centers around its compelling finishing holes. The par-3 17th serves as a fitting prelude to the demanding 18th. From an elevated tee, the 223-yard hole is visually intimidating as water covers most of the ground from tee to green. Club selection is key as a trio of bunkers guard the front of the green, and water curls around the right side to the back of the green.

A high fade is the shot most receptive to this undulated green. Because the putting surface is downhill from the tee box, expect the ball to land soft and short.

And don't forget to keep your eyes peeled for a royal procession — the King may want to play through! **BB**

**Course:** Bethpage State Park
(Black Course)

**Location:** Farmingdale, New York,
USA

**Hole:** No. 17

**Length:** 213 yards

**Par:** 3

**Designer:** Joseph Burbeck,
A.W. Tillinghast

**Course Comment:** Bethpage State
Park is a mecca for public golf,
featuring five 18-hole regulation
golf courses including the world-
renowned Black Course. This course
was the site of the U.S. Open in 2002
and will again host the U.S. Open
in 2009.

BELOW *The 17th hole on the Black
Course at Bethpage State Park,
Farmingdale, New York, USA.*

# No. **⓱** BETHPAGE STATE PARK
## (BLACK COURSE)

This par 3 on this famous golf course at this famous state park is all about
the green. But it's no easy accomplishment getting it there.

At 213 yards from the back, No. 17's putting surface is a distant
challenge. First you have to clear the bunkers guarding the front left and
front right of the green. And even if you hit the green, you have to have
enough loft to keep it there — not an easy thing to do, especially when the
weather is against you.

It's not too hard to hold the green with a 3- or 4-iron when the course is
wet. But when it's firm, it's a whole different ball game. And it's firm most
of the time.

Once you are on the green the game gets more difficult. The elevated
green is long but not too deep. It's about 30 paces deep and 70 paces wide.

There is a big swale in the middle and you could end up with a putt
going straight uphill or straight downhill depending on the pin placement.

The left side of the green is more difficult to putt than the right side. **TJ**

**Course:** Highlands Links

**Location:** Ingonish Beach, Nova Scotia, Canada

**Hole:** No. 17

**Length:** 190 yards

**Par:** 3

**Designer:** Stanley Thompson

**Course Comment:** As a tribute to the area's Celtic heritage, each hole at Highlands Links bears a Scottish name. The 17th's moniker, "Dowie Den," is an ancient ballad about a massacre in a low-lying meadow.

# No. ⑰ HIGHLANDS LINKS

At his core, Stanley Thompson was a naturalist. When routing a new design, a simple canon of the renowned Canadian's design philosophy mandated that the land, not the landowner, be the ultimate guide. "Nature must always be the architect's model," Thompson said.

It's this simple approach that produced No. 17 at the Highlands Links course. Some architects would avoid placing a relatively short par 3 so late in the line-up, concerned its straightforward simplicity would not be appropriate for late-round heroics.

Thompson, however, allowed Cape Breton's rolling terrain to dictate much of his routing and the result is a perfectly placed par 3. From the elevated tee, most players are lured into a false sense of ease by the 17th's inviting visuals. The green is open in the front left, with only a single bunker fixed in front of the right third of the putting surface.

What many players miss is the demanding angle Thompson created. The oval green is canted from front left to back right with a mere 24 paces separating the front edge from the back fringe. Short tee shots afford a player the best chance to save for par; long shots will result in either an awkward, downhill chip or a delicate sand shot from the back bunker. **RH**

## No. ⑰ DOUBLE EAGLE CLUB

**Course:** Double Eagle Club

**Location:** Galena, Ohio, USA

**Hole:** No. 17

**Length:** 355 yards

**Par:** 4

**Designer:** Tom Weiskopf, Jay Moorish

**Course Comment:** In addition to U.S. Open sectional qualifiers, Double Eagle also hosted a Shell's Wonderful World of Golf special in 2002 that featured Tom Weiskopf and Gary Player.

OPPOSITE *The 17th hole at Double Eagle Club.*

It comes as no surprise that of the dozens of courses Tom Weiskopf has designed, he lists Scotland's Loch Lomond as his favorite. After all, Weiskopf outplayed Johnny Miller down the stretch in Scotland at Troon to win the 1973 British Open.

His second favorite course, however, hits closer to home. The Ohio native teamed with Jay Moorish in 1992 to open the Double Eagle Club. Situated in Galena, Ohio, the course is located minutes from Ohio State University, where Weiskopf spent his college years alongside another golfing legend, Jack Nicklaus.

This spectacularly conditioned course has enough character to keep the most skillful players entertained. The par-4 17th, for example, has two distinct paths available from the largest tee box on the course. The conventional approach entails playing the dogleg right around a pesky trio of tall trees located in the center of the fairway.

Long-ball hitters, however, can bypass the trees and head directly over a lake positioned right of the fairway. This alternative route cuts roughly 65 yards off the hole's length.

Those who dare to drive the green have plenty to work. The putting surface is approximately 60 yards deep from front to back, which is nearly three times the size of an average Double Eagle green. Making a two-putt birdie even harder to come by, a three-foot deep valley cuts into the massive putting surface to create a myriad of subtle and not-so-subtle undulations. **BB**

## No. ⑰ ZAUDIN GOLF CLUB

**Course:** Zaudin Golf Club

**Location:** Tomares, Seville, Spain

**Hole:** No. 17

**Length:** 465 yards

**Par:** 4

**Designer:** Gary Player

**Course Comment:** Zaudin has been heralded as one of Gary Player's greatest architectural accomplishments. This is praise that the usually reserved Player agrees with despite the number of great courses he has drawn up over the years.

When you're as good a player as Gary Player was for so long, you have to learn how to finish. Great players only earn that distinction when they win — and if you can't finish, you can't win.

Player has now proven he is a great golf-course designer. And once again, he has proven he can finish.

The final two holes at the Zaudin Golf Club not only stand up to the previous 16, but stand above them. They are as good a one-two punch as you will find in the world — and that includes those found on 17 Mile Drive.

No. 17 is simply a stunning hole. One of the best in Spain or even one of the best in the world. Player has even called it one of his personal favorites.

Standing high on the elevated tee, you get the full picture of what's looming on this dogleg right. It's pretty from a scenic standpoint, but quite ugly from a scorecard standpoint. You aim your tee shot at water and must clear it to reach the very tiny island green. With all this water, the bunkers on the right have become a common host to golf balls. **TJ**

| |
|---|
| **Course:** St. Louis Country Club |
| **Location:** St. Louis, Missouri, USA |
| **Hole:** No. 17 |
| **Length:** 376 yards |
| **Par:** 4 |
| **Designer:** Charles Blair Macdonald, Seth Raynor |
| **Course Comment:** This exclusive club is home to many of the rich and famous in the St. Louis area. But it has also opened its doors to the masses, playing host to the 1947 U.S. Open and staging both men's and women's amateur events. |

# No. ⑰ ST. LOUIS COUNTRY CLUB

If you have the opportunity to play this golf course, consider yourself lucky. The St. Louis Country Club might not get the attention of an Oak Hill or Oakland Hills or Olympic Club, but it can hold its own with any golf course in the world.

Remember, some country clubs don't seek attention.

Nos. 17 and 18 are strong finishing holes to your round. This 376-yard par 4 is a pretty straightforward hole, with great scenery and course conditions as you walk from tee to green.

However, trouble lurks — there is a fairway bunker on the right side, about 130 yards out. The key to this hole is the drive. If you can hit a nice tee shot with a little fade, you should be in ideal birdie range.

The better players will hit a 3-wood off the tee and then an 8-iron into the green. Sounds easy, doesn't it?

Now for the trouble. There is a small pot bunker to the front left and another one to the back right of the green. Pot bunkers can ruin your scorecard in a hurry so make note of their locations.

The green slopes severely from right to left. **TJ**

| |
|---|
| **Course:** County Sligo Golf Club |
| **Location:** Rosses Point, Sligo, Ireland |
| **Hole:** No. 17 |
| **Length:** 455 yards |
| **Par:** 4 |
| **Designer:** Harry S. Colt |
| **Course Comment:** With so many outstanding golf courses, Ireland's "best of" is a very subjective and much debated list. But the County Sligo Golf Club, situated under the shadow of Benbulben, is a must-play on most people's Top 10. |

# No. ⑰ COUNTY SLIGO GOLF CLUB

County Sligo Golf Club is one of Ireland's great championship links. It is located on the Rosses Point peninsula about 3¾ miles from Sligo.

Established in 1894, the original nine-hole course was laid out by George Combe. He was the founding secretary of the Golfing Union of Ireland, so you're walking on sacred golfing ground.

The present championship links was designed in 1927 by architect Harry S. Colt, himself a legend. Colt created a variety of different holes challenging golfers of all skill levels.

The most famous and memorable hole on the course is called the "Gallery," a 455-yard par 4. At 455 yards, it's the longest par 4 on the course. It's also a dogleg to the left, requiring a great tee shot to get you going.

Take aim at the right side of the fairway. If you get your drive into position, get ready for one of the more difficult shots of the day. The second shot will require both length and accuracy.

Take note of the very steep front of the green. Being short here is trouble. In fact, they call the front of the green, "the valley of sin." That should be enough of a reminder not to be short. **TJ**

**Course:** Cypress Point Club

**Location:** Pebble Beach, California, USA

**Hole:** No. 17

**Length:** 393 yards

**Par:** 4

**Designer:** Alister MacKenzie

**Course Comment:** The AT&T Pebble Beach National Pro-Am was contested at Cypress Point from 1947 to 1990 before it moved to Poppy Hills in the three-course rotation.

# No. ⑰  CYPRESS POINT CLUB

When planning a trip to Cypress Point, be sure to pack an oxygen tank. This cliff-side course can literally leave a player breathless.

Located in the midst of the renowned 17 Mile Drive, Cypress Point is at or near the top of nearly every course ranking. In 1928, before securing his fate with America's beloved Augusta National, Alister MacKenzie carved out a west-coast treasure with the design of this sublime masterpiece.

After whetting a player's appetite with the inland front nine, the 6,524-yard course takes a turn toward the ocean on the back side. After completing the famed 16th, awestruck golfers head directly behind the green to the 17th tee.

There players must decide which route to take when approaching the 393-yard dogleg right. When crossing a sliver of the Pacific, one can bite off a significant amount of distance by hugging the rocky shoreline. While aiming down the left side may be the safer bet, be prepared for a lengthier second shot back across the ocean. Bunkers guarding this undulated green only add to Mother Nature's demands.

When you walk off the 17th green, take a deep breath. Cypress Point owes you one. **BB**

# No. ⓱ CONGRESSIONAL COUNTRY CLUB (BLUE COURSE)

The great thing about great golf clubs is their continuing dedication to maintaining the challenge of the original designer, even though today's players and technology sometimes make that very difficult. And, it's not just about adding length. That's the simple way. The truly great clubs stick as close to the original design as possible, yet make changes that keep even the best players honest. Such is the case at Congressional Country Club.

Rees Jones made considerable changes at Congressional in 1990, 1995, and in 1997. He took Devereux Emmet's original 1924 design (modified by Jones' father, Robert Trent Jones Sr., in 1957) and rebuilt every green and bunker, regraded many fairways to eliminate blind shots, and added considerable mounding. Some of these changes made the course more difficult, some made it more modern. But none made the course drastically different from Emmet's idea of what Congressional should be.

The 17th hole at Congressional is one of the holes that has been altered considerably. The U.S. Golf Association, as is its wont, mandated change without giving as much thought as members might to tradition and original design. When the Kemper Open was played at Congressional during the 1980s, players were able to ignore the crest of the fairway, which was originally meant to be the landing area off the tee. But the pros easily

blew it over the crest in the fairway to the downslope, leaving them with short irons into the peninsula green.

But before the 1997 U.S. Open at Congressional, the U.S. Golf Association ordered Jones to move the tees back 40 yards, forcing players to hit a much longer club on their second shots. It made the hole more difficult, but it also changed its appearance to the point that Emmet might not even recognize his own creation.

This hole isn't just about length either. It's very important to land your tee shot on the left half of the fairway, where the lies are relatively flat. Tee shots that land on the right side of the fairway are left with lies that often play havoc with the aim of your approach. The green slopes from front right to back left and the challenge is enhanced by a mound directly in the center of the green that essentially cuts it in half. Approaches on the wrong side of the green leave for some quite undesirable putts. **JB**

## No. 🄗 SEIGNOSSE

**Course:** Seignosse

**Location:** Seignosse, France

**Hole:** No. 17

**Length:** 386 yards

**Par:** 4

**Designer:** Robert Von Hagge

**Course Comment:** Seignosse's 17th hole is the only par 4 on the course without a bunker.

Seignosse Golf Club, designed by the American architect Robert Von Hagge, was built on a scenic, hilly estate near the lovely coastal city of Biarritz on France's southwest coast. Its 18 holes thread their way through pines, cork oaks, and numerous well-designed bunkers and water hazards. Though it measures only a little more than 6,300 yards from the back tees, narrow fairways, steep slopes, and contoured greens require strategic and pinpoint iron play.

The 17th hole is a dogleg left that wraps around a huge lake that begins at the landing area for drives and runs all the way down the side of the green. Placing the tee shot on the left side of the fairway leaves a preferred angle and a slightly shorter approach for the second shot, but the water encroaches on the landing area from that side, making such a play off the tee a definite risk. Draw it just a bit too much, and it will find the water. The same could be said for the approach, as the long, narrow putting surface is placed directly next to the lake, and is further guarded by overhanging trees on the right. **KA**

## No. 🄗 TURTLE BAY (PALMER COURSE)

**Course:** Turtle Bay (Palmer Course)

**Location:** Oahu, Hawaii, USA

**Hole:** No. 17

**Length:** 452 yards

**Par:** 4

**Designer:** Arnold Palmer, Ed Seay

**Course Comment:** Located on the North Shore of Oahu, the 880-acre Turtle Bay Resort recently completed $60 million in renovations and has almost five miles of beachfront that includes Kawela Bay, Kuilima Cove, and, of course, Turtle Bay.

Oahu's only 36-hole golf resort, Turtle Bay has two first-rate championship golf courses designed by two designers, Arnold Palmer and George Fazio. Both courses make their way through the tropical countryside with spectacular views of the North Shore.

The Palmer Course is a 2-for-1 deal. The front nine is more of a links-style course while the back nine meanders around the Punaho'olapa Marsh; a bird and wildlife sanctuary. The green of the 17th hole sits oceanside next to Kahujku Point, Oahu's northernmost point.

This is one of the most unique fairways you will ever encounter. While many courses line the fairway with trees from tee to green, Mr. Palmer lined his par 4 with bunkers. But the bunkers don't stay on one side.

The series of 10 bunkers begin on the left side, cut over the middle to the right side, and then cut back over the middle again closer to the green before finishing on the left side of the putting surface.

You want to aim your tee shot over the second bunker from the left. When you line up your approach shot, put this at the top of your must-remember lists: the green is not easy to hold, so put plenty of loft on the shot and then cross your fingers. If you are long, you are out of bounds — remember that as well. One more thing to remember: the bunkers are much nicer to look at than to play out of. **TJ**

**Course:** Forest Highlands Golf Club (Canyon Course)

**Location:** Flagstaff, Arizona, USA

**Hole:** No. 17

**Length:** 390 yards

**Par:** 4

**Designer:** Tom Weiskopf, Jay Morrish

**Course Comment:** Forest Highlands sits approximately 7,000 feet above sea level, adding plenty of yardage to a golfer's normal distance.

# FOREST HIGHLANDS GOLF CLUB
## (CANYON COURSE)

This hole presents golfers with an interesting dilemma as they're standing on the tee box, driver in hand. Because of a wide, scraggly creek bed that cuts diagonally across the middle of the fairway, they have the option of attempting to knock their tee shots over the hazard in an effort to get near the green, or of putting the driver back, taking a mid-iron out of their bag, and laying up short of the creek bed, leaving a much longer second shot. So which do you think most long hitters prefer?

Because of Forest Highlands' extreme elevation and its location in the Arizona high country, reaching the green is a distinct possibility for some, even at 390 yards. To get there, however, the shot must find the left side of the fairway, avoiding trees that encroach on the left but taking advantage of the left to right slope of the landing area in order to get a bounce onto the putting surface. Such a choice, however, also brings the possibility of big numbers into play, thereby giving golfers the thrilling rush that making such a delicious risk-reward decision always brings.

The question remains: will you or won't you? **KA**

**Course:** Carnoustie Golf Links

**Location:** Carnoustie, Angus, Scotland

**Hole:** No. 17

**Length:** 459 yards

**Par:** 4

**Designer:** Allan Robertson, Willie Park Jr., James Braid

**Course Comment:** In the 1931 British Open, Jose Jurado topped his tee shot into the Barry Burn, finished the hole with a six and effectively ended his hopes of winning the Open, which was won by Tommy Armour. In the same event, Mac Smith also made double bogey on No. 17, even though his ball never landed in a hazard.

**BELOW AND OPPOSITE** *Two views of the 17th hole on the Championship Course at Carnoustie Golf Links.*

# No. ⑰ CARNOUSTIE GOLF LINKS

Carnoustie Golf Links, considered one of the most challenging courses in the world, has also been the site of some of the game's great highlights. The finest performance of all might just belong to the great Ben Hogan. Carnoustie Golf Links was the climax of Ben Hogan's career — his last major championship with quite possibly his best golf. He won the 1953 British Open here the first time he played the tournament and his course record 68 (5 under par) in the final round is as close to a flawless round of golf as has ever been played. And though he vowed, "I'll be back," he never did return. Maybe he felt he had nothing left to prove.

Hogan mastered Carnoustie that historic day, and left knowing he had conquered a golf giant. But mere mortals, and even greats of the game, often leave Carnoustie humbled. The 17th hole is the kind of challenge that prevails at the links — tough, demanding, but fair if you are precise.

Nicknamed "The Island," No. 17 isn't exactly a pure island, but the meandering Barry Burn seems inescapable no matter which direction an errant shot might wander.

The tee shot must be played over an S-shaped coil of the burn and kept to the right half of the fairway. Any shot too far left will find a watery grave, and anything played too far right may find thick rough or, in extreme cases, out of bounds.

The inescapable nature of the burn becomes obvious quickly enough. Even though you have just crossed it on your tee shot, you must once again traverse the streaming water on your long approach. The green slopes left to right, and often guides even shots that appear to be sound into the craters they call bunkers just to the right of the putting surface.

This hole has managed to destroy the scorecards of some of the best players in the world. But there is a small consolation if you come away with a poor score and happen to blame it on the wind. The 18th hole runs in the exact opposite direction as No. 17. So, if the wind was your enemy on No. 17, it will be your friend on the finisher. **JB**

**Course:** Royal Lytham & St. Annes

**Location:** St. Annes-On-Sea, Lancashire, England

**Hole:** No. 17

**Length:** 462 yards

**Par:** 4

**Designer:** George Lowe

**Course Comment:** There is a plaque in the rough at the 17th hole about 175 yards from the green, signifying the spot where Bobby Jones played a magnificent recovery shot with a mashie (equivalent to a 4-iron today) on his way to the 1926 British Open Championship.

BELOW *The 17th hole at Royal Lytham & St. Annes, Lancashire, England.*

OPPOSITE *Se Ri Pak of South Korea digs out of a bunker onto the 17th green at Royal Lytham & St. Annes.*

There have been countless major moments at Royal Lytham, but there certainly was no bigger year than 1926, when King George V bestowed the "Royal" title to the club, and it hosted its first British Open Championship. Bobby Jones — a bit of golf royalty himself — won the 1926 Open.

It was 70 years and eight more Opens before another American (Tom Lehman) won a British Open at St. Annes-On-Sea, and he did so after setting the course record with a third-round 64. Lehman followed that round with a 73 he described as "gritty, not pretty," but it was enough to capture the championship.

Nestling between two busy seaside resorts, Royal Lytham is one of the most distinctive courses in the rotation of the British Open. It is a links in every sense of the word, with sandy soil and the wind blowing in from the Irish Sea.

Exposed to the elements, the trees on the course permanently lean sideways, with the wind often proving a formidable competitor in the homeward five holes of the course. Unusually, the course is set amongst a Victorian housing estate, and occupies a limited piece of land, with red-brick houses in plain view. Located nearby is the St. Annes train station with the railway line running adjacent to the first nine holes of the course.

The 17th hole is part of one of the toughest five-hole finishes in British golf. The hole is a dogleg left that is fairly flat, but its difficulty is enhanced by clusters of bunkers at the dogleg's elbow. If you stay in the middle, you will still have a lengthy, windy test, but this is a force you can deal with. However, unless you have the skill of a Bobby Jones, you probably forfeit a chance at par if you land in the rough.

The 17th is a monster of a hole, but at least it gets you one step closer to the grand Victorian clubhouse, with its oak-paneled dining room. It is a clubhouse saturated with tradition, and is a spot from which countless international events have been viewed. Nine British Opens and Arnold Palmer's first Ryder Cup in 1961 are just a couple of the footnotes in the history of Royal Lytham & St. Annes Golf Club. **JB**

## No. 🟦 **PHILADELPHIA COUNTRY CLUB**

**Course:** Philadelphia Country Club

**Location:** Gladwyne, Pennsylvania, USA

**Hole:** No. 17

**Length:** 472 yards

**Par:** 4

**Designer:** William S. Flynn, Howard C. Toomey

**Course Comment:** This club offers three nine-hole courses. Two are generally played as an 18-hole combination, and one (the Centennial Course) which is played separately. Both courses feature rolling terrain and open fairways.

In 2004, the Philadelphia Country Club hired a new golf professional. She admitted that when she gets a par on this hole she is tempted to jump up and down. And she's the pro!

The No. 2 handicap hole on the course (the pro said it's the toughest) begins with an uphill climb and bends slightly to the right. There are dense trees along the right side of the fairway (this reduces your chances of cutting the corner) and plenty of long fescue along the left side. Neither is very attractive.

There is a big hump in the middle of the fairway, which slopes back up to the green. Your tee shot should clear the hump and get down the hill if you are going to have a good shot at hitting the green in two.

Your second shot is most likely going to be a side-hill lie. And you are going to have to hit it around 200 yards to reach the green.

The green is tricky to hold, especially using a 3-wood. The green slopes severely downward on the right side and there is a severe slope upward on the left side.

Three-putts are common on this tricky green. **TJ**

---

## No. 🟦 **CARNE**

**Course:** Carne

**Location:** Carne, Belmullet, County Mayo, Ireland

**Hole:** No. 17

**Length:** 399 yards

**Par:** 4

**Designer:** Eddie Hackett

**Course Comment:** Carne was the last links course to be designed by the late Eddie Hackett and it is now believed by many who have played it to be his greatest challenge.

Named "An Muirineach," No. 17 is a 399-yard par 4 that many believe is Eddie Hackett's greatest challenge, especially from the back tees.

The nickname translates literally to "maram" or "bentgrass," which is plentiful on this hole. Also plentiful here are challenging shots.

The advice for this hole is to play smart. Play for par and not birdie, and be happy with a bogey. Some holes you can go after on this course while others you need to pull back. Consider this one of the latter.

If you can, try and get a later tee time and plan it so you are walking up the 17th fairway at sunset. You won't be disappointed by Mother Nature's golden touch.

There are four sets of tees at Carne. On the 17th hole the backs sit back at 399 yards, while the forward red tees are at 339 yards.

*Turasoireacht Iorrais* (Erris Tourism) is a local company set up to help develop and promote tourism. What better way to bring in the folks than a great golf course? **TJ**

## No. ⑰ CAPE KIDNAPPERS

**Course:** Cape Kidnappers

**Location:** Hawke's Bay, New Zealand

**Hole:** No. 17

**Length:** 463 yards

**Par:** 4

**Designer:** Tom Doak

**Course Comment:** Every hole at Cape Kidnappers has a view of the bay, and at the sixth and 15th holes it's possible to pull your approach off the very end of the earth, though it will take nearly 10 seconds of hang time for your ball to reach the ocean, 500 feet below.

You might think you left the 16th green and landed at Shinnecock Hills on Long Island. But there is no way that could have happened. What is more likely is that Shinnecock Hills traveled to New Zealand. Cape Kidnappers' owner Julian Robertson is a member at Shinnecock, so you can excuse him if he was influenced by the classic American course.

But, here, the property is so much more glorious. And Robertson brought Tom Doak along, as well.

No. 17 is an unforgettable golf hole on a course basking in memorable holes. The 463-yard par 4 is a slight dogleg right with an elevated green.

The wild grasses in front of the green add to the awesome scenery you never get tired of seeing. Staying focused on golf is hard on this course and on this hole in particular.

Here is Tom Doak's advice on playing No. 17: "No laying back here. You'll need to hit your two best shots to get home in regulation on this uphill par 4. Those uncertain of carrying the greenside bunkers can play safely to the right. If you drive in the rough it might be better to play straight ahead on the second and then pitch your third over the bunkers." **TJ**

## No. ⑰ CAPITAL GOLF CLUB

**Course:** Capital Golf Club

**Location:** Melbourne, Victoria, Australia

**Hole:** No. 17

**Length:** 437 yards

**Par:** 4

**Designer:** Peter Thomson, Michael Wolveridge, Ross Perrett, Lloyd Williams

**Course Comment:** Visitors laud the five-star facilities at Capital, which includes a stunning clubhouse and a practice area of such stellar quality that many touring pros prefer to work on their games there when they are in the Melbourne region.

Sand is the biggest feature here — sand in the form of a dozen bunkers that are visible from an enormous tee — and with the lake that comes almost immediately into play, this makes the 17th feel like a Saharan oasis.

Without the camels, of course.

The best drive at this hole, considered the toughest on the brilliantly conditioned and wonderfully designed course, is one that skirts the water hazard to an extremely tight landing area.

Fairway bunkers on the left and right put a premium on accuracy, and it is important when golfers make their second shots to clear the bunkers in front of the green. A small gap does allow for precise run-up shots from various positions on the left side of the fairway, but that is a very difficult way to go in most cases.

Better if they loft a long iron to the center of the putting surface and try to snuggle it up to the hole. **JS**

**Course:** Erinvale Golf Course

**Location:** Somerset West, South Africa

**Hole:** No. 17

**Length:** 481 yards

**Par:** 4

**Designer:** Gary Player

**Course Comment:** The course is situated on the former Erinvale Farm at the foot of the Helderberg Mountains. The views are spectacular. One can see beautiful False Bay and the Hottentots Holland mountain range in the east.

The surrounding mountains at Erinvale not only provide splendid scenery, they are also the friends of golfers there. Erinvale is hard enough to play without having to cope with any windy conditions, but, thanks to the sheltering mountains, golfers don't have to.

Erinvale is, in fact, two courses in one. The first nine holes, resting peacefully in a valley, offer a rather easy stretch despite the many bunkers and water hazards that can come into play. Holes 10 to 18, however, stretch over and around the mountains, which presents a challenge worthy of a championship golf course.

The 17th hole is the ultimate test — for any level of play. It is a long par 4 with out-of-bounds close to the right side of the fairway that stretches all the way to the green. The fairway slopes from right to left and can lead to a row of pines if the shot is struck too far left.

A rather narrow shoot between bunkers leads to an undulating green that requires concentration and poise. Remember, poise counts.

Erinvale hosted the 1996 World Cup of Golf and is the home of the South African Airways Open of the European Tour, which was won by Trevor Immelman in 2004. **TJ**

**BELOW AND OPPOSITE** *Two views of the 17th hole at Erinvale Golf Course.*

## No. 🄄 BRORA

**Course:** Brora

**Location:** Brora, Sutherland, Scotland

**Hole:** No. 17

**Length:** 430 yards

**Par:** 4

**Designer:** James Braid

**Course Comment:** Nestled up against the North Sea, the great James Braid used the natural surroundings and created a golf course that will forever stand the test of time.

Named after the lighthouse at Tarbetness, there are few better driving holes than right here at Brora. A hole for the camera as well as the golf shot.

James Braid designed the hole for two drawn shots. First at the tee, your drive must find its way to the narrow section of the fairway. It's not a big target, but an important target. You will need another draw as you take aim toward the right side of the green.

This is one of the toughest holes here and things can quickly get out of hand. Facing into the wind — which is usually strong — the fairway is tight. You must nail your drive right between a hill on the right and a series of bunkers on the left. The green is protected by bunkers and has plenty of slope to contend with.

Braid called No. 17 his favorite hole on the course. It's one of Scotland's favorites as well and it all starts from an elevated tee, where you get a splendid view of the entire golf course.

But don't let the scenery distract you from your business. Stay focused and let your caddy take the pictures. **TJ**

## No. 🄄 ROYAL MELBOURNE GOLF CLUB (WEST COURSE)

**Course:** Royal Melbourne Golf Club (West Course)

**Location:** Black Rock, Victoria, Australia

**Hole:** No. 17

**Length:** 441 yards

**Par:** 4

**Designer:** Alister MacKenzie

**Course Comment:** Interestingly, MacKenzie never saw the great West Course he designed at Royal Melbourne, spending only a couple of months in the area in late 1926 before moving on to other projects, among them the construction of Cypress Point and Augusta National.

The finish at this fine track, which opened in 1931, is among the best in the country, starting with this tough par-4 dogleg left.

It is critical that players put their drive on the right side of No. 17 to avoid the fairway bunker at the turn on the left. But they must be careful their balls do not drift too far in that direction, as that will leave them with difficult approaches that must clear a stunning bunker short and to the right of the slightly elevated green. It is that hazard, and one back and to the right of the putting surface, that give this hole its meat — and its grace — as they are beautifully crafted examples of MacKenzie's work at its devilish best.

Shots that come up a little short may trickle into a series of hollows in front of a green that is 35 yards deep, forcing players to demonstrate their chipping prowess in an effort to get up-and-down before moving onto the 18th hole, another long par 4. **JS**

## No. ⑰ TRALEE GOLF CLUB

Tralee Golf Club has plenty of history. The club was founded in 1896, and had three previous courses in the nearby town of Tralee — all of them hampered by high amounts of rainfall and left unplayable in the winter. The site that members picked for their fourth course — a magnificent links-style stretch along the Atlantic Ocean — also came with plenty of history.

Brendan the Navigator is reputed to have begun his journey toward America from these windy shores almost 1,000 years before Christopher Columbus's expedition, and Roger Casement's ill-fated landing in a German submarine came here in 1916. He was hanged for treason a few months later. A tower on the third hole dates to the 14th century, and nearby are the ruins of a 12th-century castle.

Tralee's latest course, which opened in 1984, is making its own history as one of Ireland's finest layouts, thanks to holes like No. 17. The tee shot on this dogleg right along the Atlantic must carry a gorge to reach a rugged, undulating fairway, and the approach must be hit to an elevated green perched high against a backdrop of mountains. Judge the wind correctly and avoid concentrating too much on the scenery, and you just might earn a par. **KA**

**Course:** Golden Horseshoe Golf Club
(Gold Course)

**Location:** Williamsburg, Virginia, USA

**Hole:** No. 17

**Length:** 435 yards

**Par:** 4

**Designer:** Robert Trent Jones Sr.

**Course Comment:** The Gold Course received a $4.5 million makeover in 1997 by Rees Jones, the son of the original course designer Robert Trent Jones Sr.

# No. ⑰ GOLDEN HORSESHOE GOLF CLUB
## (GOLD COURSE)

Colonial Williamsburg is a place where visitors can take a step back into America's history, where a restored Revolutionary War-era town still operates much as it did in the 18th century.

Similarly, the Golden Horseshoe Golf Club's Gold Course remains true to the roots of the game. Opened in 1963, it remains one of the best examples of traditional golf-course architecture in the world, and noted designer Robert Trent Jones Sr. called it "his finest design." Indeed, there is nothing fancy about the Gold Course's 17th hole. It is simply a long, well-designed par 4 that requires two strong, straight shots to reach the green and have a chance for par.

The tee shot must be hit to a narrow fairway that is lined by trees on both sides, likely to cost any golfer who hits a wayward drive. The uphill second shot is to a green that is protected by trees on the left and large bunkers at the front right and front left to penalize less-than-perfect approaches. The putting surface slopes from back to front, and shots that land on the front edge are likely to roll back down, so golfers should take an extra club and fire at the center of the green. **KA**

# WILD DUNES GOLF LINKS
## (LINKS COURSE)

**Course:** Wild Dunes Golf Links (Links Course)

**Location:** Isle of Palms, South Carolina, USA

**Hole:** No. 17

**Length:** 405 yards

**Par:** 4

**Designer:** Tom Fazio

**Course Comment:** Wild Dunes Resort's Links Course was closed for nine months after Hurricane Hugo hit the South Carolina coast in September 1989.

The Links Course at Wild Dunes Resort marked Tom Fazio's first solo design when it opened in 1980, and you might say it was a successful debut, helping to catapult the career of a course architect now considered one of the best ever. Fazio said that much of the requirements for golf greatness were already present on the piece of magnificent coastal property near the historic city of Charleston. "It had all the elements you could ask for — trees, water, dunes, and an ocean coast," Fazio said.

Most come into play on Wild Dunes's 17th hole, a par 4 that takes golfers for the first time out to the Atlantic. The hole contains no bunkers — unless you want to count the huge stretch of sand dunes that follows the hole's entire left side, covered by thick clumps of tall coastal grasses that will swallow any hooked shots.

Palmetto trees dot the right side of the landing area, but the real obstacle on this hole is the wind, which often gusts hard off the ocean and can affect shots in a myriad of ways. The subtly undulating fairway narrows as it reaches the green, making club selection key on the approach, as the beach awaits only several yards to the left. **KA**

**Course:** St. Andrews (Old Course)

**Location:** St. Andrews, Fife, Scotland

**Hole:** No. 17

**Length:** 461 yards

**Par:** 4

**Designer:** Old Tom Morris

**Course Comment:** The Old Course has evolved over time and was not designed by any one architect. Those who played a major role in shaping it are Daw Anderson (1850s), Old Tom Morris (1860s–1900), and Alister MacKenzie (1930s).

## No. ⓱ ST. ANDREWS (OLD COURSE)

"The Road Hole."

The most famous hole on the most famous golf course in the world. No. 17 at St. Andrews Old Course.

The oldest golf course in the world has many features that make it so special that golfers from around the world make a point of making a pilgrimage to golf's hallowed ground. Some make the trip a once-in-a-lifetime highlight. Others annually visit the holy land of the game.

But even though it is the spot where golf was played more than 600 years ago, the Old Course is far more than a historical relic that offers a call to yesteryear. It remains a fearsome test today. Just play The Road Hole. You will understand why.

The 17th at the Old Course has long held the title of the world's most famous hole. There are others that might be close, but The Road Hole will undoubtedly hold the title for at least the foreseeable future. It is a very long par 4, only 14 yards short of 475 yards — the generally accepted length of short par 5s.

Unless you are a highly skilled player, it is best to stand on the tee, soak in the history, and just play the hole as if it were a par 5. And even if you are an accomplished player, it's best to try a third-shot pitch rather than risk going into the notorious Road Bunker on the approach. If that happens, depending on how close you are to the face, a number of possibilities await — including attempting to hit backwards out of the bunker to escape.

The tee shot should go over the dark green sheds on the right, with just a slight draw and a carry of about 180 yards. To accomplish this, you should then try for the right front of the green, but don't be disappointed if you fall short. Holding this green is almost impossible from the distance you must approach from, which means a runner is the only option. But bear in mind that if you attempt to run it too far up to the left, the insatiable Road Bunkers await.

It is famous. It is historical. And it is also a wickedly tough golf hole. **JB**

## No. ⑰   DEVIL'S PULPIT GOLF CLUB

**Course:** Devil's Pulpit Golf Club

**Location:** Caledon, Ontario, Canada

**Hole:** No. 17

**Length:** 456 yards

**Par:** 4

**Designer:** Michael Hurdzan, Dana Fry

**Course Comment:** The Devil's Pulpit Golf Association, which is made up of Devil's Pulpit and its newer sister course, Devil's Paintbrush, was formed by Chris Haney and Scott Abbott, co-inventors of the popular board game Trivial Pursuit.

Located on the Niagara Escarpment, in the midst of the spectacular Caledon Hills, Devil's Pulpit was sculpted by Michael Hurdzan, who had more than 1.7 million cubic yards of dirt moved to create his masterpiece on a line of glacial hills that provide panoramic vistas of downtown Toronto and the surrounding Canadian countryside.

The 17th hole is a long par 4 that requires a long, accurate uphill tee shot. Even well-struck shots, however, often fail to reach the crest of the hill, leaving an approach of more than 200 yards.

The closer the drive is to the fairway bunker on the right, the better the angle for the approach to the green, which slopes from back to front and is guarded by a deep bunker front left.

The course is named after the Devil's Pulpit, a landmark rock that has the shape of a pulpit. According to legend, after an Indian brave stole a maiden from another tribe, the God of Lightning split the rock off from a several-hundred-foot-high cliff that forms the Credit River's south bank, leaving him stranded in his teepee, to die alone atop the rock . **KA**

## No. ⑰   OLYMPIC VIEW GOLF CLUB

**Course:** Olympic View Golf Club

**Location:** Victoria, British Columbia, Canada

**Hole:** No. 17

**Length:** 417 yards

**Par:** 4

**Designer:** Bill Robinson

**Course Comment:** The clubhouse sits on the highest point of the course, which means that the front nine play downhill, while the back nine play uphill.

Imagine being surrounded by the magnificence of the Olympic Mountains, the roar of two spectacular waterfalls, and the tranquility of twelve lakes. Well, there is no need to imagine any of this. You can experience it all just by booking a tee time at Olympic View Golf Club.

Just remember to bring a camera so that you can share part of the experience with your family and friends.

And save plenty of film for No. 17.

This hole is the most photographed hole on the course because of its Japanese garden and majestic 60-foot waterfall directly behind the green.

A tee shot down the middle of a pretty narrow fairway will put you in an ideal position to go for the pin on your second shot. If you are going to miss, miss your shot to the right because a water hazard guards the left.

The approach shot is slightly downhill so make sure that goes into your club selection process. And don't be long. That waterfall is for photos, not for playing out of. A photo of you making a birdie putt with the beautiful waterfall in the background is a much better shot than one of you trying to save bogey. **TJ**

**Course:** Barsebäck Golf & Country Club (New Course)

**Location:** Landskrona, Sweden

**Hole:** No. 17

**Length:** 440 yards

**Par:** 4

**Designer:** Ture Bruce

**Course Comment:** Needing only five points on Sunday to regain the Solheim Cup, Sweden's Catriona Matthew ended her match against Rosie Jones on the 17th hole to clinch the cup. The Swede hit her approach to nine feet and the birdie was conceded when Jones missed her par attempt.

## No. ⑰ BARSEBÄCK GOLF & COUNTRY CLUB (NEW COURSE)

A thick line of trees frames each hole at Barsebäck Golf & Country Club, creating well-defined playing corridors that seem to gently guide a player from tee to green. These towering walls of timber also act as a cloak, masking Barsebäck's single most intimidating element — wind.

Hidden behind this curtain of flora and fauna, just a short par 4 to the east of the 7,365-yard layout, lies the Baltic Sea. Weather systems generated by its cool waters are area staples, and the winds from its swirling surface dominate play at Barsebäck.

European players at the 2003 Solheim Cup already knew of Barsebäck's secret, having played the Ladies European Tour's Compaq Open in 1998 and 2000 at the seaside course. The U.S. side, however, was unaware of the layout's shrouded secret.

Few holes at Barsebäck are dominated by the wind like the par-4 17th hole. The 44-yard par 4 plays into the prevailing wind and requires a long, well-placed drive to set up a demanding second shot.

The putting surface is large enough to accept a long-iron approach but anything off-line will leave a demanding chip to a rolling green. **RH**

**Course:** Desert Highlands Golf Club

**Location:** Scottsdale, Arizona, USA

**Hole:** No. 17

**Length:** 570 yards

**Par:** 4

**Designer:** Jack Nicklaus

**Course Comment:** Desert Highlands served as home to the first two Skins Games in 1983 and 1984.

## No. ⑰ DESERT HIGHLANDS GOLF CLUB

When Desert Highlands opened in the early 1980s, it was far removed from development, a golf oasis located in the Sonoran Desert foothills outside Phoenix. In many ways, it paved the way for high-end golf development in the Scottsdale area, and today is surrounded by dozens of other top-notch desert courses.

Desert Highlands remains among the best, however, because of great Nicklaus holes like the par-4 17th. Although its downhill terrain tempts golfers to attempt to get home in two, they may be better off to wait and play for the tricky green with their third shot. Groups of pot bunkers must be avoided on the drive, and those who decide to go for the green with the second shot must carry a rugged stream that crosses the fairway as well as avoid several bunkers that protect the shallow putting surface, which slopes from left to right.

In the inaugural Skins Game played in 1983 at Desert Highlands, Gary Player made a short birdie putt on No. 17 worth $150,000 on the final day. That earned Player the title with a total of $170,000, as he defeated course designer Jack Nicklaus, Arnold Palmer, and Tom Watson. **KA**

## No. 🅗 COMMONWEALTH GOLF CLUB

**Course:** Commonwealth Golf Club

**Location:** South Oakleigh, Victoria, Australia

**Hole:** No. 17

**Length:** 337 yards

**Par:** 4

**Designer:** Sam Bennett, Charles Lane, Sloan Morpeth

**Course Comment:** Long-time club secretary Sloan Morpeth is listed as one of the designers of this Melbourne track, as he redid the 10th and 11th holes when Commonwealth acquired additional property some four decades ago. He also revamped a number of greens.

This hole plays just a hair uphill and is the perfect complement to the long par 4 that precedes it, as it is considerably shorter, at 337 yards, and much more straightforward.

A driver is often the play off the tee, though a well-struck 3-wood or long iron will work just as well. What's left after that is little more than a pitch to an undulating green that tends to throw poorly-hit putts into three-jack territory with no apology and demands deft positioning if there is to be any hope of par.

Approaching the putting surface from the proper angle is key, and that is one of the standout design features at Commonwealth. Golfers must think — and play — their way around the course, and anyone interested only in rolling up their sleeves and bombing drives will likely pay the price. **JS**

## No. 🅗 THE CARNEGIE CLUB AT SKIBO CASTLE

**Course:** The Carnegie Club at Skibo Castle

**Location:** Dornoch, Sutherland, Scotland

**Hole:** No. 17

**Length:** 304 yards

**Par:** 4

**Designer:** John Sutherland

**Course Comment:** Here is what Willie Newlands of the *Financial Times* had to say about The Carnegie Club: "An extraordinary and successful re-creation of Carnegie's multi-millionaire style of life, plus some of the best golf to be found anywhere in the world."

At 6,671 yards from the back tees, the course is not long by modern standards. But what the scorecard doesn't include is the wind. So when you add it all up, this course is challenging by modern standards or any other standards you care to use.

It's also quite scenic, taking golfers on a stroll through and around carefully preserved natural terrain. Bring a camera for a snapshot of some of the wildlife here, too. Try as you might, you will struggle to find a better setting for golf anywhere in the world.

The finishing two holes on the Carnegie Links offer a splendid one-two finishing punch.

From the elevated tee on No. 7 you get more than a view of the fairway below. You get a panoramic postcard right across the Dornoch Firth and up to the hills beyond.

You might not like the view of the fairway as much as the hill, however. There are five deep bunkers to avoid off the tee.

At only 304 yards off an elevated tee, the question comes quickly and often: can you reach the green in one? A solid drive around 245 yards is the bottom line answer. Anything short and the answer is no — and more often than not you'll end up in a bunker. **TJ**

**Course:** The Country Club

**Location:** Brookline, Massachusetts, USA

**Hole:** No. 17

**Length:** 381 yards

**Par:** 4

**Designer:** Willie Campbell

**Course Comment:** This original is simply The Country Club. It was one of the first havens for wealthy Americans to gather, socialize, and play. It's also the one that gave the name "Country Club" to thousands of other courses.

BELOW AND OPPOSITE *Two views of the 17th hole at The Country Club.*

Since we are at such an historical venue it's only appropriate we tee off with a history lesson. In the 1913 U.S. Open at The Country Club, 20-year-old Francis Ouimet, a former caddy at the course, beat two of the game's best players in a playoff that helped to establish American golfers at the forefront of the game.

The championship course, which was not around in Ouimet's time, is derived from the basic layout played by the members and the addition of some holes from the Primrose Course, another 9-hole layout.

The most historic hole is the only one on the back nine under 400 yards, the par-4, 381-yard 17th. This is a simple and short little dogleg left and is considered one the club's birdie holes — just the way the members like it.

But No. 17 does have its share of trouble. Remember, nothing is easy in golf. A bunker at the bend in the fairway is called the (Harry) Vardon bunker after it ruined his chances against Ouimet in 1913. It is the same bunker that kept Jackie Cupit from winning the Open 50 years later.

Are there better courses on the planet with better par 4s than The Country Club? If there are, the list isn't very long. **TJ**

## No. ⑰   TPC AT THE WOODLANDS

**Course:** TPC at The Woodlands

**Location:** The Woodlands, Texas, USA

**Hole:** No. 17

**Length:** 382 yards

**Par:** 4

**Designer:** Bruce Devlin, Robert Von Hagge

**Course Comment:** This eye-catching public course played host to the PGA Tour's Shell Houston Open for 17 years. The 17th hole is also rated among the toughest holes in Texas.

The 17th hole at TPC at The Woodlands plays very tough indeed. Although the hole only plays 382 yards there is trouble everywhere on No. 17 and on every shot.

The drive on this tricky par 4 is pivotal. There is water on the left and rough on the right. Many players try to smooth an iron onto the small fairway, and some even try to stretch a driver as far as they can. The safe play is an iron.

Depending on what you play off the tee you can have anywhere from 175 to inside 100 yards to the green, but each will still be over water. Also, the wind on this hole is often stronger than it appears, so hit plenty of club, especially with a right pin placement.

The green is completely surrounded by water in the front, and a bunker is awaiting behind the back middle-right of this green. The pin placement is critical to how a player must play their second shot. A front or back-left pin brings the water into play, and a back right brings the bunker into play.

As for the green itself, it resembles a dull arrowhead, with the tip facing toward the right side. Like the hole, the 17th green is very tricky. A two-putt here is very good; many players putt for birdie on this hole and walk away with a bogey. **GE**

## No. ⑰   DELAWARE SPRINGS

**Course:** Delaware Springs

**Location:** Burnet, Texas, USA

**Hole:** No. 17

**Length:** 310 yards

**Par:** 4

**Designer:** Dave Axland, Dan Proctor

**Course Comment:** This is one of the few "municipal" courses with a hole listed among our 1001, but it truly is worthy. Axland and Proctor, while not yet widely known as designers, deserve credit for keeping costs down and quality up.

Dave Axland and Dan Proctor, who worked for Ben Crenshaw's design company for more than a decade, were rewarded their first solo project at Delaware Springs. Sometimes when a course is labeled "municipal," golfers automatically assume that means "second rate." But when a good municipal works, it creates a downright cozy feeling. Axland and Proctor made it click nicely at Delaware Springs, and nowhere more quaintly and succinctly than at No. 17.

No sand. No water. A 310-yard par 4. At first glance, this is a birdie waiting to happen. But, as is often the case in this tricky game, first glances can be deceiving.

When taking a closer look at the short 17th at Delaware Springs, you will note that the green is partially hidden behind a grouping of trees to the left. Also visible is the flagstick, which is tempting to the long hitter. However, the green is canted to the right and away from the tee, so any shot struck low enough to go 310 yards almost certainly will roll off the green.

And because the green does slope to the right and the only angle in is from the left, even a safe shot off the tee presents trouble on the approach. This is a devilish little hole, and its deception is delicious. **JB**

**Course:** National Golf Links of America

**Location:** Southampton, New York, USA

**Hole:** No. 17

**Length:** 360 yards

**Par:** 4

**Designer:** Charles Blair Macdonald

**Course Comment:** The 17th green complex is one of only two on the course that aren't in their original 1906 location (No. 14 is the other). The 17th green was shifted back 35 yards in the 1920s to add length and maintain its challenge. Amazingly, it has continued to be splendidly vexing today.

# No. ⓱ NATIONAL GOLF LINKS OF AMERICA

It is common custom for a golf-course designer to make a few visits to a property, walk the lay of the land, conceptualize, and then get to the drawing board. A few more visits are made during its construction to make sure the plans are executed properly, and then it's off to the next project. But when Charles Blair Macdonald began work on The National Golf Links of America in 1906, it began a 30-year love affair of tweaking and tinkering that resulted in his lasting monument to the game.

After traveling Great Britain to study great golf features, Macdonald returned to begin work on The National Golf Links of America. So it isn't surprising that The National, as it has come to be known, includes a Redan hole (from North Berwick), a Sahara hole (from Royal St. George's), and an Alps hole (from Prestwick).

He also drew from his education and subsequent visits to St. Andrews, where the Old Course heavily influenced his thinking. This is evident by the wide fairways and large, undulating greens that he saw at the Old Course and incorporated into The National.

The National Golf Links of America is an American treasure, but it is much more than a historical landmark. The same characteristics that made it a great golf course in Macdonald's day make it an exemplary layout today. Macdonald wanted a "forever golf course," and that's just what he accomplished. No more lasting, and more wonderfully natural, testament to the game exists than at The National's 17th.

The short par 4 was even shorter before its renovation in the 1920s, but whether at a current length of 360 yards or its original incarnation at 325, this hole has never been about length. The 17th at The National, nicknamed "Peconic" (after a nearby city with a population of 1,100), has always been about angles. And the devious Macdonald didn't do much to help a player understand which angle to take.

Should a player take his tee shot to the extreme right side to get a solid angle into the green? Certainly, you say, except this tee shot must land just a trifle too close for comfort to a collection of pesky bunkers. Another option off the tee is straight down the center, which actually makes for a shorter approach shot. However, shorter doesn't always mean easier because the approach from the center of the fairway is nearly blind.

All of this decision-making is influenced heavily by wind direction. There really is no prevailing direction of the breezes at No. 17, so today's decision might be quite a bit different than yesterday's. **JB**

**Course:** Paraparaumu Beach
Golf Club

**Location:** Wellington, New Zealand

**Hole:** No. 17

**Length:** 442 yards

**Par:** 4

**Designer:** Alex Russell

**Course Comment:** Paraparaumu
Beach, a private club with 906
members that include men, women,
and juniors, has been the venue for
12 New Zealand Golf Opens and
numerous other major tournaments.

# No. ⑰ PARAPARAUMU BEACH GOLF CLUB

It was as if Alex Russell, the 1924 Australian Open champion who went on to enjoy a 23-year career in golf-course design, wanted a last hurrah to show off his skill. Paraparaumu Beach Golf Club was Russell's final work, and he took quite good advantage of the opportunity, creating a links course that was finished in 1949 and remains essentially unchanged to this day. The course used to be consistently rated as the best in the country — although Cape Kidnappers and others have come along since to displace it. Still, even though it may not be the absolute best course in New Zealand, it remains in the top three. And Russell no doubt would have been proud that his layout stood atop all New Zealand tracks for more than five decades.

The course is a traditional links built on the site of an earlier nine-hole course that was established in 1929 with a second nine added in 1937. The well-drained, undulating fairways, fierce rough, fast greens, and intimidating bunkers combine with the naturally windy coastal weather to create a truly challenging golf experience.

Nowhere on the course is the "links feel" more prevalent than at No. 17, where 21 bunkers crop up at the most inopportune moments, finding golf balls that might ordinarily have been in prime position. This is not one of those lush, green Augusta-looking holes, but don't mistake that for poor maintenance. It is just the essence of links golf, where brown, firm ground, gauging the wind, and avoiding sand and thick grass are all part of the challenge.

Paraparaumu, as a rule, is not a terribly long course, and plays even shorter than the scorecard indicates because of the hard-running fairways. But No. 17 is an exception to the rule. At 442 yards, it is about the average length of a par 4, but it plays into the wind much of the time, more than compensating for the hard ground.

The 17th offers a choice off the tee, as players gaze out to a split fairway. You can shorten the hole by using the right fairway, but then have a much harder second shot unless you naturally fade the ball to avoid the bunkers on the way to the green. Safety says use the left fairway, which calls for a long drive to be on the green in regulation.

The green slopes outward on the left, right and back, and back sides, so if you come in hot, forget about holding the surface.

Nice encore, Alex Russell. You certainly left your mark. **JB**

# No. ⑰ BEL-AIR COUNTRY CLUB

**Course:** Bel-Air Country Club

**Location:** Los Angeles, California, USA

**Hole:** No. 17

**Length:** 468 yards

**Par:** 4

**Designer:** Billy Bell Sr., George Thomas, Jack Neville

**Course Comment:** Lore has it that Ben Hogan considered Bel-Air's 17th one of the best par 4s in the world. The legend's assessment creates an interesting members' debate since some consider the par-4 closing hole the layout's best.

When it comes to recruiting, UCLA coach O.D. Vincent has a trump card that has nothing to do with star-watching or a reserved seat at Spago's.

For more than 20 years the Bruins have honed their games at Bel-Air Country Club, a demanding test that gives the team an edge on the golf course and Vincent an advantage when wooing potential players.

"[Playing at Bel-Air] is something players look at closely when they're choosing a school because it's such a great course," said Vincent.

In its entirety, Bel-Air is a persuasive tool for Vincent. But if he needed just a single reason for players to come to UCLA Vincent would probably take a potential student-athlete to Bel-Air's 17th.

The slight dogleg right begins from an elevated tee that features an expansive view of downtown Los Angeles. Tee shots are best played from left-to-right off a bunker on the left side of the fairway to set up the best approach to this well-guarded green.

The putting surface slopes gently to the left. Anything too far left, however, will ricochet down a steep hill. A pair of deep bunkers guards the right side of the green, and the opening to the putting surface is extremely narrow, making any approach a challenge. **RH**

**Course:** Quinta do Lago

**Location:** Almansil, The Algarve, Portugal

**Hole:** No. 17

**Length:** 561 yards

**Par:** 5

**Designer:** William Mitchell, Joseph Lee, Rocky Roquemore

**Course Comment:** The Portugese Open has been played at Quinta do Lago seven times, and when it is, the 17th hole actually plays as No. 8 on the C nine. This is the composite course that is formed for championship events.

# No. ⓱ QUINTA DO LAGO

Golf is a way of life at Quinta do Lago — and rightly so. Quinta do Lago has been the site of many top Portuguese events, and it is generally considered to be among the top courses in this gorgeous region of Portugal known as The Algarve.

Part of an internationally known natural park, Quinta do Lago has centuries-old scented pine forests and fresh and saltwater lakes as the setting for acres of lush fairways and manicured greens. The natural features of the terrain have been used to perfection by the trio of American architects who designed the course, and exquisite manicuring ensures quality conditions year round. The golf is one of the main attractions in the area, but just as important is the glorious climate, which is consistently beautiful. The Algarve region is also close to nearby airports, and these highlights have made it one of the fastest-growing golf destinations in the world. Quinta do Lago is among the best The Algarve has to offer.

One of the jewels of Quinta do Logo is the par-5 17th hole. The tee shot is picturesque, with lakes to the front and left of the tee, but it takes far more than beauty to make a golf hole. It also takes challenge and the call for strategy. No. 17 has all of that.

A long, straight drive is required, and if accomplished, leaves a second shot to a generous fairway, where the optimum position is on the left side. This opens up the proper angle into the green, avoiding the severe bunkers which line the right side of the slightly elevated green.

The green is not severely contoured, which is sometimes an advantage. However, this is not true of the putting surface — the contours are there, and they will affect putts. Although the slopes are very subtle, unless you've played Quinta do Lago before, or have a playing partner with local knowledge (better yet, a caddie), the green is bound to fool you into under-reading putts. And every stroke is valuable with just one hole to play. **JB**

**Course:** Royal Portrush

**Location:** Portrush, Northern Ireland

**Hole:** No. 17

**Length:** 548 yards

**Par:** 5

**Designer:** Harry S. Colt

**Course Comment:** Royal Portrush, home to two 18-hole courses and one nine-hole pitch-and-putt course, was simply called the Country Club when it was formed in May 1888.

BELOW *Graham Marsh of Australia plays his second shot on the 17th hole at Royal Portrush, July 2004.*

The philosophy is right out of Golf 101. It's so simple. But for some reason, even the smartest golfers ignore the warning signs. On this 548-yard par 5, even the experts suggest keeping Big Bertha and those other big drivers in the bag. You only need to take a look down the fairway to see why this is good, sound judgement. Then, pull out the driver and let it rip. You're going to do it anyway.

This 548-yard par 5 requires touch not power. The fairway is pretty straight, but narrows as you get closer to the green. You therefore need to keep the ball straight as you approach the green.

About 234 yards from the tee is a large bunker on the right side. Trouble continues along this side almost to the green. Your drive needs to be straight and farther than 246 yards to clear a severe slope in the fairway.

If you hit your drive about 250 or 260 yards you are still looking at about 200 yards to a very narrow green with bunkers all around.

The ideal play is to lay up just before a bunker on the left about 80 yards from the green. Then take a wedge to the putting surface. **TJ**

**Course:** Wentworth Club (West Course)

**Location:** Virginia Water, Surrey, England

**Hole:** No. 17

**Length:** 571 yards

**Par:** 5

**Designer:** Harry S. Colt

**Course Comment:** Perhaps the only golf course in the world that plays host to three professional golf tournaments every year, Wentworth stages the Cisco World Match Play Championship, the Volvo PGA Championship, and the Energis Senior Masters (played at the newer Edinburgh Course).

## No. ⑰ **WENTWORTH CLUB** (WEST COURSE)

There are no bunkers on this hole, but then there is no need for man-made protection at the signature hole on this course, built in 1927. Mother Nature provides guard of her own.

Wentworth West's 17th doglegs sharply left through trees, and it demands precision from tee to green. The drive is a test because there is out of bounds to the left and the fairway slopes severely to the right. The slightest rightward direction off the tee leads to an unstoppable trek to the deep rough and trees. And, of course, left leads to disaster as well.

The idea is to keep a tight line to the left side of the fairway on the tee shot, but if you don't get past the corner, you have to lay up on the second shot. Then you have to hit a draw off a hanging lie to a deceptive green. Sometimes, it's almost impossible to get the ball close to the hole.

The 17th is difficult enough on its own, but when you consider that it directly follows the monstrous, 481-yard par-4 16th and precedes a 531-yard, par-5 finisher, a golfer better have all his strength left as he approaches the end of his round.

Among those who have weathered the finishing storm at Wentworth are Arnold Palmer, Jack Nicklaus, Tom Weiskopf, Hale Irwin, Bill Rogers, Corey Pavin, and Mark O'Meara — all players who have won the World Match Play Championship here. **JB**

**Course:** Gulf Harbour Country Club

**Location:** Whangaparaoa, Auckland, New Zealand

**Hole:** No. 17

**Length:** 648 yards

**Par:** 5

**Designer:** Robert Trent Jones Jr.

**Course Comment:** Gulf Harbour combines two of New Zealand's sporting favorites. The course offers splendid views of waters raced during various America's Cup yachting competitions.

Set on the lovely Whangaparaoa Peninsula overlooking the scenic waters of Hauaki Gulf, Gulf Harbour Country Club, established in 1997, has quickly become one of Robert Trent Jones Jr.'s most renowned designs.

Whangaparaoa means "Bay of Whales" in the native tongue, and Gulf Harbour's 17th hole, one of the world's longest at 648 yards, is called *Taniwah*, meaning "supernatural being." It is an assessment that most golfers who have tackled this challenging par 5 would not dispute.

On the inland side of the hole is a long ridge line that separates this area from the rest of the course, and on the right are scattered indigenous trees and a magnificent view of the gulf. The dogleg-right fairway then makes its turn between large groups of bunkers on both sides of the landing area for the second shot, leaving golfers with an uphill approach to a tiered green that is set into one of the saddles along the ridge.

Only one year after its opening, Gulf Harbour played host to the 1998 World Cup of Golf, won by England's Nick Faldo and David Carter, and — rare for a par 5 — almost twice as many bogeys as birdies were recorded on its monster of a 17th hole. **KA**

**Location:** Springfield, New Jersey, USA

**Hole:** No. 17

**Length:** 630 yards

**Par:** 5

**Designer:** A.W. Tillinghast

**Course Comment:** John Daly became the first player in history to reach the 17th green in two shots, which he did with a driver and a 1-iron in the 1993 U.S. Open.

# No. ⑰ BALTUSROL (LOWER COURSE)

At the time of writing, the 17th hole at Baltusrol is the longest hole ever to be played in the U.S. Open. However, given the U.S. Golf Association's penchant for topping itself when it comes to making courses as difficult as possible for its championships, 630 yards might not hold up long.

However, this is one long hole. And it requires much more than power to succeed. Yes, your drive must be behemoth to have a shot at birdie on this hole, but it must also be accurate to have a prayer of getting into proper position for the second shot.

If you do manage to place your drive about 300 yards out, directly in the center of the fairway, then what awaits is another doozy. If you aren't John Daly, then you're looking to play this as a legitimate three-shot hole, which means you'll need to clear a mass of cross-bunkers (referred to as the Sahara Desert) at about the 420-yard mark, and then to set yourself up for the approach.

The third shot won't be long, but it must avoid five large bunkers and two smaller ones that encase the putting surface. The green is small, circular, and elevated. When looking at this hole, it is difficult to imagine how any human being, even a player as gifted and powerful as John Daly, could possibly have reached this hole in two.

Daly's achievement was among the more memorable moments at Baltusrol, but it was far from the only moments of greatness. The U.S. Open has been held at Baltusrol seven times (amazingly, on three different courses), and as you might imagine there have been dozens of dramatic shots and chases.

The historical people at Baltusrol aren't limited to the competitions themselves. Some of the most famous figures in the game — Bobby Jones, Francis Ouimet, Joe Dey, and P.J. Boatwright — have been asked to critique the courses and have played a part in shaping the grounds.

Right from the beginning, it seemed that Baltusrol was destined for greatness. When it opened on October 19, 1895, there were but 30 members. By 1898, there were more than 400, and plans for another golf course were in place. Its first major championship was the U.S. Women's Open in 1901, followed in 1903 by its first U.S. Open and its first U.S. Amateur. **JB**

**Course:** Hamburger Golf Club (Falkenstein Course)

**Location:** Hamburg, Germany

**Hole:** No. 17

**Length:** 480 yards

**Par:** 5

**Designer:** Harry S. Colt, Charles Alison, John S.F. Morrison

**Course Comment:** Native son Bernhard Langer captured his second PGA European Tour victory at the 1981 German Open at Hamburger, marking the first of his five German Open triumphs.

No. **17** **HAMBURGER GOLF CLUB**
## (FALKENSTEIN COURSE)

Hamburger Golf Club's original nine-hole layout was built in 1906, and played host to the 1914 international German championships, which were called off after the first round because of the outbreak of World War I. Following the war, the club acquired a new parcel of land, with the acclaimed English architects Colt, Alison, and Morrison hired to build the current 18-hole course, which opened in 1930.

When war broke out again, the course and surrounding landscape was damaged by bomb craters. After World War II, the club was not turned back over to members until 1950, but it has rebounded nicely and still is considered one of the country's most beautiful layouts.

Similar to the rest of the course, the par-5 17th isn't long, but is a mental challenge for golfers. The tee shot should be hit to a landing area that is protected by bunkers on each side and marks the turning point of the dogleg-left fairway, about 220 yards from the green. The second shot presents an important decision.

Try to get home in two over a 100-yard sea of thick native vegetation called heide, or hit a short lay up, setting up an easier approach to a green guarded by a long bunker on the left. **KA**

**Course:** The Oxfordshire Golf Club

**Location:** Milton Common, Thame, Oxfordshire, England

**Hole:** No. 17

**Length:** 599 yards

**Par:** 5

**Designer:** Rees Jones

**Course Comment:** During the 1996 Benson and Hedges Open on the PGA European Tour, when the winds were howling in Oxfordshire, scores from 3 to 13 were taken. And these were from the best professionals in Europe.

## No. ⑰ THE OXFORDSHIRE GOLF CLUB

The Oxfordshire Golf Club, situated in rolling English countryside, is located approximately one hour northwest of London on the outskirts of the university town of Oxford. When it opened, architect Rees Jones had this to say of his handiwork: "I want this to be a golf course that provides continuing variety and challenge day after day for players of all levels."

For the most part, Jones succeeds. But the "players of all levels" gets stretched just a bit at the wishbone-shaped 17th. This is a hole that literally turns you inside out by the shape of its fairway around a lake, and if you aren't a quality player, the damage it can do to your scorecard could be mind-boggling as well as round-ruining.

This is a wonderful hole, however, and it should be enjoyed regardless of the number you scratch into your card. This downhill par 5 requires concentration and decision-making all the way from tee to green, and if you aren't a thinking golfer, then this hole can be almost unplayable. However, if you keep your wits, it can be one of the most enjoyable holes on the course.

RIGHT *The 17th green at the Oxfordshire Golf Club, England.*

The drive needs to be long and straight; no options there. However, the second shot provides three choices. You can try a second shot over water to a small landing area protected by pot bunkers. The safer route plays around the lake and requires a longer shot partially over water. The big hitter may try for the green in two shots, but beware, a full water carry is required to the green which is also protected by sand.

An interesting aspect of the design at Oxfordshire is the layout in regard to wind influence. Each par 3 and par 5 plays in different directions, so if you are penalized because of wind going one way, you catch relief going the other. This might not seem like a major concession from the designer, but when you know No. 17 awaits, you'll take any break you can get.

One last word from Rees Jones: "The layout of The Oxfordshire flows naturally with the beautifully contoured land and was created to preserve the existing trees. This provides an environment where the player will be able to see and understand the design at work." Another classic inspired by Mother Nature herself. **JB**

**Course:** Pelican Hill Golf Club
(Ocean North Course)

**Location:** Newport Coast, California, USA

**Hole:** No. 17

**Length:** 543 yards

**Par:** 5

**Designer:** Tom Fazio

**Course Comment:** Pelican Hill played host to stars from the PGA, Senior PGA, and LPGA tours in the 1999 Diners Club Matches.

OPPOSITE *The 17th hole on the Ocean North Course at Pelican Hill Golf Club.*

# No. ⑰  PELICAN HILL GOLF CLUB
## (OCEAN NORTH COURSE)

Offering splendid views of Newport Bay and the Pacific Ocean and the name of one of the world's top course architects, it didn't take long for Pelican Hill to quickly leap to the top of the list of Southern California's most desired public golf destinations.

One look at the par-5 17th hole on Pelican Hill's Ocean North Course, and you'll understand why. Appropriately called "Gut Check," this hole requires three stomach-churning shots in order to earn par. The tee shot must be a strong one, avoiding a sprawling bunker on the right side of the fairway, which is further pinched in by an encroaching ocean inlet. The second shot also should be kept on the left side of the narrowing fairway just past the point where it doglegs right, again staying clear of fairway bunkers on each side and allowing for the best angle into the green.

The third shot is a real knee-knocker and somewhat of an optical illusion because of a lone Tonyon tree to the left and the deep blue Pacific on the horizon. Whatever you do, don't miss right, as that side of the elevated green falls off into deep bunkers and thick coastal vegetation that leads down to the water below. **KA**

---

**Course:** The Estancia Club

**Location:** Scottsdale, Arizona, USA

**Hole:** No. 17

**Length:** 560 yards

**Par:** 5

**Designer:** Tom Fazio

**Course Comment:** Like many golf clubs in Arizona, The Estancia Club was designed out of the natural surroundings and is one of the more scenic clubs in the state. It's also a generous club with wide fairways and good-sized greens.

# No. ⑰  THE ESTANCIA CLUB

The Estancia Club is an exclusive, private golf club located at the base of Pinnacle Peak in Scottsdale, Arizona. As you can imagine, a golf course in the desert at the base of a mountain offers some pretty stunning views.

But this par 5 is stunning even without the postcard views.

The tee sits up on a ridge and bends to the left into a little canyon. The big hitters can reach this in two but it takes two pretty good hits. There is no dogleg to cut, so just reach back and swing away.

The right side of the fairway is your ideal target because it gives you a better approach into the green, which you better hit or you could be in trouble. The left side of the green falls off into the desert. The right side drops off into a bunker.

Your second shot does have the advantage of being downhill, which could mean the difference in a club length and a better chance at the green.

The more average golfer should lay up. Your second shot should be directed at the flat surface about 110 yards from the green. However, don't go past this mark, or you are looking at a difficult downhill shot off a sloping fairway.

The green is very narrow and slopes hard back to front. There is also a bunker situated so far below the green that if you happen to land in it, you can't see the hole. **TJ**

**Course:** Old Head Golf Links

**Location:** Kinsale, County Cork, Ireland

**Hole:** No. 17

**Length:** 632 yards

**Par:** 5

**Designer:** Paddy Merrigan, Liam Higgins, Joe Carr

**Course Comment:** The *Lusitania*, a British cargo and passenger ship, was sunk by a German torpedo on May 7, 1915, several miles offshore of the lighthouse at the rear of Old Head's 17th green.

Old Head Golf Links, which opened in 1997, isn't one of those short, old-style links courses where the yardage is limited by its location along the coastal terrain and in a nod to the stiff ocean winds that often make holes play longer. Make no mistake, Old Head still has the spectacular views — and definitely more than its share of wind — but the course stretches 7,200 yards from the tips, making it a particularly challenging test for today's long hitters.

A perfect example is the par-5 17th, Old Head's longest hole, set on a cliff above the crashing waves of the Atlantic below and playing toward the welcoming beacon of a 150-year-old lighthouse on a hill above the green. The tee shot must carry a large stone in the center of the fairway, and the second shot must avoid the cliffs on the right, although an overly cautious second shot that strays too far left will leave a blind approach to the green. The fairway begins a dramatic slope about 175 yards from the green, requiring a downhill third shot to a putting surface set close to the cliff on the right and further protected by a large bunker at the front left. **KA**

**RIGHT AND OPPOSITE** *Two views of the 17th hole on Old Head Golf Links.*

| |
|---|
| **Course:** Cherry Hills Country Club |
| **Location:** Englewood, Colorado, USA |
| **Hole:** No. 17 |
| **Length:** 555 yards |
| **Par:** 5 |
| **Designer:** William Flynn |
| **Course Comment:** This course and hole has hosted several U.S. Opens. Ralph Guldahl (1938), Arnold Palmer (1960), and Andy North (1978) all won Opens here. This course will also host the 2005 U.S. Women's Open. |

## No. ⑰  CHERRY HILLS COUNTRY CLUB

The 555-yard, par-5 17th hole at Cherry Hills Country Club makes every player think twice. This fairly long hole leaves players two choices, to go for it in two, or hit three shots and be happy.

The first shot will probably be the easiest. A straight drive is required to a fairway with tons of landing room. Keep it to the right center just to be safe. On the left there is a row of trees, but a really bad shot must be played in order to reach them.

The second shot — decision time — should be in the area of 240-plus yards to a green surrounded by water. For the big hitter, a long iron or wood should get you there, but once again watch out for the water behind, to the left and right of the green.

For the more distance-challenged player, you should hit a mid-iron to a landing area which is about 50 yards away from the green. This is the safe play and with a nice wedged third shot you will have a good run at birdie.

The green is small and has some undulation in it. Many players say finding the right line and speed on this green is the key. With the greens usually rolling fast, tempo is the key to your birdie. **GE**

Course: Glasgow Hills Resort
& Golf Club

Location: Hunter River, Prince
Edward Island, Canada

Hole: No. 17

Length: 502 yards

Par: 5

Designer: Les Furber

Course Comment: Sitting in the
rolling hills of New Glasgow, Prince
Edward Island, Glasgow Hills Resort
& Golf Club offers spectacular
scenery unique to this area.

# No. ⑰  GLASGOW HILLS RESORT & GOLF CLUB

So what can you see that will take your breath away? How about plenty? One can view the Gulf of St. Lawrence in the background while watching the golfers from the stately clubhouse located high on the hills.

Glasgow Hills is a par-72 "World Class Signature Golf Course" ranging in length from 5,279 to 6,915 yards with four sets of tees to accommodate players of all levels. Architect Les Furber has created a spectacular golf course in a spectacular setting. You will be impressed with the great elevation changes as well as the tremendous views. But what you will remember most is the golf course itself.

Glasgow Hills is touted as a "must play" golf course on Prince Edward Island. And No. 17 is the highlight of highlights. This spectacular hole features an elevated tee box with a full view of an inviting fairway. Grab your club and let's get started.

Slightly to the left of the bunker on the right-hand side is your bull's eye, so aim for this spot. The second shot, setting up your approach shot, is the big shot. You will want every bit of help you can get from that second shot because your third shot is challenging. The green is elevated and getting some loft on your shot is the only way to hold the green. **TJ**

Course: Royal Melbourne Golf Club
(East Course)

Location: Black Rock, Victoria,
Australia

Hole: No. 17

Length: 558 yards

Par: 5

Designer: Alex Russell

Course Comment: No. 17 is so
good that it is used as part of the
acclaimed composite course at
Royal Melbourne, which was first
employed in competition in 1959,
when 12 holes from the West Course
were combined to form a Dream
Team 18 with six from the East. It has
been used for top events ever since,
and golf critics rank it among the
very best layouts in the world.

# No. ⑰  ROYAL MELBOURNE GOLF CLUB (EAST COURSE)

A par 5 of sufficient length, this hole tempts players to take out their drivers on the tee and think about going for the green in two, especially if they are successful with their first shots.

However, a barrier of fairway bunkers running diagonally from left to right and toward the putting surface can swallow up any errant — and aggressive — approaches, and that can put some very damaging doubts in minds. So can out-of-bounds on the right.

As a result, Royal Melbourne members believe the most sensible play for most players at the 17th hole involves three accurate — and reasonably safe — shots to the center of the green. In their view, any fancy play-making here is best left to the pros.

One of the beauties of the Royal Melbourne courses is that they are relatively unchanged, staying as true to the MacKenzie design and intention as possible. The 17th is one of the few with which the club has fiddled, but the changes were only minor ones. A bit of length was added prior to the playing of the Canada Cup (now known as the World Cup) there in 1959, and the cross bunker was moved closer to the green. **JS**

**Course:** Club at Eaglebrooke

**Location:** Lakeland, Florida, USA

**Hole:** No. 17

**Length:** 514 yards

**Par:** 5

**Designer:** Ron Garl

**Course Comment:** The Club at Eaglebrooke served as the official home of the Futures Tour — the developmental tour of the LPGA — from 1998 to 2003.

## No. ⑰ CLUB AT EAGLEBROOKE

From Costa Rica to Thailand to . . . Lakeland, Florida, Ron Garl has spread his award-winning touch throughout the world. In 1997 the University of Florida graduate took on a project close to home by designing the Club at Eaglebrooke, located minutes from his Lakeland office.

Reachable par 5s, rolling landscapes, extensive putting surfaces, and a unique island fairway make the challenging course a visual treat. Like many Eaglebrooke holes, attacking the par-5 17th has as much to do with course management as it does with skill.

The 514-yard dogleg right curves sharply around a body of water that sets up the two difficult finishing holes. From an elevated tee, players should first assess the wind before making their club selection.

When playing into the wind, leave the driver in the bag as the fairway begins to narrow 200 yards from the tee. There the water begins to come into play, and the fairway is pinched to 30 yards. While concentrating on avoiding the water, be careful not to draw the ball too much, as out-of-bounds begins just left of the cart path. From there, it's a three-shot hole as a 5-wood over the water will leave a wedge into the green.

On the other hand, if the hole is playing downwind, unleash a driver down the left side with a slight fade. From the fairway, be sure to aim the second shot slightly left as the downhill, sidehill lie feeds everything toward the water.

The large, undulating green offers no easy putts. But leave here with birdie and the demanding 18th loses a bit of its bite. **BB**

**Course:** The Stanwich Club

**Location:** Greenwich, Connecticut, USA

**Hole:** No. 17

**Length:** 568 yards

**Par:** 5

**Designer:** William Gordon, David Gordon

**Course Comment:** With his victory at the 2002 U.S. Mid-Amateur at Stanwich, George Zahringer became the first Mid-Amateur stroke play medalist to go on and capture the overall title.

## No. ⑰ THE STANWICH CLUB

Long known by members for its narrow, tree-lined fairways and lightning-fast greens, The Stanwich Club burst onto the national stage in 2002, when it played host to its first major amateur event, the U.S. Mid-Amateur Championship. The title was won by 49-year-old New Yorker and Stanwich member George Zahringer, who defeated fellow forty-something Jerry Courville, 43, a Connecticut native, by a 3-and-2 margin in the 36-hole final.

Stanwich's par-5 17th hole presented a challenge to competitors that week. The dogleg-left hole is lined by water on its left side and by thick stands of pine trees on the right. The drive should be kept to the right center of the fairway, as should the second shot, leaving golfers with the preferred angle into a green that is guarded by bunkers at the left and front right. The approach should be kept below the hole to avoid a tricky downhill putt, as the putting surface slopes from back to front.

For the few long hitters who attempt to reach the green in two, the water will have to be carried with the second shot — a difficult proposition. **KA**

No. **⑰** **VALDERRAMA GOLF CLUB**

**Course:** Valderrama Golf Club

**Location:** Andalucia, Spain

**Hole:** No. 17

**Length:** 490 yards

**Par:** 5

**Designer:** Robert Trent Jones Sr.

**Course Comment:** Despite all the controversy, the par-5 17th is the fourth easiest hole at Valderrama. In the World Stroke Play Championship it played at an average of 4.817. Only three holes played more easily.

The United States has Augusta National. Scotland has St. Andrews. And Spain has Valderrama. The word "classic" is reserved for the elite few and is the perfect tag for Valderrama.

The 17th hole used to be not much more than a very long par 5.

But that has changed. And so has the approach to this hole. The second shot presents the player with an interesting dilemma: try to carry the water for a birdie or eagle, or play it smart and lay up.

The answer usually depends on who you are and what you have in the golf bag. Most of the time, though, lay up wins out.

In the 1995 Volvo Masters, Miguel Angel Jimenez scored the first albatross of his life here, and the first that Valderrama had ever seen.

The high stone wall to the right of the second landing area is a true gabion, just as they were built centuries ago, usually as part of a fortification. It acts as a retaining wall and also provides a spectacular viewing platform.

Seve Ballesteros was brought in to make further improvements to Jones' design and redesign. Ballesteros left his mark, most notably on No. 17. He certainly left the hole up for debate. But the numbers don't lie. **TJ**

# Hole 18

The curtain closer. The final act. For a struggling player, the 18th tee can be a welcome sight, but, for golfers in good form, the 18th represents a conclusion to a round they might not want to end. One more hole, and it's back to reality.

Designers realize No. 18 is their final shot to impress a player, so they often save their best for last. One need look no further than this book to realize that the No. 18s of the world offer the best theater in golf. Of the 1001 entries in these pages, 108 are 18th holes — by far the most of any hole.

Whether the 18th is the most difficult on the course, the most beautiful, the most distinctive, or a combination of all of the above, it is often the most memorable.

No. 18 is both a wonderful capper to 4 ½ hours of pleasure, and a sad reminder that all the world is not a golf course. But, while the round may be finished, you will golf another day.

LEFT *The 18th hole at the Bay Hill Club & Lodge, Orlando, Florida, USA.*

**Course:** Desert Mountain Golf Club
(Geronimo Course)

**Location:** Scottsdale, Arizona, USA

**Hole:** No. 18

**Length:** 197 yards

**Par:** 3

**Designer:** Jack Nicklaus

**Course Comment:** Scottsdale boasts
one of the highest percentages of
blue-sky days in the country — good
news for those looking to get the
full Desert Mountain experience.

## No. 🔞 DESERT MOUNTAIN GOLF CLUB
### (GERONIMO COURSE)

Jack Nicklaus junkies can get their fix of Golden Bear golf at the sweeping
Desert Mountain complex. With 108 signature Nicklaus holes at their
disposal, the roughly 2,500 Desert Mountain members never lack variety.
Of the six courses located in the high Sonoran Desert, the Outlaw and
Geronimo courses are considered the most demanding tracks.

One of Geronimo's most unique characteristics is its renowned par-3
finishing hole. In addition to having a stunning clubhouse as its backdrop,
the natural beauty of the 197-yard hole is positively breathtaking.

Visually intimidating from the tee, players have to carry the ball over a
rugged canyon to an expansive green. Although the 18th is ranked No. 16 on
the course's handicap index, it's hardly considered one of Geronimo's
gentle holes. In fact, when the wind kicks up in the afternoon many players
have trouble finding the 90-foot deep putting surface.

Besides the two bunkers guarding either side, only rocks and coarse
terrain surround the two-tiered green. Players who come up short often
find the front-left bunker, which sits 15 feet below the putting surface
where it's nearly impossible to see the bentgrass green. However, those
taking too much club in an effort to assuredly clear the canyon will find
gnarly rocks and bushes a mere five feet behind the green. **BB**

OPPOSITE *The 18th hole on
the Geronimo Course at Desert
Mountain Golf Club.*

**Course:** Lindrick Golf Club

**Location:** Worksop,
Nottinghamshire, England

**Hole:** No. 18

**Length:** 210 yards

**Par:** 3

**Designer:** Tom Dunn, F.W. Hawtree

**Course Comment:** The last major
change to the Lindrick course came
more than 70 years ago, in 1932. Only
Nos. 11–13 have been changed since.

## No. 🔞 LINDRICK GOLF CLUB

Lindrick Golf Club was first laid out as a nine-hole track in 1892, and was
expanded to 18 holes two years later. It's rather unique to have a par 3 as a
finishing hole, but Lindrick's No. 18 is every bit the challenging test you
want for a final hole. There's nothing fancy about this long one-shotter,
which features Lindrick's majestic clubhouse as an imposing presence in
the background, but the tee shot must be true to avoid groups of deep
bunkers on both the front left and front right sides.

Lindrick played host to the 1957 Ryder Cup after Yorkshire industrialist
Sir Stuart Goodwin donated £10,000 toward the British Ryder Cup team.
Down 3-1 after the first day's foursomes, Great Britain and Ireland rallied to
win six of eight singles matches for a 7½ to 4½ victory over the United
States. It was Great Britain and Ireland's last victory against the American
side. Its next victory — after 13 consecutive losses — didn't come until 1985,
when players from other European countries were allowed on the team.

Other major competitions held at Lindrick Golf Club include the 1960
Curtis Cup, the 1988 Women's British Open, and the 2003 Ladies' British
Amateur Championship. **KA**

**Course:** Killarney Golf & Fishing Club (Mahony's Point Course)

**Location:** Killarney, County Kerry, Ireland

**Hole:** No. 18

**Par:** 3

**Length:** 196 yards

**Designer:** Henry Longhurst, Sir Guy Campbell

**Course Comment:** Killarney Golf Club is home to two treks worthy of a round. The Killeen Course and the Mahoney's Point Course are both considered among the top 100 courses in the British Isles. The Lackabane Course is the newest at the club and is quickly making a name for itself.

No. ⑱ **KILLARNEY GOLF & FISHING CLUB (MAHONY'S POINT COURSE)**

Killarney's nine-hole layout was expanded to 18 holes in 1939, when Henry Longhurst and Sir Guy Campbell formed what is now the basis of Mahony's Point, the first of three parkland layouts set near the splendor of the famous Lakes of Killarney and the majestic peaks of Magilicuddy's Reeks, the highest mountain range in Ireland.

A one-shot hole is a great finisher to a round of golf — and the par-3 18th at Mahony's Point certainly delivers.

The long tee shot requires a carry of 150 yards over a breathtaking corner of Lough Leane to a well-bunkered green that is beautifully framed by mature pine trees and rhododendron bushes, with the winds off the lake occasionally affecting play. Satisfying yes, but potentially devastating to the scorecard. Finishing on par will leave players positively giddy.

If you needed to be further convinced of this gem of a finish, Gene Sarazen once said of it and Mahony's Point: "When the wind blows in off the lake, even the best player in the world will be hard pressed to break 80. The 18th hole in particular, is one of the most memorable holes in golf." **KA**

## No. ⑱  MARRIOTT FOREST OF ARDEN
### (ARDEN COURSE)

**Course:** Marriott Forest of Arden (Arden Course)

**Location:** Meriden, Warwickshire, England

**Hole:** No. 18

**Length:** 211 yards

**Par:** 3

**Designer:** Donald Steel

**Course Comment:** The Forest of Arden has a long association with the European Tour, and 2003 marked the 10th tour event for the Arden Championship Course.

The Arden Course at Marriott Forest of Arden is one of the country's most spectacular challenges and also host to a succession of major international tournaments, including the 2003 British Masters.

As unique and challenging and dramatic as this golf course is, the finishing hole stands out as one of the most memorable you might ever play in England or anywhere else for that matter.

First of all, the Arden Course finishes with a par 3. That alone, is pretty bold. But we're just getting started here. This hole is as good a test as any on the golf course. A lead in a big tournament is never safe until you walk off this green.

At 211 yards, the hole is the longest par 3 on the golf course. But if you so choose, you can move up to the 207-yard (white), the 194-yard (yellow), or the 150-yard (red) tees.

One of the European Tour's most distinct signature holes, the 211-yard par 3 overlooks the fishing lakes and resort. It's a breathtaking view with a breathtaking tee shot, which requires you to carry the water.

A par here and you deserve a pint of accolades.

The par-72 course plays to 7,213 yards from the back tees. **TJ**

## No. ⑱  YOMIURI COUNTRY CLUB

**Course:** Yomiuri Country Club

**Location:** Tokyo, Japan

**Hole:** No. 18

**Length:** 224 yards

**Par:** 3

**Designer:** Seichi Inoue

**Course Comment:** Yomiuri is the long-time host for the Japan Golf Tour's season-ending tour championship, the Nippon Series JT Cup.

Yomiuri Country Club, which opened in 1964, features mountainous terrain, slick greens, and several blind shots, with wind often a factor.

The par-3 18th hole is a fine finishing test for golfers in the Japan Golf Tour's Nippon Series JT Cup played annually at Yomiuri. As is the case with many Japanese golf courses, the hole features two rotating greens, with the season of the year determining which putting surface is played. The green used most of the year — and during the tournament — is set behind a mammoth complex of five bunkers that must be carried with the tee shot.

In the 2003 Nippon Series JT Cup, No. 18 ranked as the most difficult hole by far in all four rounds, playing to an overall average of 3.370, with only 43 percent of the field hitting the green in regulation and only five birdies marked there the entire week, with none on the final two days. During the third round, the hole was especially tough, playing to a 3.560 average, with the limited 25-man field managing only 11 pars and 14 bogeys.

The elite tournament has been won by such notable Japanese players as Masashi Ozaki (1995, 1996), Shigeki Maruyama (1997), and Shingo Katayama (2000, 2002) **KA**

**Course:** Pierce Lake Golf Club

**Location:** Chelsea, Michigan, USA

**Hole:** No. 18

**Length:** 234 yards

**Par:** 3

**Designer:** Harry Bowers

**Course Comment:** You better straighten out your shot on the front nine where the fairways are nice and wide because the back tightens up quite a bit and can make you pay for hooks and slices.

## No. ⓲ PIERCE LAKE GOLF CLUB

Wooded areas, along with wetlands and tighter fairways, make the back nine at Pierce Lake Golf Club a formidable challenge. In an area — a chip shot west of Ann Arbor and just off Interstate-94 — with formidable competition at practically every exit, Pierce Lake divides its 18 holes into playable and challenging. There is something here for everyone.

They throw a curveball at you at the end of your round — instead of finishing with a more traditional par 4 or par 5, Pierce Lake tees up a par 3. And a "Piercing" par 3 at that.

At 234 yards from the back tees, you better have your 3-wood fine tuned. You have to really hit it to reach the green. Hitting it straight is another advantage.

There are five sets of tees here (remember, this course is playable for everyone) so you can play from the reds (177 yards) or the whites (183 yards) if you so choose.

Not only is there plenty of yardage between the tee and green, but the wind in your face makes this hole even longer. The green is also unique. It's very long and also very narrow.

The good news is the pin is usually set toward the front of the green. **TJ**

**Course:** East Lake Golf Club

**Location:** Atlanta, Georgia, USA

**Hole:** No. 18

**Length:** 232 yards

**Par:** 3

**Designer:** Donald Ross, George Cobb, Rees Jones

**Course Comment:** East Lake's closing hole proved to be a key turning point in Bubba Dickerson's 36-hole final match at the 2001 U.S. Amateur. Dickerson played the hole in 1 under while his opponent, Robert Hamilton, struggled to a clumsy 3 over and lost the final, 1 up, with a double bogey-5 on the 36th hole.

## No. ⓲ EAST LAKE GOLF CLUB

It is one of the most curious conclusions in the game. Golf architecture's version of a duck-billed platypus.

Not that anything is wrong with East Lake's par-3 18th. Quite the contrary actually, the par-3 18th is a weighty hole that demands equal parts strength, skill, and spirit. What's peculiar is the hole's position in the line-up. A curt yet classic conclusion to one of the finest loops in the game.

East Lake is not the only renowned course with a par-3 finish but it is arguably the genre's most venerable layout. It has hosted numerous major tournaments: including the 2001 U.S. Amateur and the 1963 Ryder Cup.

Throughout its storied past the 18th has proved to be a perfect stage for the dramatic and the dazzling.

Tee shots to the 232-yard 18th are uphill and normally into the prevailing wind. Even during the 2002 PGA Tour Championship many players used long irons or fairway woods.

A pair of deep bunkers cradle the green on the front left and right but it may be easier to save for par from their sandy depths than from above the hole. Long tee shots leave players with lengthy putts from the green's top tier, down a slippery slope. **RH**

# DORAL RESORT AND SPA
## (BLUE COURSE)

**Course:** Doral Resort and Spa
(Blue Course)

**Location:** Miami, Florida, USA

**Hole:** No. 18

**Length:** 445 yards

**Par:** 4

**Designer:** Dick Wilson,
Robert Von Hagge

**Course Comment:** What else would
you expect of the finishing hole on a
course nicknamed the Blue Monster?
It is indeed a monster, and is one of
the most challenging finishers PGA
Tour players face each year when
they visit for the Ford Championship
every March.

The Doral Resort and Spa has long been a stop on the PGA Tour, and it is one of the most respected courses on the professional circuit. Players may not come out and say they love the course, but they do respect the challenges of the Blue Monster. In the words of Ben Crenshaw: "To play well here, a player has to have all the shots."

Often, Florida courses are thought to be a bit mundane because of the naturally flat terrain on which most of them lie. But Doral has proven this wrong ever since it came into being in 1962.

Even though the course is respected, it has not rested on past merit. In fact, in 1996, Raymond Floyd led a restoration project and in 1999, Jim McLean restored the bunkers to the original Dick Wilson design. The goal was not only to restore features of the course, but to reinforce the challenge of the Blue Monster.

Water continues to be the most constant and feared hazard on the course, and the 18th hole is no exception. No. 18 is among the most recognizable holes in the world, and it often ranks as the most difficult finishing hole of all the courses played by PGA Tour professionals.

The 18th almost always plays directly into the wind, which is as odd as it sounds, is somewhat of a blessing. Because if the wind isn't directly in your face, it's more than likely going to be a left-to-right cross-wind. This is

extremely tricky because of the large lake that lies on the left-hand side, all the way down the fairway and in front of the green. If the cross-breeze is blowing you actually have to hit the ball toward the lake and let the wind carry it back to the fairway. A nervy shot, to be sure.

If you shy away from the lake too much and go right, you've got deep rough and thick trees, not to mention a difficult angle into a razor-thin green. The putting surface is bordered on the left by the lake, which never seems to be out of your mind from tee shot to final putt. The Sunday pins here are brutal. Monstrous, if you will. **JB**

# No. ⑱ LOCH LOMOND GOLF CLUB

The Club sits on the historic Clan Colquhoun estate, which is steeped in Scottish tradition dating back to the 12th century. As Scotland is known as the birthplace of golf, Loch Lomond enjoys a long history and tradition associated with the sport, yet also provides an experience uniquely its own.

Tom Weiskopf considers Loch Lomond his best work and insists the piece of property with which he had to work was the finest in the world.

No. 18 complements the rest of the course and is a perfect ending to the day. The 430-yard par 4 challenges and tempts even the best golfer. You decide how daring you want to get.

Here is what Weiskopf had to say about No. 18: "This is a great driving hole with water all the way up the left of the right-to-left dogleg.

"The player must decide how much of the angle he dares to cut off. Penal bunkers guard the right-hand side of the fairway which is only 42 yards wide and the green is not an easy one."

This isn't the longest par 4 on the course, but it's certainly a test. The narrow fairway forces you to be straight and the bunkers on the right must be avoided. **TJ**

## No. ⑱ GREYSTONE GOLF CLUB

**Course:** Greystone Golf Club

**Location:** Romeo, Michigan, USA

**Hole:** No. 18

**Length:** 451 yards

**Par:** 4

**Designer:** Jerry Matthews

**Course Comment:** Michigan is known for some outstanding and challenging golf courses, but the final three holes at Greystone — including the 18th — are as difficult as any in the state.

Named as one of the best new golf courses in the United States in 1992 by *Golf Digest* Magazine, the design incorporates hundreds of mounds, well-defined bunkers, and unique vistas. Sensitive wetlands and over 100-year-old oaks were left virtually undisturbed during construction.

Of the three final finishing holes — called the quarry holes because they were built around an old gravel pit — No. 18 is easily the most challenging. You need a long drive off the tee and it must be straight. No room for error here with out-of-bounds on the left and a lake on the right. There are some small hills on the left side — aiming for those and having your ball kick back into the fairway is a wise option.

About 125 yards from the green is a large tree on the left side. Try not to get behind this tree.

Your approach shot has water in front and is a downhill look.

The green is wide but not too deep except on the right-hand side where it is surrounded by water. If the pin is in the large part, it's not a very difficult shot. **TJ**

## No. ⑱ HUNTINGTON VALLEY COUNTRY CLUB (FLYNN COURSE)

**Course:** Huntington Valley Country Club (Flynn Course)

**Location:** Abington, Pennsylvania, USA

**Hole:** No. 18

**Length:** 434 yards

**Par:** 4

**Designer:** William Flynn, Howard Toomey

**Course Comment:** Huntingdon Valley was founded in 1897 and incorporated in 1898 as a nine-hole course, although the current William Flynn layout did not open until 1928. In 1998, the club added a third nine holes, called the Centennial Nine.

Some of William Flynn's finest works are in the Philadelphia area, and Huntingdon Valley can hold its own with any of them. The well-bunkered course is set in a secluded, wooded valley that's shaped like a bowl, with the Flynn Nine wonderfully routed along the foot of the slope. Because of the terrain, many holes feature sloping fairways and greens, leaving golfers with uneven lies on both approach shots and putts.

The dogleg-right 18th hole (actually No. 9 on the Flynn Nine Course) is considered one of the best — if not the best — finishing hole in a region that's stocked with great courses. Players who attempt to cut off as much of the corner as they can on the tee shot could find themselves hitting an approach from a nasty complex of deep bunkers just off the right side of the fairway. The best play is to the far left side of the landing area, because the fairway slopes hard from left to right. That leaves a long, uphill approach to a green that's guarded by a series of four bunkers on the right and another on the left. As if that weren't enough, the putting surface has a false front, is usually lightning quick, and has plenty of slope. **KA**

**Course:** Southern Hills Country Club

**Location:** Tulsa, Oklahoma, USA

**Hole:** No. 18

**Length:** 430 yards

**Par:** 4

**Designer:** Perry Maxwell

**Course Comment:** Southern Hills has held eight U.S. Golf Association championships here, including three U.S. Opens (1958, 1977, 2001). The PGA Tour's Tour Championship was held here in 1995 and 1996, and the PGA Championship was staged at Southern Hills in 1970, 1982, and 1994. The first nationally prominent championship held here, however, was the U.S. Women's Amateur, won by Babe Zaharias in 1946.

# No. ⑱  SOUTHERN HILLS COUNTRY CLUB

The roster of major events that have come to Southern Hills Country Club goes back some 60 years and has brought with them the best players in history. Another biggie is coming to Tulsa in 2007 when Southern Hills plays host to its fourth PGA Championship. There is a reason that the world's best events and players keep returning to the plains of Oklahoma.

This golf course, which was established in 1936, has stood the test of time and is ready for more. It is little wonder Southern Hills has endured. When the stock market crashed in 1929, oilman Waite Phillips' $50 million fortune was almost entirely spared because most of it remained completely liquid. He kindly donated the land needed to build the course and the construction of the project took place over two years from 1935 to 1936.

Without the inventive vision of Perry Maxwell, however, Southern Hills certainly couldn't have stood up to the challenges that today's technology brings. But, stand up it does.

From beginning to end, Southern Hills presents a challenge worthy of the world's best golfers, yet truly enjoyable for the rest. Nowhere is this more accurate than on the finisher, No. 18.

It is an impressive finale, and a severe test of a par 4, particularly when a championship is at stake. It is a dogleg right that demands a drive not only on the fairway, but on a plateau to the fairway's left side. To get there, your tee shot must avoid two ponds and then two bunkers, but the plateau is where you need to be to get the proper angle to the green. And still, you're left with a shot of worthy distance to the putting surface.

A long iron is the play on your approach, and even if you've landed your tee shot where you aimed, the possibility exists that the ball is not level with your feet. Given the challenge of your approach, an uneven lie adds an unwanted burden.

The green is elevated, sloping, and well protected by two large bunkers (front-left and right). Putting is a chore on the sometimes drastic slopes, and it is little wonder that this is the toughest par on the course. **JB**

**RIGHT** *Stewart Cink of the USA makes his first putt on the 18th green at Southern Hills, June 2001.*

**OPPOSITE** *The 18th hole at Southern Hills Country Club.*

**Course:** Old Memorial Golf Club

**Location:** Tampa, Florida, USA

**Hole:** No. 18

**Length:** 451 yards

**Par:** 4

**Designer:** Steve Smyers

**Course Comment:** This golf course plays well to its natural surroundings. It's cut right out of what Mother Nature provided. But at 7,236 yards, it can challenge the best of the big hitters.

# No. ⑱ OLD MEMORIAL GOLF CLUB

Many of the members at Old Memorial would rank No. 18 among the most difficult on the golf course. And some would say that it is actually the most difficult on the golf course.

The slight dogleg right has no bunkers off the tee but environmentally protected areas are on both sides. On the tee, take aim at the big oak tree and try and hit the ball over it. Or start your drive a little to the left and fade it.

If you can do either of these things, your second shot will be a nice open iron shot about 180 or 190 yards from the green. It sure sounds easy but it's anything but easy.

At about 50 yards out from the green are bunkers on the right side of the fairway. More bunkers protect both sides of the green, which is a pretty good size target and fairly flat.

Many of the greens at Old Memorial are fast, but you should have the speed down by the time you reach 18. If you don't, it won't matter what you do on this hole.

This is a pretty golf hole, as are the previous 17 at this Tampa track. This one, however, may stand alone in its challenge. **TJ**

## No. ⑱  FALLEN OAK GOLF CLUB

**Course:** Fallen Oak Golf Club

**Location:** Saucier, Mississippi, USA

**Hole:** No. 18

**Length:** 493 yards

**Par:** 4

**Designer:** Tom Fazio

**Course Comment:** Opened in November 2006, Fallen Oak is an exclusive getaway for guests of the upscale Beau Rivage Resort and Casino, just 15 miles south in Biloxi.

If you bring your camera to Fallen Oak Golf Club, make sure the batteries don't run out before you reach No. 18. The finishing hole at Fallen Oak is one great photo op. It is a tough enough hole, but it is known more for its beauty. Don't hold up the group behind you, but don't be afraid to snap a few shots.

The entire hole runs down the right side of a picturesque ravine, which provides peril to golf shots all the way down the fairway. The grand oak for which the course is named sits on the right side of the fairway, and the ideal strategy is to play right to left — using the oak as an aiming point.

There are streams, marshes, wetlands, trees, and ravines, which make for a beautiful sight, but every one of these scenic pleasures offers a hazard with which to contend. The par 4 is also full of bunkers, which are readily accessible from the elevated tee.

You actually could snap the shutter on your camera at just about every hole on the 7,487-yard course that was built by the MGM Mirage for $50 million. It is amazing to note that the course has so much natural beauty left after Hurricane Katrina ravaged it so heavily in 2005. But, now, years later, with the thousands of trees and the rest of the natural surroundings, there is no evidence of damage. **JB**

## No. ⑱  COUNTRY CLUB OF DETROIT

**Course:** Country Club of Detroit

**Location:** Grosse Point Shores, Michigan, USA

**Hole:** No. 18

**Length:** 425 yards

**Par:** 4

**Designer:** Harry S. Colt, Robert Trent Jones Sr., Arthur Hills & Associates

**Course Comment:** If Arnold Palmer is golf royalty, then this course is one of his 18-hole golf palaces. A young Palmer emerged onto the golf scene when he walked away with a victory at the 1954 U.S. Amateur at the Country Club of Detroit.

It is a flat design dotted with deep, treacherous bunkers. Trees line the fairways en route to this course's grand finale, and the wind sweeping from Lake St. Clair makes No. 18 the course's most challenging.

A tee shot up a dogleg-right fairway gets you to this par 4. Piggyback it with a sharp uphill approach shot to the elevated, well-bunkered green, and pray. It's a real doozy of a finishing hole, a rather short par 4 by today's standards, but it plays much longer than it really is due to its uphill climb.

A 50-year celebration honoring the birth of a pioneer was held here in 2004 — 30 former Amateur champions (including 2004 Master's champion Phil Mickelson) gathered for the benefit event — the Arnold Palmer Turning Point Invitational.

Prestigious, posh, and private, this course is one of the oldest in the United States. It has been a hallmark of Midwest golf since 1897. **KLL**

**Course:** Martis Camp Club

**Location:** Truckee, California, USA

**Hole:** No. 18

**Length:** 492 yards

**Par:** 4

**Designer:** Tom Fazio

**Course Comment:** Martis Camp Club, which opened in 2007, has been named to play host to the 2013 U.S. Junior Amateur Championship.

# No. ⑱ MARTIS CAMP CLUB

Slowly but surely, the Lake Truckee, California, area has taken hold as a place to visit if you're looking for more than a couple days of solid golf. It has taken a while — 50 years in fact — but the day has come.

Beginning with Incline Village in the 1960s, and then over the years came Edgewood Tahoe, Old Greenwood, Coyote Moon, Lahontan, Grays Crossing, and Timilick. And, now, the grandest of the grand has solidified Truckee as a true golf destination.

Martis Camp Club makes Truckee a worthy journey. The first 17 holes are enough to convince, but No. 18 alone might just be enough to bring you back. It is that good.

The signature hole on the course is the last. MCC's finisher is one of the most scenic holes in Northern California. It is given an advantage because it plays downhill at first, which makes every inch of the first part of the beautifully pristine fairway visible from tee.

Then comes the drama.

After the downhill portion of the fairway comes to a close, it rises to the green about 80 feet beneath a rock promontory. It is at once protective, gorgeous, and unique. The ideal play is to run the ball up to the green rather than risk hitting the promontory. And, there is plenty to see. **JB**

# No. ⑱ PABLO CREEK

**Course:** Pablo Creek

**Location:** Jacksonville, Florida, USA

**Hole:** No. 18

**Length:** 463 yards

**Par:** 4

**Designer:** Tom Fazio

**Course Comment:** This is an exclusively private course, therefore guests must be accompanied by a member in order to play this golf course. It has plenty of sand and water — but then what else would you expect in Florida?

Pablo Creek is a gorgeous course. And while the large marsh and babbling creek may not be a golfer's best friend, they make for a picturesque and tranquil surrounding.

No. 9 is as scenic a golf hole as you will find at Pablo Creek. It's what many would call the signature hole. But No. 18, while not as pretty, is just as difficult. It's a very good golf hole on a very good golf course.

From the back tees, you are going to need a good poke to even get to the fairway. You will end up in the marsh if you don't put a good 250 yards behind your drive. The landing area of the fairway is a nice plateau before a big drop downhill.

The marsh runs all along the left side from tee to green although parts of it are blocked by trees.

From about 180 yards to 60 yards before the green is all downhill. But at about 60 yards, the fairway climbs to the green. There are two bunkers along the front left of the green and one to the right.

The green is three-tiered so pay attention to pin placement. **TJ**

# No. ⑱ THE NATURAL

**Course:** The Natural

**Location:** Gaylord, Michigan, USA

**Hole:** No. 18

**Length:** 445 yards

**Par:** 4

**Designer:** Jerry Matthews

**Course Comment:** The Natural is a natural choice in the Michigan golf mecca of Gaylord. There are many upscale resort-style courses within a chip shot of The Natural, but you can't go wrong here. A fun golf course for sure.

Their saying here is "Each hole at The Natural fits perfectly into the existing terrain, making the golf course look as if it has been there for years." The 18th hole is indeed a perfect fit on this golf course. Very scenic and also very difficult. From an elevated tee you can see the wetlands winding down the right of the fairway. You can also see why this hole is the No. 1 handicap on the scorecard as it heads back to the clubhouse.

From the tee, you want to hit a slight draw to help set you up for your second shot on this par 4. The approach shot will be long and must clear the wetlands and land on a narrow green. Not an easy assignment even for the best golfer.

The green is very long with two tiers and sand traps guarding the back. The green is typical of the others at The Natural. There isn't a lot of break in them and they are basically pretty flat. But it's a fair green so trust your judgement. This is a great finishing hole on one of Michigan's northern jewels. **TJ**

**Course:** The De Vere Belfry
(Brabazon Course)

**Location:** Sutton Coldfield,
Warwickshire, England

**Hole:** No. 18

**Length:** 474 yards

**Par:** 4

**Designer:** Peter Alliss, David Thomas

**Course Comment:** The Brabazon
Course held its fourth Ryder Cup in
2002. The matches were originally
scheduled for September 2001,
but were postponed for one year
following the terrorist attacks on
New York City's World Trade Center.

**BELOW** *José Maria Olazábal of Spain
putting on the 18th hole on the
Brabazon Course at the Belfry Golf
Club, May 2000.*

**OPPOSITE** *A view of the 18th hole on
the Brabazon Course at the Belfry.*

# No. ⓲  THE DE VERE BELFRY
## (BRABAZON COURSE)

The 18th at the De Vere Belfry's Brabazon Course has been called one of the best match-play holes in all of golf. This might be because four Ryder Cup matches have played on this course and finished on this hole, creating match-play memories for a lifetime. But, most golfers, after taking in the crushing difficulty and stately views of the 18th, would call it one of the best holes, period. Match play, stroke play, recreational play, whatever. It's just a great hole.

David Thomas, course designer of the Brabazon, said dramatic golf was his goal when he molded this course. No doubt he has achieved it, particularly at the 18th, where you must carry water twice and deal with a myriad of other difficulties.

In his own words, he describes it thus: "The Brabazon has always been recognized as a good test of golf and a course where the better player is rewarded for well-executed shots . . . It's one of the most famous sports amphitheaters in the world."

Officials at the Brabazon call the 18th one of the hardest holes in golf, and standing on the tee, it's difficult to argue otherwise. The first factor you must consider is the wind, which should come as no surprise. This is England, after all. And, quite naturally, the prevailing wind is almost always in your face, coming slightly from the left. This forces a carry of nearly 260 yards over water and trees into a breeze. A drive pulled left or one that can't make the carry will end up wet and dead. And if you go too far

right off the tee, you are facing a second shot, back over the water, of perhaps 230 yards onto a severely sloping, three-tiered green protected by cavernous bunkers on either side.

The green is a course superintendent's delight. It is extremely long, and slopes from back to front, so there is as much as a four-club difference between a pin placement in the back of the putting surface and one in the front.

Thomas wanted an amphitheater, he wanted drama, and he wanted to send golfers home with something special to remember. He has accomplished it all at the superb Brabazon, particularly with its curtain-closing 18th. **JB**

**Course:** Pete Dye Golf Club

**Location:** Bridgeport, West Virginia, USA

**Hole:** No. 18

**Length:** 475 yards

**Par:** 4

**Designer:** Pete Dye

**Course Comment:** Simpson Creek comes into play on many of the holes at the Pete Dye Golf Club, but this is no creek. It's more like a river. And when it rains, the creek has some power behind it and flows pretty fast, so don't be fooled by the word creek.

A finishing hole to remember on a golf course you won't soon forget.

Most great golf courses leave you wanting more, so leave you with a lasting impression. This difficult hole scores well on both points.

You tee off on the left-hand side of Simpson Creek, which is as much as 50 feet wide at some points, so make sure you clear its waters. Only the forward tees spare you the challenge of hitting over the creek.

The fairway slopes and there is trouble on either side with a stone wall on the right and water on the left. To make matters worse there's also some thick fescue, which some like to call U.S. Open-like fescue.

Just when you think you've got past the worst, there's more. A rise in the middle of the fairway blocks you from seeing the green, and it's best to drive the cart up a ways to see exactly what you are shooting at. This blind shot makes for a fun way to finish.

The green is 44 yards deep with a lot of movement. There is a creek to the left and a deep bunker to the right. The back third of the green is almost out of play if you don't come in high enough. It's very tough to hold your ball, which most likely will roll off the green right into the creek. **TJ**

## No. ⑱  **CAPITOL HILL** (THE SENATOR COURSE)

**Course:** Capitol Hill (The Senator Course)

**Location:** Prattville, Alabama, USA

**Hole:** No. 18

**Length:** 457 yards

**Par:** 4

**Designer:** Robert Trent Jones Sr.

**Course Comment:** Capitol Hill is part of the famed Robert Trent Jones Golf Trail, a collection of courses in Alabama all designed by Jones. No. 18 at Capitol Hill's Senator layout is considered by many to be the toughest hole on the trail.

The Senator Course stands tall enough on its own to merit a visit, but when you consider that it is part of the Robert Trent Jones Golf Trail, it turns into what could be a legitimate 10-day golf adventure. And The Senator's 18th is both the finisher and the highlight of your round in Prattville.

It is the best hole on the course, and it also is the toughest. Not only is it the No. 1 handicap on the scorecard, but it also ranks in the 50 toughest golf holes played by the Nationwide Tour each year. The PGA Tour's developmental circuit plays its Tour Championship annually at The Senator, and in 2002, for example, the hole yielded just nine birdies and 50 bogeys. The par-4 hole played to an average of 4.316 strokes that year. And this by players on the cusp of qualifying for the PGA Tour cards.

This is a beautiful and tough golf hole. It doglegs left, and the landing area off the tee is protected by three bunkers on the left side. From there, a large lake runs down the left side of the fairway all the way to the green.

The putting surface is enormous, and if you land on the front and the pin is in the back you could have a putt of up to 50 yards. Chris Couch, who won the 2003 Nationwide Tour Championship despite leaving himself in such a position on No. 18, had this to say in his post-tournament news conference: "I was on the green, but I was thinking to myself, 'Putt? I've still got half a wedge.' " **JB**

# KILLARNEY GOLF & FISHING CLUB (KILLEEN COURSE)

**Course:** Killarney Golf & Fishing Club (Killeen Course)

**Location:** Mahony's Point, Killarney, Ireland

**Hole:** No. 18

**Length:** 411 yards

**Par:** 4

**Designer:** Eddie Hackett, Dr. W. O'Sullivan

**Course Comment:** Killarney Golf Club is home to two outstanding tracks, the Killeen Course and the Mahony's Point Course, both considered among the top 100 courses in the British Isles. The Lackabane Course is the newest at the club.

The flagship of the three courses, Killeen is truly one of the greatest courses in the country. At 7,080 yards it will certainly challenge the longest of hitters, and with water on almost every hole accuracy is essential.

There are differences and similarities between the Killeen and Mahony's Point Courses. One thing they have in common is that both finish with excellent holes. But while the Mahony's Point round ends with a par 3, the Killeen finishes up with a very challenging par 4.

You need a good, straight drive from the elevated tee on the 411-yard par-4 18th. It's important to be in position for your second shot. You want to create the best possible location because there isn't much room for error on the approach shot, which must carry the water to a challenging green.

The Killeen Course has many great holes, and each golfer has his or her favorite. You'll find yourself spoilt for choice.

The Killeen Course is consistently rated among the very best courses in the world and has hosted many of the major championships, including the 1991 and 1992 Irish Open Golf Championship, won both times by the great Nick Faldo. It also hosted the 1996 Curtis Cup. **TJ**

**Course:** Gary Player Country Club

**Location:** Sun City, South Africa

**Hole:** No. 18

**Length:** 483 yards

**Par:** 4

**Designer:** Gary Player

**Course Comment:** Ernie Els had 28 consecutive sub-par rounds during the Nedbank Golf Challenge before the streak ended in the first round of the 2003 event.

## No. ⑱  GARY PLAYER COUNTRY CLUB

The demanding tee shot on Gary Player Country Club's boomerang-shaped 18th hole has made many players feel their collars tighten during the annual Nedbank Challenge, as there is little margin for error on the distance of this drive. If it is hit too short, the ball won't make it to the corner on this sharp dogleg-left hole and the angle for the tricky second shot will be made that much tougher. If it goes straight but too far through the fairway, it will find trees and thick rough. If it is hit too far left, it will find more trees or a pond that must be carried on the approach.

Wherever your drive lands, the approach won't be easy. In addition to carrying the water, the ball must avoid deep bunkers at the front left and back of the small, undulating putting surface.

Three-time Nedbank Challenge winner Ernie Els (1999, 2000, 2002) clinched his dominating, eight-stroke victory in 2002 with a final-round 63 that included four birdies in the final five holes, capped off by a birdie at No. 18. But the dangers of the finishing hole were made clear to Els during the 2003 event, when he bogeyed the hole each of the final two rounds. **KA**

**BELOW** *Nick Price of Zimbabwe plays his second shot on the 18th hole of the Gary Player Course, December 2000.*

**Course:** Patriot Golf Club

**Location:** Owasso, Oklahoma, USA

**Hole:** No. 18

**Length:** 432 yards

**Par:** 4

**Designer:** Robert Trent Jones Jr.

**Course Comment:** The Patriot Golf Club, which opened in 2010, is home to the Folds of Honor Foundation scholarship program to benefit the families of U.S. troops disabled or killed in Iraq and Afghanistan. Its founder is Major Dan Rooney, the only PGA golf professional who's also a certified Air Force fighter jet pilot. For information on how to contribute, visit www.patriotgolfclub.com.

# No. ⑱ PATRIOT GOLF CLUB

Each Labor Day at Patriot Golf Club, Patriot Golf Day is held to benefit families of U.S. troops disabled or killed in Iraq and Afghanistan. So far, it has raised more than $5 million and counting.

This is an unbelievably worthy cause, and is deserving of great attention. But there is more than just fantastic charitable events taking place at Patriot Golf Club. There is also some wonderful golf.

It was important to those behind the Patriot Golf Club to bring in a renowned golf architect to make sure the golf was outstanding. Robert Trent Jones Jr. fit the bill. One of his favorite axioms deals with making sure to get the first and last holes right because of the impressions they make.

With a 150-foot launching pad at No. 1, he certainly made an impression. And, at 18, which we now discuss, he nailed it as well.

Leading to No. 18, there are dense woods and uplands prairie, limestone canyons, and lowland meadows. Such is the case at No. 18 as well. But the finishing hole adds one new element to the equation just to give one last twist to a player's round.

After the tee shot adjacent to a steep canyon, there is another shot across a canyon to a very shallow green that is protected by bunkers. It is quite a way to end a day. A great day of golf, and a great day of patriotism. **JB**

**Course:** Shoal Creek Golf Club

**Location:** Birmingham, Alabama, USA

**Hole:** No. 18

**Length:** 445 yards

**Par:** 4

**Designer:** Jack Nicklaus

**Course Comment:** Shoal Creek has played host to the 1984 and the 1990 PGA Championships and the 1986 U.S. Amateur. When the 1990 PGA Championship was held at Shoal Creek, No. 18 was the toughest-ranked hole on the course.

Nestled between Oak Mountain and Double Oak Mountain, in the rolling valleys of Birmingham, Alabama, is a golf course that is consistently rated among America's best. It has hosted major championships and endured a major controversy about its lack of integrated membership (which has since has been rectified) to maintain its rich tradition of excellent golf.

The Jack Nicklaus design offers a natural challenge from Nos. 1–18. The backdrop of Double Oak Mountain offers an awesome spectacle from anywhere on the course.

Your experience at Shoal Creek Golf Club begins even before you get on the course. The clubhouse is constructed in colonial Williamsburg style, right down to the authentic Flemish Bond brickwork. The clubhouse, pro shop, town meeting hall, and guest cottages are arranged in village fashion reminiscent of Williamsburg itself. And the crest over the clubhouse front door is a replica of that of the Governor's Palace in Williamsburg.

The golf experience is as rich in tradition as the structure's architectural style. The beginning of the experience may start in the clubhouse, but its conclusion — the 18th hole — is a final memory worth holding.

The tee box at the 18th is immersed in trees: left, right, and rear. It feels as if you are striking your tee ball from the midst of a thick forest, and there's good reason for that. You are. Escaping this natural tunnel of trees isn't actually a terribly difficult chore. Just keep it straight and start it low. But, this is where the leisurely part of the 18th hole ends.

The approach shot is an exercise in precision, for there is danger in all places except your point of aim. The green is elevated, and is higher on both the right and left than it is in the middle. There is a smattering of small traps on the right and a long strange-shaped bunker running leanly on the left. Further left is a water hazard, but you really would have to be errant to bring the water into play.

The green offers the possibility for some tantalizing pin placements. Three separate levels are available, and the approach would have to be on the same level as the pin, or else two-putts are your best hope. **JB**

## No. ⑱   **SEMINOLE GOLF CLUB**

**Course:** Seminole Golf Club

**Location:** North Palm Beach, Florida, USA

**Hole:** No. 18

**Length:** 417 yards

**Par:** 4

**Designer:** Donald Ross

**Course Comment:** The prestigious George Coleman Invitational, reserved for the country's top mid-amateur and senior amateur golfers, is held annually at Seminole.

When you think of Donald Ross, palm trees and surf probably aren't the first things that pop into your mind. But Seminole Golf Club — one of the nation's most prestigious clubs in one of the nation's most prestigious cities — is considered one of the two or three best golf-course masterpieces ever created by the renowned architect.

Seminole's strong finishing hole is one of the reasons why. It features a tee box that sits atop the dunes with stunning views of the Atlantic Ocean. The view toward the dogleg-left fairway, however, isn't quite as pleasant, as the tee shot must be played through a chute of trees to a landing area guarded by sprawling fairway bunkers at the corner.

That leaves golfers with a difficult uphill approach to a narrow green that is guarded by a deep bunker to the right and dunes to the left. As always on a links golf course, the wind can dramatically affect shots and distances from one round to the next, making club selection key.

During the prime of his career, the legendary Ben Hogan often spent several weeks at Seminole in preparation for the start of his season. No doubt Seminole's 18th hole prepared him well. **KA**

**Course:** The Olympic Club
(Lake Course)

**Location:** San Francisco, California, USA

**Hole:** No. 18

**Length:** 347 yards

**Par:** 4

**Designer:** Sam Whiting

**Course Comment:** They say this is one of the greatest finishing holes in all of golf. It's certainly one of the most photographed and painted holes in golf.

OPPOSITE *The 18th hole on the Lake Course at The Olympic Club.*

## No. ⑱ THE OLYMPIC CLUB
### (LAKE COURSE)

Nearly a third of the field during the second round of the 1998 U.S. Open at The Olympic Club made bogey or worse on the 347-yard finishing hole, the second-shortest par 4 on the course.

The players didn't like it. And the USGA didn't like it. And it might have cost The Olympic Club in the future. David Fay, then the USGA executive director, said the following year: "Clearly, if we return to Olympic for a U.S. Open, we're going to have to do something with that green."

Well, The Olympic Club had already changed the slope of the green.

But how do you think you would do on this green? It's still very challenging, especially when you're not a member of the PGA Tour. The putting problem centers on the topography. The green is very small and narrow. It also slopes severely from back to front, making any pin position in the back two-thirds of the green very tricky.

From the tee, this fairly straight hole doesn't look very difficult. It's pretty, but not intimidating. The key is to keep the second shot below the hole. The green is not only small but there are bunkers on both sides. **TJ**

---

**Course:** Lakeside Country Club
(West Course)

**Location:** KyungKi Do, Seoul, South Korea

**Hole:** No. 18

**Length:** 410 yards

**Par:** 4

**Designer:** Nakano Ryu, Iksung Yoon

**Course Comment:** Juli Inkster sank a 12-foot putt on Lakeside's 18th hole to win the 1997 Samsung World Championship, defeating Helen Alfredsson and Kelly Robbins in a sudden-death playoff.

## No. ⑱ LAKESIDE COUNTRY CLUB
### (WEST COURSE)

Similar to many holes in Japan, the finishing hole on Lakeside Country Club's West Course has two greens, each for use in different seasons. The putting surface to the right is used most of the year, making a drive to the left side of the fairway the correct play off the tee. That allows golfers to avoid a tree that encroaches on the right side of the landing area, effectively blocking the approach to the green from that angle. The front of the green is also guarded by a pot bunker that must usually be carried with the relatively short second shot.

Lakeside's West Course has played host to several top professional events, including the 1997 Samsung World Championship of Women's Golf, the Asian Tour's SK Telekom Open, and the Korean PGA Tour's Maekyung Open, and usually proves to be a tough test.

Mark Calcavecchia of the United States was one of only six players under par for the week when he won the 2004 Maekyung Open with a score of six under par. And in the 1997 Samsung World Championship, Juli Inkster of the United States tied for first with a score of eight under par over 72 holes, then prevailed in a playoff. **KA**

# SAN ROQUE GOLF CLUB
## (OLD COURSE)

**Course:** San Roque Golf Club (Old Course)

**Location:** San Roque, Spain

**Hole:** No. 18

**Length:** 428 yards

**Par:** 4

**Designer:** Dave Thomas

**Course Comment:** In the foothills of the Sierra Bermeja, the peace and natural beauty of Andalucia is complemented by a stylish retreat where five-star facilities and two 18-hole championship golf courses are enhanced by a friendly atmosphere.

Between Jerez and Marbella, almost at the tip of the Iberian peninsula, you will find the San Roque Golf Club. It's location might be secluded but the course itself is easy to locate when looking for the best courses in Europe.

Where might you find it? Near the top, of course.

Home to the Old Course and now New Course (opened in 2003), San Roque provides both the beauty and challenge you would expect to find at such a prestigious golf club.

Designed by Dave Thomas with bunkers redesigned by Spain's golf hero, Seve Ballesteros, the Old Course is rated amongst the finest in Europe.

The finishing holes stand above the rest. And 18 might just be the best.

This par 4 is a dogleg left with water along the right side. The fairway is pretty generous, so take advantage. There is a tree near the green along the left side that can come into play if you are in the left rough.

The center or right side offers a great angle into a green with some water on the right and a bunker in the back left. The green is typical for the others on the Old Course: fast, contoured, and true, rewarding well-judged putts and punishing anything else. **TJ**

**Course:** Half Moon Bay Golf Links
(Old Course)

**Location:** Half Moon Bay, California,
USA

**Hole:** No. 18

**Length:** 435 yards

**Par:** 4

**Designer:** Arnold Palmer,
Frank Duane, Arthur Hills

**Course Comment:** Half Moon
Bay's Old Course, formerly known
as the Links Course, was originally
designed in 1973. It received a
makeover by Arthur Hills in 2000.

# No. ⑱ HALF MOON BAY GOLF LINKS (OLD COURSE)

No. 18 at Half Moon Bay is a magnificent finishing hole, a challenging test that features stunning views of the Pacific, tricky ocean breezes, and a forced carry on the final approach of the round.

The hole sits high above the rocky, rugged shoreline that stretches along the entire right side of the hole, and the winds that normally blow hard off the water may actually help golfers keep their tee shots away from the cliffs. Hit too far of a drive, however, and your ball may be swallowed by a wide ravine that cuts across the fairway. The ravine must be carried for the second shot to a green that is nestled between the cliffs on the right and a hillside at the rear. The putting surface is protected by bunkers on three sides — the left, right, and rear. The bunker at the front left is a recent addition, preventing golfers from bailing out on the approach.

The hole was formerly framed by thick vegetation behind the green, but now the swanky Ritz-Carlton Half Moon Bay is an imposing presence at the left and rear — often giving golfers a gallery as they play their final shots of the day. **KA**

**Course:** Fox Meadow Golf and
Country Club

**Location:** Stratford, Prince Edward
Island, Canada

**Hole:** No. 18

**Length:** 544 yards

**Par:** 5

**Designer:** Robert Heaslip &
Associates

**Course Comment:** This golf course is
so good that they couldn't pick out
just one signature hole. So No. 7 and
No. 18 were chosen as co-signature
holes. Still, there are others worthy
of such distinction.

## No. ⓲  FOX MEADOW GOLF AND COUNTRY CLUB

This finishing hole is considered the fourth most difficult on the golf course. There are four sets of tees to soften the blow if you aren't the most skilled golfer in the world. From the red tees, this hole plays at 449 yards. Plenty of choices on the tee box.

A challenging par 5 with plenty of distance is a great way to end the round. And Fox Meadow has teed up a dandy of a hole. Hopefully your slice is long gone by now because trees are lined up all along the right side.

With two bunkers along the left side of the fairway, straight is your best option. Speaking of straight, your second shot needs to be on line as well. If you decide to lay up, watch out for the one bunker on the right side about 100 yards out.

If you are going for the green, this is a tough uphill shot with trouble (yes, more trees) along both sides of the fairway. There are also two tricky bunkers on the right and another to the left of the green.

The putting surface is no gimmie. Getting there in two is great, unless you three-putt. Then the glory fades just a bit. **TJ**

**Course:** Honors Course

**Location:** Ooltewah, Tennessee, USA

**Hole:** No. 18

**Length:** 451 yards

**Par:** 4

**Designer:** P.B. Dye, Pete Dye

**Course Comment:** The club hosted
the U.S. Amateur in 1991, and the
Curtis Cup in 1994, and the men's
NCAA Championships were held here
in 1996, won by Tiger Woods.

## No. ⓲  HONORS COURSE

The final hole on the Honors Course is a gentle dogleg to the right. Off the tee players want to favor the left center of the fairway. If you spray it to the right on this hole you will find the trees and blow any chance of making par on this hole.

The second shot on this long par 4 requires pinpoint accuracy — unless you are on the PGA Tour you will really need to concentrate on this stroke.

On the right side you have a crazy bunker, which sits some 10–15 feet below the green. You don't want to be in this bunker because it will really limit your chance at par. And on the left you have a large tree that comes into play and tends to knock balls down like an NBA shot-blocker. You can avoid the tree it you hit to the left, but it will take some luck, so try to hit the center of the green.

The putting surface on this hole is fairly big and somewhat fast. Everything feeds to the right on this hole, like any Pete Dye course, so don't think any putt will necessarily be good.

This is a classic finishing hole to a classic course, which really was created for the classic player. **GE**

**Course:** Colleton River Plantation (Dye Course)

**Location:** Bluffton, South Carolina, USA

**Hole:** No. 18

**Length:** 441 yards

**Par:** 4

**Designer:** Pete Dye

**Course Comment:** While the Nicklaus Course at Colleton River gets plenty of attention, the Pete Dye Course deserves the same accolades. Dye's 18-hole gem is perched next to a swamp right along the Colleton River.

# No. ⑱ COLLETON RIVER PLANTATION
## (DYE COURSE)

Colleton River Plantation stands alone. The 1999 *Golf Magazine* Top 100 Golf Courses in the U.S. ranking included the Dye Course, making Colleton River the only private golf community in the world to have had two courses on the same Top 100 list. And the most amazing thing is that the Dye Course was only six months old at the time. Now that's growing up in a hurry.

No. 18 provides a spectacular view and an even more spectacular way to finish. Talk about dramatic endings. This 441-yard par-4 dogleg left has everything you would expect from a thrilling conclusion. The fairway makes a slow bend to the left with water hugging the left side from tee to green. There are some very difficult bunkers in between the fairway and the water on that side. They aren't the best places to be, but at least they save you from the water. Trees can come into play on your tee shot if you slice it right. Straight is by far your best option.

A good tee shot sets you up for an iron to the green. And this green is unique to the Dye Course. It's the deepest green on this 18. But, like most of the others, it is well guarded with bunkers. **TJ**

**Course:** Inverness Club

**Location:** Toledo, Ohio, USA

**Hole:** No. 18

**Length:** 354 yards

**Par:** 4

**Designer:** Donald Ross

**Course Comment:** In a 2000 makeover of Inverness, Arthur Hills restored many features of Donald Ross's original design, reclaiming 15 feet of putting surface, returning a bunker to the left rear of the green, and replacing the first bunker on the right with three small pot bunkers.

## No. ⑱ INVERNESS CLUB

This hole's short length has always provided an opportunity for an heroic, tournament-winning birdie on the climactic final hole of the many major championships held at Inverness. However, don't be fooled: short doesn't necessarily mean easy. Bunkers line the landing area for most drives on both sides of the twisting fairway, and the nearby front of the green is also surrounded by bunkers, creating a dramatic visual from the tee. As if that weren't enough, the putting surface slopes sharply from front to back, and there is a small swale to the right of the green given the appropriate moniker of "Death Valley." No less an authority than Jack Nicklaus called No. 18 at Inverness "the hardest easy hole I've ever played."

Of course, there's one shot that has forever given Inverness' finishing hole a place in golf lore. Tied with Greg Norman on the 72nd hole, Bob Tway looked as if he had been defeated by the sand in the final round of the 1986 PGA Championship, landing in a tough position in the right-hand greenside bunker. Instead, he blasted it into the hole for a birdie, defeating Greg Norman and beginning Norman's run of bad luck in majors. **KA**

**Course:** Troon North Golf Club (Monument Course)

**Location:** Scottsdale, Arizona, USA

**Hole:** No. 18

**Length:** 444 yards

**Par:** 4

**Designer:** Tom Weiskopf, Jay Morrish

**Course Comment:** Set against the backdrop of Pinnacle Peak and the McDowell Mountains, Monument is a classic desert-style target course carved into dramatic terrain.

## No. ⑱ TROON NORTH GOLF CLUB (MONUMENT COURSE)

The sand surrounding holes leading to No. 18 (courtesy of Mother Nature, rather than the duo of architects) comes into play frequently, and there are some spectacular views from elevated spots along the route, the first being from the tee.

Length and accuracy are your friends on No. 18. Two long, precise shots are your only chances for par. The tee shot is normally played into the wind and the blazing sun, and must be aimed for the fairway's left-center, avoiding two large bunkers as the hole bends left to the clubhouse. The approach shot must carry a ravine to a large green that's protected on both sides by sand. It's a classic finish to an unconventional golf course in the heart of the high Sonoran Desert. Shapely ridges and peaks provide a backdrop that silhouettes against the setting.

Vegetation is lush and wildlife abundant, with rabbits, lizards, and the occasional coyote scurrying across a fairway. Holes that carry over dry desert washes and route around towering saguaro cacti are typical here.

Monument is young, but it is an immaculate desert golf benchmark. Quite simply, all 18 holes exist in complete harmony with the desert. **KLL**

**Course:** Valderrama Golf Club

**Location:** San Roque, Cadiz, Spain

**Hole:** No. 18

**Length:** 454 yards

**Par:** 4

**Designer:** Robert Trent Jones Sr.

**Course Comment:** In the 2003 Volvo Masters Andalucia, No. 18 played to a stroke average of 4.111, yielding 36 birdies compared with 55 bogeys and three double bogeys.

# No. ⑱   VALDERRAMA GOLF CLUB

No. 18 at Valderrama has ended the chances of many competitors in the steady stream of top professional events played at Valderrama since the 1997 Ryder Cup brought the course international notoriety in 1997.

This formidable finishing hole is a tight dogleg left lined by cork trees and thick rough. Players are tempted to hit an iron off the tee because of the narrow landing area, but that strategy will leave a long approach to a slightly crowned green that is guarded by bunkers at the front right, front left, and rear. Those who dare to attempt a drive over the trees on the left can set up an easier angle for the approach.

Native Spaniard Miguel Angel Jimenez, valiantly attempting to defeat the world's best player in front of friendly galleries in his home country, was one of those who has felt the sting of Valderrama's 18th. He bogeyed the hole twice on the final day of the 1999 World Golf Championships-American Express Championship — once on the final hole of regulation and once in a sudden-death playoff to hand the victory to Tiger Woods. In 2000, Canadian Mike Weir won by two shots at Valderrama in the American Express Championship. **KA**

| |
|---|
| **Course:** Butler National Golf Club |
| **Location:** Oak Brook, Illinois, USA |
| **Hole:** No. 18 |
| **Length:** 466 yards |
| **Par:** 4 |
| **Designer:** George Fazio, Tom Fazio |
| **Course Comment:** Few players have felt the sting of Butler National's final hole like Peter Jacobsen. In back-to-back years (1988–1989), Jacobsen came to the 18th with a chance to win the Western Open but double-bogeyed the hole both times to finish runner-up. |

# No. ⑱  BUTLER NATIONAL GOLF CLUB

For 17 years Butler National was home to the PGA Tour's Western Open and for 17 years the George and Tom Fazio-designed treasure was center-stage to some of the game's most epic duels.

In 1979 Larry Nelson stunned Ben Crenshaw in a classic playoff, and six years later Scott Verplank became the first player in the modern era to win the Western as an amateur. Throughout the years Butler National was a perfect setting for these classic duels, most of which seemed to turn and terminate at the par-4 18th.

The 466-yard hole curves to the right from the tee and then back to the left closer to the green. The drive is from an elevated tee box and must be precise, avoiding Salt Creek which runs down the left of the land area.

Long irons are usually needed for approach shots to a small putting surface that is framed by Salt Creek on three sides. Only the front right portion of the putting surface is clear of the water hazard, leaving players a narrow window through which to run a low approach shot.

The green slopes from back to front and, as more than one potential champion has learned, any birdie opportunity must come from below. **RH**

**Course:** Mount Juliet Golf Club

**Location:** Tomastown, County Kilkenny, Ireland

**Hole:** No. 18

**Length:** 433 yards

**Par:** 4

**Designer:** Jack Nicklaus

**Course Comment:** Mount Juliet opened in 1991 with a match featuring golfing legends Christy O'Connor Sr. and Jack Nicklaus.

**BELOW** *Tiger Woods of the USA hits his second shot on the 18th hole at Mount Juliet, September 2002.*

## No. ⑱ MOUNT JULIET GOLF CLUB

Mount Juliet Estate is 1,500 acres of old Irish elegance, with an elegant Georgian mansion surrounded by lush pastures and rolling woodlands along the River Nore. Hunting, fishing, and equestrian sports are all offered, but golfers will be most interested in the Jack Nicklaus-designed course that has been woven through the middle of this spectacular setting.

The 18th hole is one of the most lovely — and perilous — parkland holes in all of the British Isles. Golfers who hit a long tee shot to the center of the fairway have the best chance to fare well on an approach that's difficult at best. The second shot, which often must be hit from a downhill lie, must carry a pond directly in front of a sloping green that is built atop a stone wall and beautifully framed by a cluster of flowering trees.

Mount Juliet played host to the 2002 World Golf Championships-American Express Championship, which Tiger Woods won with an amazing 25-under-par total, and again served as host for the 2004 event. The PGA European Tour's Irish Open also was held here from 1993 to 1995, with three worthy champions: Nick Faldo, Bernhard Langer, and Sam Torrance. **KA**

**Course:** San Lorenzo

**Location:** Quinta do Lago, The Algarve, Portugal

**Hole:** No. 18

**Length:** 382 yards

**Par:** 4

**Designer:** Joe Lee

**Course Comment:** The birdlife to be found in the waters surrounding the 18th is spectacular. Just as well, because for many players that may be the only redeeming feature of this demanding par 4.

## No. ⓳ SAN LORENZO

It is probably fitting that San Lorenzo's finishing hole is defended by the waters that make up part of the Rio Formosa, a huge nature reserve that architect Joe Lee has made good use of in designing this highly acclaimed and challenging course.

The 18th is a dogleg left that calls for a tee shot to be played over water, and then a second shot that also has to be played over water. If ever a hole needed a drop zone then this is it — and it gets its fair share of use.

As with most doglegs, the more you cut off its corner the shorter the shot into the green. Of course the danger then is that the ball can end up in the water. Play for the wide part of the fairway and a longer shot into the green is called for, and the last thing you want approaching this green is a long shot.

One more thing, if ever there was a hole where you needed one more club, then this is it. Better to be at the back of the green with a long putt than risk going for the perfect shot and ending up in the water.

The 18th is a dramatic hole that can ruin a scorecard. It shouldn't really pose a problem for low handicap players, but higher handicappers could find themselves perfecting their dropping techniques. **AT**

**Course:** Bay Hill Club & Lodge

**Location:** Orlando, Florida, USA

**Hole:** No. 18

**Length:** 441 yards

**Par:** 4

**Designer:** Dick Wilson,
Arnold Palmer

**Course Comment:** In the 2001 Bay Hill Invitational, Tiger Woods held a one-shot lead on No. 18. But he hooked his drive left on No. 18, and it looked for all the world to be heading out of bounds. But Woods received a fortuitous bounce when the ball hit a fan and caromed back toward the fairway. Woods then hit a rifling 6-iron to the 18th green and sank a birdie putt to win his second straight Bay Hill Invitational.

**BELOW AND OPPOSITE** *Two views of the 18th hole at the Bay Hill Club & Lodge.*

# No. ⑱ BAY HILL CLUB & LODGE

Arnold Palmer, "The King" himself, fell in love with Orlando in 1965 when he played an exhibition at Bay Hill with a young golfer named Jack Nicklaus. Palmer shot 66 that day and was smitten with the course. He decided to make Bay Hill his winter home and, with a group of partners, purchased the club and lodge in 1970.

Although the world has since discovered Palmer's little secret in central Florida, he has not changed his mind about his adopted hometown. "I loved Bay Hill from the first time I saw it, and I loved the area," Palmer said. "Orlando is a great town and it is a wonderful place to play golf."

Palmer's club is now called Arnold Palmer's Bay Hill Club & Lodge, and luxury homes and a handsome lodge have replaced the trees that used to line the fairways. But, largely at Palmer's insistence, Bay Hill has retained its charm and beauty. Palmer is currently the primary owner along with two of his associates.

When Palmer came on board, he added his design touches to the course's original layout. Among his changes was to add some teeth to No. 18. A narrow fairway requires the tee shot to be on the left side in order to allow for an approach to the crescent-shaped green, which is protected on the right-front by a pond and on the left by two large bunkers.

The 18th has been the site of many dramatic finishing shots at the Bay Hill PGA Tour stop; among the most exciting was in 1990 when Robert Gamez holed out from the fairway with a 7-iron to finish with an eagle and win what was then called the Nestlé Invitational.

Every year, the world gets a first-hand look at Orlando golf when watching the Bay Hill Invitational. And the 18th is the capping hole on Orlando's "most famous course." This city has become enraptured with the game and can now legitimately be called a first-class golf destination. Need more proof? Just ask Arnold Palmer. He'll tell you this city, and the 18th hole at his beloved Bay Hill Club, is fit for a king. **JB**

## No. ⑱ CYPRESS POINT CLUB

**Course:** Cypress Point Club

**Location:** Pebble Beach, California, USA

**Hole:** No. 18

**Length:** 346 yards

**Par:** 4

**Designer:** Alister MacKenzie

**Course Comment:** Like most golf courses along 17 Mile Drive, wind is a big factor. The holes are difficult enough on a calm day, but throw in the wind factor and your scorecard begins to look like a mobile home after a hurricane.

When a golf course is considered by many to be the greatest in the world, there isn't room for a "bad" hole on the course. And Cypress Point, regarded by astute golf observers as one of the world's best, certainly doesn't have one. In fact, the word "bad" doesn't exist in any form at this Pacific Ocean wonderland. Of the 18 great golf holes, however, there are some that certainly stand out.

Welcome to one of those standout holes. While 15, 16, and 17 are more famous, the 346-yard par-4 No. 18 helps complete an amazing series of golf holes. Most people have read or heard about these holes, and have no doubt seen them countless times on television. But you must play them to really appreciate them.

No. 18 is a dogleg right to an elevated green. You must hit your drive by the right-hand corner group of cypress trees in order to have a clear view into the green. Otherwise, you must lay up.

Your approach shot is the big shot here. You have to carry it up over a big cypress tree that leans out over the fairway and still try to land the ball below the hole because the green is contoured into the natural terrain and severely slopes from back to front.

If it sounds hard, it's because it is hard. **TJ**

## No. ⑱ BULLE ROCK

**Course:** Bulle Rock

**Location:** Havre de Grace, Maryland, USA

**Hole:** No. 18

**Length:** 485 yards

**Par:** 4

**Designer:** Pete Dye

**Course Comment:** Welcome to one of the top courses not only in Maryland but the entire East Coast. In fact, Bulle Rock is recognized by most of the top golf magazines as one of America's premier upscale golf courses.

Here's what Joe Logan of the *Philadelphia Inquirer* said about Bulle Rock: "If you told me I could only play one golf course for the rest of my life, and I could choose between world-famous Pine Valley and Bulle Rock, well I'd need some time to think about it."

This course is spectacular. There is no other word to describe it. And the finishing hole is "Rock" solid. It doesn't get any better than this.

The hole is a dogleg left with water on the left side.

Bulle Rock has plenty of water, including three lakes. The lakes are replenished by a three-mile pipeline, which was constructed specifically for the golf course and feeds from the Susquehanna River.

Just to reach the fairway from the back tees is 214 yards. To get within 200 yards you need a drive of about 280 yards. The fairway is tight with trees at the start of the hole on the left, and all along the right side.

There is a bunker on the right side of the fairway about 100 yards from the green. Speaking of the green, it's narrow and is cut into the water. Anything long is wet, unless it rolls off the green and into the rocks which frame the putting surface. **TJ**

| |
|---|
| **Course:** Chantilly Vineuil Golf Club |
| **Location:** Chantilly, France |
| **Hole:** No. 18 |
| **Length:** 403 yards |
| **Par:** 4 |
| **Designer:** Tom Simpson |
| **Course Comment:** Chantilly's Vineuil Course has hosted the French Open a record 10 times, the last coming in 1990 when Ireland's Philip Walton edged out Bernhard Langer of Germany in a playoff. |

# No. ⑱  CHANTILLY VINEUIL GOLF CLUB

In a search for the game's most hallowed layouts, a golf historian would undoubtedly spend much of their time scouring the famous links courses of Scotland, England, and Ireland. Some courses however, disprove this general trend.

Consider, for example, Tom Simpson's Vineuil layout. Located in the Chantilly region of France — just a short, white-knuckled drive northeast of Paris — Simpson's gem is as demanding and rewarding today as it was when it opened in 1906.

Even at a lean 6,984 yards in length, Chantilly's Vineuil course has all the ingredients of a classic layout. The parkland course features contoured fairways that require more strategy than strength and angled greens that demand a well-placed drive in order to have any chance to make birdie.

Vineuil's par-4 18th is an example of Simpson's simplicity and a primary reason why the century-old layout is often compared to the game's most venerable layouts.

From the tee, the hole's length (403 yards) tempts players to hit driver but for this finish accuracy, not free-swinging power, is crucial. The best play is down the right center of the tree-lined fairway to set up the most forgiving approach to a rolling green.

Special attention should be paid to what portion of the green the hole is located. Approach shots must be positioned correctly on the putting surface, otherwise, a three-putt becomes likely. **RH**

**Course:** Royal Lytham & St. Annes

**Location:** St. Annes-on-Sea, Lancashire, England

**Hole:** No. 18

**Length:** 410 yards

**Par:** 4

**Designer:** Harry S. Colt

**Course Comment:** Here's the bad news. The fairways are narrow, the greens are small and mostly elevated, and it's windy on nearly every hole. The good news is you are playing at Royal Lytham & St. Annes.

BELOW *Michael Hoey of Ireland plays his second shot to the 18th green at Royal Lytham & St. Annes, July 2001.*

OPPOSITE *David Duval of the USA holes out on the 18th green at Royal Lytham & St. Annes, July 2001.*

# No. ⑱   ROYAL LYTHAM & ST. ANNES

Holes 16, 17, and 18 have produced some of the most memorable moments in major championship history.

But standing behind the 18th green with the grand Victorian clubhouse next to you is a special moment you will never forget. History has walked up and down that fairway, so take it all in while you can.

Take a moment and travel back to 1969. The spot you now find yourself is the same spot from which Tony Jacklin hit his "immaculate" drive during the 1969 British Open. Jacklin's win was the first for a British player since 1951 and helped recharge the game in England.

And now here you stand. Ready to recharge for one final hole. And what a way to go out. Your drive must be straight and avoid the bunkers on both sides. There are even cross-bunkers in the middle of the fairway.

The better the drive, the better your approach shot, which will usually make or break you on this hole. The green is very well protected by bunkers.

There are four sets of tees on this classic. The closest is 309 yards with the back tees set at 410 yards. **TJ**

**Course:** Quinta do Lago

**Location:** The Algarve, Portugal

**Hole:** No. 18

**Length:** 451 yards

**Par:** 4

**Designer:** William Mitchell

**Course Comment:** Quinta do Lago translates as "the farm by the lake." This course has hosted the Portuguese Open eight times.

## No. ⑱   QUINTA DO LAGO

Quinta do Lago winds through some pretty rolling country and eventually ends up back on the high ground for the final hole. This is a dogleg left par 4 that calls for an accurate tee shot to set up a chance of par. Hit the ball too far right off the tee and the ball can run through the fairway into the trees.

A long tee shot is needed since the shorter the iron into the flag, the better. The green slopes sharply from right to left and is well bunkered. Push the approach shot with the pin on the right-hand side and a hellish chip shot remains.

Those who do miss the green will hope the greenkeepers have cut the rough down, since the last shot anyone wants to play on this hole is a bunker-type explosion shot from long grass to a fast, sloping green.

Even those who hit the green will have a job two-putting since the slope of the green is such that there is no such thing as an easy two-putt unless the ball is very close. Par here is an excellent score. **AT**

**Course:** Harbour Town Golf Links

**Location:** Hilton Head Island, South Carolina, USA

**Hole:** No. 18

**Length:** 478 yards

**Par:** 4

**Designer:** Pete Dye, Jack Nicklaus

**Course Comment:** The Harbour Town Golf Links is often ranked as the top course in South Carolina, one of America's most saturated golf markets.

BELOW *A view of the 18th hole on Harbour Town Golf Links.*

OPPOSITE *Ted Purdy of the USA hits his tee shot on the 18th hole at Harbour Town Golf Links, April 2004.*

# No. ⓲ HARBOUR TOWN GOLF LINKS

Harbour Town Links, a beautiful place to play the game, is also beautifully deceptive. It is actually a relatively short golf course by today's standards, at 6,973 yards from the tips. And, when you consider it plays host each year to the PGA Tour's MCI Heritage, you'd think the pros would tear it up.

Think again.

Remember, the course might play a bit under 7,000 yards, but it is also a par 71. Length is not the issue at Harbour Town. It's all about positioning, and if you aren't hitting it straight, you will quickly find out why this course has a steep slope of 146. Brute strength is a luxury at times, but it isn't necessary here.

Unwavering consistency and unfailing accuracy are the keys to mastering Harbour Town. And, if you've kept your wits and have a decent round going by the time you get to the 18th hole, don't celebrate yet. There's a devil of a finisher waiting.

Highlighted by one of the most recognizable landmarks in golf, the red-and-white striped lighthouse, it seems stately and proper to be standing guard, because this is a hole that might leave you in need of rescue. On a course where length is not generally an issue, the 18th is an exception. It is a long par 4 that plays even longer if you take the safe approach.

The landing area on the right side is more wide open, but the direct approach is on the left side of the fairway, in a landing area that juts into Calibogue Sound, a body of water that lines the left side from tee to green. Yes, you need to be long — as on every hole at Harbour Town — but you also need to be straight. Appropriately, if you choose the more dangerous route near the water, the lighthouse is your aiming point. For all but the best of the best, it is extremely advisable to take the safer route on the right.

The green is protected on the left by the Sound and up front by a thin, long bunker. Going for the middle of the green or aiming for the pin is a risky proposition. It is more advisable to go for the right side of the green, no matter where the pin is placed. This allows you to avoid trouble, and if you happen to miss right, there is a bail-out area. This hole offers a wonderful way to finish a brilliant golf course. **JB**

**Course:** Vale do Lobo (Royal Course)

**Location:** Vale do Lobo, The Algarve, Portugal

**Hole:** No. 18

**Length:** 361 yards

**Par:** 4

**Designer:** Sir Henry Cotton, Rocky Roquemore

**Course Comment:** Vale do Lobo's 18th hole is the most photographed hole in all of Portugal, perhaps in all of Continental Europe.

## No. 🔞 VALE DO LOBO (ROYAL COURSE)

If ever a hole was proof that par 4s don't have to measure over 450 yards to be tough it is the 18th on Vale do Lobo's Royal Course. This hole should serve as a reminder to all golf-course architects that short can also mean dangerous. Look at the scorecard and the Royal's final hole looks like an easy par. Play it and that soon becomes anything but the case.

For a start the tee shot is made harder by pine trees that line both sides of the fairway. The natural tendency is to try to steer the ball through the trees. Golfers tighten up as a result and are often found playing their second shots from pine needles in amongst the trees. Even those who hit the fairway are not guaranteed to keep the ball on it. The fairway slopes from left to right, so that the ideal shot is one that starts down the right and draws back toward the center to hold the ball on the short grass.

Holding the ball on the green is no easy task either, since it falls away sharply from left to right. Any approach shot not hit with conviction can spin back down off the green leaving a tricky uphill chip shot to a sloping green. Disrespect this hole at your peril. **AT**

**Course:** Clustered Spires Golf Course

**Location:** Frederick, Maryland, USA

**Hole:** No. 18

**Length:** 468 yards

**Par:** 4

**Designer:** Ault, Clark & Associates

**Course Comment:** One of Maryland's top places to play, Clustered Spires emphasizes playability. The course offers a fun and exciting challenge to golfers of all skill levels in a timely manner.

## No. 🔞 CLUSTERED SPIRES GOLF COURSE

This hole is long. At 468 yards, you can hit your drive around 300 yards and still have a long way to go to reach the green. And from those back tees, it's a good 250 yards just to reach the fairway.

In between the tee and fairway is rough. And landing in there is a real rough way to begin this hole. But if you can't hit your drive 250 yards, you probably shouldn't be playing from the back tees anyway. There is out-of-bounds to the left and two large sycamore trees on the right.

The real fun on this hole begins (but doesn't end) at the tee. The best location to be is on the right side of the fairway. From the right, the green opens up and is a very large target to aim at.

The problem is that the fairway slopes right to left and it's not easy to keep your ball up on the right side. From the left side of the fairway, the green looks small and it's a much more difficult shot.

The green has two small bunkers on the right side and a large one along the entire left side — which comes into play when you are coming in from the left.

The green is two-tiered and three-putts are common. **TJ**

# PINEHURST
## (NO. 2 COURSE )

**Course:** Pinehurst (No. 2 Course)

**Location:** Pinehurst, North Carolina, USA

**Hole:** No. 18

**Length:** 417 yards

**Par:** 4

**Designer:** Donald Ross

**Course Comment:** *Golf Magazine* rated the No. 2 Course fourth best in the "Top 100 Courses You Can Play in the U.S."

**BELOW** *Jack Nicklaus tees off on the 18th hole on the No. 2 Course at Pinehurst Country Club, July 1994.*

The great designer Donald Ross once said of Pinehurst No. 2 that it is "the fairest test of championship golf" that he has ever designed.

No. 18 is a fantastic finish to a fantastic golf course. It's the final hole rounding off a banquet of golf. The fairway heads uphill and bends slightly left to right. Don't consider your work done if you nail the fairway on the drive. In fact, you'll have to do better than that. You not only have to hit the fairway, but you have to hit the correct side of the fairway. And which side that is depends on which side the flag is on.

A hole located on the left benefits more from a drive to the right side. If you are coming in from the right, the deep swale in the Ross green is less of a factor — and that's a good thing. A right-hand pin location means you want your tee shot to find the left side. But be aware of the danger presented by the deep fairway bunker.

Pinehurst No. 2 Course has been the site of more championships than any other course in the country. **TJ**

**Course:** Sunningdale Golf Club

**Location:** Sunningdale, Ascot, Berkshire, England

**Hole:** No. 18

**Length:** 411 yards

**Par:** 4

**Designer:** Willie Park

**Course Comment:** Built in 1910, Sunningdale's two courses are private. Visitors need a handicap certificate of 18 or better and a letter of introduction from their own club to play.

The springy turf is remarkable, and the wonderful combination of heather, bracken, pine, and silver birch makes for truly great scenic beauty. As with many of these historic golf courses, it's important to take a few moments to think of the great players and great memories that have walked this sacred ground.

The final hole is one worth remembering. Nos. 5, 10, and 15 may get more compliments, but this 411-yard dogleg right is right up there with the very best in England.

The hole slopes right to left toward plenty of awaiting gorse and rough. You can forget any chance of birdie if you land in there. The rough also waits on the left to catch any drives not hit with sufficient fade. Again, that's some serious trouble.

With the clubhouse as a backdrop, the players will hit over bunkers that break the fairway 100 yards out. The green is no sunny stroll in the country. The putting surface slopes from left to right with costly bunkers on the right side.

A great way to finish a round to remember. So when you are done, head into the clubhouse and buy a round to commemorate this time. **TJ**

## No. ⑱ COLONIAL COUNTRY CLUB

**Course:** Colonial Country Club

**Location:** Fort Worth, Texas, USA

**Hole:** No. 18

**Length:** 434 yards

**Par:** 4

**Designer:** John Bredemus, Perry Maxwell

**Course Comment:** At the 1971 Colonial, winner Gene Littler became the first player to eagle the 18th.

The finishing hole at Hogan's Alley presents contenders with a final chance at birdie — or an opportunity at disaster — in the PGA Tour's annual Colonial, which has featured a who's who list of past champions. The dogleg left features trees on both sides that can affect wayward shots. The approach must be hit with precision to a green protected by a pond on the left, a deep bunker front left, and a pair of nasty bunkers on the right.

In 1995, Tom Lehman made a 24-foot putt on No. 18 to edge Craig Parry by a stroke, only the third time in 49 years that Colonial's 72nd hole had been birdied for a victory. In 2000, Phil Mickelson clinched his two-shot victory with a long birdie putt here.

Of course, because of its well-protected fairway and green, the hole also presents the opportunity for a big number. In 1973, Bruce Crampton had led the tournament from the start, but made a double-bogey 6 on the 18th hole to lose by a stroke to Tom Weiskopf.

In 2003, when No. 1-ranked female Annika Sorenstam made her PGA Tour debut, she parred the 18th both times she played it. **KA**

## No. ⑱ WILDHORSE GOLF CLUB

**Course:** Wildhorse Golf Club

**Location:** Henderson, Nevada, USA

**Hole:** No. 18

**Length:** 398 yards

**Par:** 4

**Designer:** Bob Cupp, Hubert Green

**Course Comment:** This former host site of a PGA Tour event may not be the best course in Henderson any more but it's still very enjoyable. The locals still seem to like it, and that's usually a very good sign.

Even great golf courses require change. Even a historic venue such as Augusta National needs to adjust to the times and improve the overall "playability" of the golf course.

Wildhorse Golf Club galloped onto the golf scene in 1959. But you wouldn't recognize that golf course today. As good as it might have been, Wildhorse is strides better than it was on opening day.

Hubert Green and Bob Cupp redesigned the golf course in 1987. The results were dramatic. The Southern Nevada Golf Association rated it as the No. 1 course in 1993. But they weren't done. Maybe No. 1 wasn't good enough, but in 1996, the course was upgraded again, including the opening of a new 15,000 square foot clubhouse.

Speaking of No. 1. Check out No. 18. This 398-yard par 4 has a large water hazard on the right side of the fairway that you must deal with right away. Your tee shot must avoid the water looming on the right and find the fairway.

Don't rush your second shot. Stand over it for a moment and enjoy the view and the great challenge that lies in front of you. Water is in front and on the left of the green with a bunker between the water and the front of the green. **TJ**

**Course:** Oak Hill Country Club (East Course)

**Location:** Rochester, New York, USA

**Hole:** No. 18

**Length:** 480 yards

**Par:** 4

**Designer:** Donald Ross

**Course Comment:** Oak Hill Country Club is located in Pittsford, New York, an upscale suburb of Rochester. Rochester is the home of the Eastman Kodak Co., and you can be sure plenty of film has been used on this Donald Ross classic.

## No. ⑱  OAK HILL COUNTRY CLUB (EAST COURSE)

Donald Ross designed many notable holes on the East Course at Oak Hill Country Club — No. 7 and No. 13 are two holes that quickly come to mind, but No. 18 is a classic finisher.

With the 2003 PGA Championship visiting the course, the staff decided to add 30 yards to this dogleg-right finishing hole.

No. 18 is anything but easy. It ranked second and third most difficult in Oak Hill's two previous majors. Problems off the tee are everywhere: deep bunkers to the right and hills and trees to the left.

The bunkers are "right" where you would think they would be. "Right" at the bend of the dogleg on the right side. For you golfers with a slice, these are in the "wrong" place.

This tee shot will favor a left-to-right shot. A big drive is needed in order to have a mid- to long-iron into the green.

The green, although wide, is shallow and set right at the base of a very steep hill. Any shot hitting short of the green will not make it up this slope.

A series of bunkers protects the right side. There is also a bunker on the left side. **TJ**

## No. ⑱　THE COUNTRY CLUB

**Course:** The Country Club

**Location:** Brookline, Massachusetts, USA

**Hole:** No. 18

**Length:** 436 yards

**Par:** 4

**Designer:** Willie Campbell, Rees Jones

**Course Comment:** The Country Club has a history of hosting major events. In 1988 it hosted the U.S. Open, in 1999 it saw the U.S. win the Ryder Cup, and in 2005 it will host the PGA Championship.

As you stand on the 18th tee box looking at the clubhouse, be sure to look around, take a deep breath, and try to remember all the great shots that have been played before the ones you are about to play.

This final dogleg-left hole requires a long straight drive. The only real trouble off the tee is the out-of-bounds on the left side along with a group of fairway bunkers. The right center of the fairway is the best play here.

Also the fairway on this hole is very flat, so if you hit a low screamer you should get plenty of roll.

The second shot here is demanding. A large cross-bunker sits in front of the green, which is elevated and has a very firm putting surface. The bunkers around this green are deep, so try to stay out of them. If you find a bunker just try to play your next series of shots as if the hole from that point was a par 3 and if you happen to get up-and-down it will feel like a birdie. As for the green, which is always quick, it slopes from back to front and has some really tricky breaks in it, depending on the pin position.

This is a very famous hole and many dreams have been shattered here, so don't feel too bad if you don't make par. **GE**

# No. ⑱ MERION GOLF CLUB
## (EAST COURSE)

The tee shot on Merion Golf Club's 18th hole must carry an overgrown limestone quarry. The quarry also comes into play on the previous two holes, leaving a long second shot that may just come to rest near the site of one of the most remembered approach shots in the history of golf.

Merion's finishing hole has been immortalized by the famous photograph of Ben Hogan's amazing 1-iron onto the elevated green, protected by bunkers on the left and front right, which secured him a 72nd-hole par during the 1950 U.S. Open. Hogan, still hobbled by numerous injuries received in a horrific automobile accident in 1949, was playing his 36th hole of the day and had seen his three-stroke lead dwindle to nothing, yet somehow he saved his par on 18, then came back and easily won an 18-hole playoff the following day. The shot and subsequent victory cemented Hogan as a golf legend.

Merion's long association with national championships has produced other historic moments: Bobby Jones completed the Grand Slam here in 1930 by winning the U.S. Amateur, and in the 1971 U.S. Open, Lee Trevino beat Jack Nicklaus in an 18-hole playoff after playfully tossing a rubber snake at Nicklaus before the round began. **KA**

## WINGED FOOT GOLF CLUB
### (WEST COURSE)

**Course:** Winged Foot Golf Club (West Course)

**Location:** Mamaroneck, New York, USA

**Hole:** No. 18

**Length:** 448 yards

**Par:** 4

**Designer:** A.W. Tillinghast

**Course Comment:** This course will host the 2006 U.S. Open Championship, which will be the fifth U.S. Open to be held on the West Course.

The 18th on the West Course at Winged Foot Golf Club is considered one of the best inland finishers in the United States. This picturesque finishing hole is very hard, but despite its difficulty, you can't walk this fairway without thinking of all of the great golf that has been played before you.

The drive on this dogleg left must be straight and long. A player needs to find the fairway off the tee, because of what lies ahead. If you spray it to the left or right, you find the rough or the trees and punching out will be your best bet. There is also a bunker on the right, almost at the spot where the hole turns left. From the fairway, the historic stone clubhouse provides a picturesque backdrop, but one must focus on the approach shot.

If you go left, you will find the green-side bunker which is tough to get out of, and if you go right then you face almost as difficult a shot from the sloping terrain to the green.

As for the green itself, which is identified as one of the hardest in golf, it is a beauty. Not only does it have some severe break in it, but it is also fast, very fast. Depending on what time of the day you get to this green (which is always exposed to the sun), you may want to pay up your bets on the tee box so you can enjoy this hole. **GE**

**Course:** New St. Andrews Golf Club

**Location:** Tochigi Prefecture, Japan

**Hole:** No. 18

**Length:** 425 yards

**Par:** 4

**Designer:** Jack Nicklaus

**Course Comment:** Jack Nicklaus, the designer, had this to say about No. 18: "This is a hole, that if you made par every day of a golf tournament, you definitely should win. Because you know you'd be playing consistently well."

# No. ⓲  NEW ST. ANDREWS GOLF CLUB

Invoking the name St. Andrews in a golf course can be a dicey proposition. It is a moniker that draws attention, to be sure, which delights those in charge of marketing the property. However, when you call upon one of the most sacred names in the game, you had better back it up with some prowess. Jack Nicklaus, when he designed New St. Andrews Golf Club, knew he had to bring something special to the table.

He pulled it off splendidly, particularly at the finisher.

No. 18 is one of those golf holes that plays longer than it is marked. At 425 yards, it isn't overly long, and it doesn't depend on wind or gimmicks to give it a more lengthy feel. It's just long enough, and when you add the constraints of disconcerting mounding and bunkers, it is far more of a challenge than the yardage would indicate.

Power isn't an advantage at No. 18. In fact, it is the self-restriction of your strength that leads to success on this hole. It takes discipline to succeed here. If you hit it too far off the tee, you might think that leads to a nice, easy approach shot. But you would be mistaken, because too long of a drive puts you over the crest of the fairway and you are likely to have an awkward downhill lie. In fact, you are almost certainly going to be left with discomfort if not disaster. You will probably have to deal with some sort of uneven lie, even if you aren't over the crest, because the fairway slopes from right to left.

Because you've had to lay up off the tee, you are then left with at least a middle iron to the green, even though the hole is but 425 yards. This is no ideal, because you must come in high and soft to an elevated green. A runner is out of the question because of the moonscape of seven huge and varied bunkers along the front. And a low liner is no good because you'll run through the green and up onto a mound behind, leaving a severe downhill chip coming back (and the chance of rolling into one of those bunkers in front). **JB**

No. ⑱ **JUPITER HILLS CLUB**
**(HILLS COURSE)**

Welcome to the rollercoaster at Jupiter Hills. This 431-yard par 4 is a pretty golf hole. As in pretty to look at and pretty tough. From the tee you are looking at a 40-foot drop in elevation and to reach the level part of the fairway, you need a good 300-yard drive from the back tees.

The fairway then rolls right back up to the green. But while the slope down from the tee is gradual, the climb back up is severe.

A 431-yard par 4 is long enough, but in Florida it seems even longer. Because of the sandy soil, you don't get much roll around here. So that 300-yard tee shot is going to have to be pretty much all in the air.

There are bunkers around the green to the front right and along the hill. A big tree protects the right side of the green but shouldn't come into play unless you are in the right-side rough.

Your approach shot should be from the center or left side of the fairway.

The green has three gradual sections. The front left is low, the right side is a bit higher, and the back is the highest. **TJ**

**Course:** Spring City Golf and Lake Resort (Mountain Course)

**Location:** Kunming, China

**Hole:** No. 18

**Length:** 472 yards

**Par:** 4

**Designer:** Jack Nicklaus

**Course Comment:** In 2004, Spring City's Mountain Course was one of 219 courses designed by Jack Nicklaus, and China was one of 27 countries that has a Nicklaus course.

## No. ⑱ SPRING CITY GOLF AND LAKE RESORT (MOUNTAIN COURSE)

Kunming, the capital of China's Yunnan Province, is a land of rolling hills and glassy lakes. The city proper has a population of three million, which sounds large but really isn't overly congested compared with the rest of China. Add to that the fact that Yunnan is China's sixth-largest province with a population of about 36 million, and three million is a surprisingly small number.

Still, when you think of millions of people, you don't think about a serene ambience for golf. However, take a 30-mile drive east of the city (45 minutes from the airport), and you escape the people, the noise, and the hubbub. Here you will find Spring City Golf and Lake Resort, an ideal place to play your game of choice immersed in breathtaking scenery.

There are two courses on the property, with a Jack Nicklaus design being the original, and a Robert Trent Jones Jr. course added in 1998. The Mountain Course, designed by Nicklaus, is what started to bring golf visitors to this resort, which sprawls over thousands of acres, features five-star lodges, and every amenity you can think of — including outstanding golf.

"We wanted to design a course that complements the area's climate, enabling golfers to enjoy its splendor all year round," Nicklaus explains. "Spring City utilizes the natural undulations of the terrain, which is fairly spectacular."

This beauty includes lush green fairways framed by native pines, rock outcroppings, mountain views, and Yang Zong Hai Lake.

Nicklaus, who often saved his best performances as a player for the end of a tournament, did the same with the dramatic finishing hole at Spring City's Mountain Course.

No. 18 is as cosmetically sound as the rest of the layout, but it is more challenging — forcing players to finish with the No. 1 handicap hole on the course. It is long at 472 yards, and its difficulty is maximized by a row of bunkers on the right side of the fairway, not to mention a snaking ravine criss-crossing your path.

The deep gulley almost always results in a lost ball, but it can be avoided if you stay straight. The only time the ravine comes into play is if you land in one of the bunkers off the tee. Even an accurate tee shot, however, leaves a daunting approach. It is long, and there are several bunkers surrounding a putting surface that cants drastically from back to front. **JB**

No. **⑱**  # BLACKWOLF RUN GOLF CLUB
## (MEADOW VALLEYS COURSE)

Blackwolf Run's Meadow Valleys and Rivers courses are, by all official estimates, entirely independent entities. Both in terms of architecture and geography, the companion layouts are a study in contrasts.

The Rivers Course is fundamentally a woodlands layout, while Meadow Valleys is defined by an opening nine that has a distinct Scottish links aura.

Yet when the U.S. Golf Association awarded the 1998 U.S. Women's Open to Blackwolf Run, it was a wonderfully creative combination of the two courses that was used to host the championship. Officials started with the back nine at Meadow Valleys, which included the original 10th hole that was no longer used, and finished the championship with a combination of the front and back nines of the Rivers Course.

The USGA just recognized the obvious. The two courses are inexplicably linked and nowhere is that more evident than at Meadow Valleys' par-4 18th. The demanding hole finishes with a T-shaped putting surface that is shared with the closing hole on the Rivers Course.

Getting to that massive green, however, is no stroll in the meadow.

A river runs the length of the hole on the right and in front of the green, making the placement of the tee shot crucial. On the left, the green is 50 yards deep with a small bunker guarding the front. **RH**

**Course:** St. Leon-Rot Golf Club
(St. Leon Course)

**Location:** St. Leon-Rot, Baden-Wurttemberg, Germany

**Hole:** No. 18

**Length:** 443 yards

**Par:** 4

**Designer:** Hannes Schreiner, Dave Thomas

**Course Comment:** Tiger Woods scored a perfect 3-for-3 in the first three years that the Deutsche Bank-SAP Open was played at St. Leon-Rot (1999, 2001, 2002): three appearances, three victories.

BELOW *Tiger Woods of the USA on the 18th fairway on the St. Leon Course, May 1999.*

OPPOSITE *A view of the 18th hole on the St. Leon Course.*

## No. 🔞 ST. LEON-ROT GOLF CLUB
### (ST. LEON COURSE)

This hole provides a fitting finish to the PGA European Tour's Deutsche Bank-SAP Open TPC of Europe often held at St. Leon-Rot. The drive must find a narrow, twisting fairway and avoid a trio of bunkers on the left and a large pond on the right that runs from the preferred landing area all the way to the front of the green. The fairway turns to the right as it nears the green, and the approach must again avoid the water as well as a well-placed bunker at the left front of the putting surface.

The hole was originally the ninth hole of the club's Hannes Schreiner-designed Rot course, but was made the finishing hole of the newer Dave Thomas-designed St. Leon course in 2002. Thomas made changes to the fairway and the greenside bunkers, but the rest of the hole is as Schreiner designed it.

In his 2002 playoff victory, Tiger Woods defeated Colin Montgomerie on the 18th, when, on the third playoff hole, Montgomerie landed his drive in one of the fairway bunkers, then found the water with his approach. For the week, the hole played to a 4.089 average, giving up 1 eagle and 57 birdies to 76 bogeys and 12 double bogeys. **KA**

**Course:** Laguna National Golf and Country Club (Masters Course)

**Location:** Laguna Singapore

**Hole:** No. 18

**Length:** 411 yards

**Par:** 4

**Designer:** Dye Designs

**Course Comment:** Laguna National is regarded as one of the premier clubs in Singapore and has hosted many tournaments, including the 2004 Caltex Masters won by Colin Montgomerie, the 1997 Singapore Ladies Golf Association Amateur Ladies Open, and the 1996 Canon Singapore Open.

# No. 🔞 LAGUNA NATIONAL GOLF AND COUNTRY CLUB (MASTERS COURSE)

The two finishing holes are both above par on this outstanding golf course. After the par-3 17th, which requires a carry over water, you tee it up for the last time on the par-4 18th.

And again, water comes into play. Or at least, it can come into play.

Water rolls along the right side of the fairway from tee to green. It's always looming and always in the back of your mind. Try and block it out and stay on the fairway.

The landing area for your tee shot is fairly generous. Take advantage of the hospitality because it tightens up the rest of the way.

The hole is a dogleg right with a tough green.

The courses here are quite different and offer a variety of styles. The Master's Course offers a taste of the old Scottish course with rolling fairways and mounds. This Classic Course is more of an "American" golf course. It is a little shorter than the Master's with less water and gentler fairway mounds. The emphasis here is the all-important approach shots as the greens are strategically well guarded.

Both courses offer a variety of tees for all levels of golfers. **TJ**

Course: Royal Birkdale

Location: Southport, Merseyside, England

Hole: No. 18

Length: 475 yards

Par: 4

Designer: George Lowe, F.W. Hawtree, J.H. Taylor

Course Comment: It is on this hole that a sporting act, now known simply as "The Concession," occurred. After making a 4-foot putt for par on the final hole of the 1969 Ryder Cup with the matches tied, Jack Nicklaus conceded a 2-footer to Tony Jacklin. It was the first tie in the history of the Ryder Cup.

## No. ⑱ ROYAL BIRKDALE

Royal Birkdale will stage its ninth British Open Championship in 2008. This after hosting the 2005 British Amateur and the 2005 Women's British Open. Men, women, and children. Birkdale appeals to all golfers, regardless of age or gender.

There are many reasons why Royal Birkdale has been chosen to host so many major events. Virtually every British championship of any import has been held here and, of course, the most prestigious one of all — the British Open Championship — has been held here a total of eight times. History, atmosphere, and drama are some of the main reasons why the major events keep returning. Another reason? The 18th hole.

No. 18 at Royal Birkdale is one of the most famous finishing holes in England, which of course means it is one of the most well-known and recognizable finishers on the planet. At 475 yards, it is a very long par 4 for members, but when the world's best come here, it is actually a decent birdie opportunity to finish a round. That's if you keep it straight.

There is a tendency to push the ball right, but that's the last thing you want to do because it makes the shot to the green very difficult. Fairways are your friends on almost all golf courses, but this is particularly true at Royal Birkdale. The fairways are unusually flat for an English course, and this is the case at No. 18. The sand hills that line both sides of virtually all the fairways — including the 18th — are as treacherous as they are beautiful.

If you are in the fairway off the tee, a long-iron shot remains, with the dining-room windows of the clubhouse as your aiming point. There are six bunkers surrounding the green, but the three up front are your biggest concerns. They do allow for a runner, but it must be precise because the entrance is narrow.

If you keep it straight, hit it long, and do what you're supposed to do, this hole is fair. If you don't it can be penal. Regardless of whether you achieve par, take a moment to reflect on one of the most regal finishers in golf. **JB**

**Course:** Riviera Country Club

**Location:** Pacific Palisades, California, USA

**Hole:** No. 18

**Length:** 451 yards

**Par:** 4

**Designer:** George Thomas Jr.

**Course Comment:** One of the best approach shots to a green in the world. Imagine 5,000 people standing on that big hill behind the green as you line up that shot to the putting surface. It's a great-looking shot even without the gallery.

## No. ⑱ RIVIERA COUNTRY CLUB

Where did that come from?

That's a popular question on the No. 18 tee at the Riviera Country Club. The "that" is a hill. For the most part, this golf course is flat. But there is a good-size hill to deal with right off the tee on No. 18.

You tee off on No. 1 down a hill and then play 17 basically flat holes before climbing back up the hill on your drive on No. 18. It's a long way between peaks on this rollercoaster.

There is about a 50-foot height difference from the tee box down to the fairway on this 451-yard, par-4 finishing hole.

This isn't what you would call a severe dogleg, but the fairway does break to your right at around the 150-yard mark.

There is a small tree in front of you on the tee, and the ideal drive is just about 10 to 15 feet to the left of that tree. If you manage a little fade you will land in the center of the fairway with a nice-looking approach shot.

There are two traps about 70 yards in front of the green along the right side of the fairway. **TJ**

## No. 18  CANTERBURY GOLF CLUB

**Course:** Canterbury Golf Club

**Location:** Beachwood, Ohio, USA

**Hole:** No. 18

**Length:** 438 yards

**Par:** 4

**Designer:** Herbert Strong

**Course Comment:** From 12 feet, Ben Hogan three-putted the final hole of the 1946 U.S. Open at Canterbury to miss advancing to a playoff with eventual champion Lloyd Mangrum, Vic Ghezzi, and Byron Nelson.

It's been three decades since Canterbury Golf Club hosted its last PGA Tour major championship. The Herbert Strong-designed gem has been another victim of a technology boom that's turned drivers into titanium launch pads and golf balls into multi-layered, single-piece missiles combined with better conditioned players.

The 6,852-yard layout was deemed out of date following Jack Nicklaus's four-stroke victory at the 1973 PGA Championship, yet standing on the tee box of the par-4 18th it's hard to imagine how hot drivers or buff pros could overpower this mammoth.

From the tee, the 438-yard hole climbs a steep slope to a fairway pinched on the right by two large bunkers. The hole bends subtly to the left and tee shots too far left will be blocked by trees.

Even the most prodigious hitters will have a long-iron approach to a green that is shielded by bunkers on all sides except for a narrow opening in the front.

Although one of Canterbury's flattest putting surfaces, the 18th banks from back to front and features rounded edges that run away from the center on each side. Even the slightest spin on approach shots will catch these slopes and run off the green. **RH**

**Course:** The River Course at Virginia Tech University

**Location:** Radford, Virginia, USA

**Hole:** No. 18

**Length:** 476 yards

**Par:** 4

**Designer:** Ault, Clark & Associates

**Course Comment:** Formerly known as the River Course at Heron's Landing, this semi-private course was built in 1999, has five sets of tees, and measures over 7,000 yards.

## No. ⓲ THE RIVER COURSE AT VIRGINIA TECH UNIVERSITY

They say Virginia is for lovers. Well, The River Course at Virginia Tech University is for lovers of golf. And you are sure to fall in love with this scenic and testing 18 holes.

*Golf Magazine* is sure you will love your visit here. The magazine recently selected it as one of the best new public access courses in the United States. From the elevated tees, the majestic course wraps along 2½ miles of the majestic New River.

Welcome to No. 18. Since this is a university course, they decided to make the final hole one of the most challenging on the golf course. Let's call it your final exam. And this one is sure to make you sweat. The long par 4 is a slight dogleg right, but that's the least of your problems. The first part of your test is your drive. The fairway is narrow and there is a large bunker on the right side. Get past that and stay in the fairway and you will have aced the opener.

All along the right side of the fairway, from tee to green, is water. It's always there. And always in your mind. Block it out and keep it straight — or a little left. There is a very large bunker by the green to the front right side. So keep that approach shot straight or left.

You don't have to study too hard on this hole. Just don't be right. **TJ**

**Course:** Ocean Hammock Golf Club

**Location:** Palm Coast, Florida, USA

**Hole:** No. 18

**Length:** 468 yards

**Par:** 4

**Designer:** Jack Nicklaus

**Course Comment:** Located just a short wedge south of St. Augustine, Palm Coast Golf Resort features five splendid 18-hole golf courses: Cypress Knoll, Matanzas Woods, Ocean Hammock, Palm Harbor, and Pine Lakes.

## No. ⓲ OCEAN HAMMOCK GOLF CLUB

In 2000, Jack Nicklaus added another milestone to his career and this one required a shovel and not a golf club. Nicklaus' Ocean Hammock Golf Club was the first ocean-front course to be built in Florida since the 1920s.

And what a golf course it turned out to be. The course plays through dunes and natural ocean-front landscape where six holes overlook the ocean, including the 468-yard, par-4 18th hole.

The last four holes of the 7,201-yard, par-72 course have been nicknamed the "Bear's Claw" and are considered to be among the most memorable finishing holes anywhere.

The final hole features the ocean to your left, trouble to your right, and the target pretty much straight ahead. The green does angle off a little bit to the left, but this is in no way a dogleg.

There is a large bunker on the right side that can come into play. The perfect shot is past this bunker in the middle of the fairway. From here, you have a nice look at the ocean and an even nicer look at the green.

There is a bunker short right and one big, nasty one along the left side of the green.

Watch for the wind on your approach shot. **TJ**

**Course:** Crooked Stick Golf Club

**Location:** Carmel, Indiana, USA

**Hole:** No. 18

**Length:** 457 yards

**Par:** 4

**Designer:** Pete Dye

**Course Comment:** This course is hailed as one of Dye's finest designs. He shaped it to be worthy of world-class competition and its long history of major events proves his success. Crooked Stick has been host to memorable golf championships that include the 1993 LPGA U.S. Open; the staging of the 2005 Solheim Cup does nothing to hinder Crooked Stick's reputation.

# No. ⓲ CROOKED STICK GOLF CLUB

Crooked Stick's 18th is famous courtesy of a rookie named John Daly. He was an unknown, alternate entry to the field and his dramatic finishing-hole victory at the 1991 PGA Championship at Crooked Stick instantly put him on the map in the golf world.

That drama aside, this 457-yard, par-4 dogleg right is also a fantastic challenge. Hitting too far right will plop your ball straight into a monster of a lake. Too far left and you're in the ravine or trapped by a pot bunker. Playing for par is risky business on No. 18 — a conservative golfer has almost no shot at it.

But making par means gaining a stroke on the rest of the field.

Pete Dye etched 18 Scottish-style links holes into rolling terrain when he built Crooked Stick. He put his typically innovative stamp on the course with spacious greens and the devilish pot bunkers he's known for. Undulations make the greens plenty tough. **KLL**

## No. ⓲  THE WILSHIRE COUNTRY CLUB

**Course:** The Wilshire Country Club

**Location:** Los Angeles, Caliornia, USA

**Hole:** No. 18

**Length:** 439 yards

**Par:** 4

**Designer:** Norman Macbeth

**Course Comment:** A barranca runs through the course and comes into play on 13 holes, but especially on No. 18. On a clear day you can see some of the Los Angeles skyline on this hole.

This finishing hole is quite a seesaw. On the one hand it is very pleasing to the eye, but on the other, it is very demanding.

The drive on this 439-yard dogleg-right hole is what will give you a chance at birdie. A high, hard 260-yard cut (for right-handers) is the best approach to take.

The 15-foot-wide barranca runs along the whole left side, then it cuts back across the fairway, at about 150 yards from the green, flows down the left side of the fairway to behind the green before ending on the right side again. Bottom line: stay out of it.

If you hit it too far off the tee, you will be wet and if you go left you will also find water.

As for the second shot, a mid-iron is the common play, and many players try to aim for the middle-left of the green. Do not go left, long, or right or once again you will be taking a drop.

The green on this hole is a real gem because every year it gets flooded, which creates some new twists and turns on the putting surface. This green is always fast and if you can stay dry on this hole, hit the green in regulation, you may be able to smile on your way into the 19th hole. **GE**

## No. ⓲  THE LEGENDS

**Course:** The Legends

**Location:** Kebun, Sedenak, Malaysia

**Hole:** No. 18

**Length:** 440 yards

**Par:** 4

**Designer:** Jack Nicklaus

**Course Comment:** No. 18 is one of two holes on the course that offer two distinct approaches to the green. Even on the scorecard, there are two routes suggested. No. 6 is the other challenge that can play two different ways.

The 18th hole at The Legends might just be worth the trip to Malaysia. It is a wonderful hole with an enormously wide fairway that plays into the inquisitive golfer's hand. The fairway is 120 yards wide, but that only serves to make the challenge more perplexing.

You can play to the left side of the fairway and avoid the bunkers on the right that run from the 200-yard mark to the 250-yard mark. This is safe off the tee, but it leaves a very long second shot in. If you're feeling brutish and you're on form through the first 17 holes, then a carry over the bunkers on the right leaves a short approach and a solid shot at birdie.

There is plenty to think about when standing on the 18th tee, and it is one of the most ingeniously inventive finishers in the world. And this on a course that has offered unique characteristics throughout. The front nine rolls comfortably over rolling hills and then most of the back is wedged tightly into a valley.

The nines are distinct, but their greens are congruous. The tiny putting surfaces on both sides at The Legends average just under 6,000 square feet. And on a course that plays more than 7,000 yards, greens of this size border on torturous. **JB**

# No. ⑱ OCEAN FOREST GOLF CLUB

**Course:** Ocean Forest Golf Club

**Location:** Sea Island, Georgia, USA

**Hole:** No. 18

**Length:** 457 yards

**Par:** 4

**Designer:** Rees Jones

**Course Comment:** The back nine opens out to the ocean on this links-style course and the ocean comes into play on the final three finishing holes. The wind is very much a factor down the stretch.

**BELOW** *Jamie Elson of Great Britain and Ireland tees off on the 18th hole at Ocean Forest, August 2001.*

Just try and take your eyes off the ocean. It's not easy. What a view this golf hole tees up. The entire length of the fairway you are escorted from tee to green by the Atlantic Ocean.

And even though you've already seen it during your round of golf, you never get tired of looking. Eventually, however, you have to play some golf or the group behind you won't be too happy.

Once on the tee use that strong wind off the sea to your advantage. Play to the left side of the fairway and let the breeze bring your ball back toward the middle.

There is a bunker on the right side of the fairway about 230 yards out from the back tee along the right side. It is about 40 yards long so can come into play. Try to miss it if you can.

The ideal location is along the right side of the fairway. This gives you the best angle into the green. There is a greenside bunker to the left and one on the right that wraps around the back.

And don't be long on this hole. There is a sharp downhill slope off the back and because of the green (it slopes from back to front), it's a difficult up-and-down from there. **TJ**

**Course:** Woodhall Spa (Hotchkin Course)

**Location:** Woodhall Spa, Lincolnshire, England

**Hole:** No. 18

**Length:** 540 yards

**Par:** 4

**Designer:** S. V. Hotchkin

**Course Comment:** A nine-hole course was opened for golf on the location in 1890. S. V. Hotchkin later designed an 18-hole course and Harry Colt lengthened the course to 6,400 yards in 1914 — the same routing (although lengthened by 101 yards) that is used today.

The Woodland Spa Hotchkin Course is bunker paradise (if, of course you are not landing in them), famous for their depth and their nastiness. You can get away with some brevity off the tee in that this heathland course plays to just 6,501 yards. It really is not a tournament course, but that does not mean it isn't challenging for visitors.

With a course of more than 120 years of history, there might be a worry that it is antiquated, but this could not be further from the case. If you are not convinced, then your journey to the 540-yard 18th will give you just the memory you need to keep you coming back.

It takes a solid drive to avoid the bunkers and get enough distance to go for the green in two. If this is done, there is a chance at birdie. If it is not, then par will be quite a chore indeed. The flag is visible, from the tee, but it is far in the distance. This may add temptation from the tee to go for the "rip and grip" approach that may land players in hazards instead of fairway.

Play off the tee is perhaps the most important factor on No. 18 because the hole is fairly open the rest of the way. There is but one bunker protecting the green. Be smart off the tee, and a birdie just might await. **JB**

## No. ⑱ **MUIRFIELD LINKS**

**Course:** Muirfield Links

**Location:** Gullane, East Lothian, Scotland

**Hole:** No. 18

**Length:** 448 yards

**Par:** 4

**Designer:** Old Tom Morris, Harry S. Colt, Tom Simpson

**Course Comment:** One of the most memorable shots on Gullane's 18th (at least in modern golf) was Nick Faldo's brilliant 5-iron approach in the 1987 British Open to beat Paul Azinger by one stroke.

You think this course might have a little history? Its first 16 holes were built by hand and horse and were opened on May 3, 1891 — and this was a full 147 years after the Honourable Company of Edinburgh Golfers (who now call Muirfield home) held their first meeting on Leith Links. Of course, the 18th hole is downright modern by comparison. Along with the 17th, this hole wasn't opened until December of 1891.

Sarcasm aside, you get the idea. This is a great golf course, with a legendary history. Not to mention a wonderful finishing hole.

The landing area is extremely tight on No. 18, and it is a brutal test of nerves for competitors in the British Open Championship. The whole world is watching, it is the oldest major championship in golf, and there is a mere strip of safety on which to land.

Add to the difficulty that a draw is required to get the ball to roll toward the green, and the pressure becomes palpable, even if you happen to be watching the championship on television rather than actually attending the Open Championship. There are three bunkers on the left near where you'd like to land your drive, but if you overcompensate, there is gruff rough to the right.

The green is deep enough to afford comfort, but it is narrow enough to cause trepidation. Add to this a ridge in the middle, and it is imperative to land your approach on the same tier as the pin. **JB**

**VICTORIA NATIONAL GOLF CLUB**

**Course:** Victoria National Golf Club

**Location:** Newburgh, Indiana, USA

**Hole:** No. 18

**Length:** 432 yards

**Par:** 4

**Designer:** Tom Fazio

**Course Comment:** *Golf Digest* selected this Tom Fazio-designed jewel as its No. 1 course on its list of "Best New Private" courses for 1999. Nothing wrong with being No. 1.

Many of the members like No. 16, a par 3 with little room for error. Others say No. 9, a par 5 with a split fairway, is their favorite. And No. 17 is certainly worth mentioning. They are all worthy candidates for the most memorable hole. No one will argue with any of those selections. No. 18, a 432-yard par 4, is the ideal conclusion to this debate. It is not a clear-cut winner by any means. Just another strong contender for the crown.

The dogleg right tees up a challenging finish to a great day on the links. Like No. 17, you have water all the way up on the right side. The key here is position. If you lay up a bit off the tee you won't have to carry the deep greenside bunkers on the left side. But you will have a little longer shot into the green.

Coming in more from the right allows you to roll right onto the green. Whatever you do, avoid the lake. That's the worst decision (or outcome) of all.

The final five-hole stretch at Victoria National is tough to beat. There is plenty of variety and challenge down the home stretch. It's just a terrific conclusion to one of Indiana's top courses. **TJ**

No. **18** **ALA WAI GOLF COURSE**

**Course:** Ala Wai Golf Course

**Location:** Honolulu, Oahu, Hawaii, USA

**Hole:** No. 18

**Length:** 374 yards

**Par:** 4

**Designer:** Donald MacKay

**Course Comment:** If you want to play here, you are not alone. Make sure you have a tee time because this is one of the most popular courses in Hawaii. They average about 500 rounds per day.

The popularity of the Ala Wai golf course can be attributed to many factors, including its reasonable green fees, prime location, and the number of tourists just a step away in Waikiki.

This is what you might call a flat but sporty course. Its location though, on the perimeter of Waikiki along the Ala Wai Canal, is spectacular. Your views include — but are not limited to — Diamond Head, the Koolau mountain range, and the Waikiki skyline.

There are several challenging holes on this golf course, but it certainly isn't among the most difficult holes in Hawaii. There are, however, many scenic and fun holes.

The par-4 No. 18 is all three — challenging, scenic, and fun. This hole is last on the course, but first in memorable moments. Visitors and/or tourists will remember plenty of their visit to the famous islands, including No. 18 at Ala Wai.

Your first challenge here is at the tee. The fairway is as narrow as any on the golf course as it makes its way alongside the Ala Wai Canal. The green is very tight and there is a stream flowing right though the middle.

A birdie or even par here and you deserve some time in the 19th hole — or on the beach. **TJ**

**Course:** Frankfurter Golf Club

**Location:** Frankfurt, Hessen, Germany

**Hole:** No. 18

**Length:** 432 yards

**Par:** 4

**Designer:** Harry S. Colt, Charles Alison, John S.F. Morrison

**Course Comment:** After being heavily damaged in World War II, the Frankfurter Golf Club remained under American control from 1945 to 1955, when it was finally turned back over to members.

As a frequent host of the German Open, Frankfurter Golf Club's 18th hole required contenders to hit one last great approach if they were to earn the title. The fairway offers a relatively wide landing area for the tee shot, being protected only by a fairway bunker on the left side. But a laser-like second shot was demanded because of a difficult final-round pin, placed extremely close to a large, deep bunker at the front right of the putting surface, which slopes hard from back to front.

The German Open was held at Frankfurter for the first time in 1938, when Sir Henry Cotton captured the trophy. It also played host to three consecutive German Opens from 1987 to 1989, the final three times it served as the site for the national championship. Mark McNulty of Zimbabwe captured the second of his four German Open victories in 1987, followed by Seve Ballesteros of Spain in 1988 and Craig Parry of Australia in 1989. Parry triumphed in a sudden-death playoff over Englishman Mark James, who left his second shot above the hole. Faced with a difficult downhill first putt, he wound up three-putting to hand Parry his second PGA European Tour victory. **KA**

**Course:** TPC at Sawgrass
(Stadium Course)

**Location:** Ponte Vedra Beach, Florida,
USA

**Hole:** No. 18

**Length:** 440 yards

**Par:** 4

**Designer:** Pete Dye

**Course Comment:** The Stadium
Course at TPC at Sawgrass is
host to the PGA Tour's The Players
Championship, which has the
strongest field of any regular PGA
Tour event. In 2004, Australian Adam
Scott, 23, became the TPC's youngest
champion.

# No. ⓲ TPC AT SAWGRASS
## (STADIUM COURSE)

You'd think after finishing with one of the more famous (or is it infamous?) holes in golf, after surviving the famed island green, after carrying a fairway made purely of water, that you might get a break. You'd be wrong.

There is no time to breathe a sigh of relief after playing the 17th at the TPC at Sawgrass' Stadium Course. The 18th awaits, and this is no place to relax. In fact, if you don't have your guard up, you can put up an ugly finish to your round.

No. 18 is the third consecutive Stadium Course hole to be featured in this book, so this gives you an idea of the challenge it poses. The final triumvirate here is as demanding as golf holes come. This is one of the reasons that the PGA Tour holds its Players' Championship here. Or perhaps we should say three of the reasons.

No. 18 has been the determining factor in many TPC Championships, including the first, when Jerry Pate made birdie in 1982. When Pate jumped into the lake adjacent to the 18th green, most figured it was a celebration. But, after playing Nos. 16, 17, and 18 and surviving the torturous test, he simply may have been seeking relief.

The 18th hole is a brilliant dogleg left, which forces accuracy, length, and strategy to be employed to the very last shot of your round. Tee-to-green precision is a necessity on No. 18 because water lines the entire length of the hole to the left, and mounds (filled with spectators during the TPC) and trees line the right side.

Several grassy bunkers guard the front-right section of the green, and a horseshoe-shaped bunker awaits shots that are hit left or long. The grass behind the green is quite rough, and is best avoided. There is also a new spectator mound behind the green; sending a ball into that area is an unwise venture, whether you are a pro playing the TPC or an everyday player who just happens to be lucky enough to get on for once-in-a-lifetime Saturday Nassau. **JB**

RIGHT *The 18th hole on the Stadium Course at the Tournament Players Course at Sawgrass.*

OPPOSITE *Jeff Maggert of the USA tees off on the 18th hole of the Stadium Course, TPC at Sawgrass, March 1994.*

**Course:** Westin Mission Hills Resort (Pete Dye Course)

**Location:** Rancho Mirage, California, USA

**Hole:** No. 18

**Length:** 385 yards

**Par:** 4

**Designer:** Pete Dye

**Course Comment:** Located in the heart of the Coachella Valley and surrounded by mountains, the spectacular vistas offered by the Pete Dye Resort Course are just part of the fun. Of course, elevated greens, pot bunkers, and plenty of water can add strokes to your game, so be careful.

## No. ⑱ WESTIN MISSION HILLS RESORT (PETE DYE COURSE)

Just a short drive from downtown Palm Springs, The Westin Mission Hills Resort is a paradise set on 360 acres in Rancho Mirage where the sun almost always shines.

Along with the Dye Course, Gary Player designed a super 18-hole challenge, but few would disagree that the Dye Course is the greatest test of golf in the Coachella Valley — and that's saying something.

No. 18 on the Dye Course is the perfect conclusion to a perfect round. They don't call this a resort for nothing. Everything — and then some — you would expect from resort golf is to be found on this course. The finishing hole is a 385-yard par 4. It's not long but very wet. The fairway is narrow with water all along the left side and a deep bunker on the right side. The tee shot sets up for a nice right-to-left fade. The hole is fairly straight with a slight dogleg to the left. The green has water to the left and water behind. There is no rough on the green, just fringe and the trademark Pete Dye railroad ties, so if you miss left or long, you're in trouble. There is also a deep bunker on the right side of the green to watch out for.

With the lake and the immaculate fairway and green, No. 18 is among the most picturesque holes you will come across anywhere. **TJ**

**Course:** Arbutus Ridge Golf & Country Club

**Location:** Cobble Hill, British Columbia, Canada

**Hole:** No. 18

**Length:** 426 yards

**Par:** 4

**Designer:** Bill Robinson

**Course Comment:** While the golf is fun and challenging, there is also plenty of beauty to take in. Views from the links include Mt. Baker and Salt Spring Island.

## No. ⑱ ARBUTUS RIDGE GOLF & COUNTRY CLUB

Known as one of the top courses on scenic Vancouver Island, this course tends to back up while players ponder some very difficult choices.

There is no road map to this course or blueprint to follow so play it to your strengths. There will be plenty of chances to gamble, so pick them wisely. The smart play is often the best, but don't be shy when you think you can cut some corners.

No. 18 is the perfect finish to this splendid round of golf. The 426-yard par 4 includes, among other challenges, a 40-yard elevated green that features five tiers and a pond on the left side.

The fairway is mostly a straight shot with the green off a little to the left, where it cuts into the water. There are fairway bunkers on each side that can come into play on your tee shot, especially the one further up on the right.

Three bunkers line the right side of the green, with the first one beginning out in the fairway.

This challenging par-71, 18-hole championship course, with 6,200 yards of perfectly kept fairways, is playable virtually year round due to the temperate climate of southern Vancouver Island. **TJ**

**Course:** Verdura Golf & Spa Resort
(East Course)

**Location:** Sciacca, Sicily, Italy

**Hole:** No. 18

**Length:** 436 yards

**Par:** 4

**Designer:** Kyle Phillips

**Course Comment:** There are two
18-hole courses on the property and
a 9-hole course. Every day, one of the
18-hole courses is set up for two-ball
play and the other for four-ball play.

## No. ⑱ VERDURA GOLF & SPA RESORT
### (EAST COURSE)

It is a 45-hole collection set among olive trees and orange groves, basking alongside the breaking waves of the Mediterranean Sea. Yes, you could say that Verdura Golf & Spa Resort is a splendid setting to play a splendid game.

It is a difficult golf course on which to find a signature hole, and on such a layout sometimes it is best to look to the finishing hole.

As the staffers at Verdura say, designer Kyle Phillips came up with "a suitable climax to a superb course." The Mediterranean coastline of Sicily lines the right side of the par 4 from tee to green and the hole description calls it Europe's counterpart to Pebble Beach. But, frankly, this hole is so beautiful, it doesn't need to be compared to anything.

The sea is indeed beautiful, but it is a perilous place to play your tee shot. It is best to stay on the left side of the fairway, or at least mid-left. The fairway slopes gently, and there is a rough area to the left and three fairway bunkers as you meander down toward the green.

There is one hindrance as you approach the putting surface. There is a tiny valley, which acts as a masquerade to the green. There are two greenside bunkers, as well, so challenge comes along with the beauty of the hole. **JB**

## No. ⑱ OAKMONT COUNTRY CLUB

**Course:** Oakmont Country Club

**Location:** Oakmont, Pennsylvania, USA

**Hole:** No. 18

**Length:** 453 yards

**Par:** 4

**Designer:** Henry Fownes

**Course Comment:** This golf course is famous for many reasons, but this hole is most famous for one historical moment. Will anyone ever forget Arnold Palmer's final walk up No. 18 at Oakmont in his last U.S. Open?

So many great players have strolled up this fairway to grand applause. Grand applause on a grand golf course for players playing a grand golf hole.

The view from the tee at 18 is unlike any other on the golf course. The straight par 4 is long and challenging, as the bunkers seem to have been placed in all the right (or is it the wrong) places. In addition, the green is quite unusual, but the famous clubhouse helps restore calm to the scene.

A bad tee shot leaves you with a bad decision. Going for the green in two from any place other than the fairway is tough enough, but trying to hit that shot from the rough or a bunker is near impossible.

There is a bunker about 60 yards in front of the green that makes that decision even more difficult. Actually, it should make it easier. Lay up or risk being in the trap — still 60 yards from the green.

So, it's safe to say you want your tee shot straight with the fairway in the crosshairs.

The green at No. 18 isn't easy, either. As in it's not an easy read and it's not easy to navigate. So watch the three-putts here. **TJ**

**Course:** Atlanta Country Club

**Location:** Marietta, Georgia, USA

**Hole:** No. 18

**Length:** 509 yards

**Par:** 5

**Designer:** Willard Byrd, Joe Finger

**Course Comment:** When John Daly won the 1994 BellSouth Classic his caddie wanted him to hit 1-iron from the 18th tee in the final round. Instead, "Long John" opted for a fairway wood which he safely ripped over the oaks down the left side of the fairway. For his second shot, Daly hit 8-iron and got up-and-down for birdie to edge Nolan Henke and Brian Henninger by one stroke.

# No. ⑱ ATLANTA COUNTRY CLUB

Poll anyone familiar with Atlanta Country Club and the conversation inevitably turns to the majestic par-3 13th hole. The 13th's signature waterfall along with its dense wooded nest have been the muse for many an artist and the source of countless double-takes from awed golfers.

Visually the 13th is a postcard with plenty of pin placements. However, from a tactical vantage, Atlanta's par-5 closing hole conjures an entirely different set of images.

The 18th swings hard to the left from the tee and at 509 yards it would appear to be something of a pushover for today's prodigious players. Yet this hole is less strength and more strategy.

A pair of ominous lakes line the left side of the landing area yet tee shots played too far away from the water hazards will have to be carved around or over a stand of ancient oaks on the right.

There is plenty of room to lay up down the right side, and this may be the best option if the pin is tucked on the front left and accessible only by high approach shots. Hole locations in the back right of the bisected putting surface open the green to a longer approach and open the door for the longer hitters. **RH**

**RIGHT** *Steve Lowery of the USA on the 18th green at Atlanta Country Club, October 2002.*

**Course:** Wild Dunes Golf Links (Links Course)

**Location:** Isle of Palms, South Carolina, USA

**Hole:** No. 18

**Length:** 501 yards

**Par:** 5

**Designer:** Tom Fazio

**Course Comment:** The Links Course at Wild Dunes was Tom Fazio's first solo design. He later went on to design another layout at Wild Dune, The Harbor Course. And of course, he has gone on to design many more.

# No. ⑱  WILD DUNES GOLF LINKS
## (LINKS COURSE)

With its ambling fairways framed by majestic oaks and sweeping palms, the Links Course at Wild Dunes is as much a visual bounty as it is a challenge of golf. It is a track filled with threatening sand dunes, and they all lead up to the ocean-side 18th. Tom Fazio, in his first solo design, got it right on his first try at Wild Dunes Links. He's been in the business for more than 30 years since.

"People have a very high standard for me and my work and that's very flattering," Fazio said recently. "But we try to do the best we can from the very first day the course is open."

It is a piece of land rich in history for Tom Fazio, and it is also the site of famous war battles. Most of all, however, the 18th hole at Wild Dunes is a great finale to a fine round of golf.

The length, at just a pace over 500 yards, makes this hole reachable for players of even mid-handicap ability. This, of course, brings out the bravado in most golfers of that ilk. But the prudent play would be three nice, easy shots to the green. This method would certainly assure par, and with a solid approach might lend a shot at birdie. But, more often than not, players are going to go for this green in two. That's fine if you make it, but the risk is pretty drastic if you don't reap the reward.

The front of the green is zealously guarded by two cavernous traps, and natural heather creeps ominously close to the edges of the putting surface. The length is not your challenge on this hole, but an unsuccessful bid at the putting surface in two strokes will put you in a position where par becomes unnecessarily difficult.

The 18th is Fazio's first effort at a classic finishing hole, and his success at his first finisher proved the precursor for his career. He has gone on to design such top-of-the-line courses as Shadow Creek, Dallas National, Barton Creek, the Honors Course, courses at Pinehurst, and many others.

And it all started on this historical site in the Isle of Palms, South Carolina. **JB**

| |
|---|
| **Course:** Carton House Golf Club (Montgomerie Course) |
| **Location:** Maynooth, Co. Kildare, Ireland |
| **Hole:** No. 18 |
| **Length:** 513 yards |
| **Par:** 5 |
| **Designer:** Colin Montgomerie |
| **Course Comment:** The Montgomerie Course, designed by seven-time European Order of Merit winner Colin Montgomerie, played host to the 2005–06 Irish Open and the 2010 Seniors Open. Carton Demesne is home to Carton House Golf Club and the Golfing Union of Ireland, the oldest golfing union in the world. |

# CARTON HOUSE GOLF CLUB (MONTGOMERIE COURSE)

Even before the Montgomerie Course came along in 2003, Carton House already housed the Golfing Union of Ireland and had the respected course designed by Mark O'Meara. But when Montgomerie added his bunker-laden gem, it was the icing on the cake.

Long viewed as one of the most consistent players in European golf, it is no wonder that his golf course at Carton House should also be viewed as consistent from No. 1 to the finishing hole. It is windswept throughout, and perhaps the most consistent feature is the deep-rooted bunkers. These bunkers create a menace for players because they are strategically placed where landing areas might otherwise exist.

The 18th is a par-5 beauty, which is paralleled along the right side by Rye Water, which has players eyeing the left side all the way down. Of course, as one might imagine, there are bunkers in strategic places down the left side, so there is reason for care on both sides. The green is reachable in two, however, provided the sand is avoided.

The landing area is fairly generous, but there is rough to the right and water to the right of the rough. The green is inviting, and playable. So, if the wind is right, and you can steer clear of the menacing bunkers, a finishing birdie is within reach. Quite a nice finish to quite a round. **JB**

**Course:** Shadow Creek Golf Club

**Location:** North Las Vegas, Nevada, USA

**Hole:** No. 18

**Length:** 527 yards

**Par:** 5

**Designer:** Tom Fazio

**Course Comment:** Shadow Creek is where the stars come to play. Michael Jordan, George Clooney, Reggie Jackson, Michael Douglas, and Joe Pesci are just a few of the celebrities who have played this Vegas gem.

# No. ⑱  SHADOW CREEK GOLF CLUB

Nothing understated ever makes it in Las Vegas. Without glitz and glamour, sheen and shine, you simply won't be noticed in Sin City. Vegas mogul Steve Wynn knew this when he built his private playground for personal friends and the biggest gamblers at his casinos, so he poured $60 million into the course which features mountains, trees, manicured grounds, waterfalls, and every other extravagance you could imagine on a golf course. And, some you couldn't.

OK, so it's not exactly traditional, but, as we said earlier, if you don't go big in Las Vegas, you don't go at all. Golf purists may turn the other way when Shadow Creek admirers begin lauding the lavish club, but it is a beautiful place to play golf.

The course sits on a 350-acre site in the middle of the desert, and Tom Fazio had all the land he needed along with an unlimited budget. Every creek, lake, hillside, and waterfall was meticulously planned and carefully built. There are more than 150 tree species and it is almost impossible to believe you are in the middle of the desert, much less within driving distance of the Las Vegas strip.

With all of the opulence and extravagance, it's difficult to pick a trademark hole at Shadow Creek. Some point to the fourth, the ninth, the 15th, or the 17th, but the 527-yard 18th more than holds its own.

The tee box is set into a high ridge, and a stream flows from the green toward the tee, but is interrupted by three waterfalls before tumbling into a lake. An expansive ridge meanders from the tee up the left side before the hole doglegs at the landing area, which is about 25 feet above the water.

The second shot is best played to a second dogleg, just short of a bend in the lake. There is the option of going for the green in two, but that means a long carry over water and somehow stopping the ball on the green. The putting surface is long and narrow, and it is framed by flowers, hills, and trees.

It is a dynamic finishing hole, and it tops off one of the more unique experiences in golf. **JB**

## No. ⑱  GLEN ABBEY GOLF CLUB

**Course:** Glen Abbey Golf Club

**Location:** Oakville, Ontario, Canada

**Hole:** No. 18

**Length:** 524 yards

**Par:** 5

**Designer:** Jack Nicklaus

**Course Comment:** Billy Andrade won the 1998 Bell Canadian Open despite hitting it in the water on Glen Abbey's 18th hole, each of the final two days.

No. 18 at Glen Abbey Golf Club is a great risk-reward final hole for golfers in the numerous Bell Canadian Opens that have been held at Glen Abbey. A short par 5 by today's standards, the tee shot must find a landing area that is surrounded by no fewer than nine bunkers. Then comes the decision — lay up to the left, or hit it over the lake and try for the well-protected green in two. If you lay up for a short third shot, three bunkers line the green on the left and the ever-present water still looms on the right.

In the 2000 Bell Canadian Open, Tiger Woods found one of the numerous fairway bunkers off the tee, but proceeded to blast out with a marvelous 6-iron from 218 yards to land his ball just back of the green. He then chipped up to a foot and tapped in for birdie for a one-stroke victory over New Zealand's Grant Waite. The victory earned Woods the elusive Triple Crown — triumphs in the U.S. Open, British Open, and Canadian Open in the same calendar year, making him only the second player to accomplish the feat (Lee Trevino did it first in 1971). **KA**

## No. ⑱ CARLOW GOLF CLUB

Course: Carlow Golf Club

Location: Deerpark, County Carlow, Ireland

Hole: No. 18

Length: 482 yards

Par: 5

Designer: Cecil Barcroft, Tom Simpson

Course Comment: Ireland is deeply rooted in the historical development of this great game. Famous, historic, and excellent are adjectives you could use to describe many courses in Ireland. But No. 18 at Carlow is often considered the best No. 18 in the country.

Set in the beautiful green countryside of the Midlands, Carlow Golf Club combines links and spectacular parkland features to help create a unique and challenging round of golf.

Carlow Golf Club, which rolls through and around a wild deer park, is known for its outstanding dogleg holes, good enough to challenge even the very best golfers.

In 1998, this dramatic No. 18 hole got longer and in turn much more difficult. Because of the added yardage only the very big hitters can still cut the corner, which now requires a 250-yard carry.

Go ahead and try to cut the corner. You might regret not trying. But if you get in that rough along the left side, forget the green in two and start playing for par.

If you find the fairway, take aim at the largest putting surface on the course. But beware: two bunkers guard the sides and two others sit up front in the fairway.

Tom Simpson redesigned 10 greens and many of the bunkers, but other than that the course has pretty much stayed true to the original design, making it a great game of golf. **TJ**

## No. ⑱ LAUREL VALLEY GOLF CLUB

Course: Laurel Valley Golf Club

Location: Ligonier, Pennsylvania, USA

Hole: No. 18

Length: 537 yards

Par: 5

Designer: Dick Wilson, Arnold Palmer, Ed Seay

Course Comment: Laurel Valley was redesigned in 1988 by Arnold Palmer and Ed Seay, who have dramatically stretched the course and continue to make enhancements. Palmer is also a member of the club's board of directors and has been Laurel Valley's tournament professional since the club opened in 1958.

Formerly a par 4, Laurel Valley Golf Club's finishing hole was changed to a par 5 by Arnold Palmer and Ed Seay during the lengthening of the course. The hole's difficulty, however, has remained.

A strong tee shot down the right side of the fairway will give long hitters the opportunity to get home in two, but to do so, they must hit a high, soft fairway wood over a large lake to a wide but shallow green that's well protected by bunkers. Take the risk, but know that it has consequences. For players laying up, a mid-iron will be required to stay short of three new bunkers that Palmer and Seay placed on the left side of the fairway.

Set in western Pennsylvania's breathtaking Laurel Highlands, Laurel Valley has played host to some of golf's top professional events. Palmer captained the United States to a 21-11 victory over Great Britain and Ireland in the 1975 Ryder Cup matches; Dave Marr edged Jack Nicklaus and Billy Casper by two shots in the 1965 PGA Championship; and the 1989 U.S. Senior Open was won by Orville Moody. It also has been selected to play host to the 2005 Senior PGA Championship. **KA**

**Course:** Nantucket Golf Club

**Location:** Siasconset, Massachusetts, USA

**Hole:** No. 18

**Length:** 590 yards

**Par:** 5

**Designer:** Rees Jones

**Course Comment:** When it opened in 1998, Nantucket Golf Club had one of the country's highest initiation fees of any private club — reported to be $200,000.

# No. ⑱  NANTUCKET GOLF CLUB

Your best shot at getting a glimpse of the very private Nantucket Golf Club might be playing a round at the adjacent Siasconset Golf Club, a historic nine-hole course that dates back to 1894.

More than 100 years later, Rees Jones designed Nantucket Golf Club's championship layout, which opened in 1998 to rave reviews. In many ways, however, Nantucket holds true to the traditional New England courses built in the early 1900s, featuring square tee boxes, no cart paths, and short walks from greens to the following tees. There are also no tennis courts, no pool, and no real estate development save the clubhouse and a few cottages for members.

Set along the tiny island of Nantucket's sandy southeast corner, the course features numerous unique, rugged fairway bunkers and native, long-stemmed grasses, a combination that creates tight landing areas and gives the layout a heathland flavor. Another obstacle is the ever-present wind that often makes club selection difficult. For that reason, the course's design encourages low-running approaches.

Those fortunate enough to play Nantucket will experience a beast of a finishing hole, as the naturally undulating fairway snakes past bunkers and large mounds on the right; but it offers spectacular views of a wildlife refuge on the left. **KA**

**Course:** Pebble Beach Golf Links

**Location:** Pebble Beach, California, USA

**Hole:** No. 18

**Length:** 543 yards

**Par:** 5

**Designer:** Jack Neville, Douglas Grant, Chandler Egan

**Course Comment:** If Jack Nicklaus has his way, the 18th hole at Pebble Beach will be the last golf hole he ever plays: "If I had only one more round to play," Nicklaus said, "I would choose to play it at Pebble Beach. I've loved this course from the first time I saw it."

# No. ⑱ PEBBLE BEACH GOLF LINKS

Since 1919, No. 18 has been the finisher, the pinnacle of an American gem. Debates are inevitable when choosing America's best course, but no one could argue against Pebble Beach Golf Links playing a major role in the debate. Besides playing host to the PGA Tour's AT&T Pebble Beach National Pro-Am each year, Pebble Beach has staged four U.S. Opens. It has also held a firm and constant grip on the hearts of golfers throughout the world.

The first 17 holes are so dramatic, so beautiful, and such a perfect test of golf, that it would seem almost impossible that No. 18 could rise to the occasion of topping its predecessors. But the finisher explodes into a golf crescendo, more than meeting expectations of those lucky enough to experience Pebble Beach.

It is a golf course set on some of the most precious coastline in the world, and the 18th hugs it from start to finish. Your scorecard may be scattered with bogeys and beyond leading up to the 18th, but even though a stern test still awaits, you are presented with a vision that will stay with you forever, regardless of where your golf travels take you after playing Pebble's 18th.

But, visuals aside, take a breath and get ready to play. This is a three-shot hole, and your best bet is to hit your tee shot just to the left of two large trees in the middle of the fairway. Your first shot is struck from a tee box that juts into the Pacific onto a fairway that abuts Carmel Bay. Right-to-left cant awaits the landing of your tee shot, so it's best to aim for the trees and let nature guide your ball toward the bay.

The second shot should be placed on the left side of the fairway, which allows for the avoidance of a tree hanging over the right side of the green. This is perilous, however, because it places you right along the bay, just a few feet above the crashing waves. But this is where you must be if you want a decent third shot at the green.

The approach must carry the bunker up front, which curls around the right side and runs into a second bunker that starts mid-right and follows to the rear of the green. There is a third bunker tucked on the left side between the green and the water, but for your ball to be caught in this is actually a blessing, especially if it is headed toward Carmel Bay.

Once on the putting surface, bear in mind what you've already learned about Pebble Beach, that putts roll toward the water. But take a moment to cast your eyes toward the heavens. **JB**

**Course:** Sebonack Golf Club

**Location:** Southampton, New York, USA

**Hole:** No. 18

**Length:** 560 yards

**Par:** 5

**Designer:** Jack Nicklaus, Tom Doak

**Course Comment:** Talk about golf's high-rent district! Sebonack's 300-acre course is neighbor to the National Golf Links of America and Shinnecock Hills Golf Course.

## No. ⓲  SEBONACK GOLF CLUB

Even though the 18th hole at Sebonack is a sheer beauty that runs along the coastline, and is dotted with bunkers throughout, lined with trees, and provides some of the most stunning views of the course, co-designer Tom Doak refuses to call it the signature hole of the course: "If one hole stands out, then you haven't done a good job with the golf course," Doak insists. Fair enough, but some would argue that No. 18 is indeed a standout hole.

It seems fitting that the word "argue" comes up when discussing Sebonack's par-5 18th. The hole was a point of contention from the beginning. Sebonack founder Michael Pascucci wanted a par-5 finisher, but Doak and co-designer Jack Nicklaus wanted a long par-4. After a protracted, and often pointed, discussion, the man with the pocketbook won the argument.

On this wonderful finishing hole, there are seven bunkers from tee to green, and none are simply for cosmetic value. All come into play, if not guarded against. And, then the approach to the green — whether it be on your second or third shot — is also guarded by sand. Four bunkers surround the green. Even if you hit the putting surface, trouble could wait because there are three large undulations — front left, back right, front right — that could hurt your chances for a two putt. But, with proper care, a birdie is possible. **JB**

**Course:** Al Badia Golf Resort

**Location:** Dubai, United Arab Emirates

**Hole:** No. 18

**Length:** 536 yards

**Par:** 5

**Designer:** Robert Trent Jones Jr.

**Course Comment:** The resort is brand new and sparkling, and the course — particularly its finishing hole — is already drawing attention. Jones says the 18th at Al Badia is "among the most challenging I have conceived."

## No. ⑱ AL BADIA GOLF RESORT

You'd never guess it started as a flat piece of desert.

The par-5 18th hole, all 536 yards of it, wraps around a large central lake and the golfer's task is simple: challenge the edge of the lake as much as you dare. Not only is it an oasis in the desert, it is a hole rich in peril.

The 18th at the newly opened Al Badia is a boomerang-shaped dogleg left that requires you to use both strategy and strength.

The prevailing wind is generally at your back, making the green reachable in two. But you need to be careful because the two shots needed to reach the green both play over water. The putting surface is also protected at the back by a meandering bunker which is shared with the ninth green.

Robert Trent Jones Jr. says the hole on the bank of the Dubai Creek is one of the toughest he has designed. And this from an award-winning visionary whose company has designed more than 220 courses in 38 countries.

Just like the rugged 18th hole, Jones said the design of this course set its own demands.

"The challenge presented was to create a golf course that was equal in vision to the richness and detail of the project, but molding it into the Dubai Festival City property development," he said.

Jones is happy with the result, and he says the Al Badia course is far different to the other courses in this dry land.

"The existing courses in the Emirates are either wall-to-wall green or green and desert," he explained. "The Al Badia Golf Resort's water features create elevation change and add a calming effect, like an oasis."

One of the unique features (but not so calming) on the 18th hole is the "rivers of sand" concept, which runs throughout the Dubai Festival City course and adds texture, color, and creates elevation change.

These rivers of sand present a visually crisp hazard that, unlike a body of water, give players a chance to recover from an errant shot.

You might have a chance to recover from a shot into the rivers of sand, but it may take you longer to recover from the realization that — despite the colorful surroundings — you really are right in the middle of the desert. **JB**

## No. ⑱ THE CLUB AT CARLTON WOODS

**Course:** The Club at Carlton Woods

**Location:** Woodlands, Texas, USA

**Hole:** No. 18

**Length:** 548 yards

**Par:** 5

**Designer:** Jack Nicklaus

**Course Comment:** Nicklaus designed this course for the chosen few. The Club at Carlton Woods is part of a gated community in Woodlands, Texas, just north of Houston. If you are lucky enough to play it, you will enjoy some spectacular scenery.

You could have a terrific round of golf going at The Club at Carlton Woods, but you won't rest easy until you walk off the final green. The 18th is always on your mind as you make your way around the Nicklaus classic. Every hole is challenging, scenic, and fun to play. But 18 looms in the distance — and you know it must be at least held in check if you are going to check off successful on that scorecard.

On the tee, this is a dogleg right. You want to place your drive to a crowned landing area just left of the bunker resting along the right side of the fairway. If you can drive the ball over 300 yards, feel free to consider going for this green in two. Otherwise lay up.

Hitting this green in two requires you to carry a lake, as the fairway wraps around the right side of this. If on-in-two is your intention, you not only have to carry the lake but you also have to clear a small bunker that rests between the water and the green.

For those playing it safe, it means the hole becomes a dogleg left, as the fairway makes its way around the lake. There is a large bunker to the right front of the green and your second shot must hit a shrinking fairway.

A very tough hole. But also one with wonderful views. **TJ**

## No. ⑱ BANGKOK GOLF CLUB

**Course:** Bangkok Golf Club

**Location:** Pathumthanee, Thailand

**Hole:** No. 18

**Length:** 552 yards

**Par:** 5

**Designer:** Arnold Palmer

**Course Comment:** A classic closing hole with plenty of opportunities for last-minute dramatics, Bangkok's 18th was the stage for one of the more memorable finishes in Asian Tour history. Needing an eagle to force a playoff with Thailand's Thongchai Jaidee at the 2003 Volvo Masters of Asia, Taiwan's Lin Keng-chi's shot at three came up just short.

For a golf course replete with almost every bell and whistle known to modern architecture, it seems fitting that Bangkok Golf Club's most inspiring attribute is a no-nonsense finishing hole that challenges and charms all at once.

Bangkok Golf Club features dramatic waterfalls and huge lights to guide the way for night play, but what a player will remember and what will give one a reason to come back is the Arnold Palmer-designed 552-yard closing hole.

No. 18 twists its way back to the club's palatial clubhouse, first weaving right and then back to the left. Before players are home, however, they must avoid a pair of large fairway bunkers lingering at the end of the landing area on the right and a lake that runs down the left side.

Bangkok's thick air and an assortment of hazards will keep most from reaching the 18th green in two shots — but laying up is no easy task. Another fairway bunker sits at the left corner of the dogleg, and the putting surface is ringed by a foursome of foreboding perils.

The green is framed in front, to the left, and behind by a trio of deep bunkers, while a pond defines and defends the right-hand edge of the putting surface. **RH**

Course: Wade Hampton Golf Club

Location: Cashiers, North Carolina, USA

Hole: No. 18

Length: 555 yards

Par: 5

Designer: Tom Fazio

Course Comment: The course was named after General Wade Hampton III, who is described as a "popular and respected gentleman who distinguished himself during the War Between the States." Hampton went on to serve as a U.S. Senator and a member of President Grover Cleveland's cabinet.

# No. ⓲  WADE HAMPTON GOLF CLUB

People have been escaping to the tiny enclave of Cashiers (pronounced cash-ers) since the early 1800s, finding relief at 3,650 feet of elevation from the heat of the Lowcountry during the scorching summer months. Since 1987, there has been another opportunity for those in Cashiers — a peaceful and elegant golf course called Wade Hampton.

This mountain course may be less than 20 years old, but it attracted attention from the pundits the day it opened. It was ranked among the best golf courses in America in its first year, and it continues to show up in virtually every ranking today.

This is high praise for a course that isn't even ranked as the top layout in its state. However, when you consider Wade Hampton is ranked No. 2 in North Carolina, and also that it's right behind famed Pinehurst No. 2, that puts the ranking in proper perspective. Quite simply, Wade Hampton is a magnificent mountain course. But make sure you leave enough time on your itinerary for a peaceful drive through the mountains . . . the Smokies are nearby, and on the other side is Gatlinburg, Tennessee.

The mountain drive, of course, comes after you play Wade Hampton, and after you've challenged yourself at the 555-yard, par-5 18th hole.

Chimney Top Mountain, for which the front set of tees throughout the course are named, dwarfs you as you stand on the 18th tee. And if you choose to play the tips, you would be playing the Fazio tees, named after the course's designer. This is a beautiful finishing hole, and with the towering mountains at your back, it does nothing but add to the majesty.

It's beautiful, but it really is tough. The right rough is laced with eight bunkers, lined neatly one after the other, unavoidable for any ball hit in that direction. Lest you overcompensate for fear of the bunkers, there is a babbling creek to the left. Even if you avoid the creek off the tee, it comes back again two shots later, where you have to cross it on your approach to the green.

The putting surface is carved into the side of a hill, and is encircled by four bunkers. **JB**

## No. ⑱ ROYAL WOODBINE

**Course:** Royal Woodbine

**Location:** Toronto, Ontario, Canada

**Hole:** No. 18

**Length:** 585 yards

**Par:** 5

**Designer:** Michael Hurdzan, Dana Fry

**Course Comment:** Get used to seeing that creek. The Mimico Creek winds its way though this picturesque golf course and comes into play on every hole.

*Golf Digest* magazine quoted Royal Woodbine as "a good test and always in great shape . . . good layout, water, and tough greens . . . excellent, a real treat to play."

Royal Woodbine was very cunningly designed by Michael Hurdzan and plays 6,446 yards from the tips, winding its way up and down both sides of the Mimico Creek. There is water everywhere and plenty of islands, so bring plenty of golf balls.

It's a golf cliché, but it's the truth here: You'll need every club in your bag to successfully navigate this track, known as much for its overall conditions as for its challenging course.

Like many great courses, Royal Woodbine saves the best for last. No. 18 is a 585-yard par 5 that requires a straight tee shot to a narrow landing area. If you don't hit it straight here, cross birdie off your scorecard. Your second shot must carry the creek. If you don't, cross par off your scorecard.

The third is over a pond to a well-bunkered green, and you'll need all the help you can get to make it over the water. It's a good thing the pro shop sells golf balls and the clubhouse serves cold beer. **TJ**

**Course:** Taiheiyo Club Gotemba
(East Course)

**Location:** Gotemba-shi, Shizuoka,
Japan

**Hole:** No. 18

**Length:** 517 yards

**Par:** 5

**Designer:** Shunsuke Kato

**Course Comment:** Taiheiyo Club's
West Course played host to the
World Golf Championships-EMC
World Cup in 2001, with South
Africa's Ernie Els and Retief Goosen
winning in a four-hole playoff. Els
and Goosen and the American team
of Tiger Woods and David Duval each
made eagle on the 18th hole to get
into the playoff.

## No. ⑱  TAIHEIYO CLUB GOTEMBA
### (EAST COURSE)

Some might say Taiheiyo's finishing hole is too easy for competitors in the Sumitomo Visa Taiheiyo Masters, a Japan Golf Tour event held annually on the East Course. But that would be missing the point. The hole offers galleries plenty of drama and thrills as well as giving a contender the chance to be a hero — or a goat — when the tournament's on the line.

The tee shot must split a pair of fairway bunkers to set up the opportunity to get home in two — a shot well within reach for long hitters. But if not struck perfectly, the drive can easily find trouble — either in a pond that must be carried to reach the green, or a trio of bunkers at the left rear of the tiered putting surface.

Still, the hole — which offers a magnificent view of Mount Fuji in the background — isn't a difficult one to scale for world-class players. It played as the easiest during the 2003 Taiheiyo Masters, with a stroke average of 4.592 and more birdies (141) than pars (106) and bogeys (29) combined. Yet its risk-reward aspect might be better shown by the eight eagles and five double bogeys scored there.

Drama, thrills, and Mount Fuji. There's certainly nothing wrong with any of that. **KA**

**Course:** Rancho La Quinta
(Jones Course)

**Location:** La Quinta, California, USA

**Hole:** No. 18

**Length:** 561 yards

**Par:** 5

**Designer:** Robert Trent Jones Jr.

**Course Comment:** There are several ways to see the Santa Rosa Mountains. You could get in your car and drive around, or you can grab your golf clubs and go play the Rancho La Quinta golf course.

## No. ⑱ RANCHO LA QUINTA
### (JONES COURSE)

Sometimes it pays to be a member. That's certainly the case on the Robert Trent Jones course at Rancho La Quinta. Now don't think this is a walk in the park, but the course isn't exactly set up to penalize a slight miss or a little hook or slice. You really have to hit a bad shot to face a stiff penalty.

But that's an advantage on No. 18, a long and difficult par 5. You can really let it fly off the tee, and if you are even thinking green in two, you better get a good drive.

For most players, this is a lay-up. Trying to reach the green in two isn't worth it. Too much danger. This might be member-friendly, but a par on this hole must be earned.

The green cuts into a pond and there is water to the front. You can go over the green on your approach shot and be okay, although there is a bunker in the back.

The oval-shape green has a big hump in the middle and certainly tests the better putters. The best play is to lay up and try and reach the green safely in three. A two-putt then earns you a par. **TJ**

---

**Course:** Delta Rocky Crest Golf Club

**Location:** Mactier, Ontario, Canada

**Hole:** No. 18

**Length:** 563 yards

**Par:** 5

**Designer:** Thomas McBroom

**Course Comment:** This very popular parkland-style golf course features rolling, tree-lined fairways that are dotted with rock outcroppings from the Canadian Shield.

## No. ⑱ DELTA ROCKY CREST GOLF CLUB

Rocky Crest's 18-hole championship golf course, designed by Thomas McBroom, has earned rave reviews for its distinctive granite outcroppings, seamless routing, and log-cabin-style clubhouse.

The course made its debut at No. 4 in a 2001 ranking of Ontario's best courses. No. 18 is a challenging par-5 finishing hole. It begins with a drive over a flowering marsh to a generous fairway.

You can reach the green in two here but it is going to take two very good golf shots. Even if you hit the ideal drive off the tee and clear the rock cropping and place it perfectly on the fairway, you are still looking at a 260-yard shot to the green. That's a long way to go.

The second and third shots approach the sloping green with a view of the log-cabin-style clubhouse sitting atop giant rock outcroppings, which cut their way down to the hole from the patio to form sort of a natural amphitheater.

This dogleg right isn't the toughest hole on the course (it's the 12th handicap) but will punish a golfer getting a little too greedy or looking ahead to the cold beer on the patio. **TJ**

**Course:** Rush Creek

**Location:** Maple Grove, Minnesota, USA

**Hole:** No. 18

**Length:** 569 yards

**Par:** 5

**Designer:** Bob Cupp, John Fought

**Course Comment:** Host of the 2004 U.S. Amateur Public Links Championship, Rush Creek is considered by many as one of the top 10 courses in the state. In 1996, *Golf Digest* rated it the fourth best in Minnesota.

## No. ⑱ RUSH CREEK

Save the best for last?

Well, Rush Creek has plenty of outstanding and dramatic golf holes so picking out one isn't easy. But as far as memorable goes, the 569-yard par 5 at Rush Creek would appear on anyone's list of the best holes in Minnesota.

To really appreciate this hole you must see it from the air. It will scare you and intrigue you at the same time. But since we can't find a helicopter we will keep our feet on the ground. And yes, you still get a pretty good idea of the uniqueness and beauty of this par 5.

At 569 yards from the back tees, this hole has some length built in. You are going to have to clear the lake and wetlands off the tee — and again on your second shot. The fairway is pretty wide for your first shot but much tighter on your second. There are also rolling hills, similar to the rest of the fairways at Rush Creek.

Reaching the green in two requires a long shot over the water and marsh to a green featuring a bunker in front of it and water around the left-hand side and back.

And don't be long. The shot back to this green is very difficult. **TJ**

**LOS NARANJOS GOLF CLUB**

**Course:** Los Naranjos Golf Club

**Location:** Marbella, Malaga, Spain

**Hole:** No. 18

**Length:** 576 yards

**Par:** 5

**Designer:** Robert Trent Jones Sr.

**Course Comment:** The name Marbella means "beautiful sea" in Spanish, an appropriate name for the site of this beautiful course.

Set among scenic orange groves and palms in the midst of the well-known Golf Valley of Marbella, the Robert Trent Jones Sr.-designed Los Naranjos Golf Club, which opened in 1977, features many elevated tee boxes, large undulating greens, and an American-style finishing hole.

No. 18, a long dogleg-left par 5, features two water hazards that could conceivably come into play on all three shots. The tee shot must avoid a bunker at the outside corner of the dogleg, tempting players to cut as much of the corner as possible, but those who pull their drives long and left could find a large lake that starts at the inside corner and continues along the left side of the hole.

A wide stream then crosses the fairway a few yards short of the green, discouraging all but the longest hitters from attempting to get home in two. Most players instead choose to lay up and leave a short approach over the water to an elevated green, with the Andalucian-style clubhouse and mountains forming a majestic background. Even then, the third shot's not easy. The putting surface slopes from left to right, and is further guarded by a sprawling bunker on its left side. **KA**

# No. ⑱ KAPALUA GOLF CLUB
## (PLANTATION COURSE)

The entire golf course was built around this stunning finishing hole. And standing on the back tees with your driver in hand, you must ask yourself one question. Is this a par 6?

At 663 yards, this is by far the longest par 5 on the course. The next closest is almost 100 yards shorter. But there are options. You can play from the regular tees (585 yards) or the front tees (489 yards).

But, believe it or not, it is reachable in two. You have two advantages here. The hole is very much downhill and very much downwind, but you still need two really strong hits to get there in two.

The fairway is pretty generous to allow you to really rip it. The green is also very big, but wind is a factor on every shot here. Not only is this the longest hole here, but the most spectacular and dramatic hole when it comes to scenery. The background as you play it is amazing to say the least.

Big hitters want to find the right side of the fairway while the more conservative player will aim their second shot at the clubhouse. The green runs away from you toward the ocean. **TJ**

**Course:** Cherry Hills Country Club

**Location:** Englewood, Colorado, USA

**Hole:** No. 18

**Length:** 491 yards

**Par:** 5

**Designer:** William Flynn

**Course Comment:** The Cherry Hills Country Club has played host to many tournaments and championships over the years, including the 1938, 1960, and 1978 U.S. Opens. Arnold Palmer, who drove the 404-yard first hole, won the 1960 Open.

# No. 🔟 CHERRY HILLS COUNTRY CLUB

This hole can be one of the easiest holes on the golf course, or it can be one of the toughest. It all depends on who you are. For Tiger Woods, Ernie Els, and Phil Mickelson, this is a tough hole. For members, it's one of the easier holes.

No. 18 at Cherry Hills is a par 5 most of the time. The membership gets to play it that way, which makes it the No. 16 handicap hole.

But when the professional men roll into town, this becomes a par 4. This changes the whole ballgame.

Even the professional ladies get to play it as a par 5. The scorecard reads par 5 for the 2005 U.S. Women's Open.

There is water on the left side from tee to green and the fairway slopes from right to left. Your ideal drive is as close to the water as you can on a flat fairway. Things level off nicely over by the water.

Your second shot is uphill to a green with bunkers right and left. The green slopes back right to front left. **TJ**

---

**Course:** Glen Eagles Golf Club (No. 9 Red Course)

**Location:** Bolton, Ontario, Canada

**Hole:** No. 18

**Length:** 650 yards

**Par:** 5

**Designer:** René Muylaert

**Course Comment:** Toronto is a growing city, one of the fastest growing in the world. And the number of golf courses in the area is on the rise. But just 50 miles north of Toronto is Glen Eagles, a 27-hole public golf course that is certainly worth the drive.

# No. 🔟 GLEN EAGLES GOLF CLUB (NO. 9 RED COURSE)

First of all, there is no reaching this green in two. You could be John Daly and Tiger Woods rolled into one and you aren't getting to this green in anything less than three very good golf shots.

The tee is set back in the trees on this very difficult dogleg left. Of the 27 holes at Glen Eagles, this one is by far the toughest. There is the red No. 9 and all the other ones when it comes to difficulty. So play the red as your second nine and finish with a bang.

Trees line the fairway on both sides. There are no bunkers but they simply weren't needed here. The fairway is only about 85 yards wide, then about 10 yards of rough and then trees.

And believe it or not, this hole is actually longer than 650 yards when you consider the wind is usually in your face.

A good tee shot is about 280 yards straight. This will still leave you with 170 yards to reach the dogleg and where the fairway heads downhill. The hill eventually flattens out to a very large green. Such a large hole deserves a large green.

The green is pretty flat, but tricky, so don't take it lightly. **TJ**

**Course:** The Broadmoor Golf Club (West Course)

**Location:** Colorado Springs, Colorado, USA

**Hole:** No. 18

**Length:** 555 yards

**Par:** 5

**Designer:** Donald Ross, Robert Trent Jones Sr.

**Course Comment:** The 18th hole was lengthened prior to the 1998 PGA Cup Matches, a match-play event pitting U.S. PGA professionals with their European counterparts.

**BELOW** *An aerial view of the West Course at The Broadmoor.*

# No. ⑱ THE BROADMOOR GOLF CLUB
## (WEST COURSE)

The West Course at The Broadmoor doesn't need a whole lot of hype. Just consider that Donald Ross first designed the course in 1918 and that Robert Trent Jones Sr. added to it in 1955, and you know that you have a combination of rare talent on one property. What the pair produced 37 years apart stands proudly today as a golf-landscaping work of art.

The land Ross and later Jones had to deal with was spectacular yet difficult. Steep angles and rolling hills make for wonderful golf holes if dealt with correctly, but the architecture was not without challenge. Needless to say, Ross and Jones were up to the task. The fairways roll naturally with the hills, there are several doglegs that wind around thick trees, and many of the greens are canted severely with the natural lie of the land. And all of this offers a rare combination of city and mountain views.

The West Course generally plays tight off the tee and large, deep bunkers are numerous. The 18th hole is a microcosm of the entire West Course, featuring a little bit of everything from final tee to final green. The tee is elevated and overlooks a less-than-generous landing area that is made even more skimpy by native grasses and bunkers on either side. Pine trees and sand are companions the rest of the way, and it is just a matter of staying on the fairway. It is doubtful that many players can reach this 555-yard hole in two, but if you have the distance, then have a rip, because there is an opening up front.

The rest of the putting surface is encircled by bunkers however, with large sand traps on the right, left, and back of the green. The stately

Broadmoor Hotel serves as a backdrop, but it would be wise to ignore the scenery and concentrate on the task at hand. The green has two distinct levels, and it is crucial to land your approach on the same tier as the pin. Otherwise, you could be left with a putt that would put a distasteful cap on your round. **JB**

# No. ⑱ PALM MEADOWS GOLF CLUB

**Course:** Palm Meadows Golf Club

**Location:** Carrara, Gold Coast, Australia

**Hole:** No. 18

**Length:** 572 yards

**Par:** 5

**Designer:** Robin Nelson, Graham Marsh

**Course Comment:** At the 1990 Palm Meadows Cup, Greg Norman led after two rounds but disqualified himself because of an illegal drop he had taken from a water hazard in round one.

One of the first golf courses built along Australia's scenic Gold Coast, Palm Meadows Golf Club's signature 18th hole has that risk-reward aspect that makes such finishing holes exciting for both golfers and galleries alike.

Palm Meadows's No. 18 is a long dogleg-right par 5 that curves around a huge lake, but it offers longer hitters the chance to go for the green in two. The reward, of course, is an eagle putt, but the risk is having your ball coming up short of the green and landing in an inlet of the lake that cuts directly in front of the putting surface, and it has claimed many a golf ball. Those who keep their second shot to the left of the water will have a much shorter approach to a putting surface that is protected by three large bunkers at the front right, front left, and rear left.

At a sudden-death playoff in the 1990 Palm Meadows Cup, defending champion Curtis Strange opted for the safe route, with his opponent, Australia's Roger Davis, gambling and going for the green in two. The gamble paid off, as Davis made an eagle for the victory. **KA**

**Course:** Edgewood Tahoe Golf Club

**Location:** Stateline, Nevada, USA

**Hole:** No. 18

**Length:** 572 yards

**Par:** 5

**Designer:** George Fazio

**Course Comment:** The 1980 U.S. Amateur Public Links, won by Jodie Mudd, was the first U.S. Golf Association national championship ever held in Nevada.

# No. ⓲  EDGEWOOD TAHOE GOLF CLUB

As long-time host to the American Century Celebrity Golf Championship, Edgewood Tahoe's finishing hole, set along the south shore of Lake Tahoe, has provided thrilling — and embarrassing — moments for some of the country's most beloved sports stars and Hollywood celebrities.

A lengthy drive down the left side of the fairway will provide big hitters a chance to get home in two. But to do so they must avoid a large pond at the front left of the green, with very little room to skirt the water on the right. And even laying up produces no guarantees.

Just ask former Detroit Pistons standout Bill Laimbeer, who had a chance to win the 1991 Celebrity Golf Championship — that is, before he knocked three balls into the water. Ever since, the pond has affectionately been called Lake Laimbeer.

The 1985 U.S. Senior Open was held at Edgewood Tahoe, with Miller Barber winning his second consecutive Open crown and finishing as the only golfer to break par on the demanding layout, coming in at three under to defeat Robert De Vicenzo by four shots. Edgewood Tahoe Golf Club remains the only Nevada course to have served as host to a U.S. Golf Association national championship. **KA**

# No. ⑱  THE HARVEST GOLF CLUB

Bentgrass fairways that are kept in the best of conditions contribute to the unique character of this challenging and scenic course. The Harvest Golf Club serves up challenges for even the best golfers but it isn't designed to scare away newcomers to this great game. Hard, but fair.

Cooke has provided a full range of goodies to enjoy. There are the larger than usual undulating greens and the dramatic elevation changes. He even throws in a few dashes of sand and more than a cup of water to provide a true test.

So what do we come to at the end of this golfing banquet? No. 18. And since we're in Canada, it's sometimes served cold.

Aim for the left side of the fairway. Those "strategically placed bunkers" are all over the place here, including a series of three on the right-hand side at the bend.

There is a good-size landing area for those wishing to lay up. Remember that going for it isn't always wise, especially with two large bunkers protecting the right and left sides of the green.

The green has plenty of slope, so don't take anything for granted. **TJ**

# No. ⑱  LOOKOUT MOUNTAIN GOLF CLUB AT TAPATIO CLIFFS

What a way to finish — a long and challenging par 5. One last chance to pull out the driver and let it rip. One last chance to see the big drive soar through the Arizona blue sky and crashland on the plush green carpet better known as the fairway.

But look out for the sand. And look out for the water. And look out for the trouble that looms in the desert. Oh yeah, and look out at the mountains one last time. "Look out" seem to be the operative words on Lookout's 18th.

This elevated tee on the finishing hole gives you one of the more stunning views of the Pointe Hilton Tapatio Cliffs Resort with the mountains in the background. It's a view that you will take along for the rest of your life.

If you can put the camera down long enough to grab a golf club, you will want the driver. Because you can reach the green in two here with a good, long tee shot.

The fairway is nice and straight with a good-size landing area for your tee shot. Going for it in two is a challenge. The green cuts out into the water with a sand trap at the tip along the right side. The green is pretty much a peninsula so there isn't any room to miss. **TJ**

# CONTRIBUTORS

**Jeff Barr** has traveled the world reviewing golf courses, golf resorts and, of course, golf holes. He is an award-winning writer who oversees and writes for the travel section of *Golfweek* magazine, one of the most popular golf news magazines in America. His stories have appeared in *The Washington Post*, *The Detroit News*, *The Las Vegas Sun*, and many newspapers, magazines, and Web sites from coast to coast. *1001 Golf Holes* is his fourth book.

**Terry Jacoby**, who has been a sports editor and writer at *The Detroit News*, *The Sacramento Bee*, and the *Rochester Democrat and Chronicle*, also co-authored *Business Traveler's Guide to Golf* (Triumph Publishing, 1999). He is former managing editor of golfstation.com, a Web site based in Dallas, and has produced several regional golf course guides distributed to 100,000 homes annually. His next venture in the world of golf is marketing and public relations, where he plans to promote courses in the Midwest.

**Alistair Tait** of Hertfordshire, England, is a member of the Association of Golf Writers and is a regular contributor to *The Guardian*, *Daily Express*, *The Observer*, *Sunday Herald*, and many other British publications. He also is the European bureau chief for *Golfweek*.

Alistair is a qualified Rules of Golf referee, and is member of Woburn Golf & Country Club with a handicap of 10. He has been writing about golf since he graduated from the University of Guelph, Ontario, Canada in 1987. He is a former Deputy Editor of the UK magazine *Golf Monthly*, and previous to that, was deputy editor for *Today's Golfer* — another UK publication.

**John Steinbreder** has played — and written about — the top courses in Scotland, Ireland, Australia, Spain, Morocco, and the United States. He has authored six books and is an award-winning senior writer for *Golfweek*. Steinbreder has interviewed some of the biggest names in the game and regularly produces travel stories on the sport. His goal is to play all of the golf holes featured in this book.

**Kelle Larkin** has criss-crossed the globe as an award-winning travel writer. She has visited destinations in the Caribbean, Europe, South America, and the United States. Among the golf courses included in her stories are TPC of Sawgrass, LPGA International, as well as others in the Bahamas, Mexico, Jamaica, Florida, and throughout the United States. She has co-authored one book.

**Kevin Adams** has served as sports editor at three daily newspapers in the Carolinas, including *The Island Packet* of Hilton Head Island, South Carolina, where he annually wrote on the PGA Tour's MCI Heritage at Harbour Town Golf Links. He has covered several major golf championships, including the Masters, U.S. Open, and the Ryder Cup. Adams currently works as assistant managing editor at *Golfweek*. He has earned writing awards from the Associated Press Sports Editors and the Golf Writers Association of America.

**Beth Ann (Biff) Baldry** played golf at Florida Southern College and majored in journalism. She covers the LPGA, colleges and amateur golf for *Golfweek*. As part of her most recent golf destination writing assignment, she played Pebble Beach for the first time.

**Rex Hoggard** has reported on every level of competitive golf for six years. He is knowledgable on junior golf, colleges, professional, amateurs, and seniors. Hoggard has played and written about golf courses throughout the world, including top tracks in the United States, Mexico, the Dominican Republic, and Jamaica. Prior to joining *Golfweek*, Rex was a member of the *Orlando Sentinel*'s sports department.

**Graham Elliott**, a proud left-hander, has played many classic courses and plans on playing many more. Elliott has been playing golf since age six, is a single-digit handicapper, and the game has been part of his life for as long as he can remember. His father is a skilled player, his brother is a club professional at Winter Park Country Club, Florida, and he has worked at *Golfweek* as an assistant editor for five years.

# DESIGNER INDEX

# GENERAL INDEX

956

# PICTURE CREDITS